PEARSON CUSTOM LIBRARY

ENGLISH
MERCURY READER

COMPOSITION I
OAKLAND COMMUNITY COLLEGE, AUBURN HILLS

PEARSON

ISBN 10: 1-256-58369-3
ISBN 13: 978-1-256-58369-1

General Editors

Janice Neuleib
Illinois State University

Kathleen Shine Cain
Merrimack College

Stephen Ruffus
Salt Lake Community College

Table of Contents

Writing: A First Look

Why write? Aren't e-mail, voice mail, cellular phones fast dooming ordinary writing? Not long ago, some people thought and said so, but events haven't supported those predictions. In fact, much electronic media, such as Blogging, have increased the amount of writing people do. Although devices such as cell phones have made some writing unnecessary, the written word still flourishes both on campus and in the world of work.

Writing offers very real advantages to both writers and readers:

1. It gives writers time to reflect on and research what they want to communicate and then lets them shape and reshape the material to their satisfaction.
2. It makes communication more precise and effective.
3. It provides a permanent record of thoughts, actions, and decisions.
4. It saves the reader's time; we absorb information more swiftly when we read it than when we hear it.

Many people will expect you to write for them. College instructors ask you to write reports, research papers, and essay exams. Job hunting usually requires you to write application letters. And once you're hired, writing will probably figure in your duties. You might be asked to discuss the capabilities of new computer equipment, report on a conference you attended, or explain the advantages of new safety procedures to supervisors or staff. Perhaps you'll propose that your organization install a new security system, conduct a market survey, or develop an alternative traffic flow pattern. The ability to write will help you earn better grades, land the job you want, and advance in your career.

From Chapter 1 of *Strategies for Successful Writing*, Ninth Edition. James A. Reinking, Robert von der Osten.
Copyright © 2011 by Pearson Education, Inc. Published by Pearson Prentice Hall. All rights reserved.

1

Furthermore, writing ability yields personal benefits. You might need to defend a medical reimbursement claim that you filed with your health insurer, request clarification of an inadequate or ambiguous set of directions, or document a demand for replacement of a faulty product. Skill in writing will help you handle these matters.

As you can see, we usually write in response to a situation. This situation often determines the purpose and audience of our writing as well as its content, style, and organization. We don't, then, write in isolation but rather to communicate with others who have an interest in our message. To do an effective job, you will need to understand the different situations that can prompt a piece of writing and respond accordingly.

The Purposes of Writing

Whenever you write, some clear purpose should guide your efforts. If you don't know why you're writing, neither will your reader. Fulfilling an assignment doesn't qualify as a real writing purpose, although it may well be what sends you to your desk. Faced with a close deadline for a research paper or report, you may tell yourself, "I'm doing this because I have to." An authentic purpose, however, requires you to answer this question: What do I want this piece of writing to do for both my reader and me?

Purpose, as you might expect, grows out of the writing situation. You explore the consequences of the greenhouse effect in a report for your science instructor. You write an editorial for the college newspaper to air your frustration over inadequate campus parking. You propose that your organization replace an outdated piece of equipment with a state-of-the-art model. Clearly, your purpose stems from the writing situation.

Here are four common *general writing purposes*, two or more of which often join forces in a single piece:

To Inform   Presenting information is one of the most common writing purposes. The boating enthusiast who tells landlubber classmates how to handle a skiff plays the role of teacher, as does the researcher who summarizes the results of an investigation for coworkers. Some professional writers carve careers out of writing articles and books that fill gaps in the public's knowledge of timely topics. Instructors often ask you to write exams and papers so that they can gauge how well you have mastered the course material.

To Persuade   You probably have strong views on many issues, and these feelings may sometimes impel you to try swaying your reader. In a letter to the editor, you might attack a proposal to establish a nearby chemical waste dump. Or, alarmed by a sharp jump in state unemployment, you might write to your state senator and argue for a new job-training program.

To Express Yourself   Creative writing includes personal essays, fiction, plays, and poetry, as well as journals and diaries. But self-expression has a place in other kinds of writing too. Almost everything you write offers you a chance to display your mastery of words and to enliven your prose with vivid images and fresh turns of phrase.

To Entertain   Some writing merely entertains; some writing couples entertainment with a more serious purpose. A lighthearted approach can help your reader absorb dull or difficult material. Satire lets you expose the shortcomings of individuals, ideas, and institutions by poking fun at them. An intention to entertain can add savor to many kinds of writing.

More Specific Purposes

Besides having one or more *general purposes*, each writing project has its own *specific purpose*. Consider the difference in the papers you could write about solar homes. You might explain how readers could build one, argue that readers should buy one, express the advantages of solar homes to urge Congress to enact a tax credit for them, or satirize the solar home craze so that readers might reevaluate their plans to buy one.

Having a specific purpose assists you at every stage of the writing process. It helps you define your audience; select the details, language, and approach that best suit their needs; and avoid going off in directions that won't interest them. The following example from the newspaper *USA Today* has a clear and specific purpose.

We'll Trash *USA Today*, Too

J. Winston Porter

1   What will you do with *USA Today* after you finish reading it? If you're like most of us, you'll put the paper out with the garbage and it'll end up buried in a landfill. Over 80% of all household and commercial garbage ends up this way, and this is a problem.

2   The USA is relentlessly producing more and more trash, and we are rapidly running out of landfill space. At the same time, new landfills and incinerators are encountering local opposition. Before we are truly wallowing in waste, we need to declare a war on garbage.

3   The first battle we need to win is for public acceptance of a strategy that includes reducing the amount of waste generated and increasing the amount recycled. EPA is pushing a national goal of recycling 25% of all garbage within the next four years. But waste reduction and recycling aren't enough to stem the tide of trash that threatens to engulf us. We will continue to need safe landfilling of some garbage and incineration, preferably with energy recovery, as another option. EPA and the states are working to strengthen environmental controls on these facilities. The appropriate mix of waste reduction and recycling, landfilling and incineration should be "custom designed" by states and localities.

4   How can we all do our part? To begin with, we must recognize that we all contribute to the garbage problem. Next, we should cooperate in efforts to reduce the amount of trash requiring disposal. Finally, we must adopt new attitudes about disposal, because there will always be trash to be handled. This means that instead of simply opposing any new disposal facilities, citizens should assist in choosing the best options.

5   Recycling is the cornerstone of a sound waste-management strategy. We all have special responsibilities to make recycling work. Individuals must be willing to participate in local programs. Local governments should plan programs and operate

required facilities. States should do statewide planning and enforce their own laws and regulations. Industry should step up its recycling efforts. The federal government should provide national leadership, research and information-sharing as well as develop certain underlying regulations.

6   No one segment of society can, alone, lead us to victory in the war on garbage. Instead, we need a coordinated national effort to confront the solid-waste issue head-on.

From USA Today

Porter hints at his purpose in the first paragraph by noting that the disposal of garbage in landfills poses a problem. The last sentence of paragraph 2 states the purpose clearly. The remaining paragraphs name the strategies that he recommends to wage war on garbage and explain how individuals, government, and industry can all contribute. Everything Porter has written relates to his purpose.

Now examine the next paragraph, which does *not* have a firmly fixed specific purpose:

> Community is a sea in which people swim unconsciously, like fish. We fail to recognize our neighbors as fellow humans, and they show the same lack of fellow feeling for us. A complete lack of concern for one another is evident in today's complex society. What is community? Is it a plant? A building? A place? A state of being? Knowing what it is, we can see if such a place exists. To know community, one must realize who he or she is. Identity of a person is the first step in establishing a community.

This student writer can't decide what aspect of community to tackle. The opening sentence attempts a definition, but the next two veer onto the shortcomings of the modern community. Notice how aimlessly the thoughts drift. The vague leadoff sentence asserts "Community is a sea . . . ," but the later question "What is community?" contradicts this opening. Also, if community is a plant, a building, or a place, why must we realize who we are in order to know it? This contradictory and illogical paragraph reveals a writer groping for a purpose.

The paragraph, however, isn't a wasted effort. These musings offer several possibilities. By developing the first sentence, the writer might show some interesting similarities between community and a sea so that instead of taking community for granted, readers can see it in a new light. By pursuing the idea in the second and third sentences, the writer might show the callous nature of modern society to encourage readers to act more humanely. The last two sentences might lead to a statement on the relationship between individual and community in order to overcome the common view that the two are in conflict. A specific purpose can sometimes emerge from preliminary jottings.

The Audience for Your Writing

Everything you write is aimed at some audience—a person or group you want to reach. The ultimate purpose of all writing is to have an effect on a reader (even if that reader is you), and therefore purpose and audience are closely linked. Our discussion on this point clear by noting that your purpose can be to inform *someone* of something, to persuade *someone* to believe or do something, to express feelings or insights to *someone,* or to entertain *someone.* Any of these objectives requires that you *be able to define* that someone, the audience for your writing.

Writing operates on a delayed-action fuse, detonating its ideas in the readers' minds at a later time and place. Sometimes problems follow. In face-to-face conversations, you can observe your listeners' reactions, and whenever you note signs of hostility, boredom, or puzzlement, you can alter your tone, offer some examples, or ask a question. You can also use gestures and facial expressions to emphasize what you're saying. When you write, however, the words on the page carry your message. Once written work has left your hands, it's on its own. You can't call it back to clear up a misunderstanding or satisfy a disgruntled reader.

Establishing rapport with your audience is easy when you're writing for your friends or someone else you know a great deal about. You can then judge the likely response to what you say. Often, though, you'll be writing for people you know only casually or not at all: employers, customers, fellow townsfolk, and the like. In such situations, you'll need to assess your audience before starting to write and/or later in the writing process.

A good way to size up your readers is to develop an audience profile. This profile will emerge gradually as you answer the following questions:

1. What are the educational level, age, social class, and economic status of the audience I want to reach?
2. Why will this audience read my writing? To gain information? Learn my views on a controversial issue? Enjoy my creative flair? Be entertained?
3. What attitudes, needs, and expectations do they have?
4. How are they likely to respond to what I say? Can I expect them to be neutral? Opposed? Friendly?
5. How much do they know about my topic? (Your answer here will help you gauge whether you're saying too little or too much.)
6. What kind of language will communicate with them most effectively?

College writing assignments sometimes ask you to envision a reader who is intelligent but lacking specialized knowledge, receptive but unwilling to put up with boring or trite material. Or perhaps you'll be assigned, or choose, to write for a certain age group or one with particular interests. At other times, you'll be asked to write for a specialized audience—one with some expertise in your topic. This difference will affect what you say to each audience and how you say it.

The Effect of Audience on Your Writing

Let's see how audience can shape a paper. Suppose you are explaining how to take a certain type of X-ray. If your audience is a group of lay readers who have never had an X-ray, you might note at the outset that taking one is much like taking an ordinary photograph. Then you might explain the basic process, including the positioning of the patient and the equipment, comment on the safety and reliability of the procedure, and note how much time it takes. You probably would use few technical terms. If, however, you were writing for radiology students, you might emphasize exposure factors, film size, and required views. This audience would understand technical terms and want a detailed explanation of the procedure. You could speak to these readers as colleagues who appreciate precise information.

Audience shapes all types of writing in similar fashion, even your personal writing. Assume you've recently become engaged, and to share your news you write two letters: one to your minister, the other to your best friend back home. You can imagine the differences in details, language, and general tone of each letter. Further, think how inappropriate it would be if you accidentally sent the letter intended for one to the other. Without doubt, different readers call for different approaches.

Discourse Communities

Professionals often write as members of specific communities. For example, biologists with similar interests often exchange information about their research. The members of a community share goals, values, concerns, background information, and expectations, and this fact in turn affects how they write. Because such writing is closely tied to the interests of the community, professional articles often start with a section linking their content to previous research projects and articles. Often, too, custom dictates what information must be included, the pattern of organization, and the style the paper should follow. Throughout college, you will discover that part of learning to write is becoming familiar with the values and customs of different discourse communities. To do this, you'll need to read carefully in your major field, acquainting yourself with its current issues and concerns and learning how to write about them. As you start reading in any professional area, ask yourself these questions:

1. What are the major concerns and questions in this field?
2. What seems to be common knowledge?
3. To what works do writers regularly refer?
4. How do those in the field go about answering questions?
5. What methods do they follow?
6. Which kinds of knowledge are acceptable? Which are not?
7. What values seem to guide the field?
8. What kinds of information must writers include in papers?
9. How are different writing projects organized?
10. What conventions do writers follow?

We all, of course, belong to many different communities. Furthermore, a community can involve competing groups, conflicting values, differing kinds of writing projects, and varying approaches to writing. But as part of your growth as a writer and professional, you'll need to understand the goals and rules of any community you enter.

The following three excerpts deal with the same subject—antigens— but each explanation is geared to a different audience. Read the passages carefully; then answer the following questions:

1. What audience does each author address? How do you know?
2. Identify ways in which each author appeals to a specific audience.

1. The human body is quick to recognize foreign chemicals that enter it. "Foes" must be attacked or otherwise got rid of. The most common of these foes are chemical materials from viruses, bacteria, and other microscopic organisms. Such chemicals, when recognized by the body, are called *antigens.* To combat them, the body produces its own chemicals, protein molecules called *antibodies.* Each kind of antigen causes the production of a specific kind of antibody. Antibodies appear in the body fluids such as blood and lymph and in the body's cells.

    L. D. Hamilton, "Antibodies and Antigens," *The New Book of Knowledge*

2. [An] *antigen* [is a] foreign substance that, when introduced into the body, is capable of inducing the formation of antibodies and of reacting specifically in a detectable manner with the induced antibodies. For each antigen there is a specific antibody, the physical and chemical structure of which is produced in response to the physical and chemical structure of the antigen. Antigens comprise virtually all proteins that are foreign to the host, including those contained in bacteria, viruses, protozoa, helminths, foods, snake venoms, egg white, serum components, red blood cells, and other cells and tissues of various species, including man. Polysaccharides and lipids may also act as antigens when coupled to proteins.

    "Antigen," *Encyclopaedia Britannica*

    ———————————
    "Antigen," *Encyclopaedia Britannica,* 1974, I, 417.

3. The substance which stimulates the body to produce antibodies is designated antigen (antibody stimulator) . . .

    Most complete antigens are protein molecules containing aromatic amino acids, and are large in molecular weight and size. However, it has been demonstrated that other macromolecules, such as pure polysaccharides, polynucleotides, and lipids, may serve as complete antigens.

    However, certain other materials, incapable of stimulating antibody formation by themselves can, in association with a protein or other carrier, stimulate antibody formation and are the antigenic determinants. These determinants are referred to as *incomplete antigens* or *haptens* and they are able to react with antibodies which were produced by the determinant–protein complex.

    However, before an antigen can stimulate the production of antibodies, it must be soluble in the body fluids, must reach certain tissues in an unaltered form, and must be, in general, foreign to the body tissues. Protein taken by mouth loses its specific foreign-protein characteristics when digested in the alimentary tract. It reaches the tissues of the body as amino acids or other altered digested products of protein. Consequently, it no longer meets the requirements for antigenic behavior.

    Orville Wyss and Curtis Eklund, *Microorganisms and Man*

Just as you would not dial a telephone number at random and then expect to carry on a meaningful conversation, so you should not expect to communicate effectively without a specific audience in mind.

One other note: As you shape your paper, it is important that the writing please you as well as your audience—that it satisfy your sense of what good writing is and what the writing task requires. You are, after all, your own first reader.

The Qualities of Good Writing

Good writing is essential if you want your ideas to be taken seriously. Just as you would have trouble listening to someone with his shirt on backwards and wearing two different kinds of shoes, most readers dismiss out of hand writing that is disorganized, poorly worded, or marred by errors in grammar and spelling. In a world where most people are drowning under an information overload, few have the time or inclination to hunt through bad writing to search for quality ideas. Employers discard job seekers with poorly worded cover letters, badly written proposals are rejected, and few bother to read poorly written articles.

Three qualities—fresh thinking; a sense of style including the use of correct grammar and punctuations; and effective organization—help to ensure that a piece of prose will meet your reader's expectations.

Fresh Thinking   You don't have to astound your readers with something never before discussed in print. Genuinely unique ideas and information are rare. You can, however, freshen your writing by exploring personal insights and perceptions. Using your own special slant, you might show a connection between seemingly unrelated items, as does a writer who likens office "paper pushers" to different kinds of animals. Keep the expression of your ideas credible, however; far-fetched notions spawn skepticism.

Sense of Style   Readers don't expect you to display the stylistic flair of Maya Angelou or E. B. White. Indeed, such writing would impair the neutral tone needed in certain kinds of writing, such as technical reports and legal documents. Readers do, however, expect you to write in a clear style. And if you strengthen it with vivid, forceful words, readers will absorb your points with even greater interest. Readers also expect you to use standard grammar, spelling, and punctuation.

Effective Organization   All writing should be organized so it is easy to follow. A paper should have a beginning, a middle, and an end, that is, an introduction, a body, and a conclusion. The introduction sparks interest and acquaints the reader with what is to come. The body delivers the main message and exhibits a clear connection between ideas so that the reader can easily follow your thoughts. The conclusion ends the discussion so the reader feels satisfied rather than suddenly cut off. Overall, your paper should follow a pattern that is suited to its content and will guide the reader.

Freshness, style, and organization are weighted differently in different kinds of writing. A writer who drafts a proposal to pave a city's streets will probably attach less importance to fresh thinking than to clear writing and careful organization. On the other hand, fresh thinking can be very important in a description of an autumn forest scene.

Writing and Ethics

Think for a minute about how you would react to the following situation. You decide to vacation at a resort after reading a brochure that stressed its white-sand beach, scenic trails, fine dining, and peaceful atmosphere. When you arrive, you find the beach overgrown with weeds, the trails littered and the view unappealing, and the restaurant a greasy-spoon cafeteria. Worse, whenever you go outside, swarms of vicious black flies attack you. Wouldn't you feel cheated? Closer to home, think how you'd react if you decided to attend a college because of its distinguished faculty members only to discover upon arrival that they rarely teach on campus. The college counts on their reputations to attract students even though they are usually unavailable. Hasn't the college done something unethical?

As these examples show, good writing is also ethical writing. Like you, readers expect that what they read will be dependable information. Few if any would bother with a piece of writing that they realized was intended to deceive. A good test of the ethics of your writing is whether you would read your own work and act on the basis of it. Would you feel comfortable with it, or would you feel cheated, manipulated, deceived, or harmed in some way? By learning and practicing the principles of ethical writing, you will help ensure that your writing meets the standards your readers expect.

The Principles of Ethical Writing

- **Truthful** Writing perceived as truthful should *be* truthful. Granted, a writer may use humorous exaggeration to make us laugh, and some sales pitches may stretch the truth a bit in order to entice buyers. ("Try Nu-Glo toothpaste and add sparkle to your life.") But most readers recognize and discount such embellishments which, unlike major distortions, harm nobody. Deliberate, serious falsehoods, however, may harm not only the reader but sometimes the writer as well. Angered by the misrepresentations in the vacation brochure, you would certainly warn your friends against the resort and might even take some legal action against it.
- **Complete** Writing meant to be perceived as truthful should tell the whole truth, omitting nothing the reader needs to know in order to make informed decisions. The text should not be deliberately

incomplete so as to mislead. Suppose that a university's recruitment brochures stress that 97 percent of its students get jobs upon graduation. What the brochures don't say is that only 55 percent of the jobs are in the graduates' chosen fields despite strong employer demand for graduates in those areas. Clearly these brochures are deceptive, perhaps attracting students who would otherwise choose schools with better placement records.

- **Clear**   Writing should be clear to the reader. All of us know the frustration of trying to read a crucial regulation that is impossible to comprehend. A person who writes instructions so unclear that they result in harmful mistakes is partially responsible for the consequences. Readers have a right to expect understandable, accurate information. Thus, it would be deceptive for a group of state legislators to call a proposed bill the Public Education Enhancement Act when it would in fact bar teachers from belonging to unions.

- **No Harm**   Writing should not be intended to harm the reader. Certainly it is fair to point out the advantages of a product or service that readers might not need. Most people understand the nature of this type of advertising. But think how unethical it would be for a writer to encourage readers to follow a diet that the writer knew was not only ineffective but harmful. Think of the harm a writer might cause by attempting, deliberately, to persuade readers to try crack cocaine.

Plagiarism

Pivotal to ethics in writing is avoiding plagiarism. When you turn in a piece of writing, you designate it as your own work in your own words. If you have taken material from sources (including the Internet) without using the proper documentation, even if it is in your own words, it is plagiarism, an unacceptable practice for any writer. If you use another writer's language, even in part, without using quotation marks, you are also engaged in plagiarism. Most faculty members check carefully for plagiarism and many automatically fail a paper for academic dishonesty. Some even give the student an F for the entire course.

Why is this an important issue?

1. Other people have worked hard to develop ideas, do research, and write effectively. They deserve credit for their work when someone else uses it; it is their property. The authors of this text, for example, pay fees to use the essays of others. You would probably not like it if others used material from your papers without giving you credit.

2. Proper documentation strengthens your work since the source, often written by an expert, can add credibility to your claims if properly recognized.

3. If you take some material from a source and use it in your paper without documentation or quotation, you are falsely presenting another writer's

work as your own. It is not much different from cheating and simply presenting an entire paper purchased from the Internet as your own work.

4. You are in the process of being trained in college to be professionals. Professionals need to be ethical. You wouldn't want someone to take credit for the computer program you wrote, charge you for repairs they didn't make, or write you a ticket for a traffic violation you didn't commit. Journalists have been fired, politicians have lost elections, and companies have been sued because they have been involved in plagiarism.

5. You certainly cannot develop as a writer if your writing isn't mostly your own work.

How can you avoid plagiarism and the failing grade that often comes with it?

1. Be committed to honesty. You should make certain your writing is your own work.

2. If an assignment does not ask you to use sources but you believe information from sources would be useful, talk to your teacher. There may be a reason that you are not asked to use sources. If sources are acceptable, you may be asked to follow a specific procedure for that assignment such as turning in copies of your sources.

3. Be meticulous in documenting your sources, even if the material is in your own words, and in quoting and documenting any language that comes from another writer, even if it is only part of a sentence.

4. Carefully double-check to make certain that all the content in your text is your own and that if you used a source at all, it is documented.

5. Carefully double-check to make certain that all of your text uses your own language and that if you did use another writer's language, you used quotation marks.

6. If you are not sure about whether documentation or quotation marks are necessary, check with your teacher.

You must make a conscious effort to avoid plagiarism. Ignorance and carelessness are rarely accepted as an excuse by professors trying hard to make certain that students are graded fairly and no one gets credit for work that is not their own. If you follow the guidelines in this text and ask your teacher for help when you are confused, you will easily avoid the embarrassment and the often dire consequences of being accused of plagiarism.

Know your discourse community.

- What are shared questions?
- What counts as knowledge?
- What conventions do they follow?

Know your purpose.

- Are you going to inform, persuade, express yourself, entertain?
- What specific purpose do you want to accomplish?

Know your audience.

- What do they already know?
- Why will they read my writing?
- How are they likely to respond?
- How can I best reach them?

Apply principles of good writing.

- Write with fresh thinking that offers your own slant.
- Use a clear style in your own voice.
- Use effective organization.

Make certain your writing is ethical!

- Is your writing truthful, unslanted, complete, clear, helpful rather than harmful?
- Is your writing your own? Have you carefully avoided plagiarism?

Strategies for Successful Reading

Effective reading is not the passive process that many people imagine. On the contrary, it requires the ongoing interaction of your mind and the printed page. Bringing your knowledge and experience to bear on a piece of writing can help you assess its events, ideas, and conclusions. For example, an understanding of marriage, love, and conflict, as well as experience with divorce, can help readers comprehend an essay that explores divorce. As you read, you must also understand each point that's made, consider how the various parts fit together, and try to anticipate the direction the writing will take. Successful reading requires work. Fortunately, you can follow specific strategies to help yourself read better.

Orienting Your Reading

Different purposes require different approaches to reading. When reading for pleasure, you can relax and proceed at your own pace, slowing down to savor a section you especially enjoy, speeding up when you encounter less interesting material, and breaking off when you wish. Reading for information, for solid understanding, or to critique the writing calls for a more methodical approach. Even so there are some questions you should ask:

- **Why am I reading this material?** Is it for long-term use, as a reference for a project, as a building block to understanding more material?

From Chapter 2 of *Strategies for Successful Writing*, Ninth Edition. James A. Reinking, Robert von der Osten.

- **How well do I need to know the material in the article?** Can you look back to the article as a reference? Is there only one main point you need to know? Are you going to be tested on much of the material in depth?
- **Is some material in the article more important to me than other material?** Sometimes in doing research you may be looking for a specific bit of information that is only a paragraph in a long article. If so, you can skim for the information. In most things you read, some sections are more important than others. Often you can read to get the main points of the article and not focus on all the details. Sometimes, of course, you need to know the material in depth.
- **What will I need to do with the material from the article?** If you are looking for ideas for your own writing, you might read quickly. If you will be responsible for writing a critique of the article, you will need to read carefully and critically.
- **What kind of reading does the material suggest?** The significance, the difficulty, and the nature of the writing all can influence how you read. An easy humorous narrative can be read in a more leisurely fashion. A careful argument on an important issue merits careful attention to the main points and the evidence and may even require you to outline the argument.

Look briefly at "The Appeal of the Androgynous Man" later in this chapter. Identify three purposes you could have for reading this essay. Identify how these purposes would affect how you would read the essay and what you would look for in the essay.

A First Reading

You don't just jump in your car and take off. Usually you take a few minutes to think about where you want to go. Sometimes you even have to check your route. The same is true of effective reading. Because of the challenging nature of most college-level reading assignments, you should plan on more than one reading. A good first reading should orient you to the material.

Orient Yourself to the Background of the Essay Before you begin, scan any accompanying biographical sketch and try to determine the writer's expertise and views on the topic. Henry Jenkins' background as a university professor and director of the Comparative Media Studies graduate program at MIT along with his numerous publications on popular culture give additional weight to his article on video games "Art Form for the Digital Age." Sometimes there is material by the author or the editor on the writing of the essay. Professional essays often start with an abstract that provides a brief summary of the article. At this point you may want to judge the credibility of the source.

Use the Title as a Clue Most titles identify the topic and often the viewpoint as well. Thus "The Sweet Smell of Success Isn't All That Sweet" suggests that the author isn't overly impressed with the conventional attitudes toward success. Some titles signal the writer's primary strategy, whether it is a comparison, definition, or argument.

Skim to Get the Gist of the Article Sometimes you can just read the introductory and concluding paragraphs and the topic sentences (often the first or last sentences of paragraphs). Other times you will need to read the whole essay quickly. Try to gain an idea of the essay's main thrust, the key ideas that support it, and the ways that they are organized. In your first reading, you can skim the more difficult sections without trying to understand them fully.

Make Connections with What You Have Read When you've finished skimming the essay, and before you reread the essay, think about what you've learned and then, either by saying it to yourself or jotting it down, express it *in your own words.* You can hardly be said to understand what you've read, and you will be less likely to remember it, until you can state its essence in your own words. Go back and underline the thesis statement or, if one is not included, try to formulate one in your own words. Try to identify the strategy used by the writer. Also stop and identify what you already know about the topic and your connection to the issue. You will read more effectively if you can connect what you read to your own knowledge and interests. Jot down questions that the first reading has raised in your mind.

Reading Activities

1. Identify what you can about the background of the article "The Appeal of the Androgynous Man" from the statement about the author.
2. Write what you expect based on the title.
3. Skim the essay and then write down what you identify as the main points of the essay. Identify the essay's thesis. Jot down at least two questions you have.

Additional Readings

If the material was difficult or you need to know it well, a second or even third reading may be necessary. On the second reading, which will take more time than the first, you carefully absorb the writer's ideas.

Read Carefully and Actively Read at a pace suitable to the material. Underline significant topic sentences as well as other key sentences and ideas or facts that you find important, but keep in mind that underlining in itself doesn't ensure comprehension. Restating the ideas in your own words is more effective. Depending on your purposes, you may want to write down the main points in your own words or jot down the ideas in the margins. As you proceed, examine the supporting sentences to see how well they back up the main idea. Keep an eye out for how the essay fits together.

Consider Reading as a Kind of Conversation with the Text   Develop the habit of asking questions about facts, reasons, ideas—practically anything in the essay. Jot your queries and their answers in the margins. (You can see how a student interacted with the first page of Amy Gross's essay "The Appeal of the Androgynous Man.") Good writers anticipate your questions and answer them; and because you have posed the questions yourself, you are more likely to see the connections in the text. If the author hasn't answered your questions, there may be problems with the work. It can help to keep a reading log in a notebook or as a computer file where you jot down your ideas as you are reading.

Master Unfamiliar Words   At times, unfamiliar words can hinder your grasp of the material. Whenever you encounter a new word, circle it, use context to help gauge its meaning, check the dictionary for the exact meaning, and then record it in the margins or some other convenient place. If the writing is peppered with words you don't know, you may have to read the whole piece to figure out its general drift, then look up key words, and finally reread the material.

Take Conscious Steps to Understand Difficult Material   When the ideas of a single section prove difficult, restate the points of those sections you do understand. Then experiment by stating in your own words different interpretations of the problem section and see which one best fits the writing as a whole.

Sometimes large sections or entire texts are extremely difficult. There are several strategies you can use to help yourself.

- State the ideas that are easier for you to understand and use them as keys to unlock meanings that are difficult but not unintelligible. Save the most difficult sections until last. Don't think you have to understand everything completely. Some works take a lifetime to fully understand.
- Discuss a difficult essay with others who are reading it.
- Read simpler material on the topic.
- Go to your teacher for help. He or she may help you find background material that will make the selection easier.

Pull the Entire Essay Together   Whenever you finish a major section of a lengthy essay, express your sense of what it means. Speak it out loud or write it down. If you have trouble seeing the connections between ideas, try visually representing them. You might make an outline that states the main points followed by subpoints. For a comparison, you might create a table with the main points of the comparison side by side. You can make a drawing connecting the main ideas in a network, list the steps in an instruction, or write out the main facts.

To strengthen your grasp of material you'll need to remember for some time, try restating its main points a couple of days after the second reading. Sometimes it is helpful to explain the material to a sympathetic listener. If anything has become hazy or slipped your mind, reread the appropriate section(s). If you really must know the material, try making up your own test and giving it to yourself.

Mastering Reading Problems

Master the Problems That Interfere with Reading Many factors are important to effective reading. If your environment is too noisy, you are too tired, or you have something on your mind, you can have trouble reading. Do your reading at the time of day when you are most alert. Be sure you are in an environment that lets you concentrate and that is well lit. Try to be rested and comfortable. If you get tired, take a break for a specific time period; perhaps go for a short walk. If something else is bothering you, try to resolve the distraction or put it out of your mind. If you find the material uninteresting, try to find a connection between the topic and your interests and goals; read more actively.

If you have extensive problems reading for college, you can get help. Most colleges have courses in reading and tutors. College often requires a lot of reading, so take the steps necessary to be the most effective reader possible.

Reading Activities

1. Read "The Appeal of the Androgynous Man" a second time, continuing to write your own questions and notes in the margin.
2. Create a table with two columns comparing the all-man and the androgynous man.
3. Identify three words that you might find relatively new and find their definitions from the context and a dictionary.
4. Try explaining the article to a friend or your roommate.

Reading to Critique

In college you usually read not only to understand but also to evaluate what you read. Your instructors will want to know what you think about what you've read. Often you'll be asked whether you agree or disagree with a piece of writing. Sometimes you will be asked to write an explicit critique of what you read.

Merely because information and ideas are in print does not mean that they are true or acceptable. An essay, for example, might include faulty logic, unreasonable ideas, suspect facts, or unreliable authorities. Don't hesitate to dispute the writer's information.

- Does it match your experience?
- Do the pieces of evidence support the claim?
- Do the ideas appear reasonable?
- Are there other pieces of evidence or other works that contradict these claims?
- Do the ideas connect in a logical way?

Knowledge of the principles of argumentation and various reasoning fallacies can help you critique a piece of writing.

Reading Activities

Prepare your critique of "The Appeal of the Androgynous Man" by doing the following:

1. Identify where and how the claims don't match your experience.
2. Indicate where the evidence does not support the claims.
3. Indicate at least a few places where the ideas do not appear reasonable.
4. Identify any evidence that seems to contradict the author's claims.
5. Evaluate whether the ideas connect in a logical way.

Reading Assignments Carefully

Many students could get better grades by simply reading their assignments more carefully. In assignments, professors often indicate possible topics, suggest readers, identify the kinds of information that should and **should not** be included, set expectations on style and format, and establish procedures for the assignment such as the due date. You should read the assignment several times. Carefully note any specifications on topic, audience, organizational strategy, or style and format. Be sure to jot down procedures, such as due dates, in an assignment log or your calendar. Do not make assumptions. If you are not clear about a part of the assignment, ask your instructor.

Below is a very specific assignment; read it over carefully to determine what it requires.

Objective Description Short Assignment (50 points)

Typed final draft following the class format guide is due in class September 12. This assignment page should be turned in with your completed description:

The corner of Perry and State Street, near the Starr building has been the scene of a terrible accident. The insurance company has asked you to write a brief objective description (approximately 2 pages double spaced) of the intersection for a report for possible use in court. Your description should not try to take a position about the relative danger of the intersection but rather provide as clear a picture as possible of the situation. The description should include the arrangement of the streets including the number of lanes, the businesses located immediately around the intersection, traffic and pedestrian flow, and the timing of the lights and the effect of that timing on traffic.

Checklist:

The description should:

1. Provide the general location of the intersection.
2. Indicate their traffic function—i.e., major route from 131 into downtown Big Rapids.
3. Describe the actual roads.
4. Identify the businesses and their locations.
5. Describe traffic and pedestrian flow.
6. Detail the timing of the lights.
7. Maintain objective language.
8. Use clear, nontechnical language.

The assignment specifies the topic (a specific intersection), an audience (a court of law and an insurance company), key elements that are required as part of the description, a general style of writing (objective without taking a stance), and procedures including a deadline and format constraints. Clearly a short paper about the accident would not be acceptable since the assigned topic is the actual structure of the intersection. A style of writing that stressed the "horribly short lights that force students to scurry across like mice in front of a cat" would lose points since it takes a position and is not objective. Any description that left out any of the required elements (such as the timing of the lights) would also lose points.

Reading as a Writer

All of us who write can use reading as a springboard for improving our writing. You can do several things to make your reading especially useful.

As you read, the views of others, the experiences they relate, and the information they present often deepen your understanding of yourself, your relationships, and your surroundings. In turn, this broadened perspective can supply you with writing ideas. When possibilities surface, be sure to record them. Some writers keep a reading journal in which they summarize what they've read and jot down writing ideas that come to mind. In addition, you can take down specific ideas, facts, and perhaps even a few particularly telling quotations that you discover. You may want to incorporate this material into your writing at a later time. Carefully record the source so that you can document it properly in order to avoid plagiarism.

When you read various sources that explore the same topic or related topics, you may notice connections among their ideas. Since these connections can be fertile ground for a paper of your own, don't neglect to record them. Once you have jotted down these ideas, circle and label related thoughts. You can also draw a line linking the different thoughts to one another and to the main point that relates them. Express as a thesis statement your view of how these ideas fit together. Interacting with various sources and using their ideas to advance the purpose of your writing is a form of synthesis. When you proceed in this fashion, as in writing any paper, review your information, determine the points you want to make, and experiment until you find the order that works best. As you write, use the material from your sources as you would any support; be careful, however, to credit the authors properly in order to avoid plagiarism.

Let's see how you might use synthesis in writing an actual essay. Suppose, for example, you've read Amy Gross's "The Appeal of the Androgynous Man," Martin Gottfried's "Rambos of the Road," and Ellen Goodman's "The Company Man." You've noticed several connections among these essays. Gross describes "all-man" men who are insensitive in their treatment of women; Gottfried shows how some men need to assert their masculinity by driving aggressively; and Goodman characterizes a man who works himself to death. You might start your essay with Gross's definition of the "all-man" male and then cite some of her examples along with some of your own that identify how such a man would act. Next, you could stress that this particular concept of masculinity includes aggressiveness, then develop this point by using some illustrations from Gottfried's essay and from your own experience. Finally, you might conclude that being enslaved by such a narrow masculine role can have serious consequences and then support your view with material from Goodman's essay and your own observations. All of these ideas and examples could help you build an essay that points out how men can sometimes become desensitized or trapped, even victimized, by living according to stereotypes of masculinity. If you will be writing a paper that synthesizes material from various sources, be sure to document your sources properly.

Because writers solve problems, you'll want to pay attention to the techniques and strategies that other writers use. If you find an introduction, an organizational pattern, a transition, a certain description or comparison unusually engaging, study the writer's technique. Perhaps you can use it yourself. Similarly, observe when a piece of writing fails and try to determine why.

Reading Activities

1. Identify at least two strategies that the author used that you would find useful.
2. Identify at least two phrases that you found effective.
3. Identify at least two ideas that could spark your own writing.

AMY GROSS

both male and
female in one

The Appeal of the (Androgynous) Man

Amy Gross, a native of Brooklyn, New York, earned a sociology degree at Connecticut College. Upon graduation, she entered the world of fashion publishing and has held writing or editorial positions at various magazines, including Talk, Mademoiselle, Good Housekeeping, Elle, *and* Mirabella. *She is the newly appointed editor-in-chief of* O, the Oprah Magazine. *In our selection, which first appeared in* Mademoiselle, *Gross compares androgynous men favorably to macho "all-men."*

1   James Dean was my first androgynous man.[1] I figured I could talk to him. He was anguished and I was 12, so we had a lot in common. With only a few exceptions, all the men I have liked or loved have been a certain kind of man: a kind who doesn't play football or watch the games on Sunday, who doesn't tell dirty jokes featuring broads or chicks, who is not contemptuous of conversations that are philosophically speculative, introspective, or otherwise foolish according to the other kind of man. He is more self-amused, less inflated, more quirky, vulnerable and responsive than the other sort (the other sort, I'm visualizing as the guys on TV who advertise deodorant in the locker room). He is more like me than the other sort. He is what social scientists and feminists would call androgynous: having the characteristics of both male and female.

2   Now the first thing I want you to know about the androgynous man is that he is neither effeminate nor (hermaphroditic.) All his primary and secondary sexual characteristics are in order and I would say he's all-man, but that is just what he is not. He is more than all-man.   *both male and female sex organs*

3   The merely all-man man, for one thing, never walks to the grocery store unless the little woman is away visiting her mother with the kids, or is in the hospital having a kid, or there is no little woman. All-men men don't know how to shop in a grocery store unless it is to buy a 6-pack and some pretzels. Their ideas of nutrition expand beyond a 6-pack and pretzels only to take in steak, potatoes, scotch or rye whiskey, and maybe a wad of cake or apple pie. All-men men have absolutely no taste in food, art, books, movies, theatre, dance, how to live, what are good questions, what is funny, or anything else I care about. It's not exactly that the all-man's man is an uncouth illiterate. He may be educated, well-mannered, and on a first-name basis with fine wines. One all-man man I knew was a handsome individual who gave the impression of being gentle, affectionate, and sensitive. He sat and ate dinner one night while I was doing something endearingly feminine at the sink. At one point, he mutely held up his glass to indicate in a primitive, even ape-like, way his need for a refill. This was in 1967, before Women's Liberation. Even so, I was disturbed. Not enough to break the glass over his handsome head, not even enough to mutely indicate the whereabouts of the refrigerator, but enough to remember that moment in all its revelatory clarity. No androgynous man would ever brutishly expect to be waited on without even a "please." (With a "please," maybe.)

4   The brute happened to be a doctor—not a hard hat—and, to all appearances, couth. But he had bought the whole superman package, complete with that fragile beast, the male ego. The androgynous man arrives with a male ego

Does she favor androgynous men? What kind of appeal?

She will give a woman's perspective. She writes for and edits women's magazines.

Seems like she is going to talk about the advantages of androgynous men as compared to other men. Sees them as better.

Attempt to counter stereotype? Can't androgynous men also be effeminate?

Suggests "All-men" men reject behaviors and interests they consider feminine, but isn't she stereotyping? Are all these men like this? She seems to be exaggerating.

[1] James Dean (1931–1955) was a 1950s film star who gained fame for his portrayals of restless, defiant young men.

too, but his is not as imperialistic. It doesn't invade every area of his life and person. Most activities and thoughts have nothing to do with masculinity or femininity. The androgynous man knows this. The all-man man doesn't. He must keep a constant guard against anything even vaguely feminine (i.e., "sissy") rising up in him. It must be a terrible strain.

5   Male chauvinism is an irritation, but the real problem I have with the all-man man is that it's hard for me to talk to him. He's alien to me, and for this I'm at least half to blame. As his interests have not carried him into the sissy, mine have never taken me very far into the typically masculine terrains of sports, business and finance, politics, cars, boats and machines. But blame or no blame, the reality is that it is almost as difficult for me to connect with him as it would be to link up with an Arab shepherd or Bolivian sandalmaker. There's a similar culture gap.

6   It seems to me that the most masculine men usually end up with the most feminine women. Maybe they like extreme polarity. I like polarity myself, but the poles have to be within earshot. As I've implied, I'm very big on talking. I fall in love for at least three hours with anyone who engages me in a real conversation. I'd rather a man point out a paragraph in a book—wanting to share it with me—than bring me flowers. I'd rather a man ask what I think than tell me I look pretty. (Women who are very pretty and accustomed to hearing that they are pretty may feel differently.) My experience is that all-men men read books I don't want to see paragraphs of, and don't really give a damn what I or any woman would think about most issues so long as she looks pretty. They have a very limited use for women. I suspect they don't really like us. The androgynous man likes women as much or as little as he likes anyone.

7   Another difference between the all-man man and the androgynous man is that the first is not a star in the creativity department. If your image of the creative male accessorizes him with a beret, smock and artist's palette, you will not believe the all-man man has been seriously short-changed. But if you allow as how creativity is a talent for freedom, associated with imagination, wit, empathy, unpredictability, and receptivity to new impressions and connections, then you will certainly pity the dull, thick-skinned, rigid fellow in whom creativity sets no fires.

8   Nor is the all-man man so hot when it comes to sensitivity. He may be true-blue in the trenches, but if you are troubled, you'd be wasting your time trying to milk comfort from the all-man man.

9   This is not blind prejudice. It is enlightened prejudice. My biases were confirmed recently by a psychologist named Sandra Lipsetz Bem, a professor at Stanford University. She brought to attention the fact that high masculinity in males (and high femininity in females) has been "consistently correlated with lower overall intelligence and lower creativity." Another psychologist, Donald W. MacKinnon, director of the Institute of Personality Assessment and Research at the University of California in Berkeley, found that "creative males give more expression to the feminine side of their nature than do less creative men. . . . [They] score relatively high on femininity, and this despite the fact that, as a group, they do not present an effeminate appearance or give evidence of increased homosexual interests or experiences. Their elevated scores on femininity indicate rather an openness to their feelings and emotions, a sensitive intellect and understanding self-awareness and wide-ranging interests including many which in the American culture are thought of as more feminine. . . ."

10   Dr. Bem ran a series of experiments on college students who had been categorized as masculine, feminine, or androgynous. In three tests of the degree of nurturance—warmth and caring—the masculine men scored painfully low

(painfully for anyone stuck with a masculine man, that is). In one of those experiments, all the students were asked to listen to a "troubled talker"—a person who was not neurotic but simply lonely, supposedly new in town and feeling like an outsider. The masculine men were the least supportive, responsive or humane. "They lacked the ability to express warmth, playfulness and concern," Bem concluded. (She's giving them the benefit of the doubt. It's possible the masculine men didn't express those qualities because they didn't possess them.)

11   The androgynous man, on the other hand, having been run through the same carnival of tests, "performs spectacularly. He shuns no behavior just because our culture happens to label it as female and his competence crosses both the instrumental [getting the job done, the problem solved] and the expressive [showing a concern for the welfare of others, the harmony of the group] domains. Thus, he stands firm in his opinion, he cuddles kittens and bounces babies and he has a sympathetic ear for someone in distress."

12   Well, a great mind, a sensitive and warm personality are fine in their place, but you are perhaps skeptical of the gut appeal of the androgynous man. As a friend, maybe, you'd like an androgynous man. For a sexual partner, though, you'd prefer a jock. There's no arguing chemistry, but consider the jock for a moment. He competes on the field, whatever his field is, and bed is just one more field to him: another opportunity to perform, another fray. Sensuality is for him candy to be doled out as lure. It is a ration whose flow is cut off at the exact point when it has served its purpose—namely, to elicit your willingness to work out on the field with him.

13   Highly masculine men need to believe their sexual appetite is far greater than a woman's (than a nice woman's). To them, females must be seduced: Seduction is a euphemism for a power play, a con job. It pits man against woman (or woman against man). The jock believes he must win you over, incite your body to rebel against your better judgment: in other words—conquer you.

14   The androgynous man is not your opponent but your teammate. He does not seduce: he invites. Sensuality is a pleasure for him. He's not quite so goal-oriented. And to conclude, I think I need only remind you here of his greater imagination, his wit and empathy, his unpredictability, and his receptivity to new impressions and connections.

Writing About What You Read

Often in college you will be asked to write about what you read. This culminates in the Research Paper. However, sometimes you will have to write shorter summaries and critiques.

Writing a Summary

A summary states the main points of an essay in *your own words*. A good summary lets someone who hasn't read the essay understand what it says. A summary can be one or more paragraphs. It should

- provide a context for the essay,
- introduce the author of the essay,
- and state the thesis, (these first three elements often form the introduction of a multiparagraph summary)

- then state the main points of the essay (sometimes but not always based on the topic sentences),
- and conclude by pulling the essay together.

To prepare to write a summary, follow the steps in effective reading. A brief outline of the main points will make it easy to write a summary. Be careful to avoid using the author's exact wording without using quotation marks. Also, don't interject your views. A summary should reflect only the author's words.

A Sample Single Paragraph Summary of "The Appeal of the Androgynous Man"

What kind of man should appeal to women? According to Amy Gross, the editor-in-chief of *O* magazine, in "The Appeal of the Androgynous Man," her ideal is and the ideal of women should be the "androgynous man," a man who shares the personality characteristics of both male and female. To make her point, Amy Gross contrasts the all-man man and the androgynous man. She believes that the all-man man does not share in activities like shopping, has no taste in the arts, is imperialistic, resists anything feminine, and is interested in only exclusively male topics. Worse, she points to studies that show that more masculine men are less creative. Further, she argues that the all-man tends to see women as something to conquer rather than as partners. The androgynous man, by comparison, is very different. He does not resist things that are feminine and so shares in domestic activities, is comfortable with the arts, and can share interests with women. He is shown by studies to be more creative. Further, according to Gross, "The androgynous man is not your opponent but your teammate." As a result, she concludes that the androgynous man has the qualities that women should really look for in a man.

Writing a Critique

Often you will be asked to give your views on an essay, indicating where you agree and disagree with the author's position. Remember you can always agree with part of what a person says and disagree with other parts. A critique combines a summary of the article with your thoughtful reaction. Most critiques consist of several paragraphs. A critique usually includes

- a context for the essay
- an introduction to the author
- a statement of the essay's thesis
- the thesis for your critique
- a summary of the essay
- a statement of the points with which you agree
- a statement with reasons and evidence for your disagreement
- a conclusion

You are well prepared to write a critique if you follow the steps for reading effectively and reading critically.

A Sample Multiparagraph Critique of "The Appeal of the Androgynous Man"

1   What kind of man should appeal to women? According to Amy Gross, the editor-in-chief of O magazine, in "The Appeal of the Androgynous Man," her ideal is and the ideal of women should be the "androgynous man," a man who shares the personality characteristics of both male and female. But matters are not so simple. Amy Gross falsely divides men into two stereotyped categories. In fact, real men are much more complex.

2   To make her point, Amy Gross contrasts the all-man man and the androgynous man. She believes that the all-man man does not share in activities like shopping, has no taste in the arts, is imperialistic, resists anything feminine, and is interested in only exclusively male topics. Worse, she points to studies that show that more masculine men are less creative. Further, she argues that the all-man tends to see women as something to conquer rather than as partners. The androgynous man, by comparison, is very different. He does not resist things that are feminine and so shares in domestic activities, is comfortable with the arts, and can share interests with women. He is shown by studies to be more creative. Further, according to Gross, "The androgynous man is not your opponent but your teammate." As a result, she concludes that the androgynous man has the qualities that women should really look for in a man.

3   She is right that if the all-man male was like she said, he would truly be undesirable. No woman should want a partner who takes her for granted, doesn't share her interests, or treats her simply as someone to conquer. But is that really what men are like? My brother plays football and loves to watch it on television. He also hunts and fishes. But that isn't all he does. He plays with kittens, loves to cook, plays the guitar and sings, and secretly likes "chick flicks." As far as I can tell, he treats his girlfriend well. He seems genuinely concerned about her, will spend hours shopping with her, goes to events that interest her, and generally seems sensitive to her needs. Is he an "all-man" or an "androgynous man"? Equally a man can write poetry, love Jane Austen, cook gourmet meals, and still take women for granted. From what I have read, Pablo Picasso treated women dreadfully, even if he was a great artist. Was he an "all-man" man or an "androgynous man"?

4   Ms. Gross seems to present evidence from psychological studies that show that more masculine men are less creative than more feminine

men. Maybe so, but she doesn't give us the evidence we need to make up our own minds. How did they actually measure masculinity and femininity? How many people were tested? What did they count as creativity? Personally I have my doubts. Writers such as Ernest Hemingway and Norman Mailer were pretty masculine men and yet were still very creative. I know a lot of men who have feminine characteristics who aren't any more creative than the average person.

5   The mistake Ms. Gross makes is that she believes that women should select types of men. They shouldn't. Women date, love, and marry individual men. As a result, a woman should really be concerned about whether the man shares her interests, treats her well, has qualities she can love, and will be faithful. Where the man fits on Ms. Gross's little chart is far less important than the kind of man he is, regardless of whether he is "androgynous."

Successful Reading

Why you are reading the material.

Enjoyment	To use specific info	Responsible for the material

Read at your own pace.	Skim and then slow down at key info when you take notes.	■ Orient to background. ■ Use title as clue. ■ Skim-use intro and conclusion. ■ State the main ideas in your own words.

Read again more carefully.

- Underline topic sentences, key info.
- Write important material in own words.
- Jot down questions and ideas in margins or separate pages.

Outline if it will help you follow ideas.	As you finish major sections write down or say the major ideas.

Master more difficult material.

- Use context or look up unfamiliar words.
- State easier ideas and use them to unlock difficult material.
- Discuss material with others.
- If necessary read easier background material.

Read as a writer.

- Jot down ideas for writing.
- Identify techniques you like.
- Make a note of organizational patterns.

Writing a summary	Writing a critique

Take notes of main points. Identify any disagreements.

Planning and Drafting Your Paper

Planning and Drafting
Your Paper

Many students believe that good essays are dashed off in a burst of inspiration by born writers. Students themselves often boast that they cranked out their top-notch papers in an hour. Perhaps. But for most of us, writing is a process that takes time and work.

Writing is a flexible process. No one approach works for every writer. Some writers establish their purpose and draft a plan for carrying it out at the start of every project. Others begin with a tentative purpose or plan and discover their final direction as they write. As a project proceeds, the writer is likely to leapfrog backward and forward one or more times rather than to proceed in an orderly, straightforward sequence. Partway through a first draft, for instance, a writer may think of a new point to present, then pause and jot down the details needed to develop it. Similarly, part of the conclusion may come to mind as the writer is gathering the details for supporting a key idea.

Regardless of how it unfolds, the writing process consists of the following stages. Advancing through each stage will guide you if you have no plan or if you've run into snags with your approach. Once you're familiar with these stages, you can combine or rearrange them as needed.

Understanding the assignment
Zeroing in on a topic
Gathering information
Organizing the information
Developing a thesis statement
Writing the first draft

Types of Writers

Planners	Explorers
Start with a focused idea. Usually have a clear plan. Tend to develop existing plan.	Discover ideas while writing. Often follow out inspirations. Can develop tangents. Usually write more than final.
Can write like an outline. May tend to underdevelop. Can miss possible ideas.	Can go off on tangents. May initially lack obvious organization. Usually have more than needed.
Can benefit from additional brainstorming. May need additional development. May need to explore ideas outside plan.	May need to plan after drafting. Might need several revisions. Might need to refocus and cut.

Understanding the Assignment

Instructors differ in making writing assignments. Some specify the topic; some give you several topics to choose from; and still others offer you a free choice. Likewise, some instructors dictate the length and format of the essay, whereas others don't. Whatever the case, be sure you understand the assignment before you go any further.

Think of it this way: If your boss asked you to report on ways of improving the working conditions in your office and you turned in a report on improving worker benefits, would you expect the boss's approval? Following directions is crucial, so if you have any questions about the assignment, ask your instructor to clear them up right then. Don't be timid; it's much better to ask for directions than to receive a low grade for failing to follow them.

Once you understand the assignment, consider the project *yours*. If you are asked to describe a favorite vacation spot for a local newspaper, here is your chance to inform others about a place special to you. By asking yourself what the assignment allows you to accomplish, you can find your own purpose.

Zeroing In on a Topic

A subject is a broad discussion area: sports, college life, culture, and the like. A topic is one small segment of a subject, for example, testing athletes for drug use, Nirvana College's academic probation policy, the Web-surfing phenomenon. If you choose your own topic, pick one narrow enough so that you can develop it properly within any length limitation. Avoid sprawling, slippery issues that lead to a string of trite generalities.

In addition, choose a familiar topic or one you can learn enough about in the time available. Avoid overworked topics such as arguments about the death penalty or the legal drinking age, which generally repeat the same old points. Instead, select a topic that lets you draw upon your unique experiences and insights and offer a fresh perspective to your reader.

Strategies for Finding a Topic

Whenever your instructor assigns a general subject, you'll need to stake out a limited topic suitable for your paper. If you're lucky, the right one will come to mind immediately. More often, though, you'll need to resort to some special strategy. Here are six proven strategies that many writers use. Not all of them will work for everyone, so experiment to find those that produce a topic for you.

Tapping Your Personal Resources Personal experience furnishes a rich storehouse of writing material. Over the years, you've packed your mind with memories of family gatherings, school activities, movies, concerts, plays, parties, jobs, books you've read, TV programs, dates, discussions, arguments, and so on. All these experiences can provide suitable topics. Suppose you've been asked to write about some aspect of education. Recalling the difficulties you had last term at registration, you might argue for better registration procedures. Or if you're a hopeless TV addict who must write on some advertising topic, why not analyze video advertising techniques?

Anything you've read in magazines or journals, newspapers, novels, short stories, or textbooks can also trigger a topic. Dan Greenburg's "Sound and Fury," in which a potentially explosive situation is defused, might suggest a paper on some dangerous encounter in your past. An article reviewing the career of a well-known politician might stir thoughts of a friend's experience in running for the student council.

EXERCISE

Select five of the subjects listed below. Tapping your personal resources, name one topic suggested by each. For each topic, list three questions that you might answer in a paper.

Life on a city street	Some aspect of nature
A particular field of work	Contemporary forms of dancing
Some branch of the federal bureaucracy	Youth gangs
Concern for some aspect of the environment	Fashions in clothing
Saving money	Trendiness
Home ownership	Human rights
Schools in your town	Public transportation
Leisure activities	Childhood fears
Trends in technology	A new scientific discovery
A best-selling book	A religious experience

Keeping a Journal   Many writers, not comfortable relying on their memories, record their experiences in a journal—a private gathering of entries accumulated over time. Journal keeping provides an abundance of possible writing topics as well as valuable writing practice.

The hallmark of the journal entry is the freedom to explore thoughts, feelings, responses, attitudes, and beliefs without reservation and without concern for "doing it right." *You* control the content and length of the entry. Furthermore, depending on your instructor's preference, you usually don't have to worry about correct spelling or grammar. Journal writing does not represent a finished product but rather an exploration.

A few simple guidelines ensure effective journal entries:

1. Write in any kind of notebook that appeals to you; the content, not the package, is the important thing.
2. Write on a regular basis—at least five times a week, if possible. In any event don't write by fits and starts, cramming two weeks' entries into one sitting.
3. Write for ten to twenty minutes, longer if you have more to say. Don't aim for uniform entry length, for example, three paragraphs or a page and a half. Simply explore your reactions to the happenings in your life or to what you have read, heard in class, or seen on television. The length will take care of itself.

Let's examine a typical journal entry by Sam, a first-year composition student.

Last week went back to my hometown for the first time since my family moved away and while there dropped by the street where I spent my first twelve years. Visit left me feeling very depressed. Family home still there, but its paint peeling and front porch sagging. Sign next to the porch said house now occupied by Acme Realtors. While we lived there, front yard lush green and bordered by beds of irises. Now an oil-spattered parking lot. All

the other houses on our side of the street gone, replaced
by a row of dumpy buildings housing dry cleaner, bowling
alley, hamburger joint, shoe repair shop, laundromat. All of
them dingy and rundown looking, even though only a few
years old.

　　　　Other side of the street in no better shape. Directly across
from our house a used-car dealership with rows of junky
looking cars. No trace left of the Little League park that
used to be there. Had lots of fun playing baseball and learned
meaning of sportsmanship. To left of the dealership my old grade
school, now boarded and abandoned. Wonder about my fifth-grade
teacher Mrs. Wynick. Is she still teaching? Still able to make
learning a game, not a chore? Other side of dealership the
worst sight of all. Grimy looking plant of some sort pouring foul
smelling smoke into the air from a discolored stack. Smoke made
me cough.

　　　　Don't think I'll revisit my old street again.

This journal entry could spawn several essays. Sam might explore the causes of
residential deterioration, define sportsmanship, explain how Mrs. Wynick made
learning a game, or argue for stricter pollution control laws.

*Write journal entries over the next week or two for some of the
following items that interest you. If you have trouble finding a
suitable topic for a paper, review the entries for possibilities.*

Encounters with technology　　　　　　Developing relationships
Single or married life　　　　　　　　　Parents
Financial or occupational considerations　Ideas gained through reading

Sorting Out a Subject　　All of us sort things. We do it whenever we tackle the
laundry, clear away a sinkful of dishes, or tidy up a basement or garage. Sorting
out a subject is similar. First, we break our broad subject into categories and subcategories, then allow our minds to roam over the different items and see what
topics we can turn up. The chart shows what one student found when she
explored the general topic of public transportation.

As you'll discover for yourself, some subjects yield more topics than others; some, no topics at all.

Select two of the following subjects, then subdivide those two into five topics.

Advertising	Movies	The space program
Dwellings	Occupations	Sports
Fashions	Popular music	Television programs
Magazines	Social classes	Vacations

Asking Questions   Often, working your way through these basic questions will lead you to a manageable topic:

1. Can I define my subject?
2. Does it break into categories?
3. If so, what comparisons can I make among these categories?
4. If my subject is divided into parts, how do they work together?
5. Does my subject have uses? What are they?
6. What are some examples of my subject?
7. What are the causes or origins of my subject?
8. What impact has my subject had?

Let's convert these general questions into specific questions about telescopes, a broad general subject:

1. What is a telescope?
2. What are the different kinds of telescopes?
3. How are they alike? How do they differ?
4. What are the parts of each kind of telescope, and how do they work together?
5. What are telescopes used for?
6. What are some well-known telescopes?
7. Who invented the telescope?
8. What impact have telescopes had on human life and knowledge?

Each of these questions offers a starting point for a suitably focused essay. Question 3 might launch a paper comparing reflecting and refracting

Results of Sorting Out the Subject Public Transportation

Land			Water		Air	
Buses	Taxis	Trains	Seagoing	Lake, River	Airplanes	Helicopters
County bus services for the handicapped	Rights of passengers	The Orient Express, the Twentieth Century Limited	The Titanic	Barge Cruises	Airline deregulation	Air taxis
	Preventing crimes against drivers		Luxury liners		Overbooking flights	Cargo
Bus tours		Monorails	Theme Cruises			
Jitney buses		Preventing subway crimes	Modern sea pirates		Making air travel safer	
Improving bus terminals		Guardian Angels	Traveling by freighter		Coping with hijacking	
Designing buses to accommodate the handicapped		Amtrak	The impact of overseas flights on ship travel		Causes and prevention of jet lag	
		Japan's high-speed trains			Development of the stealth bomber	
		Deterioration of railroad track beds			Noise pollution around airports	

telescopes; question 6 might be answered in a paper about the Hubble Space Telescope and the problems with it.

Select two of the following subjects. Create general questions, then convert them into specific questions. Finally, suggest two essay topics for each of your two subjects.

Astrology	Games	Shopping malls
Books	Microorganisms	Stars
Colleges	Plays	Television
Emotions	Religions	Warships

Freewriting   The freewriting strategy snares thoughts as they race through your mind, yielding a set of sentences that you then look over for writing ideas. To begin, turn your pen loose and write for about five minutes on your general subject. Put down everything that comes into your head, without worrying about grammar, spelling, or punctuation. What you produce is for your eyes alone. If the thought flow becomes blocked, write "I'm stuck, I'm stuck . . ." until you break the mental logjam. When your writing time is up, go through your sentences one by one and extract potential topic material. If you draw a blank, write for another five minutes and look again.

The following example shows the product of one freewriting session. Drew's instructor had assigned a two- or three-page paper on technology; and since Drew is a business major, he considers a more personal technology with which he has experience, the cell phone.

> Technology, huh. What do I know about technology? Cell phones are technology? What about them? There are so many kinds. Razors, Blacberries. I love my new i-phone. It does everything, plays music, lets me text, check out U-tube, e-mail, take pictures and store them. They change people lives. But how? Well, we are always on them talking to friends, to anybody, and parents and teachers never get it. But why do we talk on them so much. Stuck, stuck, stuck. Well, I keep in touch with friends. Some are way at college. My girlfriend is always calling me. We also get lots of stuff done, like checking out my stupid bills.

This example suggests at least three papers. For people shopping for a new cell phone, Drew could identify the advantages of different types. He could write to people considering buying an i-phone about the features of the phone. He could write to those perplexed by student behavior to explain why students use cell phones so extensively.

Brainstorming   Brainstorming, a close cousin of freewriting, captures fleeting ideas in words, fragments, and sometimes sentences, rather than in a series of sentences. Brainstorming garners ideas faster than the other strategies do. But unless you move immediately to the next stage of writing, you may lose track of what some of your fragmentary jottings mean.

To compare the results of freewriting and brainstorming a topic, we've converted our freewriting example into this list, which typifies the results of brainstorming:

Types of cell phones	stores pictures
Razors	text message
Blackberries	e-mails
i-phones	why people use e-mail
plays music	to coordinate life
view u-tube	to get things done
takes pictures	to keep in touch

Return to the five subjects you selected for the previous exercise. Freewrite or brainstorm for five minutes on each one; then choose a topic suitable for a two- or three-page essay. State your topic, intended audience, and purpose.

Narrowing a familiar subject may yield not only a topic but also the main divisions for a paper on it. Drew's freewriting session uncovered several possible cell phone topics as well as a way of approaching each: classifying types of cell phones and writing about the strengths and weaknesses of each or identifying the different features of an i-phone and describing each feature and how it works or explaining each of the reasons college students use cell phones so frequently. Ordinarily, though, the main divisions will emerge only after you have gathered material to develop your topic. Drew, on considering his options, decides he doesn't know enough about types of cell phones and might get carried away when writing about the i-phone. He decides to write about the reasons college students are so attached to their cell phones.

Identifying Your Audience and Purpose

You can identify your purpose and audience at several stages in the writing process. Sometimes both are set by the assignment and guide your selection of a topic. For example, you might be asked to write the college president to recommend improvements in the school's registration system. At other times, you may have to write a draft before you can determine either. Usually, though, the selection of audience and purpose goes hand in hand with determining a topic. Think of the different types of information Drew would gather if he wrote for

(1) college students to break them of their cell phone habits, (2) college professors and parents to make cell phone use seem less peculiar, (3) a sociology professor to demonstrate how common behaviors can be explained through sociological theories.

Gathering Information

Once you have a topic, you'll need things to say about it. This supporting material can include facts, ideas, examples, observations, sensory impressions, memories, and the like. Without the proper backup, papers lack force, vividness, and interest and may confuse or mislead readers. The more support you can gather, the easier it will be for you to write a draft. Time spent gathering information is never wasted.

Strategies for Gathering Information

If you are writing on a familiar topic, much of your supporting material may come from your own head. Brainstorming is the best way to retrieve it. With unfamiliar topics, brainstorming won't work. Instead, you'll have to do some background reading. Whatever the topic, familiar or unfamiliar, talking with friends, parents, neighbors, or people knowledgeable about the topic can also produce useful ideas.

Brainstorming   Brainstorming a topic, like brainstorming a subject, yields a set of words, fragments, and occasionally sentences that will furnish ideas for the paper. Drew has decided that he wants to demonstrate to professors and parents that there are good reasons for student cell phone use. He generated the following list through brainstorming.

students open cell phones after class	weather updates
coordinating life	sending e-mails
meeting friends for study sessions	sending pictures by e-mail
arranging a lunch date	holding up a phone at a concert
getting a ride	calling when something funny happens
coordinating a team project	keeping in touch
getting things done	old friends in different colleges
resolving bill disputes	boyfriends or girlfriends
scheduling car repairs	text messaging
finding babysitters	playing music

You can see how some thoughts have led to others. For example, the first jotting, "arranging a lunch date" leads naturally to the next one, "getting a ride." and "keeping in touch" leads to "old friends in different colleges."

Branching is a helpful and convenient extension of brainstorming that allows you to add details to any item in your list. Here's how you might use this technique to approach "cell phone use":

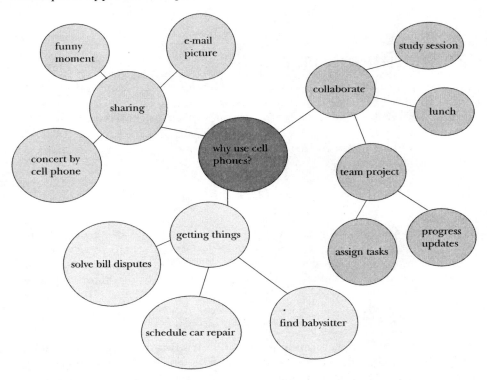

Don't worry if your brainstorming notes look chaotic and if some seem irrelevant. Sometimes the most unlikely material turns out to be the freshest and most interesting. As you organize and write your paper, you'll probably combine, modify, and omit some of the notes, as well as add others. Drew decides from his brainstorming that "playing music," "sending e-mails," and "getting weather updates" are too specific to only a few kinds of cell phones and should not be part of his paper.

Prepare a brainstorming sheet of supporting details for one of the topics you developed for the previous exercise.

Reading When you have to grapple with an unfamiliar topic, look in the library for material to develop it. Before going there, however, you will need to unearth promising references to investigate. Once you have a list of references, start searching for the books or articles. Look through each one you find and jot down information that looks useful, either as direct quotations or in your own words.

Whenever you use a direct quotation or rephrased material in your paper, you must give proper credit to the source. If you don't, you are guilty of plagiarism, a serious offense that can result in a failing grade for the course or even expulsion from college.

Talking with Others   You can expand the pool of ideas gained through brainstorming or reading by talking with some of the people around you. Imagine you're writing a paper about a taxpayers' revolt in your state. After checking the leading state newspapers at the library, you find that most of the discontent centers on property taxes. You then decide to supplement what you've read by asking questions about the tax situation in your town.

Your parents and neighbors tell you that property taxes have jumped 50 percent in the last two years. The local tax assessor tells you that assessed valuations have risen sharply and that state law requires property taxes to keep pace. She also notes that this situation is causing some people on fixed incomes to lose their homes. A city council member explains that part of the added revenue is being used to repair city streets, build a new library wing, and buy more fire-fighting equipment. The rest is going to the schools. School officials tell you they're using their extra funds to offer more vocational courses and to expand the program for learning-disabled students. As you can see, asking questions can broaden your perspective and provide information that will help you to write a more worthwhile paper.

Organizing the Information

If you have ever listened to a rambling speaker spill out ideas in no particular order, you probably found it hard to pay attention to the speech, let alone make sense of it. So, too, with disorganized writing. A garbled listing of ideas serves no one; an orderly presentation highlights your ideas and helps communication succeed.

Your topic determines the approach you take. In narrating a personal experience, such as a mishap-riddled vacation, you'd probably trace the events in the order they occurred. In describing a process, say caulking a bathtub, you'd take the reader step by step through the procedure. To describe a hillside view near your home, you might work from left to right. Or you could first paint a word picture of some striking central feature and then fan out in either direction. Other topics dictate other patterns, such as comparison and contrast, cause and effect, and illustration.

You can best organize long pieces of writing, such as library research papers, by following a formal outline. For shorter papers, however, a simple, informal system of *flexible notes* will do nicely.

The Flexible Notes System

To create a set of flexible notes, write each of your key points at the top of a separate sheet of paper. If you have a thesis statement, refer to it for your key points. Next, list under each heading the supporting details that go with that heading. Drop details that don't fit and expand points that need more support. When your sheets are finished, arrange them in the order you expect to follow in your essay. Drew's notes for the cell phone paper look like this:

Coordinating Activities

Meeting friends for a study session
Arranging a lunch date
Getting a ride
Coordinating a team project

Getting Things Done

Resolving bill disputes
Scheduling car repairs
Finding babysitters

Sharing

Sending pictures by e-mail
Holding up phone at concert
Call about something funny happening

Keeping in Touch

Old friends in different colleges
Boyfriends and girlfriends
Text messaging

Since coordinating activities, getting things done, sharing, and keeping in touch are equivalent reasons, this listing arranges them according to their probable importance—starting with the most important reason from the point of view of the audience.

Now you're ready to draft a plan showing how many paragraphs you'll have in each part of the essay and what each paragraph will cover. Sometimes the number of details will suggest one paragraph; other times you'll need a paragraph block—two or more paragraphs. Here's a plan for Drew's cell phone essay:

Coordinating Activities

Meeting for study session
Arranging a lunch date
Getting a ride
Corrdinating a team project

Getting Things Done

Resolving bill disputes
Scheduling car repairs
Finding a babysitter

Sharing

Sending pictures by e-mail
Holding up phone at concert
Calling about a funny event

Keeping in Touch

Old friends in different colleges	} By voice
Boyfriends and girlfriends	
Text messaging	} By text

These groupings suggest one paragraph about coordinating activities, one about getting things done, one about sharing, and two about keeping in touch.

Organize into flexible notes the supporting details that you prepared for the previous exercise. Arrange your note pages in a logical sequence and draft a plan showing the number and content of the paragraphs in each section.

Creating an Outline

With longer essays or if it fits your organizational style, it can be helpful to develop an outline. An outline can show you how to organize and develop your paragraphs. In an outline, you organize your essay into major units using Roman numerals (I, II, III), letters (A, B, C), and numbers to show the structure you will use in the paper. Introductions and conclusions are not usually included in the outline. There are two kinds of outlines. A topic outline simply states the main topic to be addressed in a section.

    I. Coordinating Activities
       A. Meeting friends for study sessions
          1. Setting the time
          2. Making certain everyone gets there
       B. Arranging a lunch date
          1. Deciding where everyone is meeting
          2. Arranging a ride to lunch

II. Getting Things Done
   A. Coordinating a team project
      1. Assign tasks
      2. Monitor progress
   B. Resolving bill disputes
      1. Call during business hours

Topic outlines will quickly let you know if you have enough information for a paragraph. If under one major heading, you only have one letter or under a letter only one number as in II B you may need to do more brainstorming.

In a sentence outline, you make full statements or sentences that can often be used in your paper. A sentence outline makes you think about what you really want to say.

I. Cell phones can be used to coordinate activities that would be otherwise difficult to coordinate given students' busy schedules.
   A. Cell phones can help students find out where a study session is being held.
   B. Often there is a complex schedule of classes, work, meals, and meetings to organize.
   C. Cell phones can let members of a team project keep the project on track.

To develop your outline, you take your brainstorming or notes and mark the major units as I, II, III based on the main ideas they demonstrate. Then start to develop your outline, identifying the major points for each major heading (I, II . . .) and the next major points (A, B, C). You can use your outline as a goad to additional planning as you see the holes. You should rarely have an A without a B or a 1 without a 2.

Developing a Thesis Statement

A thesis statement presents the main idea of a piece of writing, usually in one sentence. The thesis statement points you in a specific direction, helping you to stay on track and out of tempting byways. In addition, it tells your reader what to expect.

Thesis statements can emerge at several points in the writing process. If an instructor assigns a controversial topic on which you hold strong views, the statement may pop into your head right away. At other times it may develop as you narrow a subject to a topic. Occasionally, you even have to write a preliminary draft to determine your main idea. Usually, though, the thesis statement emerges after you've gathered and examined your supporting information.

As you examine your information, search for the central point and the key points that back it up; then use these to develop your thesis statement. Converting the topic to a question may help you to uncover backup ideas and write a thesis statement.

For example:

Topic: The commercial advantages of computerized data storage systems.

Question: What advantages do computerized data storage systems offer business?

Thesis statement: Computerized data storage systems offer business enormous storage capacity, cheap, instant data transmission almost anywhere, and significantly increased profits.

The thesis statement stems from the specifics the student unearthed while answering the question.

Below are some key strategies that can help you develop a thesis statement.

- Identify your main topic.
- Review your notes or research and identify the specific, major claims you want to make about your topic.
- Select those claims that will be the focus and organizational structure of the paper. You may need to outline first.
- Combine the major claim or claims with the topic in a statement that represents the main point of your paper.

Requirements of a Good Thesis Statement

Unless intended for a lengthy paper, a thesis statement *focuses on just one central point or issue.* Suppose you prepare the following thesis statement for a two- or three-page paper:

Centerville College should reexamine its policies on open admissions,

vocational programs, and aid to students.

This sprawling statement would commit you to grapple with three separate issues. At best, you could make only a few general remarks about each one.

To correct matters, consider each issue carefully in light of how much it interests you and how much you know about it. Then make your choice and draft a narrower statement. The following thesis statement would do nicely for a brief paper. It shows clearly that the writer will focus on *just one issue:*

Because of the rising demand among high school graduates for job-related

training, Centerville College should expand its vocational offerings.

A good thesis statement also *tailors the scope of the issue to the length of the paper.* No writer could deal adequately with "Many first-year college students face crucial adjustment problems" in two or three pages. The idea is too broad to yield more than a smattering of poorly supported general statements. Paring it down to "Free time is a responsibility that challenges many first-year college students," however, results in an idea that could probably be developed adequately.

A good thesis statement further provides *an accurate forecast of what's to come.* If you plan to discuss the effects of overeating, don't say, "Overeating stems from deep-seated psychological factors and the easy availability of convenience foods." Such a statement, incorrectly suggesting that the paper will focus on causes, would only mislead and confuse your reader. On the other hand, "Overeating leads to obesity, which can cause or complicate several serious health problems" accurately represents what's to follow.

Finally, a good thesis statement is *precise, often previewing the organization of the paper.* Assertions built on fuzzy, catchall words like *fascinating, bad, meaningful,* and *interesting,* or statements like "My paper is about . . ." tell neither writer nor reader what's going on. To illustrate:

- New York is a fascinating city.
- My paper is about no-fault divorce.

These examples raise a host of questions. Why does the writer find New York fascinating? Because of its skyscrapers? Its night life? Its theaters? Its restaurants? Its museums? Its shops? Its inhabitants? And what about no-fault divorce? Will the writer attack it, defend it, trace its history, suggest ways of improving it? To find out, we must journey through the paper, hoping to find our way without a roadmap sentence.

Now look at the rewritten versions of those faulty thesis statements:

- New York's art museums offer visitors an opportunity to view a wide variety of great paintings.
- Compared to traditional divorce, no-fault divorce is less expensive, promotes fairer settlements, and reflects a more realistic view of the causes of marital breakdown.

These statements tell the reader not only what points the writer will make but also the order they will follow.

In brief, your thesis statement should

- focus on just one central point or issue.
- narrow the scope of the issue to what is manageable.
- provide an accurate forecast of what is to come.
- often preview the organization of the paper.

Your thesis statement should **not**

- be too vague or general.
- include more than you can reasonably manage in a paper.
- suggest a different focus or organization than you follow in your paper.
- use clichéd and excess wording like "In this paper I will discuss . . ."

Omission of Thesis Statement

Not all papers have explicit thesis statements. Narratives and descriptions, for example, sometimes merely support some point that is unstated but nevertheless clear, and professional writers sometimes imply their thesis rather than state it openly. Nonetheless, a core idea underlies and controls all effective writing. Usually it is best to state that core idea in a thesis statement.

Changing Your Thesis Statement

Before your paper is in final form, you may need to change your thesis statement several times. If you draft the thesis statement during the narrowing stage, you might change it to reflect what you uncovered while gathering information. Or you might amend it after writing the first draft so that it reflects your additions and deletions. Drew in his first rough draft thought "In the end this cell phone mania is a necessary part of college life" was an adequate thesis statement. In revising his draft, however, he realized that it was not precise enough to direct his readers. He added a more precise statement that identified the main reasons addressed in his paper to serve as his thesis: "They use cell phones to coordinate the day's activitites, to get some business done, to share life's events, and to keep in touch."

Tentative or final, formulated early or late, the thesis statement serves as a beacon that spotlights your purpose.

1. **Write a thesis statement for the flexible notes that you developed for the previous exercise.**

2. **Reread "Requirements of a Good Thesis Statement"; then explain why each of the following does or does not qualify as an effective thesis statement for a two- or three-page essay.**

   a. My paper discusses the problem of employee absenteeism in American industry. *NO*

   b. Living on a small island offers three advantages: isolation from city problems, the opportunity to know your neighbors, and the chance to go fishing whenever you want. *yes – the three things are close enough together.*

   c. Although I don't know much about running a college, I know that Acme College is not run well. *NO*

   d. Increasing federal outlays for education will help us construct needed school buildings and create a better-trained workforce. *NO*

   e. Many people, wanting simpler and slower-paced lives, have abandoned highpaying executive positions for lower-paying, less stressful jobs. *yes*

   f. Vacationing in Britain is a nice way to spend a summer. *NO*

   g. Extending Middletown's intracity transit system will save consumers money, reduce pollution, and increase city revenues. *NO – to big of an idea*

   h. Most cable TV companies provide subscribers with several specialized-program channels. *NO – to vague*

3. **Revise the following five weak thesis statements.**

   a. The first year of college can be hard.

   b. FaceBook offers lots of features.

   c. My paper discusses the importance of writing for college students.

   d. Global warming is changing the weather.

   e. In this paper I will talk about how wireless phones do more than ever.

Writing the First Draft

Now on to the first draft of your essay. The writing should go rather quickly. After all, you have a topic you're qualified to write about, a thesis statement that indicates your purpose, enough information to develop it, and a written plan to follow. But sometimes when you sit down to write, the words won't come; and all you can do is doodle or stare at the blank page. Perhaps the introduction is the problem. Many writers are terrified by the thought of the opening paragraph. They want to get off to a good start but can't figure out how to begin. If this happens to you, additional brainstorming or freewriting can make you more comfortable and may suggest an opening. Keep in mind that any lead-in you write now can be changed later. If these suggestions don't solve your problem, skip the introduction for the time being. Once you have drafted the body of the paper, an effective opening should come more easily.

Here are some general suggestions for writing a first draft:

1. Stack your thesis statement, flexible notes, and written plan in front of you. They will start you thinking.

2. Skip every other line (double-space) and leave wide margins. Then you'll have room to revise later.

3. Write quickly; capture the drift of your thoughts. Concentrate on content and organization. Get your main points and supporting details on paper in the right sequence. Don't spend time correcting grammatical or punctuation errors, improving your language, or making the writing flow smoothly. You might lose your train of thought and end up doodling or staring again.

4. Take breaks at logical dividing points, for example, when you finish discussing a key point. Before you start to write again, scan what you've written.

Now for some specific suggestions that will help you with the actual writing:

1. Rewrite your thesis statement at the top of your first page to break the ice and build momentum.

2. Write your first paragraph, introducing your essay and stating your thesis. If you get stuck here, move on to the rest of the paper.

3. Follow your plan as you write. Begin with your first main point and work on each section in turn.

4. Look over the supporting details listed under the first heading in your flexible notes. Write a topic sentence stating the central idea of the paragraph.

5. Turn the details into sentences; use one or more sentences to explain each one. Add other related details, facts, or examples if they occur to you.

6. When you move from one paragraph to the next, try to provide a transitional word or sentence that connects each paragraph.

7. Write your last paragraph, ending your essay in an appropriate fashion. If you get stuck, set your conclusion aside and return to it later.

Writing a draft isn't always so systematic. If you are inspired, you may want to abandon your plans and simply use your first draft to explore ideas. You can always revise, so don't be overly concerned if you get off track. You might uncover some of your best material during this type of search.

Using the plan you prepared for the previous exercise, write the first draft of an essay.

Drew now uses his thesis statement and paragraph-by-paragraph plan to write the following draft. Notice that Drew, like many writers, gets off track. That is a common occurrence at this stage and can even be a step in generating new ideas. It isn't something to reject. Drew knows even as he writes that he will need to make significant revisions.

CASE HISTORY

Cell Phone Use
Rough Draft

Students open their cell phones almost before they are out of the room. It confuses professors and parents. My parents complain that young people are so wrapped up in their cell conversations that they completely miss the world around them. Why are students such non-stop cell phone users? It looks ridiculous when large numbers of college students wander around talking into their phones, ignoring the people around them. In the end this cell phone mania is a necessary part of college life.

It is hard to imagine how people managed their lives without cell phones since there seems to be so much to get done. Weren't friends going to meet after class for a study session? Where is everybody? Life in College can be crazy. We juggle complex schedules, work, meals. A quick phone call can organize it all. We arrange study sessions, confirm a lunch date, get a ride, coordinate a team project for class, and maybe even make time for a date.

Students, like everyone else, need to call about possible jobs, resolve disputes over bills, arrange to have theirs car fixed, find out the results of medical tests, and even, in some cases, find babysitters. Sometimes walking back to the dorm from a night class, students are on the phone simply to feel safer so that if anything happens they can let someone else know and perhaps get help. Cell phones let them get all this done.

Cell phones let us be together at the same time, even if we are in different places. Part of the reason for such widespread cell phone use is that instead of having to wait. A quick phone call has one person getting out of bed while another is getting out of class. Two friends seated at different ends of a stadium can enjoy the blow by blow of the action at the same time.

Continued on next page

(Continued from previous page)

Everyone likes to share. Cell phones let people share. Many phones even let you take a picture and send it by e-mail to a friend. It is because of this practice that cell phones are banned in some locker rooms and why it is dangerous to be caught in an embarrassing situation at a party. You never know what can be e-mailed to your friends or even posted to the Internet. At concerts some in the audience call up friends and then hold up the phone so that they can hear part of a concert. When something really funny is happening, anyone can with a quick call share it with someone else who would appreciate the moment. L.O.L. Cell phones allow an instant connection, a voice instant messenger.

Cell phone calls let people reach out and touch each other. Most phone calls are very short. "Hey, what's up"? "What are you doing"? "How are you"? Little information is exchanged. "Nothing much," in fact, is a common answer. What do such phone calls accomplish? They let people keep in touch with each other.

Text messaging is really a very handy way to keep in touch. Even if you can't reach the other person, you can leave a message to let you know that you are thinking about them. Other people keep in touch through MySpace or Face Book which lets friends know what is going on with each others lives, even long lost friends. Face Book can even be a great space for sharing since you can post pictures, blog your ideas, identify your favorite group or more. If anything, college students of today can be considered the in touch generation.

It must have been weird to wait an entire day before bragging to friends and family about getting the only A on a Chemistry test. It is almost impossible that students managed the complex schedule of their days before cell phones. It should not be surprising that students talk on their cell phones over nothing.

Planning and Drafting with a Computer

Using a computer with word-processing software allows you to compose, save what you write, insert new material, delete unwanted material, move sections around, and when you are ready, print copies.

Prewriting

When you are using your computer to generate ideas for your paper, do not be lulled into treating your work as a draft. If the spell and grammar check slow you down, turn them off and then turn them on again when you are writing an actual draft or proofreading. There are many ways to use your computer to generate ideas. Since you are not writing a draft but getting ideas, do not be afraid of being messy.

- Generate a list of ideas or key points you may want to make and then go back and add whatever details or ideas come to mind about those points.
- Freewrite, pull out the best ideas, and then either on the same page by inserting material or as part of different files freewrite about those ideas and repeat as necessary.
- Convert your set of questions into specific questions related to the broad subject area, and then enter them and your responses to the question into either the same page or different files for each question, depending how much material you might have.
- Keep a file or two for jotting down ideas for papers, observations about a topic, and even sentences that come to mind.
- Create a table of the main points you want to consider, such as a table for a comparison or argument, and then fill in the table with the details and ideas you will want to include in your paper.
- Use other approaches to get ideas. Some writers get ideas by discussing issues in a chat room, writing e-mails, or participating in listservs. Remember that if you take ideas from a source, you need to document the information, even if it is something you discovered in a chat room or on a listserv.

Of course, you will want to find your own techniques that work best with your style. Don't be wedded to your computer. Word-processing programs are organized in very specific text-based ways. If you are visually oriented or benefit from clustering, use regular paper and leave the computer for drafting.

Planning

Computers are excellent tools for organization. However, you should use the computer in a way that suits your own writing style. If you need to write a very rough draft without a preestablished program, let it rip. Recognize that the computer will make it easier to revise later. However, if you do benefit from a plan, you can easily create a plan on your computer and experiment with it by deleting, adding, and moving material until you have your points in the order that makes the most sense for you. You can build your draft by inserting material in the appropriate section of your plan. Some individuals who prefer formal outlines create an outline using the outline view of their program and then fill it in later. If you have created multiple files or sections as you generated ideas and made notes, you can label those sections and from this see how the ideas fit together to form a pattern.

Drafting

Do not let the final look on the screen fool you into being overly meticulous. When you are writing a draft, you know you will revise later, so you can afford to experiment. If you are writing and want to come back to a section later to develop an idea or try a different approach, mark it with an asterisk and then continue to write. You can leave gaps you fill in later. If you have more than one idea for a section, write down the other approaches, either bracketed on the same page or as a separate file. Always save each draft in a separate file, if not in a hard copy. You may want to use parts of an early draft in a later version.

Planning and Drafting Your Paper

Understand the assignment.

- Understand the topic.
- Identify key expectations.
- Make the project yours.

Find your topic.

- Talk with others.
- Keep a journal.
- Sort out the subject into categories.
- Brainstorm.

Identify audience, purpose.

Develop details.

Read, talk to others, and brainstorm.

Organize the information.

- Create labeled flexible notes.
- Develop a rough plan—a list of points in order.
- Write a quick draft to find your focus and pattern.

Develop a focused thesis.

- Focus on just one central point or issue.
- Provide an accurate forecast of what is to come.

Draft to capture your thoughts—expect to revise.

Revising and Editing Your Paper

From Chapter 4 of *Strategies for Successful Writing*, Ninth Edition. James A. Reinking, Robert von der Osten.

Revising and Editing
Your Paper

All of us at one time or another have said something careless to a friend, date, or partner and then spent the rest of the night regretting our words. In contrast, when we write we can make sure we say exactly what we mean. Good writers don't express themselves perfectly on the first try, but they do work hard at revising their initial efforts.

Just what is revision? Don't confuse it with proofreading or editing, the final stage of the writing process, where you carefully inspect your word choice, spelling, grammar, and punctuation. Revision is much more drastic, often involving an upheaval of your draft as you change its content and organization in order to communicate more effectively.

Most of what you read has been considerably altered and improved as the writers progressed through early drafts. This fact shouldn't surprise you. After all, a rough copy is merely a first attempt to jot down some ideas in essay form. No matter how well you gather and organize your material, you can't predict the outcome until you've prepared a draft. Sometimes only touch-up changes are required. More often though, despite your efforts, this version will be incomplete, unclear in places, possibly disorganized. You might even discover an entirely different idea, focus, or approach buried within it. During revision you keep changing things—your focus, approach to the topic, supporting material, and thesis statement—until the results satisfy you.

Inexperienced writers often mistakenly view initial drafts as nearly finished products rather than as experiments to alter, or even scrap, if need be. As a result, they often approach revision with the wrong attitude. To revise successfully, you need to control your ego and your fear and become your own first critical reader. Set aside natural feelings of accomplishment ("After all, I've put a great deal of thought into this") and dread ("Actually, I'm afraid of what I'll find if I look too closely"). Instead, recognize that revision offers an opportunity to upgrade your strong features and strengthen your weak ones.

Preparing to Revise

To distance yourself from your writing and sharpen your critical eye, set your first draft aside for at least a half day, longer if time permits. When you return to it, gear up for revision by jotting down your intended purpose and audience before you read your paper. These notations will help keep your changes on track. In addition, note any further ideas that have occurred to you.

The right attitude is vital to effective revision. Far too many students hastily skim their essays to reassure themselves that "Everything sounds O.K." Avoid such a quick-fix approach. If your draft appears fine on first reading, probe it again with a more critical eye. Try putting yourself in your reader's place. Will your description of a favorite getaway spot be clear to someone who has never seen it? Will your letter home asking for money really convince parents who might think they've already given you too much? Remember: If you aren't critical now, anticipating confusion and objections, your reader certainly will be later.

Read your essay at least three times, once for each of these reasons:

To improve the development of the essay as a whole

To strengthen paragraph structure and development

To sharpen sentences and words

When you finish reading your paper for content, make a final, meticulous sweep to search for errors and problems that mar your writing. Note your own special weaknesses, perhaps some problem with punctuation or a failure to provide specific support.

Considering the Whole Essay

If you inspect your draft only sentence by sentence, you can easily overlook alternative directions for your work, gaps in the text, or how the parts work together. A better approach is to step back and view the overall essay rather than its separate parts, asking questions such as "Is there any entirely new direction to take the paper, perhaps following up on a section that works especially well?" "Does the beginning mesh with the end?" "Does the essay wander?" "Has anything been left out?" In this way you can find new approaches and gauge how part and whole relate.

Use the acronym *FACT* to guide this stage of your revision.

F. Ask yourself first whether the whole essay *FITS* together, presenting a central point for a specific audience. Have you delivered what the thesis statement promises? First drafts often include paragraphs, or even large sections, that have little bearing on the main point. Some drafts contain the kernels of several different essays. Furthermore, one section of a draft might be geared to one audience (parents, for example) and another section to an entirely different audience (students, perhaps). As you read each part, verify its connection to your purpose and audience. Don't hesitate to chop out sections that don't fit, redo stray parts so they accord with your central idea, or alter your thesis statement to reflect better your supporting material. Occasionally, you might even expand one small, fertile section of your draft into an entirely new essay.

A. Whenever we write first drafts, we unwittingly leave out essential material. We often produce text based on our own knowledge and assume far too much, leaving large holes, "writer-based prose." We need to revise these drafts to produce much more complete texts that meet the needs of our readers, "reader-based prose." As we revise, we need to identify and fill these inevitable gaps. Ask yourself: "Where will the reader need more information or examples to understand my message?" "Where do I need to explain things more fully?" "What major ideas have I left out?" It can be helpful to reread your notes or do some additional brainstorming. *ADD* the appropriate sentences, paragraphs, or even pages.

C. First drafts often contain material that fits the thesis but doesn't contribute to the essay. Writing quickly, we tend to repeat ourselves, include uninteresting or uninformative examples, and crank out whole paragraphs when one clear sentence would suffice. As you revise, *CUT* away this clutter with a free hand. Such paring can be painful, especially if you're left with a skimpy text, but your message will emerge with much greater clarity. As you've probably guessed, revising a draft often requires both adding and cutting.

T. Carefully *TEST* the organization of your essay. The text should flow smoothly from point to point with clear transitions between the various ideas. Test the organization by outlining your major and minor points, then checking the results for logic and completeness. Alternatively, read the draft and note its progression. Look for spots where you can clarify connections between words and thus help your readers.

There are nine different writing strategies, each concluding with revision questions geared specifically to that strategy. Use these questions, together with the *FACT* of revision, to help you revise more effectively.

Drew carefully reconsiders his rough draft. As we indicated there, the draft needs extensive work.

FIT. While most of Drew's paper fits his audience and thesis, the material concerning the misuses of the cell phone to e-mail pictures and instant messenger slang like L.O.L. don't match his audience or purpose. It is offtrack, raises unnecessary suspicion about cell phone use, and is too informal for the audience.

ADD. If Drew really wishes to convince a skeptical audience that student cell phone use is necessary, he needs to make his examples more detailed. The material on using cell phones to be together at the same time and keeping in touch are especially scanty, but each paragraph could be more fully explained with more detailed examples.

CUT. The paragraph on text messaging may fit the topic but it is different in kind from voice communication. Cutting that paragraph will allow the paper to be more focused on a single type of cell phone use.

TEST. If the paper is going to be organized according to the order of importance to the audience, it would make sense to put a paragraph on sharing after "getting business done" and "keeping in touch" before "together at the same time." A careful review of the flow of the paragraphs shows that the third paragraph lacks a clear transitional topic sentence.

It is crucial that you view revision not as a hasty touch-up job or as a quick sweep through your draft just prior to handing it in. Instead, revision should be an ongoing process that often involves an upheaval of major sections as you see your draft through your reader's eyes and strive to write as well as you can.

As you read your own essay, note on a separate sheet of paper problems to solve, ideas to add, and changes to try. When you mark the actual essay, make your job easier by using these simple techniques:

1. To delete something, cross it out lightly; you may decide to resurrect it later.

2. To add a section of text, place a letter (*A, B, C, D*) at the appropriate spot and write the new material on a separate sheet, keyed to the letter. Make changes within sections by crossing out what you don't want and writing the replacement above it or nearby.

3. To rearrange the organization, draw arrows showing where you want things to go, or cut up your draft and rearrange the sections by taping them on new sheets of paper. Use whatever method works best for you.

When you finish revising your draft, you might want to team up with one or more classmates and read one another's work critically. The fresh eye you bring to the task can uncover shortcomings that would otherwise go unnoticed.

1. *List Drew's other options for revising this draft; then indicate the necessary changes if he had decided to write for fellow college students.*
2. *Use the FACT acronym to revise the draft you prepared for the previous exercise.*

CASE HISTORY

**Cell Phone Use
Rough Draft Marked up**

At the end of their class,
Students open their cell phones almost before they are out of the room. It con-
flip   *are greatly confused by this practice and*
fuses professors and parents. My parents complain that young people are so
Some
wrapped up in their cell conversations that they completely miss the world
Most wonder   *are compulsive*
around them. why students such non-stop cell phone users? It looks
The   *ing*
ridiculous when large numbers of college students wander around talking
may seem ridiculous to
into their phones, ignoring the people around them. In the end this cell phone
outsiders. However,
mania is a necessary part of college life.
*There are many reasons students wander around campus talking into the air.
They use cell phones to coordinate the day's activities, to get some business
done, to share life's events, and to keep in touch.*

It is hard to imagine how people managed their lives without cell phones

since there seems to be so much to get done. Weren't friends going to meet
                                       Add Ⓐ
after class for a study session? Where is everybody? Life in College can be
hectic as students   *of classes*   *and a social life*
crazy. We juggle complex schedules, work, meals. A quick phone call can

organize it all. We arrange study sessions, confirm a lunch date, get a ride,

coordinate a team project for class, and maybe even make time for a date.
Add Ⓑ
Students, like everyone else, need to call about possible jobs, resolve dis-

putes over bills, arrange to have theirs car fixed, find out the results of med-
There is often a lot to get done that has to be squeezed into a busy day.
ical tests, and even, in some cases, find babysitters. Sometimes walking back

to the dorm from a night class, students are on the phone simply to feel safer

so that if anything happens they can let someone else know and perhaps get

help. Cell phones let them get all this done. *in the time between classes or even
while walking back to their dorm, leaving them with more time for other things like
studying or going out with friends.*

Cell phones let us be together at the same time, even if we are in different

places. Part of the reason for such widespread cell phone use is that instead
We can be part of the immediate now.
of having to wait. A quick phone call has one person getting out of bed while

another is getting out of class. Two friends seated at different ends of a
Anyone can know what almost anyone else their call list is doing at any moment.
stadium can enjoy the blow by blow of the action at the same time.

Everyone likes to share. Cell phones let people share. Many phones even
moments of delight, success, and even failures with others who care.
let you take a picture and send it by e-mail to a friend. It is because of this
When a baby is expected, the soon to be grandparents
practice that cell phones are banned in some locker rooms and why it is dan-
can't wait for the call
gerous to be caught in an embarrassing situation at a party. You never know
what can be e-mailed to your friends or even posted to the internet. At concerts some in the audience call up friends and then hold up the phone so that
they can hear part of a concert. When something really funny is happening,
anyone can with a quick call share it with someone else who would appreci-
to let people experience what you
ate the moment. L.O.L. Cell phones allow an instant connection, a voice
are experiencing, whether it is excitement over a success, an idea, the finals of
instant messenger.
a sporting event, or a newscast.
Add ©

Cell phone calls let people reach out and touch each other. Most phone
calls are very short. "Hey, what's up?" "What are you doing?" "How are you?"
Little information is exchanged. "Nothing much," in fact, is a common answer.
What do such phone calls accomplish? They let people keep in touch with
each other.

Text Messaging is really a very handy way to keep in touch. Even if you
can't reach the other person, you can leave a message to let you know that you
are thinking about them. Other people keep in touch through MySpace or Face
Book which lets friends know what is going on with each others lives, even
long lost friends. Face Book can even be a great space for sharing since you
can post pictures, blog your ideas, identify your favorite group or more. If anything, college students of today can be considered the in touch generation.

It must have been weird to wait an entire day before bragging to friends and
incomprehensible
family about getting the only A on a Chemistry test. It is almost impossible
that students managed the complex schedule of their days before cell phones.
snap open   at the
It should not be surprising that students talk on their cell phones over nothing.
*drop of almost anything. The surprise would be if they kept their cell phones in
their pockets and waited. Add* ©

*What did a student do if a ride didn't show up? How did a couple share the
excitement of a concert in the moment or a good joke if they had to wait days?
Earlier generations who seem puzzled by the cell phone fever that has hit college
campuses might wonder how they might have felt without a phone, having to wait
for weeks for the mail or longer for a visit.*

Continued on next page

61

Continued from previous page

A.   A quick cell phone call to a friend reveals that the study session was moved to the student center. Does everyone have his or her part ready for the presentation speech class at 3:00 p.m.? A flurry of cell phone calls makes certain everyone is ready. Will Collin be able to meet his girlfriend this afternoon? He needs to call to see if she is still free. Where is Jennifer since she said she was picking me up in front of the Science Building?

B.   Sometimes cell phone calls get important business done. Heather needs to convince her parents that she really, really needs more money to cover the cost of books. Tim needs to contact his advisor so he can schedule for the next semester.

C.   If you got an A on a paper that you thought would get an F, you can quickly spread the celebration to anyone who would echo your joy while the feeling was still hot. Sometimes a cell phone call can make the sharing very concrete, getting someone to go outside to look at a spectacular meteor shower, getting a friend to change channels so they can see an interview with a favorite rock star, or letting family know about a terrible earthquake in China.

D.   Contact is what helps keep people close. Parents like their children to visit. Couples need to make time for each other. When people keep in touch, it lets them know that others care, lets them keep each other as important parts of their lives. Some students call their parents every day keeping the family ties tight, getting the emotional reassurance of those loving connections. Sometimes it seems like couples seem to be holding electronic hands as they walk across campus, with little room for some interloper to break up their relationships. Friends may not be able to see each other since they are going to different colleges, but a simple cell phone lets them each know the others are still friends.

CASE HISTORY

**Cell Phone Use
Second Draft**

Clarified classroom
by adding class.

      At the end of their class, students flip open their cell phones almost before they are out of the room. Professors and parents are confused by this practice. Some complain that young people are so wrapped up in their cell conversations that they completely miss the world around them. Most wonder why students are compulsive cell phone users. There are many reasons students wander around campus talking into the air. They use cell phones to coordinate the day's activities, to get some business done, to share life's events, and to keep in touch. The large number of college students wandering around talking into their phones, ignoring the people around them, may seem ridiculous to outsider. However, in the end this cell phone mania is a necessary part of college life.

It is hard to imagine how people managed their life without cell phones since there is so much to coordinate. Weren't friends going to meet after class for a study session? Where is everybody? A quick cell phone call to a friend reveals that the study session was moved to the student center. Does everyone have his or her part ready for the presentation in Speech class at 3:00 p.m.? A flurry of cell phone calls makes certain everyone is ready. Will Collin be able to meet his girlfriend this afternoon? He needs to call to see if she is still free. Where is Jennifer since she said she was picking me up in front of the Science Building? Life in College can be hectic as students juggle complex schedules of classes, work, meal times, and a social life. A quick phone call can organize it all; arrange study sessions, confirm a lunch date, arrange a ride, coordinate a team project for class, and maybe even make time for a date.

Sometimes cell phone calls get important business done. Heather needs to convince her parents that she really, really needs more money to cover the cost of books. Tim needs to contact his advisor since he needs to lift his holds so he can schedule for the next semester. Students, like everyone else, need to call about possible jobs, resolve disputes over bills, arrange to have their car fixed, find out the results of medical tests, and even, in some cases, find babysitters. There is often a lot to get done that has to be squeezed into a busy day. Sometimes walking back to the dorm from a night class, students are on the phone simply to feel safer so that if anything happens they can let some-one else know and perhaps get help. Cell phones let them get all this done in the time between classes or even while walking back to their dorm, leaving them with more time for other things like studying or going out with friends.

Everyone likes to share moments of delight, success, and even failure with others who care. When a baby is expected, the soon to be grandparents can't wait for the call. Cell phones let people share. Many phones even let you take a picture and send it by e-mail to a friend. At concerts some in the audience call up friends and then hold up the phone so that they can hear part of a concert. When something really funny is happening, anyone can with a quick call share it with someone else who would appreciate the moment. If you got an A on a paper that you thought would get an F, you can quickly spread the celebration

Continued on next page

Added thesis statement that outlines paper order.

Provided more detailed account of cell phone use helped.
Placed academic material first for audience.

Clarified what was complex.

Added a transitional thesis statement.
Added more specific examples to appeal to audience.

Added context that relates to understanding of reader. Moved sharing paragraph up to make order of material. Cut material on inappropriate use of phone picture that might offend audience. Added more concrete examples appropriate to target audience.

Continued from previous page

to anyone who would echo your joy while the feeling was still hot. Sometimes a cell phone call can make the sharing very concrete, getting someone to go outside to look at a spectacular meteor shower, getting a friend to change channels so they can see an interview with a favorite rock star, or letting family know about a terrible earthquake in China. Cell phones allow an immediate connection to let people experience what you are experiencing, whether it is excitement over a success, an idea, the finals of a sporting event, or a news event.

Cell phone calls let people stay in touch with each other. Most phone calls are very short, over before students have gotten from the classroom to the door of the building. "Hey, what's up?" "What are you doing?" "How are you?" Little information is exchanged and little is really shared. "Nothing much," in fact, is a common response. What do such phone calls accomplish? They let people keep in touch with each other. Contact is what helps keep people close. Parents like their children to visit. Couples need to make time for each other. When people keep in touch, it lets them know that others care, lets them keep each other as important parts of their lives. Some students call their parents every day keeping the family ties tight, getting the emotional reassurance of those loving connections. Sometimes it seems like couples seem to be holding electronic hands as they walk across campus, with little room for some interloper to break up their relationships. Friends may not be able to see each other since they are going to different colleges, but a simple cell phone lets them each know the others still are friends.

Part of the reason for such widespread cell phone use is that instead of having to wait, we can be part of the immediate now. A quick phone call has one person getting out of bed while another is getting out of class. Two friends seated at different ends of a stadium can enjoy the blow by blow of the action at the same time. Anyone can know what almost anyone else in their call list is doing at any moment.

It must have been lonely to wait an entire day before bragging to friends and family about getting the only A on a Chemistry test. It is almost incomprehensible that students managed the complex schedule of their days before cell phones. What did a student do if a ride didn't show up? How did people share the excitement of a concert in the moment or a good joke if they had to wait days? Earlier generations who seem puzzled by the cell phone fever that has hit college campuses might wonder how they might have felt without a phone, having to wait for weeks for the mail or longer for a visit. It should not be surprising that students snap open their cell phones at the drop of almost anything. The surprise would be if they kept their cell phones in their pockets and waited.

Adds more detailed examples appropriate to target audience.

Cut paragraph on text messages.

This paragraph still needs improvement.

Strengthening Paragraph Structure and Development

Once you finish considering the essay as a whole, examine your paragraphs one by one, applying the *FACT* approach that you used for the whole paper. Make sure each paragraph *FITS* the paper's major focus and develops a single central idea. If a paragraph needs more support or examples, *ADD* whatever is necessary. If a paragraph contains ineffective or unhelpful material, *CUT* it. *TEST* the flow of ideas from paragraph to paragraph and clarify connections, both between and within paragraphs, as necessary. Ask the basic questions in the checklist that follows about each paragraph, and make any needed revisions.

REVISION CHECKLIST FOR PARAGRAPHS

- Does the paragraph have one, and only one, central idea?
- Does the central idea help to develop the thesis statement?
- Does each statement within the paragraph help to develop the central idea?
- Does the paragraph need additional explanations, examples, or supporting details?
- Would cutting some material make the paragraph stronger?
- Would reorganization make the ideas easier to follow?
- Can the connections between successive sentences be improved?
- Is each paragraph clearly and smoothly related to those that precede and follow it?

Don't expect to escape making changes. Certain paragraphs may be stripped down or deleted, others beefed up, still others reorganized or repositioned.

EXERCISE

Here are three sample student paragraphs. Evaluate each according to the Revision Checklist for Paragraphs and suggest any necessary changes.

1. I can remember so many times when my father had said that he was coming to pick me up for a day or two. I was excited as a young boy could be at the thought of seeing my father. With all the excitement and anticipation raging inside of me, I would wait on the front porch. Minutes would seem like hours as I would wait impatiently.

2. Going to high school for the first time, I couldn't decide if I should try out for the cheerleading team or wait a year. Since I had time and had been on other

squads, I decided "why not?" I had nothing to lose but a lot to gain. Tryouts were not as hard as I thought, but I just knew I had to be on the squad. The tryout consisted of learning the routine they made up, making up your own routine, doing splits, and making a chant. Yet although these things were not that hard, I still was not sure whether I would make the team or not. The time came for the judges to make their decisions on who made the squad. Totaling the votes, they handed the results to the coach. She gave her speech that all coaches give. We were all good, but only a few could be picked for the team. As she started to read the names, I got hot. When she called my name, I was more than happy.

3. For hours we had been waiting under the overhang of an abandoned hut. None of us had thought to bring ponchos on our short hike through the woods. Soon it would be dark. Earlier in the day it had been a perfectly clear day. We all agreed that we didn't want to stand here all night in the dark, so we decided to make a dash for it.

Sharpening Sentences and Words

Next, turn your attention to sentences and words. You can improve your writing considerably by finding and correcting sentences that convey the wrong meaning or are stylistically deficient in some way. Consider, for example, the following sentences:

Just Mary was picked to write the report.
Mary was just picked to write the report.
Mary was picked to write just the report.

The first sentence says that no one except Mary will write the report; the second says that she was recently picked for the job; and the third says that she will write nothing else. Clearly, each of these sentences expresses a different meaning.

Now let's look at a second set of sentences:

Personally, I am of the opinion that the results of our membership drive will prove to be pleasing to all of us.

I believe the results of our membership drive will please all of us.

The wordiness of the first sentence slows the reader's pace and makes it harder to grasp the writer's meaning. The second sentence, by contrast, is much easier to grasp.

Like your sentences, your words should convey your thoughts precisely and clearly. Words are, after all, your chief means of communicating with your reader. Examine the first draft and revised version of the following paragraph, which describe the early morning actions of the writer's roommate. The underlined words identify points of revision.

First Draft

Coffee cup in hand, she <u>moves</u> toward the bathroom. The coffee spills <u>noisily</u> on the tile floor as she <u>reaches</u> for the light switch and <u>turns</u> it on. After <u>looking</u> briefly at the face in the mirror, she <u>walks</u> toward the bathtub.

Revised Version

Coffee cup in hand, she <u>stumbles</u> toward the bathroom. <u>Spilled</u> coffee <u>slaps</u> on the tile floor as she <u>gropes</u> for the light switch and <u>flips</u> it on. After <u>squinting</u> briefly at the face in the mirror, she <u>shuffles</u> toward the bathtub.

Note that the words in the first draft are general and imprecise. Exactly how does she move? With a limp? With a strut? With a spring in her step? And what does "noisily" mean? A thud? A roar? A sharp crack? The reader has no way of knowing. Recognizing this fact, the student revised her paragraph, substituting vivid, specific words. As a result, the reader can visualize the actions more sharply.

Don't confuse vivid, specific words with "jawbreaker words"—those that are complex and pretentious. Words should promote communication, not block it.

Reading your draft aloud will force you to slow down, and you will often hear yourself stumble over problem sections. You'll be more likely to uncover errors such as missing words, excessive repetition, clumsy sentences, and sentence fragments. Be honest in your evaluation; don't read in virtues that aren't there or that exaggerate the writing quality.

REVISION CHECKLIST FOR SENTENCES

- What sentences are not clearly expressed or logically constructed?
- What sentences seem awkward, excessively convoluted, or lacking in punch?
- What words require explanation or substitution because the reader may not know them?
- Where does my writing become wordy or use vague terms?
- Where have I carelessly omitted words or mistakenly used the wrong word?

EXERCISE

Reread paragraph 1 in the previous exercise and revise the sentence structure and word choice to create a more effective paragraph.

Writing the Introduction and Conclusion

If you've put off writing your introduction, do it now. Generally, short papers begin with a single paragraph that includes the previously drafted thesis statement, which sometimes needs to be rephrased so that it meshes smoothly with the rest of the paragraph. The introduction acquaints the reader with your topic; it should clearly signal your intention as well as spark the reader's interest.

The conclusion wraps up your discussion. Generally a single paragraph in short papers, a good ending summarizes or supports the paper's main idea.

Selecting a Title

Most essays require titles. Unless a good title unexpectedly surfaces while you are writing, wait until you finish the paper before choosing one. Since the reader must see the connection between what the title promises and what the essay delivers, a good title must be both accurate and specific.

Titling the essay "Cell Phone Use" would mislead the reader since this would seem to suggest that the essay is on how to use a cell phone. A specific title suggests the essay's focus rather than just its topic. For example, "The Reasons for College Cell Phone Fever" is clearer and more precise than simply "Cell Phone Use." The essay is about why cell phones are so extensively used, not about how they are to be used.

To engage your reader's interest, you might try your hand at a clever or catchy title, but don't get so carried away with creativity that you forget to relate the title to the paper's content. Here are some examples of common and clever titles:

Common	"Handling a Hangover"
Clever	"The Mourning After"
Common	"Selecting the Proper Neckwear"
Clever:	"How to Ring Your Neck"

Use a clever title only if its wit or humor doesn't clash with the overall purpose and tone of the paper.

Peer Evaluation of Drafts

At various points in the writing process, your instructor may ask you and your classmates to read and respond to one another's papers. Peer response often proves useful because even the best writers cannot always predict how their readers will react to their writing. For example, magazine articles designed to reduce the fear of AIDS have, in some cases, increased anxiety about the disease. Furthermore, we often have difficulty seeing the problems with our own drafts because so much hard work has gone into them. What seems clear and effective to us can be confusing or boring to our readers. Comments from our peers can frequently launch a more effective essay.

Just as the responses of others help you, so will your responses help them. You don't have the close, involved relationship with your peers' writing that you do with your own. Therefore, you can gauge their drafts objectively. This type of critical evaluation will eventually heighten your awareness of your own writing strengths and weaknesses. And knowing how to read your own work critically is one of the most important writing skills you can develop.

Responding to Your Peers' Drafts

Responding to someone else's writing is easier than you might imagine. It's not your job to spell out how to make the draft more effective, how to organize it, what to include, and what language to use. The writer must make these decisions. Your job is to *identify* problems, not *solve* them. You can do that best by responding honestly to the draft.

Some responses are more helpful than others. You don't help the writer by casually observing that the draft "looks O.K." Such a response doesn't point to problem areas; rather it suggests that you didn't read the paper carefully and critically. Wouldn't you inform a friend who was wearing clothes that looked terrible *why* they looked terrible? The same attitude should prevail about writing, something that makes a statement just as clothes do. Nor is a vague comment such as "The introduction is uninteresting" helpful. Point out *why* it is uninteresting. For instance, you might note that "The introduction doesn't interest me in the paper because it is very technical, and I get lost. I ask myself why I should read on." Here are two more examples of ineffective responses and their more effective counterparts.

Ineffective

> The paper was confusing.

Effective

> Paragraphs 2, 3, and 4 confused me. You jumped around too much. First you wrote about your experience on the first day of college, then you went on to how much you enjoyed junior high school, and finally you wrote about what you want to do for a career. I don't see how these ideas relate or why they are in the order that they are.

Ineffective

> More examples would help.

Effective

> When you indicate that college is a scary place. I get no real idea of why or how. What are the things that you think make college scary? I would like some examples.

Here are some steps to follow when responding to someone else's draft. First, read the essay from beginning to end without interruption. On a separate sheet of paper, indicate what you consider to be the main idea. The writer can then see whether the intended message has come through. Next, identify the biggest problem and the biggest strength. Writers need both negative and positive comments. Finally, reread the paper and write either specific responses to each paragraph or your responses to general questions such as the ones that follow. In either case, don't comment on spelling or grammar unless it really inhibits your reading.

PEER RESPONSE CHECKLIST

- What is the main point of this essay?
- What is the biggest problem?
- What is the biggest strength?
- What material doesn't seem to fit the main point or the audience?
- What questions has the author not answered?
- Where should more details or examples be added? Why?
- At what point does the paper fail to hold my interest? Why?
- Where is the organization confusing?
- Where is the writing unclear or vague?

As you learn the various strategies for successful writing, new concerns will arise. Questions geared to these concerns appear in the revision section that concludes the discussion of each strategy.

An Example of Peer Response in Response to "Cell Phone Use."

What is the main point of this essay?

There are many reasons students use cell phones so extensively, including to coordinate activities, get business done, share with others, keep in touch.

What is the biggest problem?

I didn't really know what was meant by this idea of the immediate now. Where did this idea come from? In what ways do we share the same now. Is this different from keeping in touch?

What is the biggest strength?

The reasons in the paper ring true to my experience, especially with the examples that are used.

What doesn't seem to fit the main point or the audience?

The material on the babysitter doesn't seem to fit or seem likely for most college students. Is walking back to *the dorm getting something done? How many students really do that? Doesn't it make you even more vulnerable?*

Where should more details or examples be added? Why?

The introduction is kind of boring. An example would make it more real. Also, more details about the now paragraph would make it clearer. Isn't the paper missing something about a really important reason which is simply that everyone is doing it?

Where is the writing unclear or vague?

The writing is pretty clear. But some places could be clearer in the intro. Which "some" and "most" do you mean? Some sentences could be tightened up like "Tim needs to contact his advisor..." Your pronouns jump around. Sometimes you use "we" and sometimes "students" and "they."

Acting on Your Peers' Responses

Sometimes you need strong nerves to act on a peer response. You can easily become defensive or discount your reader's comments as foolish. Remember, however, that as a writer you are trying to communicate with your readers, and that means taking seriously the problems they identify. Of course, you decide which responses are appropriate, but even an inappropriate criticism sometimes sets off a train of thought that leads to good ideas for revision.

As you read the final version of Drew's paper on cell phones, carefully examine the margin notes, which highlight key features of the revision. Drew added an example to the introduction to make it more interesting, added a section on how the common use of cell phones has an impact, and clarified the paragraph on "the now." He has cut the material on babysitters and walking across campus that his readers found inappropriate. He has tightened his language by sharpening his sentences and his word choice in a few places and using more consistent pronouns.

CASE HISTORY	The Reasons for College Cell Phone Fever Final Draft

Changed title to make it more focused.

At the end of their college classes, students flip open their cell phones almost before they are out of the room.

"Hey, just got out of English."

"What ya goin' to do?"

"Get some coffee and study before Biology. You?"

" Got Intro to Business in ten minutes."

"Well, see ya."

Added short conversation to make more interesting.

Continued on next page

Continued from previous page

Added sentence with more active verbs to capture scene.

Clarified the "some."

Added trend that is a later paragraph.

Clarified the word necessary by expanding idea.

Simplifies language since calls are obvious cell phones. Through out, changes language so consistently student and they, not we.

Changed language to tighten life in college to college life.

Tightened sentence by cutting wordiness.

Tightened language.

Cut the line about walking across campus at night.

Changed pronouns to be consistent.

These conversations seem far from necessary. Yet students plow their way from class to class with their cell phones glued to their ears. Professors and parents are confused by this practice. Some parents complain that young people are so wrapped up in their cell conversations that they completely miss the world around them. Many wonder why students are compulsive cell phone users. There are many reasons students wander around campus talking into the air. They use cell phones to coordinate the day's activities, to get business done, to share life's events, and to keep in touch. Part of this trend, undeniably, is that many others are also doing it. The large number of college students who wander around talking into their phones, ignoring the people around them, may seem ridiculous to outsider. However, in the end this cell phone mania is a reasonable, pleasurable, and vital part of college life.

It is hard to imagine how people managed their lives without cell phones since there is so much to coordinate. Weren't friends going to meet after class for a study session? Where is everybody? A quick call reveals that the study session was moved to the student center. Does everyone have his or her part ready for the presentation in Speech class at 3:00 p.m.? A flurry of calls makes certain everyone is ready. Will Collin be able to meet his girlfriend this afternoon? He needs to call to see if she is still free. Where is Jennifer since she said she was picking me up in front of the Science Building? College life can be hectic as students juggle classes, work, meal times, and a social life. A quick phone call can organize it all: arrange study sessions, confirm a lunch date, arrange a ride, coordinate a team project for class, and maybe even make time for a date.

Sometimes cell phone calls get important business done. Heather needs to convince her parents that she really, really needs more money to cover the cost of books. Tim needs to ask his adviser to lift his holds so he can schedule next semester's classes. Students, like everyone else, need to call about possible jobs, resolve bill disputes, arrange to have theirs car repaired, and find out medical test results. Cell phones let them get all this done in the time between classes or while walking back to their dorms, leaving them with more time for other things like studying or going out with friends.

Everyone likes to share moments of delight, success, and even failure with others who care. When a baby is expected, the expectant grandparents can't wait for the call. Cell phones let people share. At concerts, some in the audience call up friends and then hold up the phone so that they can hear part of a concert. When something really funny is happening, anyone can with a quick call share it with someone else who would appreciate the moment. If students get an unexpected A, they can quickly spread the celebration to those who would echo their joy. Sometimes a cell phone call can make the sharing very concrete, getting someone to go outside to look at a spectacular meteor shower, getting a friend to change channels to see an interview with a favorite rock star, or letting family know about a terrible earthquake in China. Cell phones allow an immediate connection to let people experience what callers are experiencing, whether it is excitement over a success, a great idea, the finals of a sporting event, or a news event.

Cell phone calls can let people stay in touch with each other. Most phone calls are very short, over before students have gotten from the classroom to the door of the building. "Hey, what's up?" "What are you doing?" "How are you?" Little information is exchanged and little is really shared. "Nothing much," in fact, is a common answer. What do such phone calls accomplish? They let people keep in touch with each other. Contact is what helps keep people close. Parents like their children to visit. Couples need to make time for each other. When people keep in touch, it lets them know that others care, lets them keep each other as important parts of their lives. Some students call their parents every day to maintain family ties while getting the emotional reassurance of those loving connections. Couples hold electronic hands as they walk across campus. Friends may not be able to see each other since they are going to different colleges, but a simple cell phone confirms their continued friendship.

A sociology professor told her class that she thought that the cell phone "created a virtual society of now." Cell phones create a feeling that all are in it together at the same time, even if in different places. Instead of having to wait to find out what might be happening, students can be part of the same now. A quick phone call has one person getting out of bed while another is getting out of class. Two friends seated at different ends of a stadium can enjoy the blow by blow of the action at the same time. Anyone can know what almost anyone else in their call list is doing at any moment. A clip from a news story on television about cosmetic surgery conveyed this perfectly. A woman is talking on her cell phone while she is undergoing liposuction. "Yeh," she declares, "I am undergoing surgery right now. No, I don't feel much, maybe just a tickle." It is hard to get more immediate than that.

All of this is made possible because others are doing it. Teenagers are notorious for doing what others are doing. Parents ask, "If your friends jumped

Continued on next page

Cut unnecessary phrase "while the feeling was still hot."

Changed from any idea to a great idea, more likely to be shared.

"Answer" is chosen as a better word than "response."

Provided a context for the paragraph. Reworded to be clearer.

Added a very specific example to make the idea clearer.

Added section on how everyone is doing this has an impact in response to peers.

Continued from previous page

Added a phrase to be memorable.

Added specific idea to explain concept.

off a bridge, would you do it too?" The answer is an embarrassing "yes," especially if the jumpers were attached to bungee cords. It would be embarrassing not to have a cell phone, ideally a razor or an iPhone or whatever is the latest trend. Everyone else seems to be talking while walking. So using cell phones right after class, between classes, during lunch, or at a concert just seems to be normal behavior—and most people want to be normal. Besides, if students are lucky enough to have good friends, their friends are probably calling them; and if friends are calling, it is important to call them back.

It must have been lonely to wait an entire day before bragging to friends and family about getting the only A on a Chemistry test. It is almost incomprehensible that students managed their complex schedules before cell phones. What did a student do if a ride didn't show up? How did people share the excitement of a concert in the moment or a good joke if they had to wait days? Earlier generations who seem puzzled by the cell phone fever that has hit college campuses might wonder how they might have felt without a phone, having to wait for weeks for the mail or longer for a visit. It should not be surprising that students snap open their cell phones at the end of class. The surprise would be if they kept their cell phones in their pockets and waited.

Of course, you decide which responses are appropriate, but even an inappropriate criticism sometimes sets off a train of thought that leads to good ideas for revisions.

ACTING ON PEER RESPONSE CHECKLIST

- Did the readers understand my main point? If not, how can I make it clearer?
- What did they see as the main problem? Can I solve it?
- What strengths did they identify that I can keep?
- What didn't fit that I need to cut or make clearer?
- Which reader's questions should I answer more completely?
- Where should I add details or examples?
- How could I make sections that lose my reader's interest more engaging or should I cut those sections?
- Why did my readers find some sections confusing? How could I reorganize those sections?
- Where could I rewrite sections to make them clearer?

Proofreading Your Draft

After revising your draft, proofread or edit it to correct errors in grammar, punctuation, and spelling. Effective proofreading is essential since even a few errors quickly detract from the credibility of your work. Since we often overlook our own errors simply because we know what we meant, proofreading can be difficult. Even after you have checked your paper using spell and grammar check, inch through your draft deliberately, moving your finger along slowly under every word. Repeat this procedure several times, looking first for errors in grammar, then for sentence errors and problems in punctuation and mechanics, and finally for mistakes in spelling. Be especially alert for problems that have plagued your writing in the past.

Effective proofreading calls for you to assume a detective role and probe for errors that weaken your writing. If you accept the challenge, you will certainly improve the quality of your finished work.

Revising with a Computer

Many writers prefer the advantages of revising on a computer. All word-processing programs allow you to write over unwanted sections of your draft, add new information, delete useless material, and move parts of the text around. Learn all the commands of your particular program and experiment to see exactly what your options are. The following practical tips will improve your efficiency:

1. Always keep a backup copy of everything. Accidentally erasing a file or losing your work to an electrical power surge is not uncommon. In addition, save copies of your earlier drafts, either as printouts or on disk; selected parts may prove useful later, and new papers sometimes sprout from old drafts. You can either save each draft under variations of your file name—"COPY A," "COPY B," "COPY C"—or keep deleted sections in specially labeled files.

2. Jot down helpful ideas or comments in your text as you revise: Enclose them with a special symbol, such as < >, and either save them in a separate file or delete them later if they serve no purpose.

3. If you struggle with a section of the text, write two or three versions and then pick your favorite. You might even open a new file, experiment freely, and then use the best version in your draft.

4. Don't allow the program to control how you revise. Don't be tempted to do what the commands make easiest: fiddle endlessly with sentences and words, never develop the essay as a whole, and move blocks of writing around indiscriminately. Avoid being electronically bewitched and make only those additions and changes that improve your writing.

5. Usually revise using a printout. If you use just the computer, you are limited to only one full screen at a time. A printed page has a different look. In addition, a printout allows you to compare several pages at once: You

can see, for example, how the second paragraph might be more effective if repositioned as paragraph 5.

6. When you finish revising, check the coherence of your draft. The writing must flow smoothly at the points where you have added, deleted, or moved sections of text. In addition, altered sentences must be clearly written and logically constructed. You can best check the essay's flow with a printout.

7. While every writer should run a spell and grammar check program before turning in work, proofreading with a word processor does have certain limitations. For example, a spelling check function can't judge whether you used the wrong word (*form* instead of *from*) or confused identical sounding but differently spelled words (*their, there, they're*). Furthermore, the unit will sometimes flag words that are not misspelled but are simply not in the computer's list. While the programs to check grammar or punctuation can offer you useful suggestions, they are intended only to give you options. **You** are still the ultimate proofreader.

8. Some programs, such as Microsoft Word (under *View, Toolbar, Reviewing*), have options to Track Changes, which let you make revisions, which then appear in color with the record of changes noted in the margin. Later you can go back and accept or reject the changes. This feature can be especially useful if you are getting peer feedback or working on a collaborative writing project.

Collaborative Writing

In many careers you'll have to work as part of a group to produce a single document. Recognizing this fact, many instructors assign collaborative writing projects. Writing as part of a group offers some advantages and poses some challenges. You can draw on many different perspectives and areas of expertise, split up the work, and enjoy the feedback of a built-in peer group. On the other hand, you must also coordinate several efforts, resolve conflicts over the direction of the project, deal with people who may not do their fair share, and integrate different styles of writing.

Even though you write as part of a group, the final product should read as though it were written by one person. Therefore, take great pains to ensure that the paper doesn't resemble a patchwork quilt. You can help achieve this goal by following the principles of good writing discussed throughout this text. Here are some suggestions for successful collaborative work:

1. Select a leader with strong organizational skills.
2. Make sure each person has every other group member's phone number and e-mail address.
3. Analyze the project and develop a work plan with clearly stated deadlines for each step of the project.
4. Assign tasks on the basis of people's interests and expertise.
5. Schedule regular meetings to gauge each person's progress.
6. Encourage ideas and feedback from all members at each meeting.

7. If each member will develop a part of the paper, submit each one's contribution to the other members of the group for peer evaluation. This can be done electronically.

8. To ensure that the finished product is written in one style and fits together as a whole, give each member's draft to one person and ask him or her to write a complete draft.

9. Allow plenty of time to review the draft so necessary changes can be made.

Collaborative writing provides an opportunity to learn a great deal from other students. Problems can arise, however, if one or more group members don't do their work or skip meetings entirely. This irresponsibility compromises everyone's grade. The group should insist that all members participate, and the leader should immediately contact anyone who misses a meeting. If a serious problem develops despite these efforts, contact your instructor.

Collaboration Using E-Mail, Instant Messenger, or Chat Rooms

Many college students use electronic communication to collaborate on writing projects. This allows you to exchange material and comments at every stage of the writing process. To illustrate, you can share

1. brainstorming ideas developed during the search for a writing topic
2. brainstorming ideas developed during the search for supporting information
3. tentative thesis statements or any general statement that will shape the document
4. individual sections of the writing project
5. copies of the entire original draft.

Whenever you use e-mail for collaborative writing, it's a good idea to designate a project leader who will ensure that all members participate and who will receive and distribute all materials. Your instructor may request copies of the e-mail exchanges in order to follow your work.

Maintaining and Reviewing a Portfolio

A portfolio is an organized collection of your writing, usually kept in a three-ring binder or folder. It's a good idea to retain all your work for each class, including the assignment sheet, your prewriting, and all your drafts. Organize this material either in the order the papers were completed or by type of assignment.

Why assemble a portfolio? Not only can a portfolio be a source of ideas for future writing, but it also allows you to review the progress of your current papers. In addition, should any confusion arise about a grade or an assignment, the contents of your portfolio can quickly clarify matters.

Some instructors will require you to maintain a portfolio. They will probably specify both what is to be included and how it is to be organized. They may use the portfolio to help you gain a better understanding of your strengths and weaknesses. Furthermore, portfolios give your instructor a complete picture of your work. Some departments collect student portfolios to assess their writing program; by reviewing student progress, instructors can determine what adjustments will make the program even more effective. Increasingly colleges may have you maintain a portfolio using a Web-based program. If your school has you maintain an electronic portfolio, you will receive clear instructions about the process. Do not be afraid to ask questions about this process.

You can review your own portfolio to gain a better understanding of your writing capabilities. Answer these questions as you look over your materials:

1. With what assignments or topics was I most successful? Why?

2. What assignments or topics gave me the most problems? Why?

3. How has my prewriting changed? How can I make it more effective?

4. How has my planning changed? How can I make it more effective?

5. What makes my best writing good? How does this writing differ from my other work?

6. What are the problem areas in my weakest writing? How does this writing differ from my other work?

7. Did·I use the checklists in the front of this text to revise my papers? Do I make significant changes on my own, in response to peer evaluation, or in response to my instructor's comments? If not, why not? What kinds of changes do I make? What changes would improve the quality of my work?

8. What organizational patterns have I used? Which ones have been effective? Why? Which ones have given me trouble? Why?

9. What kinds of introductions have I used? What other options do I have?

10. What kinds of grammar or spelling errors mar my writing? (Focus on these errors in future proofreading.)

Revising Your Paper

Prepare to revise.

- Distance yourself from your writing.
- Jot down your initial plans for your writing and ideas that came to mind.
- Talk about your paper with others.
- Read peer response and judge what makes sense.

Revise your whole essay.

- To discover new directions.
- Find what *FITS* and doesn't.
- *ADD* to develop and clarify.
- *CUT* what doesn't help.
- *TEST* the organization and restructure and add transitions.

Revise your paragraphs.

- Fit the thesis.
- Focus on central idea.
- Add detail as necessary.
- Cut what doesn't fit.
- Reorganize for easier flow.

Read out loud if it is helpful. Pay attention to where you stumble and what doesn't sound good. Slow down your reading to revise so you don't skim.

Strengthen words and sentences.

- Use more precise and vivid words.
- Make sure sentences mean what you want.
- Cut excess wordiness.

Repeat entire process or parts as needed.

Now proofread your paper.

Paragraphs

From Chapter 5 of *Strategies for Successful Writing*, Ninth Edition. James A. Reinking, Robert von der Osten.

Paragraphs

Imagine the difficulty of reading a magazine article or book if you were faced with one solid block of text. How could you sort its ideas or know the best places to pause for thought? Paragraphs help guide readers through longer pieces of writing. Some break lengthy discussions of one idea into segments of different emphasis, thus providing rest stops for readers. Others consolidate several briefly developed ideas. Yet others begin or end pieces of writing or link major segments together. Most paragraphs, though, include a number of sentences that develop and clarify one idea. Throughout a piece of writing, paragraphs relate to one another and reflect a controlling purpose. To make paragraphs fit together smoothly, you can't just sit down and dash them off. Instead, you first need to reflect on the entire essay, then channel your thoughts toward its different segments. Often you'll have to revise your paragraphs after you've written a draft.

Characteristics of Effective Paragraphs

Unity

A paragraph with unity develops one, and only one, key controlling idea. To ensure unity, edit out any stray ideas that don't belong and fight the urge to take interesting but irrelevant side trips; they only create confusion about your destination.

The following paragraph *lacks unity:*

> The Montessori Method for teaching math in the earliest grades builds on the child's natural link to physical objects and concrete learning. Spelling and reading is also taught with special materials. It was the

psychologist Piaget who recognized that there were different kinds of cognition from the concrete to the more abstract. Maria Montessori was a pioneer in applying insights into how children actually think to the classroom.

What exactly is this writer trying to say? We can't tell. Each sentence expresses a different, undeveloped idea:

1. The use of concrete materials to teach math.
2. The use of special materials to teach spelling and reading.
3. Piaget's contribution in identifying levels of intelligence.
4. Maria Montessori's contribution to education.

In contrast, the following paragraph develops and clarifies only one central idea, the Montessori Method's use of concrete materials to teach math:

> The Montessori Method for teaching math in the earliest grades builds on the child's natural link to physical objects and concrete learning. Children count out unit beads. When they reach ten unit beads, they can exchange them for a ten-bar, a line of ten linked beads. Ten ten-bars can be exchanged for one one-hundred square. By physically placing unit beads, ten-lines, and hundred-squares on a mat, children quickly learn about the units, tens, and hundreds place and how to carry. These concrete tools can also help children learn addition and subtraction. Children lay out a number like two hundred thirty six on a mat as well as the number one hundred sixty five. They add them together, counting up the five and the six to get eleven and exchanging ten unit-beads for the ten bar leaving one unit bead, adding up the now ten ten-bars and exchanging them for a hundred-square and then reading out the resulting number of four hundred and one. While the description of the procedure may sound complicated, the actual process of using these concrete materials to understand addition and carrying is easy for children to grasp.
>
> Diane Honegger

Because no unrelated ideas sidetrack the discussion, the paragraph has unity. To check your paragraphs for unity, ask yourself what each one aims to do and whether each sentence helps that aim.

After reading the next two paragraphs, answer the questions that follow.

1. The legend—in Africa—that all elephants over a large geographical area go to a common "graveyard" when they sense death is approaching led many hunters

to treat them with special cruelty. Ivory hunters, believing the myth and trying to locate such graveyards, often intentionally wounded an elephant in the hopes of following the suffering beast as it made its way to the place where it wanted to die. The idea was to wound the elephant seriously enough so that it thought it was going to die but not so seriously that it died in a very short time. All too often, the process resulted in a single elephant being shot or speared many times and relentlessly pursued until it either fell dead or was killed when it finally turned and charged its attackers. In any case, no wounded elephant ever led its pursuers to the mythical graveyard with its hoped-for booty of ivory tusks.

Kris Hurrell

2.   It is not surprising that the sale figures for CDs keep slumping since it is easier and more convenient to download the music buyers want from the Internet. The online music stores, such as i-tunes, are very easy to use with simple instructions for searching for music and making purchases. Music fans can quickly find the performers or albums of their choice, even obscure works, from the convenience of their living room without having to drive from store to store. Then they can buy either the songs or entire albums that interest them. Once downloaded they can either burn a CD to play on more traditional stereos or copy the music to an mp3 player of some kind. The effects have been devastating on the music retail industry. Major stores such as Tower Records went out of business. Barnes and Noble has cut back on the number of CDs that the chain sells. The shift to online distribution of music has had the added advantage of allowing alternative groups to present their music that they would have had trouble getting made into CDs and distributed through major chains. This also ends the potential impact of major chains such as Wal-Mart on what music is sold.

Annonymous

1. Which of these paragraphs lacks unity? Refer to the paragraphs when answering.
2. How would you improve the paragraph that lacks unity?

The Topic Sentence

The topic sentence states the main idea of the paragraph. Think of the topic sentence as a rallying point, with all supporting sentences developing the idea it expresses. A good topic sentence helps you gauge what information belongs in a paragraph, thus ensuring unity. At the same time, it informs your reader about the point you're making.

Placement of the topic sentence varies from paragraph to paragraph, as the following examples show. As you read each, note how supporting information develops the topic sentence, which is italicized.

Topic Sentence Stated First   Many paragraphs open with the topic sentence. The writer reveals the central idea immediately and then builds from a solid base.

Starting about one million years ago, the fossil record shows an accelerating growth of the human brain. It expanded at first at the rate of one cubic inch of additional gray matter every hundred thousand years; then the growth rate doubled; it doubled again; and finally it doubled once more. Five hundred thousand years ago the rate of growth hit its peak. At that time, the brain was expanding at the phenomenal rate of ten cubic inches every hundred thousand years. No other organ in the history of life is known to have grown as fast as this.

Robert Jastrow, Until the Sun Dies

_____

Robert Jastrow, *Until the Sun Dies* (New York: Norton, 1977).

Topic Sentence Stated Last   In order to emphasize the support and build gradually to a conclusion, a topic sentence can end the paragraph. This position creates suspense as the reader anticipates the summarizing remark.

An experience of my own comes handily to mind. Some years ago, when the Restaurant de la Pyramide in Vienne was without question one of the best half-dozen restaurants in the world, I visited it for the first time. After I had ordered my meal, the sommelier[wine steward] appeared to set before me a wine list of surpassing amplitude and excellence. But as I cast my eyes down this unbelievable offering of the world's most tantalizing wines, the sommelier bent over me and pointed out a wine of which I had never heard, ticketed at a price one-fifth that of its illustrious neighbors. "Monsieur," said the sommelier, "I would suggest this one. It is a local wine, a very good wine. It is not a great wine, but after all, monsieur, you are likely to pass this way only once. The great wines you will find everywhere; this wine you will find only in Vienne. I would like you to try it, while you have the opportunity." *This, to my mind, was true sophistication—on the part of M. Point for having the wine and on the part of the waiter for offering it.*

Stephen White, "The New Sophistication: Defining the Terms"

Topic Sentence Stated First and Last   Some paragraphs lead with the main idea and then restate it, usually in different words, at the end. This technique allows the writer to repeat an especially important idea.

Everything is changing. . . . This is a prediction I can make with absolute certainty. As human beings, we are constantly in a state of change. Our bodies change every day. Our attitudes are constantly evolving. Something that we swore by five years ago is now almost impossible for us to imagine ourselves believing. The clothes we wore a few years ago now look strange to us in old photographs. The things we take for granted as absolutes, impervious to change, are, in fact, constantly doing just that. Granite boulders become sand in time. Beaches erode and shape new shorelines. Our buildings become outdated and are replaced with modern structures that also will be torn down. Even those things which last thousands of years, such as the Pyramids and the Acropolis, also are changing. This simple insight is very important to grasp if you want to be a no-limit person, and are desirous of raising no-limit children. *Everything you feel, think, see, and touch is constantly changing.*

Wayne Dyer, What Do You Really Want for Your Children?

_____

Wayne Dyer, *What Do You Really Want for Your Children?* (New York: William Morrow, Inc., 1985).

Topic Sentence Stated in the Middle   On occasion, the topic sentence falls between one set of sentences that provides background information and a follow-up set that develops the central idea. This arrangement allows the writer to shift the emphasis and at the same time preserve close ties between the two sets.

Over the centuries, China has often been the subject of Western fantasy. In their own way, a number of scholars, journalists, and other travelers have perpetuated this tradition in recent years, rushing to rediscover the country after its long period of isolation. Some of these visitors, justifiably impressed by the Communists' achievements in eliminating the exploitative aspects of pre-1949 mandarin society, propagated the view that the revolution, after its initial successes, had continued to "serve the people," and that China was "the wave of the future"—a compelling alternative to the disorder and materialism of contemporary Western society. Human rights were not at issue, they argued, because such Western concepts were inapplicable to China. *In the past year, however, the Chinese have begun to speak for themselves, and they are conveying quite a different picture.* In the view of many of its own people, China is a backward and repressive nation. "China is Asia's Gulag Archipelago," an elderly Chinese scholar said to me shortly after I had arrived in China last spring. "I was in Germany right after the Second World War, and I saw the horrors of Buchenwald and other concentration camps. In a way—in its destruction of the human spirit these past two decades—China has been even worse."

David Finkelstein, "When the Snow Thaws"

David Finkelstein, "When the Snow Thaws," *The New Yorker*, Sept. 10, 1979, p. 127.

Topic Sentence Implied   Some paragraphs, particularly in narrative and descriptive writing, have no topic sentence. Rather, all sentences point toward a main idea that readers must grasp for themselves.

> [Captain Robert Barclay] once went out at 5 in the morning to do a little grouse shooting. He walked at least 30 miles while he potted away, and then after dinner set out on a walk of 60 miles that he accomplished in 11 hours without a halt. Barclay did not sleep after this but went through the following day as if nothing had happened until the afternoon, when he walked 16 miles to a ball. He danced all night, and then in early morning walked home and spent a day partridge shooting. Finally he did get to bed—but only after a period of two nights and nearly three days had elapsed and he had walked 130 miles.

John Lovesey, "A Myth Is As Good As a Mile"

John Lovesey, "A Myth Is as Good as a Mile," *Sports Illustrated*, Nov. 9, 1964.

The details in this paragraph collectively suggest a clear central idea: that Barclay had incredible physical endurance. But writing effective paragraphs without topic sentences challenges even the best writers. Therefore, control most of your paragraphs with clearly expressed topic sentences.

Identify the topic sentences in each of the following paragraphs and explain how you arrived at your decisions. If the topic sentence is implied, state the central idea in your own words.

1.   Last winter, while leafing through the <u>Guinness Book of World Records</u>, I came across an item stating that the tallest sunflower ever had been grown by G. E. Hocking, an Englishman. Fired by a competitive urge, I planted a half acre of sunflower seeds. That half acre is now a magnificent 22,000 square feet of green and gold flowers. From the elevated rear deck of my apartment, I can look out over the swaying mass of thick, hairy green stalks and see each stalk thrusting up through the darker heart-shaped leaves below and supporting

an ever-bobbing imitation of the sun. In this dwarf forest, some of the flower heads measure almost a foot in diameter. Though almost all my plants are now blooming, none will top the sixteen feet, two inches reached by Hocking's plant. My tallest is just thirteen feet even, but I don't think that's too bad for the first attempt. Next year, however, will be another matter. I plan to have an automatic watering system to feed my babies.

Joseph Wheeler

Joseph Conrad, *Lord Jim* (New York: Holt, Rinehart and Winston, 1957), p. 13.

2.　What my mother never told me was how fast time passes in adult life. I remember, when I was little, thinking I would live to be at least as old as my grandmother, who was dynamic even at ninety-two, the age at which she died. Now I see those ninety-two years hurtling by me. And my mother never told me how much fun sex could be, or what a discovery it is. Of course, I'm of an age when mothers really didn't tell you much about anything. My mother never told me the facts of life.

Joyce Susskind, "Surprises in a Woman's Life"

Joyce Susskind, "Surprises in a Woman's Life," *Vogue,* Feb. 1979, p. 252.

3.　The UN's International Labor Organization estimates that as many as 200 million children go to work rather than to school. They are in developing nations throughout the world, making everything from clothing and shoes to handbags and carpets. These children are the dark side of the new global economy, an international underclass working 12 or more hours a day, six or seven days a week. In the carpet factories of India, they are often separated from their families for years at a time. In the leather-handbag plants of Thailand, children report being forced to ingest amphetamines just to keep up their strength. In the charcoal industry of Brazil, tens of thousands of children work in a soot-drenched hell producing ingredients for steel alloys used in the manufacture of American cars. Child laborers everywhere develop arthritis and carpal tunnel syndrome from the repetitive work; their respiratory systems are damaged by inhaling toxic chemicals in poorly ventilated workshops; their posture is permanently altered by the long hours in cramped conditions. And the products they make are in homes across America, serving as a bitterly ironic commentary on what we consider a child's right to a carefree youth.

Mark Schapiro, "Children of a Lesser God"

Mark Schapiro, "Children of a Lesser God," *Harper's Bazaar,* April 1996, pp. 205–18.

4.　The first hostage to be brought off the plane was a dark little man with a bald head and a moustache so thick and black that it obliterated his mouth. Four of the masked terrorists were guarding him closely, each with a heavy rifle held ready for fire. When the group was about fifty feet from the plane, a second hostage, a young woman in flowered slacks and a red blouse, was brought out in clear view by a single terrorist, who held a pistol against the side of her head. Then the first four pushed the dark little man from them and instructed him to kneel on the pavement. They looked at him as they might an insect. But he sat there on his knees, seemingly as indifferent as if he had already taken leave of his body. The shots from the four rifles sounded faintly at the far end of the field where a group of horrified spectators watched the grisly proceedings.

Bradley Willis

Paragraphs

EXERCISE

1. Develop one of the ideas below into a topic sentence. Then write a unified paragraph that is built around it.

   a. The career (or job or profession) I want is _____ .
   b. The one quality most necessary in my chosen field is _____.
   c. The most difficult aspect of my chosen field is _____.
   d. One good example of the American tendency to waste is _____.
   e. The best (or worst) thing about fast-food restaurants is _____.
   f. The college course I find most useful (or interesting) is _____.
   g. Concentration (or substitute your own term here) is an important part of a successful golf game (or substitute your own sport) _____.
   h. The one place where I feel most at home is _____.
   i. More than anything else, owning a pet (or growing a garden) involves _____.

2. Write a topic sentence that would control a paragraph on each of the following:

   a. Preparations for traveling away from home
   b. Advantages of having your own room
   c. Some landmark of the community in which you live
   d. The price of long-distance telephone calls
   e. Registering for college courses
   f. A cherished memento or souvenir
   g. High school graduation
   h. New Year's resolutions

Adequate Development

Students often ask for guidelines on paragraph length: "Should I aim for fifty to sixty words? Seven to ten sentences? About one-fourth of a page?" The questions are natural, but the approach is wrong. Instead of targeting a particular length, ask yourself what the reader needs to know. Then supply enough information to make your point clearly. Developing a paragraph inadequately is like inviting guests to a party but failing to tell them when and where it will be held. Skimpy paragraphs force readers to fill in the gaps for themselves, a task that can both irritate and stump them. On the other hand, a paragraph stuffed with useless padding dilutes the main idea. In all cases, the reader, the information being presented, and the publication medium determine the proper amount of detail. A newspaper might feature short paragraphs including only key facts, whereas a scientific journal might have lengthy paragraphs that offer detailed development of facts.

The details you supply can include facts, figures, thoughts, observations, steps, lists, examples, and personal experiences. Individually, these bits of information may mean little, but together they clearly illustrate your point. Keep in mind, however, that development isn't an end in itself but instead advances the purpose of the entire essay. Still, less experienced writers often produce underdeveloped paragraphs. Look for places where you can specifically add a clarifying explanation, a detailed example, or a more complete account of an already provided example. You might want to take weak paragraphs and brainstorm for additional details.

Paragraphs   ·

Here are two versions of a paragraph, the first inadequately developed:

Underdeveloped Paragraph

Most of the delegates to the Constitutional Convention of 1787 feared too much democracy. As a result, they drafted the Constitution as a document outlining a limited democracy. Indeed, some of the provisions were simply undemocratic. But despite reflecting the delegates' distrust of popular rule, the Constitution did provide a framework in which democracy could evolve.

Adequately Developed Paragraph

Most of the delegates to the Constitutional Convention of 1787 feared too much democracy. As a result, they drafted the Constitution as a document outlining a limited democracy. Indeed, some of the provisions were simply undemocratic: *universal suffrage was denied; voting qualifications were left to the states; and women, blacks, and persons without property were denied the federal franchise. Until the passage of the Seventeenth Amendment in 1913, senators were not popularly elected but were chosen by state legislators.* But despite reflecting the delegates' distrust of popular rule, the Constitution did provide a framework in which democracy could evolve.

The first paragraph lacks examples of undemocratic provisions, whereas the second one provides the needed information.

Readability also helps set paragraph length. Within a paper, paragraphs signal natural dividing places, allowing the reader to pause and absorb the material presented up to that point. Too little paragraphing overwhelms the reader with long blocks of material. Too much creates a choppy effect that may seem simplistic, even irritating. To counter these problems, writers sometimes use several paragraphs for an idea that needs extended development, or they combine several short paragraphs into one.

1. Indicate where the ideas in this long block of material divide logically; explain your choices.

During the summer following graduation from high school, I could hardly wait to get to college and "be on my own." In my first weeks at State University, however, I found that independence can be tough and painful. I had expected raucous good times and a carefree collegiate life, the sort depicted in old beach movies and suggested by the selective memories of sentimental alumni. Instead, all I felt at first was the burden of increasing responsibilities and the loneliness of "a man without a country." I discovered that being independent of parents who kept at me to do my homework and expected me to accomplish certain household chores did not mean I was free to do as I pleased. On the contrary, living on my own meant that I had to perform for myself all the tasks that the family used to share. Studying became a full-time occupation rather than a nightly duty to be accomplished in an hour or two, and my college instructors made it clear that they would have little sympathy for negligence or even for my inability to do an assignment. But what was more troubling about my early college life than having to do laundry, prepare meals, and complete stacks of homework was the terrifying sense of being entirely alone. I was independent, no longer a part of the world that had seemed to confine me, but I soon realized that confinement had also meant security. I never liked the feeling that people were watching over me, but I knew that my family and friends were also watching out for me—and that's a good feeling to have. At the university no one seemed particularly to be watching, though professors constantly evaluated the quality of my work. I felt estranged from people in those first weeks of college life, desperately needing a confidant but fearful that the new and tenuous friendships I had made would be damaged if I were to confess my fears and problems. It was simply too early for me to feel a part of the university. So there I was, independent in the fullest sense, and thus "a man without a country."

2. **The following short, choppy units are inadequately developed. List some details you could use to expand one of them into a good paragraph.**

> I like living in a small town because the people are so friendly. In addition, I can always get the latest gossip from the local busybody.
>
> In a big city, people are afraid to get too friendly. Everything is very private, and nobody knows anything about anybody else.

3. **Scan the compositions you have written in other classes for paragraphs that are over- or underdeveloped. Revise any you find.**

Organization

An effective paragraph unfolds in a clear pattern of organization so that the reader can easily follow the flow of ideas. Usually when you write your first draft, your attempt to organize your thoughts will also organize your paragraphs. Writers do not ordinarily stop to decide on a strategy for each paragraph. But when you revise or are stuck, it's useful to understand the available choices. You may learn about some strategies later in your studies.

The choice you make depends upon your material and purpose in writing.

Writing Strategies   These include all of the following patterns:

Time sequence (narration)
Space sequence (description)

Paragraphs

Process analysis
Illustration
Classification
Comparison
Cause and effect
Definition
Argument

Four example paragraphs follow. The first, organized by *time sequence*, traces the final years of the Model T Ford, concluding with a topic sentence that sums up its impact.

In 1917 the Model T lost much of its attraction when its exterior appearance was drastically altered. The famous flat-sided brass radiator disappeared and the new style featured (in the words of the catalogue) "The stream-lined hood, large radiator and enclosed fan, crown fenders, black finish and nickel trimmings" ("crown fenders" would be described in England as domed mud-guards). Electric lighting and starting followed in 1919, and the model then continued with little alteration until 1927, when it was finally withdrawn. After a considerable pause it was replaced by the Model A, a very conventional machine with wire wheels, three-speed gearbox and four-wheel brakes (the "T" had never made this concession to progress and continued to the last with two minute brake drums on the back wheels only). While it was in preparation, others had taken the lead and the "A" never replaced the immortal "T" in the public fancy. Indeed, the "Tin Lizzy" or "Flivver" had become almost a national characteristic, and at the end of its eighteen years in production the total number sold was fifteen million.

Cecil Clutton and John Stanford, *The Vintage Motor-Car*

Cecil Clutton and John Stanford, *The Vintage Motor-car* (New York: Charles Scribner's Sons, 1955), p. 135.

The next paragraph, organized by *space sequence*, describes a ceramic elf, starting from the bottom and working up to the top. Other common spatial arrangements include top to bottom, left to right, right to left, nearby to far away, far away to nearby, clockwise, and counterclockwise.

The ceramic elf in our family room is quite a character. His reddish-brown slippers, which hang over the mantel shelf, taper to a slender point. Pudgy, yellow-stockinged legs disappear into a wrinkled tunic-style, olive-green jacket, gathered at the waist with a thick, brown belt that fits snugly around his roly-poly belly. His short, meaty arms hang comfortably, one hand resting on the knapsack at his side and the other clutching the bowl of an old black pipe. An unkempt, snow-white beard, dotted by occasional snarls, trails patriarch-fashion from his lower lip to his belt line. A button nose capped with a smudge of gold dust, mischievous black eyes, and an unruly snatch of hair peeking out from under his burnt-orange stocking cap complete Bartholomew's appearance.

Maria Sanchez

Paragraphs

Although descriptive paragraphs, like those developed by narration, often lack topic sentences, our example leads off with the central idea.

Here is a paragraph showing *process* development.

Making beer nuts is a quick, simple procedure that provides a delicious evening snack. You'll need six cups of raw peanuts, three cups of sugar, and one-and-one-half cups of water. To begin, combine the sugar and water in a two-quart saucepan and stir to dissolve the sugar. Next, add the peanuts and stir again until all of the peanuts are covered by the sugar-water solution. Leave the pan, uncovered, on a burner set at medium-high heat for ten to twelve minutes, until the sugar crystallizes and coats the peanuts thoroughly. Stay at the stove during the heating process and stir the mixture every two or three minutes to ensure even coating of the nuts. When the peanuts are thoroughly coated, pour them onto an ungreased cookie sheet and bake at 350 degrees for about thirty minutes, stirring and lightly salting at ten-minute intervals. Serve your beer nuts fresh out of the oven or eat them at room temperature.

Kimberlee Walters

Again, the topic sentence comes first.

The final example illustrates development by *comparison* and also proceeds from an opening topic sentence.

There is an essential difference between a news story, as understood by a newspaperman or a wire-service writer, and the newsmagazine story. The chief purpose of the conventional news story is to tell what happened. It starts with the most important information and continues into increasingly inconsequential details, not only because the reader may not read beyond the first paragraph but because an editor working on galley proofs a few minutes before press time likes to be able to cut freely from the end of the story. A newsmagazine is very different. It is written to be read consecutively from beginning to end, and each of its stories is designed, following the critical theories of Edgar Allan Poe, to create one emotional effect. The news, what happened that week, may be told in the beginning, the middle, or the end; for the purpose is not to throw information at the reader but to seduce him into reading the whole story, and into accepting the dramatic (and often political) point being made.

Otto Friedrich, "There Are 00 Trees in Russia"

Otto Friedrich, "There are 00 Trees in Russia," *Harper's Magazine*, Oct. 1964.

Order of Climax   Climactic order creates a crescendo pattern, starting with the least emphatic detail and progressing to the most emphatic. The topic sentence can begin or end the paragraph, or it can remain implied. This pattern holds the reader's interest by building suspense. On occasion, writers reverse the order, landing the heaviest punch first; but such paragraphs can trail off, leaving the reader dissatisfied.

Here is a paragraph illustrating climactic order:

> The speaking errors I hear affect me to different degrees. I'm so conditioned to hearing "It don't make any difference" and "There's three ways to solve the problem" that I've almost accepted such usage. However, errors such as "Just between you and I, Arnold loves Edna" and "I'm going back to my room to lay down" still offend my sensibility. When hearing them, I usually just chuckle to myself and walk away. The "Twin I's"—<u>irrevelant</u> and <u>irregardless</u>—are another matter. More than any other errors, they really grate on my ear. Whenever I hear "that may be true, but it's irrevelant" or "Irregardless of how much I study, I still get <u>C</u>'s," I have the urge to correct the speaker. It's really surprising that more people don't clean up their language act.
>
> Valerie Sonntag

From a magazine or newspaper article, select four paragraphs that illustrate different patterns of organization. Identify the topic sentence in each case; or if it is implied, state it in your own words. Point out the organization of each paragraph.

Coherence

Coherent writing flows smoothly and easily from one sentence and paragraph to another, clarifying the relationships among ideas and thus allowing the reader to grasp connections. Because incoherent writing fails to do this, it confuses, and sometimes even irritates, the reader.

Here is a paragraph that lacks coherence:

> I woke up late. I had been so tired the night before that I had forgotten to set the alarm. All I could think of was the report I had stayed up until 3 a.m. typing, and how I could possibly get twenty copies ready for next morning's 9 o'clock sales meeting. I panicked and ran out the door. My bus was so crowded I had to stand. Jumping off the bus, I raced back up the street. The meeting was already under way. Mr. Jackson gestured for me to come into the conference room. Inserting the first page of the report into the copier, I set the dial for twenty copies and pressed the print button. The sign started flashing CALL KEY OPERATOR. The machine was out of order. Mr. Jackson asked whether the report was ready. I pointed to the flashing red words. Mr. Jackson nodded grimly without saying anything. He left me alone with the broken machine.

This paragraph has some degree of unity: most of its sentences relate to the writer's disastrous experience with the sales report. Unfortunately, though, its many gaps in logic create rather than answer questions, and in very bumpy prose, at that. Note the gap between the third and fourth sentences. Did the writer jump out of bed and rush right out the door? Of course not, but the reader has no real clue to the actual sequence of events. Another gap occurs between the next two sentences, leaving the reader to wonder why the writer had to race up the street upon leaving the bus. And who is Mr. Jackson? The paragraph never tells, but the reader will want to know.

Now read this rewritten version, additions italicized:

> I woke up late *because* I had been so tired the night before that I had forgotten to set the alarm. All I could think of was the report I had stayed up until 3 a.m. typing, and how I could possibly get twenty copies ready for next morning's 9 o'clock sales meeting. *When I realized it was 8:30,* I panicked. *Jumping out of bed, I threw on some clothes, grabbed the report,* and ran out the door. My bus was so crowded I had to stand *and could not see out the window. Two blocks beyond my stop, I realized I should have gotten off.* "Stop!" *I cried and,* jumping off the bus, raced back up the street. *When I reached the office, it was 9:15, and* the meeting was already under way. Mr. Jackson, *the sales manager, saw me and* gestured for me to come into the conference room. *"One moment," I said as calmly as I could and hurried to the copier.* Inserting the first page of the report into it, I set the dial for twenty copies and pressed the print button. *Immediately,* the sign started flashing CALL KEY OPERATOR. The machine was out of order. *The next thing I knew,* Mr. Jackson *was at my side* asking whether the report was ready. I pointed to the flashing red words, *and* Mr. Jackson nodded grimly without saying anything. *Turning on his heel,* he *walked away and* left me alone with the broken machine.

As this example shows, correcting an incoherent paragraph may call for anything from a single word to a whole sentence or more.

Coherence derives from a sufficient supply of supporting details and your firm sense of the way your ideas go together. If you brainstorm your topic thoroughly and think carefully about the relationships between sentences, incoherence isn't likely to haunt your paragraphs.

As you write, and especially when you revise, signal connections to the reader by using *transitions*—devices that link sentences to one another. These are the most common transitional devices:

1. Connecting words and phrases
2. Repeated key words
3. Pronouns and demonstrative adjectives
4. Parallelism

You can use them to furnish links both within and between paragraphs.

Connecting Words and Phrases   Connectors clarify relationships between sentences. The following list groups them according to function:

Showing similarity: in like manner, likewise, moreover, similarly

Showing contrast: at the same time, but, even so, however, in contrast, instead, nevertheless, still, on the contrary, on the other hand, otherwise, yet

Showing results or effects: accordingly, as a result, because, consequently, hence, since, therefore, thus

Adding ideas together: also, besides, first (second, third . . .), furthermore, in addition, in the first place, likewise, moreover, similarly, too

Drawing conclusions: as a result, finally, in brief, in conclusion, in short, to summarize

Pointing out examples: for example, for instance, to illustrate

Showing emphasis and clarity: above all, after all, again, as a matter of fact, besides, in fact, in other words, indeed, nonetheless, that is

Indicating time: at times, after, afterward, from then on, immediately, later, meanwhile, next, now, once, previously, subsequently, then, until, while

Conceding a point: granted that, of course, to be sure, admittedly

Don't overload your paper with connectors. In well-planned prose, your message flows clearly with only an occasional assist from them.

In the following excerpt, which clarifies the difference between workers and workaholics, the connectors are italicized:

> My efforts to define workaholism and to distinguish workaholics from other hard workers proved difficult. *While* workaholics do work hard, not all hard workers are workaholics. Moonlighters, *for example*, may work 16 hours a day to make ends meet, but most of them will stop working when their financial circumstances permit. Accountants, *too*, seem to work non-stop, but many slow down after the April 15 tax deadline. Workaholics, *on the other hand*, always devote more time and thought to their work than their situation demands. Even in the absence of deadlines to meet, mortgages to pay, promotions to earn, or bosses to please, workaholics still work hard. What sets them apart is their attitude toward work, not the number of hours they work.
>
> Marilyn Machlowitz, "Workaholism: What's Wrong with Being Married to Your Work?"

Marilyn Machlowitz, "Workaholism: What's Wrong with Being Married to Your Work?" *Working Woman*, May 1978, p. 51.

Discussion Questions

   1. What ideas do each of the italicized words and phrases connect?
   2. What relationship does each show?

Repeated Key Words   Repeating key words, especially those that help convey a paragraph's central idea, can smooth the reader's path. The words may appear in different forms, but their presence keeps the main issues before the reader. In the following paragraph, the repetition of *majority, minority,* and *will* aids coherence, as does the more limited repetition of *government* and *interests*.

> Whatever fine-spun theories we may devise to resolve or obscure the difficulty, there is no use blinking the fact that the *will* of the *majority* is not the same thing as the *will* of all. *Majority* rule works well only so long as the *minority* is *willing* to accept the *will* of the *majority* as the *will* of the *nation* and let it go at that. Generally speaking, the *minority* will be *willing* to let it go at that so long as it feels that its essential *interests* and rights are not fundamentally different from those of the current *majority*, and so long as it can, in any case, look forward with confidence to mustering enough votes within four or six years to become itself the *majority* and so redress the balance. But if it comes to pass that a large *minority* feels that it has no such chance, that it is a fixed and permanent *minority* and that another group or class with rights and *interests* fundamentally hostile to its own is in permanent control, then *government* by *majority* vote ceases in any sense to be *government* by the *will* of the people for the good of all, and becomes *government* by the *will* of some of the people for their own *interests* at the expense of the others.
>
> Carl Becker, *Freedom and Responsibility in the American Way of Life*

Write a paragraph using one of the following sentences as your topic sentence. Insert the missing key word and then repeat it in your paragraph to help link your sentences.

1. _____ is my favorite relative.
2. I wish I had (a, an, some, more) _____.
3. _____ changed my life.
4. _____ is more trouble than it's worth.
5. A visit to _____ always depresses me.
6. Eating _____ is a challenge.
7. I admire _____.

Pronouns and Demonstrative Adjectives   Pronouns stand in for nouns that appear earlier in the sentence or in previous sentences. Mixing pronouns and their nouns throughout the paragraph prevents monotony and promotes clarity. We have italicized the pronouns in the following excerpt from an article about the writer's first visit to a gambling casino.

> There are three of *us* on this trip, two veterans of Atlantic City and *I*, a neophyte, all celebrating the fact that *we* have recently become grandmothers. One of *my* companions is the canny shopper in *our* crowd; as a bargain-hunter *she* knows the ways of the world. *I* have followed *her* through discount shops and outlet stores from Manhattan's Lower East Side to the Secaucus, New Jersey, malls. . . . Without saying a word, *she* hands *me* a plastic container of the kind that might hold two pounds of potato salad, and takes one *herself*. *She* drags *me* off to the change booth, where *she* exchanges bills for tubes of silver, careful not to let *me* see just how much. *I* do the same. Then *she* leads *me* to a clattering corner, where a neon sign winks on and off, *Quartermania*. "Let's try to find a couple of machines that only have handles," *she* says. . . .
>
> Eileen Herbert Jordan, "My Affair with the One-Armed Bandit"

Ellen Herbert Jordan, "My Affair with the One-Armed Bandit," *Modern Maturity,* July–Aug. 1995: 37, 864.

All the pronouns in the excerpt refer to the writer, her bargain-hunting friend, or the whole group.

Four demonstrative adjectives—*this, that, these,* and *those*—also help hook ideas together. Demonstratives are special adjectives that identify or point out nouns rather than describe them. Here is an example from the Declaration of Independence:

> We hold *these* truths to be self-evident, that all men are created equal, that they are endowed by their Creator with certain unalienable Rights, that among *these* are Life, Liberty, and the pursuit of Happiness. That to secure *these* rights, Governments are instituted among Men, deriving their just powers from the consent of the governed. That whenever any Form of Government becomes destructive of *these* ends, it is the Right of the People to alter or to abolish it, and to institute new Government, laying its foundation on such principles and organizing its power in such form, as to them shall seem most likely to effect their Safety and Happiness.

In a magazine, newspaper, textbook, or some other written source, find two paragraphs that use pronouns and demonstrative adjectives to increase coherence. Copy the paragraphs, underline the pronouns and demonstrative adjectives, and explain what each refers to.

Parallelism Parallelism uses repetition of grammatical form to express a series of equivalent ideas. Besides giving continuity, the repetition adds rhythm and balance to the writing. Note how the following italicized constructions tie together the unfolding definition of poverty:

> *Poverty is staying* up all night on cold nights to watch the fire, knowing one spark on the newspaper covering the walls means your sleeping children die in flames. In summer *poverty is watching* gnats and flies devour your baby's tears when he cries. The screens are torn and you pay so little rent you know they will never be fixed. *Poverty means* insects in your food, in your nose, in your eyes, and crawling over you when you sleep. *Poverty is hoping* it never rains because diapers won't dry when it rains and soon you are using newspapers. *Poverty is seeing* your children forever with runny noses. Paper handkerchiefs cost money and all your rags you need for other things. Even more costly are antihistamines. *Poverty is cooking* without food and cleaning without soap.
>
> Jo Goodwin Parker, "What Is Poverty?"

Jo Goodwin Parker, "What Is Poverty?" in George Henderson, *America's Other Children: Public Schools Outside Suburbia* (University of Oklahoma Press, 1971).

Paragraphs with Special Functions

Special-function paragraphs include introductions, transitional paragraphs, and conclusions. One-paragraph introductions and conclusions appear in short, multi-paragraph essays. Transitional paragraphs occur primarily in long compositions.

Introductions

A good introduction acquaints and coaxes. It announces the essay's topic and may directly state the thesis. In addition, it sets the tone—somber, lighthearted, angry—of what will follow. An amusing anecdote would not be an appropriate opening for a paper about political torture.

With essays, as with people, first impressions are important. If your opening rouses interest, it will draw the reader into the essay and pave the way for your ideas. If, instead, you'd like to try your hand at turning the reader away, search for a beginning that is mechanical, plodding, and dull. Your success will astonish you. Here are some bad openings:

In this paper I intend to . . .

Wars have always afflicted humankind.

As you may know, having too little time is a problem for many of us.

In the modern world of today . . .

How would you respond to these openings? Ask yourself that same question about every opening you write.

Paragraphs

Gear the length of the introduction to that of the essay. Although longer papers sometimes begin with two or more introductory paragraphs, generally the lead-in for a short essay is a single paragraph. Here are some possibilities for starting an essay. The type you select depends on your purpose, subject, audience, and personality.

A Directly Stated Thesis   This is a common type of opening, orienting the reader to what will follow. After providing some general background, the writer of our example narrows her scope to a thesis that previews the upcoming sections of her essay.

> An increasing number of midlife women are reentering the workforce, pursuing college degrees, and getting more involved in the public arena. Several labels besides "midlife" have been attached to this type of person: the mature woman, the older woman, and, more recently, the re-entry woman. By definition, she is between thirty-five and fifty-five years old and has been away from the business or academic scene anywhere from fifteen to thirty years. The academic community, the media, marketing people, and employers are giving her close scrutiny, and it is apparent that she is having a greater impact on our society than she realizes.
>
> Jo Ann Harris

A Definition   This kind of introduction works particularly well in a paper that acquaints the reader with an unfamiliar topic.

> You are completely alone in a large open space and are struck by a terrifying, unreasoning fear. You sweat, your heart beats, you cannot breathe. You fear you may die of a heart attack, although you do not have heart disease. Suppose you decide you will never get yourself in this helpless situation again. You go home and refuse to leave its secure confines. Your family has to support you. You have agoraphobia—a disabling terror of open spaces.
>
> "Controlling Phobias Through Behavior Modification"

"Controlling Phobias Through Behavior Modification." *USA Today,* August 1978.

A Quotation   A beginning quotation, particularly from an authority in the field, can be an effective springboard for the ideas that follow. Make sure any quote you use relates clearly to your topic.

> The director of the census made a dramatic announcement in 1890. The Nation's unsettled area, he revealed, "has been so broken into by isolated bodies of settlement that there can hardly be said to be a frontier line." These words sounded the close of one period of America's history. For three centuries before, men had marched westward, seeking in the forests and plains that lay beyond the settled areas a chance to begin anew. For three centuries they had driven back the wilderness as their conquest of the continent went on. Now, in 1890, they were told that a frontier line separating the settled and unsettled portions of the United States no longer existed. The west was won, and the expansion that had been the most distinctive feature of the country's past was at an end.
>
> Ray Allen Billington, "The Frontier Disappears"

Ray Allen Billington, "The Frontier Disappears," *The American Story,* ed. Earl Schenck Miers (Great Neck, NY: Channel, 1956).

Paragraphs

An Anecdote or Personal Experience   A well-told personal anecdote or experience can lure readers into the rest of the paper. Like other introductions, this kind should bear on what comes afterward. Engle's anecdote, like the stories she reviews, demonstrates that "women also have dark hearts."

> My mother used to have a little china cream and sugar set that was given to her by a woman who later killed her children with an axe. It sat cheerfully in the china cabinet, as inadequate a symbol as I have ever seen of the dark mysteries within us. Yet at least it was there to remind us that no matter how much Jesus wanted us for a sunbeam, we would still have some day to cope with a deeper reality than common sense could explain. It stood for strange cars not to get into, running shoes to wear when you were out alone at night and the backs of Chinese restaurants you were not supposed to go into.
>
> Marian Engle, review of *The Goddess and Other Women* by Joyce Carol Oates.

Marian Engle, review of *The Goddess and Other Women*, by Joyce Carol Oates, *New York Times Book Review*, Nov. 24, 1974, p. 7.

An Arresting Statement   Sometimes you can jolt the reader into attention, using content, language, or both, particularly if your essay develops an unusual or extreme position.

> It's like Pearl Harbor. The Japanese have invaded, and the U.S. has been caught short. Not on guns and tanks and battleships—those are yesterday's weapons—but on mental might. In a high-tech age where nations increasingly compete on brainpower, American schools are producing an army of illiterates. Companies that cannot hire enough skilled workers now realize they must do something to save the public schools. Not to be charitable, not to promote good public relations, but to survive.
>
> Nancy Perry, "Saving the Schools: How Business Can Help"

Nancy Perry, "Saving the Schools: How Business Can Help," from *Fortune*, Nov. 7, 1988.

Interesting Details   These details pique curiosity and draw the reader into the paper.

> It is Friday night at any of the ten thousand watering holes of the small towns and crossroads hamlets of the South. The room is a cacophony of the ping-pong-ding-ding ding of the pinball machine, the pop-fizz of another round of Pabst, the refrain of "Red Necks, White Socks and Blue Ribbon Beer" on the juke box, the insolent roar of a souped-up engine outside and, above it all, the sound of easy laughter. The good ole boys have gathered for their fraternal ritual—the aimless diversion that they have elevated into a life-style.
>
> Bonnie Angelo, "Those Good Ole Boys"

Bonnie Angelo, "Those Good Ole Boys," *Time*, Sept. 27, 1976, p. 47.

A Question   A provocative question can entice the reader into the essay to find the answer.

> When you leave your apartment or house, do you begin to feel better? If you leave for a week-long trip, do you find your head clears, your migraine disappears, dizziness stops, your aches and pains subside, depression fades away, and your entire attitude is better? If so, chemical pollution of the atmosphere in your home may be making you ill.
>
> Marshall Mandell, "Are You Allergic to Your House?"

Marshall Mandell, "Are You Allergic to Your House?" *Prevention*, Sept. 1979, p. 101.

1. Explain why each of the preceding introductions interests or does not interest you. Does your response stem from the topic or the way the author introduces it?
2. Find magazine articles with effective introductory paragraphs illustrating at least three different techniques. Write a paragraph explaining why each impresses you.

Transitional Paragraphs

In the midst of a lengthy essay, you may need a short paragraph that announces a shift from one group of ideas to another. Transitional paragraphs summarize previously explained ideas, repeat the thesis, or point to ideas that follow. In our example, Bruno Bettelheim has been discussing a young boy named Joey who has turned into a kind of human machine. After describing Joey's assorted delusions, Bettelheim signals his switch from the delusions to the fears that caused them.

> What deep-seated fears and needs underlay Joey's delusional system? We were long in finding out, for Joey's preventions effectively concealed the secret of his autistic behavior. In the meantime we dealt with his peripheral problems one by one.
> Bruno Bettelheim, "Joey: 'A Mechanical Boy'"

The following transitional paragraph looks back as well as ahead:

> Certainly these three factors—exercise, economy, convenience of shortcuts—help explain the popularity of bicycling today. But a fourth attraction sometimes overrides the others: the lure of the open road.
>
> Mike Bernstein

Conclusions

A conclusion rounds out a paper and signals that the discussion has been completed. Not all papers require a separate conclusion; narratives and descriptions, for example, generally end when the writer finishes the story or concludes the impression. But many essays benefit from a conclusion that drives the point home a final time. To be effective, a conclusion must mesh logically and stylistically with what comes earlier. A long, complex paper often ends with a summary of the main points, but any of several other options may be used for shorter papers with easy-to-grasp ideas. Most short essays have single-paragraph conclusions; longer papers may require two or three paragraphs.

Here are some cautions about writing your conclusion:

1. Don't introduce new material. Draw together, round out, but don't take off in a new direction.
2. Don't tack on an ending in desperation when the hour is late and the paper is due tomorrow—the so-called midnight special. Your reader deserves better than "All in all, skiing is a great sport" or "Thus we can see that motorcycle racing isn't for everyone."

3. Don't apologize. Saying that you could have done a better job makes a reader wonder why you didn't.

4. Don't moralize. A preachy conclusion can undermine the position you have established in the rest of your composition.

The following examples illustrate several common types of conclusion.

Restatement of the Thesis   The following conclusion reasserts Jordan's thesis that "a mood of antisocial negativism is creeping through the structure of American life, corroding our ideals, and suffocating the hopes of poor people and minorities."

> There is room for honest differences about each of these key issues, but the new negativism's overt greed and the implicit racism of its loud "No" to minority aspirations indicate that this is a poisonous movement that denies the moral ideals and human values that characterize the best in America's heritage.
>
> Vernon E. Jordan, Jr., "The New Negativism"

Vernon E. Jordan, Jr., "The New Negativism," *Newsweek*, Aug. 14, 1978, p. 13. Copyright © 1978, Newsweek, Inc.

A Summary   A summary draws together and reinforces the main points of a paper.

> There are, of course, many other arguments against capital punishment, including its high cost and its failure to deter crime. But I believe the most important points against the death penalty are the possibility of executing an innocent man, the discriminatory manner in which it is applied, and the barbaric methods of carrying it out. In my opinion, capital punishment is, in effect, premeditated murder by society as a whole. As the old saying goes, two wrongs don't make a right.
>
> Diane Trathen

A Question   The paragraph below concludes an argument that running should not be elevated to a religion, that its other benefits are sufficient. A final question often prompts the reader to think further on the topic. If your essay is meant to be persuasive, be sure to phrase a concluding question so that the way a reasonable person would answer emphasizes your point of view.

> Aren't those gifts enough? Why ask running for benefits that are plainly beyond its capacity to bestow?
>
> James Fixx, "What Running Can't Do for You"

A Quotation   A quotation can capture the essence of your thought and end the essay with authority.

> "We had no idea of the emotional involvement and the commitment of these women," Richard says. "Suddenly a constituency arose. Suddenly there are thousands and thousands of women who don't care about your moral position or mine—they want a baby."
>
> David Zimmerman, "Are Test-Tube Babies the Answer for the Childless?"

David Zimmerman, "Arc Test-Tube Babies the Answer for the Childless?" *Woman's Day*, May 1979, p. 26.

Ironic Twist or Surprising Observation

These approaches prompt the reader to think further about a paper's topic. The following paragraph points out the ironic refusal of the government to confront poverty that exists a mere ten blocks away from its offices:

> Thus, a stark contrast exists between the two cultures of 14th Street, which appears to be like an earthworm with half of its body crushed by poverty but the other half still alive, wriggling in wealth. The two are alike only in that each communicates little with the other because of the wide disparity between the lives of the people and the conditions of the environments. The devastating irony of the situation on 14th Street lies in the fact that only ten blocks away sit the very government institutions that could alleviate the poverty—the Senate, the House of Representatives, and the White House.
>
> Student Unknown

Clever or Lighthearted Ending

In our example, the writer, capitalizing on the essay's topic, ends by exaggerating the fault being criticized.

> Because using clichés is as easy as falling off a log, it goes without saying that it would be duck soup to continue in this vein till hell freezes over. However, since that would be carrying coals to Newcastle, let's ring down the curtain and bid adieu to the fair topic of the cliché. (No use beating a dead horse.)
>
> Student Unknown

Personal Challenge

A challenge often prompts the reader to take some action.

> And therein lies the challenge. You can't merely puff hard for a few days and then revert to the La-Z-Boy recliner, smugly thinking that you're "in shape." You must sweat and strain and puff regularly, week in and week out. They're your muscles, your lungs, your heart. The only care-taker they have is you.
>
> Monica Duvall

Hope or Recommendation

Both a hope and a recommendation may restate points already made in the essay or suggest actions to take in order to arrive at a solution.

> Periodically my pilot and I climb into our aircraft and head out over the Minnesota wilderness, following a succession of electronic beeps that lead to some of the last remaining wolves in the lower 48 states. We hope that the data we collect will provide a better understanding of the wolf. We especially hope that our work

will help guide authorities into a management program that will insure the perpetuation of the species in the last vestiges of its former range.

L. David Mech, "Where Can the Wolves Survive?"

I who am blind can give one hint to those who can see—one admonition to those who would make full use of the gift of sight: Use your eyes as if tomorrow you would be stricken blind. And the same method can be applied to the other senses. Hear the music of voices, the song of the bird, the mighty strains of an orchestra, as if you would be stricken deaf tomorrow. Touch each object you want to touch as if tomorrow your tactile sense would fail. Smell the perfume of flowers, taste with relish each morsel, as if tomorrow you could never smell and taste again. Make the most of every sense; glory in all the facets of pleasure and beauty which the world reveals to you through the several means of contact which Nature provides. But of all the senses, I am sure that sight must be the most delightful.

Helen Keller, "Three Days to See"

Helen Keller, "Three Days to See," *Atlantic Monthly,* Jan. 1933, p. 35.

EXERCISE

1. Explain why each of the foregoing conclusions does or does not interest you. Does your response stem from the topic or from the author's handling of it?
2. Copy effective concluding paragraphs, illustrating at least three different techniques, from magazine articles. Then write a paragraph explaining why each impresses you.

Narration: Relating Events

From Chapter 8 of *Strategies for Successful Writing*, Ninth Edition. James A. Reinking, Robert von der Osten.

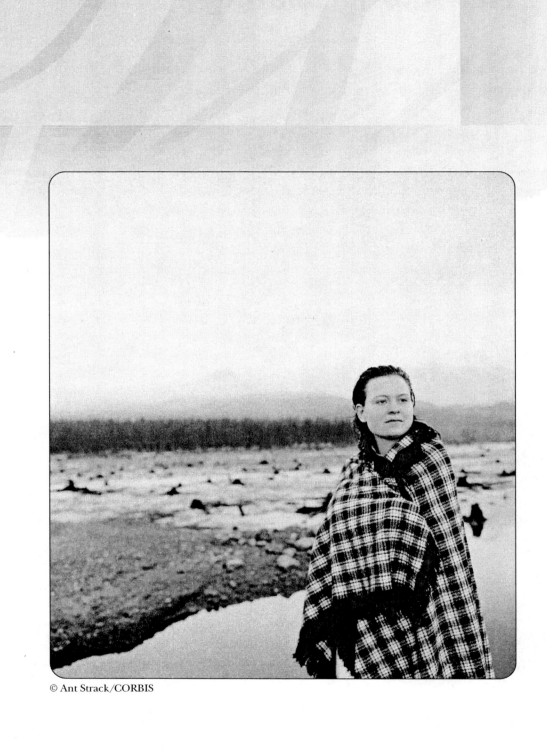

© Ant Strack/CORBIS

Narration: Relating Events

Clicking off the evening news and padding toward bed, Heloise suddenly glimpsed, out of the corner of her eye, a shadow stretching across the living room floor from under the drawn curtains.

"Wh—who's there?"

No response.

Edging backward toward the phone, her eyes riveted on the shadow, she stammered, "I–I don't have any money."

Still no answer.

Reaching the phone, she gripped the receiver and started to lift it from its cradle. Just then . . .

Just now you've glimpsed the start of a *narrative.* A narrative relates a series of events. The events may be real—as in histories, biographies, or news stories—or imaginary, as in short stories and novels. The narrative urge stirs in all of us, and like everyone else, you have responded almost from the time you began to talk. As a child, you probably swapped many stories with your friends, recounting an exciting visit to a circus or amusement park or an unusually funny experience with your pet. Today you may tell a friend about the odd happening in your biology laboratory or on the job.

Many classroom and on-the-job writing occasions call for narratives. Your English instructor might want you to trace the development of some literary character. Your history instructor might have you recap the events leading to a major war, your sociology instructor have you relate your unfolding relations with a stepparent or someone else, your psychology instructor ask you to report on society's changing attitudes toward the treatment of insanity. At work, a police officer may record the events leading to an arrest, a scientist recount the development of a research project, a nurse report on a patient's changing attitudes toward surgery, and a department manager prepare a brief history of an employee's work problems.

Purpose

A narrative, like any other kind of writing, makes a point or has a purpose. The point can either be stated or left unstated, but it always shapes the writing.

Some narratives simply tell what happened or establish an interesting or useful fact. The reporter who writes about a heated city council meeting or a lively congressional committee hearing usually wants only to set facts before the public.

Most narratives, however, go beyond merely reciting events. Writers of history and biography delve into the motives underlying the events and lives they portray, while narratives of personal experience offer lessons and insights. In the following conclusion to a narrative about an encounter with a would-be mugger, the writer offers an observation on self-respect.

> I kept my self-respect, even at the cost of dirtying my fists with violence, and I feel that I understand the Irish and the Cypriots, the Israelis and the Palestinians, all those who seem to us to fight senseless wars for senseless reasons, better than before. For what respect does one keep for oneself if one isn't in the last resort ready to fight and say, "You punk!"?
>
> Harry Fairlie, "A Victim Fights Back"

Henry Fairlie, "A Victim Fights Back," *The Washington Post*, April 30, 1978.

Action

Action plays a central role in any narrative. Other writing often only suggests action, leaving readers to imagine it for themselves:

> A hundred thousand people were killed by the atomic bomb, and these six were among the survivors. They still wonder why they lived when so many others died. Each of them counts many small items of chance or volition—a step taken in time, a decision to go indoors, catching one streetcar instead of the next—that spared him. And now each knows that in the act of survival he lived a dozen lives and saw more death than he ever thought he would see. At the time, none of them knew anything.
>
> John Hersey, *Hiroshima*

John Hersey, *Hiroshima* (New York: Modern Library, 1946), p. 4.

This passage suggests a great deal of action—the flash of an exploding bomb, the collapse of buildings, screaming people fleeing the scorching devastation—but *it does not present the action*. Narration, however, re-creates action:

> When I pulled the trigger I did not hear the bang or feel the kick—one never does when a shot goes home—but I heard the devilish roar of glee that went up from the crowd. In that instant, in too short a time, one would have thought, even for the bullet to get there, a mysterious, terrible change had come over the elephant. He neither stirred nor fell, but every line of his body had altered. He looked suddenly stricken, shrunken, immensely old, as though the frightful impact of the bullet had paralyzed him without knocking him down. At last, after what seemed a long time—it might have been five seconds, I dare say—he sagged flabbily to his knees. His mouth slobbered. An enormous senility seemed to have settled upon him. One could have imagined him thousands of years old. I fired again into the same spot. At the second shot he did not collapse but climbed with desperate slowness to his feet and stood weakly upright, with legs sagging and head drooping. I fired a third time. That was the shot that did it for him. You could see the agony of

it jolt his whole body and knock the last remnant of strength from his legs. But in falling he seemed for a moment to rise, for as his hind legs collapsed beneath him he seemed to tower upward like a huge rock toppling, his trunk reaching skywards like a tree. He trumpeted, for the first and only time. And then down he came, his belly towards me, with a crash that seemed to shake the ground even where I lay.

George Orwell, "Shooting an Elephant"

George Orwell, excerpt from "Shooting an Elephant," in *Shooting an Elephant and Other Essays,* copyright © 1950 by Sonia Brownell Orwell; renewed 1978 by Sonia Pitl-Rivers. Reprinted by permission of Harcourt, Inc.

Orwell's account offers a stark, vivid replay of the slaying, leaving nothing significant for the reader to infer.

A few words of caution are in order here. Action entails not only exotic events such as the theft of mass-destruction weapons, then the ransom demand, then the recovery of the weapons and the pursuit of the villains. A wide variety of more normal events also qualify as action: a long, patient wait that comes to nothing, an unexpected kiss after some friendly assistance, a disappointing gift that signals a failed relationship. Furthermore, the narrative action must all relate to the main point—not merely chronicle a series of events.

Conflict

The events in our lives and our world are often shaped by conflicts that need to be resolved. It should not be surprising then that conflict and its resolution, if any, are crucial to a narrative since they motivate and often structure the action. Some conflicts pit one individual against another or against a group, such as a union, company, or religious body. In others, the conflict may involve either an individual and nature or two clashing impulses in one person's head. Read the following student paragraph and note how common sense and fear struggle within the writer, who has experienced a sharp, stabbing pain in his side:

> Common sense and fear waged war in my mind. The first argued that a pain so intense was nothing to fool with, that it might indicate a serious or even life-threatening condition. Dr. Montz would be able to identify the problem and deal with it before it worsened. But what if it was already serious? What if I needed emergency surgery? I didn't want anyone cutting into me. "Now wait a minute," I said. "It's probably nothing serious. Most aches and pains aren't. I'll see the doctor, maybe get some pills, and the problem will clear up overnight. But what if he finds something major, and I have to spend the night in the hospital getting ready for surgery or recovering from it? I think I'll just ignore the pain."

> Luis Rodriguez

Point of View

Narrative writers may adopt either a first-person or third-person point of view. In first-person narratives, one of the participants tells what happened, whereas with third-person narration the storyteller stays completely out of the tale. Narratives you write about yourself use the first person, as do autobiographies. Biographies and histories use the third person, and fiction embraces both points of view.

In first-person narration, pronouns such as *I, me, mine, we,* and *ours* identify the storyteller. With the third person, the narrator remains unmentioned, and the characters are identified by nouns and such pronouns as *he, she, him,* and *her.* These two paragraphs illustrate the difference:

First-Person Narration

We would go to the well and wash in the ice-cold, clear water, grease our legs with equally cold stiff Vaseline, then tiptoe into the house. We wiped the dust from our toes and settled down for schoolwork, cornbread, clabbered milk, prayers and bed, always in that order. Momma was famous for pulling the quilts off after we had fallen asleep to examine our feet. If they weren't clean enough for her, she took the switch . . . and woke up the offender with a few aptly placed burning reminders.

Maya Angelou, "Momma's Encounter"

As this example shows, first-person narrators may refer to other characters in the narrative by using nouns and third-person pronouns:

Third-Person Narration

In the depths of the city walk the assorted human creatures who do not suspect the fate that hangs over them. A young woman sweeps happily from store to store, pushing a baby carriage along. Businessmen stride purposefully into their office buildings. A young black sulks down the sidewalks of his tenement, and an old woman tugs her shopping basket across a busy thoroughfare. The old woman is not happy: she has seen better days. Days of parks and fountains, of roses and grass, still stir in her memory. Reaching the other side, she stops and strains her neck upward, past the doorways, past the rows and rows of mirror glass, until her eyes rest on the brilliant blue sky so far away. She looks intently at the sky for a few minutes, noting every cloud that rolls past. And the jet plane. She follows the plane with her deep-socketed eyes and for some unexplainable reason suspects danger. She brings her gaze back to earth and walks away as the jet releases a large cloud of brownish-yellow gas. The gas hangs ominously in the air for a while, as if wanting to give humankind just a few more seconds. Then the cloud slowly descends to the surface, dissipating as it goes. By the time it reaches the glittering megalopolis, it is a colorless, odorless blanket of death.

Richard Latta

Identify the point of view in each of the following excerpts:

1. The bus screeched to a stop, and Pat stepped out of it and onto the sidewalk. Night enveloped the city, and a slight drizzle fell around her as she made her way to Al's office. Turning the corner, she stepped into the dark entryway. The receptionist had gone home, so she proceeded directly to the office. She knocked on the door and entered. Al, standing behind his desk and looking out the window, turned toward her with a startled look on his face.

    Jennifer Webber

2. It had really begun back in the Charlestown Prison, when Bimbi first made me feel envy of his store of knowledge. Bimbi had always taken charge of any conversation he was in, and I had tried to emulate him. But every book I picked up had few sentences which didn't contain anywhere from one to nearly all of the words that might as well have been in Chinese. When I just skipped those words, of course, I really ended up with little idea of what the book said. So I had come to the Norfolk Prison Colony still going through only book-reading motions. Pretty soon, I would have quit even these motions, unless I had received the motivation that I did.

    Malcolm X, *The Autobiography of Malcolm X*

_____

Malcolm X, *The Autobiography of Malcolm X* (New York: Ballantine Books, 1964), p. 171.

Key Events

Any narrative includes many separate events, enough to swamp your narrative boat if you try to pack them all in. Suppose you wish to write about your recent attack of appendicitis in order to make a point about heeding early warnings of an oncoming illness. Your list of events might look like this:

Awakened	Ate lunch	Entered building
Showered	Ate breakfast	Greeted fellow
Experienced acute	Opened garage door	employees
but passing pain	Started car	Began morning's work
in abdomen	Drove to work	Felt nauseated
Dressed	Parked in employee	Met with boss
Took coffee break	lot	Underwent diagnostic
Visited bathroom	Returned to work	tests
Experienced more	Began afternoon's	Had emergency
prolonged pain	work	operation
in abdomen	Collapsed at work	
Walked to cafeteria	Was rushed to hospital	

A narrative that included all, or even most, of these events would be bloated and ineffective. To avoid this outcome, identify and build your narrative around its key events—those that bear directly on your purpose. Include just enough secondary events to keep the narrative flowing smoothly, but treat them in sketchy fashion. The pain and nausea certainly qualify as key events. Here's how you might present the first attack of pain:

> My first sign of trouble came shortly after I stepped out of the shower. I had just finished toweling when a sharp pain in my lower right side sent me staggering into the bedroom, where I collapsed onto an easy chair in the corner. Biting my lip to hide my groans, I sat twisting in agony as the pain gradually ebbed, leaving me gray faced, sweat drenched, and shaken. What, I asked myself, had been the trouble? Was it ulcers? Was it a gallbladder attack? Did I have stomach cancer?

This passage convinces, not just tells, the reader that an attack has occurred. Its details vividly convey the nature of the attack as well as the reactions of the victim. As in any good narrative, the reader shares the experience of the writer, and the two communicate.

Dialogue

Dialogue, or conversation, animates many narratives, livening the action and helping draw the reader into the story. Written conversation, however, doesn't duplicate real talk. In speaking with friends, we repeat ourselves, throw in irrelevant comments, use slang, lose our train of thought, and overuse expressions like *you know, uh,* and *well.* Dialogue that reproduced real talk would weaken any narrative.

Good dialogue resembles real conversation without copying it. It features simple words and short sentences while avoiding the over-repetition of phrases like *she said* and *he replied.* If the conversation unfolds smoothly, the speaker's identity will be clear. To heighten the sense of reality, the writer may use an occasional sentence fragment, slang expression, pause, and the like, as in this passage:

> Mom was waiting for me when I entered the house.
>
> "Your friends. They've been talking to you again. Trying to persuade you to change your mind about not going into baseball. Honey, I wish you'd listen to them. You're a terrific ballplayer. Just look at all the trophies and awards you've . . ." She paused. "Joe's mother called me this morning and asked if you were playing in the game on Saturday. Davey, I wish you would. You haven't played for two weeks. Please. I want you to. For me. It would be so good for you to go and—and do what you've always . . ."
>
> "O.K., Mom, I'll play," I said. "But remember, it's just for you."
>
> Diane Pickett

Note the mother's use of the slang expression "terrific" and of sentence fragments like "your friends" and "for me" as well as the shift in her train of thought and the repetition of "and." These strategies lend an air of realism to the mother's words.

Besides making your dialogue realistic, be sure that you punctuate it correctly. Here are some key guidelines: Each shift from one speaker to another requires a new paragraph. When an expression like *he said* interrupts a single quoted sentence, set it off with commas. When such an expression comes between two complete quoted sentences, put a period after the expression and capitalize the first word of the second sentence. Position commas and periods that come at the end of direct quotations inside the quotation marks. Our example illustrates most of these guidelines.

Ethical Issues

Think how you'd react to a supervisor who wrote a narrative about the development of a new product which exaggerated his role and minimized your crucial contribution to the result. The report might cost you the opportunity for a promotion. Think of your response if you were surfing the Internet and came across a narrative about your first date that used your actual name and cast you in an unfavorable light. At the very least you would find it embarrassing. As you mull over any narrative you write, you'll want to think about several ethical issues, especially if you're depicting an actual event.

- Have I provided a truthful account that participants will recognize and accept? Deliberate falsification of someone's behavior that tarnishes that person's reputation is libel and could result in legal action.
- Would the narrative expose any participants to possible danger if it became public? Do I need to change any names in order to protect people from potential harm? Say your narrative includes someone who cooperates behind the scenes with authorities to help solve a case of cyber-vandalism. You should probably give that person a fictitious name.
- Does the narrative encourage unethical or illegal behavior? For example, extolling the delights of smoking marijuana for a teenage audience is clearly unethical.

These guidelines don't rule out exaggerated, humorous, or painfully truthful narratives. As with any kind of writing, however, narratives can impact the lives of people; as ethical writers we need to consider the possible consequences of our work.

Writing a Narrative

Planning and Drafting the Narrative

Most of the narratives you write for your composition class will relate a personal experience and therefore use the first person. On occasion, though, you may write about someone else and therefore use the third person. In either case make sure the experience you pick illustrates some point. A paper that indicates only how you violated a friend's confidence may meander along to little purpose. But if that paper is shaped by some point you wish to make—for instance, that you gained insight into the obligations of friendship—the topic can be worthwhile. To get started, do some guided brainstorming, asking yourself these questions:

- What experience in my life or that of someone I know would be worth narrating?
- What point does this experience illustrate? (Try to state the point in one or two sentences.)
- What people were involved and what parts did they play?

When you have pinpointed a topic, use further brainstorming to garner supporting material. Here are some helpful questions:

- What background information is necessary to understand the events?
- What action should I include?
- What is the nature of the conflict? Was it resolved? If so, how?
- Which events play key roles, which are secondary, and which should go unmentioned?
- Is any dialogue necessary?

Before you start to write, develop a plot outline showing the significant events in your narrative. For each one, jot down what you saw, heard, or did, and what you thought or felt.

Use the opening of your paper to set the stage for what follows. You might tell when and where the action occurred, provide helpful background information, note the incident that activated the chain of events, or identify the problem from which the action grew. If you state your main point directly, do it here or in the conclusion.

The body of the narrative should move the action forward until a turning point is about to be reached. Build the body around your key events. To avoid stranding your reader, use time signals whenever the development of the action might be unclear. Words, phrases, and clauses like *now, next, finally, after an hour,* and *when I returned* help the reader understand the sequence of events. Don't get carried away, though; a paper loaded with time signals makes the sequence seem more important than the events themselves. Finally, think about how you can best use conflict and dialogue to heighten narrative interest.

The conclusion should tie up any loose ends, settle any unresolved conflicts, and lend an air of completion to the narrative. Effective strategies to think about include introducing a surprise twist, offering a reflective summary of the events, noting your reaction to them, and discussing the aftermath of the affair.

Revising the Narrative

As you revise, ask yourself these questions:

Have I made the point, stated or unstated, that I intended?

Does all of the action relate to the main point?

Is the conflict handled appropriately?

Have I included all of the key events that relate to my purpose? Given each the right emphasis? Used time indicators where needed?

Is my point of view appropriate?

Does my dialogue ring true?

Have I considered appropriate ethical issues?

Joy Through the Tears

Brittany Coggin

Tyler Junior College

Faculty Member: Dr. Linda Gary

1   When I was growing up, there was a plaque in my grandmother's kitchen that read, "Don't get too busy making a living that you forget to make a life." My grandmother certainly followed this precept. Family was the most important thing in the world to her, and my family and I knew that we were loved.

2   As a child, I spent most days with my grandmommy while my mother was finishing school. My days were filled with baking cookies, playing games, reading stories, and making our famous mud pies. Grandmommy made time for all of this while working and taking care of all the daily chores around the house. When my mother would arrive to pick me up, it was no surprise for her to walk into the house and see Grandmommy and me prancing through the house banging pans while singing "Jingle Bells," with bright red buckets on our heads. We even called ourselves the "bucket heads."

3   My grandmother was a remarkable woman. I have always thought of her as the "center" of my family because she was. Grandmommy held high standards for her children and grandchildren, but she held even higher standards for herself. There was never a time that we did not know where she stood on an issue or where we stood with her. She had a way of holding us accountable while still leaving us in no doubt of her love for us. Although I can recall many times that I disappointed her, there was never a time that my grandmother ever disappointed me. If I thought I was in trouble and might get spanked, I usually was and did. If I thought she would be proud of me, she was. Honesty and integrity were very important to her, and she had both in abundance.

Continued on next page

Continued from previous page

4   Tragedy usually strikes when we least expect it. Nothing could have prepared me for what happened with my grandmother. She was the larger-than-life force who kept our family focused. If ever there was a problem, we took it to Grandmommy, knowing she would be able to point us in the right direction.

5   The first sign that there was a problem was when she began having excruciating pain in her legs. Her doctor thought it could be neuropathy or nerve damage because she had shingles when she was young. The doctor then sent her to a specialist, who could find nothing wrong. The following months were filled with specialist after specialist who prescribed pain medication after pain medication but could never diagnose the problem. The second clue that there was actually more to the story began when my grandmother complained that every time she ate, it felt as if her chest was on fire, and she would experience a lot of pressure in her chest. Once again, specialist after specialist could find nothing wrong. By this point, my grandmother's weight went from 125 pounds to 85 pounds. Despite the weight loss, our family doctor told her that he could find nothing wrong with her. He told her to take Tylenol and to "go home and live her life."

6   Two weeks later, she was so weak that she fell down the porch steps of our family's farmhouse. We rushed her to the hospital in Henderson, Texas. She had broken her ankle, wrist, and both of her hips when she fell. While in the hospital, the doctor ordered a "swallow study" to be completed. My aunt, who is a speech pathologist, knew the speech pathologist doing the study. She asked her to go down lower into the esophagus and to use contrast. That was when we found out that my grandmother's esophagus had completely closed and the opening into the stomach was blocked. Everything she swallowed, including any medication that was prescribed, had gathered at the end of her esophagus. By this time, she was much too weak to have the procedure to open the esophagus. Her doctor sent her to Tyler to have a procedure to remove all of the material in her esophagus and to try alternatives to surgery. During this time, the doctor finally ordered a scan, which revealed that she had lung cancer and that the cancer had metastasized to the bone.

7   This news was shocking to all of us. I had the surreal feeling that I was dreaming and that at any moment, I would wake up and my world would be as it had always been. Instead, the reality was that my world would never be the same again. Grandmommy was devastated but ready to fight.

My mom stayed with her the first night in the hospital because she had to have three rounds of chemotherapy the first night. Mom said that after each round, she and Grandmommy "high-fived." That's my Grandmommy!

8　　During this time, amazingly, it was my grandmother who gave us the strength to handle each day. Mom started graduate school that summer, so I would stay with Grandmommy while she was at school. Each day, Grandmommy seemed to lose the use of something. I found that I could handle more than I ever thought possible. I had to learn how to feed her and administer medication through a feeding tube. All I could think about was how I could not possibly do this. It was just too much and too hard. After a while, it became second nature. I can remember putting her false teeth in without thinking twice about it. When she lost all of her hair, we would play with hats and headbands. I would give her a makeover every time she had a doctor's appointment. Even when she began to lose the use of her hands, she cooked dinner for my mother. Grandmommy was disappointed with how it came out, but my mom said those were the best salmon patties she had ever eaten. That dinner was a labor of love because every step in the process involved immense pain.

9　　While this was a time of loss, it was also a time of happiness. The time I was able to spend with my grandmother drew us closer. Each moment I spent with her seemed suspended in time. Every word, facial expression, and hug became an everlasting memory. Sometimes it seemed that my whole family was in so much pain, and no one could reach out to help each other. My grandmother loved each of us so much, so she reached out to help each family member. Her love enveloped each of us, and it kept us believing that she would get better. I know that love is not tangible, but during this time, Grandmommy could look at me, and I could feel how much she loved me. In the midst of her suffering, she gave me love and comfort. In a sense, she helped prepare me for what was to come.

10　　In December 2005, my grandfather was taking Grandmommy to her doctor's appointment. After getting in the car, she collapsed and then became unconscious. I rushed to meet my family at the emergency room. When I got there, Grandmommy had regained consciousness but was not getting enough oxygen. My mother explained to her that she had pneumonia, and the doctors wanted to put her on a breathing machine until she got over it. Mom asked her to squeeze her hand if that was okay.

Continued on next page

Continued from previous page

Though Grandmommy could not speak, she squeezed my mom's hand to tell her to let the doctors go ahead with the procedure. She then went into a coma that lasted a week.

11   When she awoke, she was terrified. The doctors said that she had a severe staph infection. This scared her because her father died of a staph infection. Doctors told us she would not be able to live without the breathing machine. Grandmommy had signed an advance directive requesting that she not be allowed to live with such suffering. The days following were miserable. I did not want to lose the one person who truly understood me, but we could not let her suffer. Even without the use of her body, her mind remained alert. We would stand around the bed in her room, and she would look past us with the most beautiful smile on her face. She mouthed that she was tired, and we knew it was time. The following morning, the doctor took her off the breathing machine, and she died with her family around her.

12   My grandmother lost her battle with cancer in December 2005. While I still mourn her loss, I feel honored to have known her. Grandmommy's life will always serve as an example of how to live a life that needs no apology. She taught me that love is everlasting and that people are more important than material things. Because of her, I am stronger than I ever thought possible. I am blessed to have had this remarkable woman as my grandmother.

Discussion Questions

1. Identify the point of view of the narrative. Why is that choice of point of view important to this particular narrative?
2. What context did the writer provide before the central conflict of her grandmother's illness? What was the role of this context information?
3. Narratives depend on very specific details. What details best helped develop the character of the writer's grandmother? Why were those details effective?
4. What is the main point of this narrative? What other possible conflicts or themes might the reader have focused on? How would the narrative have to be rewritten to make that point?
5. This narrative uses very little dialogue. Would the narrative have been improved by dialogue? Where could dialogue have been added effectively?

Suggestions for Writing

1. Write a personal narrative about an experience that

   a. altered either your opinion of a friend or acquaintance or your views about some important matter;

    b. taught you a lesson or something about human nature;

    c. acquainted you with some previously unrecognized facet of your character or personality;

    d. brought about a significant change in your way of life.

    Keep in mind all the key narrative elements: purpose, action, conflict, point of view, key events, and dialogue.

2. A *maxim* is a concise statement of a generally recognized truth. Noting the key elements above, write a first-person or third-person narrative that illustrates one of the following maxims or another that your instructor approves:

    a. A little learning is a dangerous thing.

    b. The more things change, the more they stay the same.

    c. Don't judge a book by its cover.

    d. The road to hell is paved with good intentions.

    e. Pride goeth before a fall.

    f. Sometimes too much of a good thing can be wonderful.

    g. Sometimes good intentions have unexpected consequences.

3. Write a third-person narrative based on the following activities:

    a. Interview someone who works in a career area that interests you. Ask them about how they got involved in that area and write a narrative reporting the results.

    b. Find out about the history of a place that you know well and write a narrative about how the place changed.

    c. Interview someone in your class about an important event that made them who they are and write a narrative about that person.

    d. Talk to a small business owner in your area or a leader of a nonprofit group to find out how it got started in your area and write a narrative about that business or group.

CRITICAL EDGE

Sometimes writers create narratives by weaving together information from different sources. When developing a narrative about some childhood experience, you might supplement your own recollections by asking relatives and friends to supply details that you've forgotten or clear up points that have become hazy. A police officer investigating an accident questions witnesses, examines physical evidence, and uses the findings to draft an accurate report. A historian writing a biography draws upon public documents, newspaper accounts, diaries, notes of other investigators, and—depending on when the subject lived—other material such as newsreels, TV clips, and interviews in order to create a balanced portrait.

    Integrating material from several sources into a coherent piece of writing is called *synthesis*. When you synthesize, you reflect on ideas you have found in various sources, establish on your own the connections among those ideas,

Continued on next page

Continued from previous page

and then determine how the ideas and connections can advance the purpose of your writing. Thus, synthesis features independent thinking in which *you* evaluate, select, and use the material of others—which, of course, must be properly documented—to further your own purpose. Although synthesis can be challenging and does call for judgment on your part, following an effective procedure can help ensure success. Start by jotting down the main points of information from your sources and identifying where those points agree. Sometimes accounts of the same event differ. A friend's memory of your childhood experience may differ markedly from your own. A police officer may find that two witnesses disagree about how an accident happened. A historian may discover that public documents and newspapers offer different motives for an action by a biographical subject. When you encounter this type of contradiction, you'll need to weigh each position carefully in order to determine the most believable account. Then, as in developing any narrative, arrange your material in a pattern that helps make your point.

Let's say, for example, that you're narrating the history of a suburban housing development for low-income families built on land that was formerly owned by a nearby chemical plant and later was found to be contaminated by toxic chemicals. Company officials admit that wastes were buried there but insist that the chemicals were properly contained and posed absolutely no health threat. After stating the company's position, you present the findings of government investigators who analyzed soil samples from the site. These findings revealed that the containers were corroded and leaking and that the wastes included chemicals that attack the nervous system, as well as highly toxic herbicides designed for chemical warfare operations. You conclude that the company is responsible for the serious health problems that now plague the people living in the housing development. Note how the strategy of presenting the company's position early in the narrative lends added force to the point that shapes your writing—company accountability for the health of the housing development's residents.[1]

Suggestions for Writing

1. Review a number of articles in your school or local newspaper to develop a sense of journalistic style. Then interview several people about a recent event on campus or at the place you live and write a narrative that reports the event and draws on the interviews.
2. Read "Momma's Encounter" and then write a narrative that relates a particular minority experience and incorporates material from any of the three essays.
3. Takes notes from several newspaper accounts of an important or controversial event and write an account of the event that includes your notes.

---

[1]Because synthesis involves using several sources, including information from published ones, it is important to read sections on card catalogs and periodical indexes and those on handling quotations and avoiding plagiarism. As always, follow your instructor's guidelines for documenting sources.

Narration: Relating Events

Writing a Narrative

Plan the narrative.

- Identify part of topic if assigned or brainstorm personal experiences or observations for ideas.
- Talk to others to get ideas, more information, and for new perspectives.
- Read for information if needed (see Chapter 21 on documentation).

Write out main points you want to make.

Brainstorm details.

- Background information
- Actions—key conflicts
- Those involved and details
- Any dialogue

Organize narrative with plot outline.

- Let main point guide you.
- Identify the key conflict.
- List sequence of events (plot outline).
- Identify point of view: first or third.
- Identify needed context.

Revise.

Did you make your main point?
Does the action fit the main point?
Are any key events missing?
Is the point of view appropriate?
Does the dialogue ring true?
Is the narrative ethical?

Write a rough draft.

- Intro sets context, provides background, initiates action, may state main point.

- Body develops action in sequence of key event—signals transitions in time.

- Conclusion pulls together narrative, may state main point.

Proofread.

Description: Presenting Impressions

From Chapter 9 of *Strategies for Successful Writing*, Ninth Edition. James A. Reinking, Robert von der Osten.
Copyright © 2011 by Pearson Education, Inc. Published by Pearson Prentice Hall. All rights reserved.

Description: Presenting Impressions

The sound of hot dogs sizzling on a grease-spattered grill gave way to the whirling buzz of a cotton-candy machine. Fascinated, we watched as the white cardboard cone was slowly transformed into a pink, fluffy cloud. Despite their fiberglass appearance, the sticky puffs dissolved on my tongue into a sugar-like sweetness. Soon our faces and hands were gummed with a sticky mess.

You are there. Seeing, hearing, touching, tasting. This is one student writer's *description* of a small segment of a county fair. Effective description creates sharply etched word pictures of objects, persons, scenes, events, or situations. Sensory impressions—reflecting sight, sound, taste, smell, and touch—form the backbone of descriptive writing. Often, they build toward one dominant impression that the writer wants to evoke.

The human mind is not merely a logical thinking machine. Because of our emotional makeup, we react with shock to a photo of a battered victim of child abuse. We feel stirrings of nostalgia upon hearing a song from our past. We smile with satisfaction when quenching our summer thirst with tart sips from a tall, frosted drink.

Many occasions call for description. Your chemistry instructor might ask you to characterize the appearance and odor of a series of substances prepared in the laboratory; your art instructor might want you to describe a painting; your hospitality management instructor might have you portray an appealing banquet room. On the job, a realtor might write a glowing advertisement to sell a house, a nurse describe the postoperative status of a surgical incision, and a journalist describe the eruption of a volcano. All are attempts to capture the world through description.

Purpose

Sometimes description stands alone; sometimes it enriches other writing. It appears in histories and biographies, fiction and poetry, journalism and advertising, and even in technical writing. Some descriptions merely create images and mood, as when a writer paints a word picture of a boggy, fog-shrouded moor. But description can also stimulate understanding or lead to action. A historian may juxtapose the splendor of French court life with the wretchedness of a Paris slum to help explain the French Revolution. And everyone knows the persuasive power of advertising's descriptive enticements.

Description will provide effective backup for the writing you do in your composition classes, helping you to drive home your points vividly.

Sensory Impressions

Precise sensory impressions begin with close observation. If you can reexamine your subject, do it. If not, recall it to mind; then capture its features with appropriate words. When you can't find the right words, try a comparison. Ask yourself what your subject (or part of it) might be likened to. Does it smell like a rotten egg? A ripe cantaloupe? Burning rubber? Does it sound like a high sigh? A soft rustle? To come across, the comparison must be accurate and familiar. If the reader has never smelled a rotten egg, the point is lost.

Here is a passage marked by particularly vivid sight impressions:

> After our meal we went for a stroll across the plateau. The day was already drawing to a close as we sat down upon a ledge of rock near the lip of the western precipice. From where we sat, as though perched high upon a cloud, we looked out into a gigantic void. Far below, the stream we had crossed that afternoon was a pencil-thin trickle of silver barely visible in the gloaming. Across it, on the other side, the red hills rose one upon another in gentle folds, fading into the distance where the purple thumblike mountains of Adua and Yeha stretched against the sky like a twisting serpent. As we sat, the sun sank fast, and the heavens in the western sky began to glow. It was a coppery fire at first, the orange streaked with aquamarine; but rapidly the firmament expanded into an explosion of red and orange that burst across the sky sending tongues of flame through the feathery clouds to the very limits of the heavens. When the flames had reached their zenith, a great quantity of storks came flying from the south. They circled above us once, their slender bodies sleek and black against the orange sky. Then, gathering together, they flew off into the setting sun, leaving us alone in peace to contemplate. One of the monks who sat with us, hushed by the intensity of the moment, muttered a prayer. The sun died beyond the hills; and the fire withdrew.
>
> Robert Dick-Read, *Sanamu: Adventures in Search of African Art*

Robert Dick-Read, *Sanamu: Adventures in Search of African Art* (New York: E. P. Dutton, 1964), pp. 228–29.

At first, the western sky glows with "a coppery fire," which then expands into "an explosion of red and orange" that sends "tongues of flame" heavenward and then withdraws as the sun disappears. Comparisons strengthen the visual impression: the "pencil-thin" stream, the "thumblike" mountains stretching across the sky "like a twisting serpent." The familiar pencil, thumb, and serpent help us to visualize the unfamiliar landscape.

Most descriptions blend several sense impressions rather than focusing on just one. In the following excerpt, Mark Twain, reminiscing about his uncle's farm, includes all five. As you read it, note which impressions are most effective.

> As I have said, I spent some part of every year at the farm until I was twelve or thirteen years old. The life which I led there with my cousins was full of charm, and so is the memory of it yet. I can call back the solemn twilight and mystery of the

deep woods, the earthy smells, the faint odors of the wild flowers, the sheen of rain-washed foliage, the rattling clatter of drops when the wind shook the trees, the far-off hammering of woodpeckers and the muffled drumming of wood pheasants in the remoteness of the forest, the snapshot glimpses of disturbed wild creatures scurrying through the grass—I can call it all back and make it as real as it ever was, and as blessed. I can call back the prairie, and its loneliness and peace, and a vast hawk hanging motionless in the sky, with his wings spread wide and the blue of the vault showing through the fringe of their end feathers. I can see the woods in their autumn dress, the oaks purple, the hickories washed with gold, the maples and the sumachs luminous with crimson fires, and I can hear the rustle made by the fallen leaves as we plowed through them. I can see the blue clusters of wild grapes hanging among the foliage of the saplings, and I remember the taste of them and the smell. I know how the wild blackberries looked, and how they tasted, and the same with the pawpaws, the hazelnuts, and the persimmons; and I can feel the thumping rain, upon my head, of hickory nuts and walnuts when we were out in the frosty dawn to scramble for them with the pigs, and the gusts of wind loosed them and sent them down. I know the stain of blackberries, and how pretty it is, and I know the stain of walnut hulls, and how little it minds soap and water, also what grudged experience it had of either of them. I know the taste of maple sap, and when to gather it, and how to arrange the troughs and the delivery tubes, and how to boil down the juice, and how to hook the sugar after it is made, also how much better hooked sugar tastes than any that is honestly come by, let bigots say what they will.

Mark Twain, *Autobiography*

Spend some time in an environment such as one of the following. Concentrate on one sense at a time. Begin by observing what you see; then jot down the precise impressions you receive. Now do the same for impressions of touch, taste, smell, and sound.

1. The woods in the early morning
2. A city intersection
3. A restaurant or cafeteria
4. A scenic spot under a full moon
5. A storm
6. A pool or other recreation area
7. A crowded classroom or hallway
8. A construction site
9. A park or playground
10. A holiday gathering

Dominant Impression

Skillful writers select and express sensory perceptions in order to create a *dominant impression*—an overall mood or feeling such as joy, anger, terror, or distaste. This impression may be identified or left unnamed for the reader to deduce. Whatever the choice, a verbal picture of a storm about to strike, for example, might be crafted to evoke feelings of fear by describing sinister masses of clouds, cannon salvos of thunder, blinding lightning flashes, and viciously swirling wind-caught dust.

The following paragraph establishes a sense of security as the dominant impression:

> A marvelous stillness pervaded the world, and the stars together with the serenity of their rays seemed to shed upon the earth the assurance of everlasting security. The young moon recurved, and shining low in the west, was like a slender shaving thrown up from a bar of gold, and the Arabian Sea, smooth and cool to the eye like a sheet of ice, extended its perfect level to the perfect circle of a dark horizon. The propeller turned without a check, as though its beat had been part of the scheme of a safe universe; and on each side of the *Patna* two folds of water, permanent and sombre on the unwrinkled shimmer, enclosed within their straight and diverging ridges a few white swirls of foam bursting in a low hiss, a few wavelets, a few ripples, a few undulations that, left behind, agitated the surface of the sea for an instant after the passage of the ship, subsided splashing gently, calmed down at last into the circular stillness of water and sky with the black speck of the moving hull remaining everlastingly in its centre.
>
> Joseph Conrad, *Lord Jim*

The first sentence directly identifies the impression, "security," to which the "stillness" and the "serenity" contribute. Other details also do their part: the "smooth" sea, the "perfect circle" of the horizon, the "safe universe," the quick calming of the water, and the moving hull "everlastingly" in the center of water and sky.

Select one of the following topics and write a paragraph that evokes a dominant impression. Omit details that run counter to your aim.

1. A multi-alarm fire
2. A repair facility (automobile, appliance, and so on)
3. A laboratory
4. Some aspect of summer in a particular place
5. A religious service
6. A doctor's or dentist's office
7. A dark street
8. A parade or other celebration
9. Some landmark on your college campus
10. A municipal night court or small-claims court

Vantage Point

You may write a description from either a fixed or a moving vantage point. A fixed observer remains in one place and reports only what can be perceived from there. Here is how Marilyn Kluger describes the Thanksgiving morning sounds she remembers hearing from her bed as a child:

> On the last Thursday in November, I could stay in bed only until the night chill left the house, hearing first the clash of the heavy grates in the huge black iron

range, with its flowery scrolls and nickled decorations, as Mother shook down the ashes. Then, in their proper sequence, came the sounds of the fire being made—the rustle of newspaper, the snap of kindling, the rush of smoke up the chimney when Mother opened the damper, slid the regulator wide open, and struck a match to the kerosene-soaked corncobs that started a quick hot fire. I listened for the bang of the cast-iron lid dropping back into place and for the tick of the stovepipes as fierce flames sent up their heat, then the sound of the lid being lifted again as Mother fed more dry wood and lumps of coal to the greedy new fire. The duties of the kitchen on Thanksgiving were a thousand-fold, and I could tell that Mother was bustling about with a quicker step than usual.

Marilyn Kluger, "A Time of Plenty"

Marilyn Kluger, "A Time of Plenty," *Gourmet*, Nov. 1976, p. 22.

A moving observer views things from a number of positions, signaling changes in location with phrases such as "moving through the turnstile" and "as I walked around the corner." Below, H. L. Mencken takes us with him as he observes from a moving express train.

On a Winter day some years ago, coming out of Pittsburgh on one of the expresses of the Pennsylvania Railroad, I rolled eastward for an hour through the coal and steel towns of Westmoreland county. It was familiar ground; boy and man, I had been through it often before. But somehow I had never quite sensed its appalling desolation. Here was the very heart of industrial America, the center of its most lucrative and characteristic activity, the boast and pride of the richest and grandest nation ever seen on earth—and here was a scene so dreadfully hideous, so intolerably bleak and forlorn that it reduced the whole aspiration of man to a macabre and depressing joke. Here was wealth beyond computation, almost beyond imagination—and here were human habitations so abominable that they would have disgraced a race of alley cats.

I am not speaking of mere filth. One expects steel towns to be dirty. What I allude to is the unbroken and agonizing ugliness, the sheer revolting monstrousness, of every house in sight. From East Liberty to Greensburg, a distance of twenty-five miles, there was not one in sight from the train that did not insult and lacerate the eye. Some were so bad, and they were among the most pretentious—churches, stores, warehouses, and the like—that they were downright startling; one blinked before them as one blinks before a man with his face shot away. A few linger in memory, horrible even there: a crazy little church just west of Jeannette, set like a dormer-window on the side of a bare, leprous hill; the headquarters of the Veterans of Foreign Wars at another forlorn town, a steel stadium like a huge rat-trap somewhere further down the line. But most of all I recall the general effect—of hideousness without a break. There was not a single decent house within eye-range from the Pittsburgh suburbs to the Greensburg yards. There was not one that was not misshapen, and there was not one that was not shabby.

H. L. Mencken, "The Libido for the Ugly"

H. L. Mencken, "The Libido for the Ugly," Copyright 1927 by Alfred A. Knopf, Inc., and renewed 1955 by H. L. Mencken. Reprinted from *A Mencken Chrestomathy*, edited and annotated by H. L. Mencken, by permission of the publisher.

The phrase "on one of the expresses of the Pennsylvania Railroad" signals that Mencken will be a moving observer, and "From East Liberty to Greensburg" pinpoints the extent of his journey. "West of Jeannette," "another forlorn town," and "somewhere further down the line" specify the positions from which he views the church, the headquarters of the veterans' organization, and the stadium.

Whatever your vantage point, fixed or moving, report only what would be apparent to someone on the scene. If you describe how a distant mountain looks from a balcony, don't suddenly leap to a description of a mountain flower; you couldn't see it from your vantage point.

EXERCISE

1. **Writing as a fixed observer, describe in a paragraph your impressions of one of the following. Be sure to indicate your vantage point.**

    a. A post office lobby two weeks before Christmas
    b. The scene following a traffic accident
    c. A classroom when the bell rings
    d. A campus lounge
    e. An office
    f. The entrance to some building

2. **Writing as a moving observer, describe in a paragraph or two your impressions as you do one of the following things. Clearly signal your movements to the reader.**

    a. Walk from one class to another
    b. Shop in a supermarket or clothing store
    c. Walk from your home to the corner
    d. Cross a long bridge
    e. Water-ski
    f. Go through a ticket line and enter a theater, auditorium, or sports arena

Selection of Details

Effective description depends as much on exclusion as on inclusion. Don't try to pack every possible detail into your paper by providing an inventory of, for example, a room's contents or a natural setting's elements. Such an approach shows only that you can see, not write. Instead, select details that deliberately point toward the mood or feeling you intend to create. Read the following student description:

> At night, a restful stillness falls over the suburbs. . . . Everyone has vanished inside the carefully maintained homes that line the winding streets. The children have gone to bed, leaving the occasional motionless wagon or tricycle in the driveway. A light gleams in some bedroom windows. TV sets silently flicker a tranquil blue in a few living rooms. The street lamps curve protectively over the empty streets and sidewalks. The stillness is only disturbed by the brief, familiar bark of a neighbor's dog, quickly hushed, intensifying in its wake the silence that holds sway with the dark.
>
> Kim Granger

This writer evokes a sense of stillness by noting "the occasional motionless wagon or tricycle," that "TV sets silently flicker a tranquil blue," that "The street lamps curve protectively," that the dog is "quickly hushed." She ignores the car that cruises homeward, stereo booming; the husband and wife screaming at each other; the caterwauling cat fight. Mentioning these things would detract from the desired mood.

Arrangement of Details

Description, like any other writing, must have a clear pattern of organization to guide the reader and help you fulfill your purpose. Often some spatial arrangement works nicely. You might, for example, move systematically from top to bottom, left to right, front to back, nearby to far away, or the reverse of these patterns. To describe Saturday afternoon at the football game, you might start with the crowded parking lot; move into the bustling stadium; and finally zoom in on the sights, sounds, and smells of the playing field. Or if you wanted to highlight the surroundings rather than the central event, the order could be reversed. Going another route, you might start with some striking central feature and then branch out to the things around it. To capture the center of a mall, you might first describe its ornate fountain illuminated with flashing, multicolored lights, shift to the reflection of the lights on the skylight above, and end by portraying the surrounding store fronts.

Sometimes a description follows a time sequence. A writer might, for example, portray the changes in a woodland setting as winter gives way to spring and spring, in turn, yields to summer.

Ethical Issues

Imagine a police description of an auto accident that misstated the length of a car's skid marks or failed to note the icy patches of road at the scene. It might cost a blameless driver a heavy fine and a steep increase in auto insurance premiums. Imagine your disappointment and anger if you booked a weekend at a distant resort only to find it situated on an algae-covered pond instead of the beautiful lake described in the brochure. Imagine your irritation if a going-out-of-business sale described as "fabulous" turned out to offer only 10 percent price reductions. Clearly, inaccurate descriptions can create a wide range of undesirable consequences. Ask and answer these questions about your description.

- Would readers find my writing credible if they were at the scene?
- Are readers given adequate clues so that they will recognize any deliberate exaggeration?
- Will the description deceive readers in a harmful way?

You have an ethical obligation to present a reasonably accurate portrayal of your topic.

Writing a Description

Planning and Drafting the Description

If you're choosing your own topic, always select one that is familiar. Don't describe the inside of a restaurant kitchen or Old Faithful geyser in Yellowstone National Park if you've never seen either one. Instead, opt for some place where you've actually worked or a locale you've recently visited. If you keep a journal, thumb through it for possible leads.

For each potential topic that surfaces, ask yourself the following questions.

What do I want to accomplish by writing this description? Create one or more impressions? Help the reader understand something? Persuade the reader to act?

Who is my audience and why would this topic interest them?

What dominant impression will I develop?

To help gather and organize support for your topic, pose these additional questions:

What details should I include?

What sensory impressions are associated with each detail? (Jot down any words that you feel will best convey the impressions.)

How does each detail contribute to the dominant impression?

What sequence should I follow in presenting my impressions? (Map out the sequence, setting up a 1-2-3 listing or possibly a paragraph-by-paragraph plan.)

After brainstorming a list of potential details, you might use branching (below) to start accumulating sensory impressions. This illustrates how student writer Kim Swiger used branching to obtain and group the sensory impressions for a paragraph describing the sounds of her kitchen at breakfast time. Note that her grouping provided Swiger with the pattern used to organize her paragraph. Thus, the paragraph begins with stove-related sounds, moves to sounds associated with coffee-making and cooking, and ends with the sounds of mixing orange juice.

Begin your paper with an introduction that eases the reader into your topic. You might, for example, provide a historical overview, ask a provocative question, or snare the reader's attention with an arresting statement.

Develop each major feature in one or more paragraphs. Present each feature in the order you've mapped out. To ensure that the reader follows your thoughts, clearly signal any shifts in vantage point or time. As you write, aim for vivid, original language. We've all encountered writers who tell us that raindrops "pitter-patter," clouds are "fleecy white," and the sun is "a ball of fire." Such stale, worn-out language does nothing to sharpen our vision of the rain, the clouds, or the sun. The Swiger paragraph avoids this pitfall.

> Sure signs of a new day are the sounds in the kitchen as breakfast is prepared. The high sigh of the gas just before it whooshes into flame and settles into a whispering hum blends with the gurgling of the water for the morning coffee. Soon the gloop, gloop, gloop of the coffee sets up a perky beat. Then in mingles the crackle of creamy butter on a hot skillet and the shush of an egg added to the pan. Ribbons of bacon start to sizzle in the spitting grease. The soft rustle of plastic as bread is removed from its wrapper contributes to the medley. The can opener whirs, and the orange juice concentrate drops with a splat into the blender, which whizzes together the orange cylinder and splashed-in water. For minutes after the blender stops, bubbles of various sizes fizz.
>
> Kim Burson Swiger

You are there in the kitchen, hearing the carefully selected and freshly described sounds.

A word of caution about making your writing vivid. Some students are tempted to enhance their descriptions by stringing together a chain of adjectives without considering the effect on a reader. Think how you'd react if told that

> A dented, cylindrical, silver-gray, foul-smelling, overloaded trash can sat in the alley.

As you can see, more than the garbage can is overloaded here. Resist the temptation to inject similar sentences into your description. Carefully examine your adjectives and eliminate those that don't advance your purpose.

End your paper by pulling your material together in some way. If you've created an impression or mood, you might offer your reaction to it. If you want your reader to understand something, you might spell your message out. If you wish to persuade, you might urge some action.

Revising the Description

As you revise, ask the following questions:

> Have I written with a clear sense of purpose and audience in mind?
>
> Have I conveyed how my topic looks, sounds, feels, tastes, or smells? Would comparisons or more precise descriptive terms help convey my perceptions?

Have I evoked one dominant impression? Can I strengthen this impression by adding certain selected details? By eliminating details that detract from the impression?

Have I used an appropriate vantage point? If the observer is moving, have I signaled changes in location? Have I included only details that would be visible to the observer?

Have I arranged my details in an order appropriate to the topic?

Have I considered appropriate ethical issues?

SAMPLE

SAMPLE STUDENT ESSAY OF **DESCRIPTION**

My Serenity

Rachel Harvey

Ferris State University

Faculty Member: RoseAnn Shansky

1   The building blends in with the landscape, its faint yellow tinsiding disguising it from passersby on the road. As the icicles split-splop from the entryway overhang, one devious droplet sneaks into my shirt to roll down my neck. As I step into the barn, I am bombarded with the musty smell of clay dirt, sawdust, and sweet hay. The air here is more inviting than outside; it beckons me as an old friend would. I know my welcoming committee is in full swing when I hear a faint meow and a series of whinnies rising up out of the stalls. A large black-and-white barn cat, appropriately named Sylvester for his markings and ability to catch birds, stares at me with his intense yellow eyes. My boots sink into the soft dirt as I wade my way over to the worn, wooden stalls and stoop to pet the oversized feline. I stop at Dynamite Kid's stall to pay him a visit.

2   Kid stands a beautiful five feet two inches tall, with his white blond mane and tail and sleek white coat dappled with gray. As I approach him, he starts to dance, or at least a horse's version of dancing. His front legs splayed wide and rocking his weight from side to side, he resembles a flagpole in a gusty storm. I find myself giggling because he thinks I'm going to feed him; he always dances for his food. I slip into his stall and his petal-soft lips scour my hand for his treat. His teeth sound as if they're cutting bolts as he pulverizes the pea-green pellet into bits. I nuzzle up to his soft neck and inhale his aroma. The musk of a horse is unforgettable

because it's natural but so unique. This scent brings some of my most treasured memories back. Here I can forget about my ten-page paper that's due Friday and about the fight my significant other and I just had.

3   Everything seeps away from my mind as I snatch a stiff-bristled brush and start grooming him, plumes of dust rising off his back. Here it's only Kid, me, and the rustles and sighs of the other horses in their stalls. Twenty minutes later, once I've lunged and tied him, I head to the tack room to find Kid's equipment. I step into a room full of worn leather, colorful nylon, and jangling metal. I sort out his equipment: a burgundy leather bridle with a jointed bit, matching reins, and chocolate saddle trimmed with burgundy suede. The feel of chafed leather in my hand is a familiar one, both comforting and exciting. I slip the bridle over Kid's head and force the bit between his teeth. He mauls it, trying to get comfortable with the feel and taste of the harsh metal. I heft the heavy woolen saddle blanket and awkward saddle over his back to his withers and cinch it down. After some fine tuning and other adjustments, I'm sitting five foot two taller and making my way out toward the woods.

4   On top of Kid, I feel as if nothing can touch me. The rich smell of wet, rotting wood and melting snow waft over me as I pick my way through the trees. The dull colors of the landscape contrast with the white snow that is slowly but surely disappearing. The first robins are back: I can't see them, but their fluttering voices reveal their presence. Red squirrels are starting to venture out to harvest their stores of nuts, their red fur a sharp distinction from their surroundings. I steer Kid through a small depression. His feet squish into the ground, and I realize a small creek has revived. As I breathe deeply, I inhale the spring breeze picking its way over the fields. Here, spring is a timid but gay being; she will take her time in showing herself, but what she shows is wonderful and can enrapture the most stubborn of souls. I stop and close my eyes.

5   Surrounded by the countryside, I have a sense of peace and tranquility. I try my hardest to stow away this emotion, this feeling of completeness. Nature has always been able to capture my mind and whisk it away from my problems, giving me a temporary relief from the pressures of life. Kid snorts impatiently underneath me. He's eager to continue exploring, but I'm content to just stay here. After a few minutes of serenity, my cell

Continued on next page

Continued from previous page

phone blares out an excerpt of a song from George Strait, its noise a searing intrusion, and my head is violently ripped from its retreat. It's my boyfriend. I choose not to answer, trying to prolong my escape, but the spell is broken. I turn Kid back toward the barn and reality.

Discussion Questions

1. Identify details that appeal to each of the senses. Describe the dominant impression these details produce.
2. How is this description organized? Given the purpose of the essay, how effective is this pattern?
3. Where does the writer indicate movement in time and space? Does she keep the reader clearly located?
4. How effectively does the description of the phone call in the conclusion contrast with the rest of the description?

Suggestions for Writing

Choose one of the following topics or another that your instructor approves for a properly focused essay of description. Create a dominant impression by using carefully chosen, well-organized details observed from an appropriate vantage point. Try to write so that the reader actually experiences your description.

1. Holiday shopping
2. A concert of some type
3. An exercise class
4. A crafts class
5. An amusement park, a miniature or full-sized golf course, or some other type of recreational facility
6. A juice bar or coffee shop
7. A pet store or zoo
8. The lobby of a theater
9. A professional wrestling performance
10. A shopping center or minimart
11. A fast-food restaurant
12. Some type of party
13. An outdoor place of special importance to you
14. A Thanksgiving dinner
15. A reunion of some type
16. A NASCAR race
17. A video game arcade
18. An advertisement
19. A scene of environmental damage
20. A historical building or site

Most of us know that any two people are likely to see and describe the same object, place, or event differently. A motorist whose car broke down in the desert would note the impossible distances, the barrenness, the absence of human life, the blazing sun. A biologist who was well-supplied with food and water would see a rich ecosystem with a wide variety of plant life and an interesting population of insects and animals. Each would produce a different description that served a different purpose. The motorist would emphasize the grueling heat and desolation to establish the danger of the situation. The biologist would provide a detailed description of the plants, insects, and animals to advance scientific understanding of the area.

As a writer, you may occasionally need to synthesize information supplied by others when creating your own description. Suppose that you're writing a paper about the old growth forests of Oregon. You may read a naturalist's description of the ancient, rare species of trees and how the forest provides a habitat for much unique wildlife. You might also read a lumber industry study indicating that the trees are an important economic resource. You might even uncover an account by an early explorer that captures the emotions aroused by the discovery of the forest.

Armed with these and other descriptions, you could create a composite picture that captures all the different perspectives. You might start by offering the views of the Native American forest dwellers, then detail the towering majesty of the trees and the abundance of game as reported by early explorers. Next, you might turn to the accounts of early farmers, who regarded the forest as an obstacle to be cleared away, and continue by presenting the view of the forest as a lumber resource, perhaps including a description of a depleted lumbering site. To end the paper, you might note how contemporary conservationists view what remains of the forest. Collectively, this information would offer a stark portrayal of the near-total destruction of a splendid natural resource and by implication argue for preserving what is left. While this kind of writing task seems daunting, you can simplify it if you take up one perspective at a time.

Because different people are likely to see and describe the same object, place, or event differently, it's important to look critically at any description you consider for your paper. When you finish reading, ask yourself what features might have been omitted and what another slant on the material might have yielded. To illustrate, in "Once More to the Lake" E. B. White describes early morning fishing as follows: "We went fishing the first morning. I felt the same damp moss covering the worms in the bait can, and saw the dragonfly alight on the tip of my rod as it hovered a few inches from the surface of the water." If White had found fishing repugnant, he could just as easily have described the worms squiggling in the can as if they were afraid of the hook, the slimy feel of his hands after baiting the hook, the swarm of mosquitoes around his face, and the tangle in his line. Clearly, description demands choices. Different impressions and varying emphases can be selected. And like any other writer, you should carefully consider the details and slant of any description you write[1].

Suggestions for Writing

1. Select a famous U.S. landmark, such as the Grand Canyon, and read several writers' descriptions of it. After taking notes, write a description that includes their differing perspectives.
2. Rewrite a shortened version of an essay such as "Once More to the Lake" by building on the original details to create a different emphasis.
3. Interview several students to learn their impressions of your campus and weave those impressions into a descriptive essay.

---

[1]Because this type of paper includes information from published sources, it is important to read sections on card catalogs and periodical indexes and those on handling quotations and avoiding plagiarism. As always, follow your instructor's guidelines for documenting sources.

Writing a Description

Plan the description.

- Read assignment and select familiar topic.
- Identify your purpose for your description.
- Identify audience and analyze.

Brainstorm details perhaps using branching.

- Reobserve subject of paper if possible.
- Identify dominant impression.
- Select the relevant details for description.

Develop organizational strategy.

Establish **organizational strategy** and rough plan possibly ordering by space, importance, or time.

Write draft.

Intro establishes context and identifies object and reason; paragraphs of body detail major features, conclusions.

Revision often calls for additional brainstorming and possibly new observations.

Revise.

Read description critically, collect reader response, reobserve if possible.

- Be consistent with impression.
- Add details as needed.
- Cut details that don't fit.
- Test organization, and make consistent with transitions.

Proofread.

139

Process Analysis: Explaining How

From Chapter 10 of *Strategies for Successful Writing*, Ninth Edition. James A. Reinking, Robert von der Osten.

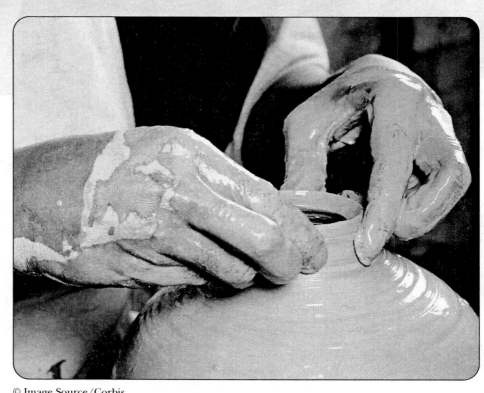

© Image Source/Corbis

Process Analysis: Explaining How

"Hey Bill, I'd like you to take a look at Mr. Gorgerise's car. He's really fuming. Says the engine's burning too much oil, running rough, and getting poor mileage. Check it out and see what you can find."

Bill begins by removing the spark plugs, hooking a remote-control starter to the starter in the car, and grounding the ignition to prevent the car's starting accidentally. Next, he fits a compression pressure gauge into the spark plug hole by cylinder number one, starts the engine, and reads and records the pressure; then he does the same for each of the other cylinders. Finally, he compares the readings with one another and the automaker's engine specs. The verdict? An excessively worn engine that needs rebuilding. Bill has carried out a *process*, just one among many that fill his workdays.

As we pursue our affairs, we perform processes almost constantly, ranging from such daily rituals as brewing a pot of coffee and flossing our teeth to taking a picture, burning a compact disc, preparing for a date, or replacing a light switch. Often we share our special technique for doing something—for example, making chicken cacciatore—by passing it on to a friend.

Many popular publications feature process analyses that help readers to sew zippers in garments, build catamarans, live within their means, and improve their wok technique. Process analysis also frequently helps you meet the writing demands of your courses. A political science instructor may ask you to explain how your state's governor won nomination, or a biology instructor may want an explanation of how bees find their way back to the hive. Another instructor may call for directions relating to some process in your field—for example, analyzing a chemical compound, taking fingerprints, or obtaining a blood sample.

On the job, a greenhouse crew leader may provide summer employees with directions for planting various kinds of shrubs and flowers. A technical writer may prepare a list of steps for workers to follow when unloading a particular solvent from a tank car. A sanitation department technician may write a brochure telling city residents how to get paper, glass, and metal trash ready for recycling.

As these examples show, a process can be nontechnical, historical, scientific, natural, or technical.

Kinds of Process Analysis Papers

Process papers fall into two categories: those intended for readers who will perform the process and those intended to explain the process for nonperformers. Papers in either category can range from highly technical and sophisticated to nonspecialized and simple.

Processes for Readers Who Will Perform Them   The audience for these papers may be technical and professional personnel who need the information to carry out a work-related task or individuals who want to perform the process for themselves.

A how-to-do-it paper must include everything the reader needs to know in order to ensure a successful outcome. Its directions take the form of polite commands, often addressing readers directly as "you." This approach helps involve readers in the explanation and emphasizes that the directions must, not merely should, be followed. Here is an illustration:

> To prepare a bacterial smear for staining, first use an inoculating loop to place a drop of distilled water on a clean glass microscope slide. Next, pass the loop and the opening of the tube containing the bacterial culture to be examined through a Bunsen burner flame to sterilize them. From the tube, remove a small bit of culture with the loop, and rub the loop in the drop of water on the slide until the water covers an area one and one-half inches long and approximately the width of the slide. Next, reflame the opening of the culture tube to prevent contamination of the culture, and then plug it shut. Allow the smear to air dry, and then pass the slide, smear side up, through the flame of the burner until it is warm to the touch. The dried smear should have a cloudy, milky-white appearance.
>
> Darryl Williams

Often each separate step is represented as a step in a numbered list to make it easier for the reader to see the separate actions that need to be completed.

Processes for Readers Who Won't Perform Them   These papers may tell how some process is or was performed or how it occurs or occurred. A paper might, for instance, detail the stages of grief, the procedure involved in an operation, the role of speech in the development of children's thinking, or the sequence involved in shutting down a nuclear reactor. These papers serve many purposes—for example, to satisfy popular curiosity; to point out the importance, difficulty, or danger of a process; or to cast a process in a favorable or unfavorable light. Even though the writers of such papers often explain their topic in considerable detail, they do not intend to provide enough information for readers to carry out the process.

Papers of this sort present the needed information without using polite commands. Sometimes a noun, a pronoun like *I, we, he, she,* or *it,* or a noun–pronoun combination identifies the performer(s). At other times, the performer remains unidentified. Three examples follow.

Pronouns Identify Performer

Thus, when I now approach a stack of three two-inch cinder blocks to attempt a breaking feat, I do not set myself to "try hard," or to summon up all my strength. Instead I relax, sinking my awareness into my belly and legs, feeling my connection with the ground. I breathe deeply, mentally directing the breath through my torso, legs, and arms. . . . When I make my final approach to the bricks, if I regard them at all they seem light, airy, and friendly; they do not have the insistent inner drive in them that I do.

Don Ethan Miller, "A State of Grace: Understanding the Martial Arts"

Don Ethan Miller, "A State of Grace: Understanding the Martial Arts," *Atlantic Monthly*, Sept. 1980. Copyright © 1980 by Don Ethan Miller.

Noun–Pronoun Combination Identifies Performers

Termites are even more extraordinary in the way they seem to accumulate intelligence as they gather together. Two or three termites in a chamber will begin to pick up pellets and move them from place to place, but nothing comes of it; nothing is built. As more join in, they seem to reach a critical mass, a quorum, and the thinking begins. They place pellets atop pellets, then throw up columns and beautiful, curving, symmetrical arches, and the crystalline architecture of vaulted chambers is created.

Lewis Thomas, "Societies as Organisms"

Lewis Thomas, excerpt from "Societies as Organisms," in *The Lives of a Cell* by Lewis Thomas. Copyright © 1971 by The Massachusetts Medical Society.

Performer Unidentified

The analyzer was adjusted so the scale read zero and was connected to the short sampling tube, which had previously been inserted into the smokestack. The sample was taken by depressing the bulb the requisite number of times, and the results were then read and recorded. The procedure was repeated, this time using the long sampling tube and sampling through the fire door.

Charles Finnie

EXERCISE

1. **Examine your favorite newspaper or magazine for examples of process analysis. Bring them to class for group discussion of which kind each represents and the writer's purpose.**
2. **Examine science textbooks and professional journals for more complex examples of process analysis. Bring your examples to class and discuss how they differ from simple instructions.**

Ethical Issues

Unclear, misleading, incomplete, or erroneous instructions written for someone to follow can spawn a wide range of unwanted consequences. Often frustration and lost time are the only results. Sometimes, though, the fallout is more serious, as in the case of a lab explosion. And in extreme cases, the outcome can be catastrophic, as when an accident occurs in a nuclear power plant. As writers, we have an ethical obligation to write clear and complete instructions. To help you do this, ask and answer the following questions when you're writing a process that the reader will perform.

- Have I used clear and unambiguous language so that the reader will not encounter unnecessary frustration and inconvenience?
- Have I clearly indicated any requirements such as time needed or additional supplies that will have to be purchased?
- Have I clearly warned readers about any possible harm they could face?

Writing a Process Analysis

Planning and Drafting the Process Analysis

As always, when the choice is yours, select a familiar topic. If you're not the outdoor type and prefer a Holiday Inn to the north woods, don't try to explain how to plan a campout. Muddled, inaccurate, and inadequate information will result. On the other hand, if you've pitched many a tent, you might want to share your technique with your readers.

Finding a suitable topic should be easy. Answer the following questions for each potential choice:

Will the reader find the process important, interesting, or useful?

Should I provide directions for the reader to follow, explain how the process takes place, or explain how others perform it?

Can I explain the process adequately within the assigned length?

Processes for Readers Who Will Perform Them   If you will develop a process for readers to follow, ponder this second set of questions to help you accumulate the details you'll need:

What separate actions make up the process? (Be especially careful not to omit any action that is obvious to you but wouldn't be to your reader. Such an oversight can ruin your reader's chances of success.)

What is the reason for each action?

What warnings will the reader need in order to perform the process properly and safely?

When you have your answers, record them in a chart similar to this one:

Action	Reason for Action	Warning
First action	First reason	First warning
Second action	Second reason	Second warning

Sometimes a reason will be so obvious no mention is necessary, and many actions won't require warnings. When you've completed the chart, review it carefully and supply any missing information. If necessary, make a revised chart.

Once you've listed the actions, group related ones to form steps, the major subdivisions of the procedure. The following actions constitute the first step—getting the fire going—of a paper explaining how to grill hamburgers:

remove grill rack   light briquets
stack charcoal briquets   spread out briquets

EXERCISE

1. **Develop a complete list of the actions involved in one of the following processes; then arrange them in an appropriate order.**

   a. Baking bread
   b. Assembling or repairing some common household device
   c. Carrying out a process related to sports
   d. Breaking a bad habit
   e. Building a fire in a fireplace
   f. Accessing the Internet

2. **Examine your favorite newspaper or magazine for examples of process analysis. Bring them to class for group discussion of how they illustrate step-by-step directions.**

Start your paper by identifying the process and arousing your reader's interest. You might, for example, note the importance of the process, its usefulness, or the ease of carrying it out. Include a list of the items needed to do the work, and note any special conditions required for a successful outcome. The paper explaining how to grill hamburgers might begin as follows:

Grilling hamburgers on an outdoor charcoal grill is a simple process that almost anyone can master. Before starting, you will need a clean grill, charcoal briquets, charcoal lighter fluid and matches, hamburger meat, a plate, a spatula, and some water to put out any flames caused by fat drippings. The sizzling, tasty patties you will have when you finish are a treat that almost everyone will enjoy.

Discussion Question

How does the writer try to induce the reader to perform the process?

Use the body of the paper to describe the process in detail, presenting each step in one or more paragraphs so that each is distinct and easily grasped.

- Present each step clearly, accurately, and fully.
- Include everything the reader needs to know.
- Note the reason for every action unless the reason is obvious.
- Flag with a cautionary warning any difficult or dangerous step or one that will result in undesirable consequences if not carried out.

- If two steps must be performed simultaneously, tell the reader at the start of the first one.
- In some places, tell readers what to expect if they have completed the instructions properly. Feedback lets readers know they are on track or that they need to redo something.

Let's see how the first step of the hamburger-grilling paper might unfold:

> The first step is to get the fire going. Remove the grill rack and stack about twenty charcoal briquets in a pyramid shape in the center of the grill. Stacking allows the briquets to burn off one another and thus produces a hotter fire. Next, squirt charcoal lighter fluid over the briquets. Wait about five minutes so that the fluid has time to soak into the charcoal. Then toss in a lighted match. The flame will burn for a few minutes before it goes out. When this happens, allow the briquets to sit for another fifteen minutes so that the charcoal can start to burn. Once the burning starts, do not squirt on any more lighter fluid. A flame could quickly follow the stream back into the can, causing it to explode. As the briquets begin to turn from pitch black to ash white, spread them out with a stick so that they barely touch one another. Air can then circulate and produce a hot, even fire, the type that makes grilling a success.

Discussion Questions

1. At what points has the writer provided reasons for doing things?
2. Where has the writer included a warning?

Some processes can unfold in *only one order*. When you shoot a free throw in basketball, for example, you step up to the line and receive the ball before lining up the shot, and you line up the shot before releasing the ball. Other processes can be carried out in an *order of choice*. When you grill hamburgers, you can make the patties either before or after you light the charcoal. If you have an option, use the order that has worked best for you.

End your paper with a few brief remarks that provide some perspective on the process. A summary of the steps often works best for longer, multi-step processes. Other popular choices include evaluating the results of the process or discussing its importance. The paper on hamburger grilling notes the results.

> Once the patties are cooked the way you like them, remove them from the grill and place them on buns. Now you are ready to enjoy a mouthwatering treat that you will long remember.

E. M. Pryzblyo

Processes for Readers Who Won't Perform Them Like how-to-do-it processes, those intended for nondoers require you to determine the steps, or for natural processes the stages, that are involved and the function of each before you start to write. In addition, since this type of essay will not enable readers to perform the process, think carefully about why you're presenting the information and let that purpose guide your writing. If, for instance, you're trying to persuade readers that the use of rabbits in tests of the effects of cosmetics should be discontinued, the choices you make in developing your steps should reflect that purpose.

To arouse your reader's interest, you might, among other possible options, begin with a historical overview or a brief summary of the whole process, or you could note its importance. The following introduction to an essay on the aging of stars provides a brief historical perspective:

> Peering through their still-crude telescopes, eighteenth-century astronomers discovered a new kind of object in the night sky that appeared neither as the pin-prick of light from a distant star nor as the clearly defined disk of a planet but rather as a mottled, cloudy disk. They christened these objects planetary nebulas, or planetary clouds.... Modern astronomers recognize planetary nebulas as the fossil wreckage of dying stars ripped apart by powerful winds....

Because the reader will not perform the process, supply only enough details in the body of the paper to provide an intelligent idea of what the procedure entails. Make sure the reader knows the function of each step or stage and how it fits into the overall process. Present each in one or more paragraphs with clear transitions between the steps or stages. The following excerpt points out the changes that occur as a young star, a red giant, begins the aging process:

> As the bloated star ages, this extended outer atmosphere cools and contracts, then soaks up more energy from the star and again puffs out: with each successive cycle of expansion and contraction the atmosphere puffs out a little farther. Like a massive piston, these pulsations drive the red giant's atmosphere into space in a dense wind that blows with speeds up to 15 miles per second. In as little as 10,000 years some red giants lose an entire sun's worth of matter this way. Eventually this slow wind strips the star down close to its fusion core.

As with processes aimed at performers, end your paper with a few remarks that offer some perspective. You might, for example, evaluate the results of the process, assess its importance, or point out future consequences. The ending of the essay on star aging illustrates the last option:

> The cloud of unanswered questions surrounding planetaries should not obscure the real insight astronomers have recently gained into the extraordinary death of ordinary stars. In a particularly happy marriage of theory and observation, astronomers have discovered our own sun's fate. With the interacting stellar winds model, they can confidently predict the weather about 5 billion years from now; very hot, with *really* strong gusts from the east.
>
> Adam Frank, "Winds of Change"

Adam Frank, excerpts from "Winds of Change," in *Discover*, June 1994, pp. 100–104.

Revising the Process Analysis

To revise, pose these questions:

> Have I written consistently for someone who will perform the process or someone who will merely understand it?
>
> If my paper is intended for performers, have I included every necessary action? Explained any purpose that is unclear? Warned about any steps that are dangerous or might be performed improperly?
>
> Are my steps presented in an appropriate order? Developed in sufficient detail?
>
> Have I considered appropriate ethical issues?

SAMPLE

STUDENT ESSAY OF **PROCESS ANALYSIS**

Basic Songwriting Techniques

Hannah Hill

Tyler Junior College

Faculty Member: Dr. Linda Gary

1   When listening to a song, one always wonders where the idea of the song comes from. What was the singer thinking, and what provoked him or her to write such a song? Songwriting is a simple technique that anyone can do if they put their hearts into it. Songs are stories put to music through the process of emotion, thought, and rhythm.

2   Emotional feelings are important when composing a good song. Start by finding a comfortable place to relax and to think freely. Perhaps a favorite room or an outdoor getaway could rid the mind of distractions. Once settled and comfortable, begin jotting down notes. Focus on feelings and emotions that are current to life or thoughts from the past that weigh heavily on the mind. For example, express how a certain situation feels or affects day-to-day life. Make it either dominantly positive or negative, but avoid mixing the emotions. Allow the mysterious secrets to flow freely. Do not be afraid to let go. Expression of the heart and mind is the most coveted form of music because it is so real. "To take an emotion and make it mean something, take other people into the feeling" is famous country singer/songwriter Kenny Chesney's initial form of songwriting ("Kenny Chesney" 1). He puts his true life on the line to create

amazing music for country fans to enjoy. Ultimately, personal experience will always draw the listener in with the passion that comes from loving to write and listen to music.

3   After putting feelings into words, a clear thought process helps to organize and put these emotions into a clear composition. Don't worry about rhyme scheme yet until all the ideas are put down and arranged. Processing through the jotted notes of life will add organization. This assembling will, in turn, add clarity of understanding for the listener. Add description and detail that brings insight of the writer out to the listener. Although life experience is the best writing utensil, it is not the only one. Add fantasy or exaggeration to liven up and add spice. Be overly emotional in certain and pertinent areas. The most important situation should show the most drama to the listener. It is common for depressing lyrics to be favored over upbeat ones. For instance, twists and turns are always more interesting than perfectly happy endings. Always remember, less is more. Take out the unnecessary, so there's not an overload of information. Leave mystery to be interpreted by the listener.

4   After modifying thoughts and before moving onto rhyme, put all information in an organized structure. Assembling begins with determining the order of the writing. Pick out the writing and separate it into sections. The first paragraph part becomes the introduction or verse one. Next is the chorus, which will repeat in between each verse. Add the second section, which becomes verse two, and repeat the chorus. If necessary, add a bridge, which is the part that intertwines but differs from the rest of the song. Then repeat the chorus one more time. Organization puts an intellectual tweak on mainstream emotions on which the song is based.

5   Finally, thoughts and feelings are translated into a potential rhythmic pattern. This is where the mainstream thinking turns into a complete thought. The story is then formed into a poetic framework. Manipulate words and sentences to contrast the feelings in the most exciting way. Be sure to avoid clichés, but add interest and uniqueness. Determine a pattern of rhyme as one would in poetry. Rhyming every other line is the most popular style of rhyme, but this is where the exotic twist of the writer can step in. However, avoid overrhyming and nonsense rhyming. Make certain that the rhyme has a reasonable flow. Form the song

Continued on next page

Continued from previous page

around individuality. This distinguishing and poetic step perfects the complete thought and finishes the writing step of song formation.

6   Writing songs can be a subtle attempt to make a statement. Songwriting is an emotional release that can be personal to both writer and listener for many different reasons. Writing of any kind should be emotionally sincere and can be very therapeutic for both writer and reader. Honest writing is always the easiest and best procedure. A passionate realization can openly interpret thoughts and feelings in an indescribable way. So get out there, write, and discover the hidden truth.

Work Cited

"Kenny Chesney: Here Comes His Life." *Cincinnati Post* 8 July 2004: T14. Infotrac Newspapers. Web. 20 Sept. 2007.

Discussion Questions

1. What is the purpose of this process essay? How does this purpose influence how the process is explained?
2. Identify the key steps the writer recommends for writing a song.
3. Identify places where the writer offers clear warnings.
4. There are many possible ways to write a song, yet the writer only suggests one approach. What are the advantages and disadvantages of this approach?
5. What changes could the writer provide to make this essay even more effective?

Suggestions for Writing

Write a process analysis on one of the topics below or one approved by your instructor. The paper may provide instructions for the reader to follow, tell how a process is performed, or describe how a process develops. Prepare a complete list of steps, arrange them in an appropriate order, and follow them as you write the body of your essay.

1. A natural process, such as erosion, that you observe or research
2. Overcoming some particular phobia
3. The stages in a technical process such as paper production
4. The stages in a student's adjustment to college
5. Creating a FaceBook page
6. Preparing for a romantic picnic in the park, on the beach, or some other place
7. Using a particular computer program
8. Registering for classes online
9. Carrying out a process related to your hobby
10. Placing an item for sale on e-Bay or bidding on e-Bay

11. Studying for an examination
12. Performing a process required by your job
13. Performing a process required by one of your classes
14. Breaking a bad habit
15. Performing a weight-training program
16. Throwing a successful party
17. The stages in some type of storm
18. The stages in a developing friendship
19. The steps in pledging a fraternity or sorority
20. The stages in becoming independent

CRITICAL EDGE

Is there only one way to study effectively, develop a marketing campaign, or cope with a demanding supervisor? No, of course not. As you've already learned, not all processes unfold in a single, predetermined order. The writing process itself illustrates this point.

If you were to think about how you write and talk with other students about their writing processes, you would learn that different writing occasions call for different approaches. When you write a letter to a good friend, you probably spend little or no time on preliminaries but start putting your thoughts on paper as they occur to you. By contrast, other kinds of correspondence, such as inquiry and claim letters, require careful planning, drafting, and perhaps rewriting.

Sometimes the same writing occasion may allow for differing procedures. If you're writing an essay for your English class, you might brainstorm for ideas, develop a detailed outline, rough out a bare-bones draft, and add details as you revise. In talking to other students with the same assignment, you might find that they prefer to write a much longer draft and then whittle it down. Still other students might do very little brainstorming or outlining but a great deal of revising, often making major changes in several drafts. Research papers present a more complex challenge, requiring that the student find and read source material, take notes, and document sources properly. Here again variations are possible: One student might prepare the list of works cited before writing the final draft, while another might perform this task last.

If you decided to synthesize your findings about student writing practices, you would, of course, need to organize your material in some fashion. Perhaps you might focus on the differences that distinguish one writing occasion from another. You could develop each occasion in a separate section by presenting the practices followed by most students while ignoring variations. A second possibility would be to report different practices used for the same writing occasion, first considering the most common practice and then describing the variations. The result might be likened to a cookbook that gives different recipes for the same dish.

Some important processes have been disputed in print, and if you wanted to investigate them you would need to consult written sources rather than talk to others. Informed disagreements exist about how the human species originated, how language developed, and how children mature. Police officers debate the best way to handle drunks, management experts the best way to motivate employees. When you investigate such controversies, determine which view is supported by the best evidence and seems most reasonable. Then, as a writer, you can present the accounts in an appropriate order and perhaps indicate which one you think merits acceptance.

Suggestions for Writing

1. Interview several students about the stages they experienced in a developing friendship and write a paper that discusses these stages. Note any discrepancies in the accounts provided by different students.
2. Research the writing process as presented in several first-year composition textbooks; after pointing out how they differ, indicate which process you prefer and why.
3. Research a controversial process, such as the extinction of the dinosaurs. After presenting different theories about the process, explain which one seems most plausible and why.

Writing a Process Analysis

Plan.

- Select a topic you know well.
- Brainstorm a list of any materials, all steps, any reasons for the steps, any warnings, and any useful feedback.
- Write out a sequence of steps in their order and double-check them for accuracy.

| Writing a **draft** for readers who will perform the action. | Writing a **draft** for readers who will not perform the action. |

| Use polite implied "you" command. | Use pronouns, identified performer, or performer unidentified. |

- Provide an intro that explains context for process. - Identify necessary materials. - Provide steps in sequence with reasons. - Offer warnings where needed. - Give periodic feedback so reader knows if work is successful.	- Provide an intro that engages readers. - Provide steps in process and reasons that they happen. - Let the reader know the function of each step and stage and how it fits the overall process.

Revise.

- Recheck each step, get peer feedback, and revise until satisfactory.
- Have you written consistently for whether the person is performing the action or just understanding it?
- Have you explained all steps, purpose, and any dangers?
- Are your steps in the appropriate order?
- Have you considered appropriate ethical issues?

Proofread.

Classification: Grouping into Categories

From Chapter 12 of *Strategies for Successful Writing*, Ninth Edition. James A. Reinking, Robert von der Osten.

© image100/Corbis.

Classification: Grouping into Categories

Help Wanted, Situations Wanted, Real Estate, Personal. Do these terms look familiar? They do if you've ever scanned the classified ads of the newspaper. Ads are grouped into categories, and each category is then subdivided. The people who assemble this layout are *classifying.* Figure 1 shows the main divisions of a typical classified ad section and a further breakdown of one of them.

As this figure indicates, grouping allows the people who handle ads to divide entries according to a logical scheme and helps readers find what they are looking for. Imagine the difficulty of checking the real estate ads if all the entries were run in the order the ads were placed.

Our minds naturally sort information into categories. Within a few weeks after their birth, infants can tell the faces of family members from those of outsiders. Toddlers learn to distinguish between cats, dogs, and rabbits. In both cases the classification rests solely on physical differences. As we mature we start classifying in more abstract ways, and by adulthood we are constantly sorting things into categories: dates or mates, eating places, oddballs, friends, investments, jobs, political views.

Classification also helps writers and readers come to grips with large or complex topics. It breaks a broad topic into categories according to some specific principle, presents the distinctive features of each category, and shows how the features vary among categories. Segmenting the topic simplifies the discussion by presenting the information in small, neatly sorted piles rather than in one jumbled and confusing heap.

Furthermore, classification helps people make choices. Identifying which groups of consumers—students, accountants, small-business owners—are most likely to buy some new product allows the manufacturer to advertise in appropriate media. Knowing the engine size, maneuverability, seating capacity, and gas mileage of typical subcompact, compact, and intermediate-size cars helps customers decide which one to buy. Examining the features of term, whole-life, and endowment insurance enables prospective buyers to select the policy that best suits their needs.

Classification: Grouping into Categories

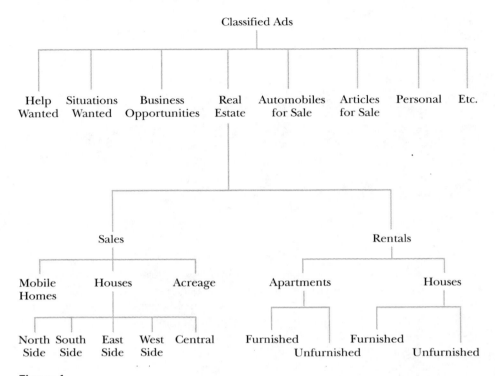

Figure 1

Because classification plays such an important part in our lives, it is a useful writing tool in many situations. Your accounting instructor may ask you to categorize accounting procedures for retail businesses. In a computer class, you may classify computer languages and then specify appropriate applications for each grouping. For an industrial hygiene class, you might categorize types of respiratory protective equipment and indicate when each type is used. On the job, a state health department employee may prepare a brochure grouping illegal drugs into categories based on their effects. The communications director of an investment firm might write a customer letter categorizing investments according to their degree of risk. An employee of a textbook publisher might prepare a catalog grouping new books by field of study.

Selecting Categories

People classify in different ways for different purposes, which generally reflect their interests. A clothing designer might classify people according to their fashion sense, a representative of the National Organization for Women according to their views on women's rights, and the Secretary of Labor according to their occupations. A college's director of housing might classify students according to their type of residence, the dean of students according to their behavior problems, and the financial aid officer according to their sources of income.

When you write a classification paper, choose a principle of classification that's suited not only to your purpose but also to your audience. To illustrate, if you're writing for students, don't classify instructors according to their manner of dress, body build, or cars they drive. These breakdowns probably wouldn't interest most students and certainly wouldn't serve their needs. Instead, develop a more useful principle of classification—perhaps by teaching styles, concern for students, or grading policies.

Sometimes it's helpful or necessary to divide one or more categories into subcategories. If you do, use just one principle of classification for each level. Both levels in Figure 2 meet this test because each reflects a single principle: place of origin for the first, number of cylinders for the second.

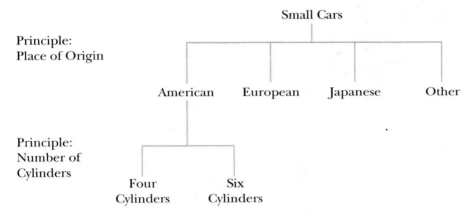

Figure 2   Proper Classification of Small Cars

Now examine Figure 3. This classification is *improper* because it groups cars in two ways—by place of origin and by kind—making it possible for one car to end up in two categories. For example, the German Porsche is both a European car and a sports car. When categories overlap in this way, confusion reigns and nothing is clarified.

Figure 3   Improper Classification of Small Cars

1. **How would each of the following people be most likely to classify the families in Anytown, USA?**

   a. The bishop of the Roman Catholic diocese in which the city is located
   b. The state senator who represents the city
   c. A field worker for the NAACP
   d. The director of the local credit bureau

2. **The following lists contain overlapping categories. Identify the inconsistent item in each list and explain why it is faulty.**

Nurses	Pictures	Electorate in Midville
Surgical nurses	Oil paintings	Republicans
Psychiatric nurses	Magazine illustrations	Democrats
Emergency room nurses	Lithographs	Nonvoters
Terminal care nurses	Watercolors	Independents
Night nurses	Etchings	

Number of Categories

Some classification papers discuss every category included in the topic. Others discuss only selected categories. Circumstances and purpose dictate the scope of the discussion. Suppose you work for the commerce department of your state and are asked to write a report that classifies the major nonservice industries in a certain city and assesses their strengths and weaknesses. Your investigation shows that food processing, furniture making, and the production of auto parts account for more than 95 percent of nonservice jobs. Two minor industries, printing and toy making, provide the rest of the jobs. Given these circumstances, you'd probably focus on the first three industries, mentioning the others only in passing. But if printing and toy making were significant industries, they too would require detailed discussion.

Developing Categories

Develop every category you include with specific, informative details that provide a clear picture of each one and help the reader grasp the distinctions and relationships among them.

Consider the student example on video games at the end of this chapter. The student does not just identify interactive simulation games as a type of games. She explains how these games are distinctive and provides a detailed example of how the games must be played. "One of the earliest of these games was an arcade game called *Dance Dance Revolution*. It requires players to match on a dance pad the moves they are instructed to do on the screen. . . . The success of this game prompted many others like *Karaoke Revolution* in which players sing popular songs into a microphone for points and *Guitar Hero* and *Donkey Konga* where players play on controllers that emulate a guitar and a set of bongos." By developing the paragraph with different examples of how interactive games are played, she builds a better understanding of that distinctive kind of game.

Ethical Issues

Classification can seem quite innocent, and yet it can cause great harm. In India, an entire group numbering millions of people was once classified as "untouchables" and so was denied the jobs and rights of other citizens. Although political progress has considerably improved the lot of these people, discrimination still hobbles their lives. In this country, many high school students have suffered the sting of being classified as "nerds" or "geeks." Clearly you'll have to evaluate the appropriateness and consequences of your classification scheme. To avoid problems, ask and answer these questions:

- Is my classification called for by the situation? It may be appropriate to classify students in a school environment according to their reading skills, but classifying factory workers in this fashion may well be inappropriate and unfair to the people involved.
- Have I avoided the use of damaging classifications? We resent stereotyping because it unjustly reduces us to some distorted general idea. No one is simply a "hillbilly" or a "jock."
- Have I applied my classification without resorting to overgeneralization? In a paper classifying student drinkers, it would be a mistake, and even harmful, to imply that all college students drink excessively.
- Could my classification promote harmful behavior? When classifying the behavior patterns of young urban dwellers, it would be unethical to present favorably the lifestyle of a group that uses hard drugs and engages in disruptive behavior at sporting events.

We are ethically responsible for the classification systems that we use in our writing. Always examine the one you use for suitability, fairness, and potential harm.

Writing a Classification

Planning and Drafting the Classification

Many topics that interest you are potential candidates for classification. If you're selecting your own topic, you might explain different kinds of rock music to novices, take a humorous look at types of teachers, or, in a more serious vein, identify types of discrimination. As always, use one or more narrowing strategies to stimulate your thinking. As possibilities come to mind, examine each one in light of these questions:

What purpose will this classification serve?

Who is my audience and what will interest them?

What are the categories of this topic?

What features distinguish my categories from one another?

Next, determine whether you'll discuss every category or only selected ones, and then set up a classification chart similar to the one following.

Category 1	**Category 2**	**Category 3**
First distinguishing feature	First distinguishing feature	First distinguishing feature
Second distinguishing feature	Second distinguishing feature	Second distinguishing feature

Such a chart helps you see the relationships among categories and provides a starting point for developing your specific details. Proceed by jotting down the details that come to mind for each distinguishing feature of every category. Then prepare a second chart with the distinguishing features and details arranged in the order you want to present them.

Begin your paper by identifying your topic and capturing your reader's attention in some way. A paper classifying hair dyes might point out their growing popularity among both men and women. One classifying snobs might offer an anecdote showing how far snobbery can go. Or you could cite a personal experience that relates to your topic. As always, circumstances dictate your choice.

In the body discuss your categories in whatever order best suits your purpose. Order of climax—least important, more important, most important—often works well. Or perhaps your topic will suggest arranging the categories by behavior, income, education, or physical characteristics. Whatever your arrangement, signal it clearly to your reader. Don't merely start the discussions of your categories by saying first . . . , second . . . , another . . . , next . . . , and the like. These words offer no hint of the rationale behind your order.

In addition, make sure the arrangement of material within the categories follows a consistent pattern. In classifying restrooms, after noting where the restroom can be found, the writer could discuss its floor, walls, and lighting, move to the furniture, and end by discussing the lavatories, soap, and toweling for each category of restroom.

The strategies for ending a classification paper are as varied as those for starting it. A paper on hair dyes might conclude by predicting their continued popularity. One on snobs might end with your recommendations for dealing with them. In other cases, you might express a hope of some kind or advise your reader to do something.

Revising the Classification

Revise your paper by pondering these questions:

Does my classification have a clear sense of purpose and audience?

Does my principle of classification accord with my purpose?

Do any of my categories overlap?

Have I chosen an appropriate number of categories?

Are these categories developed with sufficient details?

Are the categories and details arranged in an effective order?

Have I considered appropriate ethical issues?

STUDENT ESSAY FOR **CLASSIFICATION**

Types of Video Games for Children

Kyra Glass

1   Gift-giving for children and grandchildren has been getting increasingly difficult as the number of options increase. Today dolls and toy cars and board games just aren't going to cut it. Many children are used to interactive toys and toys with electronic components. Most children don't think of Monopoly or tag when they hear the word *game*; to them games are played on a television or a computer screen. Indeed, video game consoles in homes with children have become almost as ubiquitous household appliances as televisions. Most parents and grandparents are familiar with demands for *the* hot new game, but buying video games for their loved ones can be overwhelming. Many adults never had video games growing up, or if they did, video games meant *Pac Man*, *Donkey Kong*, or two plumbers named Mario and Luigi. Although these gaming icons are still available, many parents and grandparents are concerned that they are far out numbered by extremely violent or gruesome video games that they don't want their children playing. Those buying for young gamers may feel that they are stuck, that they will either be unable to buy a game or will end up with a hack-and-slash game that is too violent for younger children. In reality, there is a wide variety of fun and family-friendly games that parents or grandparents can feel good about buying for their young gaming enthusiasts. The easiest way to pick safe games is to check the ratings printed on them; anything that is rated E (for everyone) is safe for children of any age to play; anything rated E 10+ may have some mild cartoon violence but is usually acceptable for most families as well. Games that are rated Teen (T) or Mature (M) are

Continued on next page

Continued from previous page

not a good bet for younger children, and parents should research these games before giving them to their children. But checking the ratings is only the first step. There are many different categories of games with options that are appropriate for younger players: interactive simulation games, adventure/role-playing games, party games, and sports games.

2   One of the most common types of games for children or adults is adventure/role-playing games. In these games, players take on the persona of a character (or several characters) and work their way through a narrative as that character. Although there are many games of this type that aren't appropriate for younger children, a number of age-appropriate games do fall into this category. The key to finding adventure/role-playing games that are appropriate for younger players is in looking at what story the game tells and who the main characters are. A large number of games in this category are based on characters with which children are already familiar. Some of these are based on both live-action and animated children's movies. *A Series of Unfortunate Events* and *The Incredibles* inspired games of the same name, and a whole series of games based on the popular Harry Potter books and movies have been produced. Many of these games based on movies let the players go through an enhanced version of the plot of the movies or books, letting children interact with their favorite stories. Other games are based on TV cartoons like *Jimmy Neutron*, *Kim Possible*, and *SpongeBob SquarePants*, to name only a few. These games often retain the characters and themes of the shows while inventing a new narrative for players to go through in the game. Many of these games, including *Kingdom Hearts* for Play Station 2 or *Nicktoons Unite!* for GameCube, combine many characters owned by the same company such as Disney or Nickelodeon. However, there are also adventure/role-playing games with well-known and beloved characters from other children's video games. The familiar kid-friendly Mario has a role-playing game called *Paper Mario* and an adventure game called *Super Mario Sunshine*, while older children might enjoy *Sonic the Hedgehog*'s cousin in the adventure game *Shadow the Hedgehog*. When trying to choose an adventure or simulation game for a child, often the best place

to start is by picking one of the child's favorite stories or characters from movies, cartoons, and games and seeing if there is a game that features them. It is surprising how often the answer is "yes."

3   In general, the category of sports games is a pretty safe choice when picking games for children. Sports games emulate a version of a sports competition or event for the player's participation. Many different types of games fall into this category: racing games are included here, as are games based on team sports like basketball or football, extreme sports like skateboarding or motorbike racing, and individual sports like skiing or golf. Although there are some sports games that aren't appropriate for children, shoppers can usually find a game rated E for everyone in nearly any category of sports. However, although most sports games are appropriate for children, there are also, on every platform, sports games that are made especially for children to play. These games, like the adventure/role-playing games, keep the best aspects of their genre but draw on characters and environments that are familiar to children. Disney's *Extreme Skate Adventure*, on all three platforms, is a skateboarding game that allows children to create their own character or play as a familiar Disney character. They can then skate in environments from *Toy Story 2*, *The Lion King*, and *Tarzan*. Because this game is tailored to children, it allows them to pick objects such as mirrors or frying pans as well as skateboards. This is part of a series of Disney sports games including *Soccer*, *Football*, and *Basketball*, all on GameCube, and *Golf*, on Playstation 2. The ever-present Mario also has his own series of sports games for children, including *Mario Kart* racing games; *Super Mario Strikers*, a racing game; and games based on baseball, tennis, and golf. These sports franchises might be good for younger players because they are often easier to play and use familiar characters, while Madden, Fifa, or NBA sports games from Electronic Arts may be better choices for older children.

4   Interactive simulation games are an excellent choice for families because they are capable of getting children off the couch, something that many parents worry about with TV and video games. Interactive simulation games give players a hands-on experience that is as close as possible to what their character is doing in the game. One of the

Continued on next page

Continued from previous page

earliest of these games was an arcade game called *Dance Dance Revolution*. It requires players to match on a dance pad the moves they are instructed to do on the screen. Versions of this game are now available on the three main game consoles: X-Box, Playstation 2, and GameCube. The success of this game prompted many others like *Karaoke Revolution*, in which players sing popular songs into a microphone for points, and *Guitar Hero* and *Donkey Konga*, where players play on controllers that emulate a guitar or set of bongos. Most interactive simulation games require special controllers or accessories to play, and one of these accessories, the Eye Toy for Playstation 2, might change the way children think about "sitting" in front of the TV and playing video games. Eye Toy uses a USB camera so the player's body becomes the controller. Games using Eye Toy respond to the movement of the player's body to interact with the game play on screen. Eye Toy was originally packaged with the game *Play*, which featured 12 mini games that used this body motion for everything from dancing to kung fu. Since then, Eye Toy has come out with a variety of interactive games including *Play 2*, *Operation Spy*, and *AntiGrav*, as well as workout-minded games such as *Eye Toy Groove* and *Kinetic*. Interactive simulation games are the perfect choice for parents and grandparents who want to see their children physically active while having a good time.

5   Along with the concern that children spend too much time in front of the TV or on the couch, another common complaint parents have about video games is that unlike board games, they don't always encourage siblings or families to play together. That is why party games are such a great option for parents who want to be able to play along with their children and are interested in making video game time part of family time. Party games usually involve up to four players in competition and are short enough to play a round in one sitting. Most of them are made up of a series of many mini-games (short and simple games or puzzles) that are easy to learn. Most, although not all,

of these party games are styled after board games and are turn-based. A few, like *Monopoly Party*, are exactly like popular board games in video game form. Like adventure games, most party games are based on well-known children's characters. Some of these family-friendly party games are *Disney Party*, *Nickelodeon Party Blast*, *Muppets Party Cruise*, *Shrek*, *Super Party*, and *Wario Ware Inc*. These games range across a variety of console platforms, and all feature well-known characters from movies, television, and children's games. However, perhaps the best-known game in this category is the *Mario Party* series; for Game Cube, there are *Mario Parties 4 through 7*. All these games are different and feature an extensive number of levels and mini-games for families to play together.

6   There are clearly many options for parents and grandparents who want to allow their children to enjoy the same electronic entertainment as their peers while still making sure that they are playing games that are appropriate for them. Buyers can choose from a variety of sports and adventure games that allow children to play as their favorite cartoon characters from movies like Harry Potter to video game icons like Mario or Sonic. Sports games in general are usually good choices for children, but Disney and Mario series can be easier and more fun for younger children. Interactive simulation games get children on their feet dancing, singing, and moving their body to win the game. Party games allow family members to play together in board-game-like formats filled with mini-games. This account of video games is, of course, not all-inclusive, and there are other categories of games, including puzzle games, arcade games, and strategy games, that can be appropriate for children as well. The most important thing for any parent or grandparent to realize is that not all video games are the same. Becoming active in how children spend their play time and helping them choose the games that are appropriate for their age and their personality can help to make sure that they are playing games that are both fun for them and good for the family.

Discussion Questions

1. This classification paper is written to help parents or grandparents select video games for children. How do the purpose and audience of the paper influence how it was written?
2. How does the writer organize each classification section? Is this approach effective?
3. Why does the writer point out the advantage of each kind of video game? Is this appropriate for a classification?
4. In the concluding paragraph the writer indicates that there are other kinds of video games that are not discussed in the paper. How does this affect the credibility and overall effectiveness of the paper?
5. Transitions can be a difficult part of any classification. How would you evaluate the effectiveness of this writer's transitions?

Suggestions for Writing

Write a classification paper on one of the topics below or one approved by your instructor. Determine your purpose and audience, select appropriate categories, decide how many you'll discuss, develop them with specific details, and arrange them in an effective order.

1. College teachers (or college pressures)
2. Pet owners (or types of pets)
3. Herbal remedies
4. Kinds of extreme sports
5. Action movies (or romantic comedies)
6. Video games
7. Dancing
8. Reasons for surfing the Internet
9. Talk show hosts
10. Sports announcers (or fans)
11. Television reality shows (or sitcoms)
12. Alternative medicines
13. Bottled water
14. Careers in your field of interest
15. Friends
16. Dates
17. Web pages
18. Advertisements
19. Cheating (or lies)
20. Leaders

Classification provides an effective tool for organizing material into categories. But you won't always rely exclusively on your own knowledge or experience to determine or develop categories. At times you'll supplement what you bring to a writing assignment with information gained through outside reading.

Suppose that for an introductory business course, you're asked to prepare a paper that explores major types of investments. You realize that some research will be necessary. After consulting a number of books and magazines, you conclude that stocks, bonds, and real estate represent the three main categories of investments and that each category can be divided into several subcategories. Bonds, for example, can be grouped according to issuer: corporate, municipal, and U.S. Treasury securities.

At this point, you recognize that the strategy of classification would work well for this assignment. Reading further, you learn about the financial risks, rewards, and tax consequences associated with ownership. For example, U.S. Treasury securities offer the greatest safety, while corporate and municipal bonds, as well as stocks and real estate, entail varying degrees of risk depending on the financial condition of the issuer and the state of the economy. Similarly, the income from the different categories and subcategories of investments is subject to different kinds and levels of taxation. Thus, income from municipal bonds is generally tax free, income from U.S. Treasury securities is exempt from state and local taxes, and income from other kinds of investments does not enjoy such exemptions.

After assimilating the information you've gathered, you could synthesize the views expressed in your sources as well as your own ideas about investments. You might organize your categories and subcategories according to probable degree of risk, starting with the least risky investment and ending with the most risky. For your conclusion you might offer purchase recommendations for different groups of investors such as young workers, wealthy older investors, and retirees.

Before using the material of others in your writing, examine its merits. Do some sources seem more convincing than others? Why? Do any recommendations stem from self-interest? For example, a writer who seems overly enthusiastic about one type of investment may be associated with an organization that markets it. Are any sources overloaded with material irrelevant to your purpose? Which sources offer the most detail? Asking and answering questions such as these will help you write a more informed paper.

Suggestions for Writing

1. Examine the Reader essays on women's issues or health and then write a paper that draws upon these sources and classifies their content.
2. Read several authors' views on success and then write a paper that draws on these sources and classifies their content.
3. Reflect on the Reader essays that you've studied and then write a paper that presents an appropriate classification system for them, perhaps based on the writers' levels of diction, tone, or reliance on authorities.

Writing a Classification

Plan.

- Identify subject for classification.
- Establish purpose for classification.
- Identify audience.

Determine categories.

- List key categories appropriate to purpose.
- Create a table of categories and brainstorm distinguishing features and details.
- If multiple levels of categories, create a category tree.
- Test categories to make certain they are complete and not overlapping.

Consider order of categories.

- From most important to least
- From least to most important
- By key topic
- Use the table to organize

Create a rough draft.

- Intro: engage reader, identify reason for classification, establish topic.
- Body: explain and exemplify each category in order.
- Conclusion: vary.

Revise.

Gather peer feedback; test hard to see if a category is missing; try other categories.

- Does classification fit purpose?
- Do categories overlap?
- Add necessary details or categories.
- Cut categories that don't fit or help.
- Test the organization.
- Test for ethics.

Proofread.

Comparison: Showing Relationships

From Chapter 13 of *Strategies for Successful Writing*, Ninth Edition. James A. Reinking, Robert von der Osten.

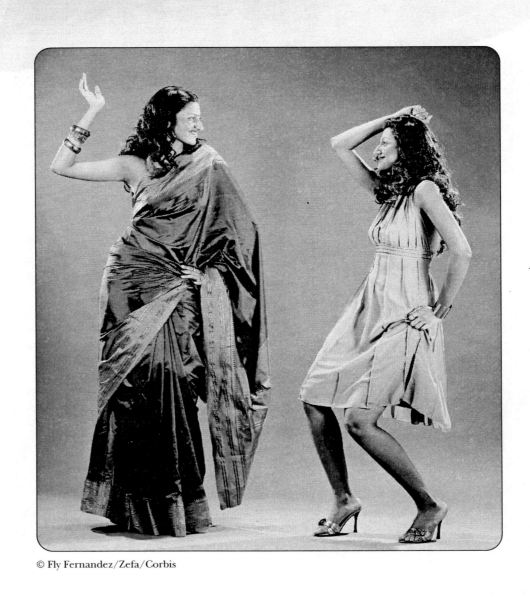

© Fly Fernandez/Zefa/Corbis

Comparison: Showing Relationships

Which candidate for senator should get my vote, Ken Conwell or Jerry Mander?
Let me know whether this new shipment of nylon thread meets specs.
Doesn't this tune remind you of an Anne Murray song?
How does high school in Australia stack up against high school in this country?

Everyone makes *comparisons*, not just once in a while but day after day. When we compare, we examine two or more items for likenesses, differences, or both.

Comparison often helps us choose between alternatives. Some issues are trivial: whether to play World of Warcraft or Warhammer, whether to order pizza or a sub sandwich. But comparison also influences our more important decisions. We weigh majoring in chemistry against majoring in physics, buying against renting, working for Microsoft against working for IBM. An instructor may ask us to write a paper comparing the features of two word-processing systems. An employer may have us weigh two proposals for decreasing employee absenteeism and write a report recommending one of them.

Comparison also acquaints us with unfamiliar things. To help American readers understand the English sport of rugby, a sportswriter might compare its field, team, rules, and scoring system with those for football. To teach students about France's government, a political science textbook might discuss the makeup and election of its parliament and the method of picking its president and premier, using our own government as a backdrop.

Both your classes and your job will call for comparison writing. Your humanities instructor may ask you to compare baroque and classical music and their contributions to later musical developments. Your psychology instructor may want you to compare two types of psychosis and assess the legal and medical ramifications of each. Your biology instructor may have you consider how the features of two kinds of body cell enable them to perform their functions. Comparisons in the workplace are common because they help people make decisions. An office manager may compare several phone systems to determine which one the company should install, a nurse assesses the condition of a patient

"WE'D LIKE TO TAKE YOU UPSTAIRS AND SHOW YOU THE REAL GRACIOUSNESS OF FRATERNITY LIFE, BUT IT'S SORT OF A RULE AROUND HERE TO WAIT UNTIL THE 'RUSHEE' IS PLEDGED."

Richard Bibler, Worthal College Cartoon. Reprinted by permission.

before and after a new medicine is given, an insurance agent points out the features of two insurance policies to highlight the advantages of one.

Selecting Items for Comparison

Any items you compare must share some common ground. For example, you could compare two golfers on driving ability, putting ability, and sand play, or two cars on appearance, gas mileage, and warranty; but you can't meaningfully compare a golfer with a car, any more than you could compare guacamole with Guadalajara or chicken with charcoal. There's simply no basis for comparison.

Any valid comparison, on the other hand, presents many possibilities. Suppose you head the music department of a large store and have two excellent salespeople working for you. The manager of the store asks you to prepare a one- or two-page report that compares their qualifications for managing the music department in a new branch store. Assessing their abilities becomes the guiding purpose that motivates and controls the writing. On the spot you can rule out points such as eye color, hair style, and religion, which have no bearing on job performance. Instead, you must decide what managerial traits the job will require and the extent to which each candidate possesses them. Your thinking might result in a list like this:

Comparison: Showing Relationships

Points of Similarity or Difference	Pat	Mike
1. Ability to deal with customers, sales skills	Excellent	Excellent
2. Effort: regular attendance, hard work on the job	Excellent	Excellent
3. Leadership qualities	Excellent	Good
4. Knowledge of ordering and accounting procedures	Good	Fair
5. Musical knowledge	Excellent	Good

This list tells you which points to emphasize and suggests Pat as the candidate to recommend. You might briefly mention similarities (points 1 and 2) in an introductory paragraph, but the report would focus on differences (points 3, 4, and 5), since you're distinguishing between two employees.

Say you want to compare two good restaurants in order to recommend one of them. List the points of similarity and difference that you might discuss. Differences should predominate because you will base your decision on them.

Developing a Comparison

Successful comparisons rest upon ample, well-chosen details that show just how the items under consideration are alike and different. Such support helps the reader grasp your meaning. Read the following two student paragraphs and note how the concrete details convey the striking differences between south and north 14th Street:

> On 14th Street running south from P Street are opulent department stores, such as Woodward and Lothrop and Julius Garfinkle, and small but expensive clothing stores with richly dressed mannequins in the windows. Modern skyscraping office buildings harbor banks and travel bureaus on the ground floors and insurance companies and corporation headquarters in the upper stories. Dotting the concretescape are high-priced movie theaters, gourmet restaurants, multilevel parking garages, bookstores, and candy-novelty-gift shops, all catering to the prosperous population of the city. This section of 14th Street is relatively clean: The city maintenance crews must clean up after only a nine-to-five populace and the Saturday crowds of shoppers. The pervading mood of the area is one of bustling wealth during the day and, in the night, calm.

> Crossing P Street toward the north, one notes a gradual but disturbing change in the scenery of 14th Street. Two architectural features assault the eyes and automatically register as tokens of trouble: the floodlights that leave no alley or doorway in shadows and the riot screens that cage in the store windows. The buildings are old, condemned,

decaying monoliths, each occupying an entire city block. Liquor stores, drugstores, dusty television repair shops, seedy pornographic bookstores that display photographs of naked bodies with the genital areas blacked out by strips of tape, discount stores smelling perpetually of stale chocolate and cold popcorn, and cluttered pawnshops—businesses such as these occupy the street level. Each is separated from the adjoining stores by a littered entranceway that leads up a decaying wooden stairway to the next two floors. All the buildings are three stories tall; all have most of their windows broken and blocked with boards or newspapers; and all reek of liquor, urine, and unidentifiable rot. And so the general atmosphere of this end of 14th Street is one of poverty and decay.

Student Unknown

Vivid details depict with stark clarity the economic differences between the two areas.

Organizing a Comparison

You can use either of two basic patterns to organize a comparison paper: block or alternating. The paper may deal with similarities, differences, or some combination of them.

The Block Pattern   The block pattern first presents all of the points of comparison for one item and then all of the points of comparison for the other. Here is the comparison of the two salespeople, Pat and Mike, outlined according to the block pattern:

  I. Introduction: mentions similarities in sales skills and effort but recommends Pat for promotion.
 II. Specific points about Mike
     A. Leadership qualities
     B. Knowledge of ordering and accounting procedures
     C. Musical knowledge
III. Specific points about Pat
     A. Leadership qualities
     B. Knowledge of ordering and accounting procedures
     C. Musical knowledge
 IV. Conclusion: reasserts that Pat should be promoted.

The block pattern works best with short papers or ones that include only a few points of comparison. The reader can easily remember all the points in the first block while reading the second.

The Alternating Pattern   The alternating pattern presents a point about one item, then follows immediately with a corresponding point about the other. Organized in this way, the Pat-and-Mike paper would look like this:

I. Introduction: mentions similarities in sales skills and effort but recommends Pat for promotion.
II. Leadership qualities
    A. Mike's qualities
    B. Pat's qualities
III. Knowledge of ordering and accounting procedures
    A. Mike's knowledge
    B. Pat's knowledge
IV. Musical knowledge
    A. Mike's knowledge
    B. Pat's knowledge
V. Conclusion: reasserts that Pat should be promoted.

For longer papers that include many points of comparison, use the alternating method. Discussing each point in one place highlights similarities and differences; your reader doesn't have to pause and reread in order to grasp them. The alternating plan also works well for short papers.

Once you select your pattern, arrange your points of comparison in an appropriate order. Take up closely related points one after the other. Depending on your purpose, you might work from similarities to differences or the reverse. Often, a good writing strategy is to move from the least significant to the most significant point so that you conclude with punch.

Using the points of comparison you selected for the previous exercise, prepare outlines for a paper organized according to the block and then the alternating pattern.

Using Analogy

An *analogy*, a special type of comparison, calls attention to one or more similarities underlying two kinds of an item that seem to have nothing in common. While some analogies stand alone, most clarify concepts in other kinds of writing. Whatever their role, they follow the same organizational pattern as ordinary comparisons.

An analogy often explains something unfamiliar by likening it to something familiar. Here is an example:

> The atmosphere of Earth acts like any window in serving two very important functions. It lets light in, and it permits us to look out. It also serves as a shield to keep out dangerous or uncomfortable things. A normal glazed window lets us keep our houses warm by keeping out cold air, and it prevents rain, dirt, and unwelcome insects and animals from coming in. . . . Earth's atmospheric window also helps to keep our planet at a comfortable temperature by holding back radiated heat and protecting us from dangerous levels of ultraviolet light.

Lester del Ray, The Mysterious Sky

Lester del Ray, *The Mysterious Shy* (New York: Chilton Book Company, 1964).

Conversely, an analogy sometimes highlights the unfamiliar in order to help illuminate the familiar. The following paragraph discusses the qualities and obligations of an unfamiliar person, the mountain guide, to shed light on a familiar practice—teaching:

> The mountain guide, like the true teacher, has a quiet authority. He or she engenders trust and confidence so that one is willing to join the endeavor. The guide accepts his leadership role, yet recognizes that success (measured by the heights that are scaled) depends upon the close cooperation and active participation of each member of the group. He has crossed the terrain before and is familiar with the landmarks, but each trip is new and generates its own anxiety and excitement. Essential skills must be mastered; if they are lacking, disaster looms. The situation demands keen focus and rapt attention: slackness, misjudgment, or laziness can abort the venture.
>
> Nancy K. Hill, "Scaling the Heights: The Teacher as Mountaineer"

Nancy K. Hill, "Scalling the Heights: The Teacher as Mountaineer," *The Chronicle of Higher Education,* June 16, 1980, p. 48.

When you develop an analogy, keep these points in mind:

1. Your readers must be well acquainted with the familiar item. If they aren't, the point is lost.
2. The items must indeed have significant similarities. You could develop a meaningful analogy between a kidney and a filter or between cancer and anarchy but not between a fiddle and a flapjack or a laser and limburger cheese.
3. The analogy must truly illuminate. Overly obvious analogies, such as one comparing a battle to an argument, offer few or no revealing insights.
4. Overextended analogies can tax the reader's endurance. A multipage analogy between a heart and a pump would likely overwhelm the reader with all its talk of valves, hoses, pressures, and pumping.

Ethical Issues

Although an old adage declares that "comparisons are odious," most people embrace comparisons except when they are unfair. Unfortunately, this situation occurs all too often. For example, advertisers commonly magnify trivial drawbacks in competitive products while exaggerating the benefits of their own merchandise. Politicians run attack ads that distort their opponents' views and demean the opponents' character. And when scientific theories clash, supporters of one view have been known to alter their findings in order to undermine the other position. Your readers expect any comparison to meet certain ethical standards. Ask and answer these questions to help ensure that those you write measure up.

- Have I avoided skewing one or both of my items in order to ensure a particular outcome?
- Are the items I'm comparing properly matched? It would be unethical to compare a student essay to a professional one in order to demonstrate the inadequacy of the former.
- If I'm using an analogy, is it appropriate? Comparing immigration officials to Nazi storm troopers is ethically odious: It trivializes the suffering and deaths of millions of Nazi victims and taints the officials with a terrible label.

Writing a Comparison

Planning and Drafting the Comparison

Don't write merely to fulfill an assignment; if you do, your paper will likely ramble aimlessly and fail to deliver a specific message. Instead, build your paper around a clear sense of purpose. Do you want to show the superiority of one product or method over another? Do you want to show how sitcoms today differ from those twenty years ago? Purpose governs the details you choose and the organization you follow.

Whether you select your own topic or write on an assigned one, answer these questions:

What purpose will my comparison serve?

Who will be my audience and why will they want to read the essay?

What points of similarity or difference will I discuss?

To develop the comparison, draw up a chart similar to this one.

Item A	Item B
First point of comparison	First point of comparison
Second point of comparison	Second point of comparison

Next, brainstorm each point in turn, recording appropriate supporting details. When you finish, stand back and ask these questions:

Do all the details relate to my purpose?

Do any new details come to mind?

In what order should I organize the details?

When you decide upon an order, copy the points of comparison and the details, arranged in the order you will follow, into a chart like the one below.

Item A	Item B
First point of comparison	First point of comparison
First detail	First detail
Second detail	Second detail
Second point of comparison	Second point of comparison

Use the introduction to identify your topic and arouse the reader's interest. If you intend to establish the superiority of one item over the other, you might call attention to your position. If you're comparing something unfamiliar with something familiar, you might explain the importance of understanding the unfamiliar item.

Organize the body of your paper according to whichever pattern—block or alternating—suits its length and the number of points you're planning to take up. If you explain something familiar by comparing it with something unfamiliar, start with the familiar item. If you try to show the superiority of one item over another, proceed from the less to the more desirable one. Note that both of the Pat-and-Mike outlines put Mike ahead of Pat, the superior candidate.

Write whatever kind of conclusion will round off your discussion effectively. Many comparison papers end with a recommendation or a prediction. A paper comparing two brands of stereo receivers might recommend purchasing one of them. A paper comparing a familiar sport, such as football, with an unfamiliar one, such as rugby, might predict the future popularity of the latter. Unless you've written a lengthy paper, don't summarize the likenesses and differences you've presented. If you've done a proper writing job, your reader already has them clearly in mind.

Revising the Comparison

Revise your paper in light of the questions that follow:

> Have I accomplished my purpose, whether to choose between alternatives or acquaint the reader with something unfamiliar?
>
> For something unfamiliar, have I shown clearly just how it is like and unlike the familiar item?
>
> Have I consistently written with my audience in mind?
>
> Have I considered all points of similarity and difference that relate to my purpose?
>
> Have I included appropriate supporting details?
>
> Are my comparisons arranged effectively?
>
> Have I considered appropriate ethical issues?

SAMPLE

STUDENT ESSAY OF **COMPARISON**

Differences between Korean and English

Sunho Lee

University of Nevada Las Vegas

Director: Vicki Homes

1   As the world undergoes globalization, English is given a great deal of weight as an official language; as a result, many people have been trying to learn English. The Korean people have also been making efforts to acquire the language; however, learning is troublesome for Korean students because English and Korean have a lot of differences. Three major differences between English and Korean give people from Korea special difficulty in learning English: accent, tense, and articles.

2   Accent is one of the obvious differences that frustrate Korean people who try to become skilled at English. For instance, *impact* can be a noun or a verb, depending on how it is stressed. When people who speak English emphasize the first syllable, *impact* is a noun. If people who use English stress the second syllable, *impact* is a verb. The Korean tongue does not use accents in this way and spells noun and verb forms completely differently. Thus distinguishing parts of speech by accent is not something familiar to Korean learners.

3   The second difference is tense, especially the present perfect tense. The present perfect tense describes actions or states that begin in the past, continue into the present, and might continue into the future. This kind of tense does not exist in Korean grammar. For example, the meanings of "I worked out" and "I have worked out" are slightly dissimilar. Of course, Korean students can interpret both meanings, yet when people who are used to speaking Korean use the present perfect tense in English, they have trouble because past and present perfect are not distinguished in the Korean language.

4   The last noticeable difference between Korean and English is the use of articles: definite and indefinite. "Ducks like to swim," "There is a duck in my bathtub," and "The duck quacked all night" are good examples. Each *ducks* or *duck* is different in these examples, but a Korean learner cannot easily see the difference between the usages. One English instructor said, "When I speak English, a bird flies to me and gives me some tips about what article I should use in this situation." This means that even native English speakers cannot define exactly how to use articles. To be sure, English grammar has some rules about how to use articles, but the number of exceptions is more than the regulations. The Korean language does not have articles; in addition, before Korean students learn English, they do not know what an article is exactly. Accordingly, for someone learning English using articles precisely is very complicated.

5   All languages have differences. Thus for a second language learner, studying English is very hard, and it is challenging to overcome the variations between the two languages. It is especially difficult because of the differences in stress, the present perfect tense, and articles. Although these features of English are not easy to understand and use, if Koreans who struggle to use English fluently study constantly, they can finally conquer English.

Discussion Questions

1. This writer decided to use a point-by-point rather than a block comparison. Was this the right decision? Why?
2. While the writer provides clear examples in English, there are no matching examples in Korean. Is this the right choice for this communication situation? Why or why not?
3. What is the audience and purpose for this essay? Does it achieve its purpose?
4. What are some of the effective organizational strategies of this essay?
5. What are the advantages and disadvantages that would result if the writer had looked at additional differences between English and Korean?

Suggestions for Writing

1. Write a properly focused comparison essay on one of the topics below or another that your instructor approves. Determine the points you will discuss and how you will develop and arrange them. Emphasize similarities, differences, or both.

   a. The representation of women, fathers, teenagers, or some other group in a 1950s or '60s sitcom and in a similar contemporary sitcom
   b. The physical or mental demands of two jobs
   c. Male and female styles of conversation
   d. Online and brick-and-morter shopping
   e. A print and an online newspaper
   f. The playing styles of two NBA or WNBA superstars
   g. Two Web servers such as AOL and Earthlink
   h. A high-pressure and a no-pressure salesperson
   i. Online and traditional dating
   j. The business or residential districts of two cities or a wealthy and a working-class residential district in the same city
   k. A favorite social spot during the day and during the evening
   l. Film and digital photography
   m. The effectiveness of two pieces of writing
   n. Traditional and extreme sports
   o. Two or more college or business Web pages
   p. Two musical groups or musical styles
   q. Two managers (or styles of managing)
   r. Authoritarian vs. permissive parenting
   s. Two or more products being considered for purchase
   t. Two or more video games

2. Develop an analogy based on one of the following sets of items or another set that your instructor approves. Proceed as you would for any other comparison.

   a. The offerings in a college catalog and a restaurant
   b. A conquering army and a swarm of locusts

c. Driving on certain highways and gambling

d. A heart and a pump

e. Writing and gardening

f. A teacher and a merchant

g. Cancer and anarchy

h. A parent and a farmer

i. A brain and a computer

j. Developing an idea and building a house

k. Succeeding at school and winning a military campaign

l. A workaholic and an alcoholic

m. A mob and a storm

n. A kidney and a filter

o. A cluttered attic and a disorderly mind

p. Reading a book and exploring a new place

q. A rock concert and a circus

r. A party and a circus

s. Casinos and robbery

t. Contemporary America and an amusement park

CRITICAL EDGE

Although you rely on your own knowledge or findings to develop many comparisons, in some cases you'll synthesize material from other sources.

Let's say that your business management instructor has asked you to prepare a report on the management styles of two high-profile chief executive officers (CEOs) at Fortune 500 companies that manufacture the same kinds of products. You realize that you'll need to do some reading in business periodicals like *Forbes*, *Fortune*, and the *Wall Street Journal* in order to complete this assignment. Your sources reveal that the first CEO favors a highly centralized managerial structure with strict limits on what can be done by all employees except top executives. The company has pursued foreign markets by establishing factories overseas and has aggressively attempted to merge with or acquire its domestic competitors. The second CEO has established a decentralized managerial structure that allows managers at various levels of the company to make key decisions. The company has also established a strong foreign presence, but it has done so primarily by entering into joint ventures with foreign firms. Most of its domestic expansion has resulted from the construction of new plants rather than from mergers or takeovers. Both CEOs have borrowed heavily to finance their companies' expansion. These three differences and one similarity are your points of comparison, which you can organize using either the block or alternating pattern. You might conclude by indicating why you prefer one of the two management styles.

After you've read the views expressed by your sources, examine them critically. Does any of the information about the two CEOs seem slanted so that it appears to misrepresent their management styles? For example, do any of the writers seem to exaggerate the positive or negative features of centralized or decentralized management? Do appropriate examples support the writers' contentions? Does any relevant information appear to be missing? Does any source contain material that isn't related to your purpose? Judging the works of others in this fashion will help you write a better report.

Suggestions for Writing

1. Read "The Case for Amnesty" and "Not Amnesty but Attrition" and then compare the views of these two writers.
2. Read several reviews of the same movie and then compare what the critics have written.
3. Write a criticism of a comparison you recently read that you thought was unreasonable.

Writing a Comparison

Plan.

- Identify items for comparison.
- Establish purpose for comparison.
- Identify and analyze audience.

Brainstorm key points of comparison.

- Brainstorm details for each comparison
- Make observations of items if possible

Test whether:
Points are complete.
Points are not
skewed.
Points meet purposes.

Create rough plan or table.

- Create table laying out points of comparison and details.
- Determine pattern: block or point by point.

Create a rough draft.

- Introduction establishes purpose for comparison and main point.
- Body develops each point of comparison with detail using pattern.
- Conclusions vary but reaffirm main point.

Revise: Gather peer responses, talk over topic, reexamine items.

- Re-brainstorm points of comparison.
- Does everything fit the purpose?
- Add additional similarities or differences as needed.
- Cut points that don't fit.
- Test organization, especially transitions that are critical.

Proofread.

Cause and Effect: Explaining Why

From Chapter 14 of *Strategies for Successful Writing*, Ninth Edition. James A. Reinking, Robert von der Osten.

Cause and Effect: Explaining Why

Cause and effect, like the two sides of a coin, are inseparably linked and together make up *causation*. Cause probes the reasons why actions, events, attitudes, and conditions exist. Effect examines their consequences. Causation is important to us because it can explain historical events, natural happenings, and the actions and attitudes of individuals and groups. It can help us anticipate the consequences of personal actions, natural phenomena, or government policies.

Everyone asks and answers questions of causation. Scott wonders why Sue *really* broke off their relationship, and Jennifer speculates on the consequences of changing her major. People wonder why child abuse and homelessness are on the rise, and millions worry about the effects of corporate cost cutting and violence in our schools.

Inevitably, therefore, you will need to write papers and reports that employ causation. Your instructors might ask you to write on topics such as the causes of the American Revolution, the consequences of white-collar crime, the reasons why so many couples are divorcing, or the effects of different fertilizers on plant growth. An employer may want a report on why a certain product malfunctions, what might happen if a community redesigns its traffic pattern, or how a school closing might affect business.

Patterns in Causal Analysis

Several organizational patterns are possible for a causal analysis. Sometimes, a single cause produces several effects. For instance, poor language skills prevent college students from keeping up with required reading, taking adequate notes, and writing competent papers and essay exams. To explore such a single cause–multiple effect relationship, construct outlines similar to the following two:

I. Introduction: identifies cause   I. Poor language skills
II. Body   II. Body
   A. Effect number 1   A. Can't keep up with required reading

B. Effect number 2
C. Effect number 3
III. Conclusion

B. Can't take adequate notes
C. Can't write competent
    papers or exams
III. Conclusion

Alternatively, you might discuss the cause after the effects are presented.

On the other hand, several causes may join forces to produce one effect. Zinc production in the United States, for example, has decreased over the last few years because it can be produced more cheaply abroad than it can here, it is being replaced on cars by plastics and lighter metals, and it cannot be recycled. Here's how you might organize a typical multiple cause–single effect paper:

I. Introduction: identifies
   effect
II. Body
    A. Cause number 1
    B. Cause number 2
    C. Cause number 3
III. Conclusion

I. Decrease in U.S. zinc production
II. Body
    A. Produced more cheaply abroad
    B. Replaced on cars by plastics,
       lighter metals
    C. Cannot be recycled
III. Conclusion

Sometimes discussion of the effect follows the presentation of causes.

At times a set of events forms a causal chain, with each event the effect of the preceding one and the cause of the following one. For example, a student sleeps late and so misses breakfast and ends up hungry and distracted, which in turn results in a poor performance on an exam. Interrupting the chain at any point halts the sequence. Such chains can be likened to a row of upright dominoes that fall one after the other when the first one is pushed. Belief in a domino theory, which held that if one nation in Southeast Asia fell to the communists all would, one after the other, helped bring about U.S. entry into the Vietnam War. Causal chains can also help explain how devices function and some social changes proceed. The following outlines typify the arrangement of a paper explaining a causal chain:

I. Introduction
II. Body
    A. Cause
    B. Effect
    C. Cause
    D. Effect
III. Conclusion

I. Introduction
II. Body
    A. Sleep late
    B. Miss breakfast
    C. Become hungry and distracted
    D. Perform poorly on exam
III. Conclusion

Papers of this kind resemble process analyses, but process is concerned with *how* the events occur, cause and effect with *why*.

In many situations the sequence of causes and effects is too complex to fit the image of a chain. Suppose you are driving to a movie on a rainy night. You approach an intersection screened by bushes and, because you have the right-of-way, start across. Suddenly a car with unlit headlights looms directly in your path. You hit the brakes but skid on the slippery pavement and crash into the other car, crumpling its left fender and damaging your own bumper. Later, as you think about the episode, you begin to sense its complexities.

Obviously, the *immediate cause* of the accident was the other driver's failure to heed the stop sign. But other causes also played roles: the bushes and unlit headlights that kept you from seeing the other car sooner; the starts and stops, speedups and slowdowns that brought the two cars to the intersection at the same time; the wet pavement you skidded on; and the movie that brought you out in the first place.

You also realize that the effects of the accident go beyond the fender and bumper damage. After the accident, a police officer ticketed the other driver. As a result of the delay, you missed the movie. Further, the accident unnerved you so badly that you couldn't attend classes the next day and therefore missed an important writing assignment. Because of a bad driving record, the other driver lost his license for sixty days. Clearly, the effects of this accident rival the causes in complexity.

Here's how you might organize a multiple cause–multiple effect essay:

Introduction	The accident
Body	Body
I. Causes	I. Causes of the accident
A. Cause number 1	A. Driver ran stop sign
B. Cause number 2	B. Bushes and unlit headlights
C. Cause number 3	impaired vision
II. Effects	C. Wet pavement caused skidding
A. Effect number 1	II. Effects of the accident
B. Effect number 2	A. Missed the movie
C. Effect number 3	B. Unnerved so missed classes
Conclusion	next day
	C. Other driver lost license
	Conclusion

In some situations, however, you might first present the effects, then turn to the causes.

1. Read the following selection and then arrange the events in a causal chain:

Although some folk societies still exist today, similar human groups began the slow process of evolving into more complex societies many millennia ago, through settlement in villages and through advances in technology and organizational structure. This gave rise to the second level of organization: civilized preindustrial, or "feudal," society. Here there is a surplus of food because of the selective cultivation of grains—and also because of the practice of animal husbandry. The food surplus permits both the specialization of labor and the kind of class structure that can, for instance, provide the leadership and command the manpower to develop and maintain extensive irrigation systems (which in turn makes possible further increases in the food supply). . . .

Gideon Sjöberg, "The Origin and Development of Cities"

2. **Trace the possible effects of the following occurrences:**

a. You pick out a salad at the cafeteria and sit down to eat. Suddenly you notice a large green worm on one of the lettuce leaves.

b. As you leave your composition classroom, you trip and break your arm.

c. Your boss has warned you not to be late to work again. You are driving to work with ten minutes to spare when you get a flat tire.

Gideon Sjoberg, "The Origin and Development of Cities," *Scientific American*, Sept. 1965, p. 55.

Reasoning Errors in Causal Analysis

Ignoring Multiple Causes

An effect rarely stems from a single cause. The person who believes that permissive parents have caused the present upsurge of venereal disease or the one who blames television violence for the climbing numbers of emotionally disturbed children oversimplifies the situation. Permissiveness and violence perhaps did contribute to these conditions. Without much doubt, however, numerous other factors also played important parts.

Mistaking Chronology for Causation

Don't assume that just because one event followed another that the first necessarily caused the second. This kind of faulty thinking feeds many popular superstitions. Horace walks under a ladder, later stubs his toe, and thinks that his path caused his pain. Sue breaks a mirror just before Al breaks their engagement; then she blames the cracked mirror. Many people once believed that the election of Herbert Hoover as president in 1928 brought on the Great Depression in 1929. Today some people believe that the testing of atomic weapons has altered our weather patterns. Don't misunderstand: One event *may* cause the next; but before you go on record with your conclusion, make sure that you're not dealing with mere chronology.

Confusing Causes with Effects

Young children sometimes declare that the moving trees make the wind blow. Similarly, some adults may think that Pam and Paul married because they fell in love, when in reality economic necessity mandated the vows, and love came later. Scan your evidence carefully in order to avoid such faulty assertions.

1. **Which of the following statements point toward papers that will focus on causes? Which point toward papers focusing on effects? Explain your answers.**

a. Most of the problems that plague newly married couples are the direct outgrowth of timidity and pride.

b. The Marshall Plan was designed to aid the economic recovery of Europe after World War II.

c. The smoke from burning poison ivy can bring on a skin rash and lung irritation.

d. Popularity in high school stems largely from good looks, a pleasing personality, participation in school activities, the right friends, and frequent dates.

2. **Identify which of the following paragraphs deals with causes, which with effects. List the causes and effects.**

a.   Color filters offer three advantages in black-and-white photography. First, a particular color will be lightened by a filter of the same color. For example, in a photograph of a red rose in a dark blue vase, both will appear almost the same shade of gray if no filter is used. However, when photographed through a red filter, the rose will appear much lighter than the vase; and through a blue filter the vase will appear much lighter than the rose. This effect can be useful in emphasizing or muting certain objects in a photograph. Second, a particular color filter will darken its complementary color in the scene. Consequently, any orange object will appear darker than normal if a blue filter is used. Finally, color filters can reduce or increase atmospheric haze. For example, in a distant aerial shot there will often be so much haze that distant detail is obscured. To eliminate haze almost entirely, the photographer can use a deep red filter. On the other hand, if more haze is desired in order to achieve an artistic effect, varying shades of blue filters can be used.

Timothy Kelly

b.   Overeating, which has become a national pastime for millions of Americans, has several roots. For example, parents who are concerned that their children get enough to eat during the growing years overfeed them and thereby establish a lifetime overeating habit. The child who is constantly praised for cleaning up his plate experiences a sort of gratification later on as he cleans up all too many plates. The easy availability of so much food is a constant temptation for many people, especially the types of food served at fast-food restaurants and merchandised in the frozen food departments of supermarkets. Equally tempting are all the snack foods constantly advertised on TV. But many people don't need temptation from the outside; their overeating arises from such psychological factors as nervousness, boredom, loneliness, insecurity, an overall discontent with life, or an aversion to exercise. Thus, overeating can actually be a symptom of psychological surrender to, or withdrawal from, the complexities and competition of modern life.

Kenneth Reichow

Ethical Issues

Causation is not immune from abuse, either accidental or deliberate. Imagine the consequences of an article that touts a new herbal remedy but fails to mention several potentially serious side effects that could harm many users. Think about the possible strain on your relationship with a friend if she unjustly suspected you of starting a vicious rumor about her. Writing cause-and-effect papers creates an ethical responsibility. Asking and answering these questions will help you meet that obligation.

- Have I tried to uncover all of the causes that might result in a particular outcome? A report blaming poor instruction alone for a high student failure rate in a certain town's public schools almost certainly overlooks such factors as oversized classes, inadequate facilities, and poor home environments.
- Have I carefully weighed the importance of the causes I've uncovered? If a few, but not most, of the classes in the school system with problems are oversized, then the report should not stress their significance.
- Have I tried to uncover and discuss every important effect, even one that might damage a case I'm trying to make? A report emphasizing the beneficial effects of jogging would be dangerously negligent if it failed to note the potential for injury.
- What would be the consequences if people act on my analysis?

Careful evaluation of causes and effects not only fulfills your writing obligation but also your ethical one.

Writing a Causal Analysis

Planning and Drafting the Causal Analysis

Because you have probably speculated about the causes and effects of several campus, local, state, or national problems, writing this type of paper should pose no great difficulty. If you choose your own topic, perhaps your personal experience will suggest something promising. Topics such as "Why I Dislike (or Like) Foreign Cars" and "How My Father's (or Someone Else's) Death Has Changed My Life" might work well. Nonpersonal topics also offer writing possibilities. For instance, "What's Behind Teenage Suicides?" and "The Impact of Global Markets on American jobs" would allow you to draw on library resources.

Answer these questions about each candidate:

What purpose will guide this writing?

Who is my audience? Will the topic interest them? Why or why not?

Shall I focus on causes, effects, or both?

Brainstorming your topic for supporting details should be easy. If you're dealing with causes, pose these questions about each one:

How significant is this cause?

Could it have brought about the effect by itself?

Does it form part of a chain?

Precisely how does it contribute to the effect?

For papers dealing with effects, substitute the following questions for the ones above:

How important is this effect?

What evidence will establish its importance?

Charting your results can help you prepare for writing the paper. To tabulate causes, use an arrangement like this one:

Cause	Contribution to Effect
First cause	Specific contribution
Second cause	Specific contribution

For effects, use this chart:

Effect	Importance
First effect	Why important
Second effect	Why important

Once your items are tabulated, examine them carefully for completeness. Perhaps you've overlooked a cause or effect or have slighted the significance of one you've already mentioned. Think about the order in which you'd like to discuss your items and prepare a revised chart that reflects your decision.

Use the opening of your paper to identify your topic and indicate whether you plan to discuss causes, effects, or both. You can signal your intention in a number of ways. To prepare for a focus on causes, you might use the words *cause, reason,* or *stem from,* or you might ask why something has occurred. To signal a paper on effects, you might use *effect, fallout,* or *impact,* or you might ask what has happened since something took place. Read these examples:

Signals causes: Midville's recent decrease in street crime stems primarily from its expanded educational program, growing job opportunities for young people, and falling rate of drug addiction.

Signals effects: Since my marriage to Rita, how has my social life changed?

At times you may choose some dramatic attention-getter. For a paper on the effects of radon, a toxic radioactive gas present in many homes, you might note that "Although almost everyone now knows about the hazards associated with smoking, eating high-cholesterol foods, and drinking excessively, few people are aware that just going home could be hazardous to one's health." If you use an arresting statement, be sure the content of your paper warrants it.

How you organize the body of the paper depends on your topic. Close scrutiny may reveal that one cause was indispensable; the rest merely played supporting roles. If so, discuss the main cause first. In analyzing your automobile mishap, which fits this situation, start with the failure of the other driver to yield the right-of-way; then fan out to any other causes that merit mentioning. Sometimes you'll find that no single cause was essential but that all of them helped matters along. Combinations of this kind lie at the heart of many social and economic concerns: inflation, depression, and urban crime rates, to name just a few. Weigh each cause carefully and rank them in importance. If your topic and purpose will profit from building suspense, work from the least important cause to the most important. Otherwise, reverse the order. For analyzing causal chains, chronological order works effectively.

If space won't permit you to deal adequately with every cause, pick out the two or three you consider most important and limit your discussion to them. To avoid giving your reader an oversimplified impression, note that other causes exist. Even if length poses no problem, don't attempt to trace every cause to some more remote cause and then to a still more remote one. Instead, determine some sensible cutoff point that accords with your purpose, and don't go beyond it.

Treat effects as carefully as you do causes. Keep in mind that effects often travel in packs, and try to arrange them in some logical order. If they occur together, consider order of climax. If one follows the other in a chainlike sequence, present them in that fashion. If space considerations dictate, limit your discussion to the most interesting or significant effects. Whatever order you choose for your paper, don't jump helter-skelter from cause to effect to cause in a way that leaves your reader bewildered.

As you write, don't restrict yourself to a bare-bones discussion of causes and effects. If, for instance, you're exploring the student parking problem on your campus, you might describe the jammed lots or point out that students often miss class because they have to drive around and look for spots. Similarly, don't simply assert that the administration's insensitivity contributes to the problem. Instead, cite examples of the college's refusal to answer letters about the situation or to discuss it. To provide statistical evidence of the problem's seriousness, you might note the small number of lots, the limited spaces in each, and the approximate number of student cars on campus.

It's important to remember, however, that you're not just listing causes and effects; you're showing the reader their connection. Let's see how one student handled this connection. After you've read "Why Students Drop Out of College," the student essay that follows in this chapter, carefully reexamine paragraph 3. Note how the sentence beginning "In many schools" and the two following it show precisely how poor study habits develop. Note further how the sentence beginning "This laxity produces" and the three following it show precisely how such poor habits result in "a flood of low grades and failure." Armed with this information, readers are better able to avoid poor study habits and their consequences.

Causal analyses can end in several ways. A paper discussing the effects of acid rain on America's lakes and streams might specify the grave consequences of failing to deal with the problem or express the hope that something will be done. Frequently, writers use their conclusions to evaluate the relative importance of their causes or effects.

Revising the Causal Analysis

Answer these questions as you revise your causal analysis:

Have I made the right decision in electing to focus on causes, effects, or both?

Have I ferreted out all important causes and effects? Mistakenly labeled something as an effect merely because it follows something else? Confused causes with effects?

Am I dealing with a causal chain? An immediate cause and several supporting causes? Multiple causes and effects?

Have I presented my causes and effects in an appropriate order?

Have I supported my discussion with sufficient details?

Have I considered appropriate ethical issues?

SAMPLE

STUDENT ESSAY OF **CAUSE AND EFFECT**

Why Students Drop Out of College

Diann Fisher

1　　Each fall a new crop of first-year college students, wavering between high hopes for the future and intense anxiety about their new status, scan college maps searching for their classrooms. They have been told repeatedly that college is the key to a well-paying job, and they certainly don't want to support themselves by flipping hamburgers or working at some other dead-end job. So, notebooks at the ready, they await what college has in store. Unfortunately many of them—indeed, over 30 percent—will not return after the first year. Why do so many students leave? There are several reasons. Some find the academic program too hard, some lack the proper study habits or motivation, others fall victim to the temptations of the college environment, and a large group leave for personal reasons.

2　　Not surprisingly, the academic shortcomings of college students have strong links to high school. In the past, a high school student who lacked the ability or desire to take a college-preparatory course could settle for a diploma in general studies and afterward find a job with

Continued on next page

Continued from previous page

decent pay. Now that possibility scarcely exists, so many poorly prepared students feel compelled to try college. Getting accepted by some
schools isn't difficult. Once in, though, the student who has taken nothing beyond general mathematics, English, and science faces serious
trouble when confronted with college algebra, first-year composition,
and biological or physical science. Most colleges do offer remedial
courses and other assistance that may help some weaker students to
survive. In spite of everything, however, many others find themselves
facing ever-worsening grade-point averages and either fail or just
give up.

3   Like academic shortcomings, poor study habits have their roots in
high school, where even average students can often breeze through with
a minimum of effort. In many schools, outside assignments are rare and
so easy that they require little time or thought to complete. To accommodate slower students, teachers frequently repeat material so many times
that slightly better students can grasp it without opening their books.
And when papers are late, teachers often don't mark them down. This
laxity produces students who can't or don't want to study, students totally
unprepared for the rigorous demands of college. There, courses may
require several hours of study each week in order to be passed with even
a C. In many programs, outside assignments are commonplace and
demanding. Instructors expect students to grasp material after one
explanation, and many won't accept late papers at all. Students who
don't quickly develop disciplined study habits face a flood of low grades
and failure.

4   Poor student motivation aggravates faulty study habits. Students
who thought high school was boring find even less allure in the more
challenging college offerings. Lacking any commitment to do well,
they shrug off assigned papers, skip classes, and avoid doing
required reading. Over time, classes gradually shrink as more
and more students stay away. With final exams upon them, some
return in a last-ditch effort to salvage a passing grade, but by then
it is too late. Eventually, repetition of this scenario forces the
students out.

5   The wide range of freedoms offered by the college environment can overwhelm even well-prepared newcomers. While students are in high school, parents are on hand to make them study, push them off to class, and send them to bed at a reasonable hour. Once away from home and parents, however, far too many students become caught up in a constant round of parties, dates, bull sessions, and other distractions that seem more fascinating than schoolwork. Again, if such behavior persists, poor grades and failure result.

6   Personal reasons also take a heavy toll on students who might otherwise complete their programs successfully. Often money problems are at fault. For example, a student may lose a scholarship or grant, fail to obtain needed work, or find that the family can no longer afford to help out. Some students succumb to homesickness; some are forced out by an illness, injury, or death in the family; and yet others become ill or injure themselves and leave to recuperate. Finally, a considerable number become disillusioned with their programs or the size, location, or atmosphere of their schools and decide not to return.

7   What happens to the students who drop out? Some re-enroll in college later, often in less demanding two- and four-year schools that offer a better chance of academic success. Of the remainder, the great bulk find civilian jobs or enlist in the armed forces. Most, whatever their choice, go on to lead productive, useful lives. In the meantime, campus newcomers need to know about the dangers that tripped up so many of their predecessors and make every effort to avoid them.

Discussion Questions

1. Identify the thesis statement in this essay.
2. Trace the causal chain that makes up paragraph 2.
3. What is the function of the first sentence in paragraph 3?
4. In which paragraphs does the writer discuss causes? Effects?

Suggestions for Writing

Use one of the following topics, or another that your instructor approves, to develop a causal analysis. Determine which causes and/or effects to consider. Scrutinize your analysis for errors in reasoning, settle on an organization, and write the essay.

1. Reasons that relationships fail
2. The effect of some friend, acquaintance, public figure, or writer on your life
3. Effects of talking on cell phones while driving
4. Effects of divorce on children
5. Why you are a _____ major
6. Causes, effects, or both of the popularity of FaceBook
7. Causes of school violence
8. Causes or effects of the popularity of casino gambling
9. Causes, effects, or both of widespread cell phone use
10. Reasons that you have a particular habit or participate in a particular sport
11. Causes or effects of sleep deprivation
12. Reasons that _____ is a popular celebrity
13. Effects of some recent Supreme Court decision or change in public policy
14. The effects of environmental concerns on our way of life
15. Causes, effects, or both of our hunger for heroes
16. Causes, effects, or both of the high cost of gasoline
17. Causes, effects, or both of drinking on college students
18. Causes of procrastination
19. Reasons that some students drop out of high school
20. Causes and effects of violence at sporting events

CRITICAL EDGE

Although nearly everyone recognizes the role of causation in human affairs, differences of opinion often surface about the causes and effects of important matters. What lies behind the widespread incivility in the United States today? Why are women more likely than men to leave management jobs? How do video games affect children? What impact does the high divorce rate have on American society? Obviously such questions lack simple answers; and as a result investigators, even when they agree on the causes and effects involved, often debate their relative importance.

Suppose your women's studies instructor has asked you to investigate the departure of women from managerial positions. A library search reveals several articles on this topic as well as a number of reasons for resigning.

Some women leave because they find it harder to advance than men do, and as a result they seldom attain senior positions. Others leave because they receive lower salaries than their male counterparts. Still others leave because of the stifling effects of corporate rigidity, unrealistic expectations, the demands of raising a family, or possibly diminished chances of marriage. Although most articles cite these causes, their relative importance is debatable. One writer, for example, emphasizes family concerns by discussing them last and at greatest length. Another puts the chief blame on obstacles to upward mobility—the existence of a "glass ceiling" that blocks women from upper-level positions along with an "old-boy network" of entrenched executives that parcels out jobs among its members.

Once you've finished your research, you're ready to synthesize the views of your sources as well as your own views. Before you start to write, though, take some time to consider carefully each cause and effect you've uncovered. Obviously you should ground your paper on well-supported and widely acknowledged causes and effects, but you might also include more speculative ones as long as you clearly indicate their secondary nature. To illustrate, one writer, while mentioning corporate rigidity as a reason that women leave management jobs, clearly labels this explanation as a theory and backs it with a single example. As you examine your material, ask yourself these critical questions as well as any others that occur to you: Does any writer exhibit obvious bias? Do the studies cited include a sufficient number of examples to be meaningful? Do the statistics appear reliable, or are some out of date, irrelevant, or skimpy? Have the writers avoided reasoning errors? Whenever you find a flaw, note where the problem lies so that you can discuss it in your writing if you choose. Such discussions often clear up common misconceptions. There are various possibilities for organizing your paper. If your sources substantially agree on the most important cause, you might begin with that one and then take up the others. A second possibility, the order-of-climax arrangement, reverses the procedure by starting with secondary causes and ending with the most significant one. You can use the same options for organizing effects. When no clear consensus exists about the relative importance of the different causes and effects, there is no best arrangement of the material.

Suggestions for Writing

1. Read three articles on the causes of a major social problem such as domestic violence and incorporate those causes and your own views in a paper.
2. Read two articles that disagree about the effects of a proposed government program such as oil and gas drilling on public land and write a paper that incorporates the writers' views and presents your own conclusions.
3. Write an essay that corrects a common misconception about the causes or effects of a matter about which you feel strongly. Possibilities might include the causes of homelessness or the impact of capital punishment on murder rates in different states.

Writing a Causal Analysis

Plan.

- Identify key topic based on assignment or personal interest.
- Identify audience and purpose.
- Decide if you are more interested in causes or effects.

Brainstorm and take notes on causes and effects.

- Read and conduct research.
- Observe.
- Talk with others for ideas.

Test causes and effects.

Are you
- missing causes or effects?
- ignoring multiple causes?
- mistaking correlation for causation?
- confusing causes and effects?

Do you have good evidence to claim something a cause or effect?

Identify most appropriate pattern.

Effects of a single cause, of a single event, a chain of effects or causes, and effects of an event.

Create a table that organizes causes or effects and provides details.

Decide on focus.

Create a rough **outline** or **plan** of pattern of cause and effect.

Write a rough draft.

- **Intro** introduces topic, reasons for analysis, focus on cause or effect.
- **Body** provides causes or effects with details and reasons, shows connections, follows pattern.
- **Conclusion** may specify consequences, warn readers, evaluate importance of cause or effect.

Revise.

Gather peer response, test analysis carefully, read more if needed, talk over with others.

- Does focus on cause or effect fit purpose and facts?
- Add missing cause or effect, detail, or evidence.
- Cut parts that don't fit.
- Evaluate accuracy of account and pattern.
- Test organization to make it clear to reader.
- Test for ethics.

Proofread.

Definition: Establishing Boundaries

From Chapter 15 of *Strategies for Successful Writing*, Ninth Edition. James A. Reinking, Robert von der Osten.

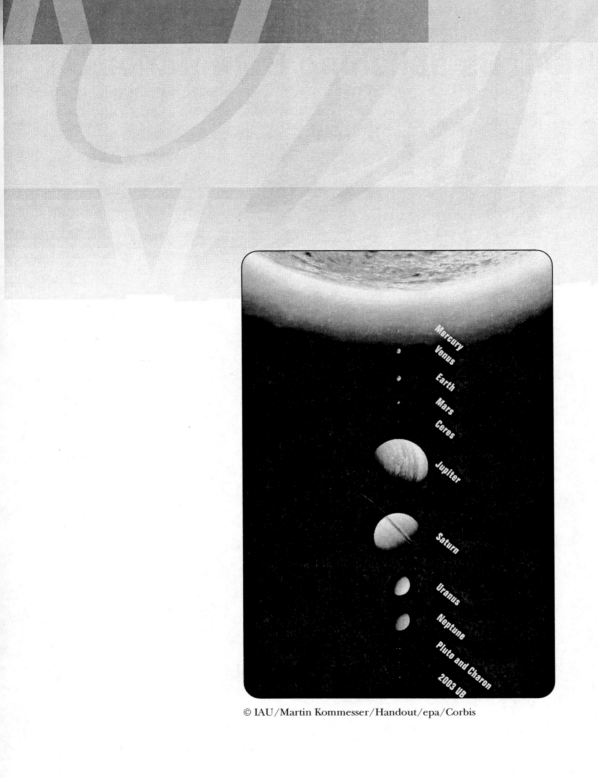

© IAU/Martin Kommesser/Handout/epa/Corbis

Definition: Establishing Boundaries

That movie was egregious.

Once the bandage is off the wound, swab the proud flesh with the disinfectant.

Speaking on statewide television, Governor Blaine called his opponent a left-winger.

Do you have questions? You're not alone. Many people would question the sentences above: "What does *egregious* mean?" "How can flesh be *proud?*" "What does the governor mean by *left-winger?* What specific policies does the opponent support that warrant this label?" To avoid puzzling and provoking your own readers, you'll often need to explain the meaning of some term. The term may be unfamiliar *(egregious)*, used in an unfamiliar sense *(proud flesh)*, or mean different things to different people *(left-winger)*. Whenever you clarify the meaning of some term, you are *defining*.

Humans are instinctively curious. We start asking about meanings as soon as we can talk, and we continue to seek, as well as supply, definitions all through life. In school, instructors expect us to explain all sorts of literary, historical, scientific, technical, and social terms. On the job, a member of a company's human resources department might prepare a brochure that explains the meaning of such terms as *corporate responsibility* and *product stewardship* for new employees. An accountant might define *statistical sampling inventory* in a report calling for a change in the inventory system. A special education teacher might write a memo explaining *learning disabled* to the rest of the staff.

When you define, you identify the features that distinguish a term, thereby putting a fence around it, establishing its boundaries, and separating it from all others. Knowing these features enables both you and your reader to use the term appropriately.

Sometimes a word, phrase, or sentence will settle a definition question. To clear up the mystery of "proud flesh," all you'd need to do is insert the parenthetical phrase "(excessively swollen and grainy)" after the word *proud*. But when you're dealing with new terms—*information superhighway* and *virtual reality* are examples—brief definitions won't provide the reader with enough information for proper understanding.

Abstract terms—those standing for things we can't see, touch, or otherwise detect with our five senses—often require extended definitions, too. It's impossible to capture the essence of *democracy* or *hatred* or *bravery* in a single sentence: The terms are too complex, and people have too many differing ideas about what they mean. The same holds true for some concrete terms—those standing for actions and things we can perceive with our five senses. Some people, for instance, limit the term *drug pusher* to full-time sellers of hard drugs like cocaine and heroin. Others, at the opposite extreme, extend the term to full- and part-time sellers of any illegal drug. Writing an argument recommending life sentences for convicted drug pushers would require you to tell just what you mean by the term so that the reader would have solid grounds for judging your position.

Types of Definitions

Three types of definition—synonyms, essential definitions, and extended definitions—serve writers' needs. Although the first two seldom require more than a word or a sentence, an extended definition can run to several pages. The three types, however, are related. Synonyms and essential definitions share space between the covers of dictionaries, and both furnish starting points for extended definitions.

Synonyms

Synonyms are words with very nearly the same meanings. *Lissome* is synonymous with *lithe* or *nimble,* and *condign* is a synonym of *worthy* and *suitable.* Synonyms let writers clarify meanings of unfamiliar words without using cumbersome explanations. To clarify the term *expostulation* in a quoted passage, all you'd have to do is add the word *objection,* in brackets, after it. Because synonyms are not identical twins, using them puts a slightly different shade of meaning on a message. For example, to "protest" and to "object" are certainly similar in many ways. Yet the claim that we "object" to the establishment of a nuclear waste site in our area fails to capture the active and sustained commitment implied in our willingness to "protest" against such a site. Still, synonyms provide a convenient means of breaking communications logjams.

Essential Definitions

An essential definition does three things: (1) names the item being defined, (2) places it in a broad category, and (3) distinguishes it from other items in that category. Here are three examples:

Item Being Defined	Broad Category	Distinguishing Features
A howdah	is a covered seat	for riding on the back of an elephant or camel.
A voiceprint	is a graphical record	of a person's voice characteristics.
To parboil	is to boil meat, vegetables, or fruits	until they are partially cooked.

Writing a good essential definition requires careful thought. Suppose your instructor has asked you to write an essential definition of one of the terms listed in an exercise, and you choose vacuum cleaner. Coming up with a broad category presents no problem: A vacuum cleaner is a household appliance. The hard part is pinpointing the distinguishing features. The purpose of a vacuum cleaner is to clean floors, carpets, and upholstery. You soon realize, however, that these features alone do not separate vacuum cleaners from other appliances. After all, carpet sweepers also clean floors, and whisk brooms clean upholstery. What then does distinguish vacuum cleaners? After a little thought, you realize that, unlike the other items, a vacuum cleaner works by suction. You then write the following definition:

> A vacuum cleaner is a household appliance that uses suction to clean floors, carpets, and upholstery.

The same careful attention is necessary to establish the distinguishing features of any essential definition.

Limitations of Essential Definitions

Essential definitions have certain built-in limitations. Because of their brevity, they often can't do full justice to abstract terms such as *cowardice, love, jealousy, power.* Problems also arise with terms that have several settled meanings. To explain *jam* adequately, you'd need at least three essential definitions: (1) a closely packed crowd, (2) preserves, and (3) a difficult situation. But despite these limitations, an essential definition can be useful by itself or as part of a longer definition. Writers often build an extended definition around an essential definition.

Pitfalls in Preparing Essential Definitions

When you prepare an essential definition, guard against these flaws:

Circular definition. Don't define a term by repeating it or changing its form slightly. Saying that a psychiatrist is "a physician who practices psychiatry" will only frustrate someone who's never heard of psychiatry. Repress circularity and provide the proper insight by choosing terms the reader can relate to, for example, "A psychiatrist is a physician who diagnoses and treats mental disorders."

Overly broad definition. Shy away from definitions that embrace too much territory. If you define a skunk as "an animal that has a bushy tail and black fur with white markings," your definition is not precise. Many cats and dogs also fit this description. But if you add "and that ejects a foul-smelling secretion when threatened," you will clear the air—of any misconceptions at least.

Overly narrow definition. Don't hem in your definition too closely, either. "A kitchen blender is a bladed electrical appliance used to chop foods" illustrates this error. Blenders perform other operations, too. To correct the error, add the missing information: "A kitchen blender is a bladed electrical appliance used to chop, mix, whip, liquefy, or otherwise process foods."

Omission of main category. Avoid using "is where" or "is when" instead of naming the main category. Here are examples of this error: "A bistro is where food and wine are served" and "An ordination is when a person is formally recognized as a minister, priest, or rabbi." The reader will not know exactly what sort of thing (a bar? a party?) a *bistro* is and may think that *ordination* means a time. Note the improvement when the broad categories are named: "A bistro is a small restaurant where both food and wine are served" and "An ordination is a ceremony at which a person is formally recognized as a minister, priest, or rabbi."

1. **Identify the broad category and the distinguishing traits in each of these essential definitions:**

   a. Gangue is useless rock accompanying valuable minerals in a deposit.
   b. A catbird is a small American songbird with a slate-colored body, a black cap, and a catlike cry.
   c. A soldier is a man or woman serving in an army.
   d. Myelin is a white, fatty substance that forms a sheath around some nerve fibers.
   e. A gargoyle is a waterspout carved in the likeness of a grotesque animal or imaginary creature and projecting from the gutter of a building.
   f. A magnum is a wine bottle that holds about two-fifths of a gallon.

2. **Indicate which of the following statements are acceptable essential definitions. Explain what is wrong with those that are not. Correct them.**

   a. A scalpel is a small knife that has a sharp blade used for surgery and anatomical dissections.
   b. A puritan is a person with puritanical beliefs.
   c. A kraal is where South African tribes keep large domestic animals.
   d. A rifle is a firearm that has a grooved barrel and is used for hunting large game.
   e. A motorcycle is a two-wheeled vehicle used mainly for human transportation.
   f. Fainting is when a person loses consciousness owing to inadequate flow of blood to the brain.

3. **Write an essential definition for each of the following terms:**

   | a. groupie | c. hit man | e. pushover |
   | b. happy hour | d. jock | f. hard grader |

Extended Definitions

Sometimes it's necessary to go beyond an essential definition and write a paragraph or whole paper explaining a term. New technical, social, and economic terms often require extended definitions. To illustrate, a computer scientist might need to define *data integrity* so that computer operators understand the importance of maintaining it. Terms with differing meanings also frequently require extended definitions. To let voters know just what he means by *left-winger*, Governor Blaine might detail the kinds of legislation his opponent favors and opposes. Furthermore, extended definition is crucial to interpretation of the law, as we see when courts clarify the meaning of concepts such as obscenity.

Extended definitions are not merely academic exercises; they are fundamental to your career and your life. A police officer needs to have a clear understanding of what counts as *reasonable grounds for search and seizure;* an engineer must comprehend the meaning of *stress;* a nuclear medical technologist had better have a solid grasp of *radiation.* And all of us are concerned with the definition of our basic rights as citizens.

Extended definitions are montages of other methods of development—narration, description, process analysis, illustration, classification, comparison, and cause and effect. Often, they also define by negation: explaining what a term *does not* mean. The following paragraphs show how one writer handled an extended definition of *sudden infant death syndrome*. The student began by presenting a case history (illustration), which also incorporated an essential definition and two synonyms.

Jane and Dick Smith were proud, new parents of an eight-pound, ten-ounce baby girl named Jenny. One summer night, Jane put Jenny to bed at 8:00. When she went to check on her at 3:00 A.M., Jane found Jenny dead. The baby had given no cry of pain, shown no sign of trouble. Even the doctor did not know why she had died, for she was healthy and strong. The autopsy report confirmed the doctor's suspicion—the infant was a victim of "sudden infant death syndrome," also known as SIDS or crib death. SIDS is the sudden and unexplainable death of an apparently healthy, sleeping infant. It is the number-one cause of death in infants after the first week of life and as a result has been the subject of numerous research studies.

Discussion Questions

1. What synonyms does the writer use?
2. Which sentence presents an essential definition?

In the next paragraph, the writer turned to negation, pointing out some of the things that researchers have ruled out about SIDS.

Although researchers do not know what SIDS is, they do know what it is *not*. They know it cannot be predicted; it strikes like a thief in the night. Crib deaths occur in seconds, with no sound of pain, and they always happen when the child is sleeping. Suffocation is *not* the cause, nor is aspiration or regurgitation. Researchers have found no correlation between the incidence of SIDS and the mother's use of birth control pills or tobacco or the presence of fluoride in water. Since it is not hereditary or contagious, only a slim chance exists that SIDS will strike twice in the same family.

Finally, the student explored several proposed causes of SIDS as well as how parents may react to the loss of their child.

As might be expected, researchers have offered many theories concerning the cause of crib death. Dr. R. C. Reisinger, a National Cancer

Institute scientist, has linked crib deaths to the growth of a common bacterium, *E. coli*, in the intestines of newborn babies. The organisms multiply in the intestines, manufacturing a toxin that is absorbed by the intestinal wall and passes into the bloodstream. Breast milk stops the growth of the organism, whereas cow's milk permits it. Therefore, Dr. Reisinger believes, bottle-fed babies run a higher risk of crib death than other babies. . . .

The loss of a child through crib death is an especially traumatic experience. Parents often develop feelings of guilt and depression, thinking they somehow caused the child's death. To alleviate such feelings, organizations have been established to help parents accept the fact that they did not cause the death.

Trudy Stelter

Ethical Issues

How we define can have devastating consequences. For centuries, the practice of defining Africans as "subhuman" helped justify the slave trade and slavery. During the 1930s and early 1940s, labeling Jews as "vermin" was used to fuel the attempt to exterminate them both in Nazi Germany and much of Western Europe. Even in the absence of malice, definition can have far-reaching effects, both good and bad. For instance, a change in the federal definition of "poverty" can increase or decrease by millions the number of individuals and households eligible for benefits such as Medicaid. Although the consequences of your writing won't approach those of the above examples, you'll nevertheless need to think about possible ethical implications. Addressing the following questions will help you do this.

- Have I carefully evaluated all of the features of my definition? In clarifying what constitutes "excessive force" by the police, it would be unfair to include the reasonable means necessary to subdue a highly dangerous suspect.
- Have I slanted my definition to reflect some prejudice? Let's say a writer opposed to casino gambling is defining "gambling addicts." The paper should focus on those who spend an excessive amount of time in casinos, bet and often lose large sums of money, and in so doing neglect family, financial, and personal obligations. It would be unfair to include those who visit casinos occasionally and strictly limit their losses.
- Have I avoided unnecessary connotations that might be harmful? A definition of teenagers that overemphasized their swift changes in mood might be unfair, perhaps even harmful, since it may influence the reactions of readers.

Writing an Extended Definition

Planning and Drafting the Extended Definition

If you choose your own topic, pick an abstract term or one that is concrete but unfamiliar to your reader. Why, for instance, define *table* when the discussion would likely bore the reader? On the other hand, a paper explaining *computer virus* might well prove interesting and informative. Use a strategy of your choice to unearth promising topics. Then answer these questions about them:

Which topic holds the most promise? Why?

What purpose will guide my writing? To clarify a technical or specialized concept? To show what the term means to me? To persuade the reader to adopt my attitude toward it? To discuss some neglected facet of it?

For what audience should I write?

Here's a helpful process to follow as you think your definition through. First, select a clear example that illustrates what you wish to define: the United States could exemplify *democracy*. Then brainstorm to uncover major identifying characteristics. For democracy your list might include majority rule, free elections, a separately elected chief executive, and basic human rights. Next, test these characteristics against other legitimate examples and retain only the characteristics that apply. Britain is clearly a democracy but doesn't have a separately elected chief executive. Finally, test the unfolding definition against a clear counterexample, perhaps the People's Republic of China. If the definition fits the example, something is wrong.

Now evaluate what methods you might use to develop your definition. Each method has its own set of special strengths, as the following list shows:

Narration. Tracing the history of a new development or the changing meaning of a term: the birth of the Internet

Description. Pointing out interesting or important features of a device, an event, or an individual: a blizzard

Process. Explaining what a device does or how it is used, how a procedure is carried out, or how a natural event takes place: an earthquake

Illustration. Tracing changes in meaning and defining abstract terms by providing examples: tyranny

Classification. Pointing out the different categories into which an item or an event can be grouped: types of romantic comedies

Comparison. Distinguishing between an unfamiliar and a familiar item: terrorist distinguished from soldier

Cause and effect. Explaining the origins and consequences of events, conditions, problems, and attitudes: disease defined by cause

Negation. Placing limitations on conditions and events and correcting popular misconceptions: why liberty isn't anarchy

Examine your topic in light of this listing and select the methods of development that seem most promising. Don't hesitate to use a method for some purpose not mentioned here. If you think that a comparison will help your reader understand some abstract term, use it.

Chart the methods of development you'll use, and then brainstorm each method in turn to gather the details that will inform the reader. When you've finished, look everything over, rearrange the details as necessary, add any new ones you think of, and prepare a revised chart. The example that follows is for a paper using four methods of development.

Narration	Classification	Process	Negation
Beginning American Democracy	Types of democracy	Election process	Not democracies
First supporting detail	First supporting detail	First supporting detail	First supporting detail
Forming a constitutional committee	Parliamentary democracy: England	Initial exploration	Single party states: Old Soviet Union
Second supporting detail	Second supporting detail	Second supporting detail	Second supporting detail
Drafting a constitution	Independent presidency: U.S.	Fund raising	Controlled elections: Egypt

Definition papers can begin in various ways. If you're defining a term with no agreed-upon meaning (for example, *conservatism*), you might note some differing views of it and then state your own. If the term reflects some new social, political, economic, or technological development (such as the *wireless Internet*), you might mention the events that brought it into being. A colloquial or slang term often lends itself nicely to an attention-getting opener. A paper defining *chutzpah* might begin by illustrating the brash behavior of someone with this trait. Often an introduction includes a short definition, perhaps taken from a dictionary. If you do include a dictionary definition, use the full name of the dictionary (*Webster's New World Dictionary* says . . .). Several dictionary titles include the word *Webster*, and unless you use the full name your reader won't know which one you mean. Draw on a dictionary definition, however, only as a last resort.

In writing the body of the paper, present the methods of development in whatever order seems most appropriate. A paper defining *drag racing* might first describe the hectic scene as the cars line up for a race, then classify the different categories of vehicles, and finally explain the steps in a race. One defining *intellectual* might start by showing the differences between intellectuals and scholars, then name several prominent intellectuals and note how their insights have altered our thinking, and conclude by trying to explain why many Americans hold intellectuals in low regard.

Definition papers can end, as well as begin, in a number of ways. If you're defining some undesirable condition or event (such as *sudden infant death syndrome*), you might express hope for a speedy solution. If you're reporting on some new development (like *information superhighway*), you might predict its economic or social impact. Often, a summary of your main points is effective. Choose whichever type of ending best supports your main idea.

Revising the Extended Definition

Use these specific questions as you revise your extended definition:

> Are my purpose and audience clear and appropriate?
>
> If I've used an essential definition, does it do what it should and avoid the common pitfalls?
>
> Are the methods of development suitable for the topic?
>
> Is the paper organized effectively?
>
> Are there other factors or examples I need to consider?
>
> Have I considered appropriate ethical issues?

SAMPLE

STUDENT ESSAY OF **DEFINITION**

Rediscovering Patriotism

Peter Wing

1   After the horrifying events of September 11, 2001, when terrorists flew jet planes into the World Trade Center and the Pentagon, killing thousands of Americans, there was a surge of patriotism. America was under attack, and as we frequently do when our nation is threatened, we rallied around the flag. Flags were pasted in the back windows of cars and the front windows of homes. So many Americans bought flags that stores were quickly sold out. It was a rare car that didn't have a United We Stand bumper sticker. Rock groups that had built their image around cynicism gleefully participated in patriotic concerts. In short, it became fashionable once again to be a flag-waving, "Star Spangled Banner"-singing, country-loving patriot.

2   These results were good, but there was also an alarming side to this newfound patriotism. Those who even suggested that American foreign policy might have contributed to the attack were branded *traitor* and were effectively silenced. People, including members of Congress, who criticized the way the war on terrorism was being conducted were

Continued on next page

Continued from previous page

lambasted as unpatriotic. In my neighborhood, those who didn't fly flags, who didn't have patriotic bumper stickers, who didn't seethe with righteous anger at America's enemy were labeled un-American. All of this raises an obvious question: What is patriotism?

3   The obvious answer is that patriotism is love for one's country. But clearly that answer is too broad. Someone could easily love the skyscrapers of Manhattan, the gorgeous vistas of the Grand Canyon, and even the cornfields of Iowa and still sell military secrets to an enemy of America, a far-from-patriotic act. Timothy McVeigh would probably have said that he loved his country, but it would be troubling to consider his attack on the Alfred P. Murrah Federal Building a patriotic act. Certainly patriotism can include an intense love for the land, an appreciation for the people that make up our nation, and a pride in the accomplishments of our country. Part of the heart-swelling quality of patriotism is the recognition of all that is great and good about our nation: the valiant role of our soldiers in World War II; the innovative spirit that forged new tech-nologies, cured diseases, and allowed Americans to journey to the moon. However, that pride would be incomplete without an appreciation for and dedication to the core principles that define this nation.

4   In the end, what is most essential to America is not our industrial wealth, our military power, or artistic works. America is defined by its initial vision, the commitment to democracy, to basic political equality for all Americans, to liberty, to the rights of the individual. Consider how odd it would be if someone's claim to patriotism were a desire for a mili-tary coup that toppled democracy to establish a more powerful military. Surely we would find someone seriously misguided who loved American industry but wanted to discard the Constitution and have only the heads of corporations serve in Congress. While there may be many aspects to patriotism, the core of American patriotism would have to be a solid commitment to the core values of the Constitution.

5   What is it, then, to have a love for and commitment to the core values of a nation? It is easy to confuse patriotism with the symbols of patriot-ism, the flag waving and anthem singing. Just as a husband who gives his wife a love poem and a diamond ring and then rushes out to cheat on her isn't really the best husband, someone who proudly flies a flag

but never votes, refuses to serve on juries, and actively discriminates is not the best patriot. Serving in the military is rightly considered one of the most distinguished acts of patriotism, and properly so. Soldiers don't just say they love their country; they risk their lives to protect the people and the principles of their nation, to preserve liberty. Just as love for a spouse isn't simply a matter of gushy greeting cards but rather concerted day-to-day action, including listening patiently to the other's problems, so patriotism lives and breathes through actions. That doesn't have to be military action but can be participation in anything that preserves and strengthens what is best about a nation. Patriotism then means voting in elections, actively participating in campaigns, writing to legislators, serving on juries, volunteering for schools, building homes for the poor, obeying laws, honoring those who serve, and criticizing things that are wrong.

6   One of the paradoxes of this notion of patriotism is that it makes it essential to criticize and even protest against government policy. It would be a poor friend who let a buddy slide into alcoholism without comment. It would be a poor patriot who would let America move away from the best it can be without action. To really love one's country is to struggle to help make that country realize its best ideals. Those who protested against segregation in America were patriots, recalling America to the fundamental commitment to equality. Many who marched against the Vietnam War were patriotic since they believed that the war violated America's commitment to justice. So too were those who felt the Vietnam War was necessary to American security, for they only wanted to protect America from a perceived communist threat. Those who objected to the way the war against terrorism was being conducted also, then, could be considered patriotic, for they too, out of a love for their country, were participating in the democratic process, raising their voice so that America would choose the best course of action. Patriotism doesn't reside in being on one side or the other of a political debate; it exists in the honest struggle to realize the best ideals of the country. Given this view, in a democracy, no group has a monopoly on patriotism.

7   That is why some of the bitter slogans of supposed patriotism—*My Country Right or Wrong* or *America: Love It or Leave It*—are just plain

Continued on next page

Continued from previous page

wrong. While it is true that patriotism would suggest that we not disown our country when it takes what we consider a misguided direction, it would surely not be patriotic to defend and support a direction we thought wrong. Those who are alarmed by the policies of the government or are deeply dissatisfied with some injustice, such as the horrible conditions of many inner-city schools, are not lacking in patriotism and have no obligation to leave. Those who complain, carp, protest, point out shortcomings are acting out of a profound patriotism. Because of their love for their country, they struggle to move the country to realize its best ideals. If there were any bumper sticker I would want to see for patriotism, it would be *Our Country: Make It the Best It Can Be.*

8   It is heartening to see the revival of patriotism. Hopefully, that patriotism will go beyond simple flag waving and dig deeper to the core meaning of patriotism where Americans together struggle to preserve and develop American ideals. Patriotism will really have taken root in America when citizens become involved in the political process, eagerly serve on juries, work to improve the lives of fellow citizens, and, surprisingly enough, raise their voices in criticism when we, as a government and a people, fall short of the very best we can become.

Discussion Questions

1. Identify the essay's essential definition.
2. What purpose do the first two paragraphs serve?
3. How does the writer develop his definition?
4. What do the first three sentences of paragraph 6 accomplish?
5. Why might the writer have decided to discuss bumper sticker slogans in the next to the last paragraph?

Suggestions for Writing

Write a properly focused extended definition using one of the following suggestions or one approved by your instructor. The term you define may be new, misused, or misunderstood or may have a disputed meaning. Develop the essay by any combination of writing strategies.

1. Integrity
2. Green technologies

3. Depression
4. School violence
5. Stress
6. Human genome
7. Extreme sports
8. Alternative rock
9. Breaking as a dance form
10. Cybervandals
11. Campus security
12. Feminist
13. Hate crimes
14. Family values
15. Some term from your field
16. Online class
17. Addiction
18. The Internet
19. The Christian Right
20. Rap music

CRITICAL EDGE

Definitions are always social creations. The way various people and communities understand and use any word determines its definition. As a result, writers who use complex words such as *justice, love,* and *charisma* to convey a message may need to consult a number of sources to determine how others have used the words. With their findings of this research in mind, the writers can stake out their own meanings of those words.

If you were writing a paper defining *dance* for a humanities class, you would probably find several conflicting meanings of the term. Frank Thiess, writing in *The Dance as an Artwork*, defines dance as the use of the body for expressive gesture. But as you mull over that definition, you realize that it is both too broad and too narrow. While some forms of dance, such as ballet, feature expressive gesture, so does pantomime or even a shaken fist; and neither of these qualifies as dance. A square dance clearly qualifies, but does it represent expressive gesture? Susanne Langer, in *Philosophy in a New Key*, defines dance as "a play of Powers made visible," pointing to the way dancers seem to be moved by forces beyond themselves. You recognize that this definition may apply to religious dance forms, that dancers sometimes appear swept away by the music, and that you yourself have experienced a feeling of power when dancing. Nevertheless, upon reflection you decide that often it's the dancer's skill that attracts us, and rarely do we dance to reveal invisible powers. Finally, you discover that Francis Sparshott, in *The Theory of the Arts*, defines dance as a rhythmical, patterned motion that transforms people's sense of their own existence according to the dance they do. As you evaluate Sparshott's contention, you decide that it has considerable merit, although you aren't convinced that every dance transforms our sense of existence. When you think about the kinds of dance you know and the various definitions you have uncovered, you conclude that each of these writers, like the blind men who felt different parts of an elephant and tried to describe it, is only partly correct. For your humanities paper, you decide to synthesize the different definitions. You might explain that all dance involves a rhythmical, patterned movement of the body for its own sake. Sometimes such movement can transform our sense of existence, as in trance dances or even waltzes. Other dances, such as story ballets, use rhythmical movements as expressive gestures that tell stories or convey emotions. Still other dances may suggest the manifestation of powers beyond the dances themselves. You proceed to explain each of these features with details drawn from both your sources and personal experience.

Carrying out this type of project requires you to look critically at the definitions of others. Do they accurately reflect the examples you know about? Do they describe examples that do not fit the definition? Are any parts of the definition questionable? Once you've answered these questions, you can then draw on the appropriate elements of the definitions to formulate your own. You might organize such a paper by developing each definition in a separate section, first presenting it in detail and then pointing out its strengths and weaknesses. In the final section, you could offer your own definition and support it with your reasoning and suitable examples.

Suggestions for Writing

1. Read the essay "Supermarket Pastoral" as well as several others on organic food that you find in the library. Reflect on the different definitions of "organic" then, drawing on your reading, offer your own definition.
2. Read "The Sweet Smell of Success . . ." and "I Have a Dream." Then write your own definition of success, taking into account the views expressed in these essays.
3. Do some reading about an abstract term like *bravery*, *democracy*, or *hatred* in at least three sources. Use the sources to develop your own definition of the term.

Definition: Establishing Boundaries

Writing a Definition

Plan.

Identify your topic, establish audience, identify purpose.

Brainstorm distinguishing characteristics, examples, examples and characteristics excluded; read, talk to others about the term, observe its use.

Test your defining features against ordinary usage; Is it too broad or too narrow?

Create a table or chart of your definition with key characteristics, examples, and exclusions.

Identify useful strategies: description, narration, process, illustration, classification, comparison, cause-effect, and negation.

Create a plan of organization or organize your table: organization may reflect strategies used or be by key defining characteristics.

Develop rough draft.

- **Intro** introduces term, reason for definition, dominant characteristic.
- **Body** presents distinctive defining characteristics.
- **Conclusion** may summarize main point, call for action, predict an outcome, stress importance.

Revise.

Gather reader responses; discuss with others; test definition against many examples; check for too general, too narrow, or circular definitions.

- Do defining characteristics fit?
- Add needed traits or examples.
- Cut unneeded elements.
- Test to make certain definition is complete and follows clear pattern.
- Test for ethics.

Proofread.

Documenting Sources

In order to acknowledge and handle sources, you must know how to (1) prepare proper bibliographical references, (2) document sources within your text, (3) handle quotations, and (4) avoid plagiarism.

The kind of information included in bibliographical references depends on the type of source and the documentation system. Two systems are in common use: the Modern Language Association (MLA) system and the American Psychological Association (APA) system. The entries that follow illustrate basic MLA and APA conventions. Both the MLA and APA systems use the hanging indent for entries in the reference list. Start the first line of each entry flush to the left margin and indent all subsequent lines five spaces.

For more information, consult the *MLA Handbook for Writers of Research Papers*, 7th ed., 2009, and the *Publication Manual of the American Psychological Association*, 6th ed., 2009. When documenting online sources, consult the Web site to supplement the information in the *Manual*. **It is important to note two changes to the MLA style for bibliographic references.**

1. The MLA now uses italics instead of underlining for idependently published works such as books, periodicals, Web sites, and television and radio broadcasts. You still use quotation marks for shorter works such as articles or poems that appear in a larger publication.

2. At the end of each entry, the MLA style now has you indicate the medium through which you retrieved it. The categories are Print, Web, CD, Peformance, etc. An electronic version of a book retrieved online would be Web, and a copy of an article retrieved from a bound volume would be Print.

From Chapter 21 of *Strategies for Successful Writing*, Ninth Edition. James A. Reinking, Robert von der Osten.

Preparing Proper MLA Bibliographic References

Books

■ A Book with One Author

Wilk, Max. *Every Day's a Matinée*. New York: Norton, 1975. Print.

■ A Book with Two Authors

Duncan, Dayton, and Ken Burns. *Lewis and Clark*. New York: Knopf, 1997. Print.

■ A Book with More than Three Authors

Alder, Roger William, et al. *Mechanisms in Organic Chemistry*. New York: Wiley, 1971. Print.   The MLA system permits the use of "et al." for four or more authors or editors (listing all authors is also permitted).

■ A Book with a Title That Includes Another Title

Set off the title of the mentioned work with quotation marks.

Tanner, John. *Anxiety in Eden: A Kierkegaardian Reading of "Paradise Lost."* Oxford: Oxford UP, 1992. Print

■ A Book with Corporate or Association Authorship

United Nations. Public Administration Div. *Local Government Training*. New York: United Nations, 1968. Print.

■ An Edition Other than the First

Turabian, Kate L. *A Manual for Writers of Term Papers, Theses, and Dissertations*. 6th ed. Chicago: U of Chicago P, 1996. Print.

■ A Book in Two or More Volumes

Bartram, Henry C. *The Cavalcade of America*. 2 vols. New York: Knopf, 1959. Print.

REPRESENTATIONS OF THE POST/HUMAN

*Monsters, aliens and others
in popular culture*

ELAINE L. GRAHAM

Rutgers University Press
New Brunswick, New Jersey

1 Author—last name first
2 Title in italics
3 City of publication followed by a colon
4 Publisher
5 Date of publication
6 Medium

Graham, Elaine L. *Representations of the Post/Human: Monsters, Aliens and Others in Popular Culture. New Brunswick: Rutgers UP*, 2002 Print.

Graham, Elaine L. Representations of The Post/Human - Monsters, Aliens and Others in Popular Culture. New Brunswick: Rutgers University Press, 2002.

---

18   SCIENCE FICTION STUDIES, VOLUME 33 (2006)

Robert Harding

Manuel Castells's Technocultural Epoch in *The Information Age*

Manual Castells writes on economy and society in the age of postmodern capital in his sociological trilogy *The Information Age,* published in 1996–98. Aiming for a "grounded theory" (Kreisler 3)—a hybridized approach that synthesizes contemporary French thought with an American empirical tradition—Castells stresses that his work is based on direct observation rather than merely "playing with words" (Kreisler 3), an approach he associates with those who "deconstruct" and abstractly theorize. As he writes at the beginning of the second volume of the trilogy, *The Power of Identity:* "This is not a book about books" (2).

In this essay, I will trace the development of what Castells calls information society. My approach involves three overlapping tracks. First, I sketch what Castells calls network "flows"—of images, wealth, and power—in global information technology. Second, I evaluate social changes arising out of the network society and how they redefine identity in both global and local contexts. Finally, I read selected science fiction texts with a view to remarking on fictional parallels with Castells's theses on informationalism.

Castells is known for his cross-cultural approach, fusing research into the information-technology revolution in the San Francisco Bay area with quantitative and qualitative data drawn from Europe, Latin America, and the Asian-Pacific Rim. In Volume 1 of *The Information Age, The Rise of Network Society,* Castells demonstrates that an information-based future will materialize in the form of a new kind of urban space: the "new global economy and the emerging informational society have indeed a new spatial form, which develops in a variety of social and geographical contexts: megacities" (*Rise* 434). He then outlines how future urban development will assume new levels of power and influence: "mega-cities articulate the global economy, link up the informational networks, and concentrate the world's power" (*Rise* 434). Castells projects this mode of development by detailing a Chinese example, the emerging "Hong Kong—Shenzen—Canton—Peral River Delta—Macau—Zhuhai metropolitan regional system" (*Rise* 436), which constitutes a massive transformation of the social world for global marketing and informational purposes.

Like sociologist Max Weber, Castells seeks to define the spirit of the age. Where Weber studied the animating force of the industrial age in the Protestant work ethic, Castells sees the ethos of the information age in the *network*. In his essay "The New Weber," Chris Freeman writes that Castells "characterises the 'informational society' as essentially a capitalist system" (156). As Castells himself puts it:

1 Author—last name first
2 Title of article in quotation marks with period inside quotation marks
3 Title of journal in italics
4 Volume number
5 Date of publication
6 First page number
7 Final page number on final page of article
8 Medium

Harding, Robert. "Manuel Castells's Technocultural Epoch in *The Information Age.*" Science Fiction Studies 33 (2006): 18-38 Print.

What Was Jim Crow?

What Was Jim Crow?

Many Blacks resisted the indignities of Jim Crow, and, far too often, they paid for their bravery with their lives.

© Dr. David Pilgrim, Professor of Sociology
Ferris State University
Sept., 2000

[1]Kennedy, Stetson. Jim Crow Guide: The Way It Was. Boca Raton: Florida Atlantic University Press, 1959/1990, pp.216–117.

[2]This list was derived from a larger list composed by the Martin Luther King, Jr., National Historic Site Interpretive Staff

http://www.ferris.edu/jimcrow/what.htm

1 Author—last name first
2 Title of article in quotation marks
3 Periodical or source location
4 Date the article was published
5 Page numbers of the article
6 Medium
7 Date it was retrieved

Pilgrim, David. "What Was Jim Crow?" *Jim Crow Museum of Racist Memorabilia. Sept. 2000: 1-8. 20 Mar. 2006.* Web. 9.

David Pilgrim, "What Was Jim Crow?" Jim Crow Museum of Racist Memorabilia, Sept. 2000, pp. 1–8. Mar 2006. http://www.ferris.edu/jimcrow/what.htm

■ A Reprint of an Older Work

Matthiessen, F. O. *American Renaissance: Art and Expression in the Age of Emerson and Whitman*. 1941. New York: Oxford UP, 1970. Print.

■ A Book with an Editor Rather than an Author

Deetz, James, ed. *Man's Imprint from the Past: Readings in the Methods of Archaeology*. Boston: Little, 1971. Print.

■ A Book with Both an Author and an Editor

Melville, Herman. *The Confidence Man*. Ed. Hershel Parker. New York: Norton, 1971. Print.

■ A Translation

Beauvoir, Simone de. *All Said and Done*. Trans. Patrick O'Brian. New York: Putnam, 1974. Print.

■ An Essay or Chapter in a Collection of Works by One Author

Woolf, Virginia. "The Lives of the Obscure." *The Common Reader, First Series*. New York: Harcourt, 1925. 111-18. Print.

■ An Essay or Chapter in an Anthology

Angell, Roger. "On the Ball." *Subject and Strategy*. Ed. Paul Eschholz and Alfred Rosa. New York: St. Martin's, 1981. 34-41. Print.

Periodicals

Periodicals include newspapers, popular magazines, and specialized occupational and scholarly journals. The basic information for a periodical article includes the name of the article's author, the name of the periodical, the title of the article, the date of publication, the page range of the entire article, and, for scholarly journals, the volume number of the periodical. The MLA system capitalizes periodical titles; however, the MLA style omits an introductory *The* from these titles.

■ An Article in a Scholarly Journal Consecutively Paged through the Entire Volume

Pfennig, David. "Kinship and Cannibalism." *Bioscience* 47 (1997): 667–75. Print.

■ An Article in a Scholarly Journal That Pages Each Issue Separately

Block, Joel W. "Sodom and Gomorrah: A Volcanic Disaster." *Journal of Geological
    Education* 23.5 (1976): 74-77. Print.

■ An Unsigned Article in a Scholarly Journal

"Baby, It's Cold Inside." *Science* 276 (1997): 537-38. Print.

■ A Signed Article in an Occupational or Popular Magazine

Gopnik, Adam. "The Good Soldier." *New Yorker* 24 Nov. 1997: 106-14. Print.

■ An Unsigned Article in an Occupational or Popular Magazine

"Robot Productivity." *Production Engineering* May 1982: 52-55. Print.

■ A Signed Article in a Daily Newspaper

Wade, Nicholas. "Germ Weapons: Deadly but Hard to Use." *New York Times* 26
    Nov. 1997, natl. ed.: A13+. Print.

■ An Unsigned Article in a Daily Newspaper

"The Arithmetic of Terrorism." *Washington Post* 14 Nov. 1997: A26. Print.

Encyclopedia Articles

When documenting familiar works, such as the *Encyclopedia Americana,* the basic
information for the MLA system includes the name of the article's author if known,
the title of the article, the name of the encyclopedia, and the date of the edition.

Sobieszek, Robert A. "Photography." *World Book Encyclopedia.* 1991 ed. Print.

The MLA system requires additional information when less familiar publications
are documented.

Fears, J. Rufus. "Emperor's Cult." *Encyclopedia of Religion.* Ed. Mircea Eliade. 16
    vols. New York: Macmillan, 1987. Print.

For an anonymous article, references begin with the article's title.

Government Documents

The basic information for a federal, state, or foreign government publication
that is documented using the MLA system includes the name of the author; the
title of the publication; the name of the government and the agency issuing

the publication; the place of publication; the name of the printing group, if known; and the date. If no author is named, begin by identifying the government and then cite the government agency as the author.

Carpenter, Russell D. *Defects in Hardened Timber.* United States. Dept. of
  Agriculture, Forest Service. Washington: GPO, 1989. Print.

United States. Environmental Protection Agency, Consumer Products Safety
  Commission. *Asbestos in the Home.* Washington: GPO, 1989. Print.

United States. Cong. Office of Technology Assessment. *The Biology of Mental
  Disorders.* 102nd Cong., 2nd sess. Washington: GPO, 1992. Print.

Other Sources

■ Book Reviews

Koenig, Rhoda. "Billy the Kid." Rev. of *Billy Bathgate*, by E. L. Doctorow. *New York*
  20 Feb. 1989: 20-21. Print.

If the review is untitled, follow the above format but omit the missing element.

■ Published Interviews

Noriega, Manuel. "A Talk with Manuel Noriega." By Felipe Hernandez. *News
  Report* 20 Mar. 1997: 28-30. Print.

■ Personal Interviews

If you conducted the interview yourself and are using the MLA system, start with the name of the person interviewed and follow it with the kind of interview and the date conducted.

Newman, Paul. Personal interview. 18 May 2001.

■ Audiovisual Media

Frankenstein. Dir. James Whale. Perf. Boris Karloff, John Boles, Colin Clive, and
  Mae Clarke. Universal, 1931. Film.

If you are interested in the contribution of a particular person, start with that person's name. Use the same model for videocassette and DVD recordings, and add release dates and distributors.

Whale, James, dir. *Frankenstein.* Perf. Boris Karloff, John Boles, Colin Clive, and
  Mae Clarke. Universal, 1931. Film.

Whale, James, dir. *Frankenstein*. Perf. Boris Karloff, John Boles, Colin Clive, and
      Mae Clarke. 1931. DVD. Universal, 1999. DVD.

■ Television and Radio Programs

Washington Week in Review. Prod. S. Ducat. PBS. WKAR, East Lansing. 6 Jan. 1995.
      Television.

Use this format when additional information is pertinent:

Peril at End House. By Agatha Christie. Adapt. Clive Exton. Dir. Renny Rye. Prod.
      Brian Eastman. Perf. David Suchet and Hugh Fraser. Mystery. Introd. Diana
      Rigg. PBS. WKAR, East Lansing. 12 Aug. 1993. Television.

■ Music and Sound Recordings

Smith, Bessie. *The World's Greatest Blues Singer*. Columbia, 1948. LP.

Smith, Bessie. "Down Hearted Blues." *The World's Greatest Blues Singer*.
      Columbia, 1948. LP.

■ CD-ROMs

Norman, J. L. "Barcelona." *Software Toolworks Multimedia Encyclopedia*. Disc 1.
      Danbury: Grolier, 1996. CD.

Online Sources

Be sure to ask your instructor which format to follow, and then use that format
consistently. Often data from the Internet are incomplete, perhaps lacking an
author, a title, or page or paragraph number. Include all the available information, but omit the correct address.

■ Books

The basic information for a book documented by the MLA system includes the
name of the author, if known; the title of the book; the place and date of original
publication, if applicable; the electronic site, if named; the date of electronic
publication if the online version has never been published in print or if it is part
of a scholarly project; the sponsor of the site; the medium by which it was
retrieved; and the date the material was retrieved.

Chaney, Walter J., William J. Diehm, and Frank Seeley. *The Second 50 Years: A*
      Reference Manual for Senior Citizens. Weed: London Circle, 1999. Web. 8
      Aug. 2000.

Locke, John. *An Essay concerning Human Understanding.* London, 1690. Inst. of
Learning Technologies. 1995. Columbia U. Web. 24 June 2000.

■ Periodicals on the World Wide Web

Periodicals online include specialized occupational and scholarly journals, popular magazines, newspapers, and newsletters. The basic information for a periodical includes the author's name, if known; the title of the article; the title of
the periodical; the volume and issue numbers, if applicable; the date the article
was published; the article's page numbers (or n. *pag.* if none are given); the
medium of the material; the date the material was retrieved; and the online
address only when necessary to find the material.

Cervetti, Nancy. "In the Breeches, Petticoats, and Pleasures of Orlando." *Journal
of Modern Literature* 20.2 (1996): n. pag. Web. 8 Jan. 1998.

Navarro, Mireya. "Women in Sports Cultivating New Playing Fields." *New York
Times on the Web* 13 Feb. 2001. Web. 22 Feb. 2001.

"No Link Found in Violence, Videos." *Boston Globe Online* 8 Aug. 2000. Web. 27
Aug. 2000.

Oakes, Jeannie. "Promotion or Retention: Which One Is Social?" *Harvard Education
Letter.* Jan.-Feb. 1999: n. pag. Web. 8 Aug. 2000.

■ Periodicals Accessed through an Online Library Service or Large Network Provider

Full-text articles are available online at libraries or at home through services such
as LexisNexis, ProQuest Direct, and America Online. Cite the author's name, if
known; the title of the article; the title of the periodical; the date the article was
published; the page numbers for the article (if the service identifies only the initial page of the article, indicate the page followed by a plus sign, 132+; if no page
is given, use *n. pag.*); the name of the database or Web site in italics; *Web* as the
medium of publication; and the date the material was accessed.

Clemetson, Lynette. "A Ticket to Private School." *Newsweek* 27 Mar. 2000: n. pag.
LexisNexis. Web. 5 May 2000.

Mayo Clinic. "Lung Cancer." 21 Feb. 2000. *America Online.* Web. 10 June 2000.

■ Encyclopedia Articles

The basic information for an encyclopedia article accessed through the Web
includes the author's name, if known; the title of the article; the name of the
encyclopedia; the date of the edition; the vendor; the medium of publication;
and the date of access.

Daniel, Ralph Thomas. "The History of Western Music." *Britannica Online: Macropaedia*. 1995. Encyclopaedia Britannica. Web. 14 June 1995.

■ Government Documents

The basic information for a government document includes the name of the author, if known; the title; the name of the government and agency issuing the document; the place of publication and printing group, if known; the date of publication; the medium of publication; the date the material was retrieved; and the online address only if necessary to find the material. If no author is given, begin by identifying the government and then give the government agency as the author.

Georgia State. Probation Div. of the Georgia Dept. of Corrections. *Alternatives to Incarceration*. 1 July 1997. Web. 3 Feb. 1998.

■ Personal Home Page

The basic information for a personal home page documented according to the MLA system includes the name of its originator, if known; the title of the site, if any (use *Home page* or other such description if no title is given); the date of the latest update, if given; the medium of publication; and the date the material was retrieved from the site.

Lanthrop, Olin. Home page. Web. 24 June 2000.

■ Newsgroups, Electronic Mailing Lists, and E-Mail

MLA gives guidelines for including newsgroups, electronic mailing lists (sometimes called Listservs), and e-mail within the Works Cited list.

Corelli, Aldo. "Colleges and Diversity." Dept. of English, U of Michigan, 20 Apr. 2003. Web. 25 Apr. 2003.

Nicholson, Brad. "Casino Gambling." Message to Jason Elridge. 2 Feb. 2001. E-mail.

Preparing Proper APA Bibliographic References

The APA has recently published its 6th edition. To better meet the challenges of online publications, APA style now recommends that the unique work you are referencing in print and electronic form be identified by the digital object identifier (DOI), a unique identification sequence assigned by the International DOI Foundation. The DOI can often be found near the copyright notices of electronic journal articles or in some cases at the top of the first page of the article. When the DOI is used, there is no need to indicate the URL of the reference.

■ Sample

Mesmer-Magnus, J. R., & DeChurch, L. A. (2009). Information sharing and team performance: A meta-analysis. *Journal of Applied Psychology, 94*(2), 535–546. doi:10.1037/a0013773

Consult with your faculty member on whether they wish you to employ the DOI with print and online sources when it is available.

Books

The APA system uses initials rather than first and middle names for authors, editors, and translators.

■ A Book with One Author

Wilk, M. (1975). *Every day's a matinée*. New York, NY: Norton.

■ A Book with Two Authors

Duncan, D., & Burns, K. (1997). *Lewis and Clark*. New York, NY: Knopf.

■ A Book with More than Three Authors

Alder, R. W., Finn, T., Bradley, M. A., and Li, A. W. (1971). *Mechanisms in organic chemistry*. New York, NY: Wiley.

The APA system gives up to and including six author or editor names in the reference list. Substitute "et al." for the seventh or more.

■ A Book with a Title That Includes Another Title

Words that would be italicized on their own should be set roman as part of an itlicized title.

Tanner, J. (1992). *Anxiety in Eden: A Kierkegaardian reading of* Paradise Lost. Oxford, England: Oxford University Press.

■ A Book with Corporate or Association Authorship

United Nations, Public Administration Division. (1968). *Local government training*. New York, NY: Author.

When the author of the work is also the publisher, the APA system uses the word "Author" following the place of publication. If the work is published by another organization, its name replaces "Author."

■ An Edition Other than the First

Turabian, K. L. (1996). *A manual for writers of term papers, theses, and dissertations* (6th ed.). Chicago, IL: University of Chicago Press.

■ A Book in Two or More Volumes

Bartram, H. C. (1959). *The cavalcade of America* (Vols. 1–2). New York, NY: Knopf.

■ A Reprint of an Older Work

Matthiessen, F. O. (1970). *American renaissance: Art and expression in the age of Emerson and Whitman.* New York, NY: Oxford University Press. (Original work published 1941)

■ A Book with an Editor Rather than an Author

Deetz, J. (Ed.). (1971). *Man's imprint from the past: Readings in the methods of archaeology.* Boston, MA: Little, Brown.

■ A Book with Both an Author and an Editor

Melville, H. (1971). *The confidence man* (H. Parker, Ed.). New York, NY: Norton. (Original work published 1857)

■ A Translation

Beauvoir, S. de. (1974). *All said and done* (P. O'Brian, Trans.). New York, NY: Putnam. (Original work published 1972)

■ An Essay or Chapter in a Collection of Works by One Author

Woolf, V. (1925). The lives of the obscure. In *The common reader, first series* (pp. 111–118). New York, NY: Harcourt Brace.

■ An Essay or Chapter in an Anthology

Angell, R. (1981). On the ball. In P. Eschholz & A. Rosa (Eds.), *Subject and strategy* (pp. 34–41). New York, NY: St. Martin's Press.

APA

Periodicals

Periodicals include newspapers, popular magazines, and specialized occupational and scholarly journals. The basic information for a periodical article includes the name of the article's author, the date of publication, the title of the article, the name of the periodical, the page range of the entire article, and, for scholarly journals, the volume number of the periodical.

■ An Article in a Scholarly Journal Consecutively Paged through the Entire Volume

Pfennig, D. (1997). Kinship and cannibalism. *Bioscience, 47,* 667–675.

■ An Article in a Scholarly Journal That Pages Each Issue Separately

Block, J. W. (1976). Sodom and Gomorrah: A volcanic disaster. *Journal of Geological Education, 23*(5), 74–77.

■ An Unsigned Article in a Scholarly Journal

Baby, it's cold inside. (1997). *Science, 276,* 537–538.

■ A Signed Article in an Occupational or Popular Magazine

Gopnik, A. (1997, November 24). The good soldier. *The New Yorker, 73,* 106–114.

■ An Unsigned Article in an Occupational or Popular Magazine

Robot productivity. (1982, May). *Production Engineering, 29,* 52–55.

■ A Signed Article in a Daily Newspaper

Wade, N. (1997, November 26). Germ weapons: Deadly but hard to use. *The New York Times,* pp. A13, A15.

■ An Unsigned Article in a Daily Newspaper

The arithmetic of terrorism. (1997, November 14). *The Washington Post,* p. A26.

Encyclopedia Articles

The APA system requires publication information for all encyclopedia citations when documenting familiar works, such as the *Encyclopedia Americana.*

Fears, J. R. (1987). Emperor's cult. In *The encyclopedia of religion* (Vol. 5, pp. 101–102). New York, NY: Macmillan.

APA

For an anonymous article, references for the APA system begin with the article's title. Position the publication date, within parentheses, after this title. The remaining format is identical to citations with an author.

Government Documents

The APA system includes the name of the author, the date of publication, and the place of publication and adds a cataloging code where one exists.

Carpenter, R. D. (1989). *Defects in hardened timber* (UCLC Puplication No. 20504424). U.S. Department of Agriculture, Forest Service. Washington, DC: Government Printing Office.

U.S. Environmental Protection Agency, Consumer Products Safety Commission. (1989). *Asbestos in the home* (SUDOCS Report No. Y3.C76/3:2/A51/989). Washington, DC: Government Printing Office.

U.S. Congress, Office of Technology Assessment. (1992). *The biology of mental disorders* (SUDOCS Report No. Y3.T22/2:2/B57/10). Washington, DC: Government Printing Office.

Other Sources
■ Book Reviews

Koenig, R. (1989, February 20). Billy the Kid [Review of the book *Billy Bathgate*]. *New York, 21,* 20–21.

If the review is untitled, follow the above format but omit the missing element.

■ Published Interviews

Hernandez, F. (1997, March 20). A talk with Manuel Noriega. *News Report, 15,* 28–30.

If the interview is untitled, follow the example above, omitting mention of a title.

■ Personal Interviews

For the APA system, a personal interview is considered personal correspondence and is not included in the References list. Instead, use an in-text parenthetical citation. Include the name of the person interviewed, the notation "personal communication," and the date: (P. Newman, personal communication, May 18, 2001).

■ Audiovisual Media

In the APA format, the citation begins with an individual's name and his or her contribution to the *motion picture* (use this term, not *film*). The country of origin (where it was made and released) is now required.

Whale, J. (Director). (1931). *Frankenstein* [Motion picture]. United States: Universal.

■ Television and Radio Programs

Ducat, S. (Producer). (1995, January 6). *Washington week in review* [Television broadcast]. Washington, DC: Public Broadcasting Service.

Use the following format when additional information is pertinent:

Exton, C. (Writer), & Rye, R. (Director). (1993). Peril at End House [Television series episode]. In B. Eastman (Producer), *Mystery*. Washington, DC: Public Broadcasting Service.

With the APA system, the name of the scriptwriter appears in the author's position, followed by the director. Any in-text references begin with the first name in the bibliographical reference (for example, Exton, 1993).

■ Music and Sound Recordings

The APA format requires identification of all formats, including a CD.

Smith, B. (1997). *The essential Bessie Smith* [CD]. New York, NY: Columbia Records.

Smith, B. (1948). Down hearted blues. On *The world's greatest blues singer* [CD]. New York, NY: Columbia Records. (Original recording February 17, 1923)

Recording dates, if different from the copyright year, follow the entry, enclosed in parentheses, with no final period.

■ Computer Software

Data Desk (Version 6.0) [Computer software]. (1997). Ithaca, NY: Data Description.

In the APA system, only specialized software or computer programs are listed in the References. Standard commercial software and languages should be cited by their proper name and version in the text itself.

■ CD-ROMs and Other Databases

Norman, J. L. (1996). Barcelona. In *Software toolworks multimedia encyclopedia* [CD-ROM]. Boston, MA: Grolier.

The APA *Manual* (6th ed.) takes the view that all aggregated databases are the same type of source, regardless of the format or manner of access (CD-ROM,

APA

library or university server, or online Web supplier). Follow the model above when you need to cite an entire CD-ROM (not a document from it). In a reference to information taken from a database (even a CD-ROM), give a "retrieval statement" containing the date you retrieved the document, article, or piece of data, as well as the full, correct name of the database. When you retrieve information from an online database, end the entry with a correct and complete URL for the specific document or version. In this case, the name of the database is omitted, unless this information will help in retrieval from a large or complex site. (See online models in the next section.)

Online Sources

The most recent edition of the *Publication Manual of the American Psychological Association* provides the APA's newest guidelines for documenting online sources. You can also consult the association's Web site for its most up-to-date information about citing electronic sources:

http://www.apastyle.org/elecref.html

Be sure to ask your instructor which format to follow and then use that format consistently. Often data from the Internet are incomplete, perhaps lacking an author, a title, or page or paragraph numbers. Include all the available information. The recommendation from the APA is that you cite document locations rather than home pages and that the referenced address actually works for that file. Remember, your goal is to allow your reader to find the source. Note the use of the DOI explained at the beginning of the section on APA References.

■ Books

Follow the general guidelines for a printed book, and conclude with appropriate electronic source information, as modeled here, or use the DOI, if known.

Locke, J. (1995). *An essay concerning human understanding*. New York, NY: Columbia University. Retrieved from http://www.ilt.columbia.edu/projects/digitexts/locke/understanding/title.html (Original work published 1690)

When some of the basic information is not provided, use whatever is available.

Chaney, W. J., Diehm, W. J., & Seeley, F. (1999). *The second 50 years: A reference manual for senior citizens*. Weed, CA: London Circle. Retrieved from http://www.londoncircle.com/2d50.html

To cite part of an electronic book, place the part's title after the date of publication. The APA also cites a chapter or section identifier following the title of the complete document.

Trochim, W. M. K. (2001). Language of research. In *The research methods knowledge base* (Foundations sec.). Cincinnati, OH: Atomic Dog. Retrieved from http://www.trochim.human.cornell.edu/kb/language.html

■ Periodicals on the World Wide Web

The APA recommends using the models for print periodicals when document-ing online articles that do not vary from their printed versions. In such cases, add [Electronic version] after the title and before the period to complete the citation. When the electronic format alters the printed version (e.g., no pagina-tion, added data or links), then cite as an online document, using a retrieval statement and the name of the database and/or the URL. APA guidelines ask for the identification of the server or the Web site in a retrieval statement only when it would be helpful in finding the source; for example, it is not necessary to state "Retrieved from the World Wide Web" since it is the most common access point to the Internet. If the DOI is available, that should be used instead of retrival data.

Cervetti, N. (1996). In the breeches, petticoats, and pleasures of Orlando. *Journal of Modern Literature, 20*(2). Retrieved from http://www.indiana.edu/~iupress /journals/mod-art2.html

Navarro, M. (2001, February 13). Women in sports cultivating new playing fields. *The New York Times on the Web.* Retrieved from http://www.nytimes.com

No link found in violence, videos. (2000, August 8). *Boston Globe Online*, p. A14. Retrieved from http://www.boston.com/dailyglobe2/no_li_nk_found_in_ violence_videos+.shtml

Oakes, J. (1999, January/February). Promotion or retention: Which one is social? *Harvard Education Letter.* Retrieved from http://www.edletter.org/past /issues/1999-jf/promotion.shtml

■ Periodicals Accessed through an Online Library Service or Large Network Provider

Increasingly, full-text articles are available online at libraries or at home through services such as LexisNexis, ProQuest Direct, and America Online. These serv-ices may or may not provide an online address for accessed material. In the APA documentation system, cite the author's name, if known; the date the article was published; the title of the article; the title of the periodical; and the page num-bers for the article, if available. Do not include the name of database.

Clemetson, L. (2000, March 27). A ticket to private school. *Newsweek.* Retrieved, from http://www.newsweek/com.icl/83469

APA style prefers that the URL that leads directly to the document file be pro-vided, following the word *from.*

■ Encyclopedia Articles

The basic information for an encyclopedia article accessed through the World Wide Web includes the author's name, if known; the date of the edition; the title of the article; the name of the encyclopedia; and the online address.

Daniel, R. T. (1995). The history of western music. In *Britannica online: Macropaedia*.

    Retrieved from http://www.eb.com:180/cgi-bin/g:DocF=macro/5004/45/0.html

■ Government Documents

The basic information for a government document includes the name of the author, if known; the date of publication; the title; a cataloging code if one is available; and the online address. If no author is given, begin by identifying the government agency as the author.

Probation Division of the Georgia Department of Corrections. (1997, July 1).

    Alternatives to incarceration (CSP Document No. 239875). Retrieved from

    http://www.harvard.edu/~innovat/aiga87.html

■ Personal Home Page

The APA *Manual* offers no specific guidelines for personal home pages. We suggest that you use the following pattern, which conforms to general APA practice. Note that the APA system includes the date of the latest Web page revision, if known, in parentheses.

Lanthrop, O. (2000, May 28). Home page. Retrieved from http://www.cognivis.com

    /olin/photos.htm

■ Newsgroups, Electronic Mailing Lists, and E-Mail

The APA format treats e-mail as personal communications, which are cited in parentheses in the text only. Newsgroups, online forums, discussion groups, and electronic mailing lists that maintain archives can be cited in the References. With these electronic forms, indicate the author's full last name and initials (screen name if the name is not available), the exact posting date, the name of the thread or blog, a label in brackets describing the type of message, "Retrieved from" followed by the name of list if not in the URL; and the address for the archived message. Categories include Online forum comment (messages posted to newsgroups, online forums, or discussion group), Electronic mailing list message (a message on an electronic mailing List or Listserve), Web log message (for a blog post), and Video file (Video blog post).

Trehub, A. (2002, January 28). Re: The conscious access hypothesis [Online forum

    comment]. Retrieved from University of Houston Psyche Discussion Forum:

    http://listserv.uh.edu/cig-bin/wa?A2=psyche-b&F=&S=&P=2334

Documenting Sources

1. Using the MLA or APA system, write a proper reference for each of the unstyled information sets that follow:

a. A book titled Gas Conditioning Fact Book. The book was published in 1962 by Dow Chemical Company in Midland, Michigan. No author is named.

b. An unsigned article titled Booze Plays a Big Role in Car Crashes. The article was published in the November 28, 1997, state edition of the Detroit News. It appears on page 2 of section C.

c. An essay written by C. Wright Mills and titled The Competitive Personality. The essay appeared in a collection of Mills's writings titled Power, Politics, and People. The collection was published in 1963 by Ballantine Books in New York. The book is edited and introduced by Irving Louis Horowitz. The essay appears on pages 263 through 273.

d. An unsigned article titled Global Warming Fears on Rise. The article was published in the October 25, 1997, issue of Newswatch magazine. It appears on pages 29 to 31.

e. A book written by Paul Theroux and titled The Kingdom by the Sea. The book was published in 1983 by the Houghton Mifflin Company in Boston.

f. A book written by Kate Chopin and titled The Awakening. The book, edited by Margaret Culley, was published in 1976 by W. W. Norton and Company in New York.

g. An article written by James E. Cooke and titled Alexander Hamilton. The article appears on pages 31 and 32 of the World Book Encyclopedia, Volume 9, published in 1996.

h. An article written by Sarah McBride and titled Young Deadbeats Pose Problems for Credit-Card Issuers. The article was published in the November 28, 1997, midwest edition of the Wall Street Journal. It appears on pages 1 and 6 of section B.

i. A book written by Magdalena Dabrowski and Rudolph Leopold and titled Egon Schiele. The book was published in 1997 by the Yale University Press in New Haven, Connecticut.

j. A book written by Jean Descola and titled A History of Spain. The book, translated by Elaine P. Halperin, was published in 1962 by Alfred A. Knopf in New York.

k. An article written by John T. Flanagan and Raymond L. Grimer and titled Mexico in American Fiction to 1850. The article was published in 1940 in a journal called Hispania. It appears on pages 307 through 318. The volume number is 23.

l. A United States government document titled Marine Fisheries Review. It was published by the National Marine Fisheries Service of the U.S. Department of Commerce in 1993 and is available from the Government Printing Office. No author is given.

m. A book written by David Kahn and titled The Codebreakers. The second edition of the book was published in 1996 by Scribner's in New York.

n. A book written by Joseph Blotner and titled Faulkner: A Biography. The book was published in two volumes in 1974 by Random House in New York.

o. An article written by Calvin Tompkins and titled The Importance of Being Elitist. The article was published in the November 24, 1997, issue of the New Yorker. It appears on pages 58 through 69.

p. A book written by Thomas Beer and titled Stephen Crane: A Study in American Letters. The book was published in 1923 and reprinted in 1972 by Octagon Books in New York.

q. A review of a book written by Jacques Barzun and titled The Culture We Deserve. The review, by Beth Winona, appeared in the March 1989 issue of American Issues magazine and was titled Barzun and Culture. It appeared on pages 46 through 50.

APA

r. An interview of playwright Neil Simon. The interview was titled Neil Simon on the New York Theater and appeared in the September 3, 1997, issue of the Long Island News, on pages C4 and C5. The interviewer was Pearl Barnes.

s. A film titled Casablanca. The film was directed by Michael Curtiz and starred Humphrey Bogart, Ingrid Bergman, Claude Rains, and Paul Henreid. It was released in 1942 by Warner Brothers.

t. A television program titled Grizzly. It appeared on WNTR, New York, on February 3, 1997. The station is part of the CBS network.

u. An online article with no author titled Robert Frost: A Reader Response Perspective. The article appears on the online journal Off the Wall and had a location of <http://www.offthewall.com/articles/backdated_bin_RobertFrost_archive.html>. The article is listed with the date May 8, 2003, but you found it on January 4, 2004.

v. An article written by May Gottchalk and titled Reconsidering Dyslexia that you accessed through a database. The article was published in the May 24, 2002, issue of Education Matters, and you retrieved the article using Wilson Select on November 22, 2003, on the Ferris State University Library Web Database Access with the address http://library.ferris.edu/databaseframes.html.

w. A personal page by Randy Cordial titled My Best Science Fiction Movies Ever. You found the Web page on May 4, 2004, at http://www.cordial.com/bestscifi.htm.

2. **Prepare a proper MLA or APA reference for each of the works you plan to use in writing your paper.**

Handling In-Text Citations

In Text

Both the MLA and APA systems use notations that appear within the text and are set off by parentheses. The systems are illustrated by the following examples.

Basic Citation Form

For the MLA system, the citation consists of the last name of the author and the page number of the publication in which the material originally appeared. The APA system identifies the last name of the author or authors and the year of publication. A page number is provided in APA both with quotations and when the information is so specific that it is important to reference the specific page.

■ Bibliographic Reference (MLA)

Rothenberg, Randall. "Life in Cyburbia." *Esquire* Feb. 1996: 56-63. Print.

■ Passage and Citation

MLA

A mania for the Internet has invaded many important aspects of our culture. Newspapers run stories on it, businesses have rushed to set up Web sites, and the Speaker of the House of Representatives has stated that even our poorest children have a stake in the Internet (Rothenberg 59).

MLA

Rothenberg states that a mania for the Internet has invaded many important aspects of our culture. Newspapers run stories on it, businesses have rushed to set up Web sites, and the Speaker of the House of Representatives has stated that even our poorest children have a stake in the Internet (59).

APA

. . . our poorest children have a stake in the Internet (Rothenberg, 1996).

APA

Rothenberg (1996) states . . . have a stake in the Internet.

■ Bibliographic Reference (MLA)

In Text

Weider, Benjamin, and David Hapgood. *The Murder of Napoleon.* New York: Congdon, 1982. Print.

■ Passage and Citation

MLA

Four different autopsy reports were filed. All the reports agreed that there was a cancerous ulcer in Napoleon's stomach, but none of them declared that the cancer was the cause of death. Nevertheless, cancer has become accepted as the cause (Weider and Hapgood 72).

APA

. . . Nevertheless, cancer has become accepted as the cause (Weider & Hapgood, 1982).

If a source has more than three authors (more than five for the APA), use "et al.," meaning "and others," for all but the first-named one.

■ Bibliographic Reference (MLA)

Baugh, Albert C., et al. *A Literary History of England.* New York: Appleton, 1948. Print.

■ Passage and Citation (MLA)

MLA

Although no one knows for certain just when Francis Beaumont and John Fletcher started collaborating, by 1610 they were writing plays together (Baugh et al. 573).

APA

. . . writing plays together (Baugh et al., 1948).

Authors with the Same Last Name

If your citations include authors with the same last name, use the initials of their first names to distinguish them.

■ Bibliographic References (MLA)

Adler, Jerry. "Search for an Orange Thread." *Newsweek* 16 June 1980: 32-34. Print.

Adler, William L. "The Agent Orange Controversy." *Detroit Free Press* 18 Dec. 1979, state ed.: B2. Print.

■ Passage and Citation

MLA

As early as 1966, government studies showed that dioxin-contaminated 2,4,5-T caused birth defects in laboratory animals. Later studies also found that this herbicide was to blame for miscarriages, liver abscesses, and nerve damage (J. Adler 32).

APA

. . . miscarriages, liver abscesses, and nerve damage (J. Adler, 1980).

Separate Works by the Same Author

If your references include two or more works by the same author, add shortened forms of the titles to your in-text citation if you follow the MLA system. But shortened book titles in italics, and use quotation marks around article and essay titles. For the APA system, use the conventional name–date–page number format. (Note: Page numbers are not always needed.)

■ Bibliographic References (MLA)

Mullin, Dennis. "After U.S. Troops Pull Out of Grenada." *US News & World Report* 14 Nov. 1983: 22-25. Print.

In Text

___. "Why the Surprise Move in Grenada—and What Next." *US News & World Report* 7 Nov. 1983: 31-34. Print.

■ Passage and Citation

MLA

As the rangers evacuated students, the marines launched another offensive at Grand Mal Bay, then moved south to seize the capital and free the governor (Mullin, "Why the Surprise" 33).

APA

. . . and free the governor (Mullin, 1983b).

As the APA example illustrates, if the two works appeared in the same year, put an "a" or a "b," without quotes, after the date to identify whether you are referring to the first or second entry for that author in the bibliography, arranged alphabetically by title.

Two Sources for the Same Citation

If two sources provide essentially the same information and you wish to mention both in one parenthetical citation, alphabetize them according to their authors' last names, list them with a semicolon between them, and position the citation as you would any other citation. (Citations in MLA style do not need to be listed alphabetically.)

■ Bibliographic References (MLA)

Bryce, Bonnie. "The Controversy over Funding Community Colleges." *Detroit Free Press* 13 Nov. 1988, state ed.: A4. Print.

Warshow, Harry. "Community College Funding Hits a Snag." *Grand Rapids Press* 15 Nov. 1988, city ed.: A2. Print.

■ Passage and Citation

MLA

In contending that a 3% reduction in state funding for community colleges would not significantly hamper their operations, the governor overlooked the fact that community college enrollment was expected to jump by 15% during the next year (Warshow A2; Bryce A4).

APA

. . . enrollment was expected to jump by 15% during the next year (Bryce, 1988; Warshow, 1988).

Unsigned References

When you use a source for which no author is given, the in-text citation consists of all or part of the title, the appropriate page numbers, and, for the APA system, the date.

■ Bibliographic Reference (MLA)

"Money and Classes." *Progressive* Oct. 1997: 10. Print.

■ Passage and Citation

MLA

According to the General Accounting Office, repairing the country's dilapidated school buildings would carry a price tag of over $110 billion. Furthermore, constructing the 6,000 buildings needed to end classroom overcrowding would cost many billions more ("Money and Classes" 10).

APA

. . . many billions more ("Money and Classes," 1997).

Citing Quotations

When the quotation is run into the text, position the citation as shown in the following examples.

■ Bibliographic Reference (MLA)

Schapiro, Mark. "Children of a Lesser God." *Harper's Bazaar* Apr. 1996: 205+.
      Print.

■ Passage and Citation

MLA

UN investigators who have studied the extent of child labor in Third World countries estimate that "as many as 200 million children go to work rather than to school . . . making everything from clothing and shoes to handbags and carpets" (Schapiro 205).

APA

". . . handbags and carpets" (Schapiro, 1996, p. 205).

With longer, indented quotations, skip one space after the end punctuation and type the reference in parentheses.

In Text

■ Bibliographic Reference (MLA)

Newhouse, John. "The Diplomatic Round: A Freemasonry of Terrorism." *New Yorker* 8 July 1985: 46-63. Print.

■ Passage and Citation

MLA

One commentator offers this assessment of why foreign terrorist groups don't operate in this country:

> The reason that America has been spared so far, apparently, is that it is less vulnerable than Europe, especially to Middle Eastern extremists. Moving in and out of most European countries isn't difficult for non-Europeans; border controls are negligible. But American customs and immigration authorities, being hyper-alert to drug traffic, tend to pay attention to even marginally doubtful people, and a would-be terrorist . . . could come under surveillance for the wrong reason. (Newhouse 63)

APA

. . . come under surveillance for the wrong reason. (Newhouse, 1985, p. 63)

Indirect Citations

In MLA style, if you use a quotation from person A that you obtained from a book or article written by person B, or you paraphrase such a quotation, put "qtd. in" before the name of the publication's author in the parenthetical reference. In APA style, name the original work in the text and, then give the secondary source in parentheses preceded by "as cited in" rather than "qtd. in."

■ Bibliographic Reference (MLA)

Klein, Joe. "Ready for Rudy." *New York* 6 Mar. 1989: 30-37. Print.

■ Passage and Citation

MLA

Rudolph Giuliani favors the death penalty for "the murder of a law-enforcement officer, mass murder, a particularly heinous killing" but would impose it only "when there is certainty of guilt well beyond a reasonable doubt" (qtd. in Klein 37).

APA

Rudolph Giuliani favors ". . . certainty of guilt well beyond a reasonable doubt" (as cited in Klein, 1989, p. 37).

Authors Identified in Text

Sometimes you'll want to introduce a paraphrase, summary, or quotation with the name of its author. In this case, the page number may be positioned immediately after the name or follow the material cited.

■ Bibliographic Reference (MLA)

Jacoby, Susan. "Waiting for the End: On Nursing Homes." *New York Times Magazine* 31 Mar. 1974, city ed.: 80+. Print.

■ Passage and Citation

MLA

Susan Jacoby (80) sums up the grim outlook of patients in bad nursing homes by noting that they are merely waiting to die.

Susan Jacoby sums up the grim outlook of patients in bad nursing homes by noting that they are merely waiting to die (80).

APA

Susan Jacoby (1974, p. 80) sums up . . .

Susan Jacoby (1974) sums up . . . waiting to die (p. 80).

1. Depending on your instructor, *using either the MLA or APA system, write a proper in-text citation for exercise 1 from the previous exercise. The type of information (info only or quote) and page number in the original source are provided: a (info p. 222), and c (a quote p. 271), and g (info p. 31), i (info only p. 221), o (a partial quote on page 60, also use same author published a different year).*
   Assume that you have not used the author's name to introduce the material you cite. Where there are multiple pages in the reference, you can select the page or pages appropriate to your citation.
2. Depending on your instructor, *using either the MLA or APA system, write a proper in-text citation for each of the bibliographic references you prepared for part 2 in the previous exercise 2. Assume that you have not used the author's name to introduce the material you cite. Where there are multiple pages in the reference, you can select the page or pages appropriate to your citation.*

Handling Quotations

Set off quotations fewer than five lines long for the MLA system (fewer than forty words long for the APA system) with quotation marks and run them into the text of the paper. For longer quotes, omit the quotation marks and indent the material ten spaces from the left margin for the MLA system (five spaces for the APA system). Double-space the typing. If you quote part or all of one paragraph, don't further indent the first line. If you quote two or more consecutive paragraphs, indent each one's first line three additional spaces for the MLA system (five for the APA system—except for the first paragraph in the quote which should not be additionally indented). Use single quotation marks for a quotation within a shorter quotation and double marks for a quotation within a longer, indented quotation. The following examples illustrate the handling of quotations. The documentation and indentation follow the MLA guidelines.

■ **Short Quotation**

Ellen Goodman offers this further observation about writers who peddle formulas for achieving success through selfishness: "They are all Doctor Feelgoods, offering placebo prescriptions instead of strong medicine. They give us a way to live with ourselves, perhaps, but not a way to live with each other" (16).

■ **Quotation within Short Quotation**

The report further stated, "All great writing styles have their wellsprings in the personality of the writer. As Buffon said, 'The style is the man'" (Duncan 49).

■ **Quotation within Longer, Indented Quotation**

Barbara Tuchman's *Proud Tower* presents a somewhat different view of the new conservative leaders:

> Besides riches, rank, broad acres, and ancient lineage, the new government also possessed, to the regret of the liberal opposition, and in the words of one of them, "an almost embarrassing wealth of talent and capacity." Secure in authority, resting comfortably on their electoral majority in the House of Commons and on a permanent majority in the House of Lords, of whom four-fifths were conservatives, they were in a position, admitted the same opponent, "of unassailable strength." (4)

Always provide some context for material that you quote. Various options exist. When you quote from a source for the first time, you might provide the author's full name and the source of the quotation, perhaps indicating the author's expertise as well. The passage just above omits the author's expertise; the passage below includes it.

Documenting Sources

Writing in *Newsweek* magazine, Riena Gross, chief psychiatric social worker at Illinois Medical Center in Chicago, said, "Kids have no real sense that they belong anywhere or to anyone as they did ten or fifteen years ago. Parents have loosened the reins, and kids are kind of floundering" (74).

Or you might note the event prompting the quotation and then the author's name.

Addressing a seminar at the University of Toronto, Dr. Joseph Pomeranz speculated that "acupuncture may work by activating a neural pain suppression mechanism in the brain" (324).

On other occasions, you might note only the author's full name and expertise.

Economist Richard M. Cybert, president of Carnegie Mellon University, offers the following sad prediction about the steel industry's future: "It will never be as large an industry as it has been. There are a lot of plants that will never come back and many laborers that will never be rehired" (43).

After first citing an author's full name, use only the last name for subsequent references.

In answering the objections of government agencies to the Freedom of Information Act, Wellford commented, "Increased citizen access should help citizens learn of governmental activities that weaken our First Amendment freedoms. Some administrative inconvenience isn't too large a price to pay for that" (137).

When quoting from a source with no author given, introduce the quotation with the name of the source.

Commenting on the problems that law enforcement personnel have in coping with computer crime, *Credit and Financial Management* magazine pointed out, "A computer crime can be committed in three hundredths of a second, and the criminal can be thousands of miles from the 'scene,' using a telephone" ("Computer Crime" 43).

Page numbers are not helpful when you cite passages from plays and poems, as these literary forms are available in many editions. When you quote from a play, identify the act, scene, and line numbers. Use Arabic numbers separated by periods. Here's how to cite Act 2, Scene 1, lines 295–300 of Shakespeare's *Othello*:

That Cassio loves her, I do well believe it;
That she loves him, 'tis apt, and of great credit:
The Moor, how be it that I endure him not,
Is of a constant, loving, noble nature;
And I dare think he'll prove to Desdemona
A most dear husband. (*Othello* 2.1.295-300)

When quoting from a short poem, use "line" or "lines" and the line number(s).

> In "Dover Beach," Matthew Arnold offers this melancholy assessment of
> the state of religion:
>
>> The Sea of Faith
>>
>> Was once, too, at the full, and round earth's shore
>>
>> Lay like the folds of a bright girdle furl'd.
>>
>> But now I only hear
>>
>> Its melancholy, long, withdrawing roar. (lines 21-25)

In quoting poetry that has been run into the text, use a slash mark(/) with a space on each side to indicate the shift from one line to the next in the original:

> In his ode "To Autumn," Keats says that autumn is the "Season of mists and
> mellow fruitfulness, / Close bosom-friend of the maturing sun" (lines 1-2).

Avoiding Plagiarism

Plagiarism occurs when a writer uses another person's material without properly acknowledging the debt. Sometimes plagiarism is deliberate, but often it happens because students simply don't understand what must be acknowledged and documented. Deliberate or not, plagiarism is absolutely unacceptable. *Any summary, paraphrase, or quotation you include in your paper must be documented as must statistics and graphics.* The only types of information escaping this requirement are those listed below:

1. *Common knowledge.* Common knowledge is information that most educated people would know. For instance, there's no need to document a statement that the Disney theme parks in California and Florida attract thousands of visitors each year. However, if you include precise daily, monthly, or yearly figures, then documentation is necessary.

2. *Your own conclusions.* As you write your paper, you'll incorporate your own conclusions at various points. (See the margin notes accompanying Keith Jacque's library research paper for examples.) Such comments require no documentation. The same holds true for your own research. If you polled students on a campus issue, simply present the findings as your own.

3. *Facts found in many sources.* Facts such as the year of Shakespeare's death, the size of the 2001 national budget surplus, and the location of the Taj Mahal need not be documented. However, where there may be disputes about the facts in question (such as the size of the 2003 deficit) or where there may be some need to enforce the credibility of your figures, provide the source for your facts. If you are not certain that something is common knowledge, indicate your source.

4. *Standard terms.* Terms widely used in a particular field require no documentation. Examples include such computer terms as *mouse, CD-ROM,* and *download.*

Any piece of information not set off with quotation marks must be in your own words. Otherwise, even though you name your source, you plagiarize by stealing the original phrasing.

The following passages illustrate the improper and proper use of source material.

Original Passage

One might contend, of course, that our country's biological diversity is so great and the land is so developed—so criss-crossed with the works of man—that it will soon be hard to build a dam anywhere without endangering some species. But as we develop a national inventory of endangered species, we certainly can plan our *necessary* development so as to exterminate the smallest number possible.

James L. Buckley, "Three Cheers for the Snail Darter,"
National Review, September 14, 1979: 1144–45. Print.

■ Plagiarism

Our country's biological diversity is so great and the land is so developed that it will soon be hard to build a dam anywhere without endangering some species. But as we develop a national inventory of endangered species, we certainly can plan our necessary development so as to exterminate the smallest number possible.

This writer clearly plagiarizes. The absence of Buckley's name and the failure to enclose his words in quotation marks create the impression that this passage is the student's own work.

■ Plagiarism

Given the extensive diversity of species in America, development such as the construction of dams is likely to endanger some species, whether it is a rare plant, a species of frog, or a rare variety of fish. By creating a database of endangered species, however, we can facilitate a planning process that will place the minimum number of species at risk.

Although this writer uses original language, the absence of documentation suggests that these ideas are the student's without any recognition of Buckley's contribution. Despite the paraphrase, this is still plagiarism.

■ Plagiarism

Our country's biological diversity is so great and the land so developed that in the near future we may pose a threat to some creature whenever we construct a dam. By developing a national inventory of endangered species, however, we can plan necessary development so as to preserve as many species as possible (Buckley 1144).

This version credits the ideas to Buckley, but the student has plagiarized by failing to put quotation marks around the phrasing (underlined here) that was copied from the original. As a result, readers will think that the passage represents the student's own wording.

■ Proper Use of Original

> America has so many kinds of plants and animals, and it is so built up, that in the near future we may pose a threat to some living thing just by damming some waterway. If, however, we knew which of our nation's plants and animals were threatened, we could use this information to preserve as many species as we can (Buckley 1144).

This student has identified the author and used her own words. As a result, no plagiarism occurs.

Plagiarism is a serious offense because it robs the original writer of recognition. Students caught plagiarizing risk failure in the course or perhaps suspension from school. Whenever you are unsure whether material requires documentation, supply a reference.

Avoiding plagiarism, from the article "The Problem with Single-Payer Plans," summarize paragraphs 11, 12, and 13; create a paraphrase of paragraph 11, and create an effective quote from material in paragraph 11. Use the original source The Hastings Center Report 38 no. 1 38-41 JA/F 2008, assuming that the material in question comes from page 39 of that report.

Indicate if each of the following statements used in a paper that drew on a reading of "The Problem with Single-Payer Plans" is plagiarism or not and why.

1. A single-payer is a system where only one party, most likely the government, pays health care costs instead of multiple private insurance companies.
2. Changes in the health care system need to consider problems with both the financing and delivery systems (Emanuel xxx).
3. One third of all doctor visits are to physicians with their own practice.
4. While the contemporary need is for chronic care, the delivery system is structured for acute care (Emanuel xxx).
5. One problem with our current finance system is that many tax payers contribute to systems like Medicaid and "yet are excluded from these programs" (Emanuel xxx).
6. The government fails to meet its responsibility for the current system since it doesn't "address key policy issues, fraud, and—for Medicaid—complex determinations of eligibility."

Reader

From Chapter 23 of *Strategies for Successful Writing*, Ninth Edition. James A. Reinking, Robert von der Osten.

NARRATION ▬ ▬ ▬ ▬ ▬ ▬ ▬ ▬ ▬

Reading Strategies

1. Read the narrative rapidly to get a feel for the story and identify the main point.
2. Identify the main conflict that moves the story forward. Identify the major characters and what they may represent.
3. Read the narrative more slowly with the main point in mind. Keep an eye on how the narrative supports the main point.

Reading Critically

1. Consider if the narrative would seem different if told from another person's point of view. Consider that point of view.
2. Ask whether the narrative really supports the author's main point. Consider what other narratives could be told about the issue and determine whether they might undermine the writer's claims.

Reading As a Writer

1. Determine the setting, conflict, characters, and development of the narrative. You might want to outline the plot to determine how it was organized.
2. Notice any particularly effective movements in the plot. If you find a useful strategy, jot it down.
3. Observe how the writer used dialogue. Make a note of any especially effective uses.

JAMES ALEXANDER THOM

The Perfect Picture[1]

James Alexander Thom (born 1933) is a native of Gosport, Indiana, where his parents were physicians, and a graduate of Butler University. Before becoming a freelance writer in 1973, he worked as an editor for the Indianapolis Star *and the* Saturday Evening Post *and as a lecturer at Indiana University. He has authored one volume of essays and several historical novels, one of which,* Panther in the Sky, *earned the Best Novel Award from the Western Writers of America. His latest novel,* The Red Heart, *appeared in 1998. He is a contributor to many magazines. "The Perfect Picture" depicts an incident and an ethical dilemma that Thom experienced as a cub reporter.*

1   It was early in the spring about 15 years ago—a day of pale sunlight and trees just beginning to bud. I was a young police reporter, driving to a scene I didn't want to see. A man, the police-dispatcher's broadcast said, had accidentally backed his pickup truck over his baby granddaughter in the driveway of the family home. It was a fatality.

Introduction: notes time, locale, and cause of action; first-person point of view

---

---

2   As I parked among police cars and TV-news cruisers, I saw a stocky white-haired man in cotton work clothes standing near a pickup. Cameras were trained on him, and reporters were sticking microphones in his face. Looking totally bewildered, he was trying to answer their questions. Mostly he was only moving his lips, blinking and choking up.

3   After a while the reporters gave up on him and followed the police into the small white house. I can still see in my mind's eye that devastated old man looking down at the place in the driveway where the child had been. Beside the house was a freshly spaded flower bed, and nearby a pile of dark, rich earth.

4   "I was just backing up there to spread that good dirt," he said to me, though I had not asked him anything. "I didn't even know she was outdoors." He stretched his hand toward the flower bed, then let it flop to his side. He lapsed back into his thoughts, and I, like a good reporter, went into the house to find someone who could provide a recent photo of the toddler.

5   A few minutes later, with all the details in my notebook and a three-by-five studio portrait of the cherubic child tucked in my jacket pocket, I went toward the kitchen where the police had said the body was.

6   I had brought a camera in with me—the big, bulky Speed Graphic which used to be the newspaper reporter's trademark. Everybody had drifted back out of the house together—family, police, reporters and photographers. Entering the kitchen, I came upon this scene:

7   On a Formica-topped table, backlighted by a frilly curtained window, lay the tiny body, wrapped in a clean white sheet. Somehow the grandfather had managed to stay away from the crowd. He was sitting on a chair beside the table, in profile to me and unaware of my presence, looking uncomprehendingly at the swaddled corpse.

8   The house was very quiet. A clock ticked. As I watched, the grandfather slowly leaned forward, curved his arms like parentheses around the head and feet of the little form, then pressed his face to the shroud and remained motionless.

9   In that hushed moment I recognized the makings of a prize-winning news photograph. I appraised the light, adjusted the lens setting and distance, locked a bulb in the flashgun, raised the camera and composed the scene in the viewfinder.

10 Every element of the picture was perfect: the grandfather in his plain work clothes, his white hair backlighted by sunshine, the child's form wrapped in the sheet, the atmosphere of the simple home suggested by black iron trivets and World's Fair souvenir plates on the walls flanking the window. Outside, the police could be seen inspecting the fatal rear wheel of the pickup while the child's mother and father leaned in each other's arms.

11 I don't know how many seconds I stood there, unable to snap that shutter. I was keenly aware of the powerful story-telling value that photo would have, and my professional conscience told me to take it. Yet I couldn't make my hand fire that flashbulb and intrude on the poor man's island of grief.

12 At length I lowered the camera and crept away, shaken with doubt about my suitability for the journalistic profession. Of course I never told the city editor or any fellow reporters about that missed opportunity for a perfect news picture.

13 Every day on the newscasts and in the papers, we see pictures of people in extreme conditions of grief and despair. Human suffering has become a spectator sport. And sometimes, as I'm watching news film, I remember that day.

14 I still feel right about what I did.

Discussion Questions

1. Thom notes in his opening paragraph that he is "driving to a scene I didn't want to see." How does this statement help explain what happens later?
2. These details, while providing the makings of a perfect picture, also highlight the horror of what has happened and through their impact on his sensitivity help influence his decision.
3. Do you think that Thom made the right decision? Why or why not?

Toward Key Insights

How have the media affected our sense of privacy?
Is their influence good or bad?
To answer these questions, consider the role of the newspaper photographer in "The Perfect Picture," TV crews at disasters, and talk shows built around very personal revelations.

Suggestion for Writing

Write a personal narrative that features a conflict over a choice between an advantageous and a morally satisfying decision. State your point directly or indirectly, and use time signals and dialogue as necessary.

DAN GREENBURG

Sound and Fury

Dan Greenburg is a native of Chicago who holds a bachelor of fine arts from the University of Illinois and a master of fine arts from UCLA. A prolific writer, he has authored over forty books, including such best sellers as How to Be a Jewish Mother, How to Make Yourself Miserable, How to Avoid Love and Marriage, *and a series of more than twenty-four children's books,* The Zack Files. *His articles have appeared in a wide and diverse range of popular magazines and been reprinted in many anthologies of humor and satire. He has been a guest on* The Today Show, Larry King Live, Late Night with David Letterman, *and other major TV talk shows. In this selection, Greenburg relates a situation in which soft words defused a potentially explosive situation.*

1   We carry around a lot of free-floating anger. What we do with it is what fascinates me.

2   My friend Lee Frank is a stand-up comedian who works regularly in New York comedy clubs. Not long ago I accompanied him to one of these places, where he was to be the late-night emcee and where I myself had once done a stand-up act in a gentler era.

3   The crowd that night was a typical weekend bunch—enthusiastic, hostile and drunk. A large contingent of inebriated young men from Long Island had decided that a comedian named Rusty who was currently on stage was the greatest

---

thing since pop-top cans and began chanting his name after almost everything he said: "Rus-TEE! Rus-TEE!"

4   My friend Lee knew he had a tough act to follow.

5   Indeed, the moment Lee walked on stage, the inebriated young men from Long Island began chanting "Rus-TEE! Rus-TEE!" and didn't give him a chance. Poor Lee, the flop sweat running into his eyes, tried every trick he knew to win them over, and finally gave up.

6   When he left the stage I joined him at the bar in the back of the club to commiserate.

7   "You did the best you could," I told him.

8   "I don't know," he said, "I could have handled it better."

9   "How?"

10   "I don't know," he said.

11   As we spoke, the young men who'd given him such a tough time trickled into the bar area. One of them spotted Lee and observed to a companion that Lee might want to do something about their heckling.

12   Lee thought he heard the companion reply, "I'm down," a casual acknowledgment that he was willing to have a fistfight. Lee repeated their remarks to me and indicated that he, too, was "down."

13   Though slight of frame, Lee is a black belt in Tae Kwon Do, has had skirmishes with three-card monte con men in Times Square, and once even captured a robber-rapist. I am also slight of frame but have had no training in martial arts. I did have one fistfight in my adult life (with a movie producer), but as Lee's best friend, I assumed that I was "down" as well.

14   Considering that there were more than a dozen of them and only two of us, the period of time that might elapse between our being "down" and our being down seemed exceedingly brief.

15   The young man who'd made the remark drifted toward Lee.

16   The eyes of everyone in the bar shifted slightly and locked onto the two men like heat-seeking missiles. Fight-or-flight adrenaline and testosterone spurted into dozens of male cardiovascular systems. Safeties snapped off figurative weapons. Red warning lights lit up dozens of DEFCON systems; warheads were armed and aimed. In a moment this bar area might very well resemble a saloon in a B grade western.

17   "How ya doing?" said Lee, his voice flat as unleavened bread, trying to make up his mind whether to be friendly or hostile.

18   "Okay," said the guy, a pleasant-looking, clean-cut kid in his mid-20s.

19   I was fascinated by what was going on between the two of them, each feeling the other out in a neutral, unemotional, slightly bemused manner. I saw no hostility here, no xenophobic loathing, just two young males jockeying for position, going through the motions, doing the dance, willing to engage at the slightest provocation. I had seen my cat do this many times when a stranger strayed onto his turf.

20   And then I had a sudden flash of clarity: These guys could either rip each other's heads off now or they could share a beer, and both options would be equally acceptable to them.

21   I'd felt close to critical mass on many occasions myself. But here, feeling outside the action, I could see clearly that it had to do with the enormous reservoir of rage that we men carry around with us, rage that seethes just under the surface and is ready to be tapped in an instant, with or without just provocation.

22   "What're you in town for?" asked Lee casually.

23   The guy was watching Lee carefully, making minuscule adjustments on his sensing and triggering equipment.

24   "It's my birthday," said the guy.

25   Lee mulled over this information for a moment, still considering all his options. Then he made his decision.

26   "Happy birthday," said Lee finally, sticking out his hand.

27   The guy studied Lee's hand a moment. Then, deciding the gesture was sincere, he took the hand and shook it.

28   "Thanks," he said, and walked back to his buddies.

29   All over the room you could hear safeties snapping on, warheads being unarmed. The incident was over, and in a moment it was as if it had never happened.

30   I felt I had just witnessed in microcosm the mechanism that triggers most acts of aggression, from gang fights to international conflagrations. It was so simple: a minor act of provocation. A decision on how to interpret it. Whether or not to escalate. And, in this particular case, a peaceful outcome. What struck me was how absolutely arbitrarily it had all been decided.

Discussion Questions

1. Discuss the appropriateness of Greenburg's title.
2. Does this essay have a stated or an unstated point? If it is stated, indicate where. If it is unstated, express it in your own words.
3. The expression "our being down" occurs twice in paragraph 14. Explain what it means in each instance.
4. Discuss the effectiveness of the figurative language in paragraph 16.
5. In paragraph 21 Greenburg credits "feeling outside the action" for helping him understand the rage involved in this situation as well as in others. Explain what he means.
6. How often do you think that the "equally acceptable" options mentioned in paragraph 20 occur in confrontations?

Toward Key Insights

What reasons can you give for the "free-floating anger" that Greenburg mentions at the outset of the essay?

How frequently and in what ways is this anger manifested?

What are some effective strategies for coping with this anger?

Suggestion for Writing

Write a narrative about a small incident that turned into a serious confrontation. Possible incidents might include an improper or reckless action of another driver, a minor disagreement with a friend or spouse, or a retaliation for an action at a sporting event. The outcome can be peaceful or otherwise.

MAYA ANGELOU

Momma's Encounter[1]

Maya Angelou has earned a reputation as one of this country's foremost black writers. Born (1928) Marguerite Johnson in St. Louis, Missouri, she spent much of her childhood in Stamps, Arkansas, the locale of our selection, where her grandmother ran a general store. Angelou has written plays, poems, and a six-part autobiography that includes I Know Why the Caged Bird Sings *(1970), from which our selection is taken. She has acted in numerous plays and has served as a television narrator, interviewer, and poet. At the January 1993 inauguration of President William Clinton, she recited a poem, "On the Pulse of Morning," that she had written especially for the occasion. In our selection, Angelou tells about an encounter in which her grandmother, whom she calls Momma, triumphs over a pack of taunting neighborhood children.*

1   "Thou shall not be dirty" and "Thou shall not be impudent" were the two commandments of Grandmother Henderson upon which hung our total salvation.

2   Each night in the bitterest winter we were forced to wash faces, arms, necks, legs and feet before going to bed. She used to add, with a smirk that unprofane people can't control when venturing into profanity, "and wash as far as possible, then wash possible."

3   We would go to the well and wash in the ice-cold, clear water, grease our legs with the equally cold stiff Vaseline, then tiptoe into the house. We wiped the dust from our toes and settled down for schoolwork, cornbread, clabbered milk, prayers and bed, always in that order. Momma was famous for pulling the quilts off after we had fallen asleep to examine our feet. If they weren't clean enough for her, she took the switch (she kept one behind the bedroom door for emergencies) and woke up the offender with a few aptly placed burning reminders.

4   The area around the well at night was dark and slick, and boys told about how snakes love water, so that anyone who had to draw water at night and then stand there alone and wash knew that moccasins and rattlers, puff adders and boa constrictors were winding their way to the well and would arrive just as the person washing got soap in her eyes. But Momma convinced us that not only was cleanliness next to Godliness, dirtiness was the inventor of misery.

5   The impudent child was detested by God and a shame to its parents and could bring destruction to its house and line. All adults had to be addressed as Mister, Missus, Miss, Auntie, Cousin, Unk, Uncle, Buhbah, Sister, Brother and a thousand other appellations indicating familial relationship and the lowliness of the addressor.

6   Everyone I knew respected these customary laws, except for the powhite-trash children.

7   Some families of powhitetrash lived on Momma's farm land behind the school. Sometimes a gaggle of them came to the Store, filling the whole room, chasing out the air and even changing the well-known scents. The children crawled over the shelves and into the potato and onion bins, twanging all the time in their sharp voices like cigarbox guitars. They took liberties in my Store that I would never dare. Since Momma told us that the less you say to whitefolks (or even powhitetrash) the better, Bailey and I would stand, solemn, quiet, in the displaced air. But if one of the playful apparitions got close to us, I pinched it.

[1]Editors' title.

Partly out of angry frustration and partly because I didn't believe in its flesh reality.

8   They called my uncle by his first name and ordered him around the Store. He, to my crying shame, obeyed them in his limping dip-straight-dip fashion.

9   My grandmother, too followed their orders, except that she didn't seem to be servile because she anticipated their needs.

10   "Here's sugar, Miz Potter, and here's baking powder. You didn't buy soda last month, you'll probably be needing some."

11   Momma always directed her statements to the adults, but sometimes, Oh painful sometimes, the grimy, snotty-nosed girls would answer her.

12   "Naw, Annie . . ."—to Momma? Who owned the land they lived on? Who forgot more than they would ever learn? If there was any justice in the world, God should strike them dumb at once!—"Just give us some extry sody crackers, and some more mackerel."

13   At least they never looked in her face, or I never caught them doing so. Nobody with a smidgen of training, not even the worst roustabout, would look right in a grown person's face. It meant the person was trying to take the words out before they were formed. The dirty little children didn't do that, but they threw their orders around the Store like lashes from a cat-o'-nine tails.

14   When I was around ten years old, those scruffy children caused me the most painful and confusing experience I had ever had with my grandmother.

15   One summer morning, after I had swept the dirt yard of leaves, spearmint-gum wrappers and Vienna-sausage labels, I raked the yellow-red dirt, and made half-moons carefully, so that the design stood out clearly and mask-like. I put the rake behind the Store and came through the back of the house to find Grandmother on the front porch in her big, wide white apron. The apron was so stiff by virtue of the starch that it could have stood alone. Momma was admiring the yard, so I joined her. It truly looked like a flat redhead that had been raked with a big-toothed comb. Momma didn't say anything but I knew she liked it. She looked over toward the school principal's house and to the right at Mr. McElroy's. She was hoping one of those community pillars would see the design before the day's business wiped it out. Then she looked upward to the school. My head had swung with hers, so at just about the same time we saw a troop of the powhitetrash kids marching over the hill and down by the side of the school.

16   I looked to Momma for direction. She did an excellent job of sagging from her waist down, but from the waist up she seemed to be pulling for the top of the oak tree across the road. Then she began to moan a hymn. Maybe not to moan, but the tune was so slow and the meter so strange that she could have been moaning. She didn't look at me again. When the children reached halfway down the hill, halfway to the Store, she said without turning, "Sister, go on inside."

17   I wanted to beg her, "Momma, don't wait for them. Come on inside with me. If they come in the Store, you go to the bedroom and let me wait on them. They only frighten me if you're around. Alone I know how to handle them." But of course I couldn't say anything, so I went in and stood behind the screen door.

18   Before the girls got to the porch I heard their laughter crackling and popping like pine logs in a cooking stove. I suppose my lifelong paranoia was born in those cold, molasses-slow minutes. They came finally to stand on the ground in front of Momma. At first they pretended seriousness. Then one of them wrapped her right arm in the crook of her left, pushed out her mouth and started to hum. I realized that she was aping my grandmother. Another said, "Naw, Helen, you ain't standing like her. This here's it." Then she lifted her chest, folded her arms and mocked that strange carriage that was Annie

Henderson. Another laughed, "Naw, you can't do it. You mouth ain't pooched out enough. It's like this."

19   I thought about the rifle behind the door, but I knew I'd never be able to hold it straight, and the .410, our sawed-off shotgun, which stayed loaded and was fired every New Year's night, was locked in the trunk and Uncle Willie had the key on his chain. Through the fly-specked screen-door, I could see that the arms of Momma's apron jiggled from the vibrations of her humming. But her knees seemed to have locked as if they would never bend again.

20   She sang on. No louder than before, but no softer either. No slower or faster.

21   The dirt of the girls' cotton dresses continued on their legs, feet, arms and faces to make them all of a piece. Their greasy uncolored hair hung down, uncombed, with a grim finality. I knelt to see them better, to remember them for all time. The tears that had slipped down my dress left unsurprising dark spots, and made the front yard blurry and even more unreal. The world had taken a deep breath and was having doubts about continuing to revolve.

22   The girls had tired of mocking Momma and turned to other means of agitation. One crossed her eyes, stuck her thumbs in both sides of her mouth and said, "Look here, Annie." Grandmother hummed on and the apron strings trembled. I wanted to throw a handful of black pepper in their faces, to throw lye on them, to scream that they were dirty, scummy peckerwoods, but I knew I was as clearly imprisoned behind the scene as the actors outside were confined to their roles.

23   One of the smaller girls did a kind of puppet dance while her fellow clowns laughed at her. But the tall one, who was almost a woman, said something very quietly, which I couldn't hear. They all moved backward from the porch, still watching Momma. For an awful second I thought they were going to throw a rock at Momma, who seemed (except for the apron strings) to have turned into stone herself. But the big girl turned her back, bent down and put her hands flat on the ground—she didn't pick up anything. She simply shifted her weight and did a hand stand.

24   Her dirty bare feet and long legs went straight for the sky. Her dress fell down around her shoulders, and she had on no drawers. The slick pubic hair made a brown triangle where her legs came together. She hung in the vacuum of that lifeless morning for only a few seconds, then wavered and tumbled. The other girls clapped her on the back and slapped their hands.

25   Momma changed her song to "Bread of Heaven, bread of Heaven, feed me till I want no more."

26   I found that I was praying too. How long could Momma hold out? What new indignity would they think of to subject her to? Would I be able to stay out of it? What would Momma really like me to do?

27   Then they were moving out of the yard, on their way to town. They bobbed their heads and shook their slack behinds and turned, one at a time:

28   "'Bye, Annie."

29   "'Bye, Annie."

30   "'Bye, Annie."

31   Momma never turned her head or unfolded her arms, but she stopped singing and said, "'Bye, Miz Helen, 'bye, Miz Ruth, 'bye, Miz Eloise."

32   I burst. A firecracker July-the-Fourth burst. How could Momma call them Miz? The mean nasty things. Why couldn't she have come inside the sweet, cool store when we saw them breasting the hill? What did she prove? And then if they were dirty, mean and impudent, why did Momma have to call them Miz?

33   She stood another whole song through and then opened the screen door to look down on me crying in rage. She looked until I looked up. Her face was a brown moon that shone on me. She was beautiful. Something had happened out

there, which I couldn't completely understand, but I could see that she was happy. Then she bent down and touched me as mothers of the church "lay hands on the sick and afflicted" and I quieted.

34   "Go wash your face, Sister." And she went behind the candy counter and hummed, "Glory, glory, hallelujah, when I lay my burden down."

35   I threw the well water on my face and used the weekday handkerchief to blow my nose. Whatever the contest had been out front, I knew Momma had won.

36   I took the rake back to the front yard. The smudged footprints were easy to erase. I worked for a long time on my new design and laid the rake behind the wash pot. When I came back in the Store, I took Momma's hand and we both walked outside to look at the pattern.

37   It was a large heart with lots of hearts growing smaller inside, and piercing from the outside rim to the smallest heart was an arrow. Momma said, "Sister, that's right pretty." Then she turned back to the Store and resumed, "Glory, glory, hallelujah, when I lay my burden down."

Discussion Questions

1. Does this narrative have a stated or an unstated point? If it is stated, indicate where. If it is unstated, express it in your own words.
2. Point out the contrast between Angelou's upbringing and that of the "powhite-trash" children. How does this contrast prepare the reader for the events that follow?
3. Explain what Angelou means in paragraph 22 when she says ". . . but I knew I was as clearly imprisoned behind the scene as the actors outside were confined to their roles."
4. Discuss the significance of the dialogue in paragraphs 28–31.
5. Suggest the significance of the pattern of hearts that Angelou draws in the front yard. Of Momma singing "Glory, glory, hallelujah, when I lay my burden down."
6. Angelou recalls that she was "around ten years old" when the encounter took place. Explain why her age was significant. How would her perception have differed had she been, say, eighteen?
7. Angelou uses the first-person point of view. Explain why third-person narration would have been inappropriate for this narrative.

Toward Key Insights

Was Momma's strategy for enduring the children's taunts the most effective approach? Why or why not?

What else could she have done?

Has she really won?

Some argue that racism should always be actively confronted since passive endurance only perpetuates it. Do you agree? If not, when and how should racism be confronted and when should it be endured?

Suggestion for Writing

Write a narrative that illustrates how a friend, an acquaintance, or a family member achieved a personal triumph through turning the other cheek.

Marta Salinas

The Scholarship Jacket

Marta Salinas has published stories in the Los Angeles Herald *and in* California Living. *She is also an environmental activist.*

1   The small Texas school that I attended carried out a tradition every year during the eighth grade graduation; a beautiful gold and green jacket, the school colors, was awarded to the class valedictorian, the student who had maintained the highest grades for eight years. The scholarship jacket had a big gold S on the left front side and the winner's name was written in gold letters on the pocket.

2   My oldest sister Rosie had won the jacket a few years back and I fully expected to win also. I was fourteen and in the eighth grade. I had been a straight A student since the first grade, and the last year I had looked forward to owning the jacket. My father was a farm laborer who couldn't earn enough money to feed eight children, so when I was six I was given to my grandparents to raise. We couldn't participate in sports at school because there were registration fees, uniform costs, and trips out of town; so even though we were quite agile and athletic, there would never be a sports school jacket for us. This one, the scholarship jacket, was our only chance.

3   In May, close to graduation, spring fever struck, and no one paid any attention in class; instead we stared out the windows and at each other, wanting to speed up the last few weeks of school. I despaired every time I looked in the mirror. Pencil thin, not a curve anywhere, I was called "Beanpole" and "String Bean" and I knew that's what I looked like. A flat chest, no hips, and a brain, that's what I had. That really isn't much for a fourteen-year-old to work with, I thought, as I absentmindedly wandered from my history class to the gym. Another hour of sweating in basketball and displaying my toothpick legs was coming up. Then I remembered my P.E. shorts were still in a bag under my desk where I'd forgotten them. I had to walk all the way back and get them. Coach Thompson was a real bear if anyone wasn't dressed for P.E. She had said I was a good forward and once she even tried to talk Grandma into letting me join the team. Grandma, of course, said no.

4   I was almost back at my classroom's door when I heard angry voices and arguing. I stopped. I didn't mean to eavesdrop; I just hesitated, not knowing what to do. I needed those shorts and I was going to be late, but I didn't want to interrupt an argument between my teachers. I recognized the voices: Mr. Schmidt, my history teacher, and Mr. Boone, my math teacher. They seemed to be arguing about me. I couldn't believe it. I still remember the shock that rooted me flat against the wall as if I were trying to blend in with the graffiti written there.

5   "I refuse to do it! I don't care who her father is, her grades don't even begin to compare to Martha's. I won't lie or falsify records. Martha has a straight A plus average and you know it." That was Mr. Schmidt and he sounded very angry. Mr. Boone's voice sounded calm and quiet.

6   "Look, Joann's father is not only on the Board, he owns the only store in town; we could say it was a close tie and—"

7   The pounding in my ears drowned out the rest of the words, only a word here and there filtered through. ". . . Martha is Mexican . . . resign . . . won't do it. . . ." Mr. Schmidt came rushing out, and luckily for me went down the opposite way toward the auditorium, so he didn't see me. Shaking, I waited a few

Marta Salinas, "The Scholarship Jacket" from *Nosotras: Latina Literature Today* by Maria del Carmen Boza, Beverly Silva, and Carmen Valle, editors. Bilingual Press/Editorial Bilingue, 1986. Tempe, Arizona. Originally from *Cuentos Chicanos: A Short Story Anthology*, Eds. Rudolfo A. Anaya and Antonio Márquez. Reprinted by permission of Bilingual Press/Editorial Bilingüe.

minutes and then went in and grabbed my bag and fled from the room. Mr. Boone looked up when I came in but didn't say anything. To this day I don't remember if I got in trouble in P.E. for being late or how I made it through the rest of the afternoon. I went home very sad and cried into my pillow that night so Grandmother wouldn't hear me. It seemed a cruel coincidence that I had over-heard that conversation.

8   The next day when the principal called me into his office, I knew what it would be about. He looked uncomfortable and unhappy. I decided I wasn't going to make it any easier for him so I looked him straight in the eye. He looked away and fidgeted with the papers on his desk.

9   "Martha," he said, "there's been a change in policy this year regarding the scholarship jacket. As you know, it has always been free." He cleared his throat and continued. "This year the Board decided to charge fifteen dollars—which still won't cover the complete cost of the jacket."

10   I stared at him in shock and a small sound of dismay escaped my throat. I hadn't expected this. He still avoided looking in my eyes.

11   "So if you are unable to pay the fifteen dollars for the jacket, it will be given to the next one in line."

12   Standing with all the dignity I could muster, I said, "I'll speak to my grand-father about it, sir, and let you know tomorrow." I cried on the walk home from the bus stop. The dirt road was a quarter of a mile from the highway, so by the time I got home, my eyes were red and puffy.

13   "Where's Grandpa?" I asked Grandma, looking down at the floor so she wouldn't ask me why I'd been crying. She was sewing on a quilt and didn't look up.

14   "I think he's out back working in the bean field."

15   I went outside and looked out at the fields. There he was. I could see him walking between the rows, his body bent over the little plants, hoe in hand. I walked slowly out to him, trying to think how I could best ask him for the money. There was a cool breeze blowing and a sweet smell of mesquite in the air, but I didn't appreciate it. I kicked at a dirt clod. I wanted that jacket so much. It was more than just being a valedictorian and giving a little thank you speech for the jacket on graduation night. It represented eight years of hard work and expecta-tion. I knew I had to be honest with Grandpa; it was my only chance. He saw me and looked up.

16   He waited for me to speak. I cleared my throat nervously and clasped my hands behind my back so he wouldn't see them shaking. "Grandpa, I have a big favor to ask you," I said in Spanish, the only language he knew. He still waited silently. I tried again. "Grandpa, this year the principal said the scholarship jacket is not going to be free. It's going to cost fifteen dollars and I have to take the money in tomorrow, otherwise it'll be given to some else." The last words came out in an eager rush. Grandpa straightened up tiredly and leaned his chin on the hoe handle. He looked out over the field that was filled with the tiny green bean plants. I waited, desperately hoping he'd say I could have the money.

17   He turned to me and asked quietly, "What does a scholarship jacket mean?"

18   I answered quickly; maybe there was a chance. "It means you've earned it by having the highest grades for eight years and that's why they're giving it to you." Too late I realized the significance of my words. Grandpa knew that I understood it was not a matter of money. It wasn't that. He went back to hoeing the weeds that sprang up between the delicate little bean plants. It was a time consuming job; sometimes the small shoots were right next to each other. Finally he spoke again.

19   "Then if you pay for it, Marta, it's not a scholarship jacket, is it? Tell your principal I will not pay the fifteen dollars."

20   I walked back to the house and locked myself in the bathroom for a long time. I was angry with Grandfather even though I knew he was right, and I was angry with the Board, whoever they were. Why did they have to change the rules just when it was my turn to win the jacket?

21   It was a very sad and withdrawn girl who dragged into the principal's office the next day. This time he did look me in the eyes.

22   "What did your grandfather say?"

23   I sat very straight in my chair.

24   "He said to tell you he won't pay the fifteen dollars."

25   The principal muttered something I couldn't understand under his breath, and walked over to the window. He stood looking out at something outside. He looked bigger than usual when he stood up; he was a tall gaunt man with gray hair, and I watched the back of his head while I waited for him to speak.

26   "Why?" he finally asked. "Your grandfather has the money. Doesn't he own a small bean farm?"

27   I looked at him, forcing my eyes to stay dry. "He said if I had to pay for it, then it wouldn't be a scholarship jacket," I said and stood up to leave. "I guess you'll just have to give it to Joann." I hadn't meant to say that; it had just slipped out. I was almost to the door when he stopped me.

28   "Martha—wait."

29   I turned and looked at him, waiting. What did he want now? I could feel my heart pounding. Something bitter and vile tasting was coming up in my mouth; I was afraid I was going to be sick. I didn't need any sympathy speeches. He sighed loudly and went back to his big desk. He looked at me, biting his lip, as if thinking.

30   "Okay, damn it. We'll make an exception in your case. I'll tell the Board, you'll get your jacket."

31   I could hardly believe it. I spoke in a trembling rush. "Oh, thank you, sir!" Suddenly I felt great. I didn't know about adrenaline in those days, but I knew something was pumping through me, making me feel as tall as the sky. I wanted to yell, jump, run the mile, do something. I ran out so I could cry in the hall where there was no one to see me. At the end of the day, Mr. Schmidt winked at me and said, "I hear you're getting a scholarship jacket this year."

32   His face looked as happy and innocent as a baby's, but I knew better. Without answering I gave him a quick hug and ran to the bus. I cried on the walk home again, but this time because I was so happy. I couldn't wait to tell Grandpa and ran straight to the field. I joined him in the row where he was working and without saying anything I crouched down and started pulling up the weeds with my hands. Grandpa worked alongside me for a few minutes, but he didn't ask what had happened. After I had a little pile of weeds between the rows, I stood up and faced him.

33   "The principal said he's making an exception for me, Grandpa, and I'm getting the jacket after all. That's after I told him what you said."

34   Grandpa didn't say anything, he just gave me a pat on the shoulder and a smile. He pulled out the crumpled red handkerchief that he always carried in his back pocket and wiped the sweat off his forehead.

35   "Better go see if your grandmother needs any help with supper."

36   I gave him a big grin. He didn't fool me. I skipped and ran back to the house whistling some silly tune.

Discussion Questions

1. Why is the scholarship jacket so important to Marta?
2. What are some of the key conflicts that are essential to the plot?
3. What is the importance of the overheard conversation in the development of the plot? How effective is it as a technique in this context?
4. Why did the school charge fifteen dollars for the scholarship jacket? How is this important to the developing theme of the narrative?
5. What is the significance of the grandfather's refusal to pay the fifteen dollars for the scholarship jacket?
6. How does the writer use very short pieces of dialogue to reveal the essential values of the characters and how they meet the situation?
7. Why doesn't the story end with the principal's statement that he will make an exception and she will get the jacket? What do the additional scenes with Mr. Schmidt and Martha's grandfather add to the narrative?
8. What is the significance of the fact that the principal calls the narrator "Martha" while her grandfather calls her "Marta"?

Toward Key Insights

Instead of simply giving the jacket to Joann in an outright act of discrimination, the school developed a policy that was likely to have the same result but seem reasonable. What policies or procedures have you observed that may seem reasonable on the surface but could simply serve to perpetuate an injustice?

The main character of this narrative is Mexican American. Is the suggestion that the scholarship jacket go to someone else based on race? Are there other social injustices that may be credited to race but have other causes?

Suggestion for Writing

Write a narrative about an injustice you experienced so that those involved in the situation could better understand what the event meant to you.

DESCRIPTION

Reading Strategies

1. Identify a thesis statement (possibly first or last paragraph) and/or a statement of purpose. Read the essay with an anticipation of what the description is intended to accomplish.
2. Don't get lost in the details. Note, possibly write in the margins, the overall impression or mood the description is evoking.
3. Decide how much of the description you need to remember. If the description is intended to create a mood, you may read quickly. If you are reading a description of rock formations for a geology class, you might want to take notes that organize the key features you need to remember under the appropriate headings.
4. Note if there is a pattern to the organization of the description. Recognizing the organizational pattern can make even dense writing easier to read.

Reading Critically

1. Identify the point of view of the description. The scene described might look very different from a different vantage point.
2. Look for how the details were selected. An emphasis on different details might have painted a very different picture.
3. Check to see if the conclusion of the essay really follows from the description. Just because a wilderness can be described as pristine doesn't mean that careful logging should be entirely banned.

Reading As a Writer

1. Identify and note down the organizational pattern if it is effective.
2. Jot down any phrases or sections that you find especially effective.
3. Examine the essay for word choice. Notice how the writer obtained the effects he or she did.

JOHN V. YOUNG

When the Full Moon Shines Its Magic over Monument Valley

John V. Young (1909–1999) was born in Oakland, California. After attending San Jose State Teachers College, he spent twelve years as a reporter and editor for several rural California newspapers, then held a series of personnel and public relations positions. In 1966, he became a full-time freelance writer, specializing in western travel pieces. His books include The Grand Canyon *(1969),* Ghost Towns of the Santa Cruz Mountains *(1979, 1984),* Hot Type and Pony Wire *(1980),* State Parks of New Mexico *(1984),* State Parks of Arizona *(1986), and* State Parks of Utah *(1989). His articles have appeared in the* New York Times *as well as in numerous travel publications. In the article that follows, he focuses on the sensations generated first by his surroundings and then by the moonrise.*

Title identifies dominant impression: magic

Introduction: paragraphs 1 and 2: identifies when, where, who, why

Touch impression

Sight impression

Comparisons

Body: paragraphs 3–8

Fixed vantage point

Sight impressions

Time signal

Sound impressions

Sight impressions

1   We were camped here in early spring, by one of those open-faced shelters that the Navajos have provided for tourists in this part of their vast tribal park on the Arizona–Utah border, 25 miles north of Kayenta. It was cool but pleasant, and we were alone, three men in a truck.

2   We were here for a purpose; to see the full moon rise over this most mysterious and lonely of scenic wonders, where fantastically eroded red and yellow sandstone shapes soar to the sky like a giant's chess pieces and where people—especially white strangers—come quickly to feel like pretty small change indeed.

3   Because all Navajo dwellings face east, our camp faced east—toward the rising sun and the rising moon and across a limitless expanse of tawny desert, that ancient sea, framed by the towering nearby twin pinnacles called The Mittens. We began to feel the magic even before the sun was fully down. It occurred when a diminutive wraith of a Navajo girl wearing a long, dark, velvet dress gleaming with silver ornaments drifted silently by, herding a flock of ghostly sheep to a waterhole somewhere. A bell on one of the rams tinkled faintly, and then its music was lost in the soft rustle of the night wind, leaving us with an impression that perhaps we had really seen nothing at all.

John V. Young. "When the Full Moon Shines Its Magic over Monument Valley," *New York Times*, March 16, 1969. Section 10, p. 1. Copyright © 1969 by John V. Young.

4   Just then, a large woolly dog appeared out of the gloom, seeming to materialize on the spot. It sat quietly on the edge of the glow from our campfire, its eyes shining like mirrors. It made no sound but when we offered food, it accepted the gift gravely and with much dignity. The dog then vanished again, probably to join the girl and her flock. We were not certain it was not part of the illusion.

Time signal
Sight impression
Comparison

5   As the sun disappeared entirely, the evening afterglow brush tipped all the spires and cliffs with magenta, deepening to purple, and the sand ripples stood out like miniature ocean waves in darkening shades of orange. Off to the east on the edge of the desert, a pale saffron glow told us the moon was about to rise behind a thin layer of clouds, slashed by the white contrail of an invisible jet airplane miles away.

Time signal
Sight impressions
Comparison
Sight impressions

6   We had our cameras on tripods and were fussing with light meters, making casual bets as to the exact place where the moon would first appear, when it happened—instant enchantment. Precisely between the twin spires of The Mittens, the enormous globe loomed suddenly, seeming as big as the sun itself, behind a coppery curtain on the rim of creation.

Sight impressions
Comparison
Vivid language

7   We were as totally unprepared for the great size of the moon as we were for its flaming color, nor could we have prepared ourselves for the improbable setting. We felt like the wizards of Stonehenge, commanding the planets to send their light through the magic orifices in line at the equinox. Had the Navajo medicine men contrived this for our benefit?

Sight impressions

8   The massive disk of the moon seemed to rise very fast at first, an optical effect magnified by the crystalline air and the flatness of the landscape between us and the distant, ragged skyline. Then it seemed to pause for a moment, as if it were pinioned on one of the pinnacles or impaled on a sharply upthrusting rocky point. Its blazing light made inky shadows all around us, split by the brilliant wedge of the moon's path between the spires. The wind had stopped. There was not a sound anywhere, nor even a whisper. If a drum had sounded just then, it would not have been out of place, I suppose, but it would have frightened us half to death.

Comparison
Sight impressions
Vivid language
Absent sound
Impression

9   Before the moon had cleared the tops of The Mittens, the show was over and the magic was gone. A thin veil of clouds spread over the sky, ending the spell as suddenly as it had come upon us. It was as if the gods had decided that we had seen enough for mere mortals on one spring night, and I must confess it was something of a relief to find ourselves back on mundane earth again, with sand in our shoes and a chill in the air.

Conclusion: time signal; renames dominant impression
Notes writer's reaction

Discussion Questions

1. How does the last sentence in paragraph 7 ("Had the Navajo medicine men contrived this for our benefit?") relate to the purpose of the essay?
2. This description takes the form of a narrative. Where does the climax occur, and how does it affect the viewers?

Touch impression

Toward Key Insights

What makes certain experiences seem magical?
How important are such magical experiences, and how might they shape our perceptions of the everyday world?

Suggestion for Writing

Select a place you know well and describe it by conveying some dominant impression that emerges during daylight hours. Settle on an appropriate vantage point and either identify the impression or allow readers to determine it for themselves.

LESLEY HAZLETON

Assembly Line Adventure[1]

Lesley Hazleton (born 1945) is a native of England who earned a B.A. degree from Manchester University and an MA degree from the Hebrew University of Jerusalem before emigrating to the United States in 1979. Hazleton is a nationally known automotive journalist with wide-ranging interests that include baseball, psychology, and politics. She has authored six nonfiction books, and her numerous shorter pieces have appeared in a variety of major newspapers and popular magazines. Our essay is excerpted from her latest book, Driving to Detroit *(1998). In it she describes her brief introduction to auto assembly line work and the lessons she learned from the experience.*

1   I'd toured many auto plants before, and physically this was not much different. That is, it was an assault on the senses: an enclosed, windowless world of harsh artificial light and hard concrete floors ringing with the discordant cacophony of industrial production. Metal rang on metal. Stamping presses clanked, power tools whined, pulleys groaned, hoists clanged, welding robots whooshed, sparks crackled, lasers beeped, compressed air hissed, bolts banged into place, trolleys rumbled down the aisles, and all the while, conveyor belts carrying cars in one stage or another of production, from bare metal frames to fully painted bodies, clattered and clanketed beside us and behind us and even over our heads.

2   At five in the afternoon, I started work, joining three other workers stationed around a huge rotating machine. Our job was to feed a robot.

3   Officially, we were preparing dashboard molds for foam injection. In fact, we were simply loading and unloading the machine for the robot, which injected the foam and then wiped its own nozzle as though it were wiping its nose—one of those infuriatingly human gestures that make you think, "Cute," and then hate yourself for having thought it.

4   This was one of the simplest tasks on the whole assembly line. Squirt some filler release into a hole. Lift a light plastic mold and place it on a protruding lip of the machine. Bang a board with your knee to drop three locks to hold the mold in place. Check the locks. Push a black button to bring the lip down into the right position for the next guy. Wait for the machine to rotate and present you with a new lip. And that was it. A ten-second job to be repeated ad infinitum.

5   Two hours later, I moved from one of the simplest jobs on the line to one of the most complicated: assembling the whole instrument panel. Steering wheel, indicator and wiper wands, gauges, dashboard line, the lot.

6   Audrey, the woman whose task it was to teach me this job, had a tough challenge ahead of her.

[1] Editors' title.

7   I guessed she was in her mid-thirties. Despite a mass of long brown curly hair, she had a boyish way to her, maybe because of the leather builder's apron she was wearing, its pockets so full of connectors and screws and bolts that it took me a while to realize she was six months pregnant.

8   "Is this your first?" I asked.

9   She burst out laughing. "Honey, I'm forty-three years old. And a grandmother. I married again not long ago, and"—she spread her arms wide and stared at her belly—"just look what happened. This sure is the last thing I ever expected."

10   "How long will you go on working?"

11   She laughed again. "Do you know how much kids cost? I'm staying right here till the day I pop."

12   She hadn't stopped working for a moment as we talked. She couldn't. The line was rolling, and it was either keep up or bring everything to a halt. We were standing *on* the line, a wide conveyor belt rumbling past an array of shelves piled high with parts, and beneath an overhead rack dangling power tools and bins of screws. On the line with us, every six feet or so, was a work-stand holding an empty dashboard shell, placed upside down on the stand so that it was easy to work on. Audrey's job was to make it into a complete instrument panel.

13   For the first few moments, standing on the moving belt was almost childishly fun. The world was reversed: you stood still and it went past you. Your mind knew it was you moving, not the world, but your senses told you otherwise. And all the time, the belt vibrated gently underfoot; if it weren't for the noise, it might even have been pleasantly sexy.

14   "Watch your head," Audrey said, and I ducked as a power wrench came dangling past my right ear. Followed by another. And yet another. Even though I reminded myself that it was me moving, not them, every time I looked up they seemed to be aiming for my brains with a certain inexorable malevolence.

15   I spent the first half-hour watching Audrey and figuring out how to stay out of the way. So far as I could make out, she had a total of some fifty separate procedures to complete in a logic-defying sequence of about three minutes. Each step had to be performed in perfect timing, so that the right parts and tools were at hand exactly when she needed them. And to add to the pressure, this job was what they called a "show-stopper."

16   Farther on down the line, the completed instrument panel would be lowered into the "smile joint"—a large lazy U going from side to side of the car's frame. If it didn't fit, the line would stop, and the whole plant would start running behind. "You can't go back and do it again," Audrey said. "You got to do it perfect the first time."

17   I knew I'd never be able to do this job. Yet Audrey seemed convinced that I was educable. She talked each movement out loud as she worked, with me following her around like a pet dog. Somehow, she convinced me to do a bit here and a bit there, until within an hour, I had the beginning of it down pat:

18   Walk six stands down the line, past other team members at different stages of the job, and read the manifest hanging on the dashboard shell. Pick up different parts from the shelves alongside the line, depending on whether this is to be a sedan or a wagon, an automatic or a manual shift. Jam a leather sheath over the sharp metal edge to the side of the module. Ease the parts into place. Snap-connect electrical wires: gray to the right, blue to the middle, white to the left.

19   So far so good. I was feeling quite proud of myself. Trouble was, this was only the beginning of the beginning.

20   The rest began to blur: Snap-connect a black fastener, then a yellow one. Don't delay. If you go too slow, the line will take you past the parts you need, and you'll have to start running back and forth for them. Pick up the steering shaft from a shelf

and ease its thirty-pound weight down through the center of the module. Arrange the wires to run over the top of the shaft. Slip on and snap a green fastener . . .

21   Or were those last two steps the other way round? "Here," said Audrey, redoing my work.

22   Okay, now pick up two bronze-colored bolts and screws, two black bolts, a circular piece, and two silver bolts from those big bins alongside the line. Insert the silver bolts. Fine. Place the bronze-colored ones in one place, the black ones in another. Great. Pull down a power wrench from the overhead line . . .

23   I grabbed for it and missed. It began to recede from me. I stretched and yanked it down just in time to tighten the bolts. I had no idea of what I was bolting to what, or why. Neither, it turned out, did Audrey.

24   Right, you've got those bolts nice and tight. Now pick different bronze-colored bolts from another bin. No, not alongside the line—right here, hanging overhead. Fine. Insert them and tighten them by hand for now. What about the wrench? Not there yet, that comes soon. First, thread the electrical wires through the back of the module and out through this flap, then loop them over and under the shaft like so, and then . . .

25   Then what? I couldn't remember. And I was only a third of the way through the job.

26   "Don't worry," said Audrey. "It takes most people four days to learn this job. You're doing real good."

27   That was sweet of her, but it didn't feel real good to me. My attention strayed for a moment, I lost a beat, and suddenly the power tools and screw bins were bearing down on me way before I was ready for them. I worked as fast as I could, one eye on my hands, the other on the dangling wrench going past. I swore, lunged for it, and yanked at the cord as though if I pulled hard enough I could pull back the whole line and slow things down to my pace. I remembered Charlie Chaplin's desperation in *Modern Times*, and suddenly there was nothing remotely funny about it. I dropped a bolt, reached for the wrong wrench, and watched pathetically as Audrey stepped in and put everything to rights. I hadn't felt quite this incompetent since I was a kid trying to thread a sewing machine at school. I never did master that.

28   Every time I thought I had the hang of it all, another two steps somehow reversed themselves in my mind, or one slipped out of existence altogether. My ears were ringing, my mind was reeling, and my hands had never felt clumsier. I began to fumble the screws, inserting them at an angle so that they wouldn't tighten properly and had to be taken out and inserted anew. Audrey was working as hard as I was by now; we stood shoulder to shoulder, me fouling things up, her fixing them.

29   And suddenly it was ten o'clock, and there was a half-hour break for lunch. Ten at night, that is. By now, I was squinting to stop from seeing double. I was convinced that if I could just work through to the end of the shift, I'd get this job down pat. But as the line came to a halt and everything stopped moving, some remote part of my brain managed to signal a weak but just decipherable message that the pressure was getting to me. It was time to call it quits before I damaged a car, or myself, or worse still, somebody else.

30   "Don't you want some lunch before you go?" said Audrey. But I was too exhausted to even look at food. I needed fresh air. And solitude. And silence. I made my excuses, stuffed my yellow Kevlar gloves into my pocket as a memento, got lost twice trying to find the way out, and finally emerged into the parking lot.

31   Never had a parking lot seemed so beautiful: so quiet, so peaceful, so serene. Even the buzzing yellow of the sodium vapor lights seemed soothing. Behind me, the plant hummed gently, its skylights glowing into the night.

Mid-shift, I was the only person out here, and I had a flash of guilt mixed with giddy freedom, the kind that comes from playing hooky.

32   I found the truck, climbed in, made to start it up. Then stopped, hand in midair, and sat staring at the instrument panel. Something was wrong. I took a moment to figure it out: I'd spent the past few hours working on upside-down instrument panels, and now I was seeing this one the right way up.

33   I reached out and examined it for its component parts, thinking of the man or the woman who'd put it together, and appreciating the way it had been done. This thing I usually took so for granted that I'd never before paid a moment's attention to it, was now an astounding piece of man-made—woman-made—complexity.

34   I started the truck and drove slowly out of the lot, wondering how long I'd keep this awareness that cars are not merely machines, but things put together by human beings, products of real men and real women doing the kind of work that would drive most people crazy. Not long enough, for sure.

Discussion Questions

1. Comment on the effectiveness of the essay's title.
2. Which of the five sensory impressions does Hazleton include? Refer to specific paragraphs when answering.
3. What is the dominant impression of this essay?
4. What time signals does Hazleton use? Refer to specific paragraphs when answering.
5. This description takes the form of a narrative with the action moving forward until a turning point is reached. Where does this turning point occur?
6. Identify the conclusion of the essay and what it accomplishes.
7. After reading Hazleton's description, how do you think you would tolerate working on an assembly line as a summer job? Discuss.

Toward Key Insights

What jobs have you done or heard about that you would consider unbearable? What characteristics make them unbearable?

What jobs have you done or heard about that you would find enjoyable? What characteristics make them enjoyable?

Suggestion for Writing

Write an essay describing your introduction to some new job. Use an appropriate number of sensory details that create a dominant impression and indicate your reaction to what you learned.

E. B. WHITE

Once More to the Lake

E. B. White (1899–1985) was born in Mount Vernon, New York, and was a graduate of Cornell University. In 1927, he joined the staff of The New Yorker, *launched just two years before, and for several decades produced a steady flow of short pieces for it. Between*

1937 and 1943, he also wrote a column, "One Man's Meat," for Harper's. *He is the author of three critically acclaimed children's books,* Stuart Little *(1945),* Charlotte's Web *(1952), and* The Trumpet of the Swan *(1970), as well as numerous adult works, including several collections of his essays and poems. In "Once More to the Lake," White creates a vivid and memorable word picture of a summer vacation that had great meaning for him and that brought him a sobering insight.*

1   One summer, along about 1904, my father rented a camp on a lake in Maine and took us all there for the month of August. We all got ringworm from some kittens and had to rub Pond's Extract on our arms and legs night and morning, and my father rolled over in a canoe with all his clothes on; but outside of that the vacation was a success and from then on none of us ever thought there was any place in the world like that lake in Maine. We returned summer after summer—always on August 1st for one month. I have since become a salt-water man, but sometimes in summer there are days when the restlessness of the tides and the fearful cold of the sea water and the incessant wind which blows across the afternoon and into the evening make me wish for the placidity of a lake in the woods. A few weeks ago this feeling got so strong I bought myself a couple of bass hooks and a spinner and returned to the lake where we used to go, for a week's fishing and to revisit old haunts.

2   I took along my son, who had never had any fresh water up his nose and who had seen lily pads only from train windows. On the journey over to the lake I began to wonder what it would be like. I wondered how time would have marred this unique, this holy spot—the coves and streams, the hills that the sun set behind, the camps and the paths behind the camps. I was sure the tarred road would have found it out and I wondered in what other ways it would be desolated. It is strange how much you can remember about places like that once you allow your mind to return into the grooves which lead back. You remember one thing, and that suddenly reminds you of another thing. I guess I remembered clearest of all the early mornings, when the lake was cool and motionless, remembered how the bedroom smelled of the lumber it was made of and the wet woods whose scent entered through the screen. The partitions in the camp were thin and did not extend clear to the top of the rooms, and as I was always the first up I would dress softly so as not to wake the others, and sneak out into the sweet outdoors and start out in the canoe, keeping close along the shore in the long shadows of the pines. I remembered being very careful never to rub my paddle against the gunwale for fear of disturbing the stillness of the cathedral.

3   The lake had never been what you would call a wild lake. There were cottages sprinkled around the shores, and it was in farming country although the shores of the lake were quite heavily wooded. Some of the cottages were owned by nearby farmers, and you would live at the shore and eat your meals at the farmhouse. That's what our family did. But although it wasn't wild, it was a fairly large and undisturbed lake and there were places in it which, to a child at least, seemed infinitely remote and primeval.

4   I was right about the tar: it led to within half a mile of the shore. But when I got back there, with my boy, and we settled into a camp near a farmhouse and into the kind of summertime I had known, I could tell that it was going to be pretty much the same as it had been before—I knew it, lying in bed the first morning, smelling the bedroom, and hearing the boy sneak quietly out and go off along the shore in a boat. I began to sustain the illusion that he was I, and therefore by simple transposition, that I was my father. This sensation persisted, kept cropping up

all the time we were there. It was not an entirely new feeling, but in this setting it grew much stronger. I seemed to be living a dual existence. I would be in the middle of some simple act, I would be picking up a bait box or laying down a table fork, or I would be saying something, and suddenly it would be not I but my father who was saying the words or making the gesture. It gave me a creepy sensation.

5   We went fishing the first morning. I felt the same damp moss covering the worms in the bait can, and saw the dragonfly alight on the tip of my rod as it hovered a few inches from the surface of the water. It was the arrival of this fly that convinced me beyond any doubt that everything was as it always had been, that the years were a mirage and there had been no years. The small waves were the same, chucking the rowboat under the chin as we fished at anchor, and the boat was the same boat, the same color green and the ribs broken in the same places, and under the floor-boards the same fresh-water leavings and debris—the dead hellgramite,[1] the wisps of moss, the rusty discarded fishhook, the dried blood from yesterday's catch. We stared silently at the tips of our rods, at the dragonflies that came and went. I lowered the tip of mine into the water, tentatively, pensively dislodging the fly, which darted two feet away, poised, darted two feet back, and came to rest again a little farther up the rod. There had been no years between the ducking of this dragonfly and the other one—the one that was part of memory. I looked at the boy, who was silently watching his fly, and it was my hands that held his rod, my eyes watching. I felt dizzy and didn't know which rod I was at the end of.

6   We caught two bass, hauling them in briskly as though they were mackerel, putting them over the side of the boat in a businesslike manner without any landing net, and stunning them with a blow on the back of the head. When we got back for a swim before lunch, the lake was exactly where we had left it, the same number of inches from the dock, and there was only the merest suggestion of a breeze. This seemed an utterly enchanted sea, this lake you could leave to its own devices for a few hours and come back to, and find that it had not stirred, this constant and trustworthy body of water. In the shallows, the dark, water-soaked sticks and twigs, smooth and old, were undulating in clusters on the bottom against the clean ribbed sand, and the track of the mussel was plain. A school of minnows swam by, each minnow with its small individual shadow, doubling the attendance, so clear and sharp in the sunlight. Some of the other campers were in swimming, along the shore, one of them with a cake of soap, and the water felt thin and clear and unsubstantial. Over the years there had been this person with the cake of soap, this cultist, and here he was. There had been no years.

7   Up to the farmhouse to dinner through the teeming, dusty field, the road under our sneakers was only a two-track road. The middle track was missing, the one with the marks of the hooves and the splotches of dried, flaky manure. There had always been three tracks to choose from in choosing which track to walk in; now the choice was narrowed down to two. For a moment I missed terribly the middle alternative. But the way led past the tennis court, and something about the way it lay there in the sun reassured me; the tape had loosened along the backline, the alleys were green with plantains and other weeds, and the net (installed in June and removed in September) sagged in the dry noon, and the whole place steamed with midday heat and hunger and emptiness. There was a choice of pie for dessert, and one was blueberry and one was apple, and the waitresses were the same country girls, there having been no passage of time, only the illusion of it as in a dropped curtain—the waitresses were still fifteen; their

---

[1]Insect used as bait.

hair had been washed, that was the only difference—they had been to the movies and seen the pretty girls with the clean hair.

8   Summertime, oh summertime, pattern of life indelible, the fade-proof lake, the woods unshatterable, the pasture with the sweetfern and the juniper forever and ever, summer without end; this was the background, and the life along the shore was the design, the cottages with their innocent and tranquil design, their tiny docks with the flagpole and the American flag floating against the white clouds in the blue sky, the little paths over the roots of the trees leading from camp to camp and the paths leading back to the outhouses and the can of lime for sprinkling, and at the souvenir counters at the store the miniature birch-bark canoes and the post cards that showed things looking a little better than they looked. This was the American family at play, escaping the city heat, wondering whether the newcomers in the camp at the head of the cove were "common" or "nice," wondering whether it was true that the people who drove up for Sunday dinner at the farmhouse were turned away because there wasn't enough chicken.

9   It seemed to me, as I kept remembering all this, that those times and those summers had been infinitely precious and worth saving. There had been jollity and peace and goodness. The arriving (at the beginning of August) had been so big a business in itself, at the railway station the farm wagon drawn up, the first smell of the pine-laden air, the first glimpse of the smiling farmer, and the great importance of the trunks and your father's enormous authority in such matters, and the feel of the wagon under you for the long ten-mile haul, and at the top of the last long hill catching the first view of the lake after eleven months of not see-ing this cherished body of water. The shouts and cries of the other campers when they saw you, and the trunks to be unpacked, to give up their rich burden. (Arriving was less exciting nowadays, when you sneaked up in your car and parked it under a tree near the camp and took out the bags and in five minutes it was all over, no fuss, no loud wonderful fuss about trunks.)

10   Peace and goodness and jollity. The only thing that was wrong now, really, was the sound of the place, an unfamiliar nervous sound of the outboard motors. This was the note that jarred, the one thing that would sometimes break the illu-sion and set the years moving. In those other summertimes all motors were in-board; and when they were at a little distance, the noise they made was a seda-tive, an ingredient of summer sleep. They were one-cylinder and two-cylinder engines, and some were make-and-break and some were jump-spark, but they all made a sleepy sound across the lake. The one-lungers throbbed and fluttered, and the twin-cylinder ones purred and purred, and that was a quiet sound too. But now the campers all had outboards. In the daytime, in the hot mornings, these motors made a petulant, irritable sound; at night, in the still evening when the afterglow lit the water, they whined about one's ears like mosquitoes. My boy loved our rented outboard, and his great desire was to achieve singlehanded mastery over it, and authority, and he soon learned the trick of choking it a little (but not too much), and the adjustment of the needle valve. Watching him I would remember the things you could do with the old one-cylinder engine with the heavy flywheel, how you could have it eating out of your hand if you got really close to it spiritually. Motor boats in those days didn't have clutches, and you would make a landing by shutting off the motor at the proper time and coasting in with a dead rudder. But there was a way of reversing them, if you learned the trick, by cutting the switch and putting it on again exactly on the final dying revolution of the flywheel, so that it would kick back against com-pression and begin reversing. Approaching a dock in a strong following breeze,

it was difficult to slow up sufficiently by the ordinary coasting method, and if a boy felt he had complete mastery over his motor, he was tempted to keep it running beyond its time and then reverse it a few feet from the dock. It took a cool nerve, because if you threw the switch a twentieth of a second too soon you would catch the flywheel when it still had speed enough to go up past center, and the boat would leap ahead, charging bull-fashion at the dock.

11   We had a good week at the camp. The bass were biting well and the sun shone endlessly, day after day. We would be tired at night and lie down in the accumulated heat of the little bedrooms after the long hot day and the breeze would stir almost imperceptibly outside and the smell of the swamp drift in through the rusty screens. Sleep would come easily and in the morning the red squirrel would be on the roof, tapping out his gay routine. I kept remembering everything, lying in bed in the mornings—the small steamboat that had a long rounded stern like the lip of a Ubangi, and how quietly she ran on the moonlight sails, when the older boys played their mandolins and the girls sang and we ate doughnuts dipped in sugar, and how sweet the music was on the water in the shining night, and what it had felt like to think about girls then. After breakfast we would go up to the store and the things were in the same place—the minnows in a bottle, the plugs and spinners disarranged and pawed over by the youngsters from the boys' camp, the fig newtons and the Beeman's gum. Outside, the road was tarred and cars stood in front of the store. Inside, all was just as it had always been, except there was more Coca-Cola and not so much Moxie and root beer and birch beer and sarsaparilla. We would walk out with a bottle of pop apiece and sometimes the pop would backfire up our noses and hurt. We explored the streams, quietly, where the turtles slid off the sunny logs and dug their way into the soft bottom; and we lay on the town wharf and fed worms to the tame bass. Everywhere we went I had trouble making out which was I, the one walking at my side, the one walking in my pants.

12   One afternoon while we were there at the lake a thunderstorm came up. It was like the revival of an old melodrama that I had seen long ago with childish awe. The second-act climax of the drama of the electrical disturbance over a lake in America had not changed in any important respect. This was the big scene, still the big scene. The whole thing was so familiar, the first feeling of oppression and heat and a general air around camp of not wanting to go very far away. In mid-afternoon (it was all the same) a curious darkening of the sky, and a lull in everything that had made life tick; and then the way the boats suddenly swung the other way at their moorings with the coming of a breeze out of the new quarter, and the premonitory rumble. Then the kettle drum, then the snare, then the bass drum and cymbals, then crackling light against the dark, and the gods grinning and licking their chops in the hills. Afterward the calm, the rain steadily rustling in the calm lake, the return of light and hope and spirits, and the campers running out in joy and relief to go swimming in the rain, their bright cries perpetuating the deathless joke about how they were getting simply drenched, and the children screaming with delight at the new sensation of bathing in the rain, and the joke about getting drenched linking the generations in a strong indestructible chain. And the comedian who waded in carrying an umbrella.

13   When the others went swimming my son said he was going in too. He pulled his dripping trunks from the line where they had hung all through the shower, and wrung them out. Languidly, and with no thought of going in, I watched him, his hard little body, skinny and bare, saw him wince slightly as he pulled up around his vitals the small, soggy, icy garment. As he buckled the swollen belt suddenly my groin felt the chill of death.

Discussion Questions

1. In paragraph 4 White says that while doing or saying things "suddenly it would be not I but my father who was saying the words or making the gesture." Explain what he means.
2. White supplies relatively little information about his son except to mention that his actions resemble White's own as a child. How do you account for this brief treatment?
3. What is the significance of the missing middle track of the road (paragraph 7) and the "nervous sound of the outboard motors" (paragraph 10)?
4. Throughout the essay White spices his descriptions with precise sensory impressions of sight, hearing, touch, taste, and smell. How do these sensory details enhance his writing?
5. On what audience would this essay likely have the largest impact?
6. White's final sentence provides an indirect statement of his main point. What is the point?

Toward Key Insights

In what ways is the lake part of E. B. White's sense of personal identity?
How and to what extent can places become part of our lives?
What kinds of circumstances or events are likely to become part of our identity?

Suggestion for Writing

Write an essay describing a place you have revisited after being absent for a number of years. Indicate what was similar and what was different and describe your reactions to the changes. Appeal to at least three of the five senses.

PROCESS ANALYSIS

Reading Strategies

1. Determine the reason you are reading the process essay. If it is to follow instructions you will need to read in one way; if it is to understand a process, you will need to proceed differently.
2. If you are going to follow the instructions, read over the process first to get an understanding of the whole. Look for specific warnings or feedback you should consider. Get an idea of what the end result should look like. Gather any equipment you will need. Then follow the process step by step, checking after each step to make certain the results you are obtaining match those described in the process.
3. If you hope to understand the process, read first quickly to get an overview of the process. As you read through more slowly, it can be very helpful to take notes outlining the major steps of the process.

Reading Critically

1. Check to see if the process could be completed differently or more effectively. Are there any cautions that are not included in the essay that might be reasonable to observe?

2. If the writer is explaining a process, is there evidence that his account is correct? Check to see that there is good reason to believe the given account. Research could show that there are competing accounts.

Reading As a Writer

1. Observe how the writer uses verbs to indicate actions.
2. Notice how the writer gets from step to step in the process. If there is a strategy you could use, make note of it.

Ian Dunbar

Fast Track to Perfection

Ian Dunbar is a veterinarian and behaviorist who has an international reputation for his "lure and reward" method of training animals. Born in England, he holds degrees from the Royal Veterinarian College of London University and in psychology from the University of California. He now heads the Center for Applied Animal Behavior at his California alma mater. Dunbar has written extensively about his speciality, coauthoring a series of volumes on different breeds of dog. In this selection, he shows readers how to apply his methods to training puppies.

1   Puppies mature at an astounding rate. Don't let yours fall behind on the developmental curve. Nearly everything a puppy needs to learn must be taught in 12 weeks—between the ages of 2 and 5 months. You can buy yourself time by knowing what and how to teach the puppy before you bring it home. Go to puppy classes, read behavior and training books, watch instructional videos and consult your veterinarian. Then raise your puppy perfectly by meeting these six training deadlines.

Deadline 1: Before You Bring Home a Puppy

2   Your puppy should be accustomed to a domestic environment before you bring it home—at around 8 weeks of age. Make sure it has been raised indoors and in close contact with people. It should be prepared for the clamor of every-day life—the noise of the vacuum cleaner, the hoopla surrounding sports programs on the television, children crying, adults arguing. Early exposure—before the pup's eyes and ears have fully opened—allows the puppy to gradually assimilate sights and sounds that otherwise might frighten.

3   The window for socializing begins to close by the time the pup turns 3 months of age, and its most impressionable learning period starts to fade by its fifth month.

Deadline 2: Puppy's First Day at Home

4   Misbehavior is the most common reason dogs end up in shelters. This is especially sad because owners can prevent most behavior problems. For instance, if you avoid leaving the pup unsupervised, it won't chew furniture and belongings or soil your house; while teeny accidents do little damage in themselves, they may set a precedent for habits in months to come.

5   When you cannot watch your pup, confine it to a crate or a puppy-proofed room, which should contain:

Marginal annotations:
- Introduction
- Warning
- Notes requirements, rewards of training a perfect dog
- Body: paragraphs 2–19
- First step and its actions
- Reason for action
- Second step and its actions
- Uses polite command, addressing reader as "you"

Ian Dunbar, "Fast Track to Perfection." *Dog Fancy* Magazine, April 1999, reprinted by permission of the author.

- a comfortable bed.
- a bowl of fresh water.
- a doggie toilet placed away from the bed and which simulates the outdoors. Lay down a sheet of linoleum and cover it with a disposable plastic sheet. Next lay newspaper or something absorbent. Top the three layers with dirt or sod to teach the pup to relieve itself on grass (or concrete slabs for city pups that relieve themselves curbside).

- Hollow chew toys with kibble inside to reward your puppy for chewing toys rather than furniture. During its first few weeks at home, a marvelous training ploy is to serve your puppy's food only in chew toys. After it's a chew toy-aholic—and has not had a chewing mishap for at least three months—begin to serve its dinner in a bowl.

6   At least every hour, release your puppy from its crate, quickly leash it and hurry it to its outdoor toilet area. Stand still and give the pup three minutes to produce. When it does, lavishly praise and offer *three* extra special treats. Freeze-dried liver treats work well because dogs love their strong smell.

7   If your puppy eliminates, it may be allowed supervised exploration of the house. If it does not eliminate, lead it back to its crate or puppy-proof room and try again in half an hour.

8   Keep up the once an hour schedule until your pup is at least 3 months old to make certain it never eliminates indoors. After 3 months of age pups start to develop the bladder control necessary for longer waits between potty breaks, but you must still be vigilant. One mistake can set a bad precedent.

9   Always reward your puppy for using its outdoors toilet area, but wait until it has completed its shots before taking it to public property; otherwise it can pick up other dogs' diseases. A pup must not walk or sniff where other dogs have been until it has developed sufficient immunity (between 3 and 4 months old).

Deadline 3: Puppy at 3 Months

10   By 3 months your pup must master socialization and basic manners. Pups that do not will have a hard time picking up these skills later in life. Unfortunately, the risk of disease means dog-to-dog socialization must wait. Meanwhile, teach your pup to be people-friendly.

11   As a general rule, your pup should socialize with at least 100 people before it is 3 months old. This is easier than it sounds. Invite eight friends over each Sunday to watch sports on the television. Each Monday invite eight different friends to watch *Ally McBeal* and *Dateline*. Catch up on outstanding social obligations by inviting family, friends and neighbors to weekly puppy parties. On another night, invite some neighborhood children. Socializing a puppy is great because it does wonders for *your* social life.

12   Show your guests how to hand feed the puppy's kibble to encourage and reward it for coming, sitting and lying down. Ask your puppy to come. Praise profusely as it approaches and offer a piece of kibble when it arrives. Back up, then do it again—and again and again. Then say "Puppy, Sit" and slowly move a piece of kibble from in front of the puppy's nose to between its eyes. As the puppy raises its nose to sniff, it will lower its rear and sit. If the puppy jumps up, you're holding the food too high. When your puppy sits, say "Good dog" and offer the kibble. Now say "Puppy, Down" and lower a piece of kibble from in front of the puppy's nose to between its forepaws. As the puppy lowers its head to follow the food, it will usually lie down. If your puppy stands, hide the kibble in your palm until it lies down. Then say "Good dog" and offer the food. Coach your

guests until each can get the puppy to come, sit and lie down three times for a piece of kibble.

13   When a puppy approaches promptly and happily, it is a sign the dog is people-friendly. Sitting and lying down on request indicates respect for the person issuing instructions. If your puppy is regularly hand-fed by guests, it will learn to enjoy people's company.

Deadline 4: Puppy at 4 1/2 Months

14   Seemingly overnight, puppies become adolescents. Enroll in a training class before yours is 14 weeks old—that is, before it starts to test your limits. A professional will teach it to stop nipping and other behavior no-no's, as well as temper its hyper-turbo energy.

15   Most puppies can start classes at 3 months. Classrooms are generally safe places; the puppies are vaccinated, the floors regularly sterilized. I advise delaying walks in public places until your puppy is 4 months old because of the risk of disease.

16   Puppy classes develop canine social savvy through play with other puppies in a controlled setting. Most classes are family-oriented, offering pups opportunities to socialize with all sorts of people—men, women and children. The number of behaviors your pup learns in its first training lesson will amaze you. Shy and fearful pups gain confidence. Bullies tone it down and become gentle. All dogs learn to come, sit and lie down when requested and listen to their owners and ignore distractions.

Deadline 5: Puppy at 5 Months

17   Take your dog everywhere—errands around town, car trips to visit friends, picnics in the park and especially to explore the neighborhood. And bring a little bag of kibble. Give a couple of pieces to each stranger who wants to meet your dog. Ask each person to offer the kibble only after your pup sits to say hello.

18   At this point, you may come to believe the canine weight-pulling record exceeds 10,000 pounds. Your dog also may begin to ignore you. A few tips:

- **Make your dog walk for its dinner.** With kibble in hand, stand still and wait for the dog to sit. Ignore everything else your dog does; it will sit eventually. When it does, say "Good dog," offer the kibble, take one giant step forward, stand still and wait for your dog to sit again. Repeat this until your dog sits each time you stop. Now take two giant steps before your stop. Then three steps, five, eight, 10, 20 and so on. *Voilà*, your dog walks calmly and attentively by your side and sits each time you stop.
- **Take a few time-outs on each walk.** Sit down, relax and allow the dog to settle down and watch the world go by. If your pup is not the sit-still type, take along a treat-stuffed chew toy as an incentive.
- **Never take your dog's sound temperament for granted.** Outdoors can be scary and offer the occasional surprise. Give your dog a piece of kibble every time a big truck, noisy motorcycle or child on a skateboard whizzes by and your dog doesn't overreact.
- **Don't make a habit of letting your dog off-leash to run and play with other dogs;** your dog may eventually refuse to come when called. Instead, take your dog's dinner to the park and, throughout its play session, call your dog every minute or so and have it sit for a couple of pieces of kibble. It will soon get the idea and its enthusiastic response will be the talk of the park.

Deadline 6: Now and Forever

19   Continue walking your dog at least once a day and take it to a dog park several times a week. Find different walks and dog parks to meet a variety of dogs and people. If your dog always sees the same people and dogs, it may regress socially and become intolerant of strangers.

20   Now enjoy life with your good-natured, well-mannered companion. Give your dog a special bone—Good dog!—and yourself a pat on the back—Good owner!

Discussion Questions

1. Point out why Dunbar's title is appropriate. Refer to the essay when answering.
2. In paragraph 18 Dunbar states that the owner might "believe the canine weight-pulling record exceeds 10,000 pounds." Explain what he means.

Toward Key Insights

Given the choice, what animal would you prefer to train? Why? What animal would you least like to train? Why?

Suggestion for Writing

Write an essay that provides directions for training a riding horse, hunting dog, or guard dog. Be sure to include the reason for any action whose purpose is not obvious and provide cautionary warnings whenever necessary.

CAROLINE GOLDMAN

Taking Carbon Down

from: Alternatives 32 no2 4 2006.

Caroline Goldman graduated with a B.A. in American Civilization and Race Relations from Brown University and earned Masters degrees in Public Administration and International Relations from Syracuse Administration. She worked for several years as a management consultant and freelance writer. She is currently the executive director for Hawkwatch International.

1   Imagine parachuting crustaceans, Millions and millions of them. This is what scientists from the British Antarctic Survey and the Centre for Coastal Studies of the University of Hull illustrated in their recent study about krill's effects on carbon sequestration.

2   Antarctic krill (Euphausia superba)—those small crustaceans that flood the Southern Ocean—have recently been recognized as a major source of carbon sinks. Scientists have known for years that krill migrate daily from the surface of the seas to the ocean's depths, but how deep they dove and how much carbon they carried with them was unknown until now.

Caroline Goldman, "Taking Carbon Down." *Alternatives Journal* 32 no2 4 2006.
Reprinted by permission of the author.

3   Each night, krill feed on phytoplankton, algae that absorb carbon through photosynthesis. As the krill dine on the phytoplankton, the carbon is passed on to them through the food chain. Bellies full, the krill fan out their legs and parachute nearly 50 metres down through the open ocean in a vertical migration, excreting waste along the way. "The waste sinks to the ocean bottom where it gets locked up in sediment," a process known as carbon sequestration, says Dr. Geraint Tarling of the British Antarctic Survey. These dives are likely an attempt to avoid the hunting whales, seals and penguins above.

4   With 50 to 150 million, tonnes of Antarctic krill making this migration approximately three times each night, 0.02 metric gigatons of carbon per year—"an amount equivalent to the annual emissions of 35 million cars" says Tarling—is transported from earth's surface to the ocean floor, an action that helps alleviate global climate change by decreasing the atmosphere's harmful overabundance of carbon.

5   For our carbon-filled air, that's good news. The bad news is that Antarctic krill populations have seen an 80 percent decline in the past 30 years, likely due to rising temperatures that lead to declining sea ice. Sea ice serves as a breeding ground for the krill's primary food source, phytoplankton, and thus in turn attracts swarms of krill, especially the larvae. As the earth's climate rises, sea ice melts away, destroying these krill nurseries—and thus much of the krill population. The warming trend also favours salps, filter-feeding gelatinous creatures that prefer warmer waters and compete with krill for phytoplankton. Salps are also known to dine on krill larvae as they rise through the water column to reach the sea ice. Most krill-dependent feeders such as whales and penguins do not eat salps, and salps do not serve the same carbon sequestration purposes that krill perform.

6   How this dramatic krill decline will affect the crustaceans' carbon sequestration abilities is as yet unknown. "Krill are not evenly spread around the Southern Ocean," says Tarling. "It is likely that krill decreases occur in some areas to a much greater extent than in others. We are just starting to calculate how the decrease in krill affects their carbon sink capacity."

Discussion Questions

1. What is the purpose of this process account of the krill?
2. What are the steps in the process by which krill remove carbon from the atmosphere?
3. How does the writer make a technically complex process more readable for non-scientific readers?
4. How does the writer use process to explain the decrease in the krill population?
5. The writer ends with an indefinite conclusion rather than a bold and stark claim. What effect does the concluding paragraph have on likely readers?

Toward Key Insights

Often it is difficult to translate complex scientific processes into accounts that are appropriate to nonexpert readers without leaving something out or oversimplifying. To what extent does this essay seem or not seem oversimplified or incomplete?

By stressing the importance of a process, it is then relatively easy to make the reader concerned about the disruption of that process. How does this writer use the positive role of krill to actually raise concerns about global warming?

Suggestions for Writing

With your teacher's permission, take a technical description of a process from a science textbook or science article and explain that process to less knowledgeable readers. Submit the original source with your essay.

Observe a natural process and write an account of that process to make an important point about the importance or destructiveness of that process. For example, a writer could observe erosion.

BETH WALD

Let's Get Vertical!

Beth Wald (born 1960) first felt the attraction of the mountains when, at age sixteen, she took a backpacking trip to Canada. A native of Minnesota, she studied botany and Russian at the University of Minnesota and then, in the mid-1980s, began a dual career as a freelance writer and photographer. Her career and her love of climbing have taken her around the world. Her articles have appeared in a variety of climbing and outdoor magazines, as have her photographs, which include environmental and cultural subjects as well as sports and travel. From 1988 to 1992, she was a contributing editor for Climbing Magazine. *In our selection, Wald acquaints potential recruits with the sport of rock climbing.*

1   Here I am, 400 feet up on the steep west face of Devil's Tower,[1] a tiny figure in a sea of petrified rock. I can't find enough footholds and handholds to keep climbing. My climbing partner anxiously looks up at me from his narrow ledge. I can see the silver sparkle of the climbing devices I've jammed into the crack every eight feet or so.

2   I study the last device I've placed, a half-inch aluminum wedge 12 feet below me. If I slip, it'll catch me, but only after a 24-foot fall, a real "screamer." It's too difficult to go back; I have to find a way up before my fingers get too tired. I must act quickly.

3   Finding a tiny opening in the crack, I jam two fingertips in, crimp them, pull hard, and kick my right foot onto a sloping knob, hoping it won't skid off. At the same time, I slap my right hand up to what looks like a good hold. To my horror, it's round and slippery.

4   My fingers start to slide. Panic rivets me for a second, but then a surge of adrenalin snaps me back into action. I scramble my feet higher, lunge with my left hand, and catch a wider crack. I manage to get a better grip just as my right hand pops off its slick hold. My feet find edges, and I regain my balance. Whipping a chock (wedge) off my harness, I slip it into the crack and clip my rope through a carabiner (oblong metal snaplink). After catching my breath, I start moving again, and the rest of the climb flows upward like a vertical dance.

5   **The Challenges and Rewards** I've tried many sports, but I haven't found any to match the excitement of rock climbing. It's a unique world, with its own language, communities, controversies, heroes, villains, and devoted followers. I've lived in vans, tepees, tents, and caves; worked three jobs to save money for expenses; driven 24 hours to spend a weekend at a good rock; and lived on beans

---

[1] A large, flat-topped rock formation, 876 feet high, in northeastern Wyoming.

Beth Wald, "Let's Get Vertical!" from *Listen: Journal of Better Living,* June 1989. Reprinted by permission.

and rice for months at a time—all of this to be able to climb. What is it about scrambling up rocks that inspires such a passion? The answer is, no other sport offers so many challenges and so many rewards.

6   The physical challenges are obvious. You need flexibility, balance, and strength. But climbing is also a psychological game of defeating your fear, and it demands creative thinking. It's a bit like improvising a gymnastic routine 200 feet in the air while playing a game of chess.

7   Climbers visit some of the most spectacular places on earth and see them from a unique perspective—the top! Because the sport is so intense, friendships between climbers tend to be strong and enduring.

8   **Anyone Can Climb** Kids playing in trees or on monkey bars know that climbing is a natural activity, but older people often have to relearn to trust their instincts. This isn't too hard, though. The ability to maintain self-control in difficult situations is the most important trait for a beginning climber to have. Panic is almost automatic when you run out of handholds 100 feet off the ground. The typical reaction is to freeze solid until you fall off. But with a little discipline, rational thinking, and/or distraction tactics such as babbling to yourself, humming, or even screaming, fear can change to elation as you climb out of a tough spot.

9   Contrary to popular belief, you don't have to be superhumanly strong to climb. Self-confidence, agility, a good sense of balance, and determination will get you farther up the rock than bulging biceps. Once you've learned the basics, climbing itself will gradually make you stronger, though many dedicated climbers speed up the process by training at home or in the gym.

10   Nonclimbers often ask, "How do the ropes get up there?" It's quite simple; the climbers bring them up as they climb. Most rock climbers today are "free climbers." In free climbing, the rope is used only for safety in case of a fall, *not* to help pull you up. (Climbing without a rope, called "free soloing," is a *very* dangerous activity practiced only by extremely experienced—and crazy—climbers.)

11   First, two climbers tie into opposite ends of a 150-foot-long nylon rope. Then one of them, the belayer, anchors himself or herself to a rock or tree. The other, the leader, starts to climb, occasionally stopping to jam a variety of aluminum wedges or other special gadgets, generically referred to as protection, into cracks in the rock. To each of these, he or she attaches a snaplink, called a carabiner, and clips the rope through. As the leader climbs, the belayer feeds out the rope, and it runs through the carabiners. If the leader falls, the belayer holds the rope, and the highest piece of protection catches the leader. The belayer uses special techniques and equipment to make it easy to stop falls.

12   When the leader reaches the end of a section of rock—called the pitch—and sets an anchor, he or she becomes the belayer. This person pulls up the slack of the rope as the other partner climbs and removes the protection. Once together again, they can either continue in the same manner or switch leaders. These worldwide techniques work on rock formations, cliffs, peaks, even buildings.

13   **Rocks, Rocks Everywhere** Some of the best climbing cliffs in the country are in the Shawangunk Mountains, only two hours from New York City. Seneca Rocks in West Virginia draws climbers from Washington, D.C., and Pittsburgh, Pennsylvania. Chattanooga, Tennessee, has a fine cliff within the city limits. Most states in the U.S. and provinces in Canada offer at least one or two good climbing opportunities.

14   Even if there are no large cliffs or rock formations nearby, you can climb smaller rocks to practice techniques and get stronger. This is called bouldering.

Many climbers who live in cities and towns have created climbing areas out of old stone walls and buildings. Ask someone at your local outdoor shop where you can go to start climbing.

15   **Get a Helping Hand** There's no substitute for an expert teacher when it comes to learning basic techniques and safety procedures. One of the best (and least expensive) ways to learn climbing is to convince a veteran climber in your area to teach you. You can usually meet these types at the local crag or climbing shop.

16   As another option, many universities and colleges, some high schools, and some YMCAs have climbing clubs. Their main purpose is to introduce people to climbing and to teach the basics. Other clubs, such as the Appalachian Mountain Club in the eastern U.S. and the Mountaineers on the West Coast, also provide instruction. Ask at your outdoor shop for the names of clubs in your area.

17   If you live in a place completely lacking rocks and climbers, you can attend one of the fine climbing schools at the major climbing area closest to you. Magazines like *Climbing, Rock & Ice,* and *Outside* publish lists of these schools. Once you learn the basics, you're ready to get vertical.

18   In rock climbing, you can both lose yourself and find yourself. Life and all its troubles are reduced to figuring out the puzzle of the next section of cliff or forgotten in the challenge and delight of moving through vertical space. And learning how to control anxiety, how to piece together a difficult sequence of moves, and how to communicate with a partner are all skills that prove incredibly useful back on the ground!

Discussion Questions

1. Discuss the effectiveness of Wald's title.
2. At the beginning of the essay, Wald notes that she is 400 feet up one side of Devil's Tower and positioned above her climbing partner. What do you think these statements accomplish?
3. In which paragraphs does Wald detail the actual process of climbing? What do the remaining paragraphs in the body of the essay accomplish?
4. Point out two places in the first four paragraphs where Wald cites reasons for her actions.
5. What attributes does Wald believe a rock climber must have? Refer to the essay when answering.
6. After reading this essay, are you ready to begin rock climbing? Does your answer stem from Wald's content, the manner of presentation, or both? Discuss.

Toward Key Insights

What challenging activities appeal to you?
What level of risk are you willing to accept in an activity?
How do you account for your attitude about taking risks?

Suggestion for Writing

Write a process paper in which you explain the attributes required and the steps involved in one of your recreational activities.

SHARI CAUDRON

Can Generation Xers Be Trained?

Shari Caudron earned a B.A. in journalism and a master's degree in human communication. She is currently pursuing an MFA in creative nonfiction. She has been a full-time freelance journalist since 1989. In this selection she presents the procedures that many businesses have found effective in training members of "Generation X."

1   If you want to know how to reach Generation Xers, eavesdrop on a training seminar conducted by Pencom International, a Denver-based company that provides training products to such restaurant chains as Denny's and Pizza Hut. You won't hear the trainers referring to restaurant patrons as "prospective customers." Instead, they're "hot targets." The trainers don't encourage new employees to "recognize and serve customers quickly." They're told to "lock on and fire." The language isn't what you'd typically find at a corporate training seminar. But, then, Generation Xers (a term they detest) aren't typical employees.

2   "These people grew up with Sonic the Hedgehog and Atari, so training has to be attention-grabbing," says Christopher O'Donnell, vice president of Pencom. "Or as Beavis would say, 'The training can't suck.'"

3   Suck indeed. Members of Generation X, those 40 million or so Americans age 20 to 33, are forcing companies to rethink and reengineer their training programs drastically. Gen Xers' values, communication styles, and life experiences are so different from those of baby boomers that traditional training doesn't stand a chance. To connect with these young employees, forget *Father Knows Best;* bring on MTV.

4   Now, before you grumble about catering to a fringe element, here's an incentive: Training geared to the needs of Generation Xers may actually be better for training all workers.

5   "This generation is spearheading change," says O'Donnell. "They're teaching us a lot about how to manage and train everyone in the workforce."

6   Granted, not all companies experience generational differences. At Dallas-based Texas Instruments, for example, employees are hired based on certain values and characteristics. That keeps TI's corporate culture harmonious and minimizes any discrepancies between workers of different generations.

7   "We don't see generational learning differences," says Ray Gumpert, manager of training and organizational effectiveness for TI's Semiconductor Group. "We recruit a certain kind of individual, so there is great consistency among TIers."

8   In *Twentysomething: Managing and Motivating Today's New Workforce* (Master Media, 1992), Claire Raines writes that companies such as Texas Instruments are the exception, not the rule. "(Though) all generations have things in common," she says, "research on Generation Xers shows that this group typically learns very differently from those that came before them."

Who Are These People Anyway?

9   To understand why and how Xers' learning styles are so different, you have to understand the characteristics that set them apart from older workers.

10   To begin with, they are the first generation to grow up with many of their parents both working. As "latchkey kids," many learned to become self-reliant. Consequently, they tend to be independent problem solvers, who are remarkably good at getting a job done on their own.

11   Many, if not most, grew up with computers at home, in school, and at arcades on weekends, so they are amazingly technoliterate. From the Internet to CD-ROMs, familiarity with new technology is just a mouse-click away.

12   In addition, Xers have been conditioned by the American culture to expect immediate gratification. Such things as automatic teller machines, pagers, and microwave ovens have taught them that they can have what they want, when they want it. In the workplace, that can mean that they expect answers and feedback now.

13   Xers came of age in an era that began with the Watergate scandal and ended with massive corporate layoffs, so they tend to distrust institutions. They don't have to be taught that there is no such thing as lifetime employment; they never expected it. Such distrust, combined with an inherent self-reliance, means that they're more likely to regard companies as places to grow, not places to grow old.

14   So, what do all of those characteristics mean for HRD professionals? Bruce Tulgan—founder of Rainmaker, a firm in New Haven, Connecticut, that helps companies recruit, motivate, and retain Generation X workers—reminds us that in the old days, the corporate approach to training was paternalistic.

15   "It used to be 'welcome to the family,'" says Tulgan. "Companies would tell employees, 'Here is your training agenda, this is the training we'll provide, and this is what you need to know.'" That approach just doesn't work with Xers. They want to know why they must learn something, before they will take the time to learn how.

16   Says Tulgan, "I'm not saying you must change the learning objectives; you must change the process." He recommends focusing on outcomes more than techniques and on what Xers are going to be able to do, not what they need to know.

17   For example, at the Orlando-based Olive Garden restaurants, training for servers had them memorize the menu and ingredients of the dishes. Now, training director Marty Fisher says that training emphasizes what servers are supposed to do with that information.

18   "We tell servers we want them to be tour guides for the menu," says Fisher. Through role play, servers can practice telling customers about each dish in appealing terms. That way, employees not only know why they are learning the ingredients, but they also know how to put the information to work.

19   At Chicago-based Anderson Consulting, trainers spend a lot of time upfront getting trainees' buy-in. According to Joe Kotey, a manager in the consulting education department, young employees have to see value in the training, or they aren't motivated to learn new skills. "Training results vary greatly, depending on how motivated a group is to learn new skills," says Kotey. "By focusing on outcomes, we show up-front why [employees] need this information."

Pushing the Right Buttons

20   Once you have the attention of Generation Xers, keep it by making training experiences meaningful, memorable, and fun. Xers are used to being entertained, having been weaned on portable CD players and Game Boy™. "We can't just pour knowledge into their heads," says Fisher. "We need to combine education with entertainment."

21   One way to keep their attention is to make training experiential. As much as possible, use all six senses, role play, and simulation learning—similar to the approaches used by NASA. Astronauts aren't expected to pilot a space shuttle without having practiced. Don't expect Xers to perform without practice.

22   For example, Andersen Consulting uses CD-ROMs during training to simulate client meetings. Using audio and video clips stored on disc, trainees can interview clients, receive phone calls, obtain advice from senior consultants, and review internal memos.

23   At the end of the computerized course, trainees have an opportunity to deliver a presentation with the findings and recommendations usually delivered to a client. "We want employees to see and feel what a client call is really like," says Roberta Menconi, training manager.

24   Classroom learning can also be made experiential. Pencom's O'Donnell remembers a training session he conducted for young employees of a Denver restaurant.

25   "I was trying to communicate the importance of seating [customers] right away, but getting nowhere. When I asked employees how long [customers] could wait comfortably before being seated, their responses ranged from three minutes to several more."

26   Frustrated, O'Donnell asked the group to time him for one minute. "I acted fidgety for a full 60 seconds while they watched. That minute went on forever and drove home the point that [customers] need to be seated immediately."

27   For a generation that grew up with more remote controls than rattles, the need to control learning is important. Xers need buttons to push. They are independent, and they're used to managing their own time. Because they're accustomed to calling the shots, they tend to resent and resist efforts to force-feed them training. To give Xers a sense of control over their learning, it's wise to provide as many options as possible where and when they can participate. That means a choice of locations and times.

28   "Because this generation is stubborn, we can't be," says O'Donnell.

29   It's even better to let Xers decide how they can learn. Tulgan tells the story of a Big Six accounting firm with a series of outstanding training courses. But they were so popular that no one could get into them.

30   Says Tulgan, "I suggested that the firm put course content on videotapes, audiotapes, and interactive CDs, and in self-paced manuals and workbooks. That puts the information into employees' hands right away and makes them accountable for learning. Generation Xers like that kind of structured self-study." Given Gen Xers' penchant for technology, computers are a natural choice for delivering training. But their ability to control has to be built into the technological solutions.

31   Menconi says that Andersen tested its first CD-ROM courses with younger employees to gauge their responses. "We discovered that they click around a lot. They want control over the paths they take. They want to stop and start at will."

32   To accommodate those needs, Andersen built sophisticated navigation systems into all of its CD-ROM–based courses.

33   Gen Xers' propensity to jump around—unlike older workers who tend to go step by step—doesn't necessarily signify a lack of attention. It's more an ability to assimilate information quickly and to focus on multiple ideas at once—called, "parallel thinking."

34   "Look at MTV or commercials," says Raines, "and you'll see four or five things going on at the same time. That drives me crazy, but these kids are used to it."

35   Companies can appeal to younger workers by developing training materials that provide multiple sources of information at once. *USA Today* and *Wired* are good examples of how to present information to Xers. Those publications combine charts, photos, text, graphics, and cartoons on a single page.

36   When making your materials more eye-catching, make sure you also keep the information simple. Don't make Gen Xers have to guess what you're trying

to say. Raines recommends highlighting key points to make the information highly scannable.

37 A note of caution: Don't go overboard and be too trendy. A few years back, the Wendy's restaurant chain created a training video, "Grill Skills," that featured a rap singer in gold lamé reviewing food-grilling techniques. The video won awards. But, after a year, it lost its effectiveness; employees saw it as outdated.

Prime Targets

38 Generation Xers—more than other employee groups—tend to make job decisions based on whether training is available. So, it may be more important that you provide them with training than how you provide it.

39 Says Tulgan, "Training departments are the ace in the hole for retaining and motivating today's workforce." That's because young employees don't envision long-term relationships with their employers, he says. They know that they must keep growing in order to stay marketable. If they don't receive training, they tend to start looking around at other jobs in other companies.

40 "In today's job market, you want to train employees to leave at any time," says Tulgan. "They won't, because they'll see working for your company as an incredible opportunity to grow and develop."

41 Terri Wolfe, director of HR at Patagonia—a Ventura, California–based clothing retailer—agrees that the biggest emerging trend among younger workers is their desire for continuous education. "We have an extensive continuing education program that a majority of our younger workers take advantage of. They're taking classes not only to advance their careers, but also because they are inherently curious."

What Generation Gap

42 What is perhaps most remarkable about training Generation Xers is that the training approaches that work well with them make sense for almost everyone, regardless of age. Here are some tips for training workers of all ages.

43 **Focus** Training should emphasize end results and place learners in control. Such training helps prepare employees for challenges on the job. After all, isn't the goal of empowerment for employees to focus on business objectives and make the necessary and appropriate decisions to achieve them? Fewer managers means that all employees have to take more responsibility for their work; learner directed training is a great way to get them used to that.

44 **Be flexible** Large-scale corporate cutbacks mean that more people are overworked and are juggling multiple demands. A flexible training schedule and choice of training resources (such as CD-ROMS, videos, and so forth) help employees fit training into their work schedules.

45 **Emphasize visuals** Create eye-catching, highly scannable training materials. Most people don't have time to read through pages of materials. Like it or not, most of us have been conditioned by the media to expect a point to be made quickly.

46 **Provide continuous education** Though younger workers have never counted on cradle-to-grave employment, older employees are also getting the message that they must prepare for unexpected events. The companies that provide continuous education are in a better position to retain productive employees.

47 "If you want to see the future of work, look into the eyes of a Generation Xer," says Tulgan. "We were shaped by the same forces that have shaped the (current) workplace and economy. We're comfortable with the new workplace because we never got accustomed to the old management style."

48 But whatever you do, don't call them "Generation Xers."

Discussion Questions

1. This process essay starts by defining Generation Xers and identifying their place in the workplace. Why is this important to the purposes of the essay?
2. Instead of offering simple concrete steps in a process, how does this essay present the process of training Generation Xers? Why is this approach most likely used?
3. Identify the key elements of the process recommended by the author. Discuss whether this approach would or would not be appealing to you.
4. What is the purpose of the writer using many different businesses as examples?
5. In the end, the author identifies some specific key principles for training Generation Xers. What are the advantages of this approach?

Toward Key Insights

To what extent are different training methods appropriate to different populations? Explore what kind of job training has been most effective for you. What were the features of that training?

Suggestion for Writing

Write a paper explaining to new employees the process of the job training they might receive at one of the places you have worked.

Select some activity you're familiar with—perhaps planning a party, programming a computer, or dieting successfully—and describe the steps involved, using appropriate comparisons and figurative language.

ILLUSTRATION

Reading Strategies

1. Read the introductory and concluding paragraphs quickly to determine the thesis for the illustration. Then read the essay quickly to get the main point of the essay. Jot down the key points of the illustration.
2. Determine, based on your own purpose for reading and the level of the essay, if it is necessary to read the essay more carefully.
3. If a more careful reading is warranted, read slowly, noticing and jotting down any key details of the illustration that make a more general point.

Reading Critically

1. Test whether the illustration really demonstrates the main point.
2. Determine whether the illustrations are typical or atypical.
3. Test the point by seeing if there are illustrations that would illuminate a different position.

Reading As a Writer

1. Identify and evaluate the kinds of examples used in the illustration.
2. Notice the strategies used to link the illustrations to a main point.
3. Identify and evaluate how the illustrations were organized (as short narratives, as descriptions) and jot down any strategies you found useful.

SABRINA RUBIN ERDELY

Binge Drinking, A Campus Killer

Sabrina Rubin Erdely is an award-winning investigative journalist based in Philadelphia. She is a Senior Writer at Philadelphia *magazine, where she has been on staff since 1995, and has contributed to a wide array of other magazines. Erdely's feature writing has earned her a number of awards, including a prestigious National Magazine Award nomination. Our selection focuses on a serious and growing problem at American colleges and universities.*

Introduction: identifies serious problem, point to be illustrated

Body: paragraphs 2–39

End of paragraph 2, paragraphs 3 and 5: first examples support main point, as do all examples

Brief examples feature different students, as do all examples, providing more evidence supporting paper's point

1 Pregame tailgating parties, post-exam celebrations and Friday happy hours—not to mention fraternity and sorority mixers—have long been a cornerstone of the collegiate experience. But on campuses across America, these indulgences have a more alarming side. For some of today's college students, binge drinking has become the norm.

2 This past February I headed to the University of Wisconsin–Madison, rated the No. 2 party school in the nation by the college guide *Princeton Review,* to see the party scene for myself. On Thursday night the weekend was already getting started. At a raucous off-campus gathering, 20-year-old Tracey Middler struggled to down her beer as fist-pumping onlookers yelled, "Chug! Chug! Chug!"

3 In the kitchen, sophomore Jeremy Budda drained his tenth beer. "I get real wasted on weekends," he explained. Nearby, a 19-year-old estimated, "I'll end up having 17, 18 beers."

4 Swept up in the revelry, these partyers aren't thinking about the alcohol-related tragedies that have been in the news. All they're thinking about now is the next party. The keg is just about empty.

5 As the 19-year-old announces loudly, these college students have just one objective: "to get drunk!"

6 The challenge to drink to the very limits of one's endurance has become a celebrated staple of college life. In one of the most extensive reports on college drinking thus far, a 1997 Harvard School of Public Health study found that 43 percent of college students admitted binge drinking in the preceding two weeks. (Defined as four drinks in a sitting for a woman and five for a man, a drinking binge is when one drinks enough to risk health and well-being.)

7 "That's about five million students," says Henry Wechsler, who co-authored the study. "And it's certainly a cause for concern. Most of these students don't realize they're engaging in risky behavior." University of Kansas Chancellor Robert Hemenway adds, "Every year we see students harmed because of their involvement with alcohol."

8 Indeed, when binge drinking came to the forefront last year with a rash of alcohol-related college deaths, the nation was stunned by the loss. There was Scott Krueger, the 18-year-old fraternity pledge at the Massachusetts Institute of Technology, who died of alcohol poisoning after downing the equivalent of

15 shots in an hour. There was Leslie Baltz, a University of Virginia senior, who died after she drank too much and fell down a flight of stairs. Lorraine Hanna, a freshman at Indiana University of Pennsylvania, was left alone to sleep off her night of New Year's Eve partying. Later that day her twin sister found her dead—with a blood-alcohol content (BAC) of 0.429 percent. (Driving with a BAC of 0.1 percent and above is illegal in all states.)

9   Experts estimate that excessive drinking is involved in thousands of student deaths a year. And the Harvard researchers found that there has been a dramatic change in why students drink: 39 percent drank "to get drunk" in 1993, but 52 percent had the same objective in 1997.

10   "What has changed is the across-the-board *acceptability* of intoxication," says Felix Savino, a psychologist at UW–Madison. "Many college students today see not just drinking but being *drunk* as their primary way of socializing."

11   The reasons for the shift are complex and not fully understood. But researchers surmise that it may have something to do with today's instant-gratification life-style—and young people tend to take it to the extreme.

12   In total, it is estimated that America's 12 million undergraduates drink the equivalent of six million gallons of beer a week. When that's combined with teenagers' need to drink secretly, it's no wonder many have a dangerous relationship with alcohol.

13   The biggest predictor of bingeing is fraternity or sorority membership. Sixty-five percent of members qualified as binge-drinkers, according to the Harvard study.

14   August 25, 1997, was meant to be a night the new Sigma Alpha Epsilon pledges at Louisiana State University in Baton Rouge would never forget, and by 8 P.M. it was certainly shaping up that way. The revelry had begun earlier with a keg party. Then they went to a bar near campus, where pledges consumed massive quantities of alcohol.

Extended example: paragraphs 14–21

15   Among the pledges were Donald Hunt, Jr., a 21-year-old freshman and Army veteran, and his roommate, Benjamin Wynne, a 20-year-old sophomore. Friends since high school, the two gamely drank the alcoholic concoctions offered to them and everyone else.

16   Before long, many in the group began vomiting into trash cans. (Donald Hunt would later allege in a lawsuit that these "vomiting stations" were set up for that very purpose, something the defendants adamantly deny.) About 9:30, incapacitated pledges were taken back to sleep it off at the frat house.

17   The 911 call came around midnight. Paramedics were stunned at what they found: more than a dozen young men sprawled on the floor, on chairs, on couches, reeking of alcohol. The paramedics burst into action, shaking the pledges and shouting, "Hey! Can you hear me?" Four couldn't be roused, and of those, one had no vital signs: Benjamin Wynne was in cardiac arrest.

18   Checking to see that nothing was blocking Wynne's airway, the paramedics began CPR. Within minutes they'd inserted an oxygen tube into his lungs, hooked up an I.V., attached a cardiac monitor and begun shocking him with defibrillation paddles, trying to restart his heart.

19   Still not responding, Wynne was rushed by ambulance to Baton Rouge General Hospital. Lab work revealed that his blood-alcohol content was an astonishing 0.588 percent, nearly six times the legal driving limit for adults—the equivalent of taking about 21 shots in an hour.

20   Meanwhile, three other fraternity pledges were undergoing similar revival efforts. One was Donald Hunt. He would suffer severe alcohol poisoning and nearly die.

21   After working furiously on Wynne, the hospital team admitted defeat. He was pronounced dead of acute alcohol poisoning.

22   One simple fact people tend to lose sight of is that alcohol is a poison—often pleasurable, but a toxin nonetheless. And for a person with little experience processing this toxin, it can come as something of a physical shock.

23   In general, a bottle of beer has about the same alcohol content as a glass of wine or shot of liquor. And the body can remove only the equivalent of less than one drink hourly from the bloodstream.

24   Many students are not just experimenting once or twice. In the Harvard study, half of binge drinkers were "frequent binge drinkers," meaning they had binged three or more times in the previous two weeks.

25   It also is assumed by some that bingeing is a "guy thing," an activity that, like cigar smoking and watching televised sports, belongs in the realm of male bonding. Statistics, however, show that the number of heavy-drinking young women is significant. Henry Wechsler's Harvard study found that a hefty 48 percent of college men were binge drinkers, and women were right behind them at 39 percent.

Extended example: paragraphs 26–32

26   Howard Somers had always been afraid of heights. Perhaps his fear was some sort of an omen. On an August day in 1997 he helped his 18-year-old daughter, Mindy, move into her dorm at Virginia Tech. As they unloaded her things in the eighth-floor room, Somers noted with unease the position of the window. It opened inward like an oven door, its lip about level with her bed. He mentioned it, but Mindy dismissed his concern with a smile.

27   "I have gone through more guilt than you can imagine," Somers says now quietly. "Things I wish I had said or done. But I never thought this would happen. Who would?"

28   Mindy Somers knew the dangers of alcohol and tried to stay aware of her limits. She'd planned not to overdo it that Friday night, since her mother was coming in that weekend to celebrate Mindy's 19th birthday on Sunday. But it was Halloween, the campus was alive with activity, and Mindy decided to stop in at several off-campus parties.

29   When she returned to her room at 3 A.M., she was wiped out enough to fall into bed fully clothed. Mindy's bed was pushed lengthwise against the long, low window. Her roommate and two other girls, who were on the floor, all slept too soundly to notice that sometime after 4 A.M. Mindy's bed was empty.

30   When the paperboy found her facedown on the grass at 6:45 A.M., he at first thought it was a Halloween prank. Police and EMTs swarmed to the scene in minutes. Somers was pronounced dead of massive chest and abdominal injuries. She had a blood-alcohol content of 0.21 percent, equal to her having drunk about five beers in one hour.

31   Police surmised that Mindy had tried to get out of bed during the night but, disoriented, had slipped out the window, falling 75 feet to her death. "It was a strange, tragic accident," Virginia Tech Police Chief Michael Jones says.

32   A terrible irony was that the week prior to Mindy's death had been Virginia Tech's annual Alcohol Awareness Week.

33   While binge drinking isn't always lethal, it does have other, wide-ranging effects. Academics is one realm where it takes a heavy toll.

34   During my trip to Wisconsin most students told me they didn't plan on attending classes the following day. "Nah, I almost never go to class on Friday. It's no big deal," answered Greg, a sophomore. According to a survey of university administrators, 38 percent of academic problems are alcohol-related, as are 29 percent of dropouts.

35   Perhaps because alcohol increases aggression and impairs judgment, it is also related to 25 percent of violent crimes and roughly 60 percent of vandalism on campus. According to one survey, 79 percent of students who had experienced unwanted sexual intercourse in the previous year said that they were under the influence of alcohol or other drugs at the time. "Some people believe that alcohol can provide an excuse for inappropriate behavior, including sexual aggression," says Jeanette Norris, a University of Washington researcher. Later on, those people can claim, "It wasn't me—it was the booze."

36   Faced with the many potential dangers, college campuses are scrambling for ways to reduce binge drinking. Many offer seminars on alcohol during freshman orientation. Over 50 schools provide alcohol-free living environments. At the University of Michigan's main campus in Ann Arbor, for instance, nearly 30 percent of undergrads living in university housing now choose to live in alcohol-free rooms. Nationwide several fraternities have announced that by the year 2000 their chapter houses will be alcohol-free.

37   After the University of Rhode Island topped the *Princeton Review* party list two years in a row, administrators banned alcohol at all student events on campus; this year URI didn't even crack the top ten. Some campuses respond even more severely, unleashing campus raids and encouraging police busts.

38   Researchers debate, however, if such "zero-tolerance" policies are helpful or if they might actually result in more secret, off-campus drinking. Other academics wonder if dropping the drinking age to 18 would take away the illicit thrill of alcohol and lower the number of kids drinking wildly. Others feel this would just create more drinking-related fatalities.

39   Whatever it takes, changing student behavior won't be easy. "What you've got here are people who think they are having fun," Harvard's Henry Wechsler explains. "You can't change their behavior by preaching at them or by telling them they'll get hurt."

40   Around 2 A.M. at UW–Madison a hundred kids congregate at a downtown intersection in a nightly ritual. One girl is trying to pull her roommate up off the ground. "I'm not that drunk," the one on the ground insists. "I just can't stand up."

Conclusion: paragraphs 40–41; returns to opening example

41   Two fights break out. A police car cruises by and the crowd thins, some heading to after-hours parties. Then maybe at 3 or 4 A.M. they'll go home to get some sleep, so they will be rested for when they start to drink again. Tomorrow night.

Discussion Questions

1. Discuss the effectiveness of Rubin Erdely's title.
2. What does Rubin Erdely accomplish in paragraphs 6–7 and in paragraphs 9–13, 22–25, and 33–38?
3. How do you account for the slang expressions found in this essay: "Chug! Chug! Chug!" in paragraph 2 and "wasted" in paragraph 3?
4. Comment on the effectiveness of the two-word sentence fragment that ends the essay.

Toward Key Insights

Why would "many college students today see not just drinking but being *drunk* as their primary way of socializing"?

What can be done to counter this mind-set?

Suggestion for Writing

Write an essay illustrating some type of benefit available on campus—perhaps academic counseling, the campus ministry, or some ethnic or racial organization. Develop your essay with several short examples or one extended one.

MARTIN GOTTFRIED

Rambos of the Road

Martin Gottfried is a native of New York City and a writer on theatrical matters. Born in 1933, he earned an A.B. degree at Columbia University and then, after attending law school, served two years in the military intelligence branch of the U.S. Army. Following his discharge in 1959, he spent four years as a music and movie critic and since 1963 has worked as a drama critic. He has authored several books on the theater as well as magazine articles on a variety of topics. In our selection, Gottfried examines the driving behavior of all too many motorists.

1 The car pulled up and its driver glared at us with such sullen intensity, such hatred, that I was truly afraid for our lives. Except for the Mohawk haircut he didn't have, he looked like Robert De Niro in "Taxi Driver," the sort of young man who, delirious for notoriety, might kill a president.

2 He was glaring because we had passed him and for that affront he pursued us to the next stoplight so as to express his indignation and affirm his masculinity. I was with two women and, believe it, was afraid for all three of us. It was nearly midnight and we were in a small, sleeping town with no other cars on the road.

3 When the light turned green, I raced ahead, knowing it was foolish and that I was not in a movie. He didn't merely follow, he chased, and with his headlights turned off. No matter what sudden turn I took, he followed. My passengers were silent. I knew they were alarmed, and I prayed that I wouldn't be called upon to protect them. In that cheerful frame of mind, I turned off my own lights so I couldn't be followed. It was lunacy. I was responding to a crazy *as* a crazy.

4 "I'll just drive to the police station," I finally said, and as if those were the magic words, he disappeared.

5 **Elbowing Fenders:** It seems to me that there has recently been an epidemic of auto macho—a competition perceived and expressed in driving. People fight it out over parking spaces. They bully into line at the gas pump. A toll booth becomes a signal for elbowing fenders. And beetle-eyed drivers hunch over their steering wheels, squeezing the rims, glowering, preparing the excuse of not having seen you as they muscle you off the road. Approaching a highway on an entrance ramp recently, I was strong-armed by a trailer truck so immense that its driver all but blew me away by blasting his horn. The behemoth was just inches from my hopelessly mismatched coupe when I fled for the safety of the shoulder.

6 And this is happening on city streets, too. A New York taxi driver told me that "intimidation is the name of the game. Drive as if you're deaf and blind. You don't hear the other guy's horn and you sure as hell don't see him."

7 The odd thing is that long before I was even able to drive, it seemed to me that people were at their finest and most civilized when in their cars. They

seemed so orderly and considerate, so reasonable, staying in the right-hand lane unless passing, signaling all intentions. In those days you really eased into highway traffic, and the long, neat rows of cars seemed mobile testimony to the sanity of most people. Perhaps memory fails, perhaps there were always testy drivers, perhaps—but everyone didn't give you the finger.

8   A most amazing example of driver rage occurred recently at the Manhattan end of the Lincoln Tunnel. We were four cars abreast, stopped at a traffic light. And there was no moving even when the light had changed. A bus had stopped in the cross traffic, blocking our paths: it was normal-for-New-York-City gridlock. Perhaps impatient, perhaps late for important appointments, three of us nonetheless accepted what, after all, we could not alter. One, however, would not. He would not be helpless. He would go where he was going even if he couldn't get there. A Wall Street type in suit and tie, he got out of his car and strode toward the bus, rapping smartly on its doors. When they opened, he exchanged words with the driver. The doors folded shut. He then stepped in front of the bus, took hold of one of its large windshield wipers and broke it.

9   The bus doors reopened and the driver appeared, apparently giving the fellow a good piece of his mind. If so, the lecture was wasted, for the man started his car and proceeded to drive directly *into the bus*. He rammed it. Even though the point at which he struck the bus, the folding doors, was its most vulnerable point, ramming the side of a bus with your car has to rank very high on a futility index. My first thought was that it had to be a rental car.

10   **Lane Merger:** To tell the truth, I could not believe my eyes. The bus driver opened his doors as much as they could be opened and he stepped directly onto the hood of the attacking car, jumping up and down with both his feet. He then retreated into the bus, closing the doors behind him. Obviously a man of action, the car driver backed up and rammed the bus again. How this exercise in absurdity would have been resolved none of us will ever know for at that point the traffic unclogged and the bus moved on. And the rest of us, we passives of the world, proceeded, our cars crossing a field of battle as if nothing untoward had happened.

11   It is tempting to blame such belligerent, uncivil and even neurotic behavior on the nuts of the world, but in our cars we all become a little crazy. How many of us speed up when a driver signals his intention of pulling in front of us? Are we resentful and anxious to pass him? How many of us try to squeeze in, or race along the shoulder at a lane merger? We may not jump on hoods, but driving the gantlet, we seethe, cursing not so silently in the safety of our steel bodies on wheels—fortresses for cowards.

12   What is it within us that gives birth to such antisocial behavior and why, all of a sudden, have so many drivers gone around the bend? My friend Joel Katz, a Manhattan psychiatrist, calls it, "a Rambo pattern. People are running around thinking the American way is to take the law into your own hands when anyone does anything wrong. And what constitutes 'wrong'? Anything that cramps your style."

13   It seems to me that it is a new America we see on the road now. It has the mentality of a hoodlum and the backbone of a coward. The car is its weapon and hiding place, and it is still a symbol even in this. Road Rambos no longer bespeak a self-reliant, civil people tooling around in family cruisers. In fact, there aren't families in these machines that charge headlong with their brights on in broad daylight, demanding we get out of their way. Bullies are loners, and they have perverted our liberty of the open road into drivers' license. They represent an America that derides the values of decency and good manners, then roam the highways riding shotgun and shrieking freedom. By allowing this to happen, the rest of us approve.

Discussion Questions

1. Identify the thesis statement of this essay.
2. What paragraphs make up the introduction? Besides starting the essay, what function do they perform?
3. Why are several examples a better choice for this essay than one extended example?
4. In what order does Gottfried arrange his examples?
5. What does Gottfried accomplish in paragraphs 11–12?
6. What function, other than ending the essay, is served by the final paragraph?

Toward Key Insights

Do you agree with Gottfried's claim that the "new America we see on the road now . . . has the mentality of a hoodlum and the backbone of a coward"? Why or why not?

Where else have you encountered macho behavior? At athletic events? At activities that generate long lines? At political demonstrations?

What conclusions can you draw about those who engage in such behavior?

Suggestion for Writing

Write an illustration essay exploring the behavior, good or bad, that you have experienced on campus, in the workplace, or while engaged in some activity such as shopping. Use several examples, arrange them in an appropriate order, and try to account for the behavior.

MATEA GOLD AND DAVID FERRELL

Going for Broke

Matea Gold, a native of Northampton, Massachusetts, earned a BA degree from UCLA and then joined David Ferrell as a staff writer for the Los Angeles Times. *Gold earned Sacramento Press Club awards in 1994 and 1995, while Ferrell was a 1996 finalist for the Investigative Reporters and Editors Award, which recognizes outstanding investigative work. The information in this article is drawn from a seven-month nationwide investigation of legalized gambling. Its case studies offer a sobering view of the consequences of gambling addiction.*

1   Rex Coile's life is a narrow box, so dark and confining he wonders how he got trapped inside, whether he'll ever get out.

2   He never goes to the movies, never sees concerts, never lies on a sunny beach, never travels on vacation, never spends Christmas with his family. Instead, Rex shares floor space in cheap motels with other compulsive gamblers, comforting himself with delusional dreams of jackpots that will magically wipe away three decades of wreckage. He has lost his marriage, his home, his Cadillac, his clothes, his diamond ring. Not least of all, in the card clubs of Southern California, he has lost his pride.

3   Rex no longer feels sorry for himself, not after a 29-year losing streak that has left him scrounging for table scraps to feed his habit. Still, he agonizes over what he has become at 54 and what he might have been.

4   Articulate, intellectual, he talks about existential philosophy, the writings of Camus and Sartre. He was once an editor at Random House. His mind is so jam-packed with tidbits about movies, television, baseball and history that card room regulars call him "Rex Trivia," a name he cherishes for the remnant of self-respect it gives him. "There's a lot of Rexes around these card rooms," he says in a whisper of resignation and sadness.

5   And their numbers are soaring as gambling explodes across America, from the mega-resorts of Las Vegas to the gaming parlors of Indian reservations, from the riverboats along the Mississippi to the corner mini-marts selling lottery tickets. With nearly every state in the union now sanctioning some form of legalized gambling to raise revenues, evidence is mounting that society is paying a steep price, one that some researchers say must be confronted, if not reversed.

6   Never before have bettors blown so much money—a whopping $50.9 billion last year—five times the amount lost in 1980. That's more than the public spent on movies, theme parks, recorded music and sporting events combined. A substantial share of those gambling losses—an estimated 30% to 40%—pours from the pockets and purses of chronic losers hooked on the adrenaline rush of risking their money, intoxicated by the fast action of gambling's incandescent world.

7   Studies place the total number of compulsive gamblers at about 4.4 million, about equal to the nation's ranks of hard-core drug addicts. Another 11 million, known as problem gamblers, teeter on the verge. Since 1990, the number of Gamblers Anonymous groups nationwide has doubled from about 600 to more than 1,200.

8   Compulsive gambling has been linked to child abuse, domestic violence, embezzlement, bogus insurance claims, bankruptcies, welfare fraud and a host of other social and criminal ills. The advent of Internet gambling could lure new legions into wagering beyond their means.

9   Every once in a while, a case is so egregious it makes headlines: A 10-day-old baby girl in South Carolina dies after being left for nearly seven hours in a hot car while her mother plays video poker. A suburban Chicago woman is so desperate for a bankroll to gamble that she allegedly suffocates her 7-week-old daughter 11 days after obtaining a $200,000 life-insurance policy on the baby.

10   But these tragedies that flash before the public eye are just lightning strokes of a roiling night storm. Far more often, compulsive gambling bends lives more subtly, less sensationally, over the course of years.

11   Gwen, one of the unseen masses trying to keep her head above water, sits on an easy chair in the living room of her worn Jefferson Park bungalow, watching the movie "Titanic" on an old TV. Her hair is uncombed and there are bags under her eyes. She puffs on a cigarette and shakes her foot nervously. On the screen, the great ship begins to founder.

12   "That's me," she says, tears rolling down her checks. "I'm sinking."

13   Gwen has just come off a three-day bender at the Hollywood Park Casino in Inglewood. She blew a paycheck, emptied out her new checking account, gambled right through her work shift. Driving home from the casino, she contemplated veering off the road, ending it all. "I just don't want to be here," she mumbles, watching Titanic's Rose and Jack struggling to hold on to a piece of driftwood in the freezing sea. "I just feel like I'm living a hopeless life. So hopeless."

14   She's written bad checks and maxed out her credit cards. One bank closed her checking account after she put too many fake deposit slips in the ATM to withdraw cash. She lies. She tells her boss she needs a salary advance because her son is in the hospital. Late on the rent, she parks a block from the house to duck the landlord. For the last eight years, this has been her life, one so empty of joy and options that the card clubs have become her only hope of filling the hole.

15   She thinks back to that night a few years ago when, desperate to recoup her gambling losses, she pilfered several thousand dollars from the safe of a restaurant where she was working. She just needed something to get herself started, she told herself. She'd pay it back with the winnings. She blew it all in one weekend.

16   Overwhelmed by guilt, she came clean with her manager. She was booked, fingerprinted and briefly thrown behind bars. "It was the worst experience of my life," she says.

17   Gwen now makes monthly $75 restitution payments to the restaurant as part of her court-ordered probation.

18   "I have hurt so many people with my gambling," says Gwen. "I have lost best friends. After all the pain I've caused everybody, the pain I caused myself, I still have the urge to gamble. I never know what I'm going to do. I'm so afraid. I'm really afraid."

19   Science has begun to uncover clues to compulsive gambling—genetic predispositions that involve chemical receptors in the brain, the same pleasure pathways implicated in drug and alcohol addiction. But no amount of knowledge, no amount of enlightenment, makes the illness any less confounding, any less destructive. What the gamblers cannot understand about themselves is also well beyond the comprehension of family members, who struggle for normality in a world of deceit and madness.

20   Money starts vanishing: $500 here, $200 there, $800 a couple of weeks later. Where is it? The answers come back vague, nonsensical. It's in the desk at work. A friend borrowed it. It got spent on family dinners, car repairs, loans to in-laws. Exasperated spouses play the sleuth, combing through pockets, wallets, purses, searching the car. Sometimes the incriminating evidence turns up—a racing form, lottery scratchers, a map to an Indian casino. Once the secret is uncovered, spouses usually fight the problem alone, bleeding inside, because the stories are too humiliating to share.

21   "Anybody who is living with a compulsive gambler is totally overwhelmed," says Tom Tucker, president of the California Council on Problem Gambling. "They're steeped in anger, resentment, depression, confusion. None of their personal efforts will ever stop a person from their [sic] addiction. And they don't really see any hope because compulsive gambling in general is such an under-recognized illness."

22   One Los Angeles woman, whose husband's gambling was tearing at her sanity, says she slept with her fists so tightly clenched that her nails sliced into her palms. She had fantasies of death—first her own, thinking he'd feel sorry for her and stop gambling. Later, she harbored thoughts of turning her rage on her husband. She imagined getting a gun, hiding in the closet and blasting him out of her life.

23   "The hurt was so bad I think I would have pulled the trigger," she says. "There were times the pain was so much I thought being in jail, or being in the electric chair, would be less than this."

24   Five years in Gam-Anon, the 12-step support group for family and friends of compulsive gamblers, has only begun to heal her. "I don't think I'm even halfway there," she says.

25   Too often, families of gambling addicts endure more than warped finances and wrecked psyches. They have come to fear for their physical safety.

26   Trena, a 42-year-old Whittier homemaker, is among them. Several months ago, after years of agony, she filed for divorce. Her husband, a manager in an industrial plant, was making decent money and took pride in his job. He had two good children and a nice home, an airy bungalow with hardwood floors and a white-brick fireplace. Inside him, though, was a fearsome need to fulfill some glossy vision.

27   Lottery keno became the rhythmic pulse of his life. For five years, Trena says, she awoke in an empty bed every weekend. Her husband would be gone by 5:30 or 6, joining other keno regulars at the neighborhood doughnut shop, watching the numbers flash on an overhead monitor. He'd shuffle home hours later, refusing to divulge his losses.

28   Trena did what tens of thousands of spouses do: She struggled desperately to pay the bills. She hid money in Cheerios boxes, books, couch cushions, under the doormat. She drew up household budgets—hundreds of them. They became her obsession. She drafted a new one almost every day, never able to get one to work.

29   Absurd dramas were played out. On paydays, when her husband's check was directly deposited into their account, they would race each other to the bank. Trena would go to one branch, he'd head to another. She would sit at the drive-up window, jamming her withdrawal slip in the pneumatic tube the moment the bank opened. If she got the money, they could pay the utilities and keep the phone connected. If not, he'd be off to the races, the casinos or the doughnut shop.

30   Like a caged animal, she threw things—smashed a clock against the wall, broke the portable TV in the bedroom. She yelled, clawed and sometimes just sank down and cried. Trena had no money for herself, for the important personal things. She got nothing for her mom on Mother's Day.

31   Increasingly reclusive, she stopped returning calls. Chit-chatting with friends seemed a frivolous distraction when dealing with foreclosure notices, filing for bankruptcy or, worse, fending off her husband's angry demands for cash.

32   He would burst into the house shouting, "Give me my money!" Pacing, following her, tipping over plants, rifling through drawers, dumping them out to try to find it. "Don't you touch my money!"

33   Joining Gam-Anon, where Trena receives emotional support from the spouses of other gamblers, has helped her deal with her decade-long ordeal. She says she is not bitter and understands that compulsive gambling is an illness.

34   While her husband now lives with his parents, she remains in their home of 19 years, a place filled with memories as wistful as they are painful.

35   With drug or alcohol abusers, there is the hope of sobering up, an accomplishment in itself, no matter what problems may have accompanied their addictions. Compulsive gamblers often see no way to purge their urges when suffocating debts suggest only one answer: a hot streak. "They have nowhere to turn—they feel cornered," says Dr. Richard J. Rosenthal, a Beverly Hills psychiatrist who founded the California Council on Problem Gambling. "Very often they are motivated by their shame into more and more desperate attempts to avoid being found out."

36   David Phillips, a UC San Diego sociology professor, studied death records from 1982 to 1988—before legalized gambling exploded across America—and found that people in Las Vegas, Atlantic City and other gambling meccas showed significantly higher suicide rates than people in non-gambling cities.

37   Rex Trivia is not about to kill himself, but like most compulsive gamblers, he occasionally thinks about it. Looking at him, it's hard to imagine he once had a promising future as a smart young New York book editor. His pale eyes are expressionless, his hair yellowish and brittle. In his fifties, his health is failing: emphysema, three lung collapses, a bad aorta, rotting teeth.

38   His plunge has been so dizzying that at one point he agreed to aid another desperate gambler in a run of bank robberies—nine in all, throughout Los Angeles and Orange counties. When the FBI busted him in 1980, he had $50,000 in cash in a dresser drawer and $100,000 in traveler's checks in his refrigerator's vegetable crisper. Rex, who ended up doing a short stint in prison, hasn't seen that kind of money since.

39   At 11 P.M. on a Tuesday night, with a bankroll of $55—all he has—he is at a poker table in Gardena. With quick, nervous hands he stacks and unstacks his $1 chips. The stack dwindles. Down $30, he talks about leaving, getting some sleep. Midnight comes and goes. Rex starts winning. Three aces. Four threes. Chips pile up—$60, $70. "A shame to go when the cards are falling my way." He checks the time: "I'll go at 2. Win, lose or draw."

40   Fate, kismet, luck—the cards keep falling. At 2 A.M., Rex is up $97. He stands, leaves his chips on the table and goes out for a smoke. In the darkness at the edge of the parking lot, he loiters with other regulars, debating with himself whether to grab a bus and quit.

41   "I should go back in there and cash in and get out of here," he says. "That's what I should do."

42   A long pause. Crushing out his cigarette, Rex turns and heads back inside. He has made his decision.

43   "A few more hands."

Discussion Questions

1. Discuss the irony of the essay's title.
2. Why do you think Gold and Ferrell repeat "never" five times in paragraph 2?
3. Identify the essay's thesis statement.
4. By referring to specific paragraphs, point out the various illustrations that the writers use in this essay.
5. Why do you think that Gold and Ferrell cite quotations at various points?
6. What do the writers accomplish by ending the selection with a continuation of the first example?

Toward Key Insights

What factors account for the explosive growth of legalized gambling?
What benefits, if any, have resulted from this growth?
How should we address the problem of compulsive gambling?

Suggestion for Writing

Write an essay illustrating addiction to television viewing or smoking. Choose an appropriate number of examples and develop them with specific details.

ELLEN GOODMAN

The Company Man

Ellen Goodman (born 1941) is a native of Massachusetts and a 1963 graduate of Radcliffe College. A journalist since graduation, she has worked as a researcher and reporter for Newsweek *magazine as well as a writer for several major newspapers and a commentator for national radio and TV shows. She has also written articles for* MS., McCall's, *and the* Village Voice. *Book-length publications include* Turning Points *(1979),* Value Judgments *(1993), and several collections of newspaper columns. Her latest book, which she co-authored with Patricia O'Brien, is entitled* I Know Just What You Mean: The Power of Friendship in Women's Lives *(2000). She has received numerous writing awards including a 1980 Pulitzer Prize for distinguished commentary. Our selection, originally a newspaper article, depicts a workaholic whose total dedication to his job killed him.*

1   He worked himself to death, finally and precisely, at 3:00 A.M. Sunday morning.

2   The obituary didn't say that, of course. It said that he died of a coronary thrombosis—I think that was it—but everyone among his friends and acquaintances knew it instantly. He was a perfect Type A, a workaholic, a classic, they said to each other and shook their heads—and thought for five or ten minutes about the way they lived.

3   This man who worked himself to death finally and precisely at 3:00 A.M. Sunday morning—on his day off—was fifty-one years old and a vice-president. He was, however, one of six vice-presidents, and one of three who might conceivably—if the president died or retired soon enough—have moved to the top spot. Phil knew that.

4   He worked six days a week, five of them until eight or nine at night, during a time when his own company had begun the four-day week for everyone but the executives. He worked like the Important People. He had no outside "extracurricular interests," unless, of course, you think about a monthly golf game that way. To Phil, it was work. He always ate egg salad sandwiches at his desk. He was, of course, overweight, by 20 to 25 pounds. He thought it was okay, though, because he didn't smoke.

5   On Saturdays, Phil wore a sports jacket to the office instead of a suit, because it was the weekend.

6   He had a lot of people working for him, maybe sixty, and most of them liked him most of the time. Three of them will be seriously considered for his job. The obituary didn't mention that.

7   But it did list his "survivors" quite accurately. He is survived by his wife, Helen, forty-eight years old, a good woman of no particular marketable skills, who worked in an office before marrying and mothering. She had, according to her daughter, given up trying to compete with his work years ago, when the children were small. A company friend said, "I know how much you will miss him." And she answered, "I already have."

8   "Missing him all these years," she must have given up part of herself which had cared too much for the man. She would be "well taken care of."

9   His "dearly beloved" eldest of the "dearly beloved" children is a hardworking executive in a manufacturing firm down South. In the day and a half before the funeral, he went around the neighborhood researching his father, asking the neighbors what he was like. They were embarrassed.

10   His second child is a girl, who is twenty-four and newly married. She lives near her mother and they are close, but whenever she was alone with her father, in a car driving somewhere, they had nothing to say to each other.

11   The youngest is twenty, a boy, a high-school graduate who has spent the last couple of years, like a lot of his friends, doing enough odd jobs to stay in grass and food. He was the one who tried to grab at his father, and tried to mean enough to him to keep the man at home. He was his father's favorite. Over the last two years, Phil stayed up nights worrying about the boy.

12   The boy once said, "My father and I only board here."

13   At the funeral, the sixty-year-old company president told the forty-eight-year-old widow that the fifty-one-year-old deceased had meant much to the company and would be missed and would be hard to replace. The widow didn't look him in the eye. She was afraid he would read her bitterness and, after all, she would need him to straighten out the finances—the stock options and all that.

14   Phil was overweight and nervous and worked too hard. If he wasn't at the office, he was worried about it. Phil was a Type A, a heart-attack natural. You could have picked him out in a minute from a lineup.

15   So when he finally worked himself to death, at precisely 3:00 A.M. Sunday morning, no one was really surprised.

16   By 5:00 P.M. the afternoon of the funeral, the company president had begun, discreetly of course, with care and taste, to make inquiries about his replacement. One of three men. He asked around: "Who's been working the hardest?"

Discussion Questions

1. Goodman says that Phil was "a perfect Type A" (paragraph 2). After reflecting on her essay, explain the characteristics of this type.
2. Why do you think Goodman doesn't supply Phil's last name or the name of the company he works for?
3. What idea is Goodman trying to present?
4. Unlike the essay by Rubin Erdely, Goodman's uses one longer illustration rather than several shorter ones. Why?
5. What is the significance of Phil's oldest son going "around the neighborhood researching his father, asking the neighbors what he was like" (paragraph 9)? Why were they embarrassed?
6. How do you account for Goodman's relatively short paragraphs?

Toward Key Insights

What social values would cause individuals to work themselves to death?
In that regard, what is the significance of the company president asking "Who's been working the hardest?"
Are these values basically good, or should we make some changes in our attitudes toward work and success? If so, what kinds of changes?

Suggestion for Writing

Using one extended example, write an essay that illustrates the lifestyle of a laid-back employee or friend. Your paper need not, of course, feature a death.

CLASSIFICATION ▬ ▬ ▬ ▬ ▬ ▬ ▬

Reading Strategies

1. Identify your purpose for reading the essay and the writer's purpose for the classification. This will determine how carefully you will need to read the selection.
2. Do not lose the big picture. Identify what is being classified—types of cars, kinds of dates—and why it is being classified.
3. Notice each of the major categories and the distinctive characteristics of each category. When this material is important to you, it can be very useful to make a table that identifies each major classification and identifies the distinctive features of each category. When carefully organized, such a table can be very helpful.

Reading Critically

1. Determine if there is reasonable evidence for the classification system or if the system is arbitrary.
2. Try to come up with an alternative classification system.
3. Check to see if the categories of the classification are clear or overlap.
4. Determine whether the defining features are distinct enough to clearly apply the system.
5. Try applying the system. Does it work?

Reading As a Writer

1. Identify how the essay establishes the characteristics of the classification system.
2. Often the transition sentences in a classification essay are awkward. Examine the transition sentences and evaluate the effectiveness of the transitions.

MARION WINIK

What Are Friends For?

Marion Winik (born 1958) is a graduate of Brown University and of Brooklyn College, where she earned a master of fine arts degree in creative writing. Since graduation, she has pursued a career in education, writing, and marketing. Her writings include poems, short stories, essays, and books, and the shorter pieces have appeared in a variety of major newspapers and popular magazines. Her book, The Lunch-Box Chronicles: Notes from the Parenting Underground *(1998), discusses her experiences in raising her sons after her husband's death. In this selection, Winik takes a humorous look at the different categories of friends and the benefits derived from each one.*

1   I was thinking about how everybody can't be everything to each other, but some people can be something to each other, thank God, from the ones whose shoulder you cry on to the ones whose half-slips you borrow to the nameless ones you chat with in the grocery line.

2   Buddies, for example, are the workhorses of the friendship world, the people out there on the front lines, defending you from loneliness and boredom. They call you up, they listen to your complaints, they celebrate your successes and curse your misfortunes, and you do the same for them in return. They hold

Introduction: indicates value of friends

Body: paragraphs 2–14

First category

---

out through innumerable crises before concluding that the person you're dating is no good, and even then understand if you ignore their good counsel. They accompany you to a movie with subtitles or to see the diving pig at Aquarena Springs. They feed your cat when you are out of town and pick you up from the airport when you get back. They come over to help you decide what to wear on a date. Even if it is with that creep.

3 What about family members? Most of them are people you just got stuck with, and though you love them, you may not have very much in common. But there is that rare exception, the Relative Friend. It is your cousin, your brother, maybe even your aunt. The two of you share the same views of the other family members. Meg never should have divorced Martin. He was the best thing that ever happened to her. You can confirm each other's memories of things that happened a long time ago. Don't you remember when Uncle Hank and Daddy had that awful fight in the middle of Thanksgiving dinner? Grandma always hated Grandpa's stamp collection; she probably left the window open during the hurricane on purpose.

4 While so many family relationships are tinged with guilt and obligation, a relationship with a Relative Friend is relatively worry-free. You don't even have to hide your vices from this delightful person. When you slip out Aunt Joan's back door for a cigarette, she is already there.

5 Then there is that special guy at work. Like all the other people at the job site, at first he's just part of the scenery. But gradually he starts to stand out from the crowd. Your friendship is cemented by jokes about co-workers and thoughtful favors around the office. Did you see Ryan's hair? Want half my bagel? Soon you know the names of his turtles, what he did last Friday night, exactly which model CD player he wants for his birthday. His handwriting is as familiar to you as your own.

6 Though you invite each other to parties, you somehow don't quite fit into each other's outside lives. For this reason, the friendship may not survive a job change. Company gossip, once an infallible source of entertainment, soon awkwardly accentuates the distance between you. But wait. Like School Friends, Work Friends share certain memories which acquire a nostalgic glow after about a decade.

7 A Faraway Friend is someone you grew up with or went to school with or lived in the same town as until one of you moved away. Without a Faraway Friend, you would never get any mail addressed in handwriting. A Faraway Friend calls late at night, invites you to her wedding, always says she is coming to visit but rarely shows up. An actual visit from a Faraway Friend is a cause for celebration and binges of all kinds. Cigarettes, Chips Ahoy, bottles of tequila.

8 Faraway Friends go through phases of intense communication, then may be out of touch for many months. Either way, the connection is always there. A conversation with your Faraway Friend always helps to put your life in perspective: when you feel you've hit a dead end, come to a confusing fork in the road, or gotten lost in some crackerbox subdivision of your life, the advice of the Faraway Friend—who has the big picture, who is so well acquainted with the route that brought you to this place—is indispensable.

9 Another useful function of the Faraway Friend is to help you remember things from a long time ago, like the name of your seventh-grade history teacher, what was in that really good stir-fry, or exactly what happened that night on the boat with the guys from Florida.

10 Ah, the Former Friend. A sad thing. At best a wistful memory, at worst a dangerous enemy who is in possession of many of your deepest secrets. But what was it that drove you apart? A misunderstanding, a betrayed confidence, an unrepaid loan, an ill-conceived flirtation. A poor choice of spouse can do in a friendship just like that. Going into business together can be a serious mistake. Time, money, distance, cult religions: all noted friendship killers. . . .

11 And lest we forget, there are the Friends You Love to Hate. They call at inopportune times. They say stupid things. They butt in, they boss you around, they embarrass you in public. They invite themselves over. They take advantage. You've done the best you can, but they need professional help. On top of all this, they love you to death and are convinced they're your best friend on the planet.

Sixth category: paragraphs 11–12

12 So why do you continue to be involved with these people? Why do you tolerate them? On the contrary, the real question is, What would you do without them? Without Friends You Love to Hate, there would be nothing to talk about with your other friends. Their problems and their irritating stunts provide a reliable source of conversation for everyone they know. What's more, Friends You Love to Hate make you feel good about yourself, since you are obviously in so much better shape than they are. No matter what these people do, you will never get rid of them. As much as they need you, you need them too.

13 At the other end of the spectrum are Hero Friends. These people are better than the rest of us, that's all there is to it. Their career is something you wanted to be when you grew up—painter, forest ranger, tireless doer of good. They have beautiful homes filled with special handmade things presented to them by villagers in the remote areas they have visited in their extensive travels. Yet they are modest. They never gossip. They are always helping others, especially those who have suffered a death in the family or an illness. You would think people like this would just make you sick, but somehow they don't.

Seventh category

Eighth category

14 A New Friend is a tonic unlike any other. Say you meet her at a party. In your bowling league. At a Japanese conversation class, perhaps. Wherever, whenever, there's that spark of recognition. The first time you talk, you can't believe how much you have in common. Suddenly, your life story is interesting again, your insights fresh, your opinion valued. Your various short-comings are as yet completely invisible.

Conclusion: memorable observation meshes stylistically with rest of essay

15 It's almost like falling in love.

Discussion Questions

  1. Comment on the effectiveness of Winik's title.
  2. Characterize the level of diction that Winik uses in her essay.
  3. What elements of Winik's essay interest you the most? What elements interest you the least?

Toward Key Insights

What traits characterize the various types of friend that you have?
In what ways are these friendships mutually beneficial?

Suggestion for Writing

Write an essay classifying the various types of people that you consider undesirable. Choose an appropriate number of categories and support them with appropriate specific details.

Scott Russell Sanders

The Men We Carry in Our Minds

Scott Russell Sanders was born (1945) in Memphis, Tennessee. After earning a B.A. degree from Brown University in 1967 and a PhD from Cambridge University in 1971, he joined the English faculty at Indiana University, where he is a full professor. Sanders is the author of numerous books of fiction and nonfiction. These books span a wide range of genres, including science fiction, historical novels, children's stories, folk tales, biographies, and personal essays. He has contributed to several essay anthologies, and his articles have appeared in literary journals and popular magazines. He has won several awards for his writing. In this essay, Sanders, in light of what he knows about the lives of working men, examines the view that power is rooted in gender.

1   The first men, besides my father, I remember seeing were black convicts and white guards, in the cottonfield across the road from our farm on the outskirts of Memphis. I must have been three or four. The prisoners wore dingy gray-and-black zebra suits, heavy as canvas, sodden with sweat. Hatless, stooped, they chopped weeds in the fierce heat, row after row, breathing the acrid dust of boll-weevil poison. The overseers wore dazzling white shirts and broad shadowy hats. The oiled barrels of their shotguns flashed in the sunlight. Their faces in memory are utterly blank. Of course those men, white and black, have become for me an emblem of racial hatred. But they have also come to stand for the twin poles of my early vision of manhood—the brute toiling animal and the boss.

2   When I was a boy, the men I knew labored with their bodies. They were marginal farmers, just scraping by, or welders, steel workers, carpenters; they swept floors, dug ditches, mined coal, or drove trucks, their forearms ropy with muscle; they trained horses, stoked furnaces, built tires, stood on assembly lines wrestling parts onto cars and refrigerators. They got up before light, worked all day long whatever the weather, and when they came home at night they looked as though somebody had been whipping them. In the evenings and on weekends they worked on their own places, tilling gardens that were lumpy with clay, fixing broken-down cars, hammering on houses that were always too drafty, too leaky, too small.

3   The bodies of the men I knew were twisted and maimed in ways visible and invisible. The nails of their hands were black and split, the hands tattooed with scars. Some had lost fingers. Heavy lifting had given many of them finicky backs and guts weak from hernias. Racing against conveyor belts had given them ulcers. Their ankles and knees ached from years of standing on concrete. Anyone who had worked for long around machines was hard of hearing. They squinted, and the skin of their faces was creased like the leather of old work gloves. There were times, studying them, when I dreaded growing up. Most of them coughed, from dust or cigarettes, and most of them drank cheap wine or whiskey, so their eyes looked bloodshot and bruised. The fathers of my friends always seemed older than the mothers. Men wore out sooner. Only women lived into old age.

4   As a boy I also knew another sort of men, who did not sweat and break down like mules. They were soldiers, and so far as I could tell they scarcely worked at all. During my early school years we lived on a military base, an arsenal in Ohio, and every day I saw GIs in the guardshacks, on the stoops of barracks, at the wheels of olive drab Chevrolets. The chief fact of their lives was boredom. Long after I left the Arsenal I came to recognize the sour smell the soldiers gave off as

that of souls in limbo. They were all waiting—for wars, for transfers, for leaves, for promotions, for the end of their hitch—like so many braves waiting for the hunt to begin. Unlike the warriors of older tribes, however, they would have no say about when the battle would start or how it would be waged. Their waiting was broken only when they practiced for war. They fired guns at targets, drove tanks across the churned-up fields of the military reservation, set off bombs in the wrecks of old fighter planes. I knew this was all play. But I also felt certain that when the hour for killing arrived, they would kill. When the real shooting started, many of them would die. This was what soldiers were *for*, just as a hammer was for driving nails.

5   Warriors and toilers: those seemed, in my boyhood vision, to be the chief destinies for men. They weren't the only destinies, as I learned from having a few male teachers, from reading books, and from watching television. But the men on television—the politicians, the astronauts, the generals, the savvy lawyers, the philosophical doctors, the bosses who gave orders to both soldiers and laborers—seemed as remote and unreal to me as the figures in tapestries. I could no more imagine growing up to become one of these cool, potent creatures than I could imagine becoming a prince.

6   A nearer and more hopeful example was that of my father, who had escaped from a red-dirt farm to a tire factory, and from the assembly line to the front office. Eventually he dressed in a white shirt and tie. He carried himself as if he had been born to work with his mind. But his body, remembering the earlier years of slogging work, began to give out on him in his fifties, and it quit on him entirely before he turned sixty-five. Even such a partial escape from man's fate as he had accomplished did not seem possible for most of the boys I knew. They joined the Army, stood in line for jobs in the smoky plants, helped build highways. They were bound to work as their fathers had worked, killing themselves or preparing to kill others.

7   A scholarship enabled me not only to attend college, a rare enough feat in my circle, but even to study in a university meant for the children of the rich. Here I met for the first time young men who had assumed from birth that they would lead lives of comfort and power. And for the first time I met women who told me that men were guilty of having kept all the joys and privileges of the earth for themselves. I was baffled. What privileges? What joys? I thought about the maimed, dismal lives of most of the men back home. What had they stolen from their wives and daughters? The right to go five days a week, twelve months a year, for thirty or forty years to a steel mill or a coal mine? The right to drop bombs and die in war? The right to feel every leak in the roof, every gap in the fence, every cough in the engine, as a wound they must mend? The right to feel, when the layoff comes or the plant shuts down, not only afraid but ashamed?

8   I was slow to understand the deep grievances of women. This was because, as a boy, I had envied them. Before college, the only people I had ever known who were interested in art or music or literature, the only ones who read books, the only ones who ever seemed to enjoy a sense of ease and grace were the mothers and daughters. Like the menfolk, they fretted about money, they scrimped and made-do. But, when the pay stopped coming in, they were not the ones who had failed. Nor did they have to go to war, and that seemed to me a blessed fact. By comparison with the narrow, ironclad days of fathers, there was an expansiveness, I thought, in the days of mothers. They went to see neighbors, to shop in town, to run errands at school, at the library, at church. No doubt, had I looked harder at their lives, I would have envied them less. It was not my fate to become a woman, so it was easier for me to see the graces. Few of them held jobs outside the home, and those who did filled

thankless roles as clerks and waitresses. I didn't see, then, what a prison a house could be, since houses seemed to me brighter, handsomer places than any factory. I did not realize—because such things were never spoken of—how often women suffered from men's bullying. I did learn about the wretchedness of abandoned wives, single mothers, widows; but I also learned about the wretchedness of lone men. Even then I could see how exhausting it was for a mother to cater all day to the needs of young children. But if I had been asked, as a boy, to choose between tending a baby and tending a machine, I think I would have chosen the baby. (Having now tended both, I know I would choose the baby.)

9   So I was baffled when the women at college accused me and my sex of having cornered the world's pleasures. I think something like my bafflement has been felt by other boys (and by girls as well) who grew up in dirt-poor farm country, in mining country, in black ghettos, in Hispanic barrios, in the shadows of factories, in Third World nations—any place where the fate of men is as grim and bleak as the fate of women. Toilers and warriors. I realize now how ancient these identities are, how deep the tug they exert on men, the undertow of a thousand generations. The miseries I saw, as a boy, in the lives of nearly all men I continue to see in the lives of many—the body-breaking toil, the tedium, the call to be tough, the humiliating powerlessness, the battle for a living and for territory.

10   When the women I met at college thought about the joys and privileges of men, they did not carry in their minds the sort of men I had known in my childhood. They thought of their fathers, who were bankers, physicians, architects, stockbrokers, the big wheels of the big cities. These fathers rode the train to work or drove cars that cost more than any of my childhood houses. They were attended from morning to night by female helpers, wives and nurses and secretaries. They were never laid off, never short of cash at month's end, never lined up for welfare. These fathers made decisions that mattered. They ran the world.

11   The daughters of such men wanted to share in this power, this glory. So did I. They yearned for a say over their future, for jobs worthy of their abilities, for the right to live at peace, unmolested, whole. Yes, I thought, yes yes. The difference between me and these daughters was that they saw me, because of my sex, as destined from birth to become like their fathers, and therefore as an enemy to their desires. But I knew better. I wasn't an enemy, in fact or in feeling. I was an ally. If I had known, then, how to tell them so, would they have believed me? Would they now?

Discussion Questions

1. Why is the essay titled "The Men *We* Carry in *Our Minds*" rather than "The Men *I* Carry in *My Mind*"?
2. Other than starting the essay, what does paragraph 1 accomplish?
3. What primary categories of men does Sanders discuss? What principle of classification does he use?
4. Sanders uses a number of comparisons, such as "zebra suits, heavy as canvas" in paragraph 1, to enhance his writing. Point out other comparisons and comment on their effectiveness.
5. The last sentence of paragraph 10 and the second, sixth, and eighth sentences of paragraph 11 are short statements. What do you think Sanders accomplishes with these statements?
6. Judging by what Sanders writes in the essay, how do you think he would answer the questions he poses in the final two sentences of paragraph 11?

Toward Key Insights

To what extent do you believe that the views expressed in the essay by the college women and Sanders reflect the views of today's college women and men? How do you account for any changes you might note?

Suggestion for Writing

Write an essay classifying the different grade school or high school teachers that you carry in your mind. Develop your categories with specific, informative details.

BERNICE MCCARTHY

A Tale of Four Learners

Bernice McCarthy, Ph.D., earned her doctorate in education and learning theory from Northwestern University. She founded About Learning, Inc., a consulting firm on educational theory and research. She has published a number of articles and presented workshops at major institutions. In this essay, she classifies learners based on THE 4MAT System® she created.

1   A young man at a midwestern middle school said of his social studies teacher, "She doesn't label us, and she helps us do all kinds of things." That student expressed very simply my evolving understanding of style since I created the 4MAT System in 1979. The way one perceives reality and reacts to it forms a pattern over time. This pattern comes to dominate the way one integrates ideas, skills, and information about people and the way one adapts knowledge and forms meaning.

2   But to learn successfully, a student also needs expertise in other learning styles; together these styles from a natural cycle of learning. That middle school teacher apparently honored the unique style that each student brought to her classroom, while helping each one do some stretching and master all the ways of learning.

3   Following are true stories about four types of learners. They illustrate how students with different learning styles experience school and why we must create opportunities for diverse learning experiences for every child.

4   Linda was in 6th grade when she hit the wall in math. She had loved school up until then. Her teachers and classmates agreed that her poetry was quite good, and her poems often appeared in local publications. But math was a problem. She couldn't connect it to anything—she simply could not see the patterns. Her teachers were not pleased with her and she longed to please them.

5   Linda went on to college, and when she was a junior, a new professor arrived on campus. The day before Linda's statistics class began, she met him in the hallway. He said, "Oh, you're Linda; I've been reading your poetry. You are going to do very well in statistics."

6   She looked at him in amazement. "How can you say that? I have such difficulty in all my math classes."

7   He smiled and answered, "I can tell from your poetry that you understand symmetry. Statistics is about symmetry. As a matter of fact, statistics is the poetry

Bernice McCarthy, "A Tale of Four Learners," from *Educational Leadership*, v. 54, March 1997, pp. 46–51.

of math." Linda went on to earn an A in that class. Her professor had connected statistics to her life and showed her the patterns (McCarthy 1996).

8   Linda is a Type 1 learner—the highly imaginative student who favors feeling and reflecting. These learners

9   ■ are at home with their feelings, people-oriented, outstanding observers of people, great listeners and nurturers, and committed to making the world a better place.

10   ■ prefer to learn by talking about experiences; listening and watching quietly, then responding to others and discussing ideas; asking questions; brainstorming; and examining relationships. They work well in groups or teams but also enjoy reading quietly.

11   ■ experience difficulty with long verbal explanations, with giving oral presentations, and with memorizing large chunks of abstract information. They dislike confusion or conflict, environments where mistakes are openly criticized, or where they cannot discuss their perceptions.

12   ■ have a cognitive style that puts perception before judgment, subjective knowledge before objective facts, and reflection before action. They prefer to make decisions based on feeling, are visual/auditory/kinesthetic, and experiential before conceptual.

13   As a Type 1 learner, Linda needed to connect math to her real life, to know why it was useful as a way of thinking and a way of formulating problems and solutions. She also needed her teachers to believe in her and to spend time with and nurture her.

14   Marcus was in 1st grade, and he loved school. Everything he longed for was present there—the teacher's loving interest, the thrill of deciphering the symbols that meant things, the things he could touch and feel, the addition problems that the teacher wrote on the chalkboard. He could always see the answers. His excitement was like that of the basketball player who knows that if he can just get his hands on the ball, he can sink it. Each question became an exciting foray into even more questions. And as his reading improved rapidly, he could not get enough of books. He welcomed the words and ideas of each new writer. He felt confident; he knew he belonged (McCarthy 1996).

15   Marcus is a Type 2 learner—the analytic student who favors reflecting and thinking. These learners

16   ■ have a knowledge-oriented style; are outstanding at conceptualizing material; analyze and classify their experiences and organize ideas; are highly organized and at home with details and data; are good at step-by-step tasks; are fascinated with structure; believe in their ability to understand; and are committed to making the world more lucid.

17   ■ prefer to learn through lectures and objective explanations, by working independently and systematically, and by reading and exchanging ideas.

18   ■ experience difficulty in noisy, high-activity environments, ambiguous situations, and working in groups. They also have trouble with open-ended assignments, as well as with presentations, role-playing, and nonsequential instructions. They have difficulty talking about feelings as well.

19   ■ have a cognitive style that is objective thinking, reflection before action, impersonal, auditory/visual/kinesthetic, conceptual over experiential. They tend to make judgments first, then support them with their perceptions.

20   As a Type 2 learner, Marcus found school an absolute joy. Testing, so frightening to Linda, was a tonic for him, a chance to prove he could do it. Because he

was naturally verbal and school is mostly a verbal challenge, he was—and continues to be—successful.

21   When Jimmy was in 2nd grade he did not like to read, and that made school difficult. He did enjoy having others read to him, and his younger brother, a 1st grader, read him stories every night. Jimmy did excel in math and art. He loved to work alone on projects and never wanted help. When he was asked to illustrate a story or build something to depict a math concept, he approached the task excitedly. He was happiest when he could solve a problem by creating a three-dimensional solution.

22   Unfortunately, Jimmy had a rigid teacher whose timing was always different from his own. Jimmy either finished too fast or took too long when he got really interested in a project. Once his teacher said in exasperation, "I didn't say you had to do your best work, Jimmy, just get it done!" When Jimmy's family bought a new VCR, they read the directions aloud to figure out how it worked. Jimmy stepped up and simply made it work. His reading problem continued into 3rd grade when he caught up with the others, but he never let it get him down—he was simply too busy doing other kinds of things (McCarthy 1996).

23   Jimmy is a Type 3 learner—the common-sense learner who favors thinking and doing. These learners

24   ■ are great problem solvers and are drawn to how things work. They are at home with tasks and deadlines, are productive and committed to making the world work better, and they believe in their ability to get the job done. They are also active and need opportunities to move around.

25   ■ prefer to learn through active problem solving; step-by-step procedures; touching, manipulating, and constructing; demonstrations; experimentation and tinkering; and competition.

26   ■ experience difficulty when reading is the primary means of learning and whenever they cannot physically test what they are told. They have trouble with verbal complexity, paradoxes or unclear choices, subtle relationships, and open-ended academic tasks. They also have difficulty expressing feelings.

27   ■ have a cognitive style that features objective thinking and facts over ideas, action before reflection, and judgment before perception. Their style is impersonal and kinesthetic/auditory/visual.

28   As a Type 3 learner, Jimmy needed to work things out in his own way, to create unique solutions to problems, and, most of all, to show what he learned by doing something concrete with it. His verbal skills did not kick in until well into the 3rd grade. Although this is not unusual with highly spatial learners, teachers treated it as an aberration. School was simply too regimented and too verbal for Jimmy. What saved him was his focus on his own learning.

29   When Leah was a high school freshman, she liked her new friends and some of her teachers. But she had a fierce need to learn, and school was not nearly exciting enough for her. She found so much of it deadening—memorizing endless facts that were totally irrelevant to her life. Leah had a wonderful spontaneity, and when it took hold of her, she focused so intensely that time became meaningless. Her teachers came to regard this spontaneity as a liability that was taking her away from the things she needed to know.

30   At first Leah persevered. Instead of preparing a juvenile justice report based on her social studies text, she asked to be allowed to go to juvenile court and see for herself, and then present her findings in a skit. Her teachers seldom agreed to her proposals, and after a while Leah stopped trying. She had natural leadership talent, which she expressed through her extra-curricular activities—the one

part of school she came to love. She graduated, but has believed ever since then that real learning does not happen in school (McCarthy 1996).

31   Leah is a Type 4 learner—the dynamic learner who favors creating and acting. These learners

32   ■ are proud of their subjectivity, at home with ambiguity and change, and great risk takers and entrepreneurs. They act to extend and enrich their experiences and to challenge the boundaries of their worlds for the sake of growth and renewal, and they believe in their ability to influence what happens. They initiate learning by looking for unique aspects of the information to learn and they sustain learning through trial and error.

33   ■ prefer to learn by self-discovery, talking, convincing others, looking for creative solutions to problems, and engaging in free flights of ideas. They also like to work independently and tackle open-ended academic tasks with lots of options, paradox, or subtle relationships. Their interpersonal skills are good.

34   ■ experience difficulty with rigid routines when they are not allowed to question. They also have trouble with visual complexity, methodical tasks, time management, and absolutes.

35   ■ have a cognitive style that is perception first with slight attention to judgment, subjective, relational, action-oriented, kinesthetic/auditory/visual, and experiential over conceptual.

36   Leah found learning for school's sake incomprehensible. As in Jimmy's case, doing was crucial to her approach. She preferred interviewing over reading, going to court to see for herself, exploring instead of hearing how others see things.

37   In any classroom, Linda, Marcus, Jimmy, Leah, and their many shades and varieties sit before the teacher—challenging and waiting to be challenged. The frustrating question is: why are some learners honored in our schools and others ignored, discouraged, or even frowned upon? Why did Marcus fare so well, while Linda, Jimmy, and Leah struggled to be accepted?

38   In my definition of learning, the learner makes meaning by moving through a natural cycle—a movement from feeling to reflecting to thinking and, finally, to acting. This cycle results from the interplay of two separate dimensions—perceiving and processing (Kolb 1984).

39   In perceiving, we take in what happens to us by (1) feeling, as we grasp our experience, and then by (2) thinking, as we begin to separate ourselves from the experience and name and classify it. The resulting concepts become our way of interpreting our world (Kegan 1982).

40   We also process experiences in two ways: by (1) reflecting on them, and then by (2) acting on those reflections. We also try things; we tinker.

41   The places in this cycle that we find most comfortable—where we function with natural ease and grace—are our learning preferences or styles, the "spins" we put on learning.

42   Unfortunately, schools tend to honor only one aspect of perceiving—thinking. This is very tough on kids whose approach to learning is predominately feeling. Linda and Leah, like many other Type 1 and 4 learners—both male and female—are naturals on the feeling end of experience. Jimmy and Marcus, the Type 2 and 3 learners, favor the thinking end.

43   As with feeling and thinking, reflecting and acting need to be in balance. But our schools favor reflecting. Marcus excelled at that, while both Jimmy and Leah needed to act. The lack of hands-on learning created difficulties for both of them.

44   Even as I define styles in my work, I caution that we must be wary of labels. Over time, and with experience, practice, and encouragement, students become

comfortable with learning styles that aren't naturally their own. Successful learners, in fact, develop multiple styles.

45   The 4MAT framework is designed to help students gain expertise in every learning style. We design lesson units as cycles built around core concepts, each of which incorporates experiencing (Type 1), conceptualizing (Type 2), applying (Type 3), and creating (Type 4). The styles answer the questions:

46   ■ Why do I need to know this? (the personal meaning of Type 1).
     ■ What exactly is this content or skill? (the conceptual understanding of Type 2).
     ■ How will I use this in my life? (the real-life skills of Type 3).
     ■ If I do use this, what possibilities will it create? (the unique adaptations of Type 4).

47   Had the teachers of Linda, Marcus, Jimmy, and Leah used the entire cycle of learning styles, including those areas in which each student needed to stretch, all four students would have acquired expertise in all facets of the cycle. They would have made personal connections to the learning, examined expert knowledge, used what they were learning to solve problems, and come up with new ways to apply the learning—both personally and in the world at large. (As it happened, the students learned to do these things on their own.)

48   In addressing the various learning styles, the 4MAT System also incorporates elements of brain research—in particular, the different ways that the right and left hemispheres of the cerebral cortex process information (Benson 1985, McCarthy 1981 and 1987, Sylvester 1995, Wittrock 1985). I call these contrasting mental operations the Left and Right Modes.

49   The Left Mode is analytical and knows those things we can describe with precision. It examines cause and effect, breaks things down into parts and categorizes them, seeks and uses language and symbols, abstracts experience for comprehension, generates theory, and creates models. It is sequential and works in time.

50   The Right Mode knows more than it can tell, filling in gaps and imagining. It is intuitive. It senses feelings; forms images and mental combinations; and seeks and uses patterns, relationships, and connections. It manipulates form, distance, and space.

51   Excellence and higher-order thinking demand that we honor both sides of the brain, teaching interactively with hands-on, real-life, messy problem solving. Learners speak in words, signs, symbols, movement, and through music. The more voices students master, the more new learning they will do. Unfortunately, however, teachers persist in lecturing and using logical, sequential problem solving most of the time.

52   In assessing student performance, traditional methods work fairly well for Type 2 learners, who like to prove themselves, and Type 3 learners, who do well on tests in general. Traditional testing doesn't work as well for Types 1 and 4, however. Type 1 learners have difficulty in formal testing situations, especially when tests are timed and call for precise answers. Type 4 learners have trouble doing things by the book and with absolutes and rigid routines when they are not allowed to ask questions.

53   Further, students change roles as they move through the learning cycle. Tests that require students to recall facts obviously do not reflect the subtlety of these changes.

54   We need assessment tools that help us understand the whole person. We must assess the students' ability to picture the concept, to experiment with the idea, to combine skills in order to solve complex problems, to edit and refine

their work, and to adapt and integrate learning. We need to know how students are connecting information to their own experiences, how they are blending expert knowledge with their own, and how creative they are. We also need some way of measuring how students reflect on material, conceptualize, and represent what they have learned through various kinds of performances.

55   Successful learning is a continuous, cyclical, lifelong process of differentiating and integrating these personal modes of adaptation. Teachers do not need to label learners according to their style; they need to help them work for balance and wholeness. Leah needs to learn the ways of Marcus; Jimmy needs Linda's ways. And all learners need encouragement to grow.

56   Learning is both reflective and active, verbal and nonverbal, concrete and abstract, head and heart. The teacher must use many instructional methods that are personally meaningful to each student. The more students can travel the cycle, the better they can move to higher-order thinking.

57   As a final note, what became of the students I described earlier? Linda directs the management division of a major human resources consulting firm. Marcus, a former professor of statistics at a prestigious university, is now president of a research firm. Jimmy will be a senior in high school this fall. He scored 100 percent on the Illinois State Math Achievement Test and achieved cum laude in the International Latin Exam. He also had his art portfolio favorably reviewed by the Art Institute of Chicago. And Leah? Leah is a pseudonym for the author of this article.

■ References

Benson, D. F. "Language in the Left Hemisphere." *The Dual Brain: Hemispheric Specialization in Humans.* Ed. D. F. Benson and E. Zaidel. New York: Guilford, 1985.

Kegan, R. *The Evolving Self: Problems and Process in Human Development.* Cambridge, MA: Harvard UP, 1982.

Kolb, D. A. *Experiential Learning: Experience as the Source of Learning and Development.* Englewood Cliffs, NJ: Prentice-Hall, 1984.

McCarthy, B. *The 4MAT System: Teaching to Learning Styles with Right/Left Mode Techniques.* Barrington, IL: Excel, Inc., 1981, 1987.

McCarthy, B. *About Learning.* Barrington, IL: Excel, Inc., 1996.

Sylvester, R. *A Celebration of Neurons: An Educator's Guide to the Human Brain.* Alexandria, VA: ASCD, 1995.

Wittrock, M. C. "Education and Recent Neuropsychological and Cognitive Research." *The Dual Brain: Hemispheric Specialization in Humans.* Ed. D. F. Benson and E. Zaidel. New York: Guilford, 1985.

Discussion Questions

1. The author starts with an example of praise for a teacher who did not "label" her students but then goes on to classify learning styles. Is this a contradiction?
2. With each type of learning style, the author follows the same pattern. What is the pattern that she uses and is it effective?

3. In paragraphs 4, 22, and 30, the author identifies the problems three out of the four sample students had in school. Why does she do this? Is it effective?

4. After discussing the four learning styles, the author discusses in paragraphs 38–48 what she identifies as the learning cycle. What is the connection between this learning cycle and how is this important in relation to the classification system?

5. It could be easy to imagine someone who had qualities of more than one learning style. Is this a problem for the writer's classification of learning styles?

6. In the conclusion the author informs us of the successes of her four example students. How is this conclusion important to the essay?

Toward Key Insights

Try to match yourself to the four learning styles. Does one learning style seem most like you? What does this say about the classification system?

What learning styles seem to dominate in most of your classes? What effects does this seem to have on the learning success of students? Do people who have different learning styles have difficulty adjusting to the dominant learning style of educational institutions?

Suggestion for Writing

Write an essay classifying teaching styles, including the different kinds of activities involved in the classroom and the different kinds of assessment.

RON GERACI

Which Stooge Are You?

Ron Geraci became a Three Stooges *fan while watching TV reruns of their movies as a youngster in southern New Jersey. Former features editor of* Men's Health, *he has written numerous articles on men's physical and emotional health for that magazine. In our selection, Geraci contends that each of the Stooges represents a different universal personality type and that recognizing our own particular type can help us avoid its pitfalls.*

1   Men spend millions of dollars on psychotherapy trying to figure out why they're unhappy, why their kids don't respect them, why women treat them like idiots. Perhaps shrinks help some men, but for many others, it's money that would have been better spent on popcorn and videotapes. To solve many of life's problems, all you really need to do is watch the *Three Stooges*.

2   We're all variations of Moe, Larry, or Curly, and our lives are often short subjects filled with cosmic slapstick. When Moe (your boss) hits Curly (your buddy) with a corporate board and then blindsides you when you try to make it all nice, you're living a Stooge moment. Here you'll find the personality type each Stooge represents. Once you determine which Stooge you are, you'll better understand the problems you bring on yourself—and how you can be a generally happier, more successful knucklehead.

3   Everyone knows more than one Moe. These men are the insufferable know-it-alls who become driving instructors, gym teachers, and divorce attorneys. The

coach who had you do pushups in front of the team? He was a Moe. So was that boss who made you carry his golf bag.

4   In short, Moes are hot-tempered men who intimidate people with verbal slaps and managerial eye pokes, according to Stuart Fischoff, Ph.D., a psychologist at California State University. "Moe has a paternalistic personality, which is pretty common among men," Fischoff says. "He treats everyone like a child and bullies people to keep them off balance." Being a temperamental loudmouth also helps Moe scare off critics who might expose his little secret: He's no smarter than the saps he terrorizes. Moe himself proved that point. Although he served up most of the nose gnashings and belly bonks in 190 shorts, he always ended up back in the mud with Larry and Curly.

5   Even if you've never actually threatened to tear somebody's tonsils out, there are a few other clues that can tag you as a Moe. First, naturally, Moes are explosive hot-heads who storm through life constantly infuriated by other people. "These men suffer from classic low frustration tolerance," says Allen Elkin, Ph.D., a psychologist in New York. "This not only makes them difficult to work with, but it also gives them high blood pressure, high cholesterol, and a much greater risk of heart attack." In fact, Moes often end up seeking counseling to control their anger, usually after it costs them a job, a marriage, or a couple of good pals. "I tell them to just get away from infuriating situations quickly," says Elkin. "Remember, you don't *have* to poke Curly in the eye because he destroyed the plumbing."

6   Second, in the likely event that a Moe manages to foul things up himself, he'll find a way to blame his mistakes on other people, says Fischoff. In *Healthy, Wealthy, and Dumb* (1938), for example, Moe breaks a $5,000 vase with a 2-by-4 and screams at Larry, "Why didn't you bring me a softer board?!"

7   Your habits on the job are the most telling signs. If you're a Moe, you're probably the hardest-driving wise guy at work. "High-strung, bossy men with Moe personalities tend to live at their jobs," says Elkin. To help stop overloading themselves with work they can't possibly finish (a common Moe peccadillo), workaholic Moes should make a list of projects they *won't do* each day—and then make sure they keep their hands off those folders.

8   Moe Howard (1897–1975) had a classic Moe personality. Even offscreen, he was the fiery, short-fused leader of the trio who made all the decisions. Of course, this put a lot of worries on Moe's shoulders. "My father was an anxiety-ridden, nervous man," says Paul Howard, Moe's son. "He didn't have much patience. He always worried about his kid brother Curly, and if Larry flubbed a line, my father could become upset and criticize him almost like a director." Larry probably shaped up fast; Moe could always put some English into the next eye gouge.

9   Now, in fairness to all men with bowl cuts and bad attitudes, there are some big advantages to having a Moe personality. "If I could choose my Stooge, I'd sure as hell be a Moe," says Fischoff. Because they're usually so domineering and assertive, Moes are often able to bark their way into leadership positions quickly. (Kennedy and Nixon were Moes; Carter is a Larry.) If you crammed all the *Fortune*-100 CEOs into one Bennigan's, you'd have Moe Central with a wet bar.

10   Another Moe perk: Women flock to you like geeks to a *Star Trek* premier. Moe is an aggressive, tenacious SOB, and women are genetically programmed to find those traits sexually attractive, says Barbara Keesling, Ph.D., a Southern California sex therapist. That's because prehistoric Moes used their superior eye-poking abilities to scare off those wise-guy tigers. It's why that Moe who gave you noogies in high school went through skirts faster than J. Edgar Hoover—and why he's probably divorced now.

11   "Moes are control freaks," says Keesling. "That can be sexually exciting at first, but women get tired of it very quickly. I know—I've dated examples of all three Stooges. I'm thankful they didn't all try to sleep in my bed at once."

12   Larry is the passive, agreeable fellow who scrapes through life by taking his licks and collecting his paycheck. "Generally, things happen *to* a Larry; he doesn't make them happen," says Alan Entin, Ph.D., a psychologist with the American Psychological Association. Larry is the ubiquitous "nice guy" who commutes to his mediocre job, congenially tries to cover Curly's ass, and spends his day trying to avoid getting whacked in the nose by Moe.

13   That's right: John Q. Taxpayer is a Larry.

14   A subtle testosterone shift, though, can make all the difference in what kind of life this lovable sap leads. Give the classic Larry a little more testicularity, and you have a good-natured man who isn't a biological doormat. He'll kick a wino off your lawn but won't fink on your free cable. That makes him a perfect coworker, neighbor, and pal.

15   But subtract a little gonad power, and a Larry can be an indecisive wimp whose greatest ambition in life is to watch *Everybody Loves Raymond.* These pitiful, wishy-washy slobs constantly get clobbered for being—as Larry put it—"a victim of soicumstance," and that typically makes them passive-aggressive, says Fischoff.

16   "A Larry doesn't have the nerve to be assertive, so he protests by not doing something," Fischoff says: not securing the ladder on the triple-bunk bed, or not mentioning that the coffee is actually rat poison. Consequently, Larrys are rarely promoted. If a Larry actually does work up the courage to ask for a raise, the Moe he works for will usually give a meaningless title upgrade—or say, "Get outta here before I murder ya."

17   To determine if you're an overly passive Larry, answer these three questions.

18   *What's new?* If you're a classic Larry, nothing is new. Your answer will be the latest yarn about the office Curly who once photocopied his own butt. "Larrys live vicariously through Moes and Curlys," says Fischoff. "They don't really have a strong identity of their own."

19   *Still dream about writing a screenplay?* "Larrys don't have a life plan," says Fischoff. They bumble from one opportunity to the next while awaiting their "break"; a Moe plots his life like a war and a Curly flatly avoids challenges.

20   *Do you weasel out of big projects?* Larrys become good at deflecting responsibility. This lets them avoid the risk of failure (and success) without looking like a bum. In *Idiots Deluxe* (1945), as Curly is being attacked by a giant bear, Moe screams, "Go out there and help him!" "The bear don't need no help!" Larry yells back.

21   The chief bonus in being a Larry, of course, is that almost everyone thinks you're a swell chum. The dames eventually warm up to you, too, although it might take a few decades. Women reeling from years of turbulent relationships with Moes and Curlys often settle down with a Larry, says Keesling, because he's a stable, predictable, okeydokey guy who won't mind heading to the 7-Eleven for tampons. That makes him husband material. "I'd date Moe and Curly, but I'd marry Larry," confided several women we asked.

22   Like most Larrys, Larry Fine (1902–1975) spent his career following Moe and his free time ducking him. "Larry and Moe weren't friends," says Lyla Budnick, Larry's sister. "Their dealings were all business." Like any good Larry, he found passive-aggressive ways to make Moe fume. "My father would be at an airport hours early," says Joan Maurer, Moe's daughter, "but Larry would show up 5 minutes before the plane took off. This made my dad very upset." For Larry, making Moe sweat in a crowded airport terminal was probably a tiny payback for the daily humiliations.

23   In *The Sweet Pie and Pie* (1941), Curly tries to throw a pie at the usual gang of rich idiots but gets nailed with a pastry each time he cocks his arm. Finally he bashes himself with the pie to deprive others of the satisfaction. This illustrates Curly's strategy for life. "These men laugh at themselves so other people can't ridicule them first," says Elkin. "It comes across as funny, but this kind of defense mechanism really stems from a large reservoir of anger and resentment."

24   Curly had what's called an oral personality, and a particularly self-destructive one. Boisterous, attention-seeking men, especially those who are secretly ashamed of something, like a beer gut or a bald head, often feel that they must perform in order to be liked, says Keesling. "These guys always come in for counseling, because they experience mood swings and addiction problems. It's what killed Curly and his modern-day version, Chris Farley."

25   Men with Curly personalities are almost always fat, says Fischoff, because they live to binge. They overdose on food, booze, gambling, drugs, or sex—and sometimes on all five in one badly soiled hotel bed. Curly, a consummate binger, even outlined his plans for a utopian life in *Healthy, Wealthy, and Dumb:* "Oh boy! Pie à la mode with beer chasers three times a day!"

26   On the job, Curlys pride themselves on providing comedic relief. "A Curly senses he's no leader, so he garners attention by being a fool," says Fischoff. This nets him no respect, but it does defuse criticism. Who can fire a guy when he's down on the carpet running in circles?

27   Just like his two nitwit cohorts, Curly Howard's offscreen personality was pretty similar to that of the Stooge he portrayed. He drank heavily, overate, and smoked several cigars a day. "He would always be out carousing and drinking, and playing the spoons in nightclubs," remembers Paul Howard, his nephew.

28   "I've heard stories that my father sometimes had to pay for the damage Curly caused while drinking," says Joan Maurer, Moe's daughter. If woo-wooing was enough to get Curly belted onscreen, can you imagine what Moe dished out over a real-life antic like this?

29   Curly's lifestyle apparently made him foggy at work, too. When he barked at women or said "nyuk-nyuk-nyuk!" it was often because he had forgotten his lines. After having a series of obvious mini-strokes (he could barely grumble out his woos in 1945's *If a Body Meets a Body)*, Curly had a career-ending stroke in 1946 and died in 1952 at age 48.

30   He had a hoot along the way, of course. Everybody loves a clown, so Curlys get plenty of party invites—and nightcaps with attractive women. "If each of the Stooges were to flirt with a woman, Curly would probably take her home, because his humor radiates confidence," Keesling says. (And what woman could resist an opener like "Hiya, Toots"?) But a Curly's neuroses usually shine through within a few dates, which explains why Curlys tend to have few long-term sex partners, says Keesling.

31   Curly Howard was married four times. "With the exception of his fourth marriage, his best relationship was with his dogs," says Paul Howard. Curly expressed his marital outlook pretty clearly in 1941's *An Ache in Every Stake,* as he shaved a lathered block of ice with a razor: "Are you married or happy?"

Discussion Questions

1. What is Geraci's purpose in writing this essay, and where is it stated?
2. Demonstrate your understanding of coherence by pointing out how paragraphs 3–6 are linked to one another. Refer to the essay when answering.

3. What audience do you think Geraci is trying to reach? Explain your answer.
4. Characterize the level of diction used in this essay. Refer to appropriate passages to support your answer.
5. Do you feel that you are a rather pure version of a Moe, Larry, or Curly, somewhat of a mixture, or that you bear little resemblance to any of them?

Toward Key Insights

How do you cope with the various personality types that you encounter at school? In your social life? On the job?

Do you think it is an oversimplification to assert that "To solve many of life's problems, all you really need to do is watch the *Three Stooges*" (paragraph 1)? Why or why not?

Suggestion for Writing

Write an essay classifying three distinctive personality types. Develop your paper with relevant, specific details and write with a specific audience in mind.

COMPARISON

Reading Strategies

1. Identify your purpose for reading the comparison and the author's purpose for the comparison. Determine how carefully you need to read the comparison.
2. Identify the items that are being compared.
3. Identify the pattern of organization (point by point or block) that is used in the comparison.
4. Read carefully to establish the points of similarities and differences. When the information might be necessary for future purposes, it can be helpful to create a table that matches similarities and differences.

Reading Critically

1. Test to see if there are any biases guiding the comparison. Does the writer show any preference or prejudice?
2. Determine if the accounts of similarities and differences are accurate or whether they are exaggerated.
3. Test to see if there are other similarities or differences that can be established. Are the items more alike or more different than the author tries to suggest?

Reading As a Writer

1. Examine how the author organized the essay. Was the organization effective in guiding the reader through the essay? Note what organizational pattern was most effective.
2. Notice the sentences that the writer uses for transitions. Jot down any useful techniques.
3. Observe how much detail was used to substantiate the comparison.

Reader

BRUCE CATTON

Grant and Lee: A Study in Contrasts

Bruce Catton (1899–1978) was a nationally recognized expert on the Civil War. Born in Petoskey, Michigan, he attended Oberlin College, then worked as a reporter for several large newspapers. Between 1942 and 1948, he held several positions in the U.S. government and then became an editor of American Heritage *magazine. His first book on the Civil War,* Mr. Lincoln's Army, *appeared in 1951 and was followed by* Glory Road *(1952) and* A Stillness at Appomattox *(1953). This last book won the Pulitzer Prize and the National Book Award and established Catton's reputation as a Civil War historian. In the years that followed, Catton continued to write books on the Civil War. In 1972 he published the auto-biographical* Waiting for the Morning Train *and in 1974* Michigan: A Bicentennial History. *In our selection, Catton points out differences as well as similarities in the two foremost adversaries of the Civil War.*

Title sets up differences

Introduction: paragraphs 1–3; background: significance of following contrasts

1 When Ulysses S. Grant and Robert E. Lee met in the parlor of a modest house at Appomattox Court House, Virginia, on April 9, 1865, to work out the terms for the surrender of Lee's Army of Northern Virginia, a great chapter in American life came to a close, and a great new chapter began.

2 These men were bringing the Civil War to its virtual finish. To be sure, other armies had yet to surrender, and for a few days the fugitive Confederate government would struggle desperately and vainly, trying to find some way to go on living now that its chief support was gone. But in effect it was all over when Grant and Lee signed the papers. And the little room where they wrote out the terms was the scene of one of the poignant, dramatic contrasts in American history.

3 They were two strong men these oddly different generals, and they represented the strengths of two conflicting currents that, through them, had come into final collision.

Body: paragraph 4 to first part, paragraph 16; alternating pattern throughout

4 Back of Robert E. Lee was the notion that the old aristocratic concept might somehow survive and be dominant in American life.

5 Lee was tidewater Virginia, and in his background were family, culture, and tradition . . . the age of chivalry transplanted to a New World which was making its own legends and its own myths. He embodied a way of life that had come down through the age of knighthood and the English country squire. America was a land that was beginning all over again, dedicated to nothing much more complicated than the rather hazy belief that all men had equal rights and should have an equal chance in the world. In such a land Lee stood for the feeling that it was somehow of advantage to human society to have a pronounced inequality in the social structure. There should be a leisure class, backed by ownership of land; in turn, society itself should be keyed to the land as the chief source of wealth and influence. It would bring forth (according to this ideal) a class of men with a strong sense of obligation to the community; men who lived not to gain advantage for themselves, but to meet the solemn obligations which had been laid on them by the very fact that they were privileged. From them the country would get its leadership; to them it could look for the higher values—of thought, of conduct, or personal deportment—to give it strength and virtue.

First difference paragraphs 4–6: Lee's background, character

6 Lee embodied the noblest elements of this aristocratic ideal. Through him, the landed nobility justified itself. For four years, the Southern states had fought a desperate war to uphold the ideals for which Lee stood. In the end, it almost seemed

Bruce Catton, "Grant and Lee: A Study in Contrasts," from *The American Story,* ed. Earl Schenck Miers. Reprinted by permission of. U.S. Capital Historical Society.

326

as if the Confederacy fought for Lee; as if he himself was the Confederacy . . . the best thing that the way of life for which the Confederacy stood could ever have to offer. He had passed into legend before Appomattox. Thousands of tired, under-fed, poorly clothed Confederate soldiers, long since past the simple enthusiasm of the early days of the struggle, somehow considered Lee the symbol of everything for which they had been willing to die. But they could not quite put this feeling into words. If the Lost Cause, sanctified by so much heroism and so many deaths, had a living justification, its justification was General Lee.

7   Grant, the son of a tanner on the Western frontier, was everything Lee was not. He had come up the hard way and embodied nothing in particular except the eternal toughness and sinewy fiber of the men who grew up beyond the mountains. He was one of a body of men who owed reverence and obeisance to no one, who were self-reliant to a fault, who cared hardly anything for the past but who had a sharp eye for the future.

Paragraphs 7–9: Grant's background, character

8   These frontier men were the precise opposites of the tidewater aristocrats. Back of them, in the great surge that had taken people over the Alleghenies and into the opening Western country, there was a deep, implicit dissatisfaction with a past that had settled into grooves. They stood for democracy not from any rea-soned conclusion about the proper ordering of human society, but simply because they had grown up in the middle of democracy and knew how it worked. Their society might have privileges, but they would be privileges each man had won for himself. Forms and patterns meant nothing. No man was born to anything, except perhaps to a chance to show how far he could rise. Life was competition.

9   Yet along with this feeling had come a deep sense of belonging to a national community. The Westerner who developed a farm, opened a shop, or set up in busi-ness as a trader could hope to prosper only as his own community prospered—and his community ran from the Atlantic to the Pacific and from Canada down to Mexico. If the land was settled, with towns and highways and accessible markets, he could better himself. He saw his fate in terms of the nation's own destiny. As its hori-zons expanded, so did his. He had, in other words, an acute dollars-and-cents stake in the continued growth and development of his country.

10   And that, perhaps, is where the contrast between Grant and Lee becomes most striking. The Virginia aristocrat, inevitably, saw himself in relation to his own region. He lived in a static society which could endure almost anything except change. Instinctively, first loyalty would go to the locality in which that society existed. He would fight to the limit of endurance to defend it, because in defend-ing it he was defending everything that gave his own life its deepest meaning.

Second difference: Lee's loyalty

11   The Westerner, on the other hand, would fight with an equal tenacity for the broader concept of society. He fought so because everything he lived by was tied to growth, expansion, and a constantly widening horizon. What he lived by would survive or fall with the nation itself. He could not possibly stand by unmoved in the face of an attempt to destroy the Union. He would combat it with everything he had, because he could only see it as an effort to cut the ground out from under his feet.

Grant's loyalty

12   So Grant and Lee were in complete contrast, representing two diametrically opposed elements in American life. Grant was the modern man emerging; beyond him, ready to come on the stage, was the great age of steel and machin-ery, of crowded cities and a restless burgeoning vitality. Lee might have ridden down from the old age of chivalry, lance in hand, silken banner fluttering over his head. Each man was the perfect champion of his cause, drawing both his strengths and his weaknesses from the people he led.

Summary of significant differences

Transition paragraph
signals switch to
similarities

First similarity

Second similarity

Third similarity: notes
order of climax

Conclusion: significance
of the meeting

13   Yet it was not all contrast, after all. Different as they were—in background, in personality, in underlying aspiration—these two great soldiers had much in common. Under everything else, they were marvelous fighters. Furthermore, their fighting qualities were really very much alike.

14   Each man had, to begin with, the great virtue of utter tenacity and fidelity. Grant fought his way down the Mississippi Valley in spite of acute personal discouragement and profound military handicaps. Lee hung on in the trenches at Petersburg after hope itself had died. In each man there was an indomitable quality . . . the born fighter's refusal to give up as long as he can still remain on his feet and lift his two fists.

15   Daring and resourcefulness they had, too; the ability to think faster and move faster than the enemy. These were the qualities which gave Lee the dazzling campaigns of Second Manassas and Chancellorsville and won Vicksburg for Grant.

16   Lastly, and perhaps greatest of all, there was the ability, at the end, to turn quickly from war to peace once the fighting was over. Out of the way these two men behaved at Appomattox came the possibility of a peace of reconciliation. It was a possibility not wholly realized, in the years to come, but which did, in the end, help the two sections to become one nation again . . . after a war whose bitterness might have seemed to make such a reunion wholly impossible. No part of either man's life became him more than the part he played in this brief meeting in the McLean house at Appomattox. Their behavior there put all succeeding generations of Americans in their debt. Two great Americans, Grant and Lee—very different, yet under everything very much alike. Their encounter at Appomattox was one of the great moments of American history.

Discussion Questions

1. Where is Catton's thesis statement?
2. Summarize the way of life that Lee stood for, and then do the same for Grant.
3. Why do the differences between Grant and Lee receive more extended treatment than the similarities? Why are the similarities discussed last?
4. How would you characterize Catton's attitude toward the two men? Refer to specific parts of the essay when answering.

Toward Key Insights

To what extent does modern society reflect the values embodied by Grant and Lee?
How would you characterize the upper class in the United States today? Does it consist
of leisured individuals who own extensive property, as Lee did, or does it have other
characteristics? Are its values the same as Lee's? If not, how are they different?
If Grant was typical of the "self-reliant" non-aristocrat, how is his contemporary
counterpart similar to and different from him?

Suggestion for Writing

*Write an essay comparing two past or present political or military figures—perhaps Abraham
Lincoln and Jefferson Davis or Dwight Eisenhower and Erwin Rommel. Try for a balanced
treatment and select an appropriate organization.*

NANCY MASTERSON SAKAMOTO

Conversational Ballgames

Nancy Masterson Sakamoto graduated Phi Beta Kappa from UCLA with a degree in English. Married to a Japanese artist and Buddhist priest, she lived in Japan for twenty-four years before moving with her husband and two sons to Honolulu in 1982. While in Japan, she was visiting professor at the University of Osaka. She gave in-service training to Japanese junior and senior high school English teachers and talks on intercultural topics, both in English and in Japanese, to various business, educational, and women's groups. In addition to her book, Polite Fictions: Why Japanese and Americans Seem Rude to Each Other, *still used as a textbook in Japanese universities, she coauthored a research project report sponsored by the Japanese Ministry of Education and wrote various articles for Japanese English-teaching publications. In Hawaii, she has been a speaker and seminar leader for many educational, business, and professional organizations. Her current position is professor of American Studies, Shitennoji Gakuen University (Hawaii branch). In this essay, she discusses the different conversational styles of Americans and Japanese, just one example of the many differences that distinguish different cultures.*

1   After I was married and had lived in Japan for a while, my Japanese gradually improved to the point where I could take part in simple conversations with my husband and his friends and family. And I began to notice that often, when I joined in, the others would look startled, and the conversational topic would come to a halt. After this happened several times, it became clear to me that I was doing something wrong. But for a long time, I didn't know what it was.

2   Finally, after listening carefully to many Japanese conversations, I discovered what my problem was. Even though I was speaking Japanese, I was handling the conversation in a western way.

3   Japanese-style conversations develop quite differently from western-style conversations. And the difference isn't only in the languages. I realized that just as I kept trying to hold western-style conversations even when I was speaking Japanese, so my English students kept trying to hold Japanese-style conversations even when they were speaking English. We were unconsciously playing entirely different conversational ballgames.

4   A western-style conversation between two people is like a game of tennis. If I introduce a topic, a conversational ball, I expect you to hit it back. If you agree with me, I don't expect you simply to agree and do nothing more. I expect you to add something—a reason for agreeing, another example, or an elaboration to carry the idea further. But I don't expect you always to agree. I am just as happy if you question me, or challenge me, or completely disagree with me. Whether you agree or disagree, your response will return the ball to me.

5   And then it is my turn again. I don't serve a new ball from my original starting line. I hit your ball back again from where it has bounced. I carry your idea further, or answer your questions or objections, or challenge or question you. And so the ball goes back and forth, with each of us doing our best to give it a new twist, an original spin, or a powerful smash.

6   And the more vigorous the action, the more interesting and exciting the game. Of course, if one of us gets angry, it spoils the conversation, just as it spoils a tennis game. But getting excited is not at all the same as getting angry. After all,

we are not trying to hit each other. We are trying to hit the ball. So long as we attack only each other's opinions, and do not attack each other personally, we don't expect anyone to get hurt. A good conversation is supposed to be interesting and exciting.

7   If there are more than two people in the conversation, then it is like doubles in tennis, or like volleyball. There's no waiting in line. Whoever is nearest and quickest hits the ball, and if you step back, someone else will hit it. No one stops the game to give you a turn. You're responsible for taking your own turn.

8   But whether it's two players or a group, everyone does his best to keep the ball going, and no one person has the ball for very long.

9   A Japanese-style conversation, however, is not at all like tennis or volleyball. It's like bowling. You wait for your turn. And you always know your place in line. It depends on such things as whether you are older or younger, a close friend or a relative stranger to the previous speaker, in a senior or junior position, and so on.

10   When your turn comes, you step up to the starting line with your bowling ball, and carefully bowl it. Everyone else stands back and watches politely, mur-muring encouragement. Everyone waits until the ball has reached the end of the alley, and watches to see if it knocks down all the pins, or only some of them, or none of them. There is a pause, while everyone registers your score.

11   Then, after everyone is sure that you have completely finished your turn, the next person in line steps up to the same starting line, with a different ball. He doesn't return your ball, and he does not begin from where your ball stopped. There is no back and forth at all. All the balls run parallel. And there is always a suitable pause between turns. There is no rush, no excitement, no scramble for the ball.

12   No wonder everyone looked startled when I took part in Japanese conversa-tions. I paid no attention to whose turn it was, and kept snatching the ball halfway down the alley and throwing it back to the bowler. Of course the conver-sation died. I was playing the wrong game.

13   This explains why it is almost impossible to get a Western-style conversation or discussion going with English students in Japan. I used to think that the prob-lem was their lack of English language ability. But I finally came to realize that the biggest problem is that they, too, are playing the wrong game.

14   Whenever I serve a volleyball, everyone just stands back and watches it fall, with occasional murmurs of encouragement. No one hits it back. Everyone waits until I call on someone to take a turn. And when that person speaks, he doesn't hit my ball back. He serves a new ball. Again, everyone just watches it fall.

15   So I call on someone else. This person does not refer to what the previous speaker has said. He also serves a new ball. Nobody seems to have paid any atten-tion to what anyone else has said. Everyone begins again from the same starting line, and all the balls run parallel. There is never any back and forth. Everyone is trying to bowl with a volleyball.

16   And if I try a simpler conversation, with only two of us, then the other per-son tries to bowl with my tennis ball. No wonder foreign English teachers in Japan get discouraged.

17   Now that you know about the difference in the conversational ballgames, you may think that all your troubles are over. But if you have been trained all your life to play one game, it is no simple matter to switch to another, even if you know the rules. Knowing the rules is not at all the same thing as playing the game.

18   Even now, during a conversation in Japanese I will notice a startled reaction, and belatedly realize that once again I have rudely interrupted by instinctively trying to hit back the other person's bowling ball. It is no easier for me to "just

listen" during a conversation, than it is for my Japanese students to "just relax" when speaking with foreigners. Now I can truly sympathize with how hard they must find it to try to carry on a Western-style conversation.

19   If I have not yet learned to do conversational bowling in Japanese, at least I have figured out one thing that puzzled me for a long time. After his first trip to America, my husband complained that Americans asked him so many questions and made him talk so much at the dinner table that he never had a chance to eat. When I asked him why he couldn't talk and eat at the same time, he said that Japanese do not customarily think that dinner, especially on fairly formal occasions, is a suitable time for extended conversation.

20   Since westerners think that conversation is an indispensable part of dining, and indeed would consider it impolite not to converse with one's dinner partner, I found this Japanese custom rather strange. Still, I could accept it as a cultural difference even though I didn't really understand it. But when my husband added, in explanation, that Japanese consider it extremely rude to talk with one's mouth full, I got confused. Talking with one's mouth full is certainly not an American custom. We think it very rude, too. Yet we still manage to talk a lot and eat at the same time. How do we do it?

21   For a long time, I couldn't explain it, and it bothered me. But after I discovered the conversational ballgames, I finally found the answer. Of course! In a Western-style conversation, you hit the ball, and while someone else is hitting it back, you take a bite, chew, and swallow. Then you hit the ball again, and then eat some more. The more people there are in the conversation, the more chances you have to eat. But even with only two of you talking, you still have plenty of chances to eat.

22   Maybe that's why polite conversation at the dinner table has never been a traditional part of Japanese etiquette. Your turn to talk would last so long without interruption that you'd never get a chance to eat.

Discussion Questions

1. Sakamoto notes in paragraph 1 that she "had lived in Japan for a while" and in paragraph 2 that she has listened "carefully to many Japanese conversations." Why does she note these facts at the outset of her essay?
2. What purpose is served by the first two sentences of paragraph 3?
3. Why do you think Sakamoto uses various games—tennis, volleyball, bowling— to help explain the differences between American and Japanese conversational styles?
4. Point out specific supporting details that help make this comparison successful.
5. For what audience is Sakamoto writing? Refer to the essay when answering.
6. Sakamoto ends paragraph 17 with the assertion that "Knowing the rules is not at all the same thing as playing the game." Explain what she means.

Toward Key Insights

In what ways other than conversational style might cultures exhibit pronounced differences?

What problems might these differences create, and how can we best deal with them?

Suggestion for Writing

Write a paper that discusses a problem that arose between you and someone else because of a difference in outlook or lifestyle and explain how you resolved the matter. Use either the block or alternating method of organization.

MARIFLO STEPHENS

Barbie Doesn't Live Here Anymore

Mariflo Stephens lives in Charlottesville, Virginia, where she writes essays and fiction. Her work appears in a number of major periodicals such as The Washington Post *and the* Virginia Quarterly Review. *This essay, from her memoir in progress,* Last One Home: Life After Oprah, *compares the place of the common Barbie doll in her and her daughter's lives to demonstrate the differences between two generations of women.*

1   I've always known there was something wrong with Barbie. She looks nice enough. And she has her own Corvette, her own band, and her own dream house. Still, I just didn't want my daughter playing with her. But how can we snub Barbie? Little girls all over Charlottesville, all over Virginia, and, yes, all over the world, seem to be spending hour after hour with her.

2   I considered relying on my own experience. When, in 1962, I was presented with my first Barbie doll, I did what all the other little girls did with their Barbies: I took her clothes off. Wow! I could hardly wait to have a pair of my very own.

3   Then I put her clothes back on. It was hard. There was a snap the size of a pinhead and Barbie hardly cooperated. I pulled the tight dress up her legs, over her hips; and it stopped right there. Had a liquid Barbie been poured into this to harden? She was stiff as stone but still smelled like new rubber. I had to put her head between my teeth to get her dress past that chest. I was exhausted. But was it ever fun, I told myself.

4   Now where were those high heels and that pair of long white gloves? I found one glove. Later my friend Jane came over to play. She took the dress off, too. We waited for something to happen. Then we went out to climb some trees. Four hours later, we told our mothers we'd had a great time playing Barbie. (This was lobbying. Jane's mother looked quizzical and noted the leaves in our hair.)

5   I was twelve in 1962, so I didn't have too many good years left for Barbie. Soon I would *be* Barbie. I was blond, wasn't I? And I would be an American teenager with no time left for playing. My time would be devoted to the serious business of dressing and dating and talking on the telephone.

6   In the months to come, I made the best of it. I spent my entire piggybank savings on Barbie clothes—sequined evening gowns, fake-fur wraps, and high heels. The outfits had themes like Barbie Goes to the Prom and Barbie Steps Out printed in a fast-moving script with exclamation marks at the end. There wasn't much to do, however, but dress and undress Barbie, and I found I had to spend most of my time looking for a lost pink high heel the size of my little fingernail.

7   Buying the clothes was the exciting part. Since I liked horses, I picked out Barbie's rodeo skirt set with white high-heeled boots and fringe. These weren't Barbie's clothes, they were mine. If I could've worn Barbie's lavender loungewear with its pink feather boa to my seventh-grade classroom, I would

have. If, that is, I could find it. Much was located under the sofa cushions, but far too late, I'm afraid.

8   Barbie retired early. I waited for my body to fill out, Barbie-style. My legs didn't grow to those proportions and neither did anything else. I got the idea that every time a teenage boy looked at me he saw only what was missing—what Barbie had that I didn't.

9   Even the blond hair didn't live up to expectations. Mine was fuzzy and its shape varied from day to day. Barbie's seemed to stay in a permanent coiffure. Evening gowns weren't even in style.

10   And not very many blondes can manage a nose that turns up that way.

11   Worst of all, Barbie doesn't do anything but lose her clothes. I had wasted a lot of money, not to mention rich fantasy time, on a false goddess.

12   When my daughter, Jane, was born, I told myself there would be no false goddesses. I didn't name her after a goddess, I named her after the girl I'd climbed trees with.

13   When relatives started to inquire about birthday gifts, I didn't say "No Barbies, please," though I wanted to. I said instead that books were very nice gifts. I mentioned there wasn't much to do with a Barbie doll except comb her hair and I was sure we'd lose those little combs.

14   Jane turned seven. She had five Barbie dolls. I didn't see her playing with them much, although every few days I would find a pink high heel somewhere. I would spot the dolls around the house—their legs splayed crazily and scarves tied around their bodies for clothes.

15   One day Jane said: "Barbies don't do anything. They don't even bend their legs when you sit them down. Their legs stick straight out." I knew she was on to something. Then we cleaned up her room. I found most of the clothes and even some of the high heels. I was pretty proud of myself. But behind me I heard Jane saying: "Let's get rid of the Barbies."

16   "Huh?"

17   "They're dumb and prissy. They clutter up everything. Let's sell them."

18   "What do you mean by 'dumb and prissy'?"

19   "They look like this," she said and raised to tiptoe and smiled maniacally. "They've got globs of blue makeup over their eyes and they can't do anything. You can't even bend their legs to sit them on a model horse."

20   I seized the moment. "What else is wrong with the Barbies?"

21   "They don't have toes. Their shoes fall off. They're always on tiptoe."

22   "That would be tiring," I said, sympathetically.

23   "They never get tired. They don't do anything."

24   "What else is wrong?"

25   "They don't wear socks or pants. Just dresses or fish-net stockings or they go barefoot. All the commercials compliment their hair, but once their hair is tangled, it never goes back."

26   "Anything else wrong?" I asked—and here she won my heart if ever there was a contest for it.

27   "They're all the same age. There are no Barbie babies and no old people."

28   "Sounds like Barbie lives in a dull world," I said.

29   "No, not dull. Dumb and prissy. Let's sell them."

30   "How much should we charge for each one?"

31   "A penny," she said disgustedly, then immediately saw her error. "No, no. A dollar."

32   "Oh," I said, seeing my own error. Just because I considered Barbie small change didn't mean everyone else did. Six Barbies went out the back door to a secondhand shop and, in a matter of minutes, six dollars came in the front door.

33   Maybe Barbie's business suit with its one-inch briefcase inspired Jane's market wisdom.

34   After all, the new Barbies are still in stores, housed in pink boxes with bold script that seems to shout: Barbie Goes to the Office! My old dolls, with their narrow eyes and puckered lips, are upstairs like other mad women of the attic, whispering: "Who stole my feather boa?"

Discussion Questions

1. This essay compares the different reactions of mother and daughter to Barbie dolls. What are the differences in their responses? What is the real point of this comparison?
2. How does this writer organize her comparison? What is the effect of this strategy?
3. Crucial to this essay is the dialogue between mother and daughter. What does the dialogue accomplish in the essay?
4. Reread the last paragraph. What point is the author trying to make in the conclusion? Is the conclusion effective?
5. How is the image of the feather boa used in the essay? What is the meaning of the feather boa for the author? What clues in the text demonstrate this meaning?

Toward Key Insights

What role do Barbies have in the developing attitudes of girls, and is that role positive or negative?
More generally, what kinds of impacts do toys have on the developing attitudes of children?

Suggestion for Writing

Compare how a toy such as video games, or how people play with a toy, has changed over a specific period of time.

Select someone of either sex whom you know well and write an essay comparing how you and the other person, as adolescents, handled such matters as peer pressure, self-image, dating, and relationships with family members. Develop the essay with relevant supporting material.

RICHARD RODRIGUEZ

Private Language, Public Language

Richard Rodriguez (born 1944) is a native of San Francisco who is of Mexican ancestry. After learning English in the elementary grades, he went on to earn a baccalaureate degree in English at Stanford University (1967) and graduate degrees at Columbia University

(1969) and the University of California at Berkeley (1975). Rejecting job offers from several major universities, he spent the next six years writing Hunger of Memory: The Education of Richard Rodriguez *(1982), a book that traces his educational odyssey.* Days of Obligation *was published in 1992, and* Brown: The Last Discovery of America *was published in 2003. His articles have appeared in a variety of scholarly magazines. In the following essay, Rodriguez explores his contrasting childhood perceptions concerning English and his native Spanish.*

1   I remember to start with that day in Sacramento—a California now nearly thirty years past—when I first entered a classroom, able to understand some fifty stray English words.

2   The third of four children, I had been preceded to a neighborhood Roman Catholic school by an older brother and sister. But neither of them had revealed very much about their classroom experiences. Each afternoon they returned, as they left in the morning, always together, speaking in Spanish as they climbed the five steps of the porch. And their mysterious books, wrapped in shopping-bag paper, remained on the table next to the door, closed firmly behind them.

3   An accident of geography sent me to a school where all my classmates were white, many the children of doctors and lawyers and business executives. All my classmates certainly must have been uneasy on that first day of school—as most children are uneasy—to find themselves apart from their families in the first institution of their lives. But I was astonished.

4   The nun said, in a friendly but oddly impersonal voice, "Boys and girls, this is Richard Rodriguez." (I heard her sound out: *Rich-heard Road-ree-guess.*) It was the first time I had heard anyone name me in English. "Richard," the nun repeated more slowly, writing my name down in her black leather book. Quickly I turned to see my mother's face dissolve in a watery blur behind the pebbled glass door.

5   Many years later there is something called bilingual education—a scheme proposed in the late 1960s by Hispanic-American social activists, later endorsed by a congressional vote. It is a program that seeks to permit non-English-speaking children, many from lower-class homes, to use their family language as the language of school. (Such is the goal its supporters announce.) I hear them and am forced to say no: It is not possible for a child—any child—ever to use his family's language in school. Not to understand this is to misunderstand the public uses of schooling and to trivialize the nature of intimate life—a family's "language."

6   Memory teaches me what I know of these matters; the boy reminds the adult. I was a bilingual child, a certain kind—socially disadvantaged—the son of working-class parents, both Mexican immigrants.

7   In the early years of my boyhood, my parents coped very well in America. My father had steady work. My mother managed at home. They were nobody's victims. Optimism and ambition led them to a house (our home) many blocks from the Mexican south side of town. We lived among *gringos* and only a block from the biggest, whitest houses. It never occurred to my parents that they couldn't live wherever they chose. Nor was the Sacramento of the fifties bent on teaching them a contrary lesson. My mother and father were more annoyed than intimidated by those two or three neighbors who tried initially to make us unwelcome. ("Keep your brats away from my sidewalk!") But despite all they achieved, perhaps because they had so much to achieve, any deep feeling of ease, the confidence of "belonging" in public was withheld from them both. They regarded the people at work, the faces in crowds, as very distant from us. They were the others, *los gringos.*

That term was interchangeable in their speech with another, even more telling, *los americanos*.

8   I grew up in a house where the only regular guests were my relations. For one day, enormous families of relatives would visit and there would be so many people that the noise and the bodies would spill out to the backyard and front porch. Then, for weeks, no one came by. (It was usually a salesman who rang the doorbell.) Our house stood apart. A gaudy yellow in a row of white bungalows. We were the people with the noisy dog. The people who raised pigeons and chickens. We were the foreigners on the block. A few neighbors smiled and waved. We waved back. But no one in the family knew the names of the old couple who lived next door; until I was seven years old, I did not know the names of the kids who lived across the street.

9   In public, my father and mother spoke a hesitant, accented, not always grammatical English. And they would have to strain—their bodies tense—to catch the sense of what was rapidly said by *los gringos*. At home they spoke Spanish. The language of their Mexican past sounded in counterpoint to the English of public society. The words would come quickly, with ease. Conveyed through those sounds was the pleasing, soothing, consoling reminder of being at home.

10   During those years when I was first conscious of hearing, my mother and father addressed me only in Spanish; in Spanish I learned to reply. By contrast, English *(inglés)*, rarely heard in the house, was the language I came to associate with *gringos*. I learned my first words of English overhearing my parents speak to strangers. At five years of age, I knew just enough English for my mother to trust me on errands to stores one block away. No more.

11   I was a listening child, careful to hear the very different sounds of Spanish and English. Wide-eyed with hearing, I'd listen to sounds more than words. First, there were English *(gringo)* sounds. So many words were still unknown that when the butcher or the lady at the drugstore said something to me, exotic polysyllabic sounds would bloom in the midst of their sentences. Often the speech of people in public seemed to me very loud, booming with confidence. The man behind the counter would literally ask, "What can I do for you?" But by being so firm and so clear, the sound of his voice said that he was a *gringo;* he belonged in public society.

12   I would also hear then the high nasal notes of middle-class American speech. The air stirred with sound. Sometimes, even now, when I have been traveling abroad for several weeks, I will hear what I heard as a boy. In hotel lobbies or airports, in Turkey or Brazil, some Americans will pass, and suddenly I will hear it again—the high sound of American voices. For a few seconds I will hear it with pleasure, for it is now the sound of *my* society—a reminder of home. But inevitably—already on the flight headed for home—the sound fades with repetition. I will be unable to hear it anymore.

13   When I was a boy, things were different. The accent of *los gringos* was never pleasing nor was it hard to hear. Crowds at Safeway or at bus stops would be noisy with sound. And I would be forced to edge away from the chirping chatter above me.

14   I was unable to hear my own sounds, but I knew very well that I spoke English poorly. My words would not stretch far enough to form complete thoughts. And the words I did speak I didn't know well enough to make into distinct sounds. (Listeners would usually lower their heads, better to hear what I was trying to say.) But it was one thing for *me* to speak English with difficulty. It was more troubling for me to hear my parents speak in public: their high-whining vowels and guttural consonants; their sentences that got stuck with "eh" and "ah" sounds; the confused syntax; the hesitant rhythm of sounds so different

from the way *gringos* spoke. I'd notice, moreover, that my parents' voices were softer than those of *gringos* we'd meet.

15   I am tempted now to say that none of this mattered. In adulthood I am embarrassed by childhood fears. And, in a way, it didn't matter very much that my parents could not speak English with ease. Their linguistic difficulties had no serious consequences. My mother and father made themselves understood at the county hospital clinic and at government offices. And yet, in another way, it mattered very much—it was unsettling to hear my parents struggle with English. Hearing them, I'd grow nervous, my clutching trust in their protection and power weakened.

16   There were many times like the night at a brightly lit gasoline station (a blaring white memory) when I stood uneasily, hearing my father. He was talking to a teenaged attendant. I do not recall what they were saying, but I cannot forget the sounds my father made as he spoke. At one point his words slid together to form one word—sounds as confused as the threads of blue and green oil in the puddle next to my shoes. His voice rushed through what he had left to say. And, toward the end, reached falsetto notes, appealing to his listener's understanding. I looked away to the lights of passing automobiles. I tried not to hear anymore. But I heard only too well the calm, easy tones in the attendant's reply. Shortly afterward, walking toward home with my father, I shivered when he put his hand on my shoulder. The very first chance that I got, I evaded his grasp and ran on ahead into the dark, skipping with feigned boyish exuberance.

17   But then there was Spanish. *Español:* my family's language. *Español:* the language that seemed to me a private language. I'd hear strangers on the radio and in the Mexican Catholic church across town speaking in Spanish, but I couldn't really believe that Spanish was a public language, like English. Spanish speakers, rather, seemed related to me, for I sensed that we shared—through our language—the experience of feeling apart from *los gringos*. It was thus a ghetto Spanish that I heard and I spoke. Like those whose lives are bound by a barrio, I was reminded by Spanish of my separateness from *los otros, los gringos* in power. But more intensely than for most barrio children—because I did not live in a barrio—Spanish seemed to me the language of home. (Most days it was only at home that I'd hear it.) It became the language of joyful return.

18   A family member would say something to me and I would feel myself specially recognized. My parents would say something to me and I would feel embraced by the sounds of their words. Those sounds said: *I am speaking with ease in Spanish. I am addressing you in words I never use with* los gringos. *I recognize you as someone special, close, like no one outside. You belong with us. In the family.*

19   *(Ricardo.)*

20   At the age of five, six, well past the time when most other children no longer easily notice the difference between sounds uttered at home and words spoken in public, I had a different experience. I lived in a world magically compounded of sounds. I remained a child longer than most; I lingered too long, poised at the edge of language—often frightened by the sounds of *los gringos,* delighted by the sounds of Spanish at home. I shared with my family a language that was startlingly different from that used in the great city around us.

21   For me there were none of the gradations between public and private society so normal to a maturing child. Outside the house was public society; inside the house was private. Just opening or closing the screen door behind me was an important experience. I'd rarely leave home all alone or without reluctance. Walking down the sidewalk, under the canopy of tall trees, I'd warily notice the—suddenly—silent neighborhood kids who stood warily watching me.

Nervously, I'd arrive at the grocery store to hear there the sounds of the *gringo*—foreign to me—reminding me that in this world so big, I was a foreigner. But then I'd return. Walking back toward our house, climbing the steps from the sidewalk, when the front door was open in summer, I'd hear voices beyond the screen door talking in Spanish. For a second or two, I'd stay, linger there, listening. Smiling, I'd hear my mother call out, saying in Spanish (words): "Is that you, Richard?" All the while her sounds would assure me: *You are home now; come closer; inside. With us.*

22   "*Sí,*" I'd reply.

23   Once more inside the house I would resume (assume) my place in the family. The sounds would dim, grow harder to hear. Once more at home, I would grow less aware of that fact. It required, however, no more than the blurt of the doorbell to alert me to listen to sounds all over again. The house would turn instantly still while my mother went to the door. I'd hear her hard English sounds. I'd wait to hear her voice return to soft-sounding Spanish, which assured me, as surely as did the clicking tongue of the lock on the door, that the stranger was gone.

24   Plainly, it is not healthy to hear such sounds so often. It is not healthy to distinguish public words from private words so easily. I remained cloistered by sounds, timid and shy in public, too dependent on voices at home. And yet it needs to be emphasized: I was an extremely happy child at home. I remember many nights when my father would come back from work, and I'd hear him call out to my mother in Spanish, sounding relieved. In Spanish, he'd sound light and free notes he never could manage in English. Some nights I'd jump up just at hearing his voice. With *mis hermanos* I would come running into the room where he was with my mother. Our laughing (so deep was the pleasure!) became screaming. Like others who know the pain of public alienation, we transformed the knowledge of our public separateness and made it consoling—the reminder of intimacy. Excited, we joined our voices in a celebration of sounds. *We are speaking now the way we never speak out in public. We are alone—together,* voices sounded, surrounded to tell me. Some nights, no one seemed willing to loosen the hold sounds had on us. At dinner, we invented new words. (Ours sounded Spanish, but made sense only to us.) We pieced together new words by taking, say, an English verb and giving it Spanish endings. My mother's instructions at bedtime would be lacquered with mock-urgent tones. Or a word like *sí* would become, in several notes, able to convey added measures of feeling. Tongues explored the edges of words, especially the fat vowels. And we happily sounded that military drum roll, the twirling roar of the Spanish *r*. Family language: my family's sounds. The voices of my parents and sisters and brother. Their voices insisting: *You belong here. We are family members. Related. Special to one another. Listen!* Voices singing and sighing, rising, straining, then surging, teeming with pleasure that burst syllables into fragments of laughter. At times it seemed there was steady quiet only when, from another room, the rustling whispers of my parents faded and I moved closer to sleep.

Discussion Questions

1. What does Rodriguez accomplish in his first four paragraphs? What connection do you see between these paragraphs and later parts of the essay?
2. What is Rodriguez's main point? Where is it stated?
3. Discuss the significance of paragraphs 7–9.
4. Why did his parents' difficulties with English cause Rodriguez such concern?

5. In paragraph 16 Rodriguez tells us that he "looked away to the lights of passing automobiles" and that he "ran on ahead into the dark . . . ." Explain these actions.
6. Rodriguez does not begin to develop his discussion of Spanish—the private language—until paragraph 17. Why do you think this discussion didn't occur earlier in the essay?
7. Explain why the concluding paragraph is effective.

Toward Key Insights

In what ways other than those noted by Rodriguez do children and their families create or inhabit private worlds that are separate from their public worlds? What are some of the benefits and problems that result from this dichotomy? How important is language to a person's identity and social world?

Suggestion for Writing

Write a comparison essay discussing some noteworthy difference between you, or some group you belong to, and the larger public. The difference may be one of race, ethnic background, religion, or lifestyle. Demonstrate clearly how the difference affects your relationship with that public.

HENRY JENKINS

Art Form for the Digital Age

Henry Jenkins is the John E. Burchard Professor of Humanities and Director of the Comparative Media Studies graduate program at MIT. His Column "The Digital Renaissance," from which this selection was taken, is featured in the journal Technology Review *monthly.*

Video games shape our culture. It's time we took them seriously.

1   LAST YEAR, AMERICANS BOUGHT OVER 215 million computer and video games. That's more than two games per household. The video game industry made almost as much money from gross domestic income as Hollywood.

2   So are video games a massive drain on our income, time and energy? A new form of "cultural pollution," as one U.S. senator described them? The "nightmare before Christmas," in the words of another? Are games teaching our children to kill, as countless op-ed pieces have warned?

No. Computer games are art—a popular art, an emerging art, a largely unrecognized art, but art nevertheless.

3   Over the past 25 years, games have progressed from the primitive two-paddles-and-a-ball Pong to the sophistication of Final Fantasy, a participatory story with cinema-quality graphics that unfolds over nearly 100 hours of play. The computer game has been a killer app for the home PC, increasing consumer demand for vivid graphics, rapid processing, greater memory and better sound. The release this fall of the Sony Playstation 2, coupled with the announcement of next-generation consoles by Nintendo and Microsoft, signals a dramatic increase in the resources available to game designers.

4   Games increasingly influence contemporary cinema, helping to define the frenetic pace and model the multi-directional plotting of Run Lola Run, providing the role-playing metaphor for Being John Malkovich and encouraging a fascination with the slippery line between reality and digital illusion in The Matrix. At high schools and colleges across the country, students discuss games with the same passions with which earlier generations debated the merits of the New American Cinema. Media studies programs report a growing number of their students want to be game designers rather than filmmakers.

5   The time has come to take games seriously as an important new popular art shaping the aesthetic sensibility of the 21st century. I will admit that discussing the art of video games conjures up comic images: tuxedo-clad and jewel-bedecked patrons admiring the latest Streetfighter, middle-aged academics pontificating on the impact of Cubism on Tetris, bleeps and zaps disrupting our silent contemplation at the Guggenheim. Such images tell us more about our contemporary notion of art—as arid and stuffy, as the property of an educated and economic elite, as cut off from everyday experience—than they tell us about games.

6   New York's Whitney Museum found itself at the center of controversy about digital art when it recently included Web artists in its prestigious biannual show. Critics didn't believe the computer could adequately express the human spirit. But they're misguided. The computer is simply a tool, one that offers artists new resources and opportunities for reaching the public; it is human creativity that makes art. Still, one can only imagine how the critics would have responded to the idea that something as playful, unpretentious and widely popular as a computer game might be considered art.

7   In 1925, leading literary and arts critic Gilbert Seldes took a radical approach to the aesthetics of popular culture in a treatise title *The Seven Lively Arts*. Adopting what was then a controversial position, Seldes argued that America's primary contributions to artistic expression had come through emerging forms of popular culture such as jazz, the Broadway musical, the Hollywood cinema and the comic strip. While these arts have gained cultural respectability over the past 75 years, each was disreputable when Seldes staked out his position.

8   Readers then were skeptical of Seldes' claims about cinema in particular for many of the same reasons that contemporary critics dismiss games—they were suspicious of cinema's commercial motivations and technological origins, concerned about Hollywood's appeals to violence and eroticism, and insistent that cinema had not yet produced works of lasting value. Seldes, on the other hand, argued that cinema's popularity demanded that we reassess its aesthetic qualities.

9   Cinema and other popular arts were to be celebrated, Seldes said, because they were so deeply imbedded in everyday life, because they were democratic arts embraced by average citizens. Through streamlined styling and syncopated rhythms, they captured the vitality of contemporary urban experience. They took the very machinery of the industrial age, which many felt dehumanizing, and found within it the resources for expressing individual visions, for reasserting basic human needs, desires and fantasies. And these new forms were still open to experimentation and discovery. They were, in Seldes' words, "lively arts."

10   Games represent a new lively art, one as appropriate for the digital age as those earlier media were for the machine age. They open up new aesthetic experiences and transform the computer screen into a realm of experimentation and innovation that is broadly accessible. And games have been embraced by a public that has otherwise been unimpressed by much of what passes for digital art. Much as the salon arts of the 1920s seemed sterile alongside the vitality and

inventiveness of popular culture, contemporary efforts to create interactive narrative through modernist hypertext or avant-garde installation art seem lifeless and pretentious alongside the creativity that game designers bring to their craft.

11   Much of what Seldes told us about the silent cinema seems remarkably apt for thinking about games. Silent cinema, he argued, was an art of expressive movement. He valued the speed and dynamism of D.W. Griffith's last-minute races to the rescue, the physical grace of Chaplin's pratfalls and the ingenuity of Buster Keaton's engineering feats. Games also depend upon an art of expressive movement, with characters defined through their distinctive ways of propelling themselves through space, and successful products structured around a succession of spectacular stunts and predicaments. Will future generations look back on Lara Croft doing battle with a pack of snarling wolves as the 21st-century equivalent of Lillian Gish making her way across the ice floes in *Way Down East*? The art of silent cinema was also an art of atmospheric design. To watch a silent masterpiece like Fritz Lang's *Metropolis* is to be drawn into a world where meaning is carried by the placement of shadows, the movement of machinery and the organization of space. If anything, game designers have pushed beyond cinema in terms of developing expressive and fantastic environments that convey a powerful sense of mood, provoke our curiosity and amusement, and motivate us to explore.

12   Seldes wrote at a moment when cinema was maturing as an expressive medium and filmmakers were striving to enhance the emotional experience of going to the movies—making a move from mere spectacle towards character and consequence. It remains to be seen whether games can make a similar transition. Contemporary games can pump us full of adrenaline, they can make us laugh, but they have not yet provoked us to tears. And many have argued that, since games don't have characters of human complexity or stories that stress the consequences of our actions, they cannot achieve the status of true art. Here, we must be careful not to confuse the current transitional state of an emerging medium with its full potential. As I visit game companies, I see some of the industry's best minds struggling with this question and see strong evidence that the games released over the next few years will bring us closer and closer to the quality of characterization we have come to expect from other forms of popular narrative.

13   In the March 6 issue *of Newsweek*, senior editor Jack Kroll argued that audiences will probably never be able to care as deeply about pixels on the computer screen as they care about characters in films: "Moviemakers don't have to simulate human beings; they are right there, to be recorded and orchestrated. . . . The top-heavy titillation of Tomb Raider's Lara Croft falls flat next to the face of Sharon Stone. . . . Any player who's moved to tumescence by digibimbo Lara is in big trouble." Yet countless viewers cry when Bambi's mother dies, and World War II veterans can tell you they felt real lust for *Esquire's* Vargas girls. We have learned to care as much about creatures of pigment as we care about images of real people. Why should pixels be different?

14   In the end, games may not take the same path as cinema. Game designers will almost certainly develop their own aesthetic principles as they confront the challenge of balancing our competing desires for storytelling and interactivity. It remains to be seen whether games can provide players the freedom they want and still provide an emotionally satisfying and thematically meaningful shape to the experience. Some of the best games—Tetris comes to mind—have nothing to do with storytelling. For all we know, the future art of games may look more like architecture or dance than cinema.

15   Such questions warrant close and passionate engagement not only within the game industry or academia, but also by the press and around the dinner table. Even Kroll's grumpy dismissal of games has sparked heated discussion and forced designers to refine their own grasp of the medium's distinctive features. Imagine what a more robust form of criticism could contribute. We need critics who know games the way Pauline Kael knew movies and who write about them with an equal degree of wit and wisdom.

16   When *The Seven Lively Arts* was published, silent cinema was still an experimental form, each work stretching the medium in new directions. Early film critics played vital functions in documenting innovations and speculating about their potential. Computer games are in a similar phase. We have not had time to codify what experienced game designers know, and we have certainly not yet established a canon of great works that might serve as exemplars. There have been real creative accomplishments in games, but we haven't really sorted out what they are and why they matter.

17   But games do matter, because they spark the imaginations of our children, taking them on epic quests to strange new worlds. Games matter because our children no longer have access to real-world play spaces at a time when we've paved over the vacant lots to make room for more condos and the streets make parents nervous. If children are going to have opportunities for exploratory play, play that encourages cognitive development and fosters problem-solving skills, they will do so in the virtual environments of games. Multi-player games create opportunities for leadership, competition, teamwork and collaboration—for nerdy kids, not just for high school football players. Games matter because they form the digital equivalent of the Head Start program, getting kids excited about what computers can do.

18   The problem with most contemporary games isn't that they are violent but that they are banal, formulaic and predictable. Thoughtful criticism can marshal support for innovation and experimentation in the industry, much as good film criticism helps focus attention on neglected independent films. Thoughtful criticism could even contribute to our debates about game violence. So far, the censors and culture warriors have gotten more or less a free ride because we almost take for granted that games are culturally worthless. We should instead look at games as an emerging art form—one that does not simply simulate violence but increasingly offers new ways to understand violence—and talk about how to strike a balance between this form of expression and social responsibility. Moreover, game criticism may provide a means of holding the game industry more accountable for its choices. In the wake of the Columbine shootings, game designers are struggling with their ethical responsibilities as never before, searching for ways of appealing to empowerment fantasies that don't require exploding heads and gushing organs. A serious public discussion of this medium might constructively influence these debates, helping identify and evaluate alternatives as they emerge.

19   As the art of games matures, progress will be driven by the most creative and forward-thinking minds in the industry, those who know that games can be more than they have been, those who recognize the potential of reaching a broader public, of having a greater cultural impact, of generating more diverse and ethically responsible content and of creating richer and more emotionally engaging stories. But without the support of an informed public and the perspective of thoughtful critics, game developers may never realize that potential.

Discussion Questions

1. What seems to be the author's main purpose in comparing video games with cinema?
2. What points of comparison does the essay make between video games and cinema? Do those points of comparison seem valid?
3. What was the rhetorical advantage of referring to Gilbert Seldes' 1925 essay in paragraph 7 and 8?
4. How is paragraph 11 organized and why is this paragraph important to the overall comparison?
5. What differences does the author point out between cinema and video games? Do these differences undercut or support his main purpose?
6. In paragraph 2, the author asks whether games teach our children to kill. Does his essay answer the question, and if it does not, does this weaken his comparison-based argument?
7. The author does not mention a lot of specific games. Why might he have made that rhetorical choice? Does it weaken his comparison?

Toward Key Insights

Often comparisons can be used to see something familiar in a new way. In this case, the author is attempting to get us to see the ways video games might be an art form. How might our idea of everyday things change if we look at advertisements as art, everyday objects as sculpture, or short messages as poetry? Are such startling comparisons appropriate or useful?

The author stresses a number of similarities between video games and cinema. That can shape our perceptions. A critical response to comparisons requires us to look for points of disagreements. In what ways may video games be significantly and forever different from cinema?

Suggestions for Writing

Write about how some other popular culture events or objects might be like art. For example, basketball could be like dance; comic books could be like visual art; extreme sports could be like ballet.

Video games such as Lara Croft have been made into movies and movies such as the Matrix *have been made into video games. Compare a specific video game with its movie counterpart.*

CAUSE AND EFFECT

Reading Strategies

1. Identify the main event that is trying to be explained or the event whose effects are being studied.
2. Determine whether the writer is identifying a chain of causes that yield a result or is considering multiple causes for the same event.
3. Be careful. In more sophisticated academic writing, authors often look at several causes that they try to show are not the real explanation. Only after ruling out some key explanations do they offer the explanation that they think is most plausible.

4. It can be helpful to make a diagram showing the connection between the causes and the effects..

Reading Critically

1. Evaluate the evidence the writer gives for the relationship between cause and effect. How does he or she prove that the cause(s) have the effect(s) in question?
2. Try to determine if there could be other causes or effects that the writer hasn't mentioned.
3. Writers often confuse "correlation" for causation. Just because something happens before or around another event doesn't mean that it is the cause of the event. Just because George W. Bush was president when the terrorists attacked the World Trade Centers does not mean that his presidency was in any way a cause of the attack. Does the writer confuse correlation and causation?

Reading As a Writer

1. Note how the writer organizes the causes and effects to keep them clear and distinct.
2. Observe what devices the writer uses to demonstrate the connection between the causes and the effects.
3. Examine how the writer pulls his or her ideas together in the conclusion.

RICHARD TOMKINS

Old Father Time Becomes a Terror

Richard Tomkins is consumer industries editor of the Financial Times, *where he has been a member of the editorial staff since 1983. He is currently based at the company's London headquarters, where he leads a team of journalists covering the consumer goods sector and writes about consumer trends. Previously, he was the* FT*'s marketing correspondent and, from 1993 to 1999, he was a correspondent in the newspaper's New York bureau, where he covered the consumer goods sector. Earlier positions in London included writing about the transport sector and corporate news. Tomkins was born in Walsall, England, in 1952. His formal education ended at the age of seventeen. Before becoming a journalist, he was a casual laborer, a factory worker, a truck driver, a restaurant cashier, a civil servant, and an assistant private secretary to a government minister. He left government service in 1978 to hitchhike around the world, and on returning to the U.K. in 1979, joined a local newspaper as a trainee reporter. He joined the* FT *as a subeditor four years later. In this selection, Tomkins discusses the time squeeze that many people are experiencing and offers a way to combat the problem.*

Introduction: paragraphs 1–8; compares the leisurely 1960s (paragraphs 1–5) with the time-stressed present.

1   It's barely 6:30 A.M. and already your stress levels are rising. You're late for a breakfast meeting. Your cell-phone is ringing and your pager is beeping. You have 35 messages in your e-mail, 10 calls on your Voicemail and one question on your mind.

2   Why was it never like this for Dick Van Dyke?

3   Somehow, life seemed much simpler in the 1960s. In *The Dick Van Dyke Show,* the classic American sitcom of the era, Rob Petrie's job as a television scriptwriter

---

Richard Tomkins, "Old Father Time Becomes a Terror," from *Financial Times*, March 20, 1999. Reprinted by permission.

was strictly nine-to-five. It was light when he left for work and light when he got home. There was no teleconferencing during his journey from the Westchester suburbs to the TV studio in Manhattan.

4   At work, deadlines loomed, but there was plenty of time for banter around the office typewriter. There was no Internet, no Voicemail, no fax machine, no CNN. The nearest Petrie came to information overload was listening to a stream of wisecracks from his colleague Buddy Sorrell about Mel, the bald producer.

5   Meanwhile, at home, Rob's wife Laura—Mary Tyler Moore—led a life of leisure. After packing little Richie off to school, she had little to do but gossip with Millie, the next-door neighbour, and prepare the evening meal. When Rob came home, the family sat down to dinner: then it was television, and off to bed.

6   Today, this kind of life seems almost unimaginable. The demands on our time seem to grow ever heavier. Technology has made work portable, allowing it to merge with our personal lives. The nine-to-five job is extinct: in the U.S. people now talk about the 24–7 job, meaning one that requires your commitment 24 hours a day, seven days a week.

7   Home life has changed, too. Laura and Millie no longer have time for a gossip: they are vice-presidents at a bank. Richie's after-school hours are spent at karate classes and Chinese lessons. The only person at home any more is Buddy, who went freelance six months ago after being de-layered by Mel.

8   New phrases have entered the language to express the sense that we are losing control of our lives. "Time famine" describes the mismatch between things to do and hours to do them in, and "multi-tasking" the attempt to reconcile the two. If multi-tasking works, we achieve "time deepening," making better use of the time available: but usually it proves inadequate, resulting in "hurry sickness" and an increasingly desperate search for "life balance" as the sufferer moves closer to break-down.

9   It was not supposed to be this way. Technology, we thought, would make our lives easier. Machines were expected to do our work for us, leaving us with ever-increasing quantities of time to fritter away on idleness and pleasure.

10   But instead of liberating us, technology has enslaved us. Innovations are occurring at a bewildering rate: as many now arrive in a year as once arrived in a millennium. And as each invention arrives, it eats further into our time.

> Body: paragraphs 10–31

11   The motor car, for example, promised unimaginable levels of personal mobility. But now, traffic in cities moves more slowly than it did in the days of the horse-drawn carriage, and we waste our lives immobilized by congestion.

> First cause and specific effects of time stress, paragraphs 10–14: technological innovations

12   The aircraft promised new horizons, too. The trouble is, it delivered them. Its very existence created a demand for time-consuming journeys that we would never previously have dreamed of undertaking—the transatlantic shopping expedition, for example, or the trip to a convention on the other side of the world.

13   In most cases, technology has not saved time, but enabled us to do more things. In the home, washing machines promised to free women from the drudgery of the laundry. In reality, they encouraged us to change our clothes daily instead of weekly, creating seven times as much washing and ironing. Similarly, the weekly bath has been replaced by the daily shower, multiplying the hours spent on personal grooming.

14   Meanwhile, technology has not only allowed work to spread into our leisure time—the laptop-on-the-beach syndrome—but added the new burden of dealing with faxes, e-mails and Voicemails. It has also provided us with the opportunity to spend hours fixing software glitches on our personal computers or filling our heads with useless information from the Internet.

15   Technology apart, the Internet points the way to a second reason why we feel so time-pressed: the information explosion.

16   A couple of centuries ago, nearly all the world's accumulated learning could be contained in the heads of a few philosophers. Today, those heads could not hope to accommodate more than a tiny fraction of the information generated in a single day.

17   News, facts and opinions pour in from every corner of the world. The television set offers 150 channels. There are millions of Internet sites. Magazines, books and CD-Roms proliferate.

18   "In the whole world of scholarship, there were only a handful of scientific journals in the 18th century, and the publication of a book was an event," says Edward Wilson, honorary curator in entymology at Harvard University's museum of comparative zoology. "Now, I find myself subscribing to 60 or 70 journals or magazines just to keep me up with what amounts to a minute proportion of the expanding frontiers of scholarship."

19   There is another reason for our increased stress levels, too: rising prosperity. As ever-larger quantities of goods and services are produced, they have to be consumed. Driven on by advertising, we do our best to oblige: we buy more, travel more and play more, but we struggle to keep up. So we suffer from what Wilson calls discontent with super abundance—the confusion of endless choice.

20   Of course, not everyone is overstressed. "It's a convenient shorthand to say we're all time-starved, but we have to remember that it only applies to, say, half the population," says Michael Willmott, director of the Future Foundation, a London research company.

21   "You've got people retiring early, you've got the unemployed, you've got other people maybe only peripherally involved in the economy who don't have this situation at all. If you're unemployed, your problem is that you've got too much time, not too little."

22   Paul Edwards, chairman of the London-based Henley Centre forecasting group, points out that the feeling of pressures can also be exaggerated, or self-imposed. "Everyone talks about it so much that about 50 percent of unemployed or retired people will tell you they never have enough time to get things done," he says. "It's almost got to the point where there's stress envy. If you're not stressed, you're not succeeding. Everyone wants to have a little bit of this stress to show they're an important person."

23   There is another aspect to all of this too. Hour-by-hour logs kept by thousands of volunteers over the decades have shown that, in the U.K., working hours have risen only slightly in the last 10 years, and in the U.S., they have actually fallen—even for those in professional and executive jobs, where the perceptions of stress are highest.

24   In the U.S., John Robinson, professor of sociology at the University of Maryland, and Geoffrey Godbey, professor of leisure studies at Penn State University, both time-use experts, found that, since the mid-1960s, the average American had gained five hours a week in free time—that is, time left after working, sleeping, commuting, caring for children and doing the chores.

25   The gains, however, were unevenly distributed. The people who benefited the most were singles and empty-nesters. Those who gained the least—less than an hour—were working couples with pre-school children, perhaps reflecting the trend for parents to spend more time nurturing their offspring.

26   There is, of course, a gender issue here, too. Advances in household appliances may have encouraged women to take paying jobs: but as we have already

noted, technology did not end household chores. As a result, we see appalling inequalities in the distribution of free time between the sexes. According to the Henley Centre, working fathers in the U.K. average 48 hours of free time a week. Working mothers get 14.

27   Inequalities apart, the perception of the time famine is widespread, and has provoked a variety of reactions. One is an attempt to gain the largest possible amount of satisfaction from the smallest possible investment of time. People today want fast food, sound bytes and instant gratification. And they become upset when time is wasted.

First general effect of time stress, paragraphs 27–28: maximizing pleasure in minimum time

28   "People talk about quality time. They want perfect moments," says the Henley Centre's Edwards. "If you take your kids to a movie and McDonald's and it's not perfect, you've wasted an afternoon, and it's a sense that you've lost something precious. If you lose some money you can earn some more, but if you waste time you can never get it back."

29   People are also trying to buy time. Anything that helps streamline our lives is a growth market. One example is what Americans call concierge services—domestic help, child care, gardening and decorating. And on-line retailers are seeing big increases in sales—though not, as yet, profits.

Second general effect: buying time

30   A third reaction to time famine has been the growth of the work-life debate. You hear more about people taking early retirement or giving up high pressure jobs in favour of occupations with shorter working hours. And bodies such as Britain's National Work-Life Forum have sprung up, urging employers to end the long-hours culture among managers—"presenteeism"—and to adopt family-friendly working policies.

Third general effect: re-evaluating jobs, long work hours

31   The trouble with all these reactions is that liberating time—whether by making better use of it, buying it from others or reducing the amount spent at work—is futile if the hours gained are immediately diverted to other purposes.

32   As Godbey points out, the stress we feel arises not from a shortage of time, but from the surfeit of things we try to cram into it. "It's the kid in the candy store," he says. "There's just so many good things to do. The array of choices is stunning. Our free time is increasing, but not as fast as our sense of the necessary."

Conclusion: paragraphs 32–36: sources of time stress; author's solution to the problem

33   A more successful remedy may lie in understanding the problem rather than evading it.

34   Before the industrial revolution, people lived in small communities with limited communications. Within the confines of their village, they could reasonably expect to know everything that was to be known, see everything that was to be seen, and do everything that was to be done.

35   Today, being curious by nature, we are still trying to do the same. But the global village is a world of limitless possibilities, and we can never achieve our aim.

36   It is not more time we need: it is fewer desires. We need to switch off the cellphone and leave the children to play by themselves. We need to buy less, read less and travel less. We need to set boundaries for ourselves, or be doomed to mounting despair.

Discussion Questions

1. Identify the thesis statement of this essay and suggest why it is located at this spot.

2. The following sentence appears in paragraph 4: "There is no Internet, no Voicemail, no fax machine, no CNN." What does the structure of this sentence accomplish?

3. Reread paragraph 14 and then suggest Tomkins's intention in using the word "opportunity."
4. Explain the meaning of "the confusion of endless choice" at the end of paragraph 19. Then suggest examples that illustrate this idea.
5. Why do you think Tomkins calls attention to groups that are unstressed (paragraph 21) and to studies showing the time gains for average Americans?

Toward Key Insights

Regarding the essay's final sentence, what type of boundaries do you think time-stressed individuals should set?

How can people establish these boundaries without sacrificing quality of life?

Suggestion for Writing

Write an essay discussing the causes and/or effects of some type of stress other than time stress. Possibilities might include academic or financial stress or the stress associated with personal relationships. Develop your paper with appropriate examples.

CAROLINE KNAPP

Why We Keep Stuff: If You Want to Understand People, Take a Look at What They Hang On To

Caroline Knapp, a humane and thoughtful writer, died at the age of 42 in 2002. She worked for the Phoenix newspapers as staff writer, editor, and contributing columnist. This essay is taken from The Merry Recluse: A Life in Essay—*a collection of some of the best of Knapp's writing.*

1 Stuff, stuff, I AM surrounded by stuff. Stuff I don't need, stuff I don't use, but stuff I feel compelled to keep. Here in my office, as I write this, I am drowning in a sea of stuff.

2 There is the stuff of procrastination—piles of letters I should answer, manuscripts I should return, memos I should file away.

3 There is the stuff of daily business—interoffice communications in one heap here, this form and that form in that heap there, bills in yet another.

4 But mostly, there is the more generalized stuff, the stuff we all hold on to for inexplicable reasons—the stuff, in other words, of which stuff is made. Old catalogs of stuff I *might* want to order someday. Old magazines I *might* want to read, or reread. Unsolicited freelance articles I *might* want to publish. And even more useless stuff, stuff with no discernible purpose or future value.

5 On one corner of a shelf hangs a bunch of ribbons, saved over the years from various packages. On another, a pile of old letters from readers that I'll no doubt never open again and never answer. On my desk, a Rolodex crammed

with numbers I'll never call (the National Association of Theater Operators? The Detroit office of the National Transportation Union? *Huh?*). In one corner, I even have a pile of envelopes containing transaction slips from the automatic teller machine that date all the way back to February 1988. That's more than three years of bank slips—stuff, pure and simple.

6   Yet in an odd way, a lot of the stuff has meaning. Granted, the significance of a pile of old ribbons may be minimal, but I think the things that people choose to hang on to, and the ways they hang on to them, are quite telling—small testimonies to the ways people organize their lives on both external and internal levels. Want to understand people a little more clearly? Look through their stuff.

. . .

7   Several years ago, as I was preparing to move out of an apartment I'd lived in for four years, I undertook my first major purge of stuff, which provided an excellent lesson in the nature of the beast. Historically, I've been a relentless pack rat, the sort of person who keeps vast numbers of relics and mementos in vast numbers of boxes around the house—ticket stubs to concerts and movies; store receipts for goods and clothing I'd long ago stopped thinking about returning; letters from people I'd long ago lost track of; even old shoes. But moving out of that particular apartment was a big step—I was leaving a place where I'd lived alone (with plenty of room for stuff) and into a new apartment—and presumably, a new life—with a man (who had much less room for stuff).

8   Accordingly, the purge was more than a logistical necessity; it also had a certain psychological value. Sure, it made sense to get rid of a lot of it: I didn't really need to hang on to that broken toaster-oven, or that tattered coat I'd stopped wearing years before. I didn't need to save the letter of acceptance from the graduate school I'd long ago decided not to attend. I didn't need the three boxes of back issues of *Gourmet* magazine. But divesting myself of all that stuff meant much more than whittling down my possessions to a manageable degree.

9   At one point, I remember going through a dresser in which I kept several pairs of jeans that I'd worn during a long and protracted struggle with anorexia. They were tiny jeans in tiny, skeletal sizes, jean with bad associations, jeans with no place in the life of someone who was trying to launch into a healthier way of living. But I'd held on to them for years and, in doing so, had held on to a set of possibilities: that I might one day need those tiny, cigarette-legged jeans again; that I might one day fit into them; and accordingly, that what I felt to be my "recovery" from anorexia might be tenuous at best, false at worst.

10   The message hidden away in that dresser drawer had to do with fear, and, needless to say, throwing out the clothes from that earlier time was an enormously healthy move: it was part of an effort to say good-bye to a person I used to be.

11   And so it is with most of our stuff: the things we keep stored away in our closets and shelves often mirror the things we hold on to inside: fears, memories, dreams, false perceptions. A good deal of that stuff in my office, for example, speaks to an abiding terror of screwing up, a fear that I might actually *need* one of those articles from one of those old magazines, or one of those old phone numbers from the Rolodex, or one of those memos or letters or whatever.

12   Lurking behind the automatic-teller-machine slips? My relentless fear of finance, and the accompanying conviction that as soon as I toss them all out, the bank will call and inform me that some huge deposit I could once verify has disappeared. Even the pile of ribbons on the shelf reflects some vague anxiety, a (comparatively minor and obsessive) worry—that one of these days, I'll have a present to wrap and (gasp) there'll be no ribbon at hand to tie it up. My mother keeps a

huge basket at home filled with nothing but rubber bands, and I'm sure she holds on to it for the same reasons: it speaks to an absolute certainty on her part that the moment she throws them away, she'll find herself in desperate need of an elastic.

13   We might need it. We might miss it. It might come back in style and we might want to wear it again. If getting rid of stuff is hard, it's because it feels like cutting off options. Or sides of ourselves. Or pieces of our history. And, the actual value of holding on to stuff notwithstanding, those things can be unsettling to give up. The movie and ticket stubs I'd kept stored away for years in my old apartment, for example, reflected good times, happy moments in relationships that I didn't want to forget; the ragged coat was a piece of clothing I'd felt pretty in, a feeling I didn't want to lose; the *Gourmet* magazines held out hopes for my (then sorely lacking) kitchen skills. Even the broken toaster-oven contained a memory—I'd bought it almost a decade earlier, with a man I'd been involved with, during a very happy year we'd lived together.

14   The trick, I suppose, is to learn to manage stuff, the same way you learn to manage fears and feelings. To throw a little logic into the heaps of stuff. To think a little rationally. Would the world really come crashing down if I tossed out some crucial phone number? Would my personal history really get tossed into the trash along with my mementos? Would I die, or even suffer a mite, without all those ribbons?

15   No, probably not. But I think I'll keep holding on to those bank slips . . . just in case.

BOSTON PHOENIX
JUNE 1991

Discussion Questions

1. What is the value of a personal reflective essay such as this one for writer and reader?
2. What is the real thesis of this essay and where is it located?
3. What role do the several paragraphs detailing the kinds of clutter the author has failed to discard play in the full essay? Why did she spend so much time describing her stuff?
4. What does the author see as the dominant cause for why people fail to discard things? How does the more general cause relate to many other more specific causes?
5. In what ways does this writer sustain a personal and even intimate tone with her readers? Is this effective?
6. How do the final two paragraphs fit the essay?

Toward Key Insights

This essay provides an excellent example of a personal reflective essay. As a result, the author's discussion of why we keep certain things is not scientific. What might be the advantages of this kind of essay over a psychological study of why people retain certain items? What are some weaknesses of this kind of writing?

In the personal reflective essay, writers share with their readers more personal elements of their thoughts and lives, such as Caroline Knapp's discussion of her past struggle with anorexia. How do such intimate revelations affect readers and their relationship with the text?

Suggestion for Writing

Write a personal reflective essay to explain what you think cause some personal behaviors or emotional states, such as procrastination or impulse shopping, for readers who may share those behaviors.

ANNE ROIPHE

Why Marriages Fail

A native of New York City, Anne Roiphe was born in 1935 and earned a BA degree from Sarah Lawrence College in 1957. In a writing career spanning more than three decades, she has produced nearly a dozen works of fiction and nonfiction centering on such matters as alienation, divorce, religious tradition, children's emotional health, and the conflicts arising from the demands of family and the desire for independence. Her many periodical articles reflect these as well as similar concerns. In this essay Roiphe examines the forces leading to marital breakup.

1   These days so many marriages end in divorce that our most sacred vows no longer ring with truth. "Happily ever after" and "Till death do us part" are expressions that seem on the way to becoming obsolete. Why has it become so hard for couples to stay together? What goes wrong? What has happened to us that close to one-half of all marriages are destined for the divorce courts? How could we have created a society in which 42 percent of our children will grow up in single-parent homes? If statistics could only measure loneliness, regret, pain, loss of self-confidence and fear of the future, the numbers would be beyond quantifying.

2   Even though each broken marriage is unique, we can still find the common perils, the common causes for marital despair. Each marriage has crisis points and each marriage tests endurance, the capacity for both intimacy and change. Outside pressures such as job loss, illness, infertility, trouble with a child, care of aging parents and all the other plagues of life hit marriage the way hurricanes blast our shores. Some marriages survive these storms and others don't. Marriages fail, however, not simply because of the outside weather but because the inner climate becomes too hot or too cold, too turbulent or too stupefying.

3   When we look at how we choose our partners and what expectations exist at the tender beginnings of romance, some of the reasons for disaster become quite clear. We all select with unconscious accuracy a mate who will recreate with us the emotional patterns of our first homes. Dr. Carl A. Whitaker, a marital therapist and emeritus professor of psychiatry at the University of Wisconsin, explains, "From early childhood on, each of us carried models for marriage, femininity, masculinity, motherhood, fatherhood and all the other family roles." Each of us falls in love with a mate who has qualities of our parents, who will help us rediscover both the psychological happiness and miseries of our past lives. We may think we have found a man unlike Dad, but then he turns to drink or drugs, or loses his job over and over again or sits silently in front of the TV just the way Dad did. A man may choose a woman who doesn't like kids just like his mother or who gambles away the family savings just like his mother. Or he may choose a

slender wife who seems unlike his obese mother but then turns out to have other addictions that destroy their mutual happiness.

4   A man and a woman bring to their marriage bed a blended concoction of conscious and unconscious memories of their parents' lives together. The human way is to compulsively repeat and recreate the patterns of the past. Sigmund Freud so well described the unhappy design that many of us get trapped in: the unmet needs of childhood, the angry feelings left over from frustrations of long ago, the limits of trust and the recurrence of old fears. Once an individual senses this entrapment, there may follow a yearning to escape, and the result could be a broken, splintered marriage.

5   Of course people can overcome the habits and attitudes that developed in childhood. We all have hidden strengths and amazing capacities for growth and creative change. Change, however, requires work—observing your part in a rotten pattern, bringing difficulties out into the open—and work runs counter to the basic myth of marriage: "When I wed this person all my problems will be over. I will have achieved success and I will become the center of life for this other person and this person will be my center, and we will mean everything to each other forever." This myth, which every marriage relies on, is soon exposed. The coming of children, the pulls and tugs of their demands on affection and time, place a considerable strain on that basic myth of meaning everything to each other, of merging together and solving all of life's problems.

6   Concern and tension about money take each partner away from the other. Obligations to demanding parents or still-depended-upon parents create further strain. Couples today must also deal with all the cultural changes brought on in recent years by the women's movement and the sexual revolution. The altering of roles and the shifting of responsibilities have been extremely trying for many marriages.

7   These and other realities of life erode the visions of marital bliss the way sandstorms eat at rock and the ocean nibbles away at the dunes. Those euphoric, grand feelings that accompany romantic love are really self-delusions, self-hypnotic dreams that enable us to forge a relationship. Real life, failure at work, disappointments, exhaustion, bad smells, bad colds and hard times all puncture the dream and leave us stranded with our mate, with our childhood patterns pushing us this way and that, with our unfulfilled expectations.

8   The struggle to survive in marriage requires adaptability, flexibility, genuine love and kindness and an imagination strong enough to feel what the other is feeling. Many marriages fall apart because either partner cannot imagine what the other wants or cannot communicate what he or she needs or feels. Anger builds until it erupts into a volcanic burst that buries the marriage in ash.

9   It is not hard to see, therefore, how essential communication is for a good marriage. A man and a woman must be able to tell each other how they feel and why they feel the way they do; otherwise they will impose on each other roles and actions that lead to further unhappiness. In some cases, the communication patterns of childhood—of not talking, of talking too much, of not listening, of distrust and anger, of withdrawal—spill into the marriage and prevent a healthy exchange of thoughts and feelings. The answer is to set up new patterns of communication and intimacy.

10   At the same time, however, we must see each other as individuals. "To achieve a balance between separateness and closeness is one of the major psychological tasks of all human beings at every stage of life," says Dr. Stuart Bartle, a psychiatrist at the New York University Medical Center.

11   If we sense from our mate a need for too much intimacy, we tend to push him or her away, fearing that we may lose our identities in the merging of marriage. One partner may suffocate the other partner in a childlike dependency.

12   A good marriage means growing as a couple but also growing as individuals. This isn't easy. Richard gives up his interest in carpentry because his wife, Helen, is jealous of the time he spends away from her. Karen quits her choir group because her husband dislikes the friends she makes there. Each pair clings to each other and are angry with each other as life closes in on them. This kind of marital balance is easily thrown as one or the other pulls away and divorce follows.

13   Sometimes people pretend that a new partner will solve the old problems. Most often extramarital sex destroys a marriage because it allows an artificial split between the good and the bad—the good is projected on the new partner and the bad is dumped on the head of the old. Dishonesty, hiding and cheating create walls between men and women. Infidelity is just a symptom of trouble. It is a symbolic complaint, a weapon of revenge, as well as an unraveler of closeness. Infidelity is often that proverbial last straw that sinks the camel to the ground.

14   All right—marriage has always been difficult. Why then are we seeing so many divorces at this time? Yes, our modern social fabric is thin, and yes the permissiveness of society has created unrealistic expectations and thrown the family into chaos. But divorce is so common because people today are unwilling to exercise the self-discipline that marriage requires. They expect easy joy, like the entertainment on TV, the thrill of a good party.

15   Marriage takes some kind of sacrifice, not dreadful self-sacrifice of the soul, but some level of compromise. Some of one's fantasies, some of one's legitimate desires have to be given up for the value of the marriage itself. "While all marital partners feel shackled at times it is they who really choose to make the marital ties into confining chains or supporting bonds," says Dr. Whitaker. Marriage requires sexual, financial and emotional discipline. A man and a woman cannot follow every impulse, cannot allow themselves to stop growing or changing.

16   Divorce is not an evil act. Sometimes it provides salvation for people who have grown hopelessly apart or were frozen in patterns of pain or mutual unhappiness. Divorce can be, despite its initial devastation, like the first cut of the surgeon's knife, a step toward new health and a good life. On the other hand, if the partners can stay past the breaking up of the romantic myths into the development of real love and intimacy, they have achieved a work as amazing as the greatest cathedrals of the world. Marriages that do not fail but improve, that persist despite imperfections, are not only rare these days but offer a wondrous shelter in which the face of our mutual humanity can safely show itself.

Discussion Questions

1. State in your own words what Roiphe means when she remarks at the end of paragraph 1, "If statistics could only measure loneliness, regret, pain, loss of self-confidence and fear of the future, the numbers would be beyond quantifying."

2. In which paragraphs does Roiphe cite expert opinion? Why do you think she includes it?

3. What is accomplished by using the short sentence "This isn't easy" in paragraph 12?

4. What additional reasons can you cite for marriage failure?

Toward Key Insights

Which of the causes of marital breakdown do you consider most important? Why? What are the most essential things that couples can do to help lower the divorce rate?

Suggestion for Writing

Write an essay explaining why certain individuals do well (or poorly) at forming friendships. Develop your causes with relevant specific details.

BELINDA LUSCOMBE AND KATE STINCHFIELD

Why We Flirt

Often writers work together to create an article, especially in journalism but also in academic settings. Belinda Luscombe has been a Senior Editor for Time *magazine since April 1999. She started in journalism at* The Daily Telegraph *in Sidney, Australia. She joined* Time *in 1995. Her work also appears in* Sports Illustrated, Fortune, Mademoiselle, Vogue, *the* New York Times *and many other publications.*

Kate Stinchfield is a productive freelance writer who often writes for Time. *Other articles by her include "Early Bird or Night Owl? Brain Scans Show the Difference." and "The Science of Risk Taking."*

This article was published in Time *in January 2008.*

1   That smile! That glance! That rapt attention! We flirt even when we don't need to. And that can be good.

2   Contrary to widespread belief, only two very specific types of people flirt: those who are single and those who are married. Single people flirt because, well, they're single and therefore nobody is really contractually obliged to talk to them, sleep with them or scratch that difficult-to-reach part of the back. But married people, they're a tougher puzzle. They've found themselves a suitable— maybe even superior—mate, had a bit of productive fun with the old gametes and ensured that at least some of their genes are carried into the next generation. They've done their duty, evolutionarily speaking. Their genome will survive. Yay them. So for Pete's sake, why do they persist with the game?

3   And before you claim, whether single or married, that you never flirt, bear in mind that it's not just talk we're dealing with here. It's gestures, stance, eye movement. Notice how you lean forward to the person you're talking to and tip up your heels? Notice the quick little eyebrow raise you make, the sidelong glance coupled with the weak smile you give, the slightly sustained gaze you offer? If you're a woman, do you feel your head tilting to the side a bit, exposing either your soft, sensuous neck or, looking at it another way, your jugular? If you're a guy, are you keeping your body in an open, come-on-attack-me position, arms positioned to draw the eye to your impressive lower abdomen?

4   Scientists call all these little acts "contact-readiness" cues, because they indicate, nonverbally, that you're prepared for physical engagement. (More general body language is known as "nonverbal leakage." Deep in their souls, all scientists

are poets.) These cues are a crucial part of what's known in human-ethology circles as the "heterosexual relationship initiation process" and elsewhere, often on the selfsame college campuses, as "coming on to someone." In primal terms, they're physical signals that you don't intend to dominate, nor do you intend to flee—both useful messages potential mates need to send before they can proceed to that awkward talking phase. They're the opening line, so to speak, for the opening line.

5   One of the reasons we flirt in this way is that we can't help it. We're programmed to do it, whether by biology or culture. The biology part has been investigated by any number of researchers. Ethologist Irenaus Eibl Eibesfeldt, then of the Max Planck Institute in Germany, filmed African tribes in the 1960s and found that the women there did the exact same prolonged stare followed by a head tilt away with a little smile that he saw in America. (The technical name for the head movement is a "cant." Except in this case it's more like "can.")

6   Evolutionary biologists would suggest that those individuals who executed flirting maneuvers most adeptly were more successful in swiftly finding a mate and reproducing and that the behavior therefore became widespread in all humans. "A lot of people feel flirting is part of the universal language of how we communicate, especially nonverbally," says Jeffry Simpson, director of the social psychology program at the University of Minnesota.

7   Simpson is currently studying the roles that attraction and flirting play during different times of a woman's ovulation cycle. His research suggests that women who are ovulating are more attracted to flirty men. "The guys they find appealing tend to have characteristics that are attractive in the short term, which include some flirtatious behaviors," he says. He's not sure why women behave this way, but it follows that men who bed ovulating women have a greater chance of procreating and passing on those flirty genes, which means those babies will have more babies, and so on. Of course, none of this is a conscious choice, just as flirting is not always intentional. "With a lot of it, especially the nonverbal stuff, people may not be fully aware that they're doing it," says Simpson. "You don't see what you look like. People may emit flirtatious cues and not be fully aware of how powerful they are."

Flirting with Intent

8   Well, some people anyway. But then there are the rest of you. You know who you are. You're the gentleman who delivered my groceries the other day and said we had a problem because I had to be 21 to receive alcohol. You're me when I told that same man that I liked a guy who knew his way around a dolly. (Lame, I know. I was caught off guard.) You're the fifty something guy behind me on the plane before Christmas telling his fortysomething seatmate how sensual her eyes were—actually, I hope you're not, because if so, you're really skeevy. My point is, once you move into the verbal phase of flirtation, it's pretty much all intentional.

9   And there are some schools of thought that teach there's nothing wrong with that. Flirtation is a game we play, a dance for which everyone knows the moves. "People can flirt outrageously without intending anything," says independent sex researcher Timothy Perper, who has been researching flirting for 30 years. "Flirting captures the interest of the other person and says 'Would you like to play?'" And one of the most exhilarating things about the game is that the normal rules of social interaction are rubberized. Clarity is not the point. "Flirting opens a window of potential. Not yes, not no," says Perper. "So we engage ourselves in this complex game of maybe." The game is not new. The first

published guide for how to flirt was written about 2,000 years ago, Perper points out, by a bloke named Ovid. As dating books go, *The Art of Love* leaves more recent publications like *The Layguide: How to Seduce Women More Beautiful Than You Ever Dreamed Possible No Matter What You Look Like or How Much You Make* in its dust. And yes, that's a real book.

10   Once we've learned the game of maybe, it becomes second nature to us. Long after we need to play it, we're still in there swinging (so to speak) because we're better at it than at other games. Flirting sometimes becomes a social fall-back position. "We all learn rules for how to behave in certain situations, and this makes it easier for people to know how to act, even when nervous," says Antonia Abbey, a psychology professor at Wayne State University. Just as we learn a kind of script for how to behave in a restaurant or at a business meeting, she suggests, we learn a script for talking to the opposite sex. "We often enact these scripts without even thinking," she says. "For some women and men, the script may be so well learned that flirting is a comfortable strategy for interacting with others." In other words, when in doubt, we flirt.

11   The thing that propels many already committed people to ply the art of woo, however, is often not doubt. It's curiosity. Flirting "is a way of testing one's mate-value and the possibility of alternatives—actually trying to see if someone might be available as an alternative," says Arthur Aron, professor of psychology at the State University of New York at Stony Brook. To evolutionary biologists, the advantages of this are clear: mates die, offspring die. Flirting is a little like taking out mating insurance.

12   If worst comes to worst and you don't still have it (and yes, I'm sure you do), the very act of flirting with someone else may bring about renewed attention from your mate, which has advantages all its own. So it's a win-win.

13   Flirting is also emotional capital to be expended in return for something else. Not usually for money, but for the intangibles—a better table, a juicier cut of meat, the ability to return an unwanted purchase without too many questions. It's a handy social lubricant, reducing the friction of everyday transactions, and closer to a strategically timed tip than a romantic overture. Have you ever met a male hairdresser who wasn't a flirt? Women go to him to look better. So the better they feel when they walk out of his salon, the happier they'll be to go back for a frequent blowout. Flirting's almost mandatory. And if the hairdresser is gay, so much the better, since the attention is much less likely to be taken as an untoward advance.

It's Dangerous Out There

14   But outside the hairdresser's chair, things are not so simple. Flirt the wrong way with the wrong person, and you run the risk of everything from a slap to a sexual-harassment lawsuit. And of course, the American virtue of plainspokenness is not an asset in an activity that is ambiguous by design. Wayne State's Abbey, whose research has focused on the dark side of flirting—when it transmogrifies into harassment, stalking or acquaintance rape—warns that flirting can be treacherous. "Most of the time flirtation desists when one partner doesn't respond positively," she says. "But some people just don't get the message that is being sent, and some ignore it because it isn't what they want to hear."

15   One of the most fascinating flirting laboratories is the digital world. Here's a venue that is all words and no body language; whether online or in text messages, nuance is almost impossible. And since text and e-mail flirting can be

done without having to look people in the eye, and is often done with speed, it is bolder, racier and unimpeded by moments of reflection on whether the message could be misconstrued or is wise to send at all. "Flirt texting is a topic everyone finds fascinating, although not much research is out there yet," says Abbey. But one thing is clear: "People are often more willing to disclose intimate details via the Internet, so the process may escalate more quickly."

16   That's certainly the case on sites like Yahoo!'s Married and Flirting e-mail group, as well as on Marriedbutplaying.com and Married-but-flirting.com. "Flirting" in this sense appears to be a euphemism for talking dirty. A University of Florida study of 86 participants in a chat room published in *Psychology Today* in 2003 found that while nearly all those surveyed felt they were initially simply flirting with a computer, not a real person, almost a third of them eventually had a face-to-face meeting with someone they chatted with. And all but two of the couples who met went on to have an affair. Whether the people who eventually cheated went to the site with the intention of doing so or got drawn in by the fantasy of it all is unclear. Whichever, the sites sure seem like a profitable place for people like the guy behind me on the pre-Christmas flight to hang out.

17   Most people who flirt—off-line at least—are not looking for an affair. But one of the things that sets married flirting apart from single flirting is that it has a much greater degree of danger and fantasy to it. The stakes are higher and the risk is greater, even if the likelihood of anything happening is slim. But the cock-tail is in some cases much headier. It is most commonly the case with affairs, therapists say, that people who cheat are not so much dissatisfied with their spouse as with themselves and the way their lives have turned out. There is little that feels more affirming and revitalizing than having someone fall in love with you. (It follows, then, that there's little that feels less affirming than being cheated on.) Flirting is a decaf affair, a way of feeling more alive, more vital, more desirable without actually endangering the happiness of anyone you love—or the balance of your bank account. So go ahead and flirt, if you can do it responsibly. You might even try it with your spouse.

A Field Guide to Flirting

Humans observed in a natural mating habitat—here, the Cock and Bull Pub in Los Angeles and Helm's Bakery in neighboring Culver City—exhibit nearly all the major flirting behaviors, whether or not they're flirting at all.

1. **Open Body Position** This come-and-get-me stance suggests the man is neither about to flee nor fight.
2. **Raised Eyebrows** Upon first seeing a potential mate, both men and women often briefly raise their eyebrows.
3. **Head Cant** Women frequently tilt their head to one side, exposing their neck, and sometimes flick their hair at the same time.
4. **Sustained Eye Contact** Men and women both hold the gaze of someone they're interested in for longer than feels quite comfortable.
5. **Leaning Forward** Both genders tend to lean in toward people they're attracted to. Sometimes they'll unconsciously point to them too, even if they're across the room.
6. **Leading Questions** A man will often ask a woman questions that allow her to show off her most attractive features.
7. **Sideways Glances** Often followed by a glance away or down and a shy smile, these coy looks are a classic flirting behavior for both sexes.

Discussion Questions

1. What are the different causes the writers identify for flirting behavior? Are those causes multiple different causes, a chain of causes, or a combination?
2. This essay was written initially for *Time*, a popular news magazine. How did that affect the style of the essay, what are some examples of this style, and how does that impact on the essay?
3. The article relies heavily on the use of experts. Based on some examples from the text, why have the writers adopted this approach? What effect does it have on the credibility of the essay?
4. Why do the writers take the time in paragraph 3 to describe physical nonverbal forms of flirting?
5. In the conclusion, the writers take a stance on flirting as a behavior. Does this conclusion follow appropriately from the rest of the essay?

Toward Key Insights

This essay assumes that there are key biological and social explanations for simple human behaviors. Does this model seem to suggest that all human behaviors can be explained? Is that good or bad?

What kinds of effects might reading such an explanation of a behavior have on readers?

Suggestion for Writing

Take a common behavior such as "small talk" or "fantasy role-playing" and either with or without research write a behavior and offer an explanation for the behavior.

DEFINITION

Reading Strategies

1. Clearly identify the term being defined.
2. Mark as you read the characteristics that are part of the defining characteristic of the concept. It can help to make a list of these defining characteristics.
3. Note specifically what the term being defined is *not* supposed to mean.
4. Observe any analogies, similes, or metaphors, noting specifically what the concept is suppose to be like.
5. Try to see if you can apply the concept.

Reading Critically

1. Check to see if the definition matches your intuition.
2. Determine if the definition is too narrow. If a person defines literature as works of fiction, the definition could leave out poetry.
3. Determine by applying the definition if it is too broad. If a person defines literature as works of writing, the definition would include phone books—a clearly unintended consequence of the definition.
4. Test if there are other available or possible definitions.

Reading As a Writer

1. Notice how the writer uses the introduction to explain the importance of the concept and the definition.

2. Identify the key strategies the writer uses to construct a definition—stating the defining characteristics, providing examples, indicating that to which the term does not apply.

3. Observe how the writer limits the definition so that it is not overapplied.

4. If the writer employs analogy, simile, or metaphor, determine how the device works in the context of the definition.

LAURENCE SHAMES

The Sweet Smell of Success Isn't All That Sweet

Laurence Shames (born 1951) is a native of Newark, New Jersey, and a graduate of New York University. After completing his education, he began a career as a nonfiction writer contributing to a variety of popular magazines and to the New York Times. *Shames's book-length publications include two nonfiction works,* The Big Time: The Harvard Business School's Most Successful Class and How It Shaped America *(1986) and* The Hunger for More *(1991), which focuses on the search for values in a world of greed. He also co-authored Peter Barton's memoir* Not Fade Away *(2003). He has also authored several fictional works, with an emphasis on detective fiction.* The Naked Detective *appeared in 2000. Shames's concern for values is apparent in this selection, which attacks contemporary attitudes about success.*

1   John Milton was a failure. In writing "Paradise Lost," his stated aim was to "justify the ways of God to men." Inevitably, he fell short of accomplishing that and only wrote a monumental poem. Beethoven, whose music was conceived to transcend Fate, was a failure, as was Socrates, whose ambition was to make people happy by making them reasonable and just. The inescapable conclusion seems to be that the surest, noblest way to fail is to set one's own standards titanically high.

Introduction: paragraphs 1–4: captures attention by ironically attacking high success standards, defending low standards

2   The flip-side of that proposition also seems true, and it provides the safe but dreary logic by which most of us live: The surest way to succeed is to keep one's strivings low—or at least to direct them along already charted paths. Don't set yourself the probably thankless task of making the legal system better; just shoot at becoming a partner in the firm. Don't agonize over questions about where your talents and proclivities might most fulfillingly lead you; just do a heads-up job of determining where the educational or business opportunities seem most secure.

3   After all, if "success" itself—rather than the substance of the achievements that make for success—is the criterion by which we measure ourselves and from which we derive our self-esteem, why make things more difficult by reaching for the stars?

4   What is this contemporary version of success really all about?

Body paragraphs 5–12

5   According to certain beer commercials, it consists in moving up to a premium brand that costs a dime or so more per bottle. Credit-card companies would have you believe success inheres in owning their particular piece of plastic.

Development by examples and brief definitions

<table>
<tr><td>Development by effect</td><td>6</td><td>If these examples sound petty, they are. But take those petty privileges, weave them into a fabric that passes for a value system and what you've got is a national mood that has vast motivating power that can shape at least the near future of the entire country.</td></tr>
</table>

Development by effect

6 If these examples sound petty, they are. But take those petty privileges, weave them into a fabric that passes for a value system and what you've got is a national mood that has vast motivating power that can shape at least the near future of the entire country.

Development by comparison, examples, and causes

7 Under the flag of success, modern-style, liberal arts colleges are withering while business schools are burgeoning—and yet even business schools are having an increasingly hard time finding faculty members, because teaching isn't considered "successful" enough. Amid a broad consensus that there is a glut of lawyers and an epidemic of strangling litigation, record numbers of young people continue to flock to law school because, for the individual practitioner, a law degree is still considered a safe ticket.

Development by effects

8 The most sobering thought of all is that today's M.B.A.'s and lawyers are tomorrow's M.B.A.'s and lawyers: Having invested so much time and money in their training, only a tiny percentage of them will ever opt out of their early chosen fields. Decisions made in accordance with today's hothouse notions of ambition are locking people into careers that will define and also limit their activities and yearnings for virtually the rest of their lives.

Development by effects and argument

9 Many, by external standards, will be "successes." They will own homes, eat in better restaurants, dress well and, in some instances, perform socially useful work. Yet there is a deadening and dangerous flaw in their philosophy: It has little room, little sympathy and less respect for the noble failure, for the person who ventures past the limits, who aims gloriously high and falls unashamedly short.

Development by effects

10 That sort of ambition doesn't have much place in a world where success is proved by worldly reward rather than by accomplishment itself. That sort of ambition is increasingly thought of as the domain of irredeemable eccentrics, of people who haven't quite caught on—and there is great social pressure not to be one of them.

Development by effects

11 The result is that fewer people are drawn to the cutting edge of noncommercial scientific research. Fewer are taking on the sublime, unwinnable challenges of the arts. Fewer are asking questions that matter—the ones that can't be answered. Fewer are putting themselves on the line, making as much of their minds and talents as they might.

Development by effect, causes, and comparison

12 The irony is that today's success-chasers seem obsessed with the idea of *not settling*. They take advanced degrees in business because they won't settle for just a so-so job. They compete for slots at law firms and investment houses because they won't settle for any but the fastest track. They seem to regard it as axiomatic that "success" and "settling" are opposites.

Conclusion: argues against contemporary notions of success

13 Yet in doggedly pursuing the rather brittle species of success now in fashion, they are restricting themselves to a chokingly narrow swath of turf along the entire range of human possibilities. Does it ever occur to them that, frequently, success is what people settle for when they can't think of something noble enough to be worth failing at?

Discussion Questions

1. Shames notes in paragraph 3 that "'success' itself—rather than the substance of the achievements that make for success—" seems to be the touchstone by which we measure our worth. What do you think he means? Why is the distinction positioned at this point?

2. Why do you think Shames ends his essay with a rhetorical question, that is, one for which no answer is expected?
3. To what extent do you agree with Shames's idea of success? Discuss.

Toward Key Insights

What evidence do you find that not all people are consumed by the desire for money? What qualities do you consider crucial to living a "good" life? To happiness?

Suggestion for Writing

Write a definition essay explaining how the popular view of responsibility, greed, marriage, single life, friendship, or some other concept needs redefining. Use whatever writing strategies advance your purpose.

MARC ZWELLING

The Blended Economy

Marc Zwelling graduated with a BS degree in journalism from Northwestern University in 1968. After graduating, he worked for Canadian Press, the Toronto Telegram, *and as public relations official for the United Steelworkers of America. He is currently president of Vector Research and Development, Inc., and conducts opinion surveys and completes feasibility studies. He has facilitated numerous workshops and written extensively about future trends. In our selection, he examines the changing nature of the business marketplace.*

1   The traditional way to innovate is to carve a specialized niche. Some building contractors specialize in renovating nineteenth-century homes. Lawyers practice trade law, criminal law, family law, labor law, immigration, copyright, or libel. Doctors can be ear-nose-throat specialists, gerontologists, or pediatricians. Specialization is efficient; specialists do their jobs faster because they know them better than non-specialists. And a niche is usually more profitable than the mass market from which someone sliced it. The trouble with a niche is that when competitors recognize it's profitable they rush in.

2   Blending is the opposite of specialization. Instead of burrowing deeper into a field or product to specialize, blending creates a new market category. The secret in the technique is to unite different, not similar, ideas, products, or services. Minivans and sport-utility vehicles, for example, grew from blending cars and trucks, creating whole new categories of consumer vehicles.

3   Companies can continually generate new ideas by blending. Most new products today are simply extrapolations of successful products, such as a faster microprocessor, a cheaper airline ticket, a smaller camera, and so on. These innovations eventually run out of possibilities. Blending different ideas instead produces limitless new directions for innovative products.

4   A food company searching for a new product for kids might think of blending different items from a list of opposites like "frozen or unfrozen," "milk or cola," "peanut butter or peanuts," "salad or soup." Perhaps kids who love peanuts would savor them in a soup. And perhaps a cola could be frozen so it would stay

Marc Zwelling, "The Blended Economy," from *The Futurist*, v. 36 no. 1 (Jan.–Feb. 2002), pp. 12–13. Reprinted by permission.

cold longer, requiring no ice. The ideas may prove impractical, nonsensical, or just plain awful, but the point is to generate more ideas because they can lead to practical products.

5   Blending also operates within social and economic trends. For instance, barriers are falling between work and leisure, devastating some retail clothing chains and department stores as employees don the same outfits at home and the office.

6   In the job market, there is vast potential to create opportunities by combining apparently unrelated occupations. Consider the number of specialists you must work with to buy or sell a house: There is a real estate agent, the loan officer, the building inspector, an insurance agent, and the mover. One specialist hands you off to another. The blending opportunity here is for, perhaps, a "home transitions" professional who can manage all these different steps.

6   Some employees may have over-specialized. Specialization narrows a worker's opportunities in a slowly growing economy and causes bottlenecks in a booming economy. Blending avoids these problems.

7   The *New York Times* recently reported unprecedented growth in the new profession of legal nurse consultant. From none a decade ago, there are more than 4,000 in America today. Blending the skills of nurses and lawyers, legal nurse consultants help lawyers in medical-related lawsuits. Blending professions is not the same as stacking one university degree on another. The legal nurse consultant is still a nurse, not a lawyer. Nurses learn enough law in training institutes to become legal nurse consultants.

8   Another example of a blended career opportunity might be an ergonomic architect—a designer and engineer with special training in child development to make safer houses for families with small children.

9   Try mixing and matching completely dissimilar occupations, such as carpenter, receptionist, software writer, investment adviser, security guard, dentist, chemical engineer, lifeguard, teacher, embalmer, chef, hairstylist, pharmacist, actor.

10   A list like this may yield few blended jobs in the literal sense, but it triggers thinking about ways to add value to products and services and differentiate businesses in super-competitive markets. For instance, a funeral home could offer caskets carved by its own carpenters. A supermarket could build customer loyalty if its meat cutters demonstrate cooking techniques. A chef with pharmaceutical training or a pharmacist with cooking skills could help customers create healthier meals using herbs and other natural supplements.

11   Career blending is most likely to develop among entrepreneurs, as attempts to blend work in traditional settings have historically met with resistance: Unions protest that management wants to make one employee do two jobs for one worker's pay. Management says unions obstruct change and efficiency.

12   Indeed, most fields resist merging and consolidating because of tradition. But since nobody can predict what the market will bear, the greater the number of innovations you can generate in products, services, and careers, the greater your chance of success.

Discussion Questions

1. In the first two paragraphs, the author contrasts blending with specialization. What might be his reason for such an approach?
2. What techniques does the writer use to define blends? How effective are those approaches?
3. What examples of blends were most effective, which least effective, and why?

Toward Key Insights

Often we are trapped in our thinking by established categories. How can blending help break us out of those established categories?

Suggestion for Writing

Create a blend of your own, perhaps even creating a new word for the blend just as brunch is a blend of breakfast and lunch. Write a short paper defining your blend.

MARTI BERCAW

Krumping

Marti Bercaw is a writer and video journalist at Social, *an online journal from which this article was taken. She loves dance and frequently writes about that topic. Other articles include "Celebrate Michael Jackson's Life and Music at University City Walk!" and "The Jabbawockeez: America's 1st Best Dance Crew."*

1   On the 3rd Saturday of every month **Tommy the Clown and Debbie Allen** have a "**Battle**" that hundreds of L.A. kids join. It is a Clowning Krumping dance war of the creative kind, organized by 2 dedicated adults who love dance, love kids and understand the power of expression through dance.

2   The location is the **Debbie Allen Dance Academy** in Culver City and the stage is a quasi-boxing ring set up in a huge studio. 500 chairs and standing-room-only space is filled to capacity by the time the show starts . . . and what a show it is!

3   Tommy the Clown serves as the Master of Ceremonies and referee with a whistle. Larry the Clown is the DJ who supplies a powerful mix of music. Ani Dizon, Tommy's manager, coordinates the whole event and process. Lil Tommy, Tommy's brother, is there to help when he is not traveling the world performing Clown and Krump Dance with his crew, and he teaches Clowning classes at D.A.D.A., too. ·

4   On stage, two girl to girl or boy to boy dancers challenge each other in a series of rounds. One opponent sits while the other performs.

5   Individual dancers "call each other out" as well as the members of a crew but it's always one performer at a time. Dancers have been as young as 4 with no limit on the high end. Everyone, even Grandparents, are welcome to battle onstage but teenagers are in the majority.

6   The audience is made up of kids, parents, grandparents and friends. The challenging dance crew changes every month, unless there is a rematch, and goes up against the current winning crew who holds onto the gold embellished championship belt until it passes to the next winner. There are cash prizes as well. The audience votes by applause at the end of each battle. Battle scores are tallied to determine the winning crew.

7   Sometimes it's clear who has won and sometimes they have to rely on an applause meter to determine the winner. It's a tough call because all the dancers are brilliant at freestyle . . . that's what it's all about.

Marti Bercaw, "Krumping." Marti Bercaw, Socal.com Writer. Reprinted by permission of the author.

About Krump

8   "Clowning" is movement invented by Tommy the Clown who developed the strange, stilted, goofy and erratic motion to entertain audiences as a clown at parties and local events around Los Angeles from as far back as 1992. Needless to say, it caught on in a big way.

9   Street dance has an evolutionary life of its own and it's very nature demands constant adaptation and change. What was once "Clowning" evolved to "Krump Dance" or Krumping. As Tommy put it, "Krumping is the dark side of Clowning." In homage to the clown, some dancers paint designs on half their face.

10   The first time I saw "Clowning/Krumping" was five years ago. Over time, it has spread to other cities in the US, Europe and Asia. "Rize," a documentary by David Lachappelle, permanently writes "Clowning" and "Krumping" into the pop history record. It will read that this dance was born in South Central Los Angeles beginning in the last decade of the century and was performed by inner city kids who, as the third generation who's offered hip hop, were hungry for something new. They made it happen.

Krump Described

11   Krumping incorporates extreme, almost impossible freestyle body motion, coordination and rhythm. Basics include chest popping, a Charlie Chaplin-esque, comic, stumbling, staccato stride and toe dance, feet that turn out, feet that turn in, arms that go wide in a ranting wave, the body jerking up and down, prancing, the torso bent from the waist that circles around the hips 360 degrees, raised arms that wrap over and around the body, the neck and head jutting forward, the mouth chattering as if in a real or silent monologue. The dance is frenzied and rapid, displaying a set of attitudes running the gamut from hostile to aggressive to seductive to comical and back again. Girls can be as good as the guys but there are fewer who compete. Their attitude can include more sexual, bump and grind elements with a flamboyant, exaggerated edge or they can have an attitude that is hard and aggressive, just like their male counterparts.

12   Krumping is not hip hop, though it uses the music and springs from the same mold. For now, it seems to stand alone as a pure urban expression.

13   It isn't pretty and it offers no apology because it tells a vivid story about being young in a hostile and dangerous world run amok. The dancer can shift from malevolent character to clown in a flash like what comes at you as you surf channels on a TV. Click, click. Life turns on a dime at the push of a button in today's world. We see the reflection in Krumping.

14   Debbie Allen and Tommy the Clown do Los Angeles a great service by providing and supporting the monthly "Battles." It is true that kids who would otherwise be involved with gangs or get into other trouble are given a creative alternative. But it is also true that these kids are already gifted, articulate about their medium and highly motivated to achieve excellence.

15   In exchange for the chance to perform, the "Clowns and Krumpers" offer everyone who cares about dance or the creation of dance form or the poetry of rap, or the embodied voice of our American culture a chance to witness art in the making.

Discussion Questions

1. What is the writer's overall purpose in writing this essay? Where is that purpose most evident?
2. Why does the author start the essay with a brief account of a specific competition?

3. What are some distinguishing features that help define Krumping?
4. The original online article had links to video clips of a Krumping competition. Where, if at all, would such video clips be helpful and why? Where would they not be needed and why?
5. In the end, the author identifies some positive features of Krumping. What impact do paragraphs 15 and 16 have on the reader?

Toward Key Insights

Increasingly, texts are being placed online where they can be supplemented by pictures as well as video and audio clips. To what extent does textual content like a definition need to stand on its own and to what extent can it depend on Web-based support material? You might want to consider the above essay as an example.

Cultural phenomenon like music and dance are especially hard to define. What are some of the challenges of defining things like Hip-Hop, Krumping, Breaking, and other similar phenomenon?

Suggestion for Writing

Take a contemporary movement such as Hip-Hop and, following the example of Marti Bercaw, write a definition paper explaining the movement.

ARGUMENT

Reading Strategies

1. Identify the background of the author if possible. Does the author bring any expertise or experience that helps make the argument more credible?
2. Read the introduction and conclusion to gain a sense of the thesis and main points of the argument.
3. Read the argument quickly to gain an overall sense of the major points of the essay and an understanding of the organizational pattern.
4. Look for the organizational pattern of the essay and keep an eye out for transition sentences. Often an author argues by first presenting the viewpoint of several other authors, then pointing out limitations of those views, then presenting his or her own position and offering support, and finally admitting possible limitations and problems with the author's position (possibly answering these objections). This pattern often confuses readers.
5. Read carefully to identify the major claims of the argument, the reasons for the author's position, and any evidence presented for any of the claims. It can be very helpful to outline an argument, making a special note of the major reasons and evidence for the claim. Note the author's approach. Is the argument mostly deductive or inductive? Does the author try to show the negative consequences of opposing views? Does the author base the argument on authority?

Reading Critically

1. Check to see if the author demonstrates any overt bias.
2. Test to determine if the reasons given really support the author's thesis.

3. Test to see if the evidence is adequate. Does the evidence support the claims? Is the source of the evidence trustworthy and unbiased? Is the evidence extensive or scanty? Could contrary evidence be offered?
4. Check the essay for informal fallacies.
5. Try to offer objections to the author's claims. Write objections in the margins or on a separate piece of paper.
6. See if you can formulate alternative conclusions to those proposed by the author.
7. Try to formulate reasons and concerns that the author may have neglected.
8. Read essays that present other viewpoints and compare.

Reading As a Writer

1. Note the organizational pattern of the argument. Identify how you might use the pattern in your arguments.
2. Examine how the writer connects the reasons with the major thesis.
3. Identify how the evidence is presented and connected as support.
4. Notice any effective word choice that helps cement the emotional argument.
5. Evaluate how the author establishes tone and ethos.
6. Examine how the author answers possible objections.

EZEKIEL J. EMANUEL

The Problem with Single-Payer Plans

Ezekiel J. Emanuel, M.D., Ph.D., is the Chair of the Department of Clinical Bioethics at the National Institutes of Health. He received his M.D. at Harvard's Medical School and his Ph.D. in Political Philosophy from Harvard University. Among his extensive publications is the book No Margin, No Mission: Health-Care Organizations and the Question of Ethical Excellence. *This article appeared in the January/February 2008 edition of the* Hastings Center Report

Identifies position to oppose	1 Many liberals in America dream about single-payer plans. Even if they acknowledge that a single-payer plan cannot be enacted, they still think it the best reform. Another proposal may be politically necessary to achieve universal coverage, but it would be a compromise, a fall-back. Single payer is the ideal.
Establishes assumption for argument	2 This is wrong. Even in theory, single payer is not the best reform option. Here's the problem: while it proposes the most radical reform of the health care financing system, it is conservative, even nostalgic, when it comes to the broken delivery system. It retains and solidifies the nineteenth century, fragmented, fee-for-service delivery system that provides profligate and bad quality care.
Establishes thesis and main argument	3 Reform of the American health care system needs to address problems with both the financing and the delivery systems. As proponents of single-payer systems note, the financing system is inequitable, inefficient, and unsustainable. There are now forty-seven million uninsured Americans, about 70 percent of whom are in families with full-time workers. Wealthy individuals receive much higher tax breaks than the poor, and insurance premiums are a larger percent of wages for those working at low wages and in small businesses. Many working poor and lower middle class Americans pay taxes to support Medicaid and
Builds Rogerian relationship with reader by agreeing with their concerns. Raises concerns about government role.	

SCHIP, yet are excluded from these programs. The employer-based and individual market parts of the financing system are inefficient because they have huge administrative costs, especially related to insurance underwriting, sales, and marketing. The government part of the finance system is inefficient because it fails to address key policy issues, fraud, and—for Medicaid—complex determinations of eligibility. Over the last three decades, health care costs have risen 2–4 percent over growth in the overall economy. Medicaid is now the largest part of state budgets, forcing states to cut other programs.

4   But the delivery system is also fraught with problems. First, it is badly fragmented. Currently, 75 percent of physicians practice in groups of eight or less. Of the one billion office visits each year, one-third are to solo practitioners, and one-third are to groups of four or fewer physicians. On average, each year Medicare beneficiaries see seven different physicians, who are financially, clinically, and administratively uncoordinated.

Identifies alternative problem with empirical support

5   A second problem is that the delivery system is structured for acute care, but the contemporary need is for chronic care. Over 133 million Americans have chronic conditions, and among Americans sixty-five and older, 75 percent have two or more chronic conditions, and 20 percent have five chronic conditions. Consequently, 70 percent of health care costs are devoted to patients with chronic conditions.

Second problem with empirical support

6   Also, the care that the system delivers is of much poorer quality than Americans realize. Use of unproven, non-beneficial, marginal, or harmful services is common. The list of offending interventions that are paid for and widely used but either unproven or of marginal benefit to patients is vast—IMRT and proton beam for early prostate cancer, CT and MRI angiograms, Epogen for chemotherapy induced anemia, Erbituax and Avastin for colorectal cancer, and drug-eluting stents for coronary artery disease. Stanford researchers recently showed that between 15 and 20 percent of prescriptions are written for indications for which there is absolutely no published data supporting their use.[1] The Dartmouth studies on variation in practices demonstrate that for many interventions, more services are not better. For instance, heart attack patients in Miami receive vastly more care than similar patients in Minnesota at 2.45 times the cost, yet have slightly worse outcomes.[2]

Identifies additional problem with delivery system using empirical support

7   In the context of reforming the American health care system, "single payer" has come to be associated with three key reforms: a single national plan for all Americans, reduced administrative costs, and negotiated prices for hospitals and physicians and perhaps for health care goods and services, such as drugs. Single-payer plans have two huge advantages.

Identifies reasons for opponent's position

8   First, single-payer plans clearly provide for universal health care coverage. Unlike Massachusetts-style individual mandate reform proposals, single-payer plans do not achieve 95 percent or 97 percent coverage, but true 100 percent coverage for all Americans.

Opposition reason—advantage

9   Second, single-payer plans enhance the efficiency of the health care financing system by eliminating the wasteful costs of insurance underwriting, sales, and marketing. This could save between $60 and $100 billion. Similarly, a single-payer plan with a formulary and negotiated prices would be able to reduce drug costs. McKinsey Global Institute has estimated that bringing drug costs in the United States down to those of other developed countries would save the U.S. system $57 billion.[3] This is a huge and real savings, enough to cover all the uninsured and probably expand the range of covered services to include dental care and other items.

Second opposition reason and empirical evidence

The problem with single-payer plans is that they have an assortment of serious structural problems. To wit:

Institutionalized fee-for-service. Single-payer plans would preserve the dysfunctional delivery system. We know two things about how to reform the delivery system. First, because no one yet has the secret formula for delivering the best quality health care, a real reform of the financing system needs to foster innovation in delivery and then measure the delivery system to find out what changes improve quality. Second, while the overall contours of reform are unknown, there is a clear need for better integration and coordination of care. Integration requires three—infrastructure, information, and incentives. Better delivery of care needs an infrastructure that coordinates doctors, hospitals, home health care agencies, and other providers administratively, fiscally, and clinically. They need to share information easily. And there have to be incentives for this coordination. It will not happen spontaneously.

The problem is that a single-payer approach uses fee-for-service reimbursement to entrench the existing delivery system. Retaining and institutionalizing the fee-for-service payment model would quash the ability to integrate care. Solo practitioners or small groups would have no incentive—financial or otherwise—for integration and coordination of care across providers.

Also, single-payer reform is hostile to the very organizations that have the financial and administrative capacity to build the infrastructure and information systems for the coordinated care delivery systems: insurance companies and health plans. If there is to be an infrastructure for integration of services, information-sharing, and incentives for collaboration, some organization has to develop and implement it. Call it what you will, that organization would look a lot like a health insurance company. (Some might argue that the Veterans Affair's health system is a single-payer system that does a great job of coordinating and integrating care. True, but it covers only thirteen million people. In essence, the VA is a big health plan, like Kaiser. There is no way a single administrative body can efficiently coordinate care for three hundred million people.) In the current system, the financial incentives for health insurance companies lead to perverse behaviors, such as avoiding sick patients. But single-payer plans eliminate not only their problems, but also their potential benefits.

Deceptive administrative savings. There is no doubt that a single-payer system would produce huge administrative savings, but low administrative costs should not be confused with low total health care costs.

Very low administrative costs in Medicare create an opening for fraud and abuse. The last assessment by the Inspector General of the Department of Health and Human Services occurred in 1996. At that time, the IG estimated that Medicare made about $23.2 billion in improper payments due to insufficient or absent documentation, incorrect billing, billing for excluded services, and other problems. In 1996, Medicare spent about $200 billion. Thus, fraud was over 10 percent of total Medicare costs. (I leave it to you to imagine why the government has not repeated this assessment in the last decade.) True, the Canadian single-payer system does not report high levels of fraud and abuse, but Canada is not the United States. Canada's population is about one-tenth that of the United States, and Canadians believe in good government.

Furthermore, a plan covering all Americans would be much larger than Medicare. It would have to process more than one billion physician visits, forty million hospitalizations, and 3.7 billion prescriptions each year. This would require sophisticated information technology, but that technology would be a major administrative cost, and keeping it updated could be politically difficult. As we have seen in the IRS and the FBI, there is great aversion to spending money on major IT upgrades.

17   Finally, monitoring the quality of care delivered to patients also constitutes an administrative expense. It is an administrative burden to systematically assess whether new technologies like cancer genetic fingerprints are in fact beneficial, whether new surgical procedures really lead to longer life, and whether new ways of preparing patients for surgery and handling intravenous lines reduce infections and hospital days.

[margin note: Additional reason assumption wrong]

18   Nothing would absolutely prohibit single-payer plans from spending more money on administration to detect fraud, improve computerization, address payment issues, and assess quality. Nothing, that is, but a strong ideological commitment to keeping administrative expenses very, very low. The war cry for single-payer plans is very low administrative costs, but repeatedly touting this advantage creates a line in the sand. Indeed, it may exacerbate the inflexibility of a single-payer plan. Because of its size, any agency administering a single-payer plan would have a built-in tendency toward inertia. Further, striving to keep administrative costs low would translate into hiring fewer people to manage the system. Fewer people would mean less expertise for addressing problems and less time to search for creative solutions. This is a prescription for inflexibility and lack of innovation.

[margin note: Negative consequences of opposition assumption]

19   **Ineffective cost-control strategies.** Efficiency savings from reduced administrative costs or cheaper drug prices should not be confused with controlling costs overall. Efficiencies, such as reducing administrative waste, are onetime savings. Controlling costs means reducing the increase in medical spending year after year. Single-payer plans use the savings from efficiencies to extend coverage to the uninsured and expand covered services without raising the total amount spent on health care. But these onetime savings do not attack the fundamental forces that drive health care cost inflation. Unless there is some mechanism to control those pressures, the onetime savings would be used up in a few years, and overall health care spending would go higher and higher. How can single-payer plans respond to this health care inflation?

[margin note: States limitation of opposition assumption]

20   There are three possible approaches. One is to "constrain the supply": use the national health plan's control to constrain the introduction and deployment of technology. A single-payer plan could decide to limit the number of MRI scanners, for example. Indeed, in the Physicians' Working Group proposal, the national health plan would negotiate with hospitals on capital expansion and could easily limit how many hospitals can build facilities for MRI scanners or new specialized surgical suites.[4] This strategy creates queuing for access to the technology. As every major country trying this has learned, queuing creates huge public resentment. People on the waiting list get furious at the central administration. Americans, especially the upper middle class, are unlikely to tolerate it.

[margin note: Identifies possible negative consequence]

21   Constraining supply also promotes gaming of the system and inequality. When technology is limited, patients—and physicians—try to jump the queue. Physicians are not great at creating priority lists based on medical need. Particularly when they have their own practices, their obligation is to their individual patients, not to ensuring that other physicians' patients get care and not to promoting the overall health of the population.

[margin note: Identifies possible negative consequence]

22   Countries that have tried this approach have found, not surprisingly, that such gaming tends to favor well-off patients. In many facets of life, well-off people have learned how to come out on top in situations where there are limits. Limits

[margin note: Empirical evidence]

on health care technology gives them one more setting in which their greater gaming skills can be deployed. A study in Winnipeg, Canada, showed that although all Canadians were legally entitled to the same services, the well-off had substantially better access to high technology services that were constrained.[5]

Negative consequence

23 A second approach, a variant of "constrain the supply," is a "low prices and fees" approach. As the only organization paying physicians, hospitals, drug companies, and other health providers, a national health plan would have a huge incentive to squeeze down on fees. This would keep costs down, and since providers would have no one else to turn to, they would have limited recourse.

Illustration of above

24 The United States government uses this low-price approach in Medicaid and Medicare. To save money, every so often Congress or the Medicare administrators roll back the fees paid to hospitals, physicians, and others. Then, just as predictably, those groups scream that they are going broke and lobby Congress to increase the fees. And so the see-saw goes on—prices rolled back and then increased after lobbying. This does not end up saving much, in part because how much is paid out depends not only on the fee or price but also on the volume—on how much is done. So one way physicians respond to lower fees is to ramp up volume; they see a lot of patients for shorter and shorter times. This is easily done because for many diseases there are no data on how often patients should be seen in the physician's office. And it is exactly how Canadian health insurance administrators kept fees low.

Empirical evidence using a single example

25 The British National Health Service used to do exactly what the Physicians' Working Group wants to do: It paid hospitals a fixed price for operating expenses and controlled capital expenditures to limit expansion and the purchase of new technologies. The result: the hospitals put off maintenance and began falling apart. They put off cleaning and became filthy. They could not buy new equipment or adapt quickly to changes in medical practice. Eventually, even the stiff-upper-lip British rebelled. The British National Health Service reversed course and recently gave hospitals the ability to make their own decisions, including decisions to raise funds or float bonds to expand or buy new technologies.

Identifies alternative assumption contrary to opposition

26 Both "constrain the supply" and "low prices and fees" are centralized, micromanaging cost control techniques. You do not have to be a die-hard capitalist to think they are bad techniques. Most left-leaning economists agree that it is better to develop incentives and let the market control costs than to have government set prices or supply.

Negative consequence

27 The third approach to cost control in a single-payer system is that adopted by Medicare in the United States: do nothing, and just pay whatever bill comes in. Let the costs go through the roof. The crisis will come later—after the current administrators and politicians are long gone. This is probably why a *New York Times* editorial said, "Even in fantasy, no one has yet come up with a way to pay for Medicare."[6]

28 These three options are what most single-payer systems in the world have done. None works, and all have long-term consequences.

Argument by analogy comparing single payer to Medicare

29 Politicized decision-making. As Michael Millenson, a health policy consultant, remarks, when single-payer advocates think about who would run the national health plan, they think of Ted Kennedy. But, he asks, what if the head were Dick Cheney? Medicare reveals what is likely to happen if we have a single-payer plan. Every Medicare decision is subject to political pressure from somewhere. When Medicare tries to lower hospital fees or equalize payments, hospitals pressure their representatives and senators for increases in payments. Patient advocacy groups lobby to have Medicare pay for their favorite technology or treatment.

Drug companies use campaign contributions—and patient advocacy groups—to prevent a Medicare formulary and forbid price negotiations that might limit their profits. The result is that Medicare decisions are made slowly, and rarely on their merits. No federal administrative agency can be completely free of political influence. But single-payer reform plans tend to ignore the importance of administrative independence.

30   The ideal reform must address not only the inequitable, inefficient, and unsustainable financing system, but also the fragmented delivery system. And it must develop a plan that creates an accountable and innovative delivery system overseen by a (relatively) independent agency that can make hard administrative choices.

■ References

[1] D. C. Radley, S. N. Finkelstein, and R. S. Stafford, "Off-Label Prescribing among Office-Based Physicians," *Archives of Internal Medicine* 166, no. 9 (2006): 1021–26.

[2] E. S. Fisher, D. E. Wennberg, T. A. Stukel, and D. J. Gottlieb, "Variations in the Longitudinal Efficiency of Academic Medical Centers." Health Affairs Web exclusive, October 7, 2004, http://content.healthaffairs.org/cgi/content/full/hlthaff.var. 19/DC3.

[3] C. Angrisano, D. Farrell, B. Kocher, M. Laboissiere, and S. Parker, "Accounting for the Cost of Health Care in the United States" (The McKinsey Global Institute, 2004), http://www.mckinsey.com/mgi/reports/pdfs/healthcare/MGI_US_HC_fullreport.pdf.

[4] "Proposal of the Physicians' Working Group for Single-Payer National Health Insurance" (Physicians for a National Health Program, 2006), http://www.pnhp.org/publications/proposal_of_the_physicians_working_group_for_singlepayer_national_health_insurance.php.

[5] D. A. Alter, A. S. Basinski, E. A. Cohen, and C. D. Naylor, "Fairness in the Coronary Angiography Queue," *Canadian Medical Association Journal* 161, no. 7 (1999): 813–17.

[6] "Talking Deficits," *New York Times* opinion, May 23, 2004.

Discussion Questions

1. In the introduction, the author clearly makes the argument political and describes the single-player plans as the dream of liberals. What is the effect of this approach? Who then is his likely audience and what is his purpose in writing this argument?

2. The author admits some of the problems with the U.S. current health care system and some advantage to single-payer systems. What effect do these admissions have on the effectiveness of the author's argument?

3. What approach does the author use to raise questions about the single-payer system? What are some strengths and weaknesses of this approach?

4. In paragraph 24, and other paragraphs, the author uses Medicaid and Medicare as examples of the possible problem with a single-payer system. Is this a fair analogy? Why?
5. In the end, the author offers no alternative solution to health care problems, except for the mention in paragraph 26 that, "it is better to develop incentives and let the market control costs than to have government set prices or supply." Does this harm the author's argument?

Toward Key Insights

One approach to any argument for a solution is to raise questions about the proposal, sometimes as a way of preserving the status quo, without offering an alternative. Is this an ethical or effective approach?

Some have said that the "perfect" is the enemy of the "better." What they mean is that everything we try to do has limitations so there can always be objections, which may make no solutions acceptable. Does this essay fall to this problem? Why or why not?

Suggestions for Writing

Based on the two articles on single-payer health care plans, and additional research if your teacher would encourage the additional research, write an argument supporting or objecting to adopting a single-payer health plan.

Focus on one specific claim of the author, such as his claim that the single-payer system has "ineffective cost-control strategies," and with additional research support or dispute his claim.

HOLLY DRESSEL

Has Canada Got the Cure?

Born in Illinois, Holly Dressel now lives in Montreal, Quebec, Canada, where she works as a researcher and writer. She has an M.A. in English from Simon Fraser University. She writes frequently for the online Yes *Magazine,* the source for this article which was adapted from Ms. Dressel's book *God Save the Queen—God Save Us All: An Examination of Canadian Hospital Care via the Life and Death of Montreal's Queen Elizabeth Hospital.*

Publicly funded health care has its problems, as any Canadian or Briton knows. But like democracy, it's the best answer we've come up with so far.

1   Should the United States implement a more inclusive, publicly funded health care system? That's a big debate throughout the country. But even as it rages, most Americans are unaware that the United States is the only country in the developed world that doesn't already have a fundamentally public—that is, tax-supported—health care system.

2   That means that the United States has been the unwitting control subject in a 30-year, worldwide experiment comparing the merits of private versus public health care funding. For the people living in the United States, the results of this

Holly Dressel, "Has Canada Got the Cure?" Reprinted from "Health Care For All" the Fall 2006 issue of *Yes! Magazine. Yes!* is a non-profit, ad-free national publication that offers positive solutions for creating a just and sustainable world.

experiment with privately funded health care have been grim. The United States now has the most expensive health care system on earth and, despite remarkable technology, the general health of the U.S. population is lower than in most industrialized countries. Worse, Americans' mortality rates—both general and infant—are shockingly high.

Different Paths

3   Beginning in the 1930s, both the Americans and the Canadians tried to alleviate health care gaps by increasing use of employment-based insurance plans. Both countries encouraged nonprofit private insurance plans like Blue Cross, as well as for-profit insurance plans. The difference between the United States and Canada is that Americans are still doing this, ignoring decades of international statistics that show that this type of funding inevitably leads to poorer public health.

4   Meanwhile, according to author Terry Boychuk, the rest of the industrialized world, including many developing countries like Mexico, Korea, and India, viscerally understood that "private insurance would [never be able to] cover all necessary hospital procedures and services; and that even minimal protection [is] beyond the reach of the poor, the working poor, and those with the most serious health problems."[1] Today, over half the family bankruptcies filed every year in the United States are directly related to medical expenses, and a recent study shows that 75 percent of those are filed by people with health insurance.[2]

5   The United States spends far more per capita on health care than any comparable country. In fact, the gap is so enormous that a recent University of California, San Francisco, study estimates that the United States would save over $161 billion every year in paperwork alone if it switched to a single-payer system like Canada's.[3] These billions of dollars are not abstract amounts deducted from government budgets; they come directly out of the pockets of people who are sick.

6   The year 2000 marked the beginning of a crucial period, when international trade rules, economic theory, and political action had begun to fully reflect the belief in the superiority of private, as opposed to public, management, especially in the United States. By that year the U.S. health care system had undergone what has been called "the health management organization revolution." U.S. government figures show that medical care costs have spiked since 2000, with total spending on prescriptions nearly doubling.[4]

Cutting Costs, Cutting Care

7   There are two criteria used to judge a country's health care system: the overall success of creating and sustaining health in the population, and the ability to control costs while doing so. One recent study published in the *Canadian Medical Association Journal* compares mortality rates in private for-profit and nonprofit hospitals in the United States. Research on 38 million adult patients in 26,000 U.S. hospitals revealed that death rates in for-profit hospitals are significantly higher than in nonprofit hospitals: for-profit patients have a 2 percent higher chance of dying in the hospital or within 30 days of discharge. The increased death rates were clearly linked to "the corners that for-profit hospitals

Side-by-Side: No Comparison

■ Canada   ■ U.S.

Canada and the U.S. used to be twins on public-health measurements. Here's how it looks after 35 years of Canadian universal health care.

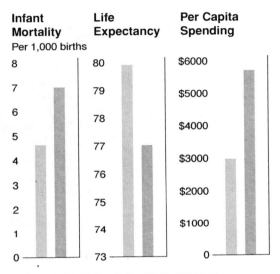

Source: World Health Organization, CIA *World Fact Book,* Centers for Disease Control

must cut in order to achieve a profit margin for investors, as well as to pay high salaries for administrators."[5]

8   "To ease cost pressures, administrators tend to hire less highly skilled personnel, including doctors, nurses, and pharmacists . . .," wrote P. J. Devereaux, a cardiologist at McMaster University and the lead researcher. "The U.S. statistics clearly show that when the need for profits drives hospital decisionmaking, more patients die."

The Value of Care for All

9   Historically, one of the cruelest aspects of unequal income distribution is that poor people not only experience material want all their lives, they also suffer more illness and die younger. But in Canada there is no association between income inequality and mortality rates—none whatsoever.

10   In a massive study undertaken by Statistics Canada in the early 1990s, income and mortality census data were analyzed from all Canadian provinces and all U.S. states, as well as 53 Canadian and 282 American metropolitan areas.[6] The study concluded that "the relationship between income inequality and mortality is not universal, but instead depends on social and political characteristics specific to place." In other words, government health policies have an effect.

11   "Income inequality is strongly associated with mortality in the United States and in North America as a whole," the study found, "but there is no relation within Canada at either the province or metropolitan area level—between income inequality and mortality."

12   The same study revealed that among the poorest people in the United States, even a one percent increase in income resulted in a mortality decline of nearly 22 out of 100,000.

13   What makes this study so interesting is that Canada used to have statistics that mirrored those in the United States. In 1970, U.S. and Canadian mortality rates calculated along income lines were virtually identical. But 1970 also marked the introduction of Medicare in Canada—universal, single-payer coverage. The simple explanation for how Canadians have all become equally healthy, regardless of income, most likely lies in the fact that they have a publicly funded, single-payer health system and the control group, the United States, does not.

Infant Mortality

14   Infant mortality rates, which reflect the health of the mother and her access to prenatal and postnatal care, are considered one of the most reliable measures of the general health of a population. Today, U.S. government statistics rank Canada's infant mortality rate of 4.7 per thousand 23rd out of 225 countries, in the company of the Netherlands, Luxembourg, Australia, and Denmark. The U.S. is 43rd—in the company of Croatia and Lithuania, below Taiwan and Cuba.

15   All the countries surrounding Canada or above it in the rankings have tax-supported health care systems. The countries surrounding the United States and below have mixed systems or are, in general, extremely poor in comparison to the United States and the other G8 industrial powerhouses.

16   There are no major industrialized countries near the United States in the rankings. The closest is Italy, at 5.83 infants dying per thousand, but it is still ranked five places higher.[7]

17   In the United States, infant mortality rates are 7.1 per 1,000, the highest in the industrialized world—much higher than some of the poorer states in India, for example, which have public health systems in place, at least for mothers and infants. Among the inner-city poor in the United States, more than 8 percent of mothers receive no prenatal care at all before giving birth.

Overall U.S. Mortality

18   We would have expected to see steady decreases in deaths per thousand in the mid-twentieth century, because so many new drugs and procedures were becoming available. But neither the Canadian nor the American mortality rate declined much; in fact, Canada's leveled off for an entire decade, throughout the 1960s. This was a period in which private care was increasing in Canadian hospitals, and the steady mortality rates reflect the fact that most people simply couldn't afford the new therapies that were being offered. However, beginning in 1971, the same year that Canada's Medicare was fully applied, official statistics show that death rates suddenly plummeted, maintaining a steep decline to their present rate.

19   In the United States, during the same period, overall mortality rates also dropped, reflecting medical advances. But they did not drop nearly so precipitously as those in Canada after 1971. But given that the United States is the richest country on earth, today's overall mortality rates are shockingly high, at 8.4 per thousand, compared to Canada's 6.5.

Rich and Poor

20   It has become increasingly apparent, as data accumulate, that the overall improvement in health in a society with tax-supported health care translates to better health even for the rich, the group assumed to be the main beneficiaries of the American-style private system. If we look just at the 5.7 deaths per thousand among presumably richer, white babies in the United States, Canada still does better at 4.7, even though the Canadian figure includes all ethnic groups and all income levels. Perhaps a one-per-thousand difference doesn't sound like much. But when measuring mortality, it's huge. If the U.S. infant mortality rate were the same as Canada's, almost 15,000 more babies would survive in the United States every year.

21   If we consider the statistics for the poor, which in the United States have been classified by race, we find that in 2001, infants born of black mothers were dying at a rate of 14.2 per thousand. That's a Third World figure, comparable to Russia's.[8]

22   But now that the United States has begun to do studies based on income levels instead of race, these "cultural" and genetic explanations are turning out to be baseless. Infant mortality is highest among the poor, regardless of race.

23   Vive la différence! Genetically, Canadians and Americans are quite similar. Our health habits, too, are very much alike—people in both countries eat too much and exercise too little. And, like the United States, there is plenty of inequality in Canada, too. In terms of health care, that inequality falls primarily on Canadians in isolated communities, particularly Native groups, who have poorer access to medical care and are exposed to greater environmental contamination. The only major difference between the two countries that could account for the remarkable disparity in their infant and adult mortality rates, as well as the amount they spend on health care, is how they manage their health care systems.

24   The facts are clear: Before 1971, when both countries had similar, largely privately funded health care systems, overall survival and mortality rates were almost identical. The divergence appeared with the introduction of the single-payer health system in Canada.

25   The solid statistics amassed since the 1970s point to only one conclusion: like it or not, believe it makes sense or not, publicly funded, universally available health care is simply the most powerful contributing factor to the overall health of the people who live in any country. And in the United States, we have got the bodies to prove it.

[1] Terry Boychuk. *The Making and Meaning of Hospital Policy in the United States and Canada.* University of Michigan Press, Ann Arbor: 1999.

[2] David U. Himmelstein, et al. *Health Affairs,* Jan.–June 2005, http://content. healthaffairs.org/cgi/reprint/hlthaff.w5.63v1

[3] Professor James Kahn, UCSF, quoted in *Harper's Magazine,* "Harper's List," Feb. 2006.

[4] National Health Expenditure Data, www.cms.hhs.gov/NationalHealthExpendData/ downloads/tables.pdf.

[5] Devereaux, Dr. P. J., et al. "A Systematic Review and Meta-Analysis of Studies Comparing Mortality between Private For-Profit and Private Not-For-Profit Hospitals," *Canadian Medical Association Journal,* May, 2002.

[6] Nancy A. Ross et al. "Relation between Income Inequality and Mortality in Canada and in the United States: Cross Sectional Assessment Using Census Data and Vital Statistics," *Statistics Canada,* reprinted in *Health Geography,* GEOG-303, ed. Nancy Ross, McGill University, 2005, pp. 109–117.

[7] *CIA World Fact Book.* www.cia.gov/cia/publications/factbook/rankorder/2091rank.html

[8] See, among many studies blaming race, Child Health USA 2003, Health Status—Infants; HRSA, with graphs such as "Breastfeeding Rates by Race/Ethnicity, 2001"; "Very Low Birth Weight Among Infants, by Race/Ethnicity 1985–2001"; http://www. mchb.hrsa.gov/chusa03.

Discussion Questions

1. The author focuses on a comparison of the relative effectiveness of the United States and Canadian health care to make her argument rather that writing a broader and more emotional argument for a single-payer system. What are the strengths and weaknesses of this approach?
2. In paragraph 7, how does the author frame her main argument? Is this approach effective?
3. This essay depends heavily on evidence. What kinds of evidence does the writer use? How does she try to make it credible? Is it effective?
4. What strategies does the writer use in her concluding paragraphs?
5. The author's argument hinges on her suggestion that the only significant difference in the U.S. and Canadian health is a result of the differences in their health insurance systems. If we assume her statistics are correct, what other explanations might there be for such differences?

Toward Key Insights

The person who sets the terms of an argument often wins. Holly Dressel defines the key issues in the health care debate as being the cost of health care delivery and the measured health of citizens. What other issues might be equally important to consider?

There are many articles in support of a single-payer system that answer most of the criticisms of this approach. This author doesn't attempt to answer possible objections. What is the effect of her refraining from tackling a wide array of issues and sticking to the comparison as a way of formulating her argument?

Suggestion for Writing

Take one of the issues the author discusses—such as the cost of health care, the infant mortality rate, or the mortality rate in general—research the topic and write an argument either supporting or disputing the claims of the author. You will want to keep an eye on the range of alternative explanations for the statistics in question.

ALAN EHRENHALT

The Misguided Zeal of the Privacy Lobby

Alan Ehrenhalt was born in 1947 in Chicago. He received an A.B. from Brandeis University and an MS from Columbia University. He was a reporter for Congressional Quarterly *and serves as executive editor of* Governing *magazine. He has written numerous articles, editorials, and books including* The Lost City: Discovering the Forgotten Virtues of Community in the Chicago of the 1950s. *In this essay, he makes the provocative argument that there have been exaggerated and even harmful demands for privacy that overcome reasonable proposals such as the one for national identity cards.*

1   My Social Security number is 349-40-7931. I don't mind telling you that largely because I'm confident you have no interest in knowing it. You won't even write it down. Of course, you could be a secret enemy of mine, eager to use any available information to discredit me in some way. But I'm not too worried about that, either. I have my share of secrets, just like anybody else, but at the moment I can't think of a single one that's vulnerable to exposure simply upon presentation of an I.D. number.

2   But I will tell you one secret belief I have that I'm usually careful not to blurt out in polite company. It's this: I think privacy is the single most overrated issue in the entire lexicon of public policy—state, local, federal or anyplace else. Of all the dangers that this society faces as it starts the new millennium, one of the most remote is the risk that America will become an Orwellian police state, watching everything citizens do and taking down every word they say. And yet people all over the country lose a lot of sleep every night worrying about it.

3   I have great admiration for George Orwell, as a writer and thinker, and as a lifelong leftist who had the courage to expose communism for the hypocritical sham it was. But in one important way, Orwell did posterity a disservice. He depicted the surveillance methods of totalitarian society so vividly and so convincingly that an entire generation of otherwise reasonable Americans has convinced itself that Big Brother is watching them even when the truth is that Big Brother has far more important ways to spend his time.

4   "They could plug in your wire whenever they wanted to," Orwell wrote a few pages into his novel, *1984*. "You had to live—did live, from habit that became instinct—in the assumption that every sound you made was overheard, and, except in darkness, every movement scrutinized."

Alan Ehrenhalt, "The Misguided Zeal of the Privacy Lobby," from *Governing*, v. 12 no. 8 (May 1999), pp. 7–8. Reprinted by permission.

5   I'm not a simpleton. I know there are governments in this century that have operated that way. The Stasi collected tons of data on the daily habits of ordinary East Germans and filed them away for later use. The KGB knew who the Soviet dissidents were almost from the moment they opened their mouths. I am also aware that even in a free society, horrible miscarriages of justice take place. Waco was indefensible. The police in a one-party dictatorship couldn't have acted any more irresponsibly.

6   But mature citizens in a civilized country are required to make distinctions between aberration and routine. Those of us who lay awake at night in America in 1999 worrying about the government's desire to snoop on them are mostly either (1) paranoid or (2) guilty of something. If there is a legitimate threat to our personal privacy these days, it comes from corporate capitalism, from the companies that make their living on the sale of information for commercial use. It doesn't come from the county commission, the legislature, or the U.S. Department of Health and Human Services.

7   But merely to say such a thing is to risk provoking shock and even ridicule among most members of the educated elite in this country. In the past generation, the idea that our precious privacy is under siege has transcended ideological differences, from the Cato institute on the right, which says "the history of government programs indicates privacy rights are violated routinely whenever expediency dictates," to Justice William O. Douglas on the left, who wrote near the end of his life that "we are rapidly entering the age of no privacy, where everyone is open to surveillance at all times, where there are no secrets from the government." Ask to see the evidence for these propositions, and you won't get much. But you will be branded as a naif, or a proto-Fascist, or both.

8   That is why I am so impressed with the courage of Amitai Etzioni, who dares to challenge the conventional wisdom in his new book, *The Limits of Privacy*. Etzioni is a reasonable man. He doesn't claim that our personal liberty is unimportant, or deny that the government possesses the technological capacity to invade it. He merely argues that we have gone overboard in our privacy obsession in recent years, and we need to tilt the balance back a few steps in the direction of common sense and provision for the common good.

9   And he offers convincing detail on why this is so. For reasons of privacy, for example, we fail to require HIV testing for mothers and infants, even though the information gained by such testing would save many of the infants' lives. We refuse to give law enforcement officials the tools to decipher encrypted computer messages, even though encryption makes systematic criminality easier to practice with each passing year. And on and on through a whole range of current public policy questions.

10   But of all the issues Etzioni takes up, none illustrates his point better than the controversy surrounding creation of a uniform identification process for American citizens.

11   The costs of not having such a system are hard to dispute. As Etzioni recounts, there are more than 30,000 fugitives from the federal criminal justice system running free on false identification. Each year, several thousand convicted sex offenders seek work in the child-care business alone. The use of fake identities by crooked taxpayers costs honest ones an amount estimated to be as much as $5 billion a year. Another $5 billion is thought to be owed by deadbeat parents fleeing their child-support responsibilities. At the end of 1997, the Secret Service reported that it had arrested nearly 10,000 people during the year for various financial crimes involving false or stolen identities, and placed the cost of that fraud to banks and legitimate credit-holders at $745 million.

12   There's no way such figures can be exact. Quite likely some of them have been inflated a little bit in the process of reporting. But if they are even roughly accurate, they make it quite clear that identity crime is a genuine problem in this country.

13   And it's a problem that could be solved relatively easily, by creating a card or other universal identifier proving that the person in search of a job or transferring money is in fact who he or she claims to be. We already use Social Security cards and numbers as a de facto identifier for many public purposes. It's just that they're easy to cheat on. How dangerous could it be to create a new version that liars would have to respect?

14   Not very dangerous at all, is the correct answer. But it's an answer that a privacy-obsessed American polity is stubbornly unwilling to consider. In 1993, when the Clinton administration included establishment of a medical "security card" as part of its national health care proposal, it soon discovered it had made a major tactical error. Anything that sounded remotely like a national I.D. card set the privacy lobby going full blast.

15   Of course, it doesn't take much to do that. Pick up any ordinary newspaper these days, and there's a good chance that somewhere within its pages you will find a warning that an identification system is merely the opening move in Big Brother's bid for absolute power. "Don't we remember the Nazi experience in Europe?" the editor *of Privacy Journal* asked in the *New York Times* a couple of years ago. "Don't we realize the dangers of allowing government to establish identity and legitimacy?"

16   Just last campaign season, a Nevada gubernatorial candidate offered up identity cards as a sign that America was "rushing headlong into becoming a socialist totalitarian society." Privacy zealots left and right are fond of repeating the warning of former California Senator Alan Cranston: ID cards are "a primary tool of totalitarian governments."

17   Well, yes, they are. So are whips, but they are not a cause of torture. So is tear gas. That doesn't make tear gas an emblem of totalitarianism. A little common sense would be useful here. If America starts to go down the road to Fascism, it won't be because people are carrying identification in their wallet. As Etzioni says, "Cards do not transform democratic societies into totalitarian ones."

18   In America in the 1990s, the obsession with privacy is more than just a simple overreaction to George Orwell or to horror stories about something that happened in Moscow or Beijing. It is a reflection of the hyperindividualism to which the political system has succumbed in the past generation or so, and the ways that prevents us from becoming civic grown-ups in a democratic society.

19   One trait that marks just about all of us during childhood and adolescence is an unremitting anxiety about what other people think of us. When we get older, if we are lucky, we begin to realize that, in fact, other people aren't thinking about us at all most of the time. Other people are worried about themselves. The rest of the world isn't watching us with a pair of binoculars. The sensible thing to do is figure out what we want to do and then go on and do it.

20   Of course, some people never figure this out, even in middle age. They go through life searching desperately for clues about the impressions they are creating—at home, at work, even among strangers on the street. They are convinced their friends and acquaintances are judging the most minute details of their lives, and making mental notes about their performance for use later.

21   It's not a very pleasant way to live, and it doesn't bear much resemblance to reality. As individuals, most of us manage to figure that out somewhere between adolescence and middle age. If we learned a similar lesson in our capacity as citizens, we would all be better off.

Discussion Questions

1. What seems to be the purpose of Ehrenhalt's essay? Is it essential for him to make a very strong argument?
2. What are Ehrenhalt's major arguments in favor of national identity cards?
3. What purpose does it serve for Ehrenhalt to indicate his social security number at the beginning of the article and then later indicate that we do use social security cards and numbers as forms of public identification?
4. In response to the argument that ID cards are the tools of totalitarian governments, Ehrenhalt answers that whips and tear gas are also tools of such governments. What is the point of his response? Is it an appropriate argumentative strategy?
5. What point does the author make in the concluding three paragraphs? How effective is this conclusion?

Toward Key Insights

Often we must make decisions weighing conflicting values. How important is privacy as a value compared to other values such as the protection of life and health?

Currently the government and companies have extensive amounts of information about us. There is also a scattered system of identification including driver's licenses and social security numbers. Would a national identification card actually decrease our liberty?

Suggestions for Writing

Write a paper arguing whether we as Americans are excessively concerned about privacy.

Write a paper on whether or not we should require HIV testing for mothers and infants.

Barbara Dority

Halt and Show Your Papers!

Barbara Dority serves as the executive director of the Washington Coalition Against Censorship. She is the president of the Humanists of Washington and edits the Secular Humanist Press. *Her columns on civil liberties appear regularly in* The Humanist Magazine. *In this selection, she argues against the use of national identity cards.*

1   The idea of a national identity (ID) card seems simple enough. Take the photographic and alphanumerical information on our birth certificates, Social Security cards, driver's licenses, and voter registration card; add a bar code, magnetic strip, fingerprint, microchip, or other biometric identifier; and display all that information (and more) on a neat plastic card no larger than a credit card. Our lives would be simplified. We'd always know for sure who we are and who everyone else really is.

2   But beneath this smooth surface lurks a complex terrain of issues and perhaps the greatest threat to personal freedom Americans have ever confronted.

Barbara Dority, "Halt and Show Your Papers!," from *The Humanist*, v. 62 no. 2 (Mar.–Apr. 2002), pp. 10–13. Reprinted by permission.

3   The concept of a national ID card has been debated in the United States for over three decades. In the past, the opposition has been strong and bipartisan and has always prevailed. Extension of the Social Security number to the status of an ID card was rejected in 1971 by the Social Security Administration. In 1976, the Federal Advisory Committee on False Identification rejected the idea of a national identifier. The Carter and Reagan administrations both went on record as opposed to a national ID system.

4   In 1996, uniform national driver's license standards—which some considered tantamount to a national ID card—were enacted into law. However, their implementation was delayed, and a permanent repeal of the proposal was contained in the FY2000 Transportation Appropriations Act signed by President Clinton. In October 1999, House Majority Leader Dick Armey's website featured an article entitled "Good Riddance to the National ID Card." Armey's accompanying statement included these words:

5   This is a classic victory of freedom over "Big Brother." Because we acted quickly, no American will have to carry a National ID Card. A national driver's license with "biometric identifiers" or social security numbers is more suited to a police state than to a free country. It took three years of hard work, but we finally laid this disturbing idea to rest.

6   Not.

7   As a result of the September 11, 2001, terrorist attacks, the debate has been renewed and elevated to a higher and much more dangerous level. Just look at this sampling of headlines from recent newspaper articles around the country:

- "Support Grows for National ID Card Proposal" (*San José Mercury News,* October 16).
- "National ID Card System Failing to Attract Supporters" (*Los Angeles Times,* October 24).
- "U.S. Security Advisor: National ID Card Not Feasible" (*NewsFactor Network,* November 8).
- "National ID Card Gaining Support" (*Washington Post,* December 17).

8   Members of Congress, security experts, and high-tech executives have rushed to endorse the idea of some new form of identification system as a critical weapon in the "fight against terrorism." Unfortunately, little of this discussion has been open to the public (no surprise there), so it has been difficult to determine where the concept currently stands in the minds of the nation's decision makers.

9   George W. Bush, thankfully, has publicly stated his opposition, saying that national ID cards are unnecessary to improve security. Richard Clarke, Bush's chief of cyberspace security, agrees and does "not think it's a very smart idea." Fierce opposition comes from a wide range of privacy advocates, the American Civil Liberties Union, and even conservative organizations like the CATO Institute, Eagle Forum, and the John Birch Society.

10   And yet, as Roger Gay headlines his article in the November 29, 2001, conservative *Toogood Reports,* perhaps "It's Too Late to Stop a National I.D. Card." Marty Abrams, an information technology specialist at the law firm Hunton and Williams and a former senior credit bureau executive, summarizes the current state of the U.S. psyche well: "We're willing to accept this immense flow of data to law enforcement and their proxies to make sure we feel safe and secure. . . . The equilibrium point has shifted as a result of September 11."

11   Most disturbingly, recent Pew Research Center and Harris polls show strong support for a national ID card by those polled: 70 percent and 68 percent, respectively. This preference is undoubtedly hinged on the assumption that such a system would largely prevent terrorists and other "evil-doers" from entering the country—an assumption that is, at best, extremely dubious.

12   Other ID card supporters include the Department of Defense (which already has such a system in place), Oracle CEO Larry Ellison (who has offered to provide the ID software for free and would be glad to offer his company's services to maintain the system and its massive databases—for a fee, of course), the American Association of Motor Vehicle Administrators (which sees this as an opportunity for a national driver's license system), the Air Transportation Association, the Justice Department, lawmakers in U.S.–Mexico border states, and all those in charge of immigration committees in Congress. To my absolute horror, even Bill of Rights champion Alan Dershowitz has recently endorsed the concept, claiming it would reduce racial profiling!

13   The single best overview I've found of the basic questions about national ID cards and concepts involved in their debate is contained on the objective "Frequently Asked Questions" (FAQ) page of the Privacy International website at www.privacy.org/pi/activities/idcard/idcard_faq.html. Its points are summarized below.

14   1. Who uses ID cards now? About a hundred countries currently utilize official, compulsory, national IDs for various purposes. These include Belgium, France, Germany, Greece, and Spain. Among the developed countries that don't have such a card are Australia, Canada, Ireland, New Zealand, Sweden, and the United States. Most countries that don't have a national universal card do have a health or social security card or other documents of identity.

15   2. What are the primary purposes of ID cards? Race, politics, and religion are often at the heart of older ID systems. Card systems have been instituted to control the threat of insurgents or political extremists, to facilitate religious discrimination, to enforce quota systems, and to allow for social engineering. The FAQ notes: "At the heart of such plans is a parallel increase in police powers. Even in democratic nations, police retain the right to demand ID on pain of detention."

16   3. What is the cost of an ID card system? The expense of implementing such a system has been at the forefront of both political and public opposition in a number of countries, including Australia, the Philippines, and the United Kingdom. Cost estimates to create and issue national ID cards in the United States are around $3 billion.

17   4. Can ID cards assist law enforcement? The usefulness of ID cards to law enforcement has been marginal. Little evidence has been advanced to demonstrate that they would either reduce the incidence of crime or enhance the success of prosecution. Police authorities in the Netherlands and the United Kingdom have stated their reluctance to administer a compulsory card that might erode relations with the public. Furthermore, forgeries would be inevitable. Obviously, the more an ID card is used, the greater the value placed on it and, consequently, the higher its value to criminal elements.

18   5. Can ID cards help to control illegal immigration? The impact of such cards on controlling illegal immigration has been patchy. The use of a

card for purposes of checking resident status depends on the police and other officials being given very broad powers to check identity—either a vastly increased level of constant checking of the entire population or a discriminatory checking procedure that would undoubtedly target minorities (numerous examples are included in the FAQ).

19   6. Which countries have rejected proposals for ID cards? The most celebrated campaign against a national ID card occurred just over a decade ago in Australia. In response to proposed legislation, tens of thousands of people took to the streets in opposition, and the government became dangerously split over the issue. The proposal caused such hostility that it was withdrawn in 1987. A similar proposal was presented in New Zealand a few years later and, under the leadership of the Auckland Council for Civil Liberties, an opposition campaign was formed and the proposal was abandoned.

20   In summary, the benefits of a national ID card are highly questionable, while the risks threaten the very heart of a free, democratic society. The national ACLU provides one of the most succinct summaries of the rights issues by boiling down the debate to five major reasons why a national ID card will keep us neither safe nor free:

21   Reason 1: A national ID card system won't solve the problem: it won't prevent terrorism. It wouldn't have thwarted any of the September 11 hijackers, for example, many of whom reportedly had identification documents on them and were in the country legally. Terrorists and criminals will continue to be able to obtain—by legal and illegal means—the documents needed to get a government ID, such as a birth certificate.

22   Reason 2: An ID card system will lead to a slippery slope of surveillance and monitoring of citizens. While such a system cannot protect us from terrorism it would create a system of internal passports that would significantly diminish the freedom and privacy of law-abiding citizens. Once put in place, it is exceedingly unlikely that such a system would be restricted to its original purpose. For example, the original Social Security Act contained strict prohibitions against using Social Security cards for unrelated purposes, but those strictures have been routinely ignored and steadily abandoned over the past fifty years. A national ID system would threaten the privacy that Americans have always enjoyed and gradually increase the control that government and business wields over everyday citizens.

23   Reason 3: A national ID card system would require the establishment of a database of all people in the United States. What happens then when an ID card is stolen? What proof may be used to decide who gets a card? The records of every individual would require continuous updating; would likely contain many errors, any one of which could render someone unemployable and possibly much worse until they get their "file" straightened out. And once created, the use of such a database would almost certainly expand. Law enforcement and other government agencies would soon ask to link into it, while employers, landlords, credit agencies, mortgage brokers, telemarketers, private investigators, civil litigants, and a long list of other parties would begin seeking access, further eroding the privacy that people have always expected in their personal lives. We already see this happening with a proposed airline security database of passenger profiles that would be designed to rate the security risk posed by each passenger.

24   Reason 4: ID cards would function as "internal passports" that monitor citizens' movements. Americans have long had a visceral aversion to building a

society in which the authorities could act like totalitarian sentries and demand "your papers please!" That everyday intrusiveness would be conjoined with the full power of modern computer and database technology. For example, if a police officer or security guard scans your ID card with a pocket barcode reader, would a permanent record be created of that check, including the time and your location? The end result could be a nation where citizens' movements inside their own country are monitored and recorded.

25   Reason 5: ID cards would foster new forms of discrimination and harassment. Rather than eliminating discrimination, as some have claimed, a national identity card would foster new forms of discrimination and harassment of anyone perceived as looking or sounding "foreign." That is exactly what happened after Congress passed the Employer Sanctions provision of the Immigration Reform and Control Act of 1985; it resulted in widespread discrimination against foreign-looking U.S. workers, especially Asians and Hispanics. A 1990 General Accounting Office study found almost 20 percent of employers engaged in such discriminatory practices. A national ID card would have the same effect on a massive scale, with Latinos, Asians, Arabs, and other minorities becoming subject to ceaseless status and identity checks from police, banks, merchants, and others. Failure to carry a national ID card would likely come to be viewed as a reason for search, detention, or arrest of minorities. The stigma and humiliation of constantly having to prove that they are U.S. citizens or legal immigrants would weigh heavily on such groups.

26   New York attorney Duncan Frissell writes in the *Sierra Times:* Most critics of a national ID card mention Hitler, police stops, and personal privacy to argue against the proposal. Those are certainly good reasons to oppose a national ID card, but they miss the idea's worst features. A national ID card is not really about identity. It is about authorization. A modern national ID system will:

27   ■ Require Americans to obtain federal government authorization to travel, work, rent or buy housing, obtain medical care, use financial services, and make many purchases.

28   ■ This federal authorization could be denied for many reasons, including database errors, a suspicious transaction profile, being a deadbeat parent, failure to pay taxes or fines, and any other social control measures Congress wishes to hang on the system.

29   ■ The system will almost certainly create an outlaw class—as large as 10 to 20% of the population—cut off from "normal" life in America. This class will include political refuseniks, as well as those whose behavior has caused the system's software to deny their transactions. This outlaw class will sustain the underground economy for the use of future terrorists (and ordinary criminals).

30   These effects are easy to predict because they've already happened on a smaller scale.

31   Robert Ellis Smith, a lawyer and privacy specialist, says the push for a national ID card is based on the false belief that there can be a simple, high-tech solution to an immensely complex problem. "One way to predict the effectiveness of a national ID number or document is to look at environments where the true identity of all residents is known: prisons, the military, many workplaces, many college campuses," he writes in a new paper about national ID cards. "And yet these places are far from crime free."

32   Ari Schwartz, a policy analyst for the Center for Democracy and Technology, supports a national ID program that is done in a way to allow individuals to

control the information held about them. But he is still concerned about the unintended consequences of a central database. "There are some measures that we should definitely be moving forward on today, and then there are some other ideas that we need to have a longer-term discussion about," he said. "This is definitely one of those longer-term ideas."

33   A similar message is offered by Peter Neumann and Lauren Weinstein, moderaters[*sic*] of the RISKS Forum (www.risks.org) and the PRIVACY Forum (www.privacyforum.org), respectively, and co-founders of People For Internet Responsibility:

34   We have noted here before that technological solutions entail risks that should be identified and understood in advance of deployment to the greatest extent possible, regardless of any panic of the moment. The purported (yet unproven) benefits of a national ID card system notwithstanding, these risks deserve to be discussed and understood in detail before any decisions regarding its adoption in any form should be made.

35   The specter of a national ID card has been cropping up in my nightmares for years. On top of the current horrifying attack on the Bill of Rights under the guise of "fighting terrorism," the potential imposition of this ultimate "Big Brother" tactic in my America leaves me in virtual despair.

36   But according to the Attorney General of the United States John Ashcroft, by writing such articles as "Invading the Bill of Rights" (*The Humanist*, November/December 2001) and this one, I'm "scaring peace-loving people with phantoms of lost liberty" and "aiding the terrorists." When I first heard this accusation, I was outraged. Upon reflection, however, I've decided I don't mind. In John Ashcroft's America, where everything is literally turned on its head, being called un-American has become the mark of a citizen who truly loves and defends the principles of the United States. (Not to mention that the company is most gratifying.)

Discussion Questions

1. What is the overall structure of the argument?
2. What are Dority's major objections to identity cards?
3. What does Dority do to demonstrate that national identity cards is a real issue? Why is this an important step in her argument?
4. Like many writers, Dority does not generate all her reasons herself but rather brings in ideas from other sources. Does the inclusion of material from the Web and ACLU weaken or strengthen the argument? How might it have been more effectively handled?
5. In paragraphs 31, 32, and 33 what is Dority's argumentative strategy? Is it effective?
6. What is the possible purpose for the conclusion? Is it effective?

Toward Key Insights

In our computerized age, the government and businesses have access to extensive amounts of information about citizens. To what extent does a national identity card pose a threat to civil liberties?

How much liberty is worth surrendering for greater security?

Suggestions for Writing

Take a stance and write an essay in support of or opposed to national identity cards.

Colleges often use identification numbers and identification cards to keep track of students. Write an essay about whether such a system infringes on students.

MARTIN LUTHER KING, JR.

I Have a Dream

Martin Luther King, Jr. (1929–1968) has earned lasting fame for his part in the civil rights struggles of the 1950s and 1960s. Born in Atlanta, Georgia, he was ordained a Baptist minister in his father's church in 1947. A year later, he graduated from Morehouse College, then went on to take a Bachelor of Divinity degree at Crozier Theological Seminary (1951) and a PhD in philosophy at Boston University (1954), after which he accepted a pastorate in Montgomery, Alabama. King's involvement with civil rights grew when he organized and led a boycott that succeeded in desegregating Montgomery's bus system. In 1957, he founded and became the first president of the Southern Christian Leadership Conference and assumed a leading role in the civil rights movement. King advocated a policy of nonviolent protest based on the beliefs of Thoreau and Gandhi and never veered from it despite many acts of violence directed at him. The success of King's crusade helped bring about the passage of the Civil Rights Act of 1964 and the Voting Rights Act of 1965 and won him the Nobel Peace Prize in 1964. King was assassinated on April 4, 1968, in Memphis. Since then, his birthday, January 15, has been made a national holiday. The speech "I Have a Dream" was delivered August 28, 1963, at the Lincoln Memorial in Washington, D.C., before a crowd of 200,000 people who had gathered to commemorate the centennial of the Emancipation Proclamation and to demonstrate for pending civil rights legislation. It stands as one of the most eloquent pleas ever made for racial justice.

1   I am happy to join with you today in what will go down in history as the greatest demonstration for freedom in the history of our nation.

2   Five score years ago, a great American, in whose symbolic shadow we stand today, signed the Emancipation Proclamation. This momentous decree came as a great beacon light of hope to millions of Negro slaves who had been seared in the flames of withering injustice. It came as a joyous daybreak to end the long night of their captivity.

3   But one hundred years later, the Negro still is not free; one hundred years later, the life of the Negro is still sadly crippled by the manacles of segregation and the chains of discrimination; one hundred years later, the Negro lives on a lonely island of poverty in the midst of a vast ocean of material prosperity; one hundred years later, the Negro is still languishing in the corners of American society and finds himself in exile in his own land.

4   So we've come here today to dramatize a shameful condition. In a sense we've come to our nation's capital to cash a check. When the architects of our republic wrote the magnificent words of the Constitution and the Declaration of Independence, they were signing a promissory note to which every American was to fall heir. This note was the promise that all men, yes, black men as well as

white men, would be guaranteed the unalienable rights of life, liberty, and the pursuit of happiness.

5   It is obvious today that America has defaulted on this promissory note in so far as her citizens of color are concerned. Instead of honoring this sacred obligation, America has given the Negro people a bad check; a check which has come back marked "insufficient funds." But we refuse to believe that the bank of justice is bankrupt. We refuse to believe that there are insufficient funds in the great vaults of opportunity of this nation. And so we've come to cash this check, a check that will give us upon demand the riches of freedom and the security of justice.

6   We have also come to this hallowed spot to remind America of the fierce urgency of now. This is no time to engage in the luxury of cooling off or to take the tranquilizing drug of gradualism. Now is the time to make real the promises of democracy; now is the time to rise from the dark and desolate valley of segregation to the sunlit path of racial justice; now is the time to lift our nation from the quicksands of racial injustice to the solid rock of brotherhood; now is the time to make justice a reality for all of God's children. It would be fatal for the nation to overlook the urgency of the moment. This sweltering summer of the Negro's legitimate discontent will not pass until there is an invigorating autumn of freedom and equality.

7   Nineteen sixty-three is not an end, but a beginning. And those who hope that the Negro needed to blow off steam and will now be content will have a rude awakening if the nation returns to business as usual. There will be neither rest nor tranquility in America until the Negro is granted his citizenship rights. The whirlwinds of revolt will continue to shake the foundations of our nation until the bright day of justice emerges.

8   But there is something that I must say to my people, who stand on the worn threshold which leads into the palace of justice. In the process of gaining our rightful place, we must not be guilty of wrongful deeds. Let us not seek to satisfy our thirst for freedom by drinking from the cup of bitterness and hatred. We must forever conduct our struggle on the high plain of dignity and discipline. We must not allow our creative protests to degenerate into physical violence. Again and again we must rise to the majestic heights of meeting physical force with soul force. The marvelous new militancy, which has engulfed the Negro community, must not lead us to a distrust of all white people. For many of our white brothers, as evidenced by their presence here today, have come to realize that their destiny is tied up with our destiny. And they have come to realize that their freedom is inextricably bound to our freedom. We cannot walk alone. And as we walk, we must make the pledge that we shall always march ahead. We cannot turn back.

9   There are those who are asking the devotees of Civil Rights, "When will you be satisfied?" We can never be satisfied as long as the Negro is the victim of the unspeakable horrors of police brutality; we can never be satisfied as long as our bodies, heavy with the fatigue of travel, cannot gain lodging in the motels of the highways and the hotels of the cities; we cannot be satisfied as long as the Negro's basic mobility is from a smaller ghetto to a larger one; we can never be satisfied as long as our children are stripped of their selfhood and robbed of their dignity by signs stating "For White Only"; we cannot be satisfied as long as the Negro in Mississippi cannot vote and a Negro in New York believes he has nothing for which to vote. No! No, we are not satisfied, and we will not be satisfied until "justice rolls down like waters and righteousness like a mighty stream."

10   I am not unmindful that some of you have come here out of great trials and tribulations. Some of you have come fresh from narrow jail cells. Some of you have come from areas where your quest for freedom left you battered by the

storms of persecution and staggered by the winds of police brutality. You have been the veterans of creative suffering. Continue to work with the faith that unearned suffering is redemptive. Go back to Mississippi. Go back to Alabama. Go back to South Carolina. Go back to Georgia. Go back to Louisiana. Go back to the slums and ghettos of our Northern cities, knowing that somehow this situation can and will be changed. Let us not wallow in the valley of despair.

11   I say to you today, my friends, that even though we face the difficulties of today and tomorrow, I still have a dream. It is a dream deeply rooted in the American dream. I have a dream that one day this nation will rise up and live out the true meaning of its creed, "We hold these truths to be self-evident, that all men are created equal." I have a dream that one day on the red hills of Georgia, sons of former slaves and the sons of former slave owners will be able to sit down together at the table of brotherhood. I have a dream that one day even the state of Mississippi, a state sweltering with the heat of injustice, sweltering with the heat of oppression, will be transformed into an oasis of freedom and justice. I have a dream that my four little children will one day live in a nation where they will not be judged by the color of their skin, but by the content of their character.

12   I HAVE A DREAM TODAY!

13   I have a dream that one day down in Alabama—with its vicious racists, with its Governor having his lips dripping with the words of interposition and nullification—one day right there in Alabama, little black boys and black girls will be able to join hands with little white boys and white girls as sisters and brothers.

14   I HAVE A DREAM TODAY!

15   I have a dream that one day every valley shall be exalted, every hill and mountain shall be made low. The rough places will be plain and the crooked places will be made straight, "and the glory of the Lord shall be revealed, and all flesh shall see it together."

16   This is our hope. This is the faith that I go back to the South with. With this faith we will be able to hew out of the mountain of despair, a stone of hope. With this faith we will be able to transform the jangling discords of our nation into a beautiful symphony of brotherhood. With this faith we will be able to work together, to pray together, to struggle together, to go to jail together, to stand up for freedom together, knowing that we will be free one day. And this will be the day. This will be the day when all of God's children will be able to sing with new meaning, "My country 'tis of thee, sweet land of liberty, of thee I sing. Land where my fathers died, land of the pilgrim's pride, from every mountain side, let freedom ring." And if America is to be a great nation, this must become true.

17   So let freedom ring from the prodigious hilltops of New Hampshire; let freedom ring from the mighty mountains of New York; let freedom ring from the heightening Alleghenies of Pennsylvania; let freedom ring from the snowcapped Rockies of Colorado; let freedom ring from the curvaceous slopes of California. But not only that. Let freedom ring from Stone Mountain of Georgia; let freedom ring from Lookout Mountain of Tennessee; let freedom ring from every hill and mole hill of Mississippi. "From every mountainside, let freedom ring."

18   And when this happens, and when we allow freedom to ring, when we let it ring from every village and every hamlet, from every state and every city, we will be able to speed up that day when all of God's children, black men and white men, Jews and Gentiles, Protestants and Catholics, will be able to join hands and sing in the words of the old Negro spiritual: "Free at last. Free at last. Thank God Almighty, we are free at last."

Discussion Questions

1. Why do you think King begins with a reference to Lincoln?
2. Does this speech have a stated or an implied proposition? What is the proposition?
3. What does King hope to accomplish by the speech? How does he go about achieving his aim(s)?
4. What is the audience for the speech?
5. How does King organize his speech? How does this organization advance his purpose?
6. Which type(s) of argumentative appeal does King use? Cite appropriate parts of the speech.
7. What kinds of stylistic devices does King use? Where do they occur? How do they increase the effectiveness of the speech?

Toward Key Insights

To what extent do people of all races relate to King's message today? Explain your answer.

Suggestion for Writing

Write an essay calling for some major social or political change. For example, you might recommend that the country enact national health insurance, institute a peacetime draft, ban smoking in all public places, amend the Constitution to ban or legalize abortions, establish federally funded day-care centers for working parents, or offer all workers a thirty-day leave of absence without pay.

WILLIAM RASPBERRY

A Journalist's View of Black Economics[1]

William Raspberry (born 1935) grew up in Okolona, Mississippi, and received his education at Indiana Central College, where he earned a Bachelor of Science degree in 1958. In college, he worked as a reporter for the Indianapolis Recorder *and following graduation continued with that publication until he entered the army. In 1962, after his military service, he began working for the* Washington Post, *an association that continues to the present. Raspberry now authors a nationally syndicated column dealing with current issues, such as criminal justice and minority concerns. In this selection Raspberry argues that black Americans should spend less time blaming their problems on racial injustice and more time creating businesses and programs to help solve these problems.*

1   I am intensely interested in the subject of the economics of black America. However, I am neither a businessman, an economist, nor a social scientist. I'm a "newspaper guy."

[1]William Raspberry, "A Journalist's View of Black Economics," © 1990, Washington Post Writers Group. Reprinted with permission.

2   That's not an apology. I like being a newspaper guy, and I like to think I'm a pretty good one. I point it out simply to warn you up front that what you will hear from me is neither economic analysis nor nuts-and-bolt business proposals. I like to think about things in general and my proposal is that we ought to approach this subject in this fashion.

3   **Myths About Race.** One of the things I would like us to think about is a myth: a myth that has crippled black America, sent us off on unpromising directions, and left us ill-equipped to deal with either political or economic reality.

4   That myth is that race is of overriding importance, that it is a determinant not just of opportunity but also of potential, a reliable basis for explaining political and economic realities, a reasonable way of talking about geopolitics, and the overwhelming basis on which to deal with the relationships between us.

5   When I refer to race-based explanations of the plight of black America as myth, I do not mean to suggest that all such explanations are false. My reference is to the definition of myth as a "traditional account of unknown authorship, ostensibly with a historical basis, but serving usually to explain some observed phenomenon."

6   The historical basis of our preoccupation with race is easy enough to see. America did not invent slavery. Slavery as an institution predates the Bible. But American slavery was peculiarly race-based. Since slavery is the basis for the very presence of black people in America, small wonder that race has assumed such importance in our mythology.

7   But slavery was more than just involuntary, unpaid servitude. Unlike other populations, to whom enslavement seemed a reasonable way of dealing with conquered enemies, America was never happy with the concept of one group of human beings holding another group of human beings in bondage. I suppose it was taken as a sin against God. But rather than forgo the economic benefits of slavery, American slaveholders resolved the dilemma by defining blacks not as fellow human beings but more like beasts of burden. There is nothing ungodly about a man requiring unremunerated work of an animal. Didn't God give man dominion over the animals?

8   Now it may have been that Africans were a special kind of animal: capable of thought, and human language, and even worship. But as long as whites could persuade themselves that blacks were not fully human, they could justify slavery.

9   Thus was born and reinforced the myth of inherent white superiority, which later became the basis for racial separation, for Jim Crow laws, for unequal opportunity and all sorts of evil. Nor is it just among whites that the myth survives . . . .

10   The myth that blacks cannot prevail in intellectual competition, that Chinese youngsters cannot play basketball, that Jews are specially vulnerable to guilt trips—these are negative myths whose acceptance has led to failure because they feed the assumption that failure is inevitable.

11   Objective reality is the arena in which we all must perform. But the success or failure of our performance is profoundly influenced by the attitudes—the myths—we bring to that reality.

12   Two things flow from the racism-is-all myth that we have used to account for our difficulties. The first is that it puts the solution to our difficulties outside our control. If our problems are caused by racism, and their solutions dependent on ending racism, our fate is in the hands of people who, by definition, don't love us.

13   **A Skewed Definition of Civil Rights.** The second outcome of the myth is our inclination to think of our problems in terms of a failure of racial justice. "Civil

390

rights," which once referred to those things whose fair distribution was a governmental responsibility, now refers to any discrepancy. Income gaps, education gaps, test-score gaps, infant-mortality gaps, life-expectancy gaps, employment gaps, business-participation gaps—all now are talked about as "civil rights" issues.

14   The problems indicated by all these gaps are real. But describing them as "civil rights" problems steers us away from possible solutions. The civil rights designation evokes a sort of central justice bank, managed by the government, whose charge is to ladle out equal portions of everything to everybody. It prompts us to think about our problems in terms of inadequate or unfair distribution. It encourages the fallacy that to attack racism as the source of our problems is the same as attacking our problems. As a result, we expend precious resources—time, energy, imagination, political capital—searching (always successfully) for evidence of racism, while our problems grow worse.

15   Maybe I can make my point clearer by reference to two other minorities. The first group consists of poor whites. There are in America not just individuals but whole pockets of white people whose situation is hardly worse than our own.

16   And yet these poor whites have their civil rights. They can vote, live where their money permits them to live, eat where their appetites and their pocketbooks dictate, work at jobs for which their skills qualify them. And yet they are in desperate straits. It doesn't seem to occur to us that the full grant and enforcement of our civil rights would leave black Americans in about the same situation that poor white people are now in. That isn't good enough for me.

17   There is another minority whose situations may be more instructive. I refer to recently arrived Asian-Americans. What is the difference between them and us? Certainly it isn't that they have managed to avoid the effects of racism. Neither the newly arrived Southeast Asians nor the earlier arriving Japanese-Americans, Chinese-Americans, and Korean-Americans are loved by white people. But these groups have spent little of their time and energy proving that white people don't love them.

18   **Opportunity Knocks: Who Answers?** The difference between them and us is our operating myths. Our myth is that racism accounts for our shortcomings. Theirs is that their own efforts can make the difference, no matter what white people think.

19   They have looked at America as children with their noses pressed to the window of a candy store: if only I could get in there, boy, could I have a good time. And when they get in there, they work and study and save and create businesses and job opportunities for their people.

20   But we, born inside the candy store, have adopted a myth that leads us to focus only on the maldistribution of the candy. Our myth leads us into becoming a race of consumers, when victories accrue to the producers.

21   Interestingly enough, this is a fairly recent phenomenon. There was a time when we, like the more recent arrivals in this country, sought only the opportunity to be productive, and we grasped that opportunity under circumstances far worse—in law, at least—than those that obtain now.

22   Free blacks and former slaves, though denied many of the rights that we take for granted today, were entrepreneurial spirits. They were artisans and inventors, shopkeepers and industrialists, financiers and bankers. The first female millionaire in America was Madame C. J. Walker. At least two companies founded at the turn of the century are now on the *Black Enterprise* list of the 100 top black firms in the country.

23   Black real estate operatives transformed white Harlem into a haven for blacks. The early 1900s saw the founding of a number of all-black towns: Mound Bayou, Mississippi; Boley, Oklahoma; Nicodemus, Kansas; and others.

24   Boley at one time boasted a bank, twenty-five grocery stores, five hotels, seven restaurants, a waterworks, an electricity plant, four cotton gins, three drug stores, a bottling plant, a laundry, two newspapers, two colleges, a high school, a grade school, four department stores, a jewelry store, two hardware stores, two ice cream parlors, a telephone exchange, five churches, two insurance agencies, two livery stables, an undertaker, a lumber yard, two photography studios, and an ice plant [from J. DeSane, *Analogies and Black History: A Programmed Approach*]. Not bad for an all-black town of 4,000.

25   As Robert L. Woodson observed in his book, *On the Road to Economic Freedom,* "The Harlem and Boley experiences, which matched aggressive black entrepreneurial activity with the self-assertion drive of the black masses, was multiplied nationwide to the point that, in 1913, fifty years after Emancipation, black America had accumulated a personal wealth of $700 million.

26   "As special Emancipation Day festivals and parades were held that year in cities and towns across the country, blacks could take pride in owning 550,000 homes, 40,000 businesses, 40,000 churches, and 937,000 farms. The literacy rate among blacks climbed to a phenomenal 70 percent—up from 5 percent in 1863."

27   **Over-learning the Civil Rights Lesson.** What has happened since then? A lot of things, including a good deal of success that we don't talk much about. But among the things that have happened are two that have created problems for us. First is the overemphasis on integration, as opposed to desegregation and increased opportunity. Hundreds of thriving restaurants, hotels, service outlets, and entertainment centers have gone out of business because we preferred integration to supporting our own painstakingly established institutions. Indeed, aside from black churches and black colleges, little remains to show for that entrepreneurial spurt of the early decades of this century.

28   The other thing that has happened is that we over-learned the lessons of the civil rights movement. That movement, brilliantly conceived and courageously executed, marked a proud moment in our history. The upshot was that black Americans, for the first time in our sojourn here, enjoy the full panoply of our civil rights.

29   Unfortunately, that period also taught us to see in civil rights terms things that might more properly be addressed in terms of enterprise and exertion rather than in terms of equitable distribution. Even when we speak of business now, our focus is on distribution: on set-asides and affirmative action.

30   **Entrepreneurs and Self-Help.** Our 1960s success in making demands on government has led us to the mistaken assumption that government can give us what we need for the next major push toward equality. It has produced in us what Charles Tate of the Booker T. Washington Foundation recently described as a virtual antipathy toward capitalism.

31   Even middle-class blacks seldom talk to their children about going into business. Instead our emphasis is on a fair distribution of jobs in business created and run by others. We ought to have a fair share of those jobs. But the emphasis, I submit, ought to be finding ways to get more of us into business and thereby creating for ourselves the jobs we need.

32   That is especially true with regard to the so-called black underclass who tend to reside in areas abandoned by white businesses.

33   In addition to figuring out ways of getting our unemployed to jobs that already exist, we need to look for ways to encourage blacks in those abandoned neighborhoods to create enterprises of their own. What I have in mind are not merely the shops and Mom & Pop stores that we still patronize (but whose owners are far likelier to be Vietnamese or Koreans than blacks), but also an entrepreneurial approach to our social problems.

34   I am not suggesting that government has no role in attacking these problems. It has a major role. What I am suggesting is that we need to explore ways of creating government-backed programs that instead of merely making our problems more bearable go in the direction of solving those problems. We are forever talking about the lack of day care as an impediment to work for welfare families. But why aren't we lobbying for legislation that would relax some of the anti-entrepreneurial rules and permit some of the money now spent on public welfare to be used to establish child-care centers run by the neighbors of those who need the care? Why aren't we looking for ways to use the funds that are already being expended to create small jitney services to transport job-seekers to distant jobs?

35   **Success Is the Goal** I said at the beginning that I am not a theoretician, but I do have one little theory that may have some relevance to our subject. It is this: When people believe that their problems can be solved, they tend to get busy solving them—partly because it is the natural thing to do and partly because they would like to have the credit. When people believe that their problems are beyond solution, they tend to position themselves so as to avoid blame for their nonsolution.

36   Now none of the black leadership will tell you that they think the problems we face are beyond solution. To do so would be to forfeit their leadership positions. But their behavior, if my theory is correct, suggests their pessimism.

37   Let me offer an example of what I am talking about. Take the woeful inadequacy of education in the predominantly black central cities. Does the black leadership see the ascendancy of black teachers and school administrators and the rise of black politicians to positions of local leadership as assets to be used in improving those dreadful schools? Rarely. What you are more likely to hear are charges of white abandonment, white resistance to integration, white conspiracies to isolate black children even when the schools are officially desegregated. In short, white people are responsible for the problem.

38   But if the youngsters manage to survive those awful school systems and make their way to historically black colleges—that is, if the children begin to show signs that they are going to make it—these same leaders sing a different song. Give our black colleges a fair share of public resources, they say, and we who know and love our children will educate them.

39   The difference, I submit, is that they believe many of our high school students won't succeed, and they conspire to avoid the blame for their failure. But they believe that most of our college youngsters will make it, and they want to be in position to claim credit for their success.

40   I suspect something like that is happening in terms of our economic well-being. Many of us are succeeding, in an astonishing range of fields, and the leadership does not hesitate to point out—with perfect justification—that our success is attributable to the glorious civil rights movement: that black exertion and courage made our success possible.

41   But many of us aren't succeeding. Teenage pregnancy, dope trafficking, lawlessness, and lack of ambition make us doubt that they ever will succeed. But do our leaders suggest that the reasons have to do with the inadequacy of the civil rights movement, or with any lack of exertion and courage on the part of the

leadership? No. When we see failure among our people, and have reason to believe that the failure is permanent, our recourse is to our mainstay myth: Racism is the culprit. Mistakenly, we credit black pride for our successes and blame prejudice for our shortfalls.

42   I leave it to others to suggest the specifics by which we will move to increase the economic success of black America. I will tell you only that I believe it can be done—not only because it is being done by an encouraging number of us, but also because it has been done by earlier generations who struggled under circumstances of discrimination, deprivation, and hostility far worse than anything we now face.

43   My simple suggestion is that we stop using the plight of the black underclass as a scourge for beating up on white racists and examine both the black community and the American system for clues to how we can transform ourselves from consumers to producers.

44   I used to play a little game in which I would concede to members of the black leadership the validity of the racism explanation. "Let's say you're exactly right, that racism is the overriding reason for our situation, and that an all-out attack on racism is our most pressing priority," I'd tell them.

45   "Now let us suppose that we eventually win the fight against racism and put ourselves in the position now occupied by poor whites. What would you urge that we do next?"

46   "Pool our resources? Establish and support black businesses? Insist that our children take advantage of the opportunities that a society free of racism would offer? What should be our next step?"

47   "Well, just for the hell of it, why don't we pretend that the racist dragon has been slain already—and take that next step right now?"

Discussion Questions

1. Explain why Raspberry identifies himself as a "newspaper guy" in paragraph 1.
2. Why do you think Raspberry offers a precise definition of "myth" in paragraph 5?
3. Reread paragraphs 13 and 14 and point out specifically how Raspberry's views differ from those of Martin Luther King, Jr., in "I Have a Dream."
4. Discuss the effectiveness of the analogy Raspberry uses in paragraphs 19–20.
5. Cite three places in the essay where Raspberry states an idea and uses specific examples to clarify its meaning.
6. What writing strategy does Raspberry use to develop paragraphs 21–29?
7. Paragraphs 44–47 function as Raspberry's conclusion. Indicate why you think the conclusion is or is not effective.
8. Raspberry's and King's arguments were both delivered as speeches, King's in 1963 and Raspberry's in 1989. Which argument seems more effective? Does your answer stem from the content, effectiveness of presentation, or both?

Toward Key Insights

Raspberry makes an "entrepreneurial approach" seem like a relatively simple solution to widespread black poverty and related problems. What difficulties might such an approach face?

Is Raspberry right in suggesting that black Americans need to spend less time blaming racial injustice for their problems and more time creating businesses and enterprises? Why or why not?

Suggestion for Writing

Develop an argument that proposes how a minority group can best enhance its economic prosperity. Use whatever types of evidence seem appropriate.

NATHAN THORNBURGH

The Case for Amnesty

Nathan Thornburgh has been a Senior Editor for Time *magazine from 2000 to the present. He is author of a number of articles including "The Fallout from a Deportation" and "Dropout Nation." This article was published in* Time *in 2007.*

1   Amnesty has emerged as the pariah term of the immigration debate, disavowed even by those who believe in its goals. But what are the alternatives to letting illegals stay? Deporting millions? Devising other punishments? Doing nothing at all? Few places have struggled with these questions as much as rural Beardstown, Ill., where an April immigration raid at the town's largest employer exposed a community that is both dependent on its undocumented workers and deeply resentful of their presence. Why legalizing the illegals makes sense for Beardstown—and for America.

1. Amnesty Can Work Politically

2   One day before the June 5 Republican debate, Senator John McCain tried to preempt the coming criticism. He knew he would spend the debate flanked by nine candidates waiting to rip into the Senate compromise bill he helped write, which calls for a salve of legalization, border security and guest-worker programs. So in a Miami speech on June 4, he sought to distance himself from the *a* word. "Critics of the bill attack this as amnesty," he said. "(But) we impose fines, fees and other requirements as punishment." The bill, he said, is not amnesty.

3   Yes, it is. Whether you fine illegal aliens or stick them in English classes or make them say a hundred Hail Marys, at the end of the day, illegals would be allowed to stay and become citizens under this bill. That's amnesty. And that's a good thing for America. The estimated 12 million illegals are by their sheer numbers undeportable. More important, they are too enmeshed in a healthy U.S. economy to be extracted.

4   Yet the word *amnesty* was still used as a cudgel at the GOP debate—McCain's rivals clobbered him with the term, and he turned it on them as well, saying that doing nothing is "silent and de facto amnesty." Why are the bill's supporters so skittish about the word? If the past five years of immigration debate have taught us anything, it's that railing against the illegal invasion is easy, popular and effective. Now politicians are being roasted for conceding a reality: illegal or not, most of those 12 million are here to stay.

5   The heat extends from President George W. Bush to McCain and all the way down to the mayor of Beardstown, where a decade of intense immigration has

turned a nearly all-white town into a place in which 72% of the prekindergarten class is Hispanic. "If I got up and said I'm gonna run each and every Mexican out of town on a donkey, the voters here would cheer me on," says Mayor Bob Walters. "But I'm not going to say that. It's not our job to deport them all, and it's not the right thing to do."

6   Many of Beardstown's white residents were pleased by the federal raid on the massive pork-processing plant at the edge of town, owned by multinational meatpacker Cargill Meat Solutions (the April 4 operation targeted a subcontractor that was cleaning the plant, not Cargill itself). The raids netted 62 people, most of whom were sent to federal detention centers that night and later deported. "It's good they got those people," Oscar Cluney, 18, told me as he hung out with his friends in the parking lot of the local Save-a-Lot store. "The whole situation here makes me kind of mad."

7   And a lot of voters are upset too—but they are deeply conflicted about the right solution. A recent Gallup poll found that 60% of people who were following the bill closely were opposed to it. But an April *USA Today/Gallup* poll found that just 14% of respondents wanted to send illegal immigrants home with no chance of returning to the U.S. The public seems confused about the definition of amnesty.

8   Politicians are tapping into the public's uncertainty. In the June 5 GOP debate, Rudy Giuliani summed up the bill's problem this way: "It's a typical Washington mess," he said. He's right, of course, but not for the reasons he thinks. Rather, the bill is a mess because it doesn't fully embrace its most important aim: amnesty. Instead, it is laden with punitive measures—designed to evoke a certain toughness—that will at most just keep illegals from participating. Amnesty, as defined by its opponents, has come to mean getting forgiveness for free. But under the Senate's current compromise, the path for illegals is not anything close to easy. Under the compromise, the 12 million would face a 13-year process including $5,000 in fines per person, benchmarks for learning English and an onerous "touchback" provision that calls for the head of each household to leave job and family behind and return to his or her home country for an indeterminate amount of time to queue up for the final green card. Nothing free about that.

9   The touchback clause is partly designed to insulate the bill from criticism that amnesty would be unfair to those waiting in line to come legally. But that's a false comparison. If people are frustrated, as they should be, by the fact that some eligible immigrants have been waiting for citizenship for as many as 28 years, then by all means, fix that problem. Streamline the process for legal immigration. But don't blame that red-tape nightmare on the millions of low-wage illegals already here, who form a very different (and vastly more populous) group.

2. Amnesty Won't Depress Wages—Globalization Has Already Done That

10   Before you talk about amnesty, it makes sense to address the anger that many citizens feel. Across the U.S., Americans feel squeezed and threatened by the newcomers. Part of the anxiety is undeniably race based. Fox News's Bill O'Reilly leavened his reluctant support for the Senate bill with warnings that it "drastically alters" a country that is already "one-third minority." Others worry about language preservation. Republican Congressman Tom Tancredo of Colorado gave a breathless defense of the English language at the GOP debate, saying that bilingualism has failed other countries and that the U.S. was fast headed in that direction. Yes, it's true: Mexicans speak Spanish. Relax. Mexicans also know that English is the key to getting ahead in the U.S. When Beardstown

opened a bilingual program for all the kids in the elementary school, Hispanic parents were as worried as white parents about missing out on an English-only education. Assimilation is slow, but it is inevitable. Beardstown was settled in the 19th century by unapologetically German immigrants, but you won't hear so much as a gesundheit uttered there today. What is lacking, in Beardstown as in Washington, is faith in America's undimmed ability to metabolize immigrants from around the world, to change them more than they change the U.S.

11   Economic anxiety animates much of the resistance to amnesty, particularly from the left. Real wages have been stagnant for nearly three decades throughout the U.S., and for a place like working-class Beardstown, having to deal with a huge new influx of Spanish-speaking workers seems like adding insult to economic injury. But if times are tough in rural America, are illegal immigrants to blame? It turns out that the truly good jobs left Beardstown long before the Mexicans came. In the mid-'80s, the Cargill plant was owned by Oscar Mayer. Walters was the union representative at the plant back then, and he says it offered good jobs and good benefits, but globalization and other corporate pressures caught up with them. The company shuttered and sold the plant in 1987. Five months later, it reopened under a new owner, with lower wages and fewer benefits. "The starting wage went from $11 an hour to $7.50," says Walters. "The meatpacking industry ought to be ashamed of what they did to towns like ours."

12   The first Hispanics didn't come to work at Cargill en masse until years later. And as Cargill likes to point out, more white workers work at the factory than before. The plant has in fact grown, thanks in large part to hardworking migrants, not just from Mexico but from more than 20 other countries. The business seems robust for the time being. The workforce is unionized again. Salaries are creeping up. A new Wal-Mart Supercenter is on the way. Cargill's strength has turned Beardstown into, if not a boomtown, at least a place that investors are paying attention to. And the town is leading its pitch with the fact that it has a large Hispanic workforce, a bellwether for economic growth. "That's all I need to tell them," says Steve Twaddle, the county's director of economic development. "Businesses understand."

13   That progress, in Beardstown and in similar towns throughout the U.S., is imperiled by illegality. Cargill has long struggled to rid its rolls of illegal workers who are using false documentation. Most notably, a rumor that another raid was imminent swept through the night shift last month. Those workers who had false papers had to make a decision: stay and risk detention and deportation if the rumor were true, or leave and expose themselves as illegal workers. Cargill wouldn't comment on the incident, but locals say that dozens fled the plant that night and were fired or quit after having outed themselves by leaving.

14   It is not easy to replace them. Meatpacking is a hard job at any salary. There's plenty of new technology in the meatpacking industry, but no machine has yet been invented to take over some of the toughest positions, like the role of gut snatcher, whose sole job is to tug the offal out of each freshly killed hog that comes down the line.

15   The economics of immigration remain a mysterious science. Everyone has a pet study proving immigration suppresses wages or it builds economies. A less malleable truth is that many towns, like many companies, are faced with a stark choice in the global economy: grow or die. So Beardstown is growing, a healthy economy surrounded by dying rural towns. The U.S. is in the same situation. For all the stresses of immigration, it is the only industrialized nation with a population that is growing fast enough and skews young enough to provide the kind of

workforce that a dynamic economy needs. The illegals are part of the reason for that, and amnesty ensures that competitive advantage.

3. Amnesty Won't Undermine the Rule of Law

16   Google "This is a nation of laws," and you'll find a thousand online Cassandras warning that our failure to prosecute illegals is an invitation to anarchy. They are right about the U.S. being a nation of laws. But our legal system is not a house of cards, one flick away from collapse. U.S. jurisprudence has in fact always been a series of hedged bets, weighing the potential harm of a violation against the costs of enforcement. That's why people get arrested for assault but not for jaywalking. It's time to think seriously about exactly where the act of illegal immigration lies in the spectrum of criminality. Consider the complicity of U.S. employers ranging from multinational corporations to suburbanites looking for gardeners. Factor in the mixed signals that lax law enforcement sent to would-be immigrants throughout the '80s and '90s, and the crime should rank as a misdemeanor, not a felony. Even if we step up border enforcement in the future—as we should—it is true that for a long time, crossing the Rio Grande was akin more to jaywalking than breaking and entering.

17   Sure, there is a very real national-security threat in having a porous border. But a large—if unquantifiable—percentage of the people crossing that line illegally are not newcomers but rather people who have already established lives in the U.S. and would qualify for amnesty. If they were legalized and free to circulate, we could concentrate on the serious criminals and terrorists crossing the border, not a worker going back to his family.

18   In Beardstown, amnesty would also help authorities tackle crime. Right now, they spend a lot of their energy sorting out who is who in the community because illegals present local police with a bewildering maze of identities. The illegals of Beardstown work under one name and go to church under another. Parents give their kindergartners fake names to use in school. "We are absolutely unable to identify our own people," says Walters. It sounds counterintuitive, but with immigration, forgiving a crime may be the best way to restore law and order.

4. Amnesty Won't Necessarily Add to the Social-Services Burden

19   Many of the undesirable traits of illegal populations stem in large part from the simple fact that they are illegal. They use expensive emergency rooms because they lack insurance or are afraid a primary-care doctor might create a paper trail. They often don't file tax returns because of the same fear, and they turn to welfare or other social services because their illegal status consigns them to the lowest rung of the economy. We infantilize undocumented workers by relegating them to second-class status, and then we chastise them for being dependent on the nanny state.

20   "(White people) think we have it easy, that we don't pay taxes," says Fernanda, 19, whose parents were deported in the April raid. "They don't know how hard it is to get ahead here."

21   Fernanda has been in the U.S. since the eighth grade and graduated last year from Beardstown Middle/High School. Those five years of public education represent a significant investment by the U.S. government. And what's the return on that investment? Fernanda had dreams of going to college to study nursing, and Beardstown badly needs bilingual nurses. But she's illegal, and after the deportation of her parents, she has to support the entire family. So she's looking for work at local hog farms, a manual-labor job that does not make the most of her talents. "There's a great human potential in this town that doesn't see the light of day because of the legal status," says community organizer Julio Flores.

22   Some would argue that Fernanda should not have been schooled on our dime in the first place. But the reality is that Fernanda is here in the U.S. to stay. She's not going back to Mexico. Amnesty would offer millions like her a fighting chance at self-sufficiency and social mobility.

5. Amnesty Doesn't Have to Spawn Even More Illegal Immigration

23   A popular reading of recent history holds that the amnesty of 1986, which offered a path to citizenship for 3 million illegals, sparked the much larger wave of unlawful immigration that followed. According to that logic, the '86 amnesty showed would-be migrants from around the world that the U.S. was weak-willed and would eventually relent and give citizenship to its illegals. Duly encouraged, Mexicans and others stormed our borders with unprecedented vigor.

24   Illegal immigration did soar, but that's not why. Studies show that the valleys and peaks in migration have depended far less on changes in policy or policing and far more on the basic economic conditions in the U.S. and Mexico. If you want to truly tamp down illegal immigration, you could induce a recession in the U.S. A better idea might be to help Mexico create more jobs that pay better. A recent Council on Foreign Relations study found that when Mexican wages drop 10% relative to U.S. wages, attempts to cross the border illegally rise 6%. As complex and corrupt as the Mexican economy is, we ignore it at our peril.

25   While Mexico patches itself up, at least the security options are better today than in 1986. There is both the political will and the technology to make enforcement a serious part of any amnesty plan. National ID cards, real employer verification, high-tech border controls can all aid in making sure that this would be the last amnesty of this size.

26   Over fried catfish at the Riverview restaurant, Walters says he calls the feds about illegals in his town a few times a month. But he is tired of the hassle and ready for legalization. "If I could wave a magic wand, I'd rather have no Hispanics and have this town be like it was in the '50s. But that's just not going to happen," he says. "Amnesty is touchy, but we can't keep doing nothing."

27   The need for action is one thing that unites all the presidential candidates. And the coalition for immigration reform is strong enough—and wide enough—to take principled stands. The President, much of the Democratic Party, and a clutch of GOP lawmakers all support legalization. It's not too much to hope that together they could make a frank and forceful argument for amnesty and win over a conflicted nation.

Discussion Questions

1. Like many arguments, this one is written at a particular time in relation to ongoing situations, such as the 2007–08 primary season to which this article makes mention. Does the article manage to have an impact beyond its specific context and if so how?

2. The argument starts by identifying a lot of the political difficulty surrounding the idea of amnesty for illegal immigrants and yet embraces the term and idea of amnesty. Why does the author do this? Is this approach effective?

3. Much of the argument attempts to answer common objections to amnesty. Why does the author adopt this approach? What kinds of reasons or evidence does he use to answer these objections? Is it effective?

4. The author makes few positive arguments for amnesty. Where does the writer make such supportive arguments? Are they effective? Why or why not?

Toward Key Insights

The author approaches this issue as if it were simply a matter of measuring the benefits and harm of granting amnesty. Others approach the issue as one of principle: "we need to enforce the law or the concept of law is meaningless." Is there any way these two approaches can find common ground to carry on the discussion? Has the author achieved such a common ground?

The author attempts to assure the reader that granting "amnesty" will not result in harmful consequences. The problem of induction is that a few cases do not guarantee future results. Does he provide sufficient evidence to make this case? What would be necessary for him to make a convincing case for you as a reader?

Suggestion for Writing

Take one of the issues that the author addresses such as "amnesty won't undermine the rule of law" and argue for and against the author's position.

MARK KRIKORIAN

Not Amnesty but Attrition

Mark Krikorian is the Executive Director of the Center for Immigration Studies, a Washington D.C. think-tank that argues for stricter immigration policy. He is a regular contributor to National Review *and has also published articles in* The Washington Post, New York Times, *and* Commentary. *He is the author of* The New Case against Immigration, Both Legal and Illegal. *This article was Published in the* National Review *in March 2004.*

1   The issue of what to do about illegal aliens living in the United States is often presented as a Hobson's choice: either launch mass roundups to arrest and deport 9-million-plus people, or define away the problem through legalization.

2   The second option—amnesty—is the one President Bush chose in his January 7 speech on immigration. It also underlies many congressional proposals, from the McCain-Kolbe-Flake and Hagel-Daschle bills in the Senate to the House Democratic leadership's plan unveiled in late January.

3   Few among the political elite entertain any alternative. At a recent panel discussion on the president's immigration proposal, Margaret Spellings, the president's chief domestic-policy adviser, reacted with a demure chuckle to the suggestion that we enforce the law.

4   The commentariat is more explicit. Not content to politely ignore the notion of enforcing the law, the *Wall Street Journal,* for instance, has flatly asserted that it's not possible, a "fantasy" of the "extreme," "nativist," and "restrictionist" Right. Meanwhile, the Manhattan Institute's Tamar Jacoby wrote in *The New Republic* of "futile law enforcement" and how "the migrant flow is inevitable."

5   Fortunately for America there is a third way, between the politically impossible and disruptive approach of mass roundups on one hand, and the surrender of our sovereignty by the open-borders Left and its libertarian fellow-travelers on the other. This third way is attrition, squeezing the illegal population through

Mark Krikorian, "Not Amnesty, but Attrition." From *National Review* 56 no5 38-41 Mr 22 2004. Reprinted by permission.

consistent, across-the-board law enforcement to bring about an annual reduction in the illegal population rather than the annual increases we have seen for more than a decade. Over a few years, the number of illegal aliens would drop significantly, shrinking the problem from a crisis to a manageable nuisance.

Of Velvet Fists . . .

6   This isn't just a wonkish daydream. There is significant churn in the illegal population, which we can use to our advantage. According to a 2003 INS report, thousands of people stop being illegal aliens each year. From 1995 to 1999, an average of 165,000 a year went back home; the same number got some kind of legal status, about 50,000 were deported, and 25,000 died, for a total of more than 400,000 people each year subtracted from the resident illegal population. The problem is that the average inflow of new illegal aliens was nearly 800,000, swamping the outflow and creating an average annual increase of close to 400,000.

7   The solution, then, is to increase the number of people leaving the illegal population and to reduce the number of new illegal settlers, so that there is an annual decline in the total number. This is a measured, Burkean approach to the problem. It doesn't aspire to an immediate, magical solution to a long-brewing crisis, but rather helps us back out of an untenable situation that we helped create through our inattention to the law.

8   This begs the natural question: "But aren't we already enforcing the law?" If not, as a *Wall Street Journal* editorial has asked, "Then what is it we've been doing for 20 years now?" The answer lies in the old Soviet joke: "We pretend to work and they pretend to pay us."

9   Since 1986, Congress has passed muscular immigration laws and then made sure that they were not enforced. In that year, the Immigration Reform and Control Act (IRCA) was enacted, which traded an illegal-alien amnesty for a first-ever ban on the employment of illegal aliens. The point was to demagnetize the strong pull of good jobs—the main reason illegals come here in the first place.

10   More than 2.7 million illegals got legalized up front, with promises of tighter enforcement in the future. But the law itself was hobbled such that it became unworkable. Only if employers had a means of verifying the legal status of new hires against Social Security or INS databases could the law succeed—but Congress refused to require the INS to start developing such a system. Instead, employers were expected to do the verifying themselves, by examining a bewildering array of easily forged documents, and then they were threatened with discrimination lawsuits by the Justice Department if they looked too hard. It would be hard to imagine a system more obviously intended to fail.

11   Eventually, even this handicapped setup was sabotaged. After catching flak for workplace raids, the INS in 1998 decided to try a new approach to enforcing the hiring ban. Instead of raiding individual employers, Operation Vanguard sought to identify illegal workers at all the meatpacking plants in Nebraska through audits of personnel records. The INS then asked to interview those employees who appeared to be unauthorized—and the illegals ran off. The procedure was remarkably successful, and was meant to be repeated every two or three months until the whole industry was weaned from dependence on illegal labor.

12   Local police were very pleased with the results, but employers and politicians vociferously criticized the very idea of enforcing the immigration law. Nebraska governor Mike Johanns organized a task force to oppose the operation; the meat packers and the ranchers hired his predecessor, Ben Nelson, to lobby on their behalf; and, in Washington, Sen. Chuck Hagel made it his mission

in life to pressure the Justice Department to stop. The INS took the hint, and all but gave up on enforcing the hiring ban nationwide.

13   Nor is this the only example of tough-looking laws that go unenforced. In 1996 Congress passed a large immigration bill, which included a provision that sought to punish long-term illegal residence by barring illegals from future re-entry for three or ten years, depending on the length of the initial unlawful stay. Its scope was limited in any case, since it applied only to people who actually left the country and then tried to return, but it was denounced at the time by the usual suspects as "radical" and "draconian." But an examination of the law's results shows that, in its first four years, the bar prevented fewer than 12,000 people from re-entering the United States.

14   Even the expansion of border enforcement follows this pattern of ineffectuality. The Border Patrol has doubled in size since 1996, accounting for the lion's share of increased resources for enforcement. Its 10,000 agents are better equipped and doing a better job than ever before. But since, as any agent will tell you, the Border Patrol alone can't control illegal immigration, there's little danger that such increased capacity will actually curtail the flow. Again, it's a policy that appears tough, but isn't—a velvet fist in an iron glove.

Networking

15   Why does this happen? It is a manifestation of the yawning gap between public and elite opinion on immigration. The laws need to look tough, with promises of robust enforcement, to satisfy public concerns. But immigration's relatively low political importance for most people ensures that the elite preference for loose enforcement will be satisfied in the end.

16   But isn't the elite right in this case? Isn't immigration inevitable? Hardly. No one wakes up in Paraguay and decides, "Today, I will move to Sheboygan!" Immigration can take place only if there are networks of relatives, friends, and countrymen directing immigrants to a particular place. And these networks are a creation of government policy, either through proactive measures or through permitting networks to grow through non-enforcement of the law.

17   As an example, look at the Philippines and Indonesia. Both are populous, poor countries on the other side of the world, and yet the 2000 Census found about 19 times more Filipino immigrants in the United States than Indonesians, 1.4 million versus 73,000. Why? Because we ruled the Philippines for 50 years as a colony and maintained a major military presence there for another 50 years, allowing extensive networks to develop, whereas we have historically had little to do with Indonesia.

18   Granted, interrupting such networks is harder than creating them, but it is not impossible—after all, the trans-Atlantic immigration networks from the turn of the last century were successfully interrupted, and atrophied completely. And, to move beyond theory, the few times we actually tried to enforce the immigration law, it worked—until we gave up for political reasons.

19   During the first several years after the passage of the IRCA, illegal crossings from Mexico fell precipitously, as prospective illegals waited to see if we were serious. Apprehensions of aliens by the Border Patrol—an imperfect measure but the only one available—fell from more than 1.7 million in FY 1986 to under a million in 1989. But then the flow began to increase again as the deterrent effect of the hiring ban dissipated, when word got back that we were not serious about enforcement and that the system could be easily evaded through the use of inexpensive phony documents.

20   As I've written in these pages before, when we stepped up immigration enforcement against Middle Easterners (and only Middle Easterners) in the

wake of 9/11, the largest group of illegals from that part of the world, Pakistanis, fled the country in droves to avoid being caught up in the dragnet.

21   And in an inadvertent enforcement initiative, the Social Security Administration in 2002 sent out almost a million "no-match" letters to employers who filed W-2s with information that was inconsistent with SSA's records. The intention was to clear up misspellings, name changes, and other mistakes that had caused a large amount of money paid into the system to go uncredited. But, of course, most of the problem was caused by illegal aliens lying to their employers, and thousands of illegals quit or were fired when they were found out. The effort was so successful at denying work to illegals that business and immigrant-rights groups organized to stop it, and won a 90 percent reduction in the number of letters to be sent out.

War of Attrition

22   We know that when we actually enforce the law, eroding the illegal-immigration population is possible. So what would a policy of attrition look like? It would have two key components. The first would include more conventional enforcement—arrests, prosecutions, deportations, asset seizures, etc. The second would require verification of legal status at a variety of important choke points, to make it as difficult and unpleasant as possible to live here illegally.

23   As to the first, the authorities need to start taking immigration violations seriously. To use only one example, people who repeatedly sneak across the border are supposed to be prosecuted and jailed, and the Border Patrol unveiled a new digital fingerprint system in the mid '90s to make tracking of repeat crossers possible. The problem is that short-staffed U.S. attorneys' offices kept increasing the number of apprehensions needed before they would prosecute, to avoid actually having to prosecute at all.

24   It would be hard to exaggerate the demoralizing effect that such disregard for the law has on the Homeland Security Department's staff. Conversely, the morale of immigration workers would soar in the wake of a real commitment to law enforcement. We've already seen a real-world example of this, too. I met with deportation officers in a newly formed "fugitive operations team" in Southern California who, unlike other immigration personnel I have spoken with, were actually excited about their jobs. They still have gripes, but the clear political commitment to locating and deporting fugitive aliens communicates to them that their work is genuinely valued by their superiors all the way up to the White House.

25   Other measures that would facilitate enforcement include hiring more U.S. attorneys and judges in border areas, to allow for more prosecutions; passing the CLEAR Act, which would enhance cooperation between federal immigration authorities and state and local police; and seizing the assets, however modest, of apprehended illegal aliens.

26   But these and other enforcement measures will not remove most of the illegal population—the majority of illegals will have to be persuaded to deport themselves. Unlike at the visa office or the border crossing, once aliens are inside the United States, there's no physical place, no choke point at which to examine whether someone should be admitted. The solution is to create "virtual choke points"—events that are necessary for life in a modern society but are infrequent enough not to bog down the business of society.

27   This is the thinking behind the law banning the employment of illegal aliens—people have to work, so requiring proof of legal status upon starting a

job would serve as such a virtual choke point. As discussed above, in the absence of a verification mechanism, such a system couldn't succeed. But the president signed into law at the end of last year a measure to re-authorize and expand the verification pilot programs that immigration authorities have been experimenting with since the mid 1990s.

28   Building on this fledgling system, we need to find other instances in which legal status can be verified, such as getting a driver's license, registering an automobile, opening a bank account, applying for a car loan or a mortgage, enrolling children in public schools, and getting a business or occupational license.

29   An effective strategy of immigration law enforcement requires no booby traps, no tanks, no tattoos on arms—none of the cartoonish images invoked in the objections raised routinely by the loose-borders side. The consistent application of ordinary law-enforcement tools is all we need. "Consistent," though, is the key word. Enforcement personnel—whether Border Patrol agents, airport inspectors, or plainclothes investigators—need to know that their work is valued, that their superiors actually want them to do the jobs they've been assigned, and that they will be backed up when the inevitable complaints roll in.

30   And, finally, this isn't root-canal Republicanism, bitter medicine we swallow for the greater good. Enforcement of the immigration law may not be popular among the elite, but actual voters across the political spectrum are all for it. As Alan Wolfe wrote in *One Nation, After All*, the difference between legal and illegal immigrants "is one of the most tenaciously held distinctions in middle-class America; the people with whom we spoke overwhelmingly support legal immigration and express disgust with the illegal variety."

31   If only our political leadership felt the same way.

Discussion Questions

1. Why does the author not argue directly against amnesty but rather on how a program of attrition can work?
2. What is the main organization of the author's argument? Is the argument simple or complex? How does this influence the effectiveness of the argument?
3. What kinds of evidence does the author use mostly? How does this evidence affect the credibility of the argument?
4. Why does the author use the examples of the Philippines and Indonesia? How does this strengthen and/or weaken his argument?
5. What is the function of paragraph 29 in the author's argument?

Toward Key Insights

Many in creating an argument seek to tackle all of the issues in the debate. This argument focuses on one narrow aspect of the debate. What are the advantages and disadvantages in focusing on one very specific issue or option?

Whenever we argue, we make assumptions which can be questioned in turn. Since the essay focuses very specifically on attrition as a strategy to reduce the number of illegal immigrants, what objections might someone raise to this approach that don't concern the strategy in question?

Suggestion for Writing

Perhaps with some research, write an argument for/or against using a verification system such as enrolling children in public schools to serve as a choke point. Consider what steps would be necessary to make such a system work.

Identify and argue for or against one of the assumptions of the writer. For example, someone could argue that it would simply be harmful to the economy to use attrition to move out illegal immigrants who are already productive workers.

MIXING THE WRITING
STRATEGIES

Reading Strategies

1. When skimming, identify the main point the author is attempting to make.
2. To orient your reading, note in the margins the strategy the reader is using.
3. Focus on how the points fit together to develop the author's thesis.

Reading Critically

1. Test whether the claims throughout the text really support the thesis.
2. Evaluate the claims based on the critical reading strategy appropriate to the technique being used.
3. Judge whether the writer's strategies are appropriate to the point he or she is making.

Reading As a Writer

1. Identify how the writer effectively changes from strategy to strategy.
2. Look to determine how the writer connects each strategy to the main thesis.
3. Read the conclusion carefully to determine how the writer pulls a complex essay back together to make his or her main point.

Most essays mix various writing strategies for assorted purposes. This section features three examples. The discussion questions following the Sullivan and Tannen essays direct your attention to the strategies these writers use as well as other relevant aspects of the essays.

MICHAEL POLLAN

Supermarket Pastoral

Michael Pollan received an MA in English from Columbia University. He has been a contributing writer to The New York Time Magazine *since 1987. His writing has won a number of awards, including the Global Award for Environmental Journalism. He has published many articles and several books. This selection is from his 2006 book* The Omnivore's Dilemma: A Natural History of Four Meals *published by Penguin Press.*

Michael Pollan, "Supermarket Pastoral." From *The Omnivore's Dilemma: A Natural History of Four Meals.* New York: Penguin Books, 2006. pp. 134-139. Reprinted by permission.

1   I enjoy shopping at Whole Foods nearly as much as I enjoy browsing a good bookstore, which, come to think of it, is probably no accident. Shopping at Whole Foods is a literary experience, too. That's not to take anything away from the food, which is generally of high quality, much of it "certified organic" or "humanely raised" or "free range." But right there, that's the point. It's the evocative prose as much as anything else that makes this food really special, elevating an egg or chicken breast or a bag of arugula from the realm of ordinary protein and carbohydrates into a much headier experience, one with complex aesthetic, emotional, and even political dimensions. Take the "range-fed" sirloin steak I recently eyed in the meat case. According to the brochure on the counter, it was formerly part of a steer that spent its days "living in beautiful places" ranging from "plant-diverse, high-mountain meadows to thick aspen groves and miles of sagebrush-filled flats." Now a steak like that has got to taste better than one from Safeway, where the only accompanying information comes in the form of a number: the price I mean, which you can bet will be considerably less. But I'm evidently not the only shopper willing to pay more for a good story.

2   With the growth of organics and mounting concerns about the wholesomeness of industrial food, storied food is showing up in supermarkets everywhere these days, but it is Whole Foods that consistently offers the most cutting-edge grocery lit. On a recent visit I filled my shopping cart with eggs "from cage-free vegetarian hens," milk from cows that live "free from unnecessary fear and distress," wild salmon caught by Native Americans in Yakutat, Alaska (population 833), and heirloom tomatoes from Capay Farm ($4.99 a pound), "one of the early pioneers of the organic movement." The organic broiler I picked up even had a name: Rosie, who turned out to be a "sustainably farmed" "free-range chicken" from Petaluma Poultry, a company whose "farming methods strive to create harmonious relationships in nature, sustaining the health of all creatures and the natural world." Okay, not the most mellifluous or even meaningful sentence, but at least their heart's in the right place.

3   In several corners of the store I was actually forced to choose between subtly competing stories. For example, some of the organic milk in the milk case was "ultrapasteurized," an extra processing step that was presented as a boon to the consumer, since it extends shelf life. But then another, more local dairy boasted about the fact they had said no to ultrapasteurization, implying that their product was fresher, less processed, and therefore more organic. This was the dairy that talked about cows living free from distress, something I was beginning to feel a bit of myself by this point.

4   This particular dairy's label had a lot to say about the bovine lifestyle: Its Holsteins are provided with "an appropriate environment, including shelter and a comfortable resting area, . . . sufficient space, proper facilities and the company of their own kind." All this sounded pretty great, until I read the story of another dairy selling raw milk—completely unprocessed—whose "cows graze green pastures all year long." Which made me wonder whether the first dairy's idea of an appropriate environment for a cow included, as I had simply presumed, a pasture. All of a sudden the absence from their story of that word seemed weirdly conspicuous. As the literary critics would say, the writer seemed to be eliding the whole notion of cows and grass. Indeed, the longer I shopped in Whole Foods, the more I thought that this is a place where the skills of a literary critic might come in handy—those, and perhaps also a journalist's.

5   Wordy labels, point-of-purchase brochures, and certification schemes are supposed to make an obscure and complicated food chain more legible to the consumer. In the industrial food economy, virtually the only information that travels along the food chain linking producer and consumer is price. Just look at the

---

Margin annotations:

Narrative to establish context

Illustration of claim

Comparison

Illustration

Illustration

Effect

Illustration

"Eliding" is a literary critic's term for cutting out or avoiding a word

Cause

Comparison

typical newspaper ad for a supermarket. The sole quality on display here is actually a quantity: tomatoes $0.69 a pound; ground chuck $1.09 a pound; eggs $0.99 a dozen—special this week. Is there any other category of product sold on such a reductive basis? The bare-bones information travels in both directions, of course, and farmers who get the message that consumers care only about price will themselves care only about yield. This is how a cheap food economy reinforces itself.

6   One of the key innovations of organic food was to allow some more information to pass along the food chain between the producer and the consumer—an implicit snatch of narrative along with the number. A certified organic label tells a little story about how a particular food was produced, giving the consumer a way to send a message back to the farmer that she values tomatoes produced without harmful pesticides or prefers to feed her children milk from cows that haven't been injected with growth hormones. The word "organic" has proved to be one of the most powerful words in the supermarket: Without any help from government, farmers and consumers working together in this way have built an $11 billion industry that is now the fastest growing sector of the food economy.

7   Yet the organic label itself—like every other such label in the supermarket—is really just an imperfect substitute for direct observation of how a food is produced, a concession to the reality that most people in an industrial society haven't the time or the inclination to follow their food back to the farm, a farm which today is apt to be, on average, fifteen hundred miles away. So to bridge that space we rely on certifiers and label writers and, to a considerable extent, our imagination of what the farms that are producing our food really look like. The organic label may conjure an image of simpler agriculture, but its very existence is an industrial artifact. The question is, what about the farms themselves? How well do they match the stories told about them?

8   Taken as a whole, the story on offer in Whole Foods is a pastoral narrative in which farm animals live much as they did in the books we read as children, and our fruits and vegetables grow in well-composted soils on small farms much like Joel Salatin's. "Organic" on the label conjures up a rich narrative, even if it is the consumer who fills in most of the details, supplying the hero (American Family Farmer), the villain (Agribusinessman), and the literary genre, which I've come to think of as Supermarket Pastoral. By now we may know better than to believe this too simple story, but not much better, and the grocery store poets do everything they can to encourage us in our willing suspension of disbelief.

9   Supermarket Pastoral is a most seductive literary form, beguiling enough to survive in the face of a great many discomfiting facts. I suspect that's because it gratifies some of our deepest, oldest longings, not merely for safe food, but for a connection to the earth and to the handful of domesticated creatures we've long depended on. Whole Foods understands all this better than we do. One of the company's marketing consultants explained to me that the Whole Foods shopper feels that by buying organic he is "engaging in authentic experiences" and imaginatively enacting a "return to a utopian past with the positive aspects of modernity intact." This sounds a lot like Virgilian pastoral, which also tried to have it both ways. In *The Machine in the Garden* Leo Marx writes that Virgil's shepherd Tityrus, no primitive, "Enjoys the best of both worlds—the sophisticated order of art and the simple spontaneity of nature." In keeping with the pastoral tradition, Whole Foods offers what Marx terms "a landscape of reconciliation" between the realms of nature and culture, a place where, as the marketing consultant put it, "people will come together through organic foods to get back to the origin of things"—perhaps by sitting down to enjoy one of the microwaveable organic TV dinners (four words I never expected to see conjoined) stacked in the frozen food case. How's that for having it both ways?

407

Effect

Description

Effect

Cause

Comparison

Narrative

Argument-Reason

Argument-Reason

10   Of course the trickiest contradiction Whole Foods attempts to reconcile is the one between the industrialization of the organic food industry of which it is a part and the pastoral ideals on which that industry has been built. The organic movement, as it was once called, has come a remarkably long way in the last thirty years, to the point where it now looks considerably less like a movement than a big business. Lining the walls above the sumptuously stocked produce section in my Whole Foods are full-color photographs of local organic farmers accompanied by text blocks setting forth their farming philosophies. A handful of these farms— Capay is one example—still sell their produce to Whole Foods, but most are long gone from the produce bins, if not yet the walls. That's because Whole Foods in recent years has adopted the grocery industry's standard regional distribution system, which makes supporting small farms impractical. Tremendous warehouses buy produce for dozens of stores at a time, which forces them to deal exclusively with tremendous farms. So while the posters still depict family farmers and their philosophers, the produce on sale below them come primarily from the two big corporate organic growers in California, Earthbound Farm and Grimmway Farms, which together dominate the market for organic fresh produce in America. (Earthbound alone grows 80% of the organic lettuce sold in America.)

11   As I tossed a plastic box of Earthbound prewashed spring mix salad into my Whole Foods cart, I realized that I was venturing deep into the belly of the industrial beast Joel Salatin had called "the organic empire." (Speaking of my salad mix, another small, beyond organic farmer, a friend of Joel's, had told me he "wouldn't use the stuff to make compost"—the organic purist's stock insult.) But I'm not prepared to accept the premise that industrial organic is necessarily a bad thing, not if the goal is to reform a half-trillion-dollar food system based on chain supermarkets and the consumer's expectations that food be convenient and cheap.

12   And yet to the extent that the organic movement was conceived as a critique of industrial values, surely there comes a point when the process of industrialization will cost organic its soul (to use a word still uttered by organic types without irony), when Supermarket Pastoral becomes more fiction than fact: another lie told by marketers.

13   The question is, has that point been reached, as Joel Salatin suggests? Just how well does Supermarket Pastoral hold up under close reading and journalistic scrutiny?

Discussion Questions

1. This section of a book uses several strategies. What strategy is dominant? How does this strategy match the main point of this essay?
2. What is the effect of the author starting and returning to a narrative of his own shopping trip at Whole Foods?
3. In several places the author specifically talks about words and phrases. What are some of the words and phrases the writer discusses? Why is it important for him to talk about this language usage?
4. In paragraph 4 the author deliberately uses a sentence fragment. Is this use of a fragment effective? Why or why not?
5. This section ends in paragraph 13 with questions. Of course, the author goes on to answer these questions in the material that follows this selection. Out of context, is this conclusion effective? What do you think based on the earlier content of this text will be the answer to his questions? What evidence leads you to that conclusion?

Toward Key Insights

A large number of essays and a fair amount of college classes spend time discussing the language people use. Based on this essay, why is this discussion of language important?

In this text, the author discusses the importance of using the skills of the literary critic. Why does he think such skills are important to understanding a supermarket? Where else might the skills of the literary critic be useful?

This essay lays out the Supermarket Pastoral as one narrative used to sell food. What other narratives can you identify that are used to sell products?

Suggestions for Writing

Visit a supermarket, a toy store, a car dealership or observe several advertisements, then write an essay explaining the narrative used to sell the products.

Identify an area of life where the talk about the experience and the experience don't match and write a paper that compares the language and the reality, offering an explanation for the language and an account of the effect that the language has on those who hear or read it.

DEBORAH A. SULLIVAN

Social Bodies: Tightening the Bonds of Beauty

Deborah A. Sullivan teaches sociology at Arizona State University. She is the coauthor of Labor Pains: Modern Midwives and Home Birth, *in addition to a number of articles. The selection here is taken from the first chapter of her book* Cosmetic Surgery: The Cutting Edge of Commercial Medicine in America. *In this section she examines the reasons for and changing meanings of tattooing.*

1   Every culture has some customs that prescribe deliberately changing a body's natural appearance (Brain 1979). The methods, however, are diverse and particular to a culture at a specific period of time. Paints, for example, are used to decorate bodies in many cultures, but the pigments, patterns, permanency, and purpose of each culture's body customs vary widely. Only a nineteenth-century Bedouin woman could appreciate the eroticism of painting the whites of a man's eyes blue. While she would have regarded her own culture's customs as highly "civilized," she probably would have thought the full body designs of Aboriginal Australians, American Indians, and Africans savage. Like eighteenth-century European explorers, she might have considered the tattooing and tooth-blackening in the Pacific region bizarre, and found the deeply carved black spirals and curves on Maori faces frightening and repulsive. It is no more likely that she could have discerned the beauty intended by the African and South American tribes who create elaborate patterns of raised scars, insert large lip plates and ear and nose plugs, and file teeth to sharp points. Nor is it likely that she could have appreciated the charm of Chinese women's bound "lotus" feet,

Padaung women's elongated necks, or Western women's constricted waists during the Victorian era and augmented breasts in recent decades. Instead, in the implausible circumstance that a nineteenth-century Bedouin woman was exposed to such body customs, she probably would have regarded them as barbaric mutilations, much as contemporary Americans' view of female circumcision, which she might have considered normal.

2   The diversity of body customs has led anthropologists (e.g., Douglas 1970; Strathern 1996) to conclude that a body is both a physical and a symbolic artifact, forged by nature and by culture at a particular moment in history. Social institutions, ideology, values, beliefs, and technology transform a physical body into a social body. The resulting social body bears the imprint of the more powerful elements of its cultural context. Bodies, therefore, provide important clues to the mechanics of society.

3   There are many well-documented examples of the cultural construction of a social body. Although some body customs may be merely decorative, many, if not most, have social significance. Cultures in which female circumcision is common are strongly patriarchal and pronatalist. Women in these traditional cultures are believed to be weak and incapable of controlling their sexual urges. They are allowed little contact with men outside their families and are expected to hide their bodies from public view. Their social roles are circumscribed to child care and domestic functions. They receive little education and are economically dependent on men and politically powerless. They are socialized by their mothers to believe that removal of external female genitalia is a religious obligation that promotes purity, cleanliness, and fertility and that unexcised women are unattractive and beastly. Their identities as desirable women depend on the submission of their physical bodies to the dictates of social norms. The custom embodies their inferior status.

4   As female circumcision illustrates, the body can be a site for the expression of power in a culture. It also is used to communicate group membership, individual status, and social identity, along with associated beliefs and values. The body is often ritually modified in connection with major life transitions. In the Australian Aboriginal culture, for example, one or two front teeth are removed at puberty. Some time later boys are painted white, secluded, and circumcised to symbolize their passage into the world of men. At the end of the ceremony, they are painted red to celebrate their reentry into society as young men with all the corresponding rights and expectations of their new status. In some tribes young men undergo a subincision ceremony in which their urethra is split open before they marry and assume full adult male rights. Rites of passage between life stages in many other cultures are marked by ritualized patterns of scarification, piercing, and tattooing. These same techniques are used to proclaim more permanent kinds of social status, such as gender and social class, as are head molding and other body modifications.

5   Using the body to communicate power, group membership, individual status, and social identity is not limited to exotic non-Western societies. It is ubiquitous in modern societies as well. American sailors, prisoners, bikers, and other gang members have tattooed their bodies throughout most of the twentieth century. Clinton Sanders (1989) argues that they use this particular body custom, considered vulgar by most middle-class, middle-aged Americans, to proclaim their resistance to conventional social norms of appearance and behavior. Their preference for death symbols, predatory animals, insulting and salacious images further enhances their rebellious statement.

6   After the mid-1960s the shock value of tattoos made them popular among some younger artistic individuals looking for attention and innovative, creative

modes of expression. By the 1980s they were de rigueur among heavy metal and rap performers seeking a following among adolescents and young adults based on flaunting the conventional values and beliefs of their parents and other authority figures. Punks, freaks, Goths, skinheads, stoners, tweakers, and other disaffected young adults who identified with the counterculture heroes of their generation went to shops with names like Hierarchy, Crawling Squid, and Pigments of Imagination to record their sense of alienation on their bodies.

7   The meaning of tattoos changed in the 1990s. They became a badge of youth. Professional athletes, middle-class college students, blue-collar workers, and even some suburban housewives marked their bodies with tribal patterns, Kanji lettering, and sexy butterflies and flowers. As the shock value of tattoos declined, the most alienated subgroups added other forms of body modifications to advertise their contempt for middle-class conventions. They pierced their ears, noses, eyebrows, lips, tongues, nipples, navels, and genitalia with safety pins, barbells, studs, and various rings. These cultural pioneers established Internet news groups to share information about techniques, complications, public reaction, and erotic effects. Pop singers and other media celebrities adopted less extreme versions of this new body custom to advertise their hip identity. High school girls turned nose studs and navel rings into a fashion statement, undermining their deviance value. Those seeking a body symbol of resistance capable of generating strong public revulsion experimented with more extreme forms of self-stigmatization, such as scalp implants and scarification, to proclaim their marginalized status.

8   Tattooing and piercing at the end of the twentieth century appear to have much in common with previous fashion fads that visually differentiated each young generation over the course of the twentieth century, although some cultural observers (e.g., Polhemus and Randall 1996) find deeper meaning in these trends. They suggest the practices express a yearning for continuity, community, and commitment in a fragmented postmodern culture where ritual is rare and anomie prevails. Tattooing and piercing offer more permanent ways of recording life transitions and one's place in society.

9   All body customs, whether temporary, like tweezing eyebrows and clipping nose hair, or more permanent, like tattoos and cosmetic surgery, are forms of self-creation. They are an effort to achieve a desired identity and connection with a reference group—marginal, hip, or mainstream. The process of reincarnation is universal.

10   Kim Hewitt (1997) additionally argues that body customs, particularly painful ones, can be used as part of a self-chosen health ritual. She theorizes that the physiological effects of pain can stimulate at least a temporary reprieve from numbing feelings of alienation (118). The acute awareness of feeling alive induced by pain has the potential to replace psychological fragmentation with holistic integration and a euphoric feeling of self-mastery. She claims that young women who starve and cut their bodies, like the punks and other marginalized subgroups who customize their bodies in extreme ways, are not only rebelling against societal constrictions, they also are trying to reclaim control of their bodies and establish individuality and autonomy. Other body customs, including female bodybuilding (Heywood 1998) and cosmetic surgery (Davis 1995), have been similarly interpreted as methods of psychological healing and cultural empowerment.

11   Those with a more Foucauldian perspective, such as Susan Bordo (1993, 1997), argue that such "disciplinary" body customs are outward manifestations of internalized cultural oppression. The discipline comes from an awareness of prevailing values, beliefs, norms and voluntary self-surveillance. Consequently, the

sense of power experienced by disciplining one's own body, whether to resist prevailing cultural dictates with tattoos and piercings or successfully conform to them with diets and cosmetic surgery, is merely a personal achievement that lacks political effect to change the culture. Instead, as Rosemary Gillespie (1996) points out, customs such as cosmetic surgery perpetuate wider social inequalities.

12   This debate raises perennial philosophical questions about the nature of social control and the extent of free will. It also raises contemporary concerns that interpreting personal behavior as victimization deprives individuals of agency and castes them as gullible cultural dupes. My own perspective is similar to that of Bordo. Respect for the right of competent adults to make decisions about their own bodies should not blind us to the impact of the larger cultural and social context in which personal choices occur. My aim is to bring the structural aspects of this context, aspects that construct cosmetic surgery, into sharper focus. This larger cultural and social context influences individual body choices, gives them social meaning, and makes some, like cosmetic surgery, common enough to be considered body customs.

■ Works Cited

Bardo, Susan. *Unbearable Weight: Feminism, Western Culture, and the Body.* Berkeley: U of California Press, 1993.

Bordo, Susan. "Braveheart, Babe, and the Body: Contemporary Images of the Body." In *Twilight Zone: The Hidden Life of Cultural Images from Plato to O.J.,* ed. Susan Bordo. Berkeley: U of California Press, 1997.

Brain, Robert. *The Decorated Body.* London: Hutchinson, 1979.

Davis, Kathy. *Reshaping the Female Body: The Dilemma of Cosmetic Surgery.* New York: Routledge, 1995.

Douglas, Mary. *Natural Symbols: Explorations in Cosmology.* New York: Pantheon, 1970.

Gillespie, Rosemary. 1996. "Women, the Body, and Brand Extension in Medicine: Cosmetic Surgery and the Paradox of Choice." *Women and Health* 24: 69–85.

Hewitt, Kim. *Mutilating the Body: Identity in Blood and Ink.* Bowling Green, Ohio: Bowling Green State U Popular Press, 1997.

Heywood, Leslie. 1998. *Bodymakers: A Cultural Anatomy of Women's Body Building.* New Brunswick, NJ: Rutgers U Press.

Polhemus, Ted, and Housk Randall. *The Customized Body.* New York: Serpent's Tale, 1996.

Sanders, Clinton. *Customizing the Body: The Art and Culture of Tatooing.* Philadelphia: Temple UP, 1989.

Strathern, Andrew. 1996. *Body Thoughts.* Ann Arbor: Michigan Press.

Discussion Questions

1. Identify the author's thesis statement. Explain as fully as possible what the author means by the thesis statement.

2. What are the advantages of the author's using many examples of body modification? How does that help make her point?
3. In the introduction, the author starts by describing the possible reaction of a nineteenth-century Bedouin woman to a variety of body modifications. What are the effects of this approach?
4. Why does the author discuss the changing meaning of tattooing?
5. This selection not only illustrates the author's thesis but does so by specifying possible causes for body modification. Identify the causes the author discusses. Do those that apply to modern tattooing seem correct to you?
6. This section from a chapter of a book draws on a variety of sources and is extensively documented. What effect does this have on the essay?
7. In the conclusion of this selection, the author raises a number of broader questions. What role do these questions play given that this selection is part of the first chapter of a book? Are they effective here where they are serving as a conclusion?

Toward Key Insights

Tattooing, piercing, and scarification are increasingly common practices. What reasons do you see for these practices?

Are those who participate in such practices "cultural dupes" who blindly follow cultural expectations or free individuals who make personal choices?

Suggestion for Writing

Write a paper that illustrates a cultural practice that you think is significant, such as the crucial role of music in the life of many college students and teens.

DEBORAH TANNEN

Gender Gap in Cyberspace[1]

Deborah Tannen born 1945) earned a B.S. degree from the State University of New York in 1966 and a PhD from the University of California in 1979. She is now a member of the linguistics department of Georgetown University. Tannen has authored a number of books on speaking and writing as well as numerous shorter pieces that have appeared in the New York Times, Newsweek, People, *and the* Harvard Business Review. *In this selection, Tannen investigates the causes and effects of the differing male and female attitudes toward e-mail.*

1   I was a computer pioneer, but I'm still something of a novice. That paradox is telling.

2   I was the second person on my block to get a computer. The first was my colleague Ralph. It was 1980. Ralph got a Radio Shack TRS-80, I got a used Apple

II +. He helped me get started and went on to become a maven, reading computer magazines, hungering for the new technology he read about, and buying and mastering it as quickly as he could afford. I hung on to old equipment far too long because I dislike giving up what I'm used to, fear making the wrong decision about what to buy, and resent the time it takes to install and learn a new system.

3   My first Apple came with videogames; I gave them away. Playing games on the computer didn't interest me. If I had free time I'd spend it talking on the telephone to friends.

4   Ralph got hooked. His wife was often annoyed by the hours he spent at his computer and the money he spent upgrading it. My marriage had no such strains—until I discovered E-mail. Then I got hooked. E-mail draws me the same way the phone does: it's a souped-up conversation.

5   E-mail deepened my friendship with Ralph. Though his office was next to mine, we rarely had extended conversations because he is shy. Face to face he mumbled so, I could barely tell he was speaking. But when we both got on E-mail, I started receiving long, self-revealing messages: we poured our hearts out to each other. A friend discovered that E-mail opened up that kind of communication with her father. He would never talk much on the phone (as her mother would), but they have become close since they both got online.

6   Why, I wondered, would some men find it easier to open up on E-mail? It's a combination of the technology (which they enjoy) and the obliqueness of the written word, just as many men will reveal feelings in dribs and drabs while riding in the car or doing something, which they'd never talk about sitting face to face. It's too intense, too bearing-down on them, and once you start you have to keep going. With a computer in between, it's safer.

7   It was on E-mail, in fact, that I described to Ralph how boys in groups often struggle to get the upper hand whereas girls tend to maintain an appearance of cooperation. And he pointed out that this explained why boys are more likely to be captivated by computers than girls are. Boys are typically motivated by a social structure that says if you don't dominate you will be dominated. Computers, by their nature, balk; you type a perfectly appropriate command and it refuses to do what it should. Many boys and men are incited by this defiance: "I'm going to whip this into line and teach it who's boss! I'll get it to do what I say!" (and if they work hard enough, they always can). Girls and women are more likely to respond, "This thing won't cooperate. Get it away from me!"

8   Although no one wants to think of herself as "typical"—how much nicer to be *sui generis*—my relationship to my computer is—gulp—fairly typical for a woman. Most women (with plenty of exceptions) aren't excited by tinkering with the technology, grappling with the challenge of eliminating bugs or getting the biggest and best computer. These dynamics appeal to many men's interest in making sure they're on the top side of the inevitable who's-up-who's-down struggle that life is for them. E-mail appeals to my view of life as a contest for connections to others. When I see that I have fifteen messages, I feel loved.

9   I once posted a technical question on a computer network for linguists and was flooded with long dispositions, some pages long. I was staggered by the generosity and the expertise, but wondered where these guys found the time—and why all the answers I got were from men.

10   Like coed classrooms and meetings, discussions on E-mail networks tend to be dominated by male voices, unless they're specifically women-only, like single-sex schools. Online, women don't have to worry about getting the floor (you just send a message when you feel like it), but, according to linguists Susan Herring and Laurel Sutton, who have studied this, they have the usual problems of having their messages ignored or attacked. The anonymity of public networks frees a small number of men to send long, vituperative, sarcastic messages that many other men either can tolerate or actually enjoy, but that turn most women off.

11   The anonymity of networks leads to another sad part of the E-mail story: there are men who deluge women with questions about their appearance and invitations to sex. On college campuses, as soon as women students log on, they are bombarded by references to sex, like going to work and finding pornographic posters adorning the walls.

12   Most women want one thing from a computer—to work. This is significant counterevidence to the claim that men want to focus on information while women are interested in rapport. That claim I found was most often true in casual conversation, in which there is no particular information to be conveyed. But with computers, it is often women who are more focused on information, because they don't respond to the challenge of getting equipment to submit.

13   Once I had learned the basics, my interest in computers waned. I use it to write books (though I never mastered having it do bibliographies or tables of contents) and write checks (but not balance my checkbook). Much as I'd like to use it to do more, I begrudge the time it would take to learn.

14   Ralph's computer expertise costs him a lot of time. Chivalry requires that he rescue novices in need, and he is called upon by damsel novices far more often than knaves. More men would rather study the instruction booklet than ask directions, as it were, from another person. "When I do help men," Ralph wrote (on E-mail, of course), "they want to be more involved. I once installed a hard drive for a guy, and he wanted to be there with me, wielding the screwdriver and giving his own advice where he could." Women, he finds, usually are not interested in what he's doing; they just want him to get the computer to the point where they can do what they want.

15   Which pretty much explains how I managed to be a pioneer without becoming an expert.

Discussion Questions

1. Does Tannen deal with causes, effects, or both? Refer to the essay when answering.
2. Characterize the level of diction in this essay.
3. Why do you think Tannen cites the two linguists in paragraph 10?
4. Point out the connecting devices that link the paragraphs in this essay.
5. What additional strategies does Tannen use?
6. Does your experience in cyberspace bear out Tannen's assertion about a gender gap? Discuss, citing specific examples.

Toward Key Insights

How do you account for the differences that Tannen describes? Do you believe that
they are inborn or stem mainly from cultural patterns?

What steps might be taken to lessen these differences?

Suggestion for Writing

*Write an essay exploring how gender affects dating done through the Internet. Support your
essay with relevant, specific details.*

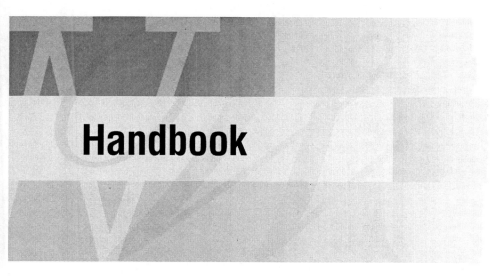

Handbook

Sentence Elements

Learning the parts of English sentences won't in itself improve your writing, but it will equip you to handle errors at the sentence level. Before you can identify and correct unwarranted shifts from past to present time, for example, you need to know about verbs and their tenses. Similarly, recognizing and correcting pronoun case errors require a knowledge of what pronouns are and how they are used. In this section we first cover subjects and predicates, then complements, appositives, and the parts of speech, and finally phrases and clauses.

Subjects and Predicates

The subject of a sentence tells who or what it is about. A *simple subject* consists of a noun (that is, a naming word) or a noun substitute. A *complete subject* consists of a simple subject plus any words that limit or describe it.

The predicate tells something about the subject and completes the thought of the sentence. A *simple predicate* consists of one or more verbs (words that show action or existence); a *complete predicate* includes any associated words also. In the following examples the simple subjects are underlined once and the simple predicates twice. The subjects and predicates are separated with slash marks.

> <u>William</u>/<u>laughed</u>.
>
> <u>Mary</u>/<u>has moved</u>.
>
> <u>Sarah</u>/<u>painted</u> the kitchen.
>
> The <u>student</u> over there in the corner/<u>is majoring</u> in art.

Complex subjects can be very long; it is helpful to be able to pick the simple subject out of a complex subject.

> The <u>storms</u> in March, which dropped a record rain fall in a one week time, <u>resulted</u> in fierce floods.

From Chapter 24 of *Strategies for Successful Writing*, Ninth Edition. James A. Reinking, Robert von der Osten.

A sentence can have a compound subject (two or more separate subjects), a compound predicate (two or more separate predicates), or both.

The <u>elephants</u> and their <u>trainer</u>/<u>bowed</u> to the audience and <u>left</u> the ring.

Sentences that ask questions don't follow the usual simple subject–simple predicate order. Instead, the word order may be changed slightly.

When questions use forms of the verb *be* (*is, am, are*), the verb appears before the subject while the rest of the predicate still follows the subject.

Is/<u>Angela</u>*/an experienced mountain climber?*

When the sentences include auxiliary, or helping, verbs, the auxiliary is moved in front of subject while the rest of the predicate remains in the same place.

Has/<u>a package</u>*/arrived yet for me?*

Sometimes a question word such as *when, why, who,* and *where* appears in front of the sentence with the helping verb.

When will/<u>we</u>*/be allowed to park on campus?*

Sometimes certain types of phrases and clauses can fall between the subject and the predicate. These should not be confused with the subject. They are usually easy to detect since they can be moved elsewhere in the sentence. The subject is underlined.

<u>My dog</u>/, *since he has gotten old,* simply lies around the house.

<u>My dog</u>/ simply lies around the house *since he has gotten old.*

Sometimes a phrase that is not part of the subject can introduce the sentence. This phrase can also usually be moved.

After we have repaired the rock wall,/ <u>we</u>*/*will begin to plant the new flowers.
<u>We</u>/will begin to plant the new flowers *after we have repaired the rock wall.*

Usage Considerations Because subjects are such important sentence elements, think carefully about each one you write so that your sentences won't be vague or misleading. Read the example below:

Our government has failed to enact a national value-added tax.

This statement can be expressed more precisely:

Congress has failed to enact a national value-added tax.

The *president* has vetoed the proposed national value-added tax.

Paying close attention to subjects lets you present your ideas more accurately and clearly.

EXERCISE

Place a slash mark between the complete subject and the complete predicate; then underline the simple subject once and the verb(s) twice. If a subject comes between an auxiliary verb and the main verb, set it off with two slash marks. If a phrase that is not the subject comes between the subject and the predicate, set it off with two slash marks.

1. Boston is one of my favorite cities.
2. My brother built a barn for his horses.
3. The cup of coffee on the counter is mine.
4. Do you know how to design a Web page?
5. The driver of the pickup truck backed into my car and then sped away.
6. The psychology final, though it was very long, was not very hard.
7. Bulimia and anorexia are disorders that affect too many young women.
8. If you plan to make a purchase using the Internet, you should make sure that the site is secure.
9. Where can visitors to the campus park their cars?
10. The advice that we scorned in our youth may seem like wisdom in our old age.

Complements

A complement is a word or word group that forms part of the predicate and helps complete the meaning of the sentence. Anything that comes after the verb is usually a complement. There are many kinds of complement, including phrases and clauses that will be reviewed later in this chapter.

- I think *that Copland was the quintessential American composer.*
- Robert hesitated *to trap the ground hog behind his house.*
- We were late *because our car would not start.*

Four common complements of traditional grammar are direct objects, indirect objects, subject complements, and object complements.

A *direct object* names whatever receives, or results from, the action of a verb.

The millwright repaired the *lathe.* (Direct object receives action of verb *repaired.*)

Hilary painted a *picture.* (Direct object results from action of verb *painted.*)

They took *coffee* and *sandwiches* to the picnic. (Direct objects receive action of verb *took.*)

An *indirect object* identifies someone or something that receives whatever is named by the direct object.

Doris lent *me* her calculator. (Indirect object *me* receives *calculator,* the direct object.)

Will and Al bought their *boat* new sails. (Indirect object *boat* receives *sails,* the direct object.)

An indirect object can be converted to a prepositional phrase that begins with *to* or *for* and follows the direct object.

noun

Doris lent her calculator *to me.*

Will and Al bought new sails *for their boat.*

A *subject complement* follows a linking verb—one that indicates existence rather than action. It renames or describes the subject.

Desmond is a *carpenter.* (Complement *carpenter* renames subject *Desmond.*)

The lights are too *bright* for Percy. (Complement *bright* describes subject *lights.*)

An *object complement* follows a direct object and renames or describes it.

The council named Donna *treasurer.* (Object complement *treasurer* renames direct object *Donna.*)

The audience thought the play *silly.* (Object complement *silly* describes direct object *play.*)

If a word is an object complement, you can form a short test sentence using *is.*

Donna is *treasurer.*

The play is *silly.*

Usage Considerations Like subjects, direct objects can be revised for greater precision, as these examples show:

John sent *a gift.*

John sent *a giant coloring book as a birthday gift.*

Often, you can carry the revision one step further by adding an indirect object, subject complement, or other complement to the sentence.

John sent his *niece* a giant coloring book as a birthday gift. (Indirect object added.)

Appositives

An appositive is a noun or word group serving as a noun that follows another noun or noun substitute and expands its meaning. Appositives may be restrictive or nonrestrictive. Restrictive appositives distinguish whatever they modify from other items in the same class. They are written without commas.

My sister *Heidi* is a professional golfer. (Appositive *Heidi* distinguishes her from other sisters.)

I have just read a book by the novelist *Henry James.* (Appositive *Henry James* distinguishes him from other novelists.)

Nonrestrictive appositives provide more information about whatever they modify. This sort of appositive is set off by a pair of commas except at the end of a sentence; then it is preceded by a single comma.

Anatoly Karpov, *the Russian chess player,* was interviewed on TV. (Appositive names *Karpov's* occupation.)

noun

Todd plans to major in paleontology, *the study of fossils.* (Appositive defines *paleontology.*)

Usage Considerations   When a brief definition is necessary, appositives can help you improve your sentences.

John Cage wrote hundreds of pieces for prepared piano.

John Cage, *a twentieth-century avant-garde composer,* wrote hundreds of pieces for prepared pianos, *instruments with odds and ends stuck between their strings to provide unusual effects.*

Don't, however, clutter your writing with appositives that provide unneeded information; the overload will impede and irritate your reader.

Identify each italicized item as a direct object (DO), an indirect object (IO), a subject complement (SC), an object complement (OC), or an appositive (AP).

1. Will and Allison purchased new furniture for their *apartment.*
2. The critics considered the movie *a masterpiece.*
3. The milk tasted *rancid.*
4. Robert Heinlein, a science fiction *writer,* thought that writers should tell an interesting story.
5. Jasmine completed her research *paper* two weeks ahead of the due date.
6. John sent his wife *candy* and *flowers* for Valantine's Day.
7. Some find bad manners *unacceptable.*
8. My roommate, a terrible *procrastinator,* finally relaxed after he turned in his paper.
9. Mr. Hanley offered *me* a job.
10. Darrel is a fine young *man.*

Parts of Speech

Traditional English grammar classifies words into eight parts of speech: *nouns, pronouns, verbs, adjectives, adverbs, prepositions, conjunctions,* and *interjections.* This section discusses these categories as well as verbals, phrases, and clauses, which also serve as parts of speech.

It is important to recognize that words that may look like one part of speech can function as another part of speech. For example, the verb *swim* can function as a noun. *Swimming* is good for your health. To identify a word as a part of speech is to identify how it functions in a sentence.

Traditional grammar defined nouns as words that name persons, places, things, conditions, ideas, or qualities. Most nouns can take a plural (book, books), possessive (Andy, Andy's), or article (bench, the bench).

Proper Nouns

Some nouns, called *proper nouns*, identify one-of-a-kind items like the following and are commonly capitalized.

France	New Years
Pacific Ocean	North Dakota
Pulitzer Prize	World Series
Spirit of St. Louis	Wyandotte Corporation
Declaration of Independence	Miami-Dade Junior College

Common Nouns

Common nouns name general classes or categories of items. Some common nouns are *abstract* and name a condition, idea, or quality that we can't experience with our five senses. *Abstract nouns* often cannot accept the plural; we cannot usually say we have *envys*. *Concrete nouns* identify something that we can experience with one or more of our senses and usually have plural forms.

Abstract Nouns	**Concrete Nouns**
arrogance	man
fear	bicycle
liberalism	desk
sickness	cartoon
understanding	smoke

Count and Non-Count Nouns

Most nouns identify things we can count and such nouns usually can take the plural form: *three bananas, a book, two children.* Some nouns, including many abstract nouns, cannot accept a plural: *coffee, water, bread.*

Usage Considerations   Good writing demands precise, potent nouns. If you carefully select your nouns, you can sharpen your message. Ill-chosen nouns, on the other hand, suggest poor thinking. Note how the vague word *freedom* robs the following sentence of any specific meaning:

Our *freedom* needs to be protected.

What did the writer have in mind? Here are a few possibilities:

Our *right to own guns* needs to be protected.
Our *private behavior* needs to be protected.
Our *national sovereignty* needs to be protected.

Even when meaning does not present problems, sentences can be sharpened by careful attention to nouns. Note the greater precision of the second sentence below:

Our *dog* has a savage bite.
Our *pit bull* has a savage bite.

Identify the nouns in the following sentences. Indicate if they are proper nouns (PN) or common nouns (CN), count nouns (count) non-count nouns (non-count), or collective nouns (coll). Clearly a noun can belong to more than one category.

1. Josh downloaded the new song by Rufus Wainwright from the Internet.
2. Americans want to be secure from terrorist attacks without surrendering their fundamental liberties.
3. Students quickly develop an addiction to coffee as they try to survive night-long cram sessions.
4. Our football team had an excellent season even if we didn't make it to a bowl game.
5. Math, especially algebra, is a subject that gives many students a fair amount of difficulty.
6. The water in the Gulf of Mexico can be uncomfortably warm by August.
7. Whether you agree or disagree with the views of the organization, the National Rifle Association has played an important role in the debate over how we should understand the Second Amendment.
8. Our understanding of the human genetic code has exploded in the last decade.
9. As everyone knows, Bill Clinton came from a town called *Hope.*
10. Human cloning is a very disturbing possibility for many citizens.

Pronouns

Pronouns are a special class of words that can fit the place of nouns in a sentence and sometimes can be seen as taking the place of a noun in a sentence. Pronouns can help you avoid the awkward repetition of nouns.

Personal Pronouns Personal pronouns refer to identifiable persons or things. Personal pronouns have different cases. The subjective case is used when the pronoun serves as the subject of the sentence or clause. *I helped Steve.* The objective case is used when the pronoun is the object of a verb or preposition. *Steve helped **me**. We spoke about **him**.* The possessive case shows possession or ownership. *That is **my** briefcase. My, your, our,* and *their* always precede nouns, as in *their car. Mine, hers, ours, yours,* and *theirs* do not precede nouns, as in *That book is mine. His* and *its* may or may not precede nouns.

	Subjective	**Objective**	**Possessive**
Singular			
First person	I	me	my, mine
Second person	you	you	your, yours
Third person	he, she, it	him, her, it	his, her, hers, its
Plural			
First person	we	us	our, ours
Second person	you	you	your, yours
Third person	they	them	their, theirs

Relative Pronouns   A relative pronoun relates a dependent clause—a word group that has a subject and a predicate but cannot function as an independent sentence—to a noun or pronoun, called an antecedent, in the main part of the sentence.

The relative pronouns include the following:

who	whose	what	whoever	whichever
whom	which	that	whomever	whatever

Who in its various forms refers to people, *which* to things, and *that* to either people or things.

> Mary Beth Cartwright, *who* was arrested last week for fraud, was Evansville's "Model Citizen" two years ago. (The antecedent of *who* is *Mary Beth Cartwright*.)
>
> He took the electric razor, *which* needed a new cutting head, to the repair shop. (The antecedent of *which* is *electric razor*.)
>
> David Bullock is someone *whom* we should definitely hire. (The antecedent of *whom* is *someone*.)
>
> Montreal is a city *that* I've always wanted to visit. (The antecedent of *that* is *city*.)

Which typically introduces nonrestrictive clauses, that is, clauses that provide more information about whatever they modify.

> The palace, *which* was in bad condition a century ago, is finally going to be restored. (Clause adds information about palace.)

That is typically used in other situations, especially to introduce restrictive clauses: those that distinguish the things they modify from others in the same class.

> The used car *that* I bought last week at Honest Bill's has already broken down twice. (Clause distinguishes writer's used car from others.)

Interrogative Pronouns   Interrogative pronouns introduce questions. All of the relative pronouns except *that* also function as interrogative pronouns.

who	which	whoever	whichever
whom	what	whomever	whatever
whose			

> *What* is the matter?
>
> *Who* asked you?
>
> *Whatever* do you mean?

When *what, which,* and *whose* are followed by nouns, they act as adjectives, not pronouns.

> *Which* movie should we see?

Demonstrative Pronouns   As their name suggests, demonstrative pronouns point things out. There are four such pronouns.

this	these
that	those

This and its plural *these* identify recent or nearby things.

> *This* is the play to see.
>
> *These* are the times that try men's souls.

That and its plural *those* identify less recent or more distant things.

> *That* is Mary's house across the road.
>
> *Those* were very good peaches you had for sale last week.

Reflexive and Intensive Pronouns

A reflexive pronoun is used when the pronoun refers back to a noun in the same clause. An intensive pronoun lends emphasis to a noun or pronoun. The two sets of pronouns are identical.

myself	herself	ourselves
yourself	itself	yourselves
himself	oneself	themselves

> My father cut *himself* while shaving. (reflexive pronoun)
>
> The president *himself* has asked me to undertake this mission. (intensive pronoun)

Don't substitute a reflexive pronoun for a personal pronoun.

Faulty	*Jill* and *myself* are going to a movie.
Revision	*Jill* and *I* are going to a movie.
Faulty	*Give the tickets to John and myself.*
Revision	*Give the tickets to John and me.*

Sometimes you'll hear people say things like "He made it *hisself*," "They're only fooling *theirself*," or "They bought *theirselves* sodas." Such forms are nonstandard. Say "himself" and "themselves" instead.

Indefinite Pronouns

These pronouns refer to unidentified persons, places, or things. One group of indefinite pronouns consistently acts as pronouns.

anybody	everything	one
anyone	nobody	somebody
anything	no one	someone
everybody	nothing	something
everyone		

A second group may function as either pronouns or adjectives.

all	any	most	few	much
another	each	either	many	neither

Here are some examples:

> *Everyone* is welcome. (indefinite pronoun)
> *Many* are called, but *few* are chosen. (indefinite pronouns)
> *Many* men but only a *few* women attend the Air Force Academy. (adjectives)

Reciprocal Pronouns The two reciprocal pronouns show an interchange of action between two or more parties. *Each other* is used when two parties interact, *one another* when three or more do.

> Pam and Patty accidentally gave *each other* the same thing for Christmas. (two persons)
> The members of the football team joyfully embraced *one another* after their victory. (more than two persons)

Usage Considerations Many students handle pronouns carelessly, damaging the clarity of their writing. Problems include letting the same pronoun stand for different nouns or using a pronoun where detailed, vivid language would be more effective. The following passage illustrates poor pronoun usage:

> My brother loves fly fishing. He thinks *it* is the only way to spend a summer weekend. In fact, whenever he's off work, he'll do *it*.

Rewritten as follows, the passage has been notably improved:

> My brother loves fly fishing. He thinks that *wading a stream and casting leisurely for trout* is the only way to spend a summer weekend. In fact, whenever he's off work, he *can be found up to his hips in water, offering his hand-tied flies to the waiting rainbows.*

EXERCISE

Identify each pronoun in the following sentences and indicate its type (personal, relative, interrogative, demonstrative, reflexive, intensive, indefinite, reciprocal). If it is a personal pronoun, indicate if it is in the subjective (S), objective (O), or possessive (P) case.

1. Anyone who wants to be successful needs to be able to use the Internet.
2. John helped himself to my copy of *The Canterbury Tales*.
3. Which fraternity did he say he was considering joining?
4. The black Subaru that is parked at the back of the lot is mine.
5. This is the kind of day that I really enjoy.
6. The president himself will teach one of the classes in political science.
7. We will all be more likely to succeed as writers if we help each other by offering our honest responses to drafts.
8. We greatly appreciate the kindness that you have shown our daughter.
9. Despite his bad back, Brian offered to help us move.
10. The prospect for manned space flights to Mars and Venus, which looked so promising in the '70s, became increasingly less likely until today they seem only a remote possibility.

Verbs

A verb indicates action or existence. Main verbs fall into two classes: *action verbs* and *linking verbs.* A very different type of verb is the *auxiliary* (or *helping*) verb, which adds specific kinds of meaning to the main verb.

Action Verbs As its name suggests, an action verb expresses action. Some action verbs are transitive, others intransitive. A *transitive* verb has a direct object that receives or results from the action and rounds out the meaning of the sentence.

> The photographer *took* the picture.

Without the direct object, this sentence would not express a complete thought. In contrast, an *intransitive* verb requires no direct object to complete the meaning of the sentence.

> Lee Ann *gasped* loudly.
> Little Tommy Tucker *sings* for his supper.

Many action verbs can play both transitive and intransitive roles, depending on the sentences they are used in.

> Kari *rode* her bicycle into town. (transitive verb)
> Karl *rode* in the front seat of the car. (intransitive verb)

Linking Verbs A linking verb shows existence or a state of affairs such as taste rather than action. Linking verbs are often followed by subject complements that reflect back on the subject of the sentence.

> Ms. Davis *is* our new director. (Complement *director* renames subject Ms. Davis.)
> The soup *was* lukewarm. (Complement *lukewarm* describes subject *soup.*)

The most common linking verbs are forms of the verb *to be* (is, are, am, was, were, be, being, been.) Likewise, verbs such as *seem, become, appear, remain, feel, look, smell, sound,* and *taste* function as linking verbs when they do not indicate actual physical action. In such cases, they are followed by adjectives. Here is an example:

> Harry looked *angry.*

When such verbs do indicate physical action, they function as action verbs and are followed by adverbs.

> Harry looked *angrily* at the referee.

Linking verbs can also be followed by adverb phrases of place or time.

> Your dinner is *on the table* (adverb phrase of place).
> The meeting will be *at 8:00 A.M.* (adverb phrase of time).

vbs

Auxiliary Verbs   Auxiliary (helping) verbs accompany action or linking verbs and provide information about time, possibility, or obligation, or establish the passive. *Have, be,* and *do* can function as both auxiliary and main verbs.

The auxiliary verbs *have (has, had)* and *be (is, are, was, were)* can provide information about time.

> Carol *has* repaired your computer.
>
> Carol *is* reformatting your hard drive.

The auxiliary verb *do* is inserted to form the negative or a question when there is no other auxiliary.

> Ellen *did* not resign.
>
> *Did* Ellen resign?

Auxiliary verbs called modals show time, obligation, possibility, or ability: *shall, should, will, would, can, could, may, might.*

With questions, the auxiliary verb is often moved to the front.

> *Will* Ellen *resign?*

Identify each verb or auxiliary in the following sentences and indicate whether it is a main verb (MV) or auxiliary (AUX).

1. An explosion rocked the apartment building and scattered debris in all directions.
2. We should be considering ways that we can improve the quality of our lives.
3. Americans have been buying CD players at a tremendous rate.
4. Did you ask Jennifer if she has her digital camera in her backpack?
5. With genetic screening we can identify individuals who are at higher risk for many serious diseases.
6. An espresso doesn't always taste good but it is always an eye-opener.
7. Beethoven's string quartets have stood the test of time as masterpieces that are rivaled only by Bartok's works in the genre.
8. It is almost impossible today to tune an engine yourself without the sophisticated computer equipment found in auto shops.
9. Advertisements can be an art form when they are created with imagination and aesthetic vision.
10. If yesterday's wildest dreams are today's reality, will today's wildest dreams be tomorrow's reality?

Usage Considerations   Energetic writing requires precise verbs. Don't take verbs for granted; revise them as necessary to strengthen a sentence. Note the improved precision of the second example.

> I *gave* the maître d' a ten-dollar bill.
>
> I *slipped* the maître d' a ten-dollar bill.

Tense   Verbs change in form to show distinctions in time. Every main verb has two basic tenses: present and past.

The *present tense* shows present condition and general or habitual action, indicates permanent truths, tells about past events in the historical present, and sometimes denotes action at some definite future time.

Verbs in the present tense must agree with their subjects. If the subject of a verb is a singular noun or pronoun (*he, she, it*), add *s* or *es* (if the word ends with an *s* or *ch* sound, as in *talks* or *teaches*). If the subject is plural or a second-person pronoun (*you*), the verb takes no ending (*talk, teach*).

Helen *looks* beautiful in her new gown. (present condition)

John *works* on the eighteenth floor. (general action)

I *brush* my teeth each morning. (habitual action)

The earth *rotates* on its axis. (permanent truth)

On November 11, 1918, the guns *fall* silent, and World War I *comes* to an end. (historical present)

Monday, I *begin* my new job. (future action)

The past tense shows that a condition existed or an action was completed in the past. This verb tense leaves the time indefinite, but surrounding words may specify it. Most verbs are regular and form the past tense by adding *-ed: talk, talked*. Some verbs are irregular and form the past by changing the vowel: *stand, stood*. A very few verbs do not change forms at all in creating the past: *set, set*.

Paul *was* angry with his noisy neighbors. (past condition, time indefinite)

Sandy *received* a long letter yesterday. (past action, time specified by *yesterday*)

Past Participle   In addition to the basic tenses, there is a *past participle* form of the main verb that is used to form the perfect form of the verb phrase and the passive voice. For most verbs, the past participle form is identical with the past tense in form.

Present	Past	Past Participle
talk	talk**ed**	talk**ed**
stand	st**oo**d	st**oo**d
set	set	set

Some verbs have different past forms and past participles. This can often lead to errors where less experienced writers often use the regular past (*He has **swam** this river before*) when the past participle form is required (*he has **swum** this river before*). Below is a table of many but not all of the irregular verbs for your reference.

Present Infinitive	Past	Past Participle	Present Infinitive	Past	Past Participle
arise	arose	arisen	blow	blew	blown
be	was, were	been	break	broke	broken
become	became	become	choose	chose	chosen
bite	bit	bitten	come	came	come
do	did	done	grow	grew	grown
draw	drew	drawn	hide	hid	hidden

Present Infinitive	Past	Past Participle	Present Infinitive	Past	Past Participle
drink	drank	drunk	know	knew	known
drive	drove	driven	ride	rode	riden
eat	ate	eaten	see	saw	seen
fall	fell	fallen	shake	shook	shaken
fly	flew	flown	slay	slew	slain
freeze	froze	frozen	speak	spoke	spoken
get	got	gotten	spring	sprang	sprung
give	gave	given	write	wrote	written

Time and Verb Forms

In addition to the tenses in English, many other forms of the verb express time.

Future Time   *Future time* is frequently indicated by the auxiliary modals *shall* or *will* with the present tense form of the verb.

> You *will feel* better after a good night's sleep. (future condition)

> I *shall attend* the concert next week. (future action)

Perfect Verb Forms   The perfect form of a verb is formed by a form of the auxiliary verb *have* and the past participle of the verb.

The *present perfect* tense is formed with *has* or *have* and the past participle of the main verb. It shows that a past condition or action, or its effect, continues until the present time.

> The players *have been* irritable since they lost the homecoming game. (Condition continues until present.)

> Juanita *has driven* a United Parcel Service truck for five years. (Action continues until present.)

> William *has repaired* the snow blower. (Effect of action continues until present although the action itself was completed in the past.)

The *past perfect* tense combines *had* and the past participle of the main verb. It refers to a past condition or action that was completed before another past condition or action.

> He *had been* in the army two years when the war ended. (Past perfect condition occurred first.)

> Vivian moved into the house that she *had built* the summer before. (Past perfect action occurred first.)

The *future perfect* tense is formed from the verbs *shall have* or *will have* plus the past participle of the main verb. It shows that a condition or an action will have been completed at some time in the future. Surrounding words specify time.

Our sales manager *will have been* with the company ten years next July. (Condition will end.)

By the end of this year, I *shall have written* the great American novel. (Action will be completed.)

Progressive Verb Forms   Each verb form, including the basic tenses, has a *progressive form* that indicates action in progress. The progressive is always indicated by some form of the verb *to be* followed by a present participle (or progressive), a verb that ends in *-ing*.

Present progressive	I am running.
Past progressive	I was running.
Future progressive	I will be running.
Present perfect progressive	I have been running.
Past perfect progressive	I had been running.
Future perfect progressive	I will have been running.

An easy way to identify the form of the verb phrase is to use the following formula.

(modal) + (have + en/ed) + (be + ing) + main verb
     Perfect   *Progressive*

Simply read the first available tense. If the modal is *will* then that designates future time. Then if *have, has,* or *had* is present, the verb phrase is *perfect*. If a form of *be* is present and the main verb ends with *ing,* then the verb phrase is progressive.

will	have	been	living
Future	*Perfect*	*Progressive*	

Usage   While most students use regular tenses and the progressive accurately, many less experienced writers do not always use the perfect verb form where appropriate. This is acceptable in informal writing; it is not acceptable for most formal writing.

Not acceptable   Jim *studied* accounting for the last three years. (This suggests that the action is over and done with.)

Acceptable   Jim *has studied* accounting for the last three years. (The present perfect verb form shows that the action comes right up to the present and may not be finished yet.)

Voice   Transitive verbs have two voices: active and passive. A verb is in the *active voice* when the subject carries out the action named by the verb.

Barry *planned* a picnic. (Subject *Barry* performs action.)

A verb is in the *passive voice* when the subject receives the action. The performer may be identified in an accompanying phrase or go unmentioned.

A picnic *was planned* by Barry. (The phrase *by Barry* identifies the performer.)

The picnic *was canceled.* (The performer goes unmentioned.)

A passive construction always uses a form of *to be* and the past participle of an action verb. Like other constructions, the passive may show past, present, or future time.

Amy *is paid* handsomely for her investment advice. (present tense)

I *was warned* by a sound truck that a tornado was nearby. (past tense)

I *will be sent* to Ghana soon by the Peace Corps. (future tense)

I *have been awarded* a sizable research grant. (present perfect tense)

The city *had been shelled* heavily before the infantry moved in. (past perfect tense)

By the end of this month, the site for our second factory *will have been chosen.* (future perfect tense)

To convert a sentence from the passive to the active voice, make the performer the subject, the original subject the direct object, and drop the form of *to be.*

The treaty *was signed* by the general. (passive)

The general *signed* the treaty. (active)

Technical and scientific writing commonly uses the passive voice to explain processes since it focuses on the objective observation or the action rather than the agent who can vary and should be irrelevant to the result. Other kinds of writing, however, avoid the passive voice except when it is desirable to not identify the one performing the action or when the action is more significant than the actor.

EXERCISE

Identify each verb group in the following sentences, indicate its form (present, past, future, present perfect, past perfect, future perfect, and any of the progressive forms), and note any use of the passive voice.

1. Devon broke his leg when he was thrown from his horse.
2. Deidra has managed our money for the last several years.
3. The Chicago Symphony is performing Mahler's *Resurrection Symphony.*
4. We will have completed the repairs on your computer by next Friday.
5. John finally bought the used BMW convertible that he had coveted for the past year.
6. Computers will be placed in every classroom as soon as the funds are available.
7. Maria has been acting in Shakespeare plays every summer since she first moved to Michigan.
8. At last the ceiling in the McCracken Building has been repaired.
9. The faculty had been consulted before the new attendance policy was implemented.
10. The future will bring many surprising changes.

Mood The mood of a verb shows whether the writer regards a statement as a

1. fact
2. command or request
3. wish, possibility, condition contrary to fact, or the like.

English has three moods: the indicative, imperative, and subjunctive.

A sentence in the *indicative mood* states a real or supposed fact or asks a question.

Nancy *graduates* from high school tomorrow.

We *lived* in Oakmont when Rachel was born.

He *had been* a sailor during the war.

Has Joe *asked* anyone to the prom yet?

Most verbs are used in the indicative mood.

A sentence in the *imperative mood* delivers a command or makes a request.

Leave the room immediately! (command)

Please *turn* the CD player down. (request)

The subject of a sentence in the imperative mood is always *you*. Although ordinarily unstated, the subject sometimes appears in the sentence.

You leave the room immediately!

The *subjunctive mood* is used

1. in *if, as if,* and *as though* clauses to express a wish, a possibility, or an action or a condition contrary to fact
2. in *that* clauses expressing orders, demands, requests, resolutions, proposals, or motions
3. with modal auxiliaries to express wishes, probability, possibility, permission, requirements, recommendations, suggestions, and conditions contrary to fact.

To express a present or future wish, possibility, condition or action in an *if, as if,* or *as though* clause, use *were* with any personal pronoun or noun serving as the subject of the clause.

If only Stan *were* less gullible! (present wish contrary to fact)

Even if Kay *were* to explain, Mary wouldn't believe her. (future possibility)

Arthur is behaving as if he *were* a millionaire (present condition contrary to fact)

To express a wish, possibility, or condition contrary to past facts, use *had been* or *had* plus the past participle of an action verb.

If the engine *had been lubricated*, the bearing wouldn't have burned out. (past condition contrary to fact)

Alice looked as if she *had lost* her best friend. (condition expressed in clause occurs before action of verb *looked*)

When writing *that* clauses expressing orders, demands, requests, resolutions, proposals, or motions, use *be* or the present plural form of an action verb.

I move that they *be* rewarded for their bravery.

The group proposed that Margaret *go* to the scene of the accident and *inspect* it personally.

In other *that* clauses, use the appropriate indicative form of the verb.

I know that they *were* rewarded for their bravery.

The group believed that Margaret *had gone* to the scene of the accident and *inspected* it personally.

The modal auxiliaries include the helping verbs *can, could, may, might, must, shall, will, would, should,* and *ought to*. The examples below illustrate the meanings they can express.

1. Wishes *(could, would)*
   I wish I *could* shimmy like my sister Kate.
   The Republicans wish the Democrats *would* go away and vice versa.
2. Probability *(should)*
   Because I've studied diligently, I *should* do better on my next chemistry test.
3. Possibility *(may, might, can, could)*
   Low inflation *could* cause our stock market to soar.
   I *might* stay up to watch the eclipse of the moon tonight.
4. Permission *(can, may)*
   The public *can* use these tennis courts every afternoon.
   You *may* leave as soon as you've finished filing these folders.
5. Requirements *(must)*
   The landlord has raised our rent again; we *must* find another apartment.
6. Recommendations, suggestions *(should, ought to)*
   Randy *should* see a doctor about his chest pains.
   All of us *ought to* exercise regularly.
7. Conditions contrary to fact *(could)*
   If only I *could* live my life over!

For each of the following sentences, identify the mood as indicative (IND), imperative (IMP), or subjunctive (SUB):

1. See your doctor before starting a strenuous exercise program.
2. The tired runner staggered across the finish line.
3. These new cell phones should prove very popular.
4. Let me know what you think of this novel.
5. Hang gliding is a great sport for anyone unafraid of heights.
6. If you practiced more, you could become an outstanding pianist.
7. The latest unemployment figures should help calm inflation fears.

8. Stop talking right now or leave the class.
9. This movie could have been shortened by fifteen minutes without harming the story.
10. Who wants to play Scrabble this evening?

Adjectives

An adjective *modifies* a noun or pronoun by describing it, limiting it, or otherwise making its meaning more exact.

> The *brass* candlestick stood next to the *fragile* vase. (*Brass* modifies *candlestick*, and *fragile* modifies *vase*.)

> The cat is *long-haired* and *sleek*. (*Long-haired* and *sleek* modify *cat*.)

There are three general categories of adjectives: limiting, descriptive, and proper.

Limiting Adjectives   A limiting adjective identifies or points out the noun or pronoun it modifies. It may indicate number or quantity. Several categories of pronouns can serve as limiting adjectives, as can numbers and nouns.

> *Whose* briefcase is on the table? (interrogative adjective)

> The couple *whose* car was stolen called the police. (relative adjective)

> *This* restaurant has the best reputation for gourmet food. (demonstrative adjective)

> *Some* people have no social tact at all. (indefinite adjective)

> Sally swerved *her* car suddenly to avoid an oncoming truck. (possessive adjective)

> *Three* people entered the lecture hall late. (number as adjective)

> The *schoolgirl* look is fashionable this year. (noun as adjective)

Descriptive Adjectives   A descriptive adjective names a quality, characteristic, or condition of a noun or pronoun. Two or more of these adjectives, members of the largest category of adjectives, may modify the same noun or pronoun.

> The *yellow* submarine belongs to the Beatles.

> He applied *clear* lacquer to the tabletop.

> The *slim, sophisticated* model glided onto the runway.

> The child was *active, happy*, and *polite*.

Proper Adjectives   A proper adjective is derived from a proper noun and is always capitalized.

> Harwell is a *Shakespearean* actor.

Articles as Adjectives   Articles appear immediately before nouns and can therefore be considered adjectives. There are three articles in English: *a, an,* and *the*. *The* points to a specific item; *a* and *an* do not. *A* precedes words beginning with consonant sounds; *an* precedes words with vowel sounds, making pronunciation easier.

> *The* right word at *the* right moment can save a friendship. (Definite articles suggest there is one right word and one right moment.)

> *A* right word can save a friendship. (Indefinite article suggests there are several right words.)

> I think I'd like *an* apple with my lunch. (No particular apple is specified.)

Sometimes the definite article refers to a class of items.

> *The* tiger is fast becoming an endangered species.

Context shows whether such a sentence refers to particular items or entire classes.

Comparison with Adjectives   Adjectives can be used to show comparison. When two things are compared, shorter adjectives usually add *-er* and longer adjectives add *more*. When three or more things are compared, shorter adjectives usually add *-est* and longer ones add *most*.

> John is *taller* than Pete. (short adjective comparing two things)

> Sandra seems *more engaged* than Jill today. (long adjective comparing two things)

> John is the *tallest* of the three brothers. (short adjective comparing three things)

> Sandra is the *most engaged* student in the class. (longer adjective comparing more than three things)

Some adjectives, like the examples below, have irregular forms for comparisons.

> good—better—best

> bad—worse—worst

Don't use the *-est* form of the shorter adjective to compare just two things.

> *Faulty*   This is the *smallest* of the two castles.

Instead, use the *-er* form.

> *Revision*   This is the *smaller* of the two castles.

Position of Adjectives   Most adjectives come immediately before the words they modify. In a few set expressions (for example, heir *apparent*), the adjective immediately follows the word it modifies. Similarly, adjective pairs sometimes appear in a follow-up position for added emphasis (The rapids, *swift* and *dangerous*, soon capsized the raft). Sometimes adjectives also serve as subject complements and follow their subjects (The puppy was *friendly*).

Usage Considerations   Some students overuse adjectives, especially in descriptions, but most underuse them. Review your sentences carefully to see where adding or cutting adjectives can increase the impact of your writing.

My Buick is the talk of my friends.

My *old, dilapidated, rusty, fenderless 1970* Buick is the talk of my friends.

My *rusty, fenderless 1970* Buick is the talk of my friends.

The first sentence lacks adjectives that show why the car is discussed. The second sentence overcorrects this fault by including two adjectives that repeat the information provided by the others. The final sentence strikes the proper balance.

Determiners   There is a category of words that are sometimes classified with adjectives that limit the noun or pronoun but do not name a quality or characteristic of the noun or pronoun.

Three sailboats raced around the island.

While we know how many sailboats are involved, there is no descriptive content added to the concept of sailboats.

There are many different kinds of determiners.

Determiners	**Name**
a, an	Indefinite article
the	Definite article
this, that, these, those	Demonstrative
one, two, three, four, five	Cardinal number
first, second, third, fourth	Ordinal number
my, our, your, his, her, hers, its, their	Possessive pronoun
some, any, no, every, another, enough,	Indefinite pronoun
either, neither, all, both, each, less,	Possessive noun
other, many, more, most, few, several	
Tom's, Mary's	

With the indefinite article a/an, *a* precedes words beginning with consonant sounds; *an* precedes words with a vowel sound to make pronunciation easier.

Identify the adjectives and determiners in the following sentences.

1. The climbers seemed very tiny as they rappelled down the sheer cliff.
2. Janine's paper offered an insightful and well-supported argument.
3. Fresh grapefruit juice can be a tart but tasty breakfast beverage.
4. In some Medieval cathedrals there were statues representing the seven deadly sins.
5. Many expeditions to climb Mt. Everest were defeated more by the inhospitable environment than by the actual challenges of the climb.

6. A good educational environment can be made better by smaller classes.
7. After the chilly air conditioning in the restaurant, Christy was grateful to step out into the warm, damp summer air.
8. Cody's sleek new convertible looked ready to fly around tight corners.
9. The black Focus seemed to pulse with the loud, heavy beat of the rock music.
10. Many Canadian writers are better known than most American critics would like to admit.

Adverbs

An adverb modifies a verb, an adjective, another adverb, or a whole sentence. Adverbs generally answer questions such as "How?" "When?" "Where?" "How often?" and "To what extent?"

> The floodwaters receded *very* slowly. (Adverb modifies adverb and answers the question "How?")

> My sister will visit me *tomorrow*. (Adverb modifies verb and answers the question "When?")

> The coach walked *away* from the bench. (Adverb modifies verb and answers the question "Where?")

> The tire is *too* worn to be safe. (Adverb modifies adjective and answers the question "To what extent?")

> The teller is *frequently* late for work. (Adverb modifies adjective and answers the question "How often?")

> *Unfortunately*, the game was canceled because of rain. (The adverb modifies the whole sentence but does not answer any question.)

Formation of Adverbs Most adverbs are formed by adding *-ly* to adjectives.

> The wind is *restless*. (*Restless* is an adjective modifying *wind*.)

> He walked *restlessly* around the room. (*Restlessly* is an adverb modifying *walked*.)

> Many common adverbs, however (*almost, never, quite, soon, then, there,* and *too*), lack *-ly* endings.

> I *soon* realized that pleasing my boss was impossible.

> This movie is *too* gruesome for my taste.

> Furthermore, some words such as *better, early, late, hard, little, near, only, straight,* and *wrong* do double duty as either adjectives or adverbs.

> We must have taken a *wrong* turn. (*Wrong* is an adjective modifying the noun *turn*.)

> Where did I go *wrong*? (*Wrong* is an adverb modifying the verb *go*.)

Comparison with Adverbs   Like adjectives, adverbs can show comparison. When two things are compared, adverbs add *more*. When three or more things are compared, *most* is used.

> Harold works *more* efficiently than Don. (adverb comparing two people)
>
> Of all the people in the shop, Harold works the *most* efficiently. (adverb comparing more than two people)

Some adverbs, like some adjectives, use irregular forms for comparisons.

> well—better—best
>
> much—more—most

Position of Adverbs   Adverbs are more movable than any other part of speech. Usually, adverbs that modify adjectives and other adverbs appear next to them to avoid confusion.

> Her *especially* fine tact makes her a welcome guest at any party. (Adverb *especially* modifies adjective *fine.*)
>
> The novel was *very* badly written. (Adverb *very* modifies adverb *badly.*)

Adverbs that modify verbs, however, can often be shifted around in their sentences without causing changes in meaning.

> *Quickly*, he slipped through the doorway.
>
> He slipped *quickly* through the doorway.
>
> He slipped through the doorway *quickly*.

Usage Considerations   You can often sharpen the meaning of a sentence by adding a well-chosen adverb.

> The student squirmed in his chair.
>
> The student squirmed *anxiously* in his chair.

Including the adverb *anxiously* in the second sentence shows the mental state of the student.

> Be careful, however, not to overuse adverbs because they can bog down your writing.

EXERCISE

Identify the adverbs in the following sentences:

1. Three friends slowly but steadily hiked up the mountain trail.
2. Everyone agreed that it was too hot to mow the lawn.
3. While the screenplay was exceptionally well written, the movie itself was poorly directed and badly miscast.
4. The violins entered too early but no one but the conductor really noticed.
5. We should meet tomorrow to plan our camping trip.

6. Some people are strangely attracted to unusually dangerous activities.
7. The two planes came nearer to each other than anyone would like.
8. Few people compete more fiercely than Phillip.
9. Gradually but persistently erosion will wear away a mountain.
10. Ms. Draco patiently explained to the class how they could approach the assignment more imaginatively.

Prepositions

A preposition links its object—a noun or noun substitute—to some other word in the sentence and shows a relationship between them. The relationship is often one of location, time, means, or reason or purpose. The word group containing the preposition and its object makes up a prepositional phrase.

The new insulation *in* the attic keeps my house much warmer now. (Preposition *in* links object *attic* to *insulation* and shows location.)

We have postponed the meeting *until* tomorrow. (Preposition *until* links object *tomorrow* to *postponed* and shows time.)

The tourists traveled *by* automobile. (Preposition *by* links object *automobile* to *traveled* and shows means.)

Warren swims *for* exercise. (Preposition *for* links object *exercise* to *swims* and shows reason or purpose.)

The following list includes the most common prepositions, some of which consist of two or more words:

about	before	except	on
above	behind	for	onto
across	below	from	out of
after	beside	in	over
against	between	instead of	since
along with	by	into	through
among	by reason of	like	to
around	contrary to	near	toward
at	down	next to	under
because of	during	of	with
			without

Many of these combine to form additional prepositions: *except for, in front of, by way of, on top of,* and the like.

Some words that are usually used as prepositions such as *up, on,* and *in* can also function as a different part of speech called a *verb particle.* Here are two examples.

The instructor let Jeff make *up* the test.

The officer turned *in* his best friend.

The verb particle is closely associated with the verb and is a part of its meaning. If a word is a verb particle, it can usually be moved after the noun.

The instructor let Jeff make the test *up.*

The officer turned his best friend *in.*

Usage Considerations It is easy to use a small group of prepositions over and over in your writing. This habit often results in imprecise or misleading sentences. To avoid this problem, think carefully about your choice of prepositions as you revise. Read the following example:

> He walked *by* the railroad tracks on his way home.

Note that two interpretations are possible.

> He walked *along* the railroad tracks on his way home.
>
> He walked *past* the railroad tracks on his way home.

Clearly you would use the preposition that conveys your intended meaning.

Identify the prepositions (P) and their objects (O) in the following sentences:

1. Angela searched her house for a book of poems by Rilke.
2. Dave and Silvia traveled across America on a motorcycle.
3. Because of the hurricane, the causeway from the Florida Keys was closed.
4. Contrary to everyone's expectation, Barry decided to go into advertising instead of theater.
5. Before her first class, Carrie likes to swim twenty-five laps in the school's pool.
6. The two boys hid for several hours in the woods behind their house.
7. In his paper on cloning, James cut through the confusion about the topic and clearly presented the arguments for each side of the issue.
8. Almost out of gas, Janine's car raced across the finish line in first place.
9. A good listener sometimes needs to hear the message behind the words.
10. I always hated it when trapeze artists flew through the air without a net beneath them.

Conjunctions

Conjunctions serve as connectors, linking parts of sentences or whole sentences. These connectors fall into three groups: coordinating conjunctions, subordinating conjunctions, and conjunctive adverbs.

Coordinating Conjunctions Coordinating conjunctions connect terms of equal grammatical importance: words, word groups, and simple sentences. These conjunctions can occur singly (*and, but, or, nor, for, yet, so*) or in pairs called correlative conjunctions (*either—or, neither—nor, both—and,* and *not only—but also*). The elements that follow correlative conjunctions must be parallel, that is, have the same grammatical form.

> Tom *and* his cousin are opening a coffee shop. (Coordinating conjunction connects nouns.)
>
> Shall I serve the tea in the living room *or* on the veranda? (Coordinating conjunction connects phrases.)

I am going to Europe this summer, *but* Marjorie is staying home. (Coordinating conjunction connects simple sentences.)

Amy *not only* teaches English *but also* writes novels. (Correlative conjunctions connect parallel predicates.)

You can study nursing *either* at Ferris State University *or* at DeWitt College. (Correlative conjunctions connect parallel phrases.)

Friendship is *both* pleasure *and* pain. (Correlative conjunctions connect parallel nouns.)

Subordinating Conjunctions

Like relative pronouns, subordinating conjunctions introduce subordinate clauses, relating them to independent clauses, which can stand alone as complete sentences. Examples of subordinating conjunctions include *because, as if, even though, since, so that, whereas,* and *whenever.*

I enjoyed the TV program *because* it was so well acted. (Conjunction connects *it was so well acted* to rest of sentence.)

Whenever you're ready, we can begin dinner. (Conjunction connects *you're ready* to rest of sentence.)

Conjunctive Adverbs

These connectors resemble both conjunctions and adverbs. Like conjunctions, they serve as linking devices between elements of equal rank. Like adverbs, they function as modifiers, showing such things as similarity, contrast, result or effect, addition, emphasis, time, and example.

The job will require you to travel a great deal; *however,* the salary is excellent.

Sean cares nothing for clothes; *in fact,* all of his socks have holes in their toes.

The following list groups the most common conjunctive adverbs according to function:

Similarity: likewise, similarly

Contrast: however, nevertheless, on the contrary, on the other hand, otherwise

Result or effect: accordingly, as a result, consequently, hence, therefore, thus

Addition: also, furthermore, in addition, in the first place, moreover

Emphasis or clarity: in fact, in other words, indeed, that is

Time: afterward, later, meanwhile, subsequently

Example: for example, for instance, to illustrate

Conjunctive adverbs should not be confused with coordinating conjunctions. Unlike conjunctions and more like adverbs, conjunctive adverbs can move, often to create a specific emphasis.

The job will require you to travel a great deal; the salary, *however,* is excellent.

The job will require you to travel a great deal; *however,* the salary is excellent.

Sean cares nothing for clothes; all of his socks, *in fact,* have holes in their toes.

Sean cares nothing for clothes; *in fact,* all of his socks have holes in them.

Because conjunctive adverbs can move, the second independent clause must be treated as a complete sentence and either be joined to the previous independent clause with a semicolon or be separated by a period.

Usage Considerations   You can add variety and precision to your writing by varying the conjunctions you use. If you consistently rely on the conjunction *because*, try substituting *as* or *since*. Likewise, you may periodically replace *if* with *provided that*. The right conjunction shows the realtionship among ideas.

When you have choppy sentences, try combining them by using a conjunction.

You can buy smoked salmon at Sally's Seafoods. You can buy it at Daane's Thriftland as well.

You can buy smoked salmon *either* at Sally's Seafoods *or* at Daane's Thriftland.

The revision is much smoother than the original sentence pair.

Interjections

An interjection is an exclamatory word used to gain attention or to express strong feeling. It has no grammatical connection to the rest of the sentence. An interjection is followed by an exclamation point or a comma.

Hey! Watch how you're driving! (strong interjection)

Oh, is the party over already? (mild interjection)

Identify the coordinating conjunctions (CC), subordinating conjunctions (SC), conjunctive adverbs (CA), and interjections (I) in the following sentences:

1. There is evidence that the polar ice caps are receding; however, scientists do not yet know the probable impact of this event.
2. Neither term limits nor campaign reform will take money out of politics.
3. Since there has been an increase in the alligator population, some lawmakers think the ban on alligator hide products should be lifted.
4. Rats! My computer ate my report.
5. Most companies work hard to secure their Internet sites, but hackers can usually find their way around these safeguards.
6. Extensive resources have been committed to the war on drugs; nevertheless, illegal narcotics continue to flow into this country.
7. After Barbara got the promotion, she took all her coworkers out to celebrate.
8. Basketball and racquetball are both excellent aerobic activities.
9. You can either enjoy a brisk game of tennis or relax in the hot tub.
10. Most people like to snack while they watch television.

Phrases and Clauses

Phrases

A phrase is a group of words that lacks a subject and a predicate and serves as a single part of speech. This section discusses four basic kinds of phrase: *prepositional, participial, gerund,* and *infinitive.* The last three are based on participles, gerunds, and infinitives, verb forms known as verbals. A fifth type of phrase, the verb phrase, consists of sets of two or more verbs (*has fixed, had been sick, will have been selected,* and the like).

Prepositional Phrases A prepositional phrase consists of a preposition, one or more objects, and any associated words. These phrases serve as adjectives or adverbs.

> The picture *over the mantel* was my mother's. (prepositional phrase as adjective)

> He bought ice skates *for himself.* (prepositional phrase as adverb modifying verb)

> The toddler was afraid *of the dog.* (prepositional phrase as adverb modifying adjective)

> Our visitors arrived late *in the day.* (prepositional phrase as adverb modifying another adverb)

Frequently, prepositional phrases occur in series. Sometimes they form chains in which each phrase modifies the object of the preceding phrase. At other times some or all of the phrases may modify the verb or verb phrase.

> John works *in a clothing store/ on Main Street/ during the summer.*

Here the first and third phrases serve as adverbs modifying the verb *works* and answering the questions "Where?" and "When?" while the second phrase serves as an adjective modifying *store* and answering the question "Where?"

On occasion, especially in questions, a preposition may be separated from its object, making the phrase difficult to find.

> Dr. Perry is the person *whom* I've been looking *for.*

> *What* are you shouting *about?*

Participial Phrases A participial phrase consists of a participle plus associated words. Participles are verb forms that, when used in participial phrases, function as adjectives or adverbs. A present participle ends in *-ing* and indicates an action currently being carried out. A past participle ends in *-ed, -en,-e, -n, -d,* or *-t* and indicates some past action.

> The chef *preparing dinner* trained in France. (present participial phrase as adjective)

> The background, *sketched in lightly,* accented the features of the woman in the painting. (past participial phrase as adjective)

> She left *whistling a jolly melody.* (present participial phrase as adverb)

A perfect participial phrase consists of *having* or *having been* plus a past participle and any associated words. Like a past participial phrase, it indicates a past action.

Having alerted the townspeople about the tornado, the sound truck returned to the city garage. (perfect participial phrase)

Having been alerted to the tornado, the townspeople sought shelter in their basements. (perfect participial phrase)

Some participial phrases that modify persons or things distinguish them from others in the same class. These phrases are written without commas. Other phrases provide more information about the persons or things they modify and are set off with commas.

The man *fixing my car* is a master mechanic. (Phrase distinguishes man fixing car from others.)

Mr. Welsh, *fatigued by the tennis game*, rested in the shade. (Phrase provides more information about Mr. Welsh.)

Gerund Phrases   A gerund phrase consists of a gerund and the words associated with it. Like present participles, gerunds are verb forms that end in *-ing*. Unlike participles, though, they function as nouns rather than as adjectives or adverbs.

Kathryn's hobby is *collecting stamps*. (gerund phrase as subject complement)

Kathryn's hobby, *collecting stamps*, has made her many friends. (gerund phrase as appositive)

He devoted every spare moment to *overhauling the car*. (gerund phrase as object of preposition.)

Infinitive Phrases   An infinitive phrase consists of the present principal part of a verb preceded by *to (to fix, to eat)*, together with any accompanying words. These phrases serve as adjectives, adverbs, and nouns.

This looks like a good place *to plant the shrub*. (infinitive phrase as adjective)

Lenore worked *to earn money for college*. (infinitive phrase as adverb)

My goal is *to have my own business some day*. (infinitive phrase as noun)

Gerunds can often be substituted for infinitives and vice versa.

To repair this fender will cost two hundred dollars. (infinitive phrase as subject)

Repairing this fender will cost two hundred dollars. (gerund phrase as subject)

At times the *to* in an infinitive is omitted following verbs such as *make, dare, let*, and *help*.

Kristin didn't dare *(to) move* a muscle.

The psychiatrist helped me *(to) overcome* my fear of flying.

Verbals Not in Phrases   Participles, gerunds, and infinitives can function as nouns, adjectives, or adverbs, even when they are not parts of phrases.

That *sunbathing* woman is a well-known model. (participle as adjective)

Dancing is fine exercise. (gerund)

The children want *to play*. (infinitive as noun)

If you're looking for a job, Sally is the person *to see*. (infinitive as adjective)

I'm prepared *to resign*. (infinitive as adverb)

Usage Considerations   Phrases can often clarify or develop the information in a sentence or combine choppy sentences.

Original	My brother is fishing.
Revision	My brother is fishing *for trout just below Barnes Dam on Sidewinder Creek*. (prepositional phrases added)
Original	The boat barely made shore.
Revision	The boat, *listing heavily and leaking badly*, barely made shore. (participial phrases added)

To avoid ponderous sentences, don't, however, weigh them down with phrases, as in the following example:

My brother is fishing for trout just below Barnes Dam on Sidewinder Creek *near Perry Pass in the mountains of Central Colorado*.

Testing a Phrase's Function

To determine whether a phrase is functioning as noun, adjective, or adverb, try a substitution test; if a common noun (something, someone, or it), adjective or adjective phrase, or adverb fits, that demonstrates the function of the phrase.

Walking at a brisk pace is excellent exercise. (gerund phrase)

Something is excellent exercise. (noun phrase)

I am prepared *to finish the job*. (infinitive phrase)

I am prepared *completely*. (adverb phrase)

He was a man *of unusual craftiness*. (prepositional phrase)

He was a *crafty* man. (adjective phrase)

Identify the italicized phrases as prepositional, participial, gerund, or infinitive and indicate whether each is used as a noun, an adjective, or an adverb.

1. *Sleeping in late* can be one of the great pleasures of a holiday.
2. The students waited *for ten minutes* before they left.
3. *Racing around the corner*, Tim crashed into another student and sent her sprawling.
4. The employees were afraid that there was a plan *to lay off a third of the workforce*.
5. The grass *in the backyard* had grown so long that it was impossible to cut with a lawnmower.

6. The company has decided *to go forward* with the direct marketing campaign.
7. Our guest speaker has written a book about *kayaking around New Zealand.*
8. Most high school students cannot wait *to graduate.*
9. David broke his leg *skiing in Colorado.*
10. We cheered as Joan, *panting with exhaustion,* crossed the finish line.

Clauses

A clause is a word group that includes a subject and a predicate. An *independent clause,* sometimes called a main clause, expresses a complete thought and can function as a simple sentence. A *subordinate clause,* or dependent clause, cannot stand by itself. Subordinate clauses may serve as nouns, adjectives, or adverbs.

Noun Clauses   A noun clause can serve in any of the ways that ordinary nouns can.

> *What the neighbor told John* proved to be incorrect. (noun clause as subject)

> The woman asked *when the bus left for Spokane.* (noun clause as direct object)

> I'll give a reward to *whoever returns my billfold.* (noun clause as object of preposition *to*)

Noun clauses normally begin with one of the following words:

Relative	Pronouns	Interrogative Pronouns
who	whoever	when
whom	whomever	why
whose	that	where
what	whatever	how
which	whichever	whether

The complementizer *that* is sometimes omitted from the beginning of a clause that acts as a direct object.

> Dr. Kant thinks *(that) he knows everything.*

If a clause is serving as a noun, you can replace it with the word *something* or *someone,* and the sentence will still make sense.

> Dr. Kant thinks *something.*

If the clause is serving as an adjective or an adverb, making the substitution turns the sentence into nonsense.

> The person *who wins the lottery* will receive two million dollars.

> The person *someone* will receive two million dollars.

Adjective Clauses   Like ordinary adjectives, adjective clauses, often called *relative clauses,* modify nouns and noun substitutes.

Give me one reason *why you feel the way you do.* (Adjective clause modifies noun.)

I'll hire anyone *that Dr. Stone recommends.* (Adjective clause modifies pronoun.)

Generally, adjective clauses begin with one of the following words:

Relative Pronouns	**Relative Adverbs**
who	when
whom	where
whose	why
what	after
which	before
that	

Sometimes the word that introduces the clause can be omitted.

The chair *(that) we ordered last month* has just arrived. (pronoun *that* omitted but understood)

The man *(whom) we were talking to* is a movie producer. (pronoun *whom* omitted but understood)

Sometimes, too, a preposition comes ahead of the introductory pronoun.

The grace *with which Nelson danced* made the onlookers envious.

An adjective clause may be restrictive and distinguish whatever it modifies from others in the same class, or it may be nonrestrictive and provide more information about whatever it modifies.

Flora wiped up the cereal *that the baby had spilled.* (restrictive clause)

Harriet Thomas, *who was born in Alaska,* now lives in Hawaii. (nonrestrictive clause)

As these examples show, restrictive clauses are not set off with commas, but nonrestrictive clauses are.

Adverb Clauses   These clauses modify verbs, adjectives, adverbs, and sentences, answering the same questions that ordinary adverbs do.

You may go *whenever you wish.* (Adverb clause modifies verb.)

Sandra looked paler *than I had ever seen her look.* (Adverb clause modifies adjective.)

Darryl shouted loudly *so that the rescue party could hear him.* (Adverb clause modifies adverb.)

Unless everyone cooperates, this plan will never succeed. (Adverb clause modifies whole sentence.)

The word or word group that introduces an adverb clause is always a subordinating conjunction. Here are the most common of these conjunctions, grouped according to the questions they answer.

When? after, as, as soon as, before, since, until, when, whenever, while

Where? where, wherever

How? as if, as though

Why? as, because, now that, since, so that

Under what conditions? although, if, once, provided that, though, unless

To what extent? than

Occasionally in an adverb clause, the omission of one or more words won't hurt its meaning. Such a construction is called an *elliptical clause.*

> *While (he was) making a sandwich,* Garth hummed softly. (*he was* omitted but understood)

Unlike noun and adjective clauses, adverb clauses can often be moved about in their sentences.

> Garth hummed softly *while (he was) making a sandwich.*

Usage Considerations

Like phrases, clauses can help develop sentences as well as smooth out choppiness.

Original	The old grandfather clock ticked loudly through the night.
Revision	The old grandfather clock *that my great-aunt gave me before she died* ticked loudly through the night. (Clause adds information.)
Original	The chemistry professor insisted on lab safety. He had been hurt in a lab explosion the previous year.
Revision	The chemistry professor, *who had been hurt in a lab explosion the previous year,* insisted on lab safety. (Clause adds smoothness.)

To avoid clumsiness, avoid overloaded sentences like the one below:

> The old grandfather clock that my great-aunt gave me before she died *and that I took with me to England when my company transferred me there for two years* ticked loudly through the night.

Identify the italicized clauses as noun, adjective, or adverb.

1. Brad pulled a muscle in his back *while he was lifting weights.*
2. The astronauts *who landed on the moon* should still be household names.
3. Some astronomers suggested *that Pluto should not be considered a planet.*
4. Jody Singleton was touched by the cards *her students sent her.*
5. *Although coffee shops would seem like the quintessential small business,* some companies have turned America's coffee habit into multimillion dollar chains.
6. *Whoever decorated this house* has an excellent eye.
7. Andrea was pleased to find out that her new employer used the kind of accounting software *on which she had been trained.*

8. The Concorde, *which offers supersonic trips across the Atlantic,* has been much less popular than was originally expected.
9. *While she was waiting at the check-in counter of the airport,* Jasmine was able to read two chapters in her history text.
10. Many companies like to go *where the labor costs and taxes are lowest.*

Coordination and Subordination

Coordination and subordination are ways to rank ideas in sentences. Coordination makes ideas equal; subordination makes them unequal. To understand coordination and subordination, you need to know about four kinds of sentences: simple, compound, complex, and compound–complex.

Simple Sentences   A simple sentence has one subject and one predicate. Some simple sentences consist merely of a single noun and a single verb.

> Millicent shouted.

Others include elements such as compound subjects, compound verbs, direct objects, indirect objects, and subject complements.

> Jim and Sue have bought a car. *(compound subject, direct object)*

> Lucretia Borgia smiled and mixed her guests a cocktail. *(compound verb, indirect object, direct object)*

> Autumn is a sad season. *(subject, complement)*

Compound Sentences   A compound sentence contains two or more independent clauses, each holding the same (coordinate) rank. As a result, the idea in the first clause receives the same emphasis as the idea in the second.

In some cases, a comma and a coordinating conjunction *(and, but, or, nor, for, yet, so)* link successive clauses.

> Name the baby Huey, *or* I'll cut you out of my will.

> The audience was young, friendly, and responsive, *so* it cheered for each speaker.

In others, a semicolon and a conjunctive adverb *(for example, however, in fact, likewise, meanwhile, instead,* and the like) furnish the connection.

> Tod wants to see the play; *in fact,* he's talked about it for weeks.

> Today, many young women do not rush into marriage and motherhood; *instead,* they spend several years establishing careers.

Finally, a writer may omit any connecting word and separate the clauses with a semicolon.

> The sky grew pitch black; the wind died; an ominous quiet hung over the whole city.

> Be sure to read this Hemingway novel; it suggests how to cope gracefully with pressure.

As the preceding sentences show, compound sentences allow writers to express simple relationships among simple ideas. However, such sentences have one important limitation: It is impossible to highlight one particular idea. To do this, we need complex sentences.

Complex Sentences   A complex sentence has one independent clause and one or more dependent clauses. Relegating an idea to a dependent clause shows that the writer wishes it to receive less emphasis than the idea in the main clause. In the following examples the dependent clauses are italicized.

> *Because the young, friendly audience was responsive*, it cheered for each speaker.

> *After the dance was over*, Arthur collapsed on the sofa.

> *Once they had reached the lakeshore*, the campers found a level spot *where they could pitch their tent.*

Unlike compound sentences, complex ones allow writers to vary the emphasis of ideas.

> *While I watered the grass*, I discussed stock options with Liz.

> I watered the grass *while I discussed stock options with Liz.*

The first sentence emphasizes the talk with Liz, the second watering the lawn.

Compound–Complex Sentences   This type of sentence features two or more independent clauses and one or more dependent clauses. Here are two examples with the dependent clauses italicized:

> Ms. Harris works as an investment manager, and Mr. Williams, *who lives next door to her*, owns a jewelry store.

> *If you are to communicate properly*, your thoughts must be clear and correct; thoughts are wasted *when language is muddled.*

Label the independent and dependent clauses in the sentences below. Then identify each sentence as simple, compound, complex, or compound–complex.

1. A career in broadcasting requires good verbal skills, an extensive wardrobe, and a pleasant smile.
2. Because its bag was too full, the vacuum cleaner backfired, leaving the room dirtier than it had been.
3. Leave your boots in the back hall, please.
4. When Tom arrived home, his roommate asked him where he had really gone; six hours seemed too long a time to spend in the library.
5. My orange tree blossomed last week; however, the grapefruit trees have withered, probably because of the freeze last month.

6. Kites make good gifts for children; even if a child already has a kite, a second one will come in handy if the first one becomes tangled in a tree.

7. It's risky to confide in a coworker because one can never be sure that the confidence will be kept.

8. I know why he moved here: He likes having the only dental practice in this part of the state.

9. The pencil and the stapler are on the table next to the window in Mr. Brigg's office.

10. Don't add bleach to your load of colored shirts; the colors will fade and the fibers weaken.

Editing to Correct Sentence Errors

Accepted usage improves the smoothness of your prose, makes your writing easier to understand, and demonstrates that you are a careful communicator. These assets, in turn, increase the likelihood that the reader will accept your ideas.

When you've finished revising the first draft of a piece of writing, edit it with a critic's eye to ensure that you eliminate errors. Circle sentences or parts of them that are faulty or suspect. Then check your circled items against this section of the Handbook, which deals with the most common errors in college writing.

Revising Sentence Fragments

A sentence fragment is a group of words that fails to qualify as a sentence but is capitalized and punctuated as if it were a sentence. To be a sentence, a word group must (1) have a subject and a verb and (2) make sense by itself. The first of the following examples has a subject and a verb; the second does not. Neither makes sense by itself.

> If you want to remain.
> His answer to the question.

Methods of Revision   Eliminating a sentence fragment is not hard. Careful reading often shows that the fragment goes with the sentence that comes just before or just after it. And sometimes two successive fragments can be joined. Note how we've corrected the fragments (italicized) in the following pairs:

Faulty	*Having been warned about the storm.* We decided to stay home.
Revision	Having been warned about the storm, we decided to stay home.
Faulty	*After eating.* The dog took a nap.
Revision	After eating, the dog took a nap.
Faulty	Sally went to work. *Although she felt sick.*
Revision	Sally went to work although she felt sick.
Faulty	Dave bought a new suit. *Over at Bentley's.*
Revision	Dave bought a new suit over at Bentley's.

Faulty	*That bronze clock on the mantel. Once belonged to my grandmother.*
Revision	*That bronze clock on the mantel once belonged to my grandmother.*

Joining a fragment to a sentence or to another fragment works only if the problem is simply one of mispunctuation. If the fragment stems from an improperly developed thought, revise the thought into correct sentence form.

Punctuating Your Corrections   When you join a fragment to the following sentence, you need not place a comma between the two unless the fragment has six or more words or if omitting a comma might cause a misreading. When joining a fragment to the preceding sentence, omit a comma unless there is a distinct pause between the two items. The preceding examples illustrate these points.

Intentional Fragments   Fragments are commonly used in conversation and the writing that reproduces it. Professional writers also use fragments to gain special emphasis or create special effects.

Connected Discourse Exercise

Identify and correct the sentence fragments in the following letter:

Dear Phone Company:

Recently I received a phone bill for over $500. While I do use the phone fairly extensively. Most of the calls I make are local ones. In this case, many of the calls on my bill were to other countries. Including a phone call to New Delhi, India. I can hardly be held responsible for these calls. Especially since I don't know anyone who lives overseas. Since the only long-distance call I made was to Kalamazoo, Michigan. I have deducted the charges for all the other long-distance calls from my bill and am sending you the balance. In order to prevent this type of error from happening again. Would you please have a representative determine why these charges appeared on my bill?

Sincerely,

Desperate

Ten main clauses paired with fragments are shown below. In each case identify the sentence (S) and the fragment (F) and then eliminate the fragment.

1. I would like you to meet Janine Lee. One of my good friends from high school.
2. Jason and Steve bought several posters. To spruce up their dorm room walls.
3. In order to get tickets to the concert. We had to stand in line for hours.
4. After we finish studying for our math test. We plan to go out for pizza.

5. The road to Cedar Lake will be closed for months. Because the flood has washed away the bridge over the Rouge River.

6. Carol bought the new computer. That she had wanted for months.

7. If the debate team lives up to its potential. We are sure to win the state finals.

8. There are several ways for companies to save on energy costs. One of them energy recycling.

9. Kristen first searched the library for information for her report. And then turned to the Internet for additional material.

10. Pleased by the amount of the painting he had already completed. John allowed himself a two-hour break to watch the football game.

Revising Run-On Sentences and Comma Splices

A run-on, or fused, sentence occurs when one sentence runs into another without anything to mark their junction. A comma splice occurs when only a comma marks the junction. These errors lead your readers to think that you are hasty or careless. Here are several examples:

Run-on sentence	Laura failed to set her alarm she was late for work.
Comma splice	Violets are blooming now, my lawn is covered with them.
Run-on sentence	Rick refused to attend the movie he said he hated horror shows.
Comma splice	Perry watched the road carefully, he still missed his turn.
Run-on sentence	Janet worked on her term paper her friend studied for a calculus test.
Comma splice	Janet worked on her term paper, her friend studied for a calculus test.

Testing for Errors   To check out a possible comma splice or fused sentence, read what precedes and follows the comma or suspected junction and see whether the two parts can stand alone as sentences. If *both parts* can stand alone, there is an error. Otherwise, there is not.

Darryl is a real troublemaker, someday he'll find himself in serious difficulty.

Examination of the parts preceding and following the comma shows that each is a complete sentence:

Darryl is a real troublemaker.

Someday he'll find himself in serious difficulty.

The writer has therefore committed a comma splice that needs correction.

Methods of Revision You can correct run-on sentences and comma splices in several ways.

1. Create two separate sentences.

    Revision Violets are blooming now. My lawn is covered with them.

    Revision Rick refused to attend the movie. He said he hated horror shows.

2. Join the sentences with a semicolon.

    Revision Violets are blooming now; my yard is covered with them.

    Revision Rick refused to attend the movie; he said he hated horror shows.

3. Join the sentences with a comma and a coordinating conjunction *(and, but, or, nor, for, yet, so)*.

    Revision Laura failed to set her alarm, *so* she was late for work.

    Revision Perry watched the road carefully, *but* he still missed his turn.

4. Join the sentences with a semicolon and a conjunctive adverb.

    Revision Laura failed to set her alarm; *consequently,* she was late for work.

    Revision Violets are blooming now; *in fact,* my yard is covered with them.

5. Introduce one of the sentences with a subordinating conjunction.

    Revision *Because* Laura failed to set her alarm, she was late for work.

    Revision Janet worked on her term paper *while* her friend studied for a calculus test.

As our examples show, you can often correct an error in several ways.

Connected Discourse Exercise

Identify and correct the comma splices and run-on sentences in the following letter:

Dear Desperate:

We are sorry to hear that you are having difficulty paying your bill, it is, however, your responsibility. Unfortunately we have no way to prevent you from making overseas calls, you have to curb your own tendency to reach out and touch your friends. Following your instructions, we are sending a technician to remove your phone. Please be home this Friday morning he will arrive then. Even though we will remove your phone, you are still responsible for the unpaid portion of your bill, it is your financial obligation. We would dislike referring this matter to a collection agency, it could ruin your credit rating.

Sincerely,

Your friendly phone representative

Indicate whether each item is correct (C), is a run-on sentence (RO), or contains a comma splice (CS) and then correct the faulty items.

1. Our company's Internet-based sales are up twenty percent; however, our store sales are down thirty percent.
2. Our computer assistants have only had three weeks of training, you cannot expect them to know the answer to every technical question.
3. Ellen worked very hard on her report she really earned her A.
4. The research on the effect of T.V. violence on children remains inconclusive, but still most of us would think that excessive exposure to images of violence would be harmful.
5. Alternative forms of punishment such as home incarceration have proven very effective, nevertheless prison is still the standard punishment for most nonviolent crimes.
6. The photographer accidentally exposed his film to the light as a result all our wedding pictures were ruined.
7. Jason got a terrific tan, he spent the winter break in Florida.
8. While tuberculosis is a terrible disease, it is rare and usually can be treated with antibiotics.
9. Many doctors' offices want to decrease costs they increasingly use physician assistants.
10. We have carefully reviewed your proposal for flexible work hours, we think it would improve employee satisfaction.

Creating Subject–Verb Agreement

A verb should agree in number with its subject. Singular verbs should have singular subjects, and plural verbs should have plural subjects.

Correct   My *boss* is a grouch. (singular subject and verb)

Correct   The *apartments have* two bedrooms. (plural subject and verb)

Ordinarily, matching subjects and verbs causes no problems. The following special situations, however, can create difficulties.

Subject and Verb Separated by a Word Group   Sometimes a word group that includes one or more nouns comes between the subject and the verb. When this happens, match the verb with its subject, not a noun in the word group.

Correct   Our *basket* of sandwiches *is* missing.

Correct   Several *books* required for my paper *are* not in the library.

Correct   *Mr. Schmidt,* along with his daughters, *runs* a furniture store.

Correct   The old *bus,* crammed with passengers, *was* unable to reach the top of the hill.

Two Singular Subjects   Most singular subjects joined by *and* take a plural verb.

Correct   The *couch* and *chair were* upholstered in blue velvet.

Sentences like the one above almost never cause problems. With subjects like *restoring cars* and *racing motorcycles,* however, singular verbs are often mistakenly used.

Faulty   *Restoring cars* and *racing motorcycles consumes* most of Frank's time.

Revision   *Restoring cars* and *racing motorcycles consume* most of Frank's time.

When *each* or *every* precedes the subjects, use a *singular* verb in place of a plural.

Correct   Every *book* and *magazine was* badly water-stained.

Singular subjects joined by *or, either—or,* or *neither—nor* also take singular verbs.

Correct   A *pear* or an *apple is* a good afternoon snack.

Correct   Neither *rain* nor *snow slows* our letter carrier.

Finally, use a singular verb when two singular subjects joined by *and* name the same person, place, or thing.

Correct   My *cousin* and business *partner is* retiring next month.

Cousin and *partner* refer to the same person.

One Singular and One Plural Subject   When one singular subject and one plural subject are joined by *or, either—or,* or *neither—nor,* match the verb with the closer of the two.

Correct   Neither *John* nor his *parents were* at home.

Correct   Neither his *parents* nor *John was* at home.

As these examples show, the sentences are usually smoother when the plural subject follows the singular.

Collective Nouns As Subjects   Collective nouns (*assembly, class, committee, family, herd, majority, tribe,* and the like) are singular in form but stand for groups or collections of people or things. Ordinarily, collective nouns are considered to be singular and therefore take singular verbs.

Correct The *class* is writing a test.

Correct The *herd was* clustered around the water hole.

Sometimes, though, a collective noun refers to the separate individuals making up the grouping, and then it requires a plural verb.

Correct The *jury are* in dispute about the verdict.

Sentences in Which the Verb Comes Ahead of the Subject Sentences that begin with words such as *here, there, how, what,* and *where* fall into this category. With such sentences, the verb must agree with the subject that follows it.

Correct Here *is* my *house.*

Correct Where *are* my *shoes?*

Correct There *is* just one *way* to solve this problem.

Correct There *go* my *chances* for a promotion.

Connected Discourse Exercise

Identify and correct the subject–verb agreement errors in the following letter:

Regional Accounts Manager:

One of your area phone representatives have seriously misread a letter I submitted with my bill. I refused to pay for long-distance overseas calls since neither I nor my roommate know anyone who lives overseas. Instead of deducting the calls from my bill, she sent someone to remove my phone. Now my phone, along with many of my valuable possessions, have been removed. Unfortunately the technician, whom I allowed into my apartment only after carefully checking his credentials, were a thief. He locked me in a closet and cleared out the apartment. I have called the police, but I also expect the phone company to reimburse me for my losses. There is only two choices. Either the stolen items or a check covering the loss need to be sent to me immediately. Otherwise I am afraid I will be forced to sue. A jury are sure to rule in my favor. In addition, I expect to find that those overseas calls has been deducted from my bill.

Sincerely,

Desperately Desperate

Choose the correct verb form from the pair in parentheses.

1. The library, along with many of the books, (*was, were*) severely damaged by the storm.
2. Congress (*retains, retain*) the right to control the country's purse strings.
3. A house with two baths and four bedrooms (*is, are*) for sale in my neighborhood.
4. What (*does, do*) these new printers cost?
5. A van or three cars (*is, are*) needed to drive the wrestling team to the meet.
6. Each of these suggestions (*has, have*) a lot of merit.
7. John Finch and his assistant (*plans, plan*) to review the contract with you next Friday.
8. There (*is, are*) a few advantages to carefully planning your work schedule.
9. Every piece of clothing and bedding (*has, have*) to be washed in scalding water.
10. Each of our employees (*knows, know*) the answer to the most common questions about our product.

Achieving Pronoun–Antecedent Agreement

The antecedent of a pronoun is the noun or pronoun to which it refers. Just as subjects should agree with their verbs, pronouns should agree with their antecedents: singular antecedents require singular pronouns, and plural antecedents require plural pronouns. Ordinarily, you will have no trouble matching antecedents and pronouns. The situations below, however, can cause problems.

Indefinite Pronouns As Antecedents   Indefinite pronouns include words like *each, either, neither, any, everybody, somebody,* and *nobody.* Whenever an indefinite pronoun is used as an antecedent, the pronoun that refers to it should be singular.

> *Faulty*   *Neither* of the actors had learned *their* lines.

> *Revision*   *Neither* of the actors had learned *his* lines.

As the revised example shows, this rule applies even when the pronoun is followed by a plural noun.

When the gender of the antecedent is unknown, you may follow it with *his or her,* or if this results in awkwardness, rewrite the sentence in the plural.

> *Correct Anyone* who has studied *his or her* assignments properly should do well on the test.

> *Correct Those* who have studied *their* assignments properly should do well on the test.

Occasionally, a ridiculous result occurs when a singular pronoun refers to an indefinite pronoun that is obviously plural in meaning. When this happens, rewrite the sentence to eliminate the problem.

Faulty   *Everybody* complained that the graduation ceremony had lasted too long, but I didn't believe *him.*

Revision   Everybody complained that the graduation ceremony had lasted too long, but I didn't agree.

Two Singular Antecedents   Two or more antecedents joined by *and* ordinarily call for a plural pronoun.

Correct   Her briefcase and umbrella were missing from *their* usual place on the hall table.

When *each* or *every* precedes the antecedent, use a singular pronoun.

Incorrect   Every college and university must do *their* best to provide adequate student counseling.

Correct   Every college and university must do *its* best to provide adequate student counseling.

Singular antecedents joined by *or, either—or,* or *neither—nor* call for singular pronouns.

Correct   Neither Carol nor Irene had paid *her* rent for the month.

Applying this rule can sometimes yield an awkward or foolish sentence. When this happens, rewrite the sentence to avoid the problem.

Faulty   Neither James nor Sally has finished *his or her* term project.

Revision   James and Sally have not finished *their* term projects.

Singular antecedents joined by *and* that refer to the same person, place, or thing use a singular pronoun.

Correct   My *cousin* and business *partner is* retiring to *her* condo in Florida next month.

Singular and Plural Antecedents   If one singular and one plural antecedent are joined by *or, either—or,* or *neither—nor,* the pronoun agrees with the closer one.

Correct   Either Terrence James or the Parkinsons will let us use *their* lawn mower.

Correct   Either the Parkinsons or Terrence James will let us use *his* lawn mower.

Sentences of this sort are generally smoother when the plural subject follows the singular.

Collective Nouns As Antecedents   When a collective noun is considered a single unit, the pronoun that refers to it should be singular.

Correct   The *troop* of scouts made *its* way slowly through the woods.

pa agr

Handbook

When the collective noun refers to the separate individuals in the group, use a plural pronoun.

Correct   The *staff* lost *their* jobs when the factory closed.

Connected Discourse Exercise

Identify and correct the pronoun–antecedent agreement errors in the following letter:

Dear Desperately Desperate:

We were sorry to hear about the theft from your apartment. Apparently a gang of con artists recently had their base of operations in your city. It posed as repair technicians and presented false credentials to anyone expecting their phone to be repaired. Someone also must have intercepted your mail and written their own response since we have no record of any previous letter from you. Clearly neither the representative you mentioned nor the phony phone technician could have held their position with our company. Every one of our technicians must provide us with their fingerprints and take periodic lie detector tests. Further, none of our representatives will answer correspondence since it is not a part of their job description. For these reasons, we do not believe we are responsible for your losses. However, a review of our records shows that you owe $500; we have included a copy of the bill in case you have misplaced the original.

Sincerely,

Accounts Manager

Choose the right pronoun from the pair in parentheses.

1. Company rules require every memo and letter to receive (*its, their*) correct authorization number.
2. Neither the Grangers nor Tom Cauldwell knew (*his, their*) lines by opening night.
3. After weeks of deliberation, the jury finally reached (*its, their*) decision.
4. Maria and Tim completed (*his or her, their*) project by the deadline.
5. Either Roderick or Shannon will present (*his or her, their*) personalized invitation to our special sale.
6. Either Sally or the Randalls will lend us (*her, their*) punch bowl for our party.
7. The class rushed into the computer room and took (*his or her, their*) seats.
8. Everybody has been assigned (*his or her, their*) own log-on name and password.
9. Every one of the women in our police force has proved that (*she, they*) can handle the duties of an officer.
10. Either Richard or Frank will be able to offer you (*his, their*) help in planning the science fiction film festival.

Using Effective Pronoun Reference

Any pronoun except an indefinite pronoun should refer to just one noun or noun substitute—its antecedent. Reference problems result when the pronoun has two or more antecedents, a hidden antecedent, or no antecedent. These errors can cause mixups in meaning as well as ridiculous sentences.

More Than One Antecedent The following sentences lack clarity because their pronouns have two possible antecedents rather than just one:

Faulty   Take the screens off the windows and wash *them*.

Faulty   Harry told Will that *he* was putting on weight.

The reader can't tell whether the screens or the windows should be washed or who is putting on weight.
  Sometimes we see a sentence like this one:

Faulty   If the boys don't eat all the Popsicles, put *them* in the freezer.

In this case, we know it's the Popsicles that should be stored, but the use of *them* creates an amusing sentence.
  Correct these faults by replacing the pronoun with a noun or by rephrasing the sentence.

Revision   Wash the windows after you have taken off the screens.

Revision   Take off the screens so that you can wash the windows.

Revision   Harry told Will, "I am (you are) putting on weight."

Revision   Put any uneaten Popsicles in the freezer.

Hidden Antecedent An antecedent is hidden if it takes the form of an adjective rather than a noun.

Faulty   The movie theater is closed today, so we can't see *one*.

Faulty   As I passed the tiger's cage, it lunged at me.

To correct this fault, replace the pronoun with the noun used as an adjective or switch the positions of the pronoun and the noun and make any needed changes in their forms.

Revision   The theater is closed today, so we can't see a movie.

Revision   As I passed its cage, the tiger lunged at me.

No Antecedent A no-antecedent sentence lacks any noun to which the pronoun can refer. Sentences of this sort occur frequently in everyday conversation but should be avoided in formal writing. The examples below illustrate this error:

Faulty   The lecture was boring, but *they* took notes anyway.

Faulty   On the news program, *it* told about a new crisis in the Persian Gulf.

To set matters right, substitute a suitable noun for the pronoun or reword the sentence.

Revision   The lecture was boring, but the students took notes anyway.

Revision   The news program told about a new crisis in the Persian Gulf.

Sometimes *this, that, it,* or *which* will refer to a whole idea rather than a single noun. This usage is acceptable provided the writer's meaning is obvious, as in this example:

pr ref

Correct   The instructor spoke very softly, *which* meant we had difficulty hearing him.

Problems occur, however, when the reader can't figure out which of two or more ideas the pronoun refers to.

Faulty   Ginny called Sally two hours after the agreed-upon time and postponed their shopping trip one day. *This* irritated Sally .very much.

What caused Sally to be irritated—the late call, the postponement of the trip, or both? Again, rewording or adding a clarifying word will correct the problem.

Revision   Ginny called Sally two hours after the agreed-upon time and postponed their shopping trip one day. *This tardiness* irritated Sally very much.

Revision   Ginny called Sally two hours after the agreed-upon time and postponed their shopping trip one day. Ginny's *change of plans* irritated Sally very much.

The first of these examples illustrates the addition of a clarifying word; the second illustrates rewriting.

Connected Discourse Exercise

Identify and correct any faulty pronoun references in the following memorandum:

To: Director of Food Services, Groan University

From: Vice President of College Services

Date: February 19, 20__ __

Subject: Student Complaints about Cafeteria

Complaints about food quality and cafeteria hours are common but easily resolved. They can be extended by simply installing vending machines. It might not make for a nutritious meal, but it certainly will undercut some of the dissatisfaction. Of course, no matter how good the food, they will complain. Still, you can partially defuse those complaints by having students list their major concerns and then meeting them. Of course, you can always increase student satisfaction by purchasing a soft ice cream machine and offering it for dessert.

Indicate whether each sentence is correct (C) or contains a faulty pronoun reference (F) and then correct the faulty sentences.

1. When Al accidentally slammed down on his car's accelerator instead of the brake, it roared forward into the intersection.
2. They have informed me that we have seen a 15 percent increase in sales this month.
3. When the supervisor walked by the water cooler, they stopped talking.
4. I like trout fishing because it is very relaxing.
5. Since I knew that our employees found their chairs uncomfortable, I replaced them with new ones.
6. In the report, it suggested that we needed to be more attentive to employee suggestions.
7. Because the batting cap hurt his head, Fred removed it.
8. Frank told his best friend that his wife wanted to spend more time with him.
9. At Electronic City, they sell many brands of computers.
10. Janine asked Caroline if she could rewrite her paper for her English class.

Managing Shifts in Person

Pronouns can be in the first person, second person, or third person. *First-person* pronouns identify people who are talking or writing about themselves, *second-person* pronouns identify people being addressed directly, and *third-person* pronouns identify persons or things that are being written or spoken about. The following table sorts pronouns according to person:

First Person	Second Person	Third Person
I	you	he
me	your	she
my	yours	it
mine	yourself	his
we	yourselves	her
us		hers
our		its
ours		one
ourselves		they
		their
		theirs
		indefinite pronouns

All nouns are in the third person. As you revise, be alert for unwarranted shifts from one person to another.

Faulty	I liked *my* British vacation better than *my* vacation in France and Italy because *you* didn't have language problems.
Revision	I liked *my* British vacation better than *my* vacation in France and Italy because *I* didn't have language problems.
Faulty	Holidays are important to *everyone*. They boost *your* spirits and provide a break from *our* daily routine.
Revision	Holidays are important to *everyone*. They boost *one's* spirits and provide a break from *one's* daily routine.
Faulty	The taller the *golfer*, the more club speed *you* will have with a normally paced swing.
Revision	The taller the *golfer*, the more club speed *he* or *she* will have with a normally paced swing.

As these examples show, the shift can occur within a single sentence or when the writer moves from one sentence to another.

Some shifts in person, however, are warranted. Read the following correct sentence:

Correct	*I* want *you* to deliver these flowers to Ms. Willoughby by three o'clock. *She* needs them for a party.

Here the speaker identifies himself or herself (*I*) while speaking directly to a listener *(you)* about someone else *(she)*. In this case, shifts are needed to get the message across.

Connected Discourse Exercise

Identify and correct the unwarranted shifts in person in the following paragraph:

Good health is clearly important to you. But it is one's responsibility to ensure our own good health. You can start with simple exercises. We would like to provide you with a low impact aerobics DVD for only $15. We guarantee that the more out of shape the customer, the quicker you will notice the benefits. The way our bodies feel affects the quality of one's lives. Let our tape help you to a better life.

Indicate whether the sentence is correct (C) or contains an unwarranted shift in person (S). Correct faulty sentences.

1. After the teacher collected our essays, she told the students that she would return the graded papers on Wednesday.

2. For someone to be successful in today's marketplace, you need to have adequate technical skills.

3. If you each will bring the results of your assigned research to the next meeting, we will be ready to begin working on our collaborative report.

4. Because our tickets were in the nosebleed section of the stadium, many of the fans felt they would have been better off watching the football game on TV.

5. If you want theater tickets, I will be glad to purchase them on my way home from work.

6. Anyone who would like to purchase the discounted Caribbean cruise tickets should place your order by May 15.

7. We enjoy living in the Grand Rapids area very much; you have access to theater, sporting events, and fine dining.

8. On major holidays, most Americans travel long distances, often at great inconvenience, to visit our relatives.

9. If you would like to learn to kayak, novices can usually get free lessons from the people who sell kayaks.

10. In our attempt to determine whether there has been an increase in tornado activity over the last twenty years, the researchers collected data on storm sightings and damage reports.

case

Using the Right Pronoun Case

Case means the changes in form that a personal pronoun undergoes to show its function in a sentence. English has three cases: the *subjective*, the *nonsubjective* (objective), and the *possessive*. The following chart shows the different forms:

Subjective Form	Nonsubjective Form	Possessive Form
I	me	my, mine
he	him	his
she	her	her, hers
we	us	our, ours
you	you	your, yours
they	them	their, theirs
who	whom	whose

The subjective case is used for subjects and subject complements, the nonsubjective for direct objects, indirect objects, and objects of prepositions. The possessive case shows ownership and is also used with gerunds.

The following pointers will help you select the proper pronoun as you revise.

We and Us Preceding Nouns   Nouns that serve as subjects take the pronoun *we*. Other nouns take the pronoun *us*.

| Correct | *We* tourists will fly home tomorrow. (*We* accompanies the subject.) |
| Correct | The guide showed *us* tourists through the cathedral. (*Us* accompanies a nonsubject.) |

If you can't decide which pronoun is right, mentally omit the noun and read the sentence to yourself, first with one pronoun and then with the other. Your ear will indicate the correct form.

My mother made (*we, us*) children vanilla pudding for dessert.

Omitting *children* shows immediately that *us* is the right choice.

> *Correct*   My mother made *us* children vanilla pudding for dessert.

Pronouns Paired with Nouns   When such a combination serves as the subject of a sentence or accompanies the subject, use the subject form of the pronoun. When the combination plays a nonsubject role, use the nonsubject form of the pronoun.

> *Correct*   Arlene and *I* plan to join the Peace Corps. (*I* is part of the compound subject.)
>
> *Correct*   Two people, Mary and *I*, will represent our school at the meeting. (*I* is part of a compound element accompanying the subject.)
>
> *Correct*   The superintendent told Kevin and *him* that they would be promoted soon. (*Him* is part of a compound nonsubject.)
>
> *Correct*   The project was difficult for Jeffrey and *him* to complete. (*Him* is part of a compound nonsubject.)

Again, mentally omitting the noun from the combination will tell you which pronoun is correct.

Who and Whom in Dependent Clauses   Use *who* for the subjects of dependent clauses; otherwise use *whom*.

> *Correct*   The Mallarys prefer friends *who are interested in the theater.* (*Who* is the subject of the clause.)
>
> *Correct*   Barton is a man *whom very few people like.* (*Whom* is not the subject of the clause.)

A simple test will help you decide between *who* and *whom.* First, mentally isolate the dependent clause. Next, block out the pronoun in question and then insert *he* (or *she*) and *him* (or *her*) at the appropriate spot in the remaining part of the clause. If *he* (or *she*) sounds better, *who* is right. If *him* (or *her*) sounds better, *whom* is right. Let's use this test on the sentence below:

The woman *who(m) Scott is dating* works as a mechanical engineer. Scott is dating (*she, her*).

Clearly *her* is correct; therefore, *whom* is the proper form.

> *Correct*   The woman *whom Scott is dating* works as a mechanical engineer.

Pronouns As Subject Complements   In formal writing, pronouns that serve as subject complements always take the subject form.

> *Correct*   It is *I*.
>
> *Correct*   It was *she* who bought the old Parker mansion.

This rule, however, is often ignored in informal writing.

> It's *her*.
>
> That's *him* standing over by the door.

Comparisons Using *than* or *as . . . as*   Comparisons of this kind often make no direct statement about the second item of comparison. When the second naming word is a pronoun, you may have trouble choosing the right one.

> Harriet is less outgoing than (*they, them*).
>
> My parents' divorce saddened my sister as much as (*I, me*).

Not to worry. Expand the sentence by mentally supplying the missing material. Then try the sentence with each pronoun and see which sounds right.

> Harriet is less outgoing than (*they, them*) are.
>
> My parents' divorce saddened my sister as much as it did (*I, me*).

Obviously *they* is the right choice for the first sentence, and *me* is the right choice for the second one.

> *Correct*   Harriet is less outgoing than *they* are.
>
> *Correct*   My parents' divorce saddened my sister as much as it did *me*.

Pronouns Preceding Gerunds   Use the possessive form of a pronoun that precedes a gerund.

> I dislike *their* leaving without saying goodbye.
>
> Ted can't understand *her* quitting such a good job.

This usage emphasizes the action named by the gerund instead of the person or persons performing it. Thus, in the above sentences, the possessive form of the pronoun signals that it's the *leaving* the writer dislikes and the *quitting* that Ted can't understand. The persons involved are secondary.

When the pronoun precedes a participle, it should be in the nonsubject case. The emphasis is then on the actor rather than the action.

> Jennifer caught *them* listening to records instead of studying.

In this example, Jennifer caught the listeners, not the listening.

If you have trouble deciding between the nonsubject and possessive forms of a pronoun, ask yourself whether you want to emphasize the action or the actor; then proceed accordingly.

case

Connected Discourse Exercise

Identify and correct the pronoun case errors in the following paragraph:

Between my brother and I, we are always able to pull at least five good-sized trout a day from the creek behind our house. Us rural trout fishermen just seem to have the knack. Of course, those city fishermen whom insist on employing artificial flies won't appreciate our methods even if they can't do as well as us. We just let our bait, usually a juicy worm, float downstream to the waiting trout. Of course, my brother won't let the fishing interfere with him sleeping. In fact, it was him that developed the idea of looping the line around his toe so that he would wake up when a trout took the bait. Others have told my brother and I that this method is dangerous, but neither of us has lost a toe yet. Of course, the people who we invite to dinner don't complain about our methods, and they seem to enjoy the fish.

Choose the right form of the pronoun for each of the following sentences. For the purpose of this exercise, assume that there would have been the appropriate pronoun antecedent in the sentence preceding the one that is shown.

1. No one is as pleased as (*I, me*) by John's recent promotion to assistant vice president.
2. There is no excuse for (*him, his*) yelling at us in public.
3. The newspaper's editor praised Marge and (*I, me*) for our coauthored article on women in the military.
4. Randy has a better grasp of European history than (*I, me*).
5. Megan is one student (*who, whom*) I believe really understands the importance of writing well.
6. (*We, Us*) Americans pride ourselves on our individuality.
7. The conductor decided that Marie and (*I, me*) should sing a duet at the next recital.
8. Rilke is the poet (*who, whom*) I like best.
9. The judge told (*we, us*) contestants that we would be called when it was our turn.
10. The manager of the movie theater gave Tom and (*I, me*) four free passes.

Creating Consistency in Showing Time

Inconsistencies occur when a writer shifts from the past tense to the present or vice versa without a corresponding shift in the time of the events being described. The following paragraph contains an uncalled-for shift from the present tense to the past:

> As *The Most Dangerous Game* opens, Sanger Rainsford, a famous hunter and author, and his old friend Whitney are standing on the deck of a yacht and

discussing a mysterious island as the ship passes near it. Then, after everyone else has gone to bed, Rainsford manages to fall overboard. He swims to the island and ends up at a chateau owned by General Zaroff, a refugee from the Communist takeover in Russia. Zaroff, bored with hunting animals, has turned to hunting humans on his desert island. Inevitably, Rainsford is turned out into the jungle to be hunted down. There were [shift to past tense] actually four hunts over a three-day period, and at the end of the last one, Rainsford jumped into the sea, swam across a cove to the chateau, and killed Zaroff in the general's own bedroom. Afterward he sleeps [shift back to present tense] and decides "he had never slept in a better bed."

The sentence with the unwarranted shift in tense should read as follows:

There are actually four hunts over a three-day period, and at the end of the last one, Rainsford jumps into the sea, swims across a cove to the chateau, and kills Zaroff in the general's own bedroom.

The time shift in the quotation part of the final sentence is justified because the sleeping has occurred before Rainsford's thoughts about it.

A second kind of inconsistency results when a writer fails to distinguish the immediate past from the less immediate past. The following sentence illustrates this error:

Faulty   Mary *answered* all thirty test questions when the class ended.

This sentence indicates that Mary completed all thirty test questions during the final instant of the class, an impossibility. When you detect this type of error in your writing, determine which action occurred first and then correct the error by adding *had* to the verb. In this case, the first verb needs correcting:

Revision   Mary *had answered* all thirty test questions when the class ended.

Besides adding *had*, you may sometimes need to alter the verb form.

Faulty   Before he turned twenty, John *wrote* two novels.

Revision   Before he turned twenty, John *had written* two novels.

Connected Discourse Exercise

Identify and correct any inconsistencies in showing time in the following passage:

There is no better time to go swimming than at night. The summer after I had graduated from high school, I worked for a landscaping company. After a sweaty day mowing lawns and digging up gardens, all of us who worked there would jump into the back of Dick's old pickup and rattle out to Woods Lake. It is just dark as we arrive. The moon is beautiful, reflected in that black

time

mirror set in a frame of hills. We stumble down a small, sandy hill to the beach, where we strip off our dusty jeans and sweaty shirts before plunging into the cool reflection of stars.

mis
adj/adv

Indicate whether each sentence is correct (C) or contains an unwarranted shift (S) in tense. Then correct the faulty sentences.

1. A thin wisp of smoke drifts from under the hood, and then the engine burst into flames.
2. After Kyra finishes checking the computers for viruses, she will load the new software.
3. Jason took on many projects but finishes few of them.
4. After I finished preparing dinner, I went for a long walk.
5. As Charlie laid pieces of the model on the table, his wife picks them up.
6. As soon as the snow falls, we break out our cross-country skis.
7. David is building his own house but found it harder work than he anticipated.
8. While Robert applies the adhesive, David carefully positioned the floor tiles.
9. Tonya stood in line for the movie tickets while Doug searches for a parking space.
10. Although it started to rain heavily, Debbie continues to mow the lawn.

Using Adjectives and Adverbs Effectively

Inexperienced writers often use adjectives when they should use adverbs and also confuse the comparative and superlative forms of these parts of speech when making comparisons.

Misusing Adjectives for Adverbs   Although most adjectives can be misused as adverbs, the following seven, listed with the corresponding adverbs, cause the most difficulty.

Adjectives	Adverbs
awful	awfully
bad	badly
considerable	considerably
good	well
most	almost
real	really
sure	surely

The following sentences show typical errors:

Faulty   Bryan did *good* in his first golf lesson. (*good* mistakenly used to modify verb *did*)

Faulty   *Most* every graduate from our auto service program receives several job offers. (*most* mistakenly used to modify adjective *every*)

Faulty   The speech was delivered *real* well. (*real* mistakenly used to modify adverb *well*)

Because adverbs modify verbs, adjectives, and other adverbs, and adjectives modify nouns and noun substitutes, the above sentences clearly require adverbs.

Revision   Bryan did *well* in his first golf lesson.

Revision   *Almost* every graduate from our auto service program receives several job offers.

Revision   The speech was delivered *really* well.

In one notable case, an adverb is commonly misused as an adjective.

Faulty   I feel *badly* about providing the wrong phone number. (*Badly* is mistakenly used as a subject complement.)

Revision   I feel *bad* about providing the wrong phone number.

If you can't decide whether a sentence requires an adjective or an adverb, determine the part of speech of the word being modified and proceed accordingly.

Confusing the Comparative and Superlative Forms in Comparisons The comparative form of adjectives and adverbs is used to compare two things, the superlative form to compare three or more things. Adjectives with fewer than three syllables generally add *-er* to make the comparative form and *-est* to make the superlative form (tall, tall*er*, tall*est*). Adjectives with three or more syllables generally add *more* to make the comparative and *most* to make the superlative (enchanting, *more* enchanting, *most* enchanting), as do most adverbs of two or more syllables (loudly, *more* loudly, *most* loudly).

When making comparisons, beginning writers sometimes mistakenly use double comparatives or double superlatives.

Faulty   Harry is *more taller* than James. (double comparative)

Faulty   The Chrysler Building has the *most splendidest* lobby I've ever seen. (double superlative)

The correct versions read as follows:

Revision   Harry is *taller* than James.

Revision   The Chrysler Building has the *most splendid* lobby I've ever seen.

In addition, writers may erroneously use the superlative form, rather than the comparative form, to compare two things.

Faulty   Barry is the *richest* of the two brothers.

Faulty   Jeremy is the *most talented* of those two singers.

Here are the sentences correctly written:

Revision   Barry is the *richer* of the two brothers.

Revision   Jeremy is the *more talented* of those two singers.

Reserve the superlative form for comparing three or more items.

Correct   Barry is the *richest* of the three brothers.

Correct   Jeremy is the *most talented* of those four singers.

Connected Discourse Exercise

Identify and correct the adjective–adverb errors in the following paragraph:

This year our football team is outstanding. Spike Jones, our quarterback, has been playing real good this past season. Stan Blunder, the most talented of our two ends, hasn't dropped a pass all season. The team can most always count on Stan to catch the crucial first-down pass. Of course, the team wouldn't be where it is today without John Schoolyard's good coaching. He has made this team much more better than it was even a year ago. Only the kicking team has done bad this season. Of course, with this most wonderfulest offense, the defensive players haven't gotten much practice. The good news is, then, that we can sure expect to watch some terrific college football for years to come.

For each of the following sentences, choose the proper word from the pair in parentheses:

1. The milk in the refrigerator tastes (*bad, badly*).
2. Old science fiction movies can be (*real, really*) funny to watch because of the clumsy special effects and stilted dialogue.
3. Steve did (*good, well*) on his history project.
4. The Vandorns have the (*prettiest, most prettiest*) house in the development.
5. Dana is the (*quieter, quietest*) of our three children.
6. Terry hurt his knees (*bad, badly*) playing football.
7. The Mustang is the (*less, least*) expensive of the two sports cars you are considering.
8. (*Most, Almost*) all of our employees make use of the day care facility we provide on the premises.
9. It is (*real, really*) important to read the entire manual.
10. The Powermax is the (*stronger, strongest*) of the three kinds of garage door openers we sell.

Placing Modifiers Correctly

A misplaced modifier is a word or word group that is improperly separated from the word it modifies. When separation of this type occurs, the sentence often sounds awkward, ridiculous, or confusing.

Usually, you can correct this error by moving the modifier next to the word it is intended to modify. Occasionally, you'll also need to alter some of the phrasing.

Faulty   There is a bicycle in the basement *with chrome fenders.* (The basement appears to have chrome fenders.)

Faulty   David received a phone call from his uncle *that infuriated him.* (The uncle appears to have infuriated David.)

Revision   There is a bicycle *with chrome fenders* in the basement.

Revision   David received an *infuriating* phone call from his uncle. (Note the change in wording.)

In shifting the modifier, don't inadvertently create another faulty sentence.

Faulty   Fritz bought a magazine with an article about Michael Jackson *at the corner newsstand.* (The article appears to tell about Jackson's visit to the corner newsstand.)

Faulty   Fritz bought a magazine *at the corner newsstand* with an article about Michael Jackson. (The corner newsstand appears to have an article about Jackson.)

Revision   *At the corner newsstand,* Fritz bought a magazine with an article about Michael Jackson.

As you revise, watch also for *squinting modifiers*—that is, modifiers positioned so that the reader doesn't know whether they are supposed to modify what comes ahead of them or what follows them.

Faulty   The man who was rowing the boat *frantically* waved toward the onlookers on the beach.

Is the man rowing frantically or waving frantically? Correct this kind of error by repositioning the modifier so that the ambiguity disappears.

Revision   The man who was *frantically* rowing the boat waved toward the onlookers on the beach.

Revision   The man who was rowing the boat waved *frantically* toward the onlookers on the beach.

EXERCISE

Indicate whether each sentence is correct (C) or contains a misplaced modifier (MM). Correct faulty sentences.

mm

1. Jason handed his report to his teacher neatly tucked into a binder.
2. The girl driving past the school wildly waved at her friends.
3. The dancers practiced Swan Lake for a month before the performance.
4. I tossed the rainbow trout to my brother still hooked firmly in the mouth.
5. Most companies do not like placing managers in charge of employees who are inexperienced.
6. There is a computer in our classroom that beeps loudly at the most unexpected times.
7. You can learn about recent volcanic eruptions at your local library.
8. Steve devoured greasy barbecued spareribs wearing a new suit.
9. The instructor reminded students on the last day of classes to turn in their twenty-page paper.
10. Stacey found beautiful and inexpensive macramé wall hangings for her dorm room in the Bahamas.

dm

Revising Dangling Modifiers

A dangling modifier is a phrase or clause that lacks clear connection to the word or words it is intended to modify. As a result, sentences are inaccurate, often comical. Typically, the modifier leads off the sentence, although it can also come at the end.

Sometimes the error occurs because the sentence fails to specify who or what is modified. At other times, the separation is too great between the modifier and what it modifies.

Faulty   *Walking in the meadow*, wildflowers surrounded us. (The wildflowers appear to be walking in the meadow.)

Faulty   Dinner was served *after saying grace.* (The dinner appears to have said grace.)

Faulty   *Fatigued by the violent exercise*, the cool shower was very relaxing. (The cool shower appears to have been fatigued.)

The first of these sentences is faulty because the modifier is positioned too far away from *us*. The other two are faulty because they do not identify who said grace or found the shower relaxing.

You can correct dangling modifiers in two basic ways. First, leave the modifier unchanged and rewrite the main part of the sentence so that it begins with the term actually modified. Second, rewrite the modifier so that it has its own subject and verb, thereby eliminating the inaccuracy.

Revision   *Walking in the meadow*, we were surrounded by wildflowers. (The main part of the sentence has been rewritten.)

Revision   *As we walked in the meadow*, wildflowers surrounded us. (The modifier has been rewritten.)

Revision   *Dinner was served after we had said grace.* (The modifier has been rewritten.)

Revision   *Fatigued by the violent exercise*, Ted found the cool shower very relaxing. (The main part of the sentence has been rewritten.)

Revision   *Because Ted was fatigued by the violent exercise*, the cool shower was very relaxing. (The modifier has been rewritten.)

Ordinarily, either part of the sentence can be rewritten, but sometimes only one part can.

Indicate whether each sentence is correct (C) or contains a dangling modifier (DM). Correct faulty sentences.

1. After listening to a tape of Orson Welles' radio broadcast of *The War of the Worlds*, I understood why many who tuned into the middle of the broadcast panicked.
2. The baseball game will start after singing *The Star-Spangled Banner*.
3. Looking at the night sky, a million stars seemed to smile down on us.
4. Driving with his emergency brake on, Matt wore down the brake pads.
5. Having scored 100 percent on the pretest, the teacher placed two students in the next level math class.
6. Picasso was known to leave customers waiting for several days, painting furiously.
7. John cataloged his CD collection, listing each CD in a database.
8. Sitting on the back porch, a black bear shuffled across the lawn to raid our garbage cans.
9. Please send an e-mail to the project head listing your concerns.
10. Rushing over the banks, Main Street was soon under three feet of water.

Maintaining Parallelism

Nonparallelism results when equivalent ideas follow different grammatical forms. One common kind of nonparallelism occurs with words or word groups in pairs or in a series.

Faulty   Althea enjoys *jogging, biking,* and *to swim.*

Faulty   The superintendent praised the workers *for their productivity* and *because they had an excellent safety record.*

Faulty   The banner was *old, faded,* and *it had a rip.*

Note how rewriting the sentences in parallel form improves their smoothness.

Revision   Althea enjoys *jogging, biking,* and *swimming.*

Revision   The superintendent praised the workers for *their productivity* and *their excellent safety record.*

Revision   The banner was *old, faded,* and *ripped.*

Nonparallelism also occurs when correlative conjunctions *(either—or, neither—nor, both—and,* and *not only—but also)* are followed by unlike elements.

Faulty   That sound *either* <u>was a thunderclap</u> *or* <u>an explosion</u>.

Faulty   The basement was *not only* <u>poorly lighted</u> *but also* <u>it had a foul smell</u>.

Ordinarily, repositioning one of the correlative conjunctions will solve the problem. Sometimes, however, one of the grammatical elements must be rewritten.

Revision   That sound was *either* <u>a thunderclap</u> *or* <u>an explosion</u>. (*Either* has been repositioned.)

Revision   The basement was *not only* <u>poorly lighted</u> *but also* <u>foul smelling</u>. (The element following *but also* has been rewritten.)

Indicate whether each sentence is correct (C) or nonparallel (NP). Correct faulty sentences.

1. The cause of the fire either was faulty wiring or an overloaded outlet.
2. After graduation, Marci will be moving to Chicago and work for a large public relations firm.
3. For spring break, Steve and his friends plan to visit either New Orleans or Orlando.
4. A good candidate for social work enjoys talking with people, helps solve problems, and seeing projects through to their conclusion.
5. This course will involve reading a number of short stories, and you will need to turn in weekly journal responses.
6. Although he was an excellent auto mechanic, Andy could neither repair air conditioning units nor car stereos.
7. Canton chicken balls are sweet, tangy, and satisfying.
8. In my spare time, I enjoy reading, canoeing, and to play the piano.
9. As stage manger, Susan had to design, construct, and maintain the set for the school play.
10. As a reference librarian, Colin is responsible for instructing students in how to perform database searches, helping researchers find the material they need, maintaining the reference section, and he also manages the patent collection.

Revising Faulty Comparisons

A faulty comparison results if you (1) mention one of the items being compared but not the other, (2) omit words needed to clarify the relationship, or (3) compare different sorts of items. Advertisers often offend in the first way.

Faulty   Irish tape has better adhesion.

With what other tape is Irish tape being compared? Scotch tape? All other transparent tape? Mentioning the second term of a comparison eliminates reader guesswork.

Revision   Irish tape has better adhesion than any other transparent tape.

Two clarifying words, *other* and *else*, are frequently omitted from comparisons, creating illogical sentences.

Faulty   Sergeant McNabb is more conscientious than any officer in his precinct.

Faulty   Stretch French is taller than anyone on his basketball team.

The first sentence is illogical because McNabb is one of the officers in his precinct and therefore cannot be more conscientious than any officer in the precinct. Similarly, because French is a member of his basketball team, he can't be taller than anyone on his team. Adding *other* to the first sentence and *else* to the second corrects matters.

Revision   Sergeant McNabb is more conscientious than any *other* officer in his precinct.

Revision   Stretch French is taller than anyone *else* on his basketball team.

Comparing unlike items is perhaps the most common kind of comparison error. Here are two examples:

Faulty   The cities in California are larger than North Dakota.

Faulty   The cover of this book is much more durable than the other book.

The first sentence compares the cities of California with a state, while the second compares the cover of a book with a whole book. Correction consists of rewriting each sentence so that it compares like items.

Revision   The cities in California are larger than *those in* North Dakota.

Revision   The cover of this book is much more durable than *that of* the other book.

Connected Discourse Exercise

Identify and correct the misplaced modifiers, dangling modifiers, nonparallelism, and faulty comparisons in the following memorandum:

TO: All Residence Hall Advisors in Knuckles Hall

FROM: John Knells, Residency Hall Director

DATE: March 13, 20__ __

SUBJECT: Noise in Residence Hall

Recently I received a report from a student that deeply disturbed me. Apparently, after quiet hours students still have visitors in their rooms, are playing their stereos loudly, and are even staging boxing matches in the halls. The student who wrote me desperately tries to study. However, he is often forced to leave his room disturbed by the noise. He was not the only one to complain. You should know that we have had more complaints about Knuckles Hall than any dorm on campus. Since discussing this problem with you at the last staff meeting, things haven't seemed to get any better. The rules are not only poorly enforced but also they are completely ignored. Your job performance is worse than the students. If you don't improve immediately, I will be forced to dismiss you.

EXERCISE

Indicate whether each sentence is correct (C) or contains a faulty comparison (FC). Correct the faulty comparison.

1. *Death of a Salesman* is performed more often than any American play.
2. The power of today's laptop computers is much greater than the large defense department mainframes of the 1950s.
3. This quarter's earning report shows significantly greater net profits.
4. The Sunday brunch at the 1913 room is much more elegant than the Eatery.
5. Of the two quarterbacks, Allen has a stronger throwing arm than Tom.
6. In contrast to your car, I usually get 40 miles to the gallon.
7. The winters in North Dakota are much worse than Maine.
8. Our new ice cream shop offers many more flavors.
9. The paint on the front of the house is much lighter than the back.
10. Professor Hinkley has published many more articles than the other members of his department.

Editing to Correct Faulty Punctuation and Mechanics

Punctuation marks indicate relationships among different sentence elements. As a result, these marks help clarify the meaning of written material. Similarly, a knowledge of mechanics—capitalization, abbreviations, numbers, and italics—helps you avoid distracting inconsistencies.

This part of the Handbook covers the fundamentals of punctuation and mechanics. Review it carefully when you edit your final draft.

Apostrophes

Apostrophes (') show possession, mark contractions, and indicate plurals that are singled out for special attention.

Possession   Possessive apostrophes usually show ownership *(Mary's cat)*. Sometimes, though, they identify the works of creative people *(Hemingway's novels)* or indicate an extent of time or distance *(one hour's time, one mile's distance)*.

Possessive apostrophes are used with nouns and with pronouns like *someone, no one, everybody, each other,* and *one another.* The possessive form is easily recognized because it can be converted to a prepositional phrase beginning with *of.*

The collar of the dog

The whistle of the wind

The intention of the corporation

The birthday of Scott

To show possession with pronouns like those above, singular nouns, and plural nouns that do not end in an *s,* add an apostrophe followed by an *s.*

Someone's car is blocking our drive. (possessive of pronoun *someone*)

The *manager's* reorganization plan will take effect next week. (possessive of singular noun *manager*)

The *women's* lounge is being redecorated. (possessive of plural noun *women*)

Sentences that make comparisons sometimes include two possessives, the second coming at the very end. In such cases, be sure to use an apostrophe with the second possessive.

Birmingham's football team is much better than *Central's.*

With singular nouns that end in *s*, the possessive is sometimes formed by merely adding an apostrophe at the end *(James' helmet)*. The preferred usage, however, is *'s (James's helmet)* unless the addition of the *s* would make it awkward to pronounce the word.

Moses's followers entered the Promised Land. (awkward pronunciation of *Moses's*)

Moses' followers entered the Promised Land. (nonawkward pronunciation of *Moses'*)

Plural nouns ending in *s* form the possessive by adding only an apostrophe at the end.

All the *ladies'* coats are on sale today. (possessive of plural noun *ladies*)

The *workers'* lockers were moved. (possessive of plural noun *workers*)

To show joint ownership by two or more persons, use the possessive form for the last-named person only. To show individual ownership, use the possessive form for each person's name.

Ronald and *Joan's* boat badly needed overhauling. (joint ownership)
Laura's and *Alice's* term projects are almost completed. (individual ownership)

Hyphenated nouns form the possessive by adding *'s* to the last word.

My *mother-in-law's* house is next to mine.

Never use an apostrophe with the possessive pronouns *his, hers, whose, its, ours, yours, theirs.*

This desk is *his;* the other one is *hers.* (no apostrophes needed)

Contractions Contractions of words or numbers omit one or more letters or numerals. An apostrophe shows exactly where the omission occurs.

Wasn't that a disappointing concert? (contraction of *was not*)

Around here, people still talk about the blizzard of *'79.* (contraction of *1979*)

Don't confuse the contraction *it's,* meaning *it is* or *it has,* with the possessive pronoun *its,* which should never have an apostrophe. If you're puzzled by an *its* that you've written, try this test. Expand the *its* to *it is* or *it has* and see whether the sentence still makes sense. If it does, the *its* is a contraction and needs the apostrophe. If the result is nonsense, the *its* is a possessive pronoun and does not get an apostrophe. Here are some examples:

Its awfully muggy today.

Its been an exciting trip.

Every dog has *its* day.

The first example makes sense when the *its* is expanded to *it is*.

It is awfully muggy today.

The second makes sense when the *its* is expanded to *it has*.

It has been an exciting trip.

Both of these sentences therefore require apostrophes.

It's awfully muggy today.

It's been an exciting trip.

The last sentence, however, turns into nonsense when the *its* is expanded.

Every dog has *it is* day.

Every dog has *it has* day.

In this case, the *its* is a possessive pronoun and requires no apostrophe.

Every dog has *its* day.

Plurals   To improve clarity, the plurals of letters, numbers, symbols, and words being singled out for special attention are written with apostrophes.

Mind your *p*'s and *q*'s. (plurals of letters)

Your *5*'s and *6*'s are hard to tell apart. (plurals of numbers)

The formula was sprinkled with [Φ] '*s* and [σ] '*s*. (plurals of symbols)

Don't use so many *however*'s and *therefore*'s in your writing. (plurals of words)

Apostrophes can be used, though they are not needed, to form the plurals of abbreviations.

How many *CD*'s (or *CDs*) do you own? (plurals of abbreviation for *compact discs*)

When no danger of confusion exists, an *s* alone will suffice.

During the late *1960s*, many university students demanded changes in academic life.

Connected Discourse Exercise

Supply, delete, or relocate apostrophes as necessary in the following memorandum:

TO: The Records Office Staff
FROM: The Assistant Registrar
DATE: January 27, 20__ __
SUBJECT: Faulty Student Transcripts

Recently, we have had too many student complaints' about handwritten transcripts. Apparently its hard to tell the B's and D's apart. One staff members' handwriting is totally illegible. This staffs carelessness is unacceptable. Someone's even gone so far as to write grade change's in pencil, which allows students to make changes. This can't continue. In a short time, John and Mary's student assistants will be typing the past transcripts into our new computer system. Once grades are entered, the computers ability to generate grade reports will solve this problem. Until that time, lets make an effort to produce clear and professional-looking transcripts.

Supply apostrophes where necessary to correct the following sentences:

1. This years winter promises to be significantly more severe than last years.
2. Everyones office will be furnished with the newest ergonomic chairs and work spaces.
3. Were attempting to determine how our students needs can best be met.
4. When you are writing numbers quickly by hand, its important to keep your *7s* and *1s* very distinct.
5. Somebodys purse was left in Dean Smiths office.
6. Once everybodys research has been presented, well be better able to reach a decision.
7. Cindys computer program was much more efficient than her peers programs.
8. There are two *Rs* and two *Ss* in the word "embarrassment."
9. Lets determine what caused the schools mainframe computer to fail before we panic.
10. Every city has its own charms that are available for the informed visitors delight.

Commas

Since commas (,) occur more frequently than any other mark of punctuation, it's vital that you learn to use them correctly. When you do, your sentence structure is clearer, and your reader grasps your meaning without having to reread.

Handbook

Commas separate or set off independent clauses, items in a series, coordinate adjectives, introductory elements, places and dates, nonrestrictive expressions, and parenthetical expressions.

Independent Clauses   When you link two independent clauses with a coordinating conjunction (*and, but, or, nor, for, yet,* or *so*), put a comma in front of the conjunction.

Arthur is majoring in engineering, *but* he has decided to work for a clothing store following graduation.

The water looked inviting, *so* Darlene decided to go for a swim.

Don't confuse a sentence that has a compound predicate with a sentence that consists of two independent clauses.

Tom watered the garden and mowed the lawn. (single sentence with compound predicate)

Tom watered the garden, *and* Betty mowed the lawn. (sentence with two independent clauses)

Here's a simple test. Read what follows the comma. Unless that part can stand alone as a sentence, don't use a comma.

Items in a Series   A series consists of three or more words, phrases, or clauses following on one another's heels. Whenever you write a series, separate its items with commas.

Sarah, Paul, and *Mary* are earning A's in advanced algebra. (words in a series)

Nancy strode *across the parking lot, through the revolving door,* and *into the elevator.* (phrases in a series)

The stockholders' report said *that the company had enjoyed record profits during the last year, that it had expanded its work force by 20 percent,* and *that it would soon start marketing several new products.* (clauses in a series)

Coordinate Adjectives   Use commas to separate coordinate adjectives—those that modify the same noun or noun substitute and can be reversed without altering the meaning of the sentence.

Andrea proved to be an efficient, cooperative employee.

Andrea proved to be a cooperative, efficient employee.

When reversing the word order wrecks the meaning of the sentence, the adjectives are not coordinate and should be written without a comma.

Many new brands of videocassette recorders have come on the market lately.

Reversing the adjectives *many* and *new* would turn this sentence into nonsense. Therefore, no comma should be used.

Introductory Elements   Use commas to separate introductory elements—words, phrases, and clauses—from the rest of the sentence. When an introductory element is short and the sentence will not be misread, you can omit the comma.

comma

Correct	After bathing, Jack felt refreshed.
Correct	Soon I will be changing jobs.
Correct	Soon, I will be changing jobs.
Correct	When Sarah smiles her ears wiggle.
Correct	When Sarah smiles, her ears wiggle.

The first example needs a comma; otherwise, the reader might become temporarily confused.

After bathing Jack . . .

Always use commas after introductory elements of six or more words.

Correct	Whenever I hear the opening measure of Beethoven's *Fifth Symphony,* I get goose bumps.

Places and Dates   Places include mailing addresses and geographical locations. The following sentences show where commas are used:

Sherry Delaney lives at 651 Daniel Street, Memphis, Tennessee 38118.

I will go to Calais, France, next week.

Morristown, Oklahoma, is my birthplace.

Note that commas appear after the street designation and the names of cities, countries, and states, except when the name of the state is followed by a zip code.

Dates are punctuated as shown in the following example:

On Sunday, June 9, 1991, Elaine received a degree in environmental science.

Here, commas follow the day of the week, the day of the month, and the year.

With dates that include only the month and the year, commas are optional.

Correct	In July 1989 James played chess for the first time.
Correct	In July, 1989, James played chess for the first time.

Nonrestrictive Expressions   A nonrestrictive expression supplies added information about whatever it modifies. This information, however, is *nonessential* and does not affect the basic meaning of the sentence. The two sentences below include nonrestrictive expressions:

Senator Conwell, *the senior senator from this state,* faces a tough campaign for reelection.

My dog, *frightened by the thunder,* hid under my bed while the storm raged.

If we delete the phrase *the senior senator from this state* from the first sentence, we still know that Senator Conwell faces a tough reelection battle. Likewise, if we delete *frightened by the thunder* from the second sentence, we still know that the dog hid during the storm.

comma

Restrictive expressions, which are written *without commas*, distinguish whatever they modify from other persons, places, or things in the same category. Unlike nonrestrictive expressions, they are almost always *essential* sentence elements. Omitting a restrictive expression alters the meaning of the sentence, and the result is often nonsense.

Any person *caught stealing from this store* will be prosecuted.

Dropping the italicized part of this sentence leaves us with the absurd statement that any person, not just those caught stealing, faces prosecution.

Parenthetical Expressions   A parenthetical expression is a word or a word group that links one sentence to another or adds information or emphasis to the sentence in which it appears. Parenthetical expressions include the following:

Clarifying phrases

Names and titles of people being addressed directly

Abbreviations of degree titles

Echo questions

"Not" phrases

Adjectives that come after, rather than before, the words they modify

The examples that follow show the uses of commas:

All of Joe's spare time seems to center around reading. Kevin, *on the other hand*, enjoys a variety of activities. (phrase linking two sentences)

Myra Hobbes, *our representative in Seattle*, is being transferred to Spokane next month. (clarifying phrase)

I think, *Jill*, that you'd make a wonderful teacher. (name of person addressed directly)

Tell me, *Captain*, when the cruise ship is scheduled to sail. (title of person addressed directly)

Harley Kendall, *Ph.D.*, will be this year's commencement speaker. (degree title following name)

Alvin realizes, *doesn't he*, that he stands almost no chance of being accepted at West Point? (echo question)

Mathematics, *not home economics*, was Tammy's favorite high school subject. ("not" phrase)

The road, *muddy and rutted*, proved impassable. (adjectives following word they modify)

Punctuating Conjunctive Adverbs   Writers often mistakenly punctuate conjunctive adverbs with commas and create, as a result, a comma splice.

Floridians do not have the heating bills of their Northern neighbors, however, they do have extensive air-conditioning bills.

comma

Conjunctive adverbs actually do not join sentences and can actually be moved, revealing the underlying comma splice.

Floridians do not have the heating bills of their Northern neighbors, they do, however, have extensive air-conditioning bills.

To fix such comma splices, join the sentences with a semicolon or punctuate with a period and start a new sentence.

Floridians do not have the heating bills of their Northern neighbors; however, they do have extensive air-conditioning bills.

Floridians do not have the heating bills of their Northern neighbors. However, they do have extensive air-conditioning bills.

Connected Discourse Exercise

Add or delete commas as necessary in the following letter:

Dear Loy Norrix Knight:

While we know you will be busy this summer we hope you will take time to join us for the twenty-five-year reunion of the graduating class of 1987. The reunion will include a cocktail hour a buffet dinner and a dance. For your entertainment we are going to bring in a professional band and a band starring some of your good, old high school chums. John Mcleary who is now a well-known professional nightclub performer will serve as the emcee. Do you remember him hosting our senior-year assemblies?

Yes many of your former, hardworking teachers will be at the reunion. You can thank them for the difference they made in your life or you can tell them what you've thought of them all these years. This reunion will also be your opportunity to catch up on the lives of your former friends find out what that old flame now looks like and brag a little about your own successes. And if you are really lucky you might even be able to sneak a dance with your high school prom partner.

We hope you will make plans, to join us here at the Kalamazoo Hilton on July 28, 2002, at 7 P.M. Wear your best 1980s-style clothes. Remember revisiting the past can be fun.

Sincerely,

The Reunion Committee

Supply commas as necessary to correct the following sentences:

1. Let us know Ms. Granger when you would like to enjoy your free stay at Rolling Hills Resort.

2. The landscapers killed the existing grass rototilled the ground added new topsoil and sprayed the prepared ground with hydroseed.

3. If you are interested in making a tax-deductible donation to the Stratford Festival please write Carla Darma treasurer at 165 University Avenue Suite 700 Toronto Ontario Canada M5H 3B8.

4. The day was unusually beautiful so Mr. Collins decided to hold his class on the Romantic poets outside.

5. Standing in the long winding line for hours on a hot muggy New York summer day Tom was able to get discount tickets to one of the most popular musicals.

6. Mr. Carlin was hired by our New York office on March 25 1997 and was supposed to report to work in our Nome Alaska office three months after his hiring date.

7. Before eating raccoons carefully wash their paws.

8. Despite the many kinds of electronic entertainment available today many people continue to prefer to read a good book.

9. Your fireplace which is cracked in several places will need to be repaired before you can use it.

10. When it is performed well *Waiting for Godot* considered by many to be a masterpiece of existential theater is actually quite humorous.

Semicolons

The main use of the semicolon (;) is to separate independent clauses, which may or may not be connected with a conjunctive adverb. Other uses include separating

two or more series of items

items containing commas in a single series

independent clauses that contain commas and are connected with a coordinating conjunction.

Independent Clauses   The examples that follow show the use of semicolons to separate independent clauses.

The fabric in this dress is terrible; its designer must have been asleep at the swatch. (no conjunctive adverb)

Steve refused to write a term paper; *therefore*, he failed the course. (conjunctive adverb *therefore* joining independent clauses)

Conjunctive adverbs can occur within, rather than between, independent clauses. When they do, set them off with commas.

Marsha felt very confident. Jane, *on the other hand*, was nervous and uncertain. (conjunctive adverb within independent clause)

To determine whether a pair of commas or a semicolon and comma are required, read what comes before and after the conjunctive adverb. Unless both sets of words can stand alone as sentences, use commas.

Two or More Series of Items   With sentences that have two or more series of items, writers often separate the series with semicolons in order to lessen the chances of misreading.

> My duties as secretary include typing letters, memos, and purchase orders; sorting, opening, and delivering mail; and making plane and hotel reservations for traveling executives.

The semicolons provide greater clarity than commas would.

Comma-Containing Items within a Series   When commas accompany one or more of the items in a series, it's often better to separate the items with semicolons instead of commas.

> The meal included veal, which was cooked to perfection; asparagus, my favorite vegetable; and brown rice, prepared with a touch of curry.

Once again, semicolons provide greater clarity than additional commas.

Independent Clauses With Commas and a Coordinating Conjunction
Ordinarily, a comma is used to separate independent clauses joined by a coordinating conjunction. When one or more of the clauses have commas, however, a semicolon provides clearer separation.

> The long black limousine pulled up to the curb; and Jerry, shaking with excitement, watched the President alight from it.

The semicolon makes it easier to see the two main clauses.

Connected Discourse Exercise

Add and delete semicolons as appropriate in the following letter. You may have to substitute semicolons for commas.

Dear Student:

Our college, as you are well aware, has been going through a number of changes, and these developments, both in the registration system and the curriculum, will continue next year. In the end these improvements will only benefit you; but we know that many of you have been anxious about the exact nature of the changes. To answer your questions, we have arranged an open forum with Linda Peters, president of the college, Drake Stevens, the registrar, and Jerry Mash, vice-president of academic affairs. The meeting will be held in Johnston Hall; 2 P.M.; March 23. Please come with your questions, this is your opportunity to put your fears to rest.

Sincerely,

John X. Pelle

Dean of Students

Supply semicolons wherever they are necessary or desirable in the following sentences. You may have to substitute semicolons for commas. If a sentence is correct, write C.

1. When he visits the main office, Mr. Harmon would like to meet with the vice president of marketing, Carol Chaffe, the personnel director, Carl Hart, and the vice president of finance, Mary Angelo.

2. Donald Nathanson, a clinical psychologist, has written an insightful book on shame, and other psychologists, who at first were very critical of his work, have begun to use his ideas in their practice.

3. E-mail is a crucial part of most businesses; in fact, some companies have replaced all memos with electronic communication.

4. This year a number of new musicals have opened on Broadway, it promises to be an exciting theater season.

5. The reading for the course was eclectic, including *The Invisible Man*, a science fiction novel, *Shane*, a western, and *Antigone*, a classic Greek play.

6. Computers can crash at any time, therefore, it is important to back up your data frequently.

7. Sales have decreased significantly this past year, we are likely to see an equivalent drop in our profits.

8. The landscaper planted carpet juniper, canby pachistima, and English ivy for ground cover, rhododendron, pyracantha, and pieris for shrubs, and a blue spruce, a Japanese black pine, and a maple for trees.

9. Chess, a game played by millions, can sharpen your mind, and now there are computer programs, most very inexpensive, that can help you learn the game.

10. We will offer sales training this summer in Lansing, Michigan, Ames, Iowa, and Minneapolis, Minnesota.

Periods, Question Marks, and Exclamation Points

Since periods, question marks, and exclamation points signal the ends of sentences, they are sometimes called *end marks*. In addition, periods and question marks function in several other ways.

Periods   Periods (.) end sentences that state facts or opinions, give instructions, make requests that are not in the form of questions, and ask indirect questions—those that have been rephrased in the form of a statement.

Linda works as a hotel manager. (Sentence states fact.)

Dean Harris is a competent administrator. (Sentence states opinion.)

Clean off your lab bench before you leave. (Sentence gives instruction.)

Please move away from the door. (Sentence makes request.)

I wonder whether Ruthie will be at the theater tonight. (Sentence asks indirect question.)

Periods also follow common abbreviations as well as a person's initials.

Mr.	Sr.	P.M.
Mrs.	B.C.	lb.
Jr.	A.D.	St.
Dr.	A.M.	Corp.

Mark J. Valentini, Ph.D., has consented to head the new commission on traffic safety.

Writers today often omit periods after abbreviations for the names of organizations or government agencies, as the following examples show:

ABC	FBI	IRS
ACLU	FHA	NAM
AFL-CIO	GM	USAF

An up-to-date college dictionary will indicate whether a certain abbreviation should be written without periods.

Periods also precede decimal fractions and separate numerals standing for dollars and cents.

0.81 percent	$5.29
3.79 percent	$0.88

Question Marks   A question mark (?) ends a whole or a partial sentence that asks a direct question (one that repeats the exact words of the person who asked it).

Do you know how to operate this movie projector? (whole sentence asking a direct question)

Has Cinderella scrubbed the floor? Swept the hearth? Washed the dishes? (sentence and sentence parts asking direct questions)

Dr. Baker—wasn't she your boss once?—has just received a promotion to sales manager. (interrupting element asking a direct question)

The minister inquired, "Do you take this woman to be your lawful wedded wife?" (quotation asking a direct question)

A question mark may be used to indicate uncertainty.

Jane Seymour (1509?–1537), third wife of Henry VIII, was a lady in waiting to his first two wives.

Exclamation Points   Exclamation points (!) are used to express strong emotion or especially forceful commands.

Darcy! I never expected to see you again!
Sam! Turn that radio down immediately!
Help! Save me!

Use exclamation points sparingly; otherwise, they will quickly lose their force.

.?!

Connected Discourse Exercise

Add, change, or remove end marks as necessary. You may want to do some slight rewording.

It was horrifying, the mob of screaming fans grabbed Jack Slitherhips as he left the concert hall. Soon all I could see were his arms reaching for help. But it never came. Why do fans act this way. I am left wondering whether they love or hate their idols? They tore the clothes off Slitherhips, they tore out patches of his hair, someone even snatched his false teeth. Is this any way to treat a fading rock star. Jack is now in the hospital in a complete body cast; when I finally got to see him, he mumbled that he was giving up show business, he plans to settle down on a small farm. Who can blame him?

Supply periods, question marks, or exclamation points wherever they are necessary. You may have to change existing punctuation marks. If a sentence is correct, write C.

1. Be sure to proofread your paper before you submit it for a grade.
2. Sigmund Freud—isn't he now generally dismissed by many psychologists—really established the concept of the unconscious.
3. The sales tax in our state was raised to 65 percent.
4. Great we will have to buy another candle.
5. Carla used to study until 2 A.M. every night.
6. When you shopped for a new computer, did you consider what programs you wanted to run, set a budget for yourself, check the reliability of the different brands.
7. The engineer wanted to know how much stress would be placed on the beams.
8. Has Dr Stevens read the research on the most recent anti-clotting medication.
9. Run for your life, the tiger has escaped from the zoo.
10. Be sure to check your e-mail as soon as you start work.

Colons, Dashes, Parentheses, and Brackets

Colons, dashes, parentheses, and brackets separate and enclose, thereby clarifying relationships among the various parts of a sentence.

Colon Colons (:) introduce explanations and anticipated lists following words that could stand alone as a complete sentence.

His aim in life is grandiose: to corner the market in wheat. (explanation)

Three students have been selected to attend the conference: Lucille Perkins, Dan Blakely, and Frank Napolis. (list)

Three factors can cause financial problems for farmers: (1) high interest rates, (2) falling land values, and (3) a strong dollar, which makes it difficult to sell crops abroad. (numbered list)

The first of the following sentences is incorrect because the words preceding the colon can't stand alone as a sentence:

Faulty   The tools needed for this job include: a hacksaw, a file, and a drill.

Revision   The tools needed for this job include a hacksaw, a file, and a drill.

Colons also frequently introduce formal quotations that extend beyond a single sentence.

The speaker stepped to the lectern and said: "I am here to ask for your assistance. Today several African nations face a food crisis because drought has ruined their harvests. Unless we provide help quickly, thousands of people will die of starvation."

In such situations, the material preceding the quotation need not be a complete sentence.

Colons also separate hours from minutes (8:20 A.M.), salutations of business letters from the body of the letters (Dear Ms. Stanley:), titles of publications from subtitles (*The Careful Writer: A Guide to English Usage*), numbers indicating ratios (a 3:2:2 ratio), and chapter from verse in biblical references (Luke 6:20–49).

Dashes   Like colons, dashes (—) set off appositives, lists, and explanations but are used in less formal writing. A dash emphasizes the material it sets off.

Only one candidate showed up at the political rally—Jerry Manders. (appositive)

The closet held only three garments—an out-at-the-elbows sports coat, a pair of blue jeans, and a tattered shirt. (list)

I know what little Billy's problem is—a soiled diaper. (explanation)

Dashes set off material that interrupts the flow of thought within a sentence.

Her new car—didn't she get it just three months ago?—has broken down twice.

Similarly, dashes are used to mark an interrupted segment of dialogue.

"I'd like to live in England when I retire."

"In England? But what will your wife—?"

"My wife likes the idea and can hardly wait for us to make the move."

Dashes set off parenthetical elements containing commas, and a dash can set off comments that follow a list.

The comedian—short, fat, and squeaky-voiced—soon had everyone roaring with laughter. (parenthetical element with commas)

A brag, a blow, a tank of air—that's what Senator Conwell is. (comment following a list)

Type a dash as two unspaced hyphens and leave no space between it and the words on either side of it.

Parentheses   Parentheses () are used to enclose numbers or letters that designate the items in a formal list and to set off incidental material within sentences. Except in the kind of list shown in the first example below, a comma does not usually precede a parenthesis.

Each paper should contain (1) an introduction, (2) several paragraphs developing the thesis statement, and (3) a conclusion.

Some occupations (computer programming, for example) may be overcrowded in ten years.

If the material in parentheses appears within a sentence, don't use a capital letter or period, even if the material is itself a complete sentence.

The growth of genetic engineering (one cannot foresee its consequences) worries some people today.

If the material in parentheses is written as a separate sentence, however, then punctuate it as you would a separate sentence.

Paula's angry outburst surprised everyone. (She had seemed such a placid person.)

If the material in parentheses comes at the end of a sentence, put the final punctuation after the closing parenthesis.

This company was founded by Willard Manley (1876–1951).

In contrast to dashes, parentheses de-emphasize the material they enclose.

Brackets   In quoted material, brackets [] enclose words or phrases that have been added to make the message clearer. They are also used with the word *sic* (Latin for "thus") to point out errors in quoted material.

"This particular company [Zorn Enterprises, Inc.] pioneered in the safe disposal of toxic wastes," the report noted. (The bracketed name is added to the original.)

"[John Chafin's] expertise in science has made him a popular figure on the lecture circuit," his friend stated. (The bracketed name replaces *his* in the original.)

"The principle [sic] cause of lung cancer is cigarette smoking," the article declared. (the word *principal* is misspelled "principle" in the original.)

To call attention to an error, follow it immediately with the bracketed *sic*. The reader will then know that the blame rests with the original writer, not with you.

: – () []

Connected Discourse Exercise

Supply any necessary or appropriate colons, dashes, parentheses, and brackets in the following letter:

Wayout Auto Company

We at Oldfield Sales a subsidiary of Jip, Inc., have had a serious problem with the cars we ordered from your company for leasing to our customers who will probably never return to us again. Two major parts fell off while the cars were sitting in the customers' driveways the exhaust system and the transmission. If this had happened while they were driving thank goodness it didn't, our customers could have been killed. Just imagine what that especially once it got into the newspapers would have done to our business. We must hold you to your claim that "while our cars are the cheepest sic on the market, we garuntee sic every car we sell." We expect immediate reimbursement for all the cars we purchased from you plus one million dollars to cover the damage to our reputation. A menace, a rip-off, a bad business deal, that's what your cars are. If you don't issue a formal recall for all your vehicles by 5:30 P.M., Friday, July 23, we will be forced to forward this matter to the federal government.

Sincerely,

Ken Swindelle

Service Manager

Supply colons, dashes, parentheses, and brackets wherever they are necessary.

1. Many former Presidents Millard Fillmore, for example have been largely forgotten by most Americans.
2. Our international sales have outperformed domestic sales by an 83 ratio.
3. The newspaper headline read, "Piece sic deal broken."
4. Among our social ills, one condition seems to be the source of many other problems poverty.
5. The new library better considered an information center will have over fifty computers with full Internet capability.
6. Our city area offers many advantages to businesses a skilled workforce, a well-developed infrastructure, and low taxes.
7. His Friedrich Nietzsche's *Thus Spoke Zarathustra* should be very familiar to anyone interested in the history of ideas.
8. In early June every elementary school student's thoughts turn to one thing summer vacation.
9. Mozart, Miles Davis, The Talking Heads his tastes certainly are eclectic.
10. The activities at the Pine Tree Resort include horseback riding, kayaking, swimming, water skiing, and much more.

Quotation Marks

Quotation marks (" ") set off direct quotations, titles of short written or broadcast works, subdivisions of books, and expressions singled out for special attention.

Direct Quotations   A direct quotation repeats a speaker's or writer's exact words.

> "Tell me about the movie," said Debbie. "If you liked it, I may go myself."

> The placement director said, "The recruiter for Procter and Gamble will be on campus next Thursday to interview students for marketing jobs." (spoken comment)

> "The U.S. trade deficit is expected to reach record levels this year," the *Wall Street Journal* noted. (written comment)

> Jackie said the party was "a total flop."

As these sentences show, a comma or period that follows a direct quotation goes inside the quotation marks. When a quotation is a sentence fragment, the comma preceding it is omitted.

When an expression like "he said" interrupts a quoted sentence, use commas to set off the expression. When the expression comes between two complete quoted sentences, use a period after the expression and capitalize the first word of the second sentence.

> "Hop in," said Jim. "Let me give you a ride to school."

> "Thank you," replied Kelly, opening the car door and sliding into the front seat.

> "I can't remember," said Jim, "when we've had a worse winter."

Titles of Short Works and Subdivisions of Books   These short works include magazine articles, essays, short stories, chapters of books, one-act plays, short poems, songs, and television and radio episodes.

> The article was titled "The Real Conservatism." (article)

> Last night I read John Cheever's "The Enormous Radio," "Torch Song," and "The Swimmer." (short stories)

> Many John Denver fans consider "Take Me Home, Country Roads" to be his greatest piece of music. (song)

> The unsuccessful TV show *Pursued* ended its brief run with a segment titled "Checkmate." (TV episode)

Here, as with direct quotations, a comma or period that follows a title goes inside the quotation marks.

Expressions Singled Out for Special Attention   Writers who wish to call the reader's attention to a word or symbol sometimes put it within quotation marks.

The algebraic formula included a "π," a "Θ," and a "Δ."

"Bonnets" and "lifts" are British terms for car hoods and elevators.

More frequently, however, these expressions are printed in italics.

Again, any commas and periods that follow expressions set off by quotation marks go inside the marks.

Quotation Marks Within   Quotation Marks When a direct quotation or the title of a shorter work appears within a direct quotation, use single quotation marks (' ').

"I heard the boss telling the foreman, 'Everyone will receive a Christmas bonus,'" John said.

The instructor told the class, "For tomorrow, read Ernest Hemingway's 'The Killers.'"

Note that the period goes inside of both the single and double quotation marks.

Positioning of Semicolons, Colons, and Question Marks   Position semicolons and colons that come at the end of quoted material after, not before, the quotation marks.

Marcia calls Francine "that greasy grind"; however, I think Marcia is simply jealous of Francine's abilities.

There are two reasons why I like "Babylon Revisited": the characters are interesting and the writing is excellent.

When a question mark accompanies a quotation, put it outside the quotation marks if the whole sentence rather than the quotation asks the question.

Why did Cedric suddenly shout, "This party is a big bore"?

Put the question mark inside the quotation marks if the quotation, but not the whole sentence, asks a question or if the quotation asks one question and the whole sentence asks another.

Marie asked, "What college is your brother planning to attend?" (The quoted material, not the whole sentence, asks the question.)

Whatever possessed him to ask, "What is the most shameful thing you ever did?" (The whole sentence and the quoted material ask separate questions.)

Connected Discourse Exercise

Use quotation marks correctly in the following paragraph:

Mr. Silver recently lectured our class on Stephen Crane's The Bride Comes to Yellow Sky. One thing we shouldn't forget, Mr. Silver insisted, is that the town is deliberately named Yellow Sky. What is the significance of

Crane's choice of the words Yellow Sky? Mr. Silver pointed out a number of possible associations, including cowardice, the setting sun, the open expanse of the West, freedom, the sand in the concluding passage. The story, Mr. Silver stated, is drenched in color words. For example, he pointed out, in the first three paragraphs alone Crane mentions vast flats of green grass, brick-colored hands, new black clothes, and a dress of blue cashmere.

Supply properly positioned quotation marks wherever they are necessary.

1. Some linguists think that the quintessential American ok may have come from the African waka.
2. My favorite piece of jazz music is St. James Infirmary.
3. What did Yeats mean by the line in his famous poem The Second Coming, Things fall apart, the center cannot hold?
4. Carl Thomas described the performance as extremely intense.
5. I managed to read Faulkner's short story The Bear, Jennifer sighed, but I don't really know what I want to say about it in my paper for English.
6. Why do so many student writers consistently confuse effect with affect?
7. In response to the Great Depression, Franklin Roosevelt declared The only thing we have to fear is fear itself; however, many families who had lost their homes and couldn't even earn enough for food really did have something to fear.
8. Yiddish words like mishugana and kibitz have come to be used outside the Jewish community.
9. In his closing argument, the defense attorney asked the jury, How would any one of us act if accused of a crime we knew we didn't commit?
10. Henry Ford supposedly called history bunk.

Hyphens

Hyphens (-) are used to join compound adjectives and nouns, compound numbers and word-number combinations, and certain prefixes and suffixes to the words with which they appear. In addition, hyphens help prevent misreadings and awkward combinations of letters or syllables and are used to split words between two lines.

Compound Adjectives   Hyphens are often used to join separate words that function as single adjectives and come before nouns. Typical examples follow:

Howard is a very *self-contained* person.

The *greenish-yellow* cloud of chlorine gas drifted toward the village.

Betty's *devil-may-care* attitude will land her in trouble someday.

When the first word of the compound is an adverb ending in *-ly* or when the compound adjective follows the noun it modifies, no hyphen is used.

The *badly* burned crash victim was rushed to the hospital.

The color of the chlorine gas was *greenish yellow.*

When two or more compound adjectives modify the same last term, the sentence will flow more smoothly if that term appears just once, after the last item in the series. The hyphens accompanying the earlier terms in the series are kept, however.

Many seventeenth-, eighteenth-, and nineteenth-century costumes are on display in this museum.

Compound Nouns   Hyphenated nouns include such expressions as the following:

secretary-treasurer	good-for-nothing
sister-in-law	man-about-town

Here is a sentence with hyphenated nouns:

Denton is *editor-in-chief* of the largest newspaper in this state.

Compound Numbers and Word–Number Combinations   Hyphens are used to separate two-word numbers from twenty-one to ninety-nine and fractions that have been written out.

Marcy has worked *twenty-one* years for this company.

One-fourth of my income goes for rent.

Similarly, hyphens are used to separate numerals from units of measurement that follow them.

This chemical is shipped in *50-gallon* drums.

Prefixes and Suffixes   A prefix is a word or set of letters that precedes a word and alters its meaning. A suffix is similar but comes at the end of the word. Although most prefixes are not hyphenated, the prefixes *self-* and *all-* do get hyphens, as does the suffix *-elect.* Also the prefix *ex-* is hyphenated when it accompanies a noun.

This stove has a *self-cleaning* oven.

Let Claire Voyant, the *all-knowing* soothsayer, read your future in her crystal ball.

Ethel is the *chairperson-elect* of the club.

Several *ex-teachers* work in this department.

A prefix used before a capitalized term is always hyphenated.

The *ex-FBI* agent gave an interesting talk on the operations of that agency.

Preventing Misreadings and Awkward Combinations of Letters and Syllables

Hyphens help prevent misreadings of certain words and also break up awkward combinations of letters and syllables between certain prefixes and suffixes and their core words.

The doctor *re-treated* the wound with a new antibiotic. (The hyphen prevents the misreading *retreated.*)

The company plans to *de-emphasize* sales of agricultural chemicals. (The hyphen prevents the awkward repetition of the letter *e* in *deemphasize.*)

Between Syllables

Whenever you have to split a word between two lines, place a hyphen at the end of the first line to show the division. The word is always broken, and the hyphen inserted, between syllables. (Any good dictionary shows the syllable divisions of each word it includes.) Never divide a one-syllable word or leave two letters to be placed on the second line, even if those two letters constitute a syllable.

EXERCISE

Supply hyphens wherever they are necessary. If the sentence is correct, write C.

1. The piece of music ended with bird like sounds made by the entire woodwind section.
2. In this brokerage firm we follow sound investment strategies rather than chase after will o' the wisp schemes.
3. It can be sobering for the president elect to learn the full requirements of the job.
4. The union negotiators were forced to retreat from their initial demands.
5. One fifth of the shipment of fresh tomatoes turned out to be spoiled.
6. The classical radio station can be received by anyone within a 100 mile radius of its broadcasting tower.
7. In this class, we will study nineteenth and twentieth century American authors.
8. Emerson thought that it was important for people to be self reliant.
9. Once the power came back on, I had to recreate the file.
10. The Gundersons have been married for thirty five years.

cap

Capitalization

Capitalize the first word in any sentence, the pronoun *I*, proper nouns and adjectives, titles used with names, and the significant words in literary and artistic titles.

Proper Nouns

A proper noun names one particular person, group of persons, place, or thing. Such nouns include the following:

Persons

Organizations

Racial, political, and religious groups

Countries, states, cities, and streets
Companies and buildings
Geographical locations and features
Days, months, and holidays
Trademarks
Languages
Ships and aircraft
Abbreviations for academic degrees
Sacred writings and pronouns standing for God and Jesus
Titles used in place of names

The sentences below show the capitalization of proper nouns:

Sigmund works for the *National Psychoanalytical Institute,* an organization that has done much to advance the science of psychiatry.

How much does this roll of *Saran Wrap* cost?

Gwen Greene moved to *Paris, France,* when her father became the consul there.

On *Friday, December* 10, 1993, *Michael Jordan* visited our city.

Larry has a master of arts degree, and his sister has a *Ph.D.*

My father works for the *Ford Motor Company,* but I work for *Daimler Chrysler.*

Do not capitalize words like *institute, college, company,* or *avenue* unless they form part of a proper name. Likewise, do not capitalize the names of courses unless they start a sentence, are accompanied by a course number, or designate a language.

I have a 95 average in *Economics* 112 but only a 73 average in sociology.

Harry plans to take intermediate *German* in his junior year.

Do you plan to attend *Drew College* or some other college?

Proper Adjectives Adjectives created from proper nouns are called proper adjectives. Like the nouns themselves, they should be capitalized.

Lolita Martinez, our class valedictorian, is of *Mexican* ancestry. (*Mexican* is derived from the proper noun *Mexico.*)

Abbreviations As a general rule, capitalize abbreviations only if the words they stand for are capitalized.

Milton DeWitt works for the *IRS.* (*IRS* is capitalized because *Internal Revenue Service* would be.)

The flask holds 1,500 *ml* of liquid. (The abbreviation *ml* is not capitalized because *milliliters* would not be.)

cap

A few abbreviations are capitalized even though all or some of the words they stand for aren't. Examples include TV (television) and VCR (videocassette recorder).

Personal Titles   Capitalize a personal title if it precedes a name or is used in place of a name. Otherwise, do not capitalize.

> The division is under the command of *General* Arnold Schafer.

> Tell me, *Doctor*, do I need an operation?

> The *dean* of our engineering division is Dr. Alma Haskins.

> Many writers capitalize titles of high rank when they are used in place of names.

> The *President* will sign this bill tomorrow.

> The *president* will sign this bill tomorrow.

Either usage is acceptable.

Titles of Literary and Artistic Works   When citing the titles of publications, pieces of writing, movies, television programs, paintings, sculptures, and the like, capitalize the first and last words and all other words except *a, an, the*, coordinating conjunctions, and one-syllable prepositions.

> Last week I played *Gone with the Wind* on my VCR and read Christopher Isherwood's *Goodbye to Berlin*. (the preposition *with*, the article *the*, and the preposition *to* are not capitalized.)

> John is reading a book called *The Movies of Abbott and Costello*. (The preposition *of* and the coordinating conjunction *and* are not capitalized. *The* is capitalized because it is the first word of the title.)

> Although I'm no TV addict, I used to watch every episode of *Murder, She Wrote*. (All of the words in the title are capitalized.)

Note that the titles of literary and artistic works are italicized.

Identify any word or abbreviation that should be capitalized in the following sentences:

1. Every friday at 1:00 P.M. the computer support team meets to review the problems that occurred during the previous week.
2. Any student of mexican history will soon see how radically different that history has been from american history.
3. Though many consider it a liberal organization, the aclu has actually protected the right to free speech of many extremely conservative groups.
4. Many students in the rotc choose to take history 321: american military history to satisfy their humanities requirement.
5. A student has a right to be proud upon earning an a.a.s. or a b.s. degree.

6. All requests for sabbatical leave must be submitted to dean Styron by october 1.
7. Though many consider latin a dead language, others continue to study it since so many great classical works were written in that language.
8. Your request for a leave of absence cannot be approved by professor Murphy.
9. Students of roman literature should be familiar with ovid's *metamorphoses*.
10. During World War II, dr. Johnson served on the u.s. submarine eel.

Abbreviations

Items that are abbreviated include certain personal titles, names of organizations and agencies, Latin terms, and specific and technical terms.

Personal Titles   Abbreviate *Mister, Doctor,* and similar titles when they come just ahead of a name, and *Junior, Senior,* and degree titles when they follow names.

> Will *Mr.* Harry Babbitt please come to the front desk?

> Arthur Compton, *Sr.*, is a well-known historian; his son, Arthur Compton, *Jr.*, is a television producer.

> This article on marital discord was written by Irma Quarles, *Ph.D.*

Names of Organizations and Agencies   Many organizations and agencies are known primarily by their initials rather than their full names. Several examples follow:

AAA	FBI	NBC
CARE	FHA	NATO
CIA	IBM	UNESCO

Latin Terms   Certain Latin terms are always abbreviated; others are abbreviated when used with dates or times.

> e.g. (*exempli gratia:* for example)

> i.e. (*id est:* that is)

> etc. (*et cetera:* and [the] others)

> vs. or v. (*versus:* against)

> A.D. (*anno Domini:* in the year of our Lord)

> A.M. or a.m. (*ante meridiem:* before noon)

> P.M. or p.m. (*post meridiem:* after noon)

> The play starts at 8 P.M.

> Many writers (*e.g.*, Dylan Thomas and Truman Capote) have had serious problems with alcohol.

For consistency with A.D., the term "before Christ" is abbreviated as B.C.

ab

Scientific and Technical Terms   For brevity's sake, scientists and technicians abbreviate terms of measurement that repeatedly occur. Terms that the reader would not know are written out the first time they are used, and they are accompanied by their abbreviation in parentheses. Unfamiliar organizations and agencies that are mentioned repeatedly are handled in like manner.

The viscosity of the fluid measured 15 centistokes (cs) at room temperature. Common practice calls for writing such abbreviations without periods unless they duplicate the spelling of some word.

Standard dictionaries list common abbreviations. When you don't recognize one, look it up. Use abbreviations sparingly in essays. If you're unsure about what is appropriate, don't abbreviate.

Supply abbreviations wherever they are necessary or are customarily used.

1. Despite extensive competition, International Business Machines continues to be a major player in the computer industry.
2. We are pleased that Mister Jones has decided to join our firm.
3. Dissolve 1 gram of NaCl in 20 milliliters of water.
4. The freezing point of water at sea level is 32° Fahrenheit (0° Celsius).
5. Since its start, the National Broadcasting Company has been strongly committed to its news programming.
6. Doctor Baxter has been doing extensive research on nanotechnology, supported by a National Science Foundation grant.
7. Carl Thorton, Junior, will offer a workshop on how to save for retirement.
8. Many composers who are now seen as giants of classical music (*exempli gratia*, Mozart and Beethoven) died paupers.
9. After Friday's performance of Shakespeare's *Midsummer Night's Dream*, Carol Brice, Doctor of Philosophy, will discuss the use of nature imagery in the play.
10. Crimes that cross state boundaries are often investigated by the Federal Bureau of Investigation.

Numbers

Some instructors ask their students to use figures for numbers larger than ninety-nine and to spell out smaller numbers.

Boise is *100* miles from here.

Boise is *ninety-nine* miles from here.

Other instructors prefer that students switch to figures beginning with the number ten.

My son will be *nine* years old on his next birthday.

My son will be *10* years old on his next birthday.

With either practice, the following exceptions apply.

Numbers in a Series   Write all numbers in a series the same way regardless of their size.

Gatsby has *64* suits, *110* shirts, and *214* ties.

In just one hour the emergency room personnel handled *two* stabbings, *five* shootings, and *sixteen* fractures.

We have *150* salespeople, *51* engineers, and *7* laboratory technicians.

Dates   Use figures for dates that include the year.

February *14, 1985* or 14 February 1935 (not February 14th, 1985)

When the date includes the day but not the year, you may use figures or spell out the number.

June 9

June ninth

the ninth of June

Page Numbers and Addresses   Use figures for page numbers and street numbers in addresses.

Check the graph.

I live at *111* Cornelia Street, and my office is at *620* Fifth Avenue.

Numbers Beginning Sentences   Spell out any number that begins a sentence. If this requires three or more words, rephrase the sentence so that the number comes after the opening and numerals can be used.

The year *1989* was a good year for this wine.

Sixty thousand fans jammed the stadium.

An army of *265,000* troops assaulted the city. (If this number began the sentence, five words—an excessive number—would be needed to write it out.)

Decimals, Percentages, Times   Use figures for decimals and percentages as well as for expressions of time that are accompanied by A.M. or P.M.

The shaft has a *0.37*-inch diameter.

Last year the value of my house jumped *25* percent.

The plane leaves here at *9:50* A.M. and reaches New Orleans at *2:30* P.M.

One Number Following Another   When a number-containing term that denotes a unit of weight or measurement comes immediately after another number, spell out the first number, if smaller than 100, and use numerals for the second one. If the first number is larger than 100, use numerals for it and spell out the second one.

We ordered *six 30*-gallon drums of solvent for the project.

The supplier shipped us *600 thirty*-gallon drums by mistake.

Identify any miswriting of numbers in the following sentences and rewrite these numbers correctly:

1. The supermarket ordered five hundred five-pound bags of sugar.
2. The Whitney Museum of American Art is at Nine Hundred and Forty-Five Madison Avenue, New York City.
3. The holes that the automated system drilled in the brackets were off by two hundredths of an inch.
4. The first memo warning the company of the problem was dated May fifteenth, 1993.
5. There will be a meeting at three-thirty P.M., May fifth, to discuss our new marketing plan.
6. Our local library has 658 CDs, 132 videocassettes, and sixty-three computer programs.
7. 8,000 people usually subscribe to our symphony orchestra series.
8. There are a number of serious editing errors on page thirty-nine of the report.
9. Over the last year, sales have increased by twenty-three percent.
10. We found that only 3 computers needed to be upgraded.

Italics

Italics are used for the titles of longer publications, the names of vehicles and vessels, foreign words and phrases, and expressions singled out for special attention. Use underlining to represent italics when hand writing or typing papers.

Titles of Longer Publications and Artistic Works These items may include the following:

books	record albums	long musical works and poems
magazines	paintings	plays
newspapers	movies	sculptures

Quotation marks are used for the titles of articles, short stories, short poems, one-act plays, and other brief pieces of writing.

Last night I finished F. Scott Fitzgerald's *The Great Gatsby* and read two articles in *The New Yorker.* (book, magazine)

Michelangelo's *David* is surely one of the world's greatest sculptures. (sculpture)

The *Detroit Free Press* had praise for the revival of Tennessee Williams's play *The Glass Menagerie.* (newspaper, play)

Stephen Vincent Benét's poem *John Brown's Body* won a Pulitzer Prize in 1929. (book-length poem)

Do not use italics when naming the Bible and its parts or other religious works such as the Torah and Koran.

Joanna's favorite book of the Bible is the Book of Ecclesiastes, part of the Old Testament.

Names of Vehicles and Vessels   Names of particular airplanes, ships, trains, and spacecraft are italicized.

The plane in which Charles Lindbergh flew over the Atlantic Ocean was named *The Spirit of St. Louis.*

Foreign Expressions   Use italics to identify foreign words and phrases that have not yet made their way into the English language.

The writer has a terribly pessimistic *weltanschauung.* (philosophy of life)

This season, long skirts are the *dernier cri.* (the latest thing)

When such expressions become completely assimilated, the italics are dropped. Most dictionaries use an asterisk (*), a dagger (†), or other symbol to identify expressions that need italicizing.

Expressions Singled Out for Special Attention   These include words, letters, numerals, and symbols.

The Greek letter *pi* is written π.

I can't tell whether this letter is meant to be an *a* or an *o* or this number a *7* or a *9*.

In England, the word *lorry* means truck.

Quotation marks sometimes replace italics for this purpose.

Connected Discourse Exercise

Use hyphens, capitalization, abbreviations, numbers, and italics properly in the following passage:

Because I can speak Russian fluently, I was recruited by the central intelligence while still at Boston college. I suspected that it was professor Hogsbottom, a Political Science teacher, who had suggested that they consider me. After all, he had been a General during World War II and still had connections with the intelligence community. It turned out that my brother in law was responsible; he was an ex FBI agent. Soon I was an american spy

ital

located, of all places, in England. Who would suspect that we had to spy on the english? For 3 years I posed as a british aristocrat who was a general bon vivant and man about town. I went by the alias of Mister Henry Higgins, Junior. Everyone, of course, wanted to know if I had seen My Fair Lady. Personally I thought the whole thing was a monty python type of joke until I found a position in the british secret service. Who could have believed the british kept so many secrets from their american allies? For twenty one years I spied on the british without anyone suspecting that I was an all american boy. I did find out recently, however, that because of my fluent russian they had suspected me of being a russian spy and had been feeding me false information all along.

Supply italics wherever they are necessary.

1. The British often use the word lift to refer to an elevator.
2. Arthur Miller's Death of a Salesman is considered by many critics to be the great American tragedy.
3. Linguists consider b to be voiced and p to be unvoiced.
4. Given the quality of the movie version, it takes a considerable amount of courage to produce a stage version of the musical West Side Story.
5. The delight many people take in the discomfort of characters in situation comedies suggests that all of us may be subject to some schadenfreude.
6. The USS Enterprise was the first nuclear aircraft carrier.
7. I have always fantasized about taking a ride on the Orient Express, which figured so prominently in a mystery by Agatha Christie.
8. There are few artistic statements against war that are stronger than Picasso's Guernica.
9. There has been a very conscious effort to make Scientific American available to a larger segment of the reading public.
10. It is a shame that so few students read Dostoevsky's Crime and Punishment as part of their education.

Spelling

"Why the big deal about accurate spelling?"
"Does it really make that much difference if I have an *i* and an *e* turned around or if I omit a letter when spelling a word?"

Students frequently question the importance of proper spelling. Perhaps the answer is suggested by the following sentence, taken from a student essay:

I spent over seven hours *studing* one day last week.

The omission of a *y* in *studing* changes the person from one who is studious to one who is a dreamer. Not only does inaccurate spelling smack of carelessness, but also it sometimes drastically alters meaning.

Although there is no sure-fire way of becoming a good speller, you can minimize the difficulties by learning basic spelling rules, applying helpful spelling tips, and memorizing the proper spelling of troublesome words.

Spelling Rules

The following four rules should ease spelling pains.

Rule 1 If a word has the double vowels* *ie* or *ei* and the combination has a long *e* sound (as in *me*), use *ie* except after *c*. If the combination has an *a* sound, use *ei*.

ie (as long *e*)	*ei* after *c*	*ei* (as long *a*)
relieve	deceive	freight
belief	receive	neighbor
grieve	receipt	reign
piece	perceive	weigh

The main exceptions to this rule include *either, financier, leisure, neither, seize, species,* and *weird.*

Rule 2 If a one-syllable word (example: *sin*) ends in a single consonant preceded by a single vowel, double the consonant before adding a suffix

---

*The vowels are *a, e, i, o,* and *u.* The consonants are the remaining letters of the alphabet.

"Dear Mom. Wud you belive I lost my job at the offise today? I gess sumwun thair doesnt like me."

From Recess Time, The Best Cartoons from The Kappan, edited by Kristin Herzog. ©1983 Bardulf Ueland. Reprinted by permission of the Estate of Bardulf Ueland.

that starts with a vowel. Apply the same rule with a word of two or more syllables (example: *admit*) if the final syllable is 0accented and ends with a single consonant preceded by a vowel.

Words with Single Syllables	Words with Two or More Syllables
rig—rigged	admit—admittance
sin—sinned	control—controller
stop—stopping	equip—equipped

If the accent does not fall on the last syllable, do not double the final consonant.

audit—audited   chatter—chattered
counsel—counselor   simmer—simmering

Rule 3 If a word ends in *y* preceded by a single consonant, change the *y* to an *i* unless you are adding the suffix *-ing*.

y changed to *i*	*y* retained
beauty—beautiful	copy—copying
fury—furious	defy—defying
easy—easily	dry—drying
vary—various	vary—varying

sp

Rule 4 If a word ends in a silent *e*, the *e* is usually dropped when a suffix starting with a vowel is added.

blue—bluish   fame—famous
dense—density   grieve—grievous

In a few cases, the *e* is retained to avoid pronunciation difficulties or confusion with other words.

dye—dyeing (not dying)   singe—singeing (not singing)
shoe—shoeing (not shoing)

The *e* is also retained when it is preceded by a soft *c* sound (pronounced like the letter *s*) or a soft *g* sound (pronounced like the letter *j*) and the suffix being added starts with an *a* or an *o*.

peace—peaceable   courage—courageous
change—changeable   manage—manageable

Helpful Spelling Tips

Here are some tips that can further improve your spelling:

1. Examine each problem word carefully, especially prefixes (*au*dience, *au*dible), suffixes (superintend*ent*, descend*ant*), and double consonants (sate*ll*ite, roo*mm*ate, and co*ll*apsible).   ·
2. Sound out each syllable carefully, noting its pronunciation. Words like *height, governor,* and *candidate* are often misspelled because of improper pronunciation.
3. Make a list of your problem words and review them periodically. Concentrate on each syllable and any unusual features (ar*ct*ic, ambig*uous*).
4. Use any crutches that will help: there is *gain* in *bargain;* to *breakfast* is to *break a fast;* a disease causes *dis-ease.*
5. When you copy anything from the blackboard or a textbook, copy it carefully. Writing a word correctly helps you to spell it correctly the next time.
6. Buy a good collegiate dictionary and look up the words you don't know how to spell.
7. If you have a word processor that has a spell checker, use it. But a word of caution: Don't rely exclusively on this tool. Your spell checker may not distinguish between *to* and *too, their* and *there,* and similar sound-alike words. The ultimate spell checker is you.

List of Troublesome Words

Students frequently misspell the words in the following list. Study these words carefully until the correct spelling becomes automatic. Then have a friend read them to you while you write them down. Tag the ones you misspell and whenever you revise a paper, check especially for these words.

abandoned	allotted	barbiturate	commit
abbreviate	allowed	beautiful	commitment
absence	all right	beggar	committed
absorb	already	believe	committee
absorption	although	beneficial	committing
absurd	altogether	benefit	comparatively
academy	always	benefited	competent
accelerate	amateur	biscuit	competition
accept	ambiguous	boundary	concede
access	among	bourgeois	conceive
accessible	analysis (analyses)	breathe	condemn
accident	analyze	Britain	condescend
accidentally	anonymous	bulletin	confident
accommodate	anxiety	bureau	congratulations
accomplish	apartment	bureaucracy	connoisseur
accumulate	apparent	business	conqueror
accustom	appearance	cafeteria	conscience
achieve	appreciate	calendar	conscientious
achievement	appropriate	camouflage	conscious
acknowledge	architecture	campaign	consistency
acknowledgment	arctic	candidate	consistent
acquaintance	argue	carburetor	conspicuous
acquire	arguing	carriage	contemptible
acquit	argument	carrying	continuous
acquitted	arithmetic	casual	controversy
address	ascent	category	convenience
advice	assassin	causal	convenient
advise	assent	ceiling	coolly
aerial	assistance	cellar	cooperate
aggravate	assistant	cemetery	corollary
aggravated	athlete	changeable	corps
aggression	athletics	changing	corpse
aggressive	attempt	characteristic	correlate
aging	attendance	chauffeur	counterfeit
alcohol	average	chief	courteous
allege	bachelor	colloquial	criticism
alleviate	balance	colonel	criticize
alley(s)	balloon	column	cruelty
allot	barbarous	commission	curiosity

curriculum	enthusiastic	heroes	manual
dealt	environment	hindrance	marriage
deceit	equal	hygiene	mathematics
deceive	equip	hypocrisy	mattress
decent	equipment	hysterical	meant
decision	equipped	illiterate	medicine
defendant	equivalent	illogical	medieval
defense	especially	illusion	mediocre
definite	exaggerate	immediate	melancholy
definitely	exceed	implement	miniature
dependent	excellent	impromptu	minute
descendant	except	inadequate	miscellaneous
descent	excerpt	incident	mischievous
describe	excess	incidentally	misspell
description	excitement	independent	modifies
desert	exercise	indict	modify
desirable	existence	indispensable	modifying
despair	experience	individual	moral
desperate	extraordinary	inevitable	morale
dessert	extremely	infinitely	mortgage
develop	fallacy	ingenious	mosquitoes
development	familiar	ingenuous	muscle
difference	fascinate	innocent	mysterious
dilemma	fascist	intelligent	necessary
disappear	February	interest	neither
disastrous	fiery	interfere	nevertheless
discernible	finally	irresistible	niece
disciple	financier	irresponsible	noticeable
discipline	foreign	jeopardy	obedience
discussion	foreword	judgment	occasion
disease	forfeit	judicial	occasionally
dissatisfied	forward	knowledge	occur
dissipate	friend	knowledgeable	occurred
dominant	fulfill	laboratory	occurrence
drunkenness	gaiety	legitimate	occurring
echoes	gases	leisure	official
ecstasy	gauge or gage	library	omission
efficiency	genius	license	omit
efficient	genuine	lightning	omitted
eighth	government	loneliness	omitting
eligible	grammar	loose	opinion
eliminate	guarantee	lose	opponent
embarrass	guard	magnificent	opportunity
emphasis	handkerchief	maintain	optimistic
employee	harass	maintenance	original
engineer	height	maneuver	outrageous

pamphlet
parallel
paralysis
parliament
particularly
pastime
patent
peaceable
perceive
perfectible
perform
permanent
permissible
perseverance
persuade
physical
physician
picnic
picnicked
playwright
pleasant
pleasurable
politician
possess
possession
possible
potatoes
practice
precede
precedent
precious
predominant
preference
preferred
prejudice
preparation
privilege
probably
procedure
proceed
professor
prominent
pronounce
pronunciation
propaganda
propagate

propeller
prophecy
prophesy
prostate
prostrate
protein
psychiatry
psychology
pursue
pursuit
quantity
questionnaire
quiet
quite
quiz
quizzes
realize
receipt
receive
recipe
recognizable
recommend
refer
reference
referring
reign
relevant
relieve
religious
remembrance
reminisce
reminiscence
reminiscent
rendezvous
repellent
repentance
repetition
representative
resemblance
resistance
restaurant
rhetoric
rhyme
rhythm
roommate
sacrifice

sacrilege
sacrilegious
safety
salary
sandwich
scarcely
scene
scenic
schedule
science
secretary
seize
sensible
separate
sergeant
severely
siege
similar
simultaneous
sincerely
skeptical
skiing
skillful
skis
society
sophomore
source
specifically
specimen
sponsor
spontaneous
statistics
steely
strategy
studying
subtle
subtlety
subtly
succeed
success
successful
succinct
suffrage
superintendent
supersede
suppose

suppress
surprise
syllable
symmetry
sympathize
synonym
synonymous
tangible
tariff
technical
technique
temperament
temperature
temporary
tenant
tendency
thorough
thought
through
traffic
trafficking
tragedy
tranquillity or
   tranquility
transcendent
transcendental
transfer
transferred
transferring
translate
tries
truly
twelfth
tyrannical
tyranny
unanimous
unconscious
undoubtedly
unmistakable
unnecessary
until
unwieldy
urban
urbane
usage
useful

sp

using	vengeance	Wednesday	worshiped or
usual	victorious	weird	worshipped
usually	village	whether	wreak
vacancy	villain	whole	wreck
vacillate	waive	wholly	writing
vacuum	warrant	wield	written
valuable	warring	wintry	yield
vegetable	weather	wiry	

Glossary of Word Usage

The English language has many words and expressions that confuse writers and thereby lessen the precision and effectiveness of their writing. These troublesome items include the following:

Word pairs that sound alike or almost alike but are spelled differently and have different meanings

Word pairs that do not sound alike but still are often confused

Words or phrases that are unacceptable in formal writing

The following glossary identifies the most common of these troublemakers. Familiarize yourself with its contents. Then consult it as you revise your writing if you have even the slightest doubt about the proper use of a word, phrase, or expression.

a, an   Use *a* with words beginning with a consonant sound (even if the first written letter is a vowel); use *an* with words beginning with a vowel or a vowel sound.

a brush, *a* student, *a* wheel, *a* risky situation, *a* once-in-a-lifetime opportunity

an architect, *an* apple, *an* unworthy participant, *an* interesting proposal, *an* honest politician

accept, except   *Accept* is a verb meaning "to receive" or "to approve." *Except* is used as a verb or a preposition. As a verb, *except* means "to take out, exclude, or omit." As a preposition, it means "excluding," "other than," or "but not."

She *accepted* the bouquet of flowers.

Linda excepted Sally from the list of guests. (verb)

All of Linda's friends *except* Sally came to the party. (preposition)

access, excess   *Access* is a noun meaning "means or right to enter, approach, or use." In the computer field it is a verb meaning "gain entrance to." *Excess* is an adjective meaning "too much; more than needed; lack of moderation."

I have *access* to a summer cottage this weekend.

The code permits users to *access* the computer.

The airline booked an *excess* number of passengers on that flight.

adapt, adopt   To *adapt* is "to adjust," often by modification. To *adopt* is "to take as one's own."

He *adapted* to the higher elevations of the Rocky Mountains.

She *adopted* the new doctrine expounded by the prophet.

adverse, averse   *Adverse* is an adjective meaning "unfavorable." *Averse* is an adjective meaning "disinclined" or "feeling distaste for."

> *Adverse* circumstances caused the ceremony to be postponed.

> Martha was *averse* to naming all the guilty children.

advice, advise   *Advice* is a noun meaning "a recommendation about how to deal with a situation or problem." *Advise* is a verb meaning "to recommend or warn."

> The young man followed his sister's *advice.*

> Mr. Smith *advised* John to buy 10,000 shares of the stock.

affect, effect   Although both words may function as nouns and verbs, usually *affect* is a verb and *effect* is a noun. The verb *affect* means "to influence, cause a change in, or arouse the emotions of." The noun *affect* is a technical term in psychology and refers to feeling. The noun *effect* means "result or outcome." The verb *effect* means "to bring about or achieve."

> His speech *affected* me greatly. (verb)

> The *effect* of the announcement was felt immediately. (noun)

> The doctor was soon able to *effect* a cure. (verb)

aggravate   *Aggravate* is a verb meaning "to intensify or make worse" an existing situation. The use of *aggravate* to mean "annoy" or "anger" is colloquial.

> *Colloquial*   Susan's behavior at the dance really *aggravated* me.

> *Standard*   Marcy's interference only *aggravated* the conflict between Bill and Nadine.

ain't   This nonstandard term for *isn't, aren't, hasn't,* or *haven't* is unacceptable in college writing.

all ready, already   *All ready* means "completely prepared" or "everyone is ready." *Already* means "previously, even now, even then."

> The scouts are *all ready* for the camp out.

> When we arrived we found he had *already* gone.

> The report is *already* a week overdue.

all right, alright   *Alright* is a nonstandard spelling of *all right* and is not acceptable in college writing.

all together, altogether   *All together* means "all in one place" or "in unison." *Altogether* is an adverb meaning "completely, entirely."

> The family was *all together* at the wedding.

> *All together*, men, push!

> Mr. Doe is *altogether* at fault for writing the letter.

allusion, delusion, illusion   An *allusion* is an indirect reference. A *delusion* is a mistaken belief, often part of a psychological condition. An *illusion* is a deceptive appearance presented to the sight or created by the imagination.

> In his sermon, the minister made many *allusions* to the New Testament.

> He suffers from the *delusion* that he is a millionaire.

> They wore makeup to give the *illusion* of beauty.

a lot, alot   *Alot* is an erroneous spelling of the two words *a lot*. The phrase *a lot* is usually colloquial; in formal writing replace it with "many."

already   See *all ready, already.*

alright   See *all right, alright.*

alternately, alternatively   *Alternately* means "occurring by turns, one after the other." *Alternatively* means "providing a choice between two items."

> The U.S. flag has seven red and six white stripes, arranged *alternately.*

> Highway 44 offers the most direct route to Junction City. *Alternatively,* Highway 88 is much more scenic.

altogether   See *all together, altogether.*

among,   between   Use *between* when referring to two things and *among* when referring to more than two.

> He divided the candy *between* Allan and Stephanie.

> He divided the candy *among* the five children.

amoral, immoral   *Amoral* means "neither moral nor immoral; morally neutral." *Immoral* means "contrary to the moral code."

> The movie, which takes no clear position on the behavior it depicts, seems curiously *amoral.*

> Murder is an *immoral* act.

amount, number   *Amount* refers to total quantities, things in bulk, or weight. *Number* refers to countable things. Never use *amount* when referring to people.

> Cassandra inherited a large *amount* of money.

> Cassandra now has a large *number* of friends.

an, a   See *a, an.*

and/or   Although often used in commercial and legal documents, this combination should be avoided in other writing.

angry, mad   *Mad* means "insane," although it is often used colloquially to mean "annoyed" or "angry." To be precise, use *mad* only to mean insane.

> *Colloquial*   I was *mad* at Debbie.
>
> *Standard*   I was *angry* with Debbie.

any, any other   Do not use *any* when you mean *any other*. Using *any* in the following example would mean that Theresa is more qualified than herself:

> Theresa is more qualified than *any other* candidate.

anyone, any one   *Anyone* means "any person." *Any one* means "any single person or thing."

> I can whip *anyone* in this room.

> I saw three movies last week but didn't like *any one* of them.

appraise, apprise   *Appraise* means "to determine the value of something." *Apprise* means "to notify" or "to tell."

usage

519

The jeweler *appraised* the gold brooch at $1,500.

Having been *apprised* of the situation, the family priest was able to reconcile the parents and the children.

apt, liable, likely   Both *apt* and *liable* express a tendency or inclination. *Liable* suggests something unpleasant or likely to result in legal action. It should be used only when the event may have unpleasant consequences.

We are *liable* to miss the train.

My lawyer said that I was *liable* for the damage my car had caused.

If the probable consequences are not unpleasant, *apt* is the better word.

I am *apt* to buy books if we go to the shopping center.

Likely merely implies strong probability.

Sandra is *likely* to pass this course without difficulty.

around   *Around* is colloquial use for "approximately" or "about."

Colloquial	She arrived *around* 10:00 P.M.
	The blouse cost *around* $15.
Standard	She arrived at *approximately* 10:00 P.M.
	The blouse cost *about* $15.

as   *As* is frequently used as a weak substitute for *because, since, when,* and *while.*

Weak	She ran out of the house *as* it was on fire.
Better	She ran out of the house *because* it was on fire.

As should not be used in place of *whether* or *that.*

Nonstandard	I don't know *as* I like her.
Standard	I don't know *that* I like her. I don't know *whether* I like her.

as, like   *As* may be used as a conjunction that introduces an adverb clause, but *like* should not be used this way.

Unacceptable	*Like* my father always said, "You can fool some of the people all of the time."
Standard	*As* my father always said, "You can fool some of the people all of the time."

Like may, however, be used as a preposition.

In times *like* this, it's hard not to despair.

Any woman *like* Sally can expect a successful career in business.

assure, ensure, insure   To *assure* is "to make safe from risk, to guarantee" or "to convince." *Ensure* and *insure* can be variant spellings meaning "to make certain." *Insure,* however, is now generally associated with the business of insurance.

The counselor tried to *assure* the students that they had made a wise choice.

The captain *assured* them that they would be rescued.

The father, wanting to *ensure* his son's college education, applied for a federally *insured* loan.

averse   See *adverse, averse.*

awful, awfully   In everyday speech, *awful* is used to describe things disagreeable or objectionable: "an *awful* movie," "an *awful* character." *Awfully* is used colloquially as an intensifier: "*awfully* nice," "*awfully* bad." Unless they are used to mean "solemnly impressive," however, both words should be avoided in formal writing.

The *awful* majesty of the cathedral silenced the chattering tourists.

awhile, a while   *A while,* consisting of the noun *while* and the article *a,* means "a period of time." *Awhile* is an adverb meaning "for a short time."

Dinner will be served in *a while.*

Sit *awhile* and tell me the latest gossip.

bad, badly   *Bad* is an adjective. *Badly* is an adverb. *Badly* is colloquial when used to mean "very much."

Unacceptable	She feels *badly* about her mistake.
	Tom behaved *bad* at the circus.
Colloquial	I want a new car *badly.*
Standard	She feels *bad* about her mistake. (adjective as subject complement)
	Tom behaved *badly* at the circus. (adverb)
	I want a new car *very much.*

being as, being that   When used as substitutes for *because* or *since,* these expressions are nonstandard.

Nonstandard	*Being that* I was the first in line, I was able to purchase choice tickets.
Standard	*Because* I was first in line, I was able to purchase choice tickets.

beside, besides   Both words are prepositions, but they have different meanings. *Beside* means "at the side of," and *besides* means "in addition to."

Sheila and Bill sat *beside* the trailer to eat their lunch.

Besides Harvey, Seymour is coming to dinner.

between   See *among, between.*

breath, breathe   *Breath* is a noun and *breathe* is its verb counterpart.

Nicole stepped outside the stuffy cabin for a *breath* of fresh air.

The cabin was so stuffy that Nicole could hardly *breathe.*

broke   *Broke,* when used to mean "without money," is colloquial.

Colloquial	Because Shelley was *broke,* she had to miss the movie.
Standard	Because Shelley *had no money,* she had to miss the movie.

can, may   *Can* refers both to permission and to the ability to do something, while *may* refers to permission only.

I think I *can* pass the exam on Friday. (ability)

My mother says I *can* go to the movies. (permission)

May I take the test next Monday? (permission)

usage

When used to denote permission, *can* lends a less formal air to writing than does *may*.

cannot, can not   The use of *cannot* is preferred unless the writer wishes to italicize the *not* for emphasis.

> You *cannot* expect a raise this year.

> No, you can *not* expect a raise this year.

can't hardly   This nonstandard form for *cannot, can't,* or *can hardly* is unacceptable in college writing.

can't help but   In college writing, this colloquial phrase should be revised to the simpler *I can't help* or *I cannot help.*

> *Colloquial*   I *can't help but* wish that I were going to the concert.

> *Standard*   I *can't help* wishing that I were going to the concert.

capital, capitol   *Capital* means "a city that serves as a seat of government." *Capitol* means "a building in which a state legislature meets" or "the building in which Congress meets."

> Dover is the *capital* of Delaware.

> The *capitol* in Dover is popular with visitors.

Capital can also refer to wealth or assets, to an offense punishable by death, or to something excellent or first-rate.

> My *capital* consists entirely of stocks and bonds.

> Murder is a *capital* crime in this state.

> That's a *capital* suggestion!

censor, censure   To *censor* is "to judge"—literature, movies, letters, and the like—and to decide what material is unfit to be read or seen. To *censure* is "to judge harshly" or "find fault with."

> The warden *censored* all the prisoners' mail.

> The judge *censured* Clyde's criminal behavior.

childish, childlike   Both of these terms mean "like a child." *Childish,* however, has a negative connotation.

> He is fifty-two years old, but he behaves in a *childish* manner.

> Jon's face has a *childlike* quality that everyone likes immediately.

cite, sight, site   *Cite* means "to mention or quote as an example," *sight* means "to see" or "a view," and *site* means "a location."

> Cheryl *cited* Abraham Lincoln's Emancipation Proclamation in her talk.

> He was able to *sight* the enemy destroyers through the periscope.

> The building *site* is a woody area south of town.

climactic, climatic   *Climactic* is an adjective that means "of, being, or relating to a climax." *Climatic* is an adjective meaning "of or relating to a climate."

> Riding the roller coaster was the *climactic* event of Alice's day.

> The *climatic* features of Arizona are desirable to many people.

usage

complement, compliment   Both words can act as nouns or verbs. As a noun, *complement* means "something that completes or makes up the whole." As a verb, it means "to complete or perfect." As a noun, *compliment* means "a flattering or praising remark." As a verb, it means "to flatter or praise."

> A *complement* of navy personnel boarded the foreign freighter. (noun)

> This fruit will *complement* the meal nicely. (verb)

> Scott paid Sara Jane a lovely *compliment* at the time of her graduation. (noun)

> Mother *complimented* me for cleaning my room. (verb)

conscience, conscious   *Conscience* refers to the sense of moral right or wrong. *Conscious* refers to the awareness of one's feelings or thoughts.

> Edgar's *conscience* forced him to return the money.

> Basil was not *conscious* of his angry feelings.

Do not confuse *conscious* with *aware;* although these words are similar in meaning, one is *conscious* of feelings or actions but *aware* of events.

contemptible, contemptuous   *Contemptible* means "deserving of contempt." *Contemptuous* means "displaying contempt."

> Peter's drunkenness is *contemptible.*

> Mary is *contemptuous* of Peter's drunkenness.

continual, continuous   *Continual* means "frequently or regularly repeated." *Continuous* means "uninterrupted."

> The telephone's *continual* ringing made the morning a nightmare.

> His wound caused him *continuous* pain for a week.

could have, could of   *Could of* is an unacceptable substitute for *could have* because a preposition cannot substitute for a verb.

> *Nonstandard*   I *could of* gone with my parents to Portugal.

> *Standard*   I *could have* gone with my parents to Portugal.

council, counsel   A *council* is a group of people that governs or advises. *Counsel* can be used as both a noun and a verb. The noun means "advice," and the verb means "to advise."

> The city *council* meets on the second Tuesday of every month.

> The lawyer's *counsel* was sound. (noun)

> The psychologist *counsels* many abused children. (verb)

couple   *Couple* denotes two things and should not be used to refer to more than that number.

criteria, criterion   *Criterion* is always singular; *criteria* always plural.

> The primary *criterion* for performing this job is manual dexterity.

> Manual dexterity is but one of many *criteria* on which you will be judged.

cute   *Cute,* an overused colloquialism, should be avoided; it has too many connotations to be used precisely in writing.

usage

data   *Data* is the plural of *datum*. Although *data* is sometimes used with a singular verb, this use is considered incorrect.

Standard	These *data* are incorrect.
Unacceptable	This *data* is incorrect.

definite, very definite   Since *definite* means "precise" or "unmistakable," *very definite* is repetitive. One really cannot be more definite than *definite*.

delusion   See *allusion, delusion, illusion*.

desert, deserts, dessert   *Desert* is land that is arid. With the accent on the last syllable, it is a verb meaning "to abandon." *Deserts* means "that which is deserved." *Dessert* is food served after dinner.

The Sonoran *desert* is full of plant life.

You'll get your just *deserts* if you *desert* me now.

They had cheesecake for *dessert* every Thursday night.

device, devise   *Device* is a noun meaning "a mechanical contrivance, gadget, or tool." *Devise* is a verb meaning "to plan or invent."

This new *device* gives us better gas mileage.

We must *devise* a new approach to our problem.

different from, different than   *Different from* is preferred over *different than*.

His ideas on marriage were *different from* those of his wife.

Different than is accepted, however, when a clause follows and the *from* construction would be wordy.

Acceptable	Susan looks *different than* she did last summer.
Wordy	Susan looks *different from* the way she looked last summer.

discreet, discrete   To be *discreet* means to be "prudent, tactful, or careful of one's actions." *Discrete* means "distinct or separate."

Jack was always *discreet* when he talked to his grandparents.

When two atoms of hydrogen combine with one atom of oxygen, they are no longer *discrete* entities.

disinterested, uninterested   A person who is *disinterested* is impartial or unbiased. A person who is *uninterested* is indifferent or not interested.

We need a *disinterested* judge to settle the dispute.

Joe is completely *uninterested* in sports.

don't   This contraction for *do not* should never be used with singular subjects such as *he, she,* or *it*. Instead, use *doesn't*, the contraction for *does not*, with singular subjects.

Nonstandard	*Don't* he know how to spell? That mistake *don't* help your image. She *don't* think of anyone except herself.
Standard	*Doesn't* he know how to spell? That mistake *doesn't* help your image. She *doesn't* think of anyone except herself.

due to   *Due to* has always been acceptable following a linking verb.

>   Her success was *due to* hard work.

Purists, however, object to *due to* when it is used in other situations, especially in introductory phrases.

>   *Due to* the many requests we have had, not everyone who wishes tickets will receive them.

In such cases, you may wish to recast the sentence.

>   *Because* we have had so many requests, not everyone who wishes tickets will receive them.

effect   See *affect, effect.*

e.g.   This abbreviation, from the Latin *exempli gratia,* means "for example." Avoid using it except in comments in parentheses and in footnotes, and always follow it with a comma.

elicit, illicit   *Elicit* is a verb that means "to draw forth." *Illicit* is an adjective meaning "not permitted."

>   A good professor can always *elicit* responses from students.

>   He was engaged in many types of *illicit* activities.

emigrate, immigrate   When people *emigrate,* they move out of a country. When people *immigrate,* they move into a country.

>   The family *emigrated* from Poland.

>   Many Russians *immigrated* to America.

eminent, imminent   *Eminent* means "prominent," whereas *imminent* means "about to happen."

>   Niels Bohr was an *eminent* physicist.

>   Our instruments show that an earthquake is *imminent.*

ensure   See *assure, ensure, insure.*

enthused, enthusiastic   *Enthused* is a colloquial word and should not be used in place of *enthusiastic.*

>   *Colloquial*   John was *enthused* about the prospects for jobs in his hometown.

>   *Standard*   John was *enthusiastic* about the prospects for jobs in his hometown.

especially, specially   The term *especially* means "particularly, notably." *Specially* means "for a specific purpose."

>   He is an *especially* talented pianist.

>   He was *specially* chosen to represent his group.

et al.   This expression, from the Latin *et alia,* means "and others," referring to people. Ordinarily, the abbreviation should be used only in footnotes and bibliographic entries.

etc.   This abbreviation, from the Latin *et cetera,* means "and other things" and is used in reference to objects rather than people. It should be avoided except in comments in parentheses or in footnotes. It should never be preceded by *and.*

everyone, every one   *Everyone* means "every person." *Every one* means "every particular person or thing."

usage

Everyone who wants to go to the ball game should let me know today.

If you carefully check *every one* of your paragraphs, you can improve your writing.

except   See *accept, except.*

excess   See *access, excess.*

explicit, implicit   *Explicit* means "clearly expressed" or "straightforward." *Implicit* means "implied" or "understood without direct statement."

You must state your needs *explicitly* if you want them fulfilled.

When I took on the project, I made an *implicit* commitment to see it through.

extant, extent   *Extant* is an adjective meaning "still existing." *Extent* is a noun meaning "scope, size, range, limit."

The dodo bird is no longer *extant.*

From Nevada to Colorado is the *extent* of my travels.

farther, further   The traditional distinction is that *farther* refers to physical distance and *further* to distance in time. Only *further* should be used to mean "additional" or "additionally."

In the race for the Muscular Dystrophy Association, Janet ran *farther* than Cindy.

If you think *further* on the matter, I am certain we can reach an agreement.

Let me make one *further* point.

fewer, less   *Fewer* refers to countable items. *Less* refers to quantity or degree.

Mrs. Smith has *fewer* dogs than cats.

There is *less* money in Joan's checking account than in Stanley's.

Jack was *less* ambitious in his later years.

Never use *less* to refer to people.

> *Nonstandard*   *Less* people were there than I expected.
>
> *Standard*   *Fewer* people were there than I expected.

flaunt, flout   To *flaunt* is "to display in a showy way." To *flout* is "to express contempt" or "to show scorn."

Jay *flaunted* his handsome physique before all his friends.

Jerrold *flouted* the convention of dressing for dinner by arriving in tennis shoes.

formally, formerly   *Formally* means "according to established forms, conventions, and rules; ceremoniously." *Formerly* means "in the past."

The ambassador *formally* greeted his dinner guests.

Formerly, smallpox was one of our most serious diseases.

funny   *Funny* refers to something that is amusing. In college writing it should not be used to mean "odd" or "unusual."

> *Colloquial*   I felt *funny* visiting my old fourth-grade classroom.
>
> *Standard*   I felt *odd* visiting my old fourth-grade classroom.

usage

further   See *farther, further.*

get   *Get,* in any of its many colloquial senses, should not be used in writing.

> *Colloquial*   Her way of looking at a man really *gets* me.
> I'll *get* him if it's the last thing I do.

> *Standard*   Beth will *get* at least a *B* in this course.

good and   Replace this colloquial phrase with *very.*

> *Colloquial*   She is *good and* tired of the cafeteria food.

> *Standard*   She is *very* tired of the cafeteria food.

good, well   Do not mistakenly use *good* as an adverb when an adjective is required.

> *Unacceptable*   John did *good* on his first test.

> *Standard*   John is making *good* progress on his report.
> John is a *good* student.

Well can be used as an adjective meaning "in good health." Otherwise it should always be used as an adverb.

> Last week I had a bad cold, but now I am *well.* (adjective)

> John did *well* on his first test. (adverb)

got, gotten   Both are acceptable past-participle forms of the verb *to get.*

had ought, hadn't ought   Both are incorrect in formal writing. The correct forms are *ought* and *ought not.*

> I *ought* to start studying.

> You *ought not* to cut class again.

hanged, hung   People may be *hanged.* Objects may be *hung.*

> The prisoner was *hanged* at noon.

> Mavis *hung* the picture in the dining room.

hisself, theirself, theirselves   These are nonstandard forms of *himself* and *themselves.*

hopefully   *Hopefully* means "in a hopeful manner." In informal speaking, it is used to mean "it is hoped" or "I hope," but this usage is not correct in formal writing. (Compare this with *carefully,* which means "in a careful manner"; no one uses *carefully* to mean "it is cared.")

> *Colloquial*   *Hopefully,* it will not rain during the class picnic.

> *Standard*   Sally walked *hopefully* into the boss's office to ask for a raise.

hung   See *hanged, hung.*

i.e.   This abbreviation, meaning "that is," comes from the Latin *id est.* Avoid using it except in comments in parentheses or footnotes, and always follow it with a comma.

usage

if, whether   *If* is used to introduce adverb clauses, where it means "assuming that."

> *If* I finish my report on time, I'll attend the concert with you.

> *If* and *whether* are often used interchangeably to introduce noun clauses that follow verbs such as *ask, say, doubt, know,* and *wonder.* In formal writing, however, *whether* is preferred.

>> *Less Desirable* I don't know *if* we'll be able to see the North Star tonight.

>> *More Desirable* I don't know *whether* we'll be able to see the North Star tonight.

illicit   See *elicit, illicit.*

illusion   See *allusion, delusion, illusion.*

immigrate   See *emigrate, immigrate.*

imminent   See *eminent, imminent.*

immoral   See *amoral, immoral.*

impact   Although *impact* is sometimes used in colloquial speech as a verb meaning "affect," this use is unacceptable in college writing.

> *Colloquial*   This new law will greatly *impact* political campaigning.

> *Standard*   This new law will greatly *affect* political campaigning.

implicit   See *explicit, implicit.*

imply, infer   To *imply* is "to indicate indirectly or give implication." To *infer* is "to conclude from facts, evidence, or indirect suggestions."

> Jack *implied* that he wanted a divorce when he told his wife that all marriages come to an end.

> Doris *inferred* that Jack wanted a divorce when he told her all marriages come to an end.

As these examples indicate, speakers and writers imply; listeners and readers infer.

incidence, incidents   *Incidents* are separate, countable experiences. *Incidence* refers to the rate at which something occurs.

> Two *incidents* during childhood led to her reclusiveness.

> The *incidence* of cancer in Japan is less than that in the United States.

incredible, incredulous   *Incredible* means "fantastic, unbelievable." *Incredulous* means "skeptical, disbelieving."

> That she could run so fast seemed *incredible.*

> Why is Bill wearing that *incredulous* look?

infer   See *imply, infer.*

ingenious, ingenuous   *Ingenious* means "clever and inventive." *Ingenuous* means "unsophisticated and innocent."

> Sue presented an *ingenious* solution to our problem.

> Mary's *ingenuous* comments amused everyone in the room.

in regards to   This is an incorrect use of *in regard to.*

insure   See *assure, ensure, insure.*

inter-, intra-   *Inter-* means "between or among." *Intra-* means "within."

> From Chicago to Milwaukee is an *interstate* drive of approximately ninety miles.

> From San Francisco to Los Angeles is an *intrastate* drive of about 400 miles.

in terms of   Avoid this vague, overused expression.

> *Vague*   *In terms of* the price he is asking, I would not recommend
>   purchasing Tom's car.

> *Preferred*   *Because* of the price he is asking, I would not recommend
>   purchasing Tom's car.

irregardless   This nonstandard form of *regardless* includes the repetitive elements of *ir* and *less*, both of which mean "without."

is when, is where   *Is when* properly refers only to time.

> April *is when* our lilac bush blooms.

Is where properly refers only to place.

> Athens *is where* I met him.

The following sentences are *faulty* because of poorly phrased predicates which indicate that muckraking is a place and an abscess is a time:

> Muckraking *is where* someone investigates corporate or governmental abuses of power.

> An abscess *is when* some spot in body tissue fills with pus.

These sentences should be rephrased to eliminate the faulty assertion.

> Muckraking is the investigation of corporate or governmental abuses of power.

> An abscess occurs when some spot in body tissue fills with pus.

its, it's, its'   *Its* is a possessive pronoun. *It's* is a contraction of *it is* or *it has*.

> The gold chair was ruined, for someone had torn *its* seat.

> *It's* all I have to offer. (It is all I have to offer.)

> *It's* been a difficult day. (It has been a difficult day.)

> There is no correct use for *its'*.

kind of, sort of   In college writing, these are unacceptable substitutes for *somewhat*, *rather*, or *slightly*.

> *Colloquial*   She is *sort of* angry.
>   I am *kind of* glad she went away.

> *Standard*   She is *somewhat* angry.
>   I am *rather* glad she went away.

When *kind* and *sort* refer to a type, use them with singular nouns and verbs. With their plural forms, *kinds* and *sorts*, use plural nouns and verbs.

> *Unacceptable*   These *kind* of exams are difficult.

> *Standard*   This *kind* of exam is difficult.
>   These *kinds* of exams are difficult.

usage

529

In such constructions, be certain that *kind of* or *sort of* is essential to your meaning. Otherwise, these phrases are unnecessary.

later, latter   *Later* refers to time; *latter* points out the second of two items. If more than two items are listed, use *last* to refer to the final one.

He arrived at the party *later* than he was expected.

Although Professors Stein and Patterson both lectured during the course, only the *latter* graded the final exam.

Of my three cats, Sheba, Tiger, and Spot, only the *last* still needs the vaccination.

lay, lie   *Lie* means "to recline" or "to remain in a particular position." It never takes a direct object. *Lay* means "to place" and always takes a direct object. These verbs are often confused, in part because the past tense of *lie* is *lay*. (The past tense of *lay* is *laid*.)

If I *lie* here a minute, I shall feel better.

Lay the book on the table, please.

As I *lay* asleep, a robber entered my apartment and stole my stereo.

He *laid* a hand on her shoulder.

leave, let   *Leave* means "to depart," and *let* means "to allow." Never use *leave* when *let* is meant.

Nonstandard   **Leave** him figure it out alone.

Standard   **Let** him figure it out alone.

lend, loan   Traditionally, *loan* has been classed as a noun and *lend* as a verb. Today, the use of *loan* as a verb is so commonplace that it is accepted as colloquial English.

Standard   I have applied for a *loan* so that I can buy a car. (noun)

Please *lend* me your class notes. (verb)

Colloquial   Please *loan* me your class notes. (verb)

less   See *fewer, less*.

let   See *leave, let*.

liable   See *apt, liable, likely*.

lie   See *lay, lie*.

like   See *as, like*.

likely   See *apt, liable, likely*.

literally   The word *literally* means "restricted to the exact, stated meaning." In formal writing, use *literally* only to designate factual statements.

Colloquial   It was 65°, but I was *literally* freezing.

Standard   Our dog was *literally* foaming at the mouth.
It was 65°, but I was *very* cold.

loan   See *lend, loan*.

loose, loosen, lose   *Loose* can be used as both a verb and an adjective. As a verb, it means "untie or unfasten"; as an adjective, it means "unattached, unrestrained, not confined." *Loosen* is a verb meaning "undo or ease." *Lose* can be used only as a verb meaning "mislay, fail to win, unable to maintain."

He *loosed* the restraints on the tiger. (verb)

One should wear *loose* clothing when bowling. (adjective)

When will Mrs. Brady *loosen* her control over young Tom? (verb)

You would *lose* your nose if it were not attached to your face. (verb)

lots, lots of   *Lots* and *lots of* colloquially mean "many, much, a large amount, or a great amount." Avoid these expressions in college writing.

> *Colloquial*   I've spent *lots of* money in my life.
>
> *Standard*   I have spent *much* money in my life.

mad   See *angry, mad.*

many, much   *Many* is used when referring to countable items; *much* is used when referring to an indefinite amount or to abstract concepts.

There are *many* students in the biology class.

How did Betty learn so *much* in so little time?

may   See *can, may.*

may be, maybe   *May be* is always used as a verb phrase. *Maybe* is an adverb meaning "perhaps."

I *may be* chairman of the board by next June.

Maybe we will see Jim at home.

medium, media   *Medium* is the singular form of this word; *media* is the plural.

Television is the *medium* I use most to get the news.

The *media* have given extensive coverage to the brain transplant story.

much   See *many, much.*

myself   *Myself* is an intensive and a reflexive pronoun; it cannot substitute for a personal pronoun such as *I* or *me.*

> *Unacceptable*   Four other students and *myself* founded the club.
>
> *Standard*   Four other students and *I* founded the club.

nice   *Nice* is an adjective suggesting delicacy, precision, subtlety, accuracy, the ability to discriminate, or the need for great care.

These two seemingly identical proposals actually have several *nice* differences.

This author's short stories have a *nice* touch.

Nice as a term of approval meaning "pleasing, enjoyable, attractive" is too generalized for use in college writing.

not hardly   This is a nonstandard variation of *hardly* and is inappropriate in college writing.

number   See *amount, number.*

of between, of from, off of   Eliminate the unnecessary *of* from these colloquial phrases.

Colloquial	There was a crowd *of between* three and four thousand people at the contest. Get *off of* my property!
Standard	The crowd at the contest numbered *between* three and four thousand people. Get *off* my property!

on account of   When used to begin an adverb clause, this is a nonstandard substitute for *because*.

Nonstandard	The team was unable to practice *on account of* everyone was still upset over Tuesday's loss.
Standard	The team was unable to practice *because* everyone was still upset over Tuesday's loss.

When *on account of* precedes a single word or a phrase, it is considered colloquial.

Colloquial	The game was called *on account of* rain.

over, more than   *Over* should not be substituted for *more than;* if *more than* fits the phrase, use it.

Nonstandard	My brother likes ice cream *over* cake.
Standard	My brother likes ice cream *more than* cake.

passed, past   *Passed* is a verb designating activity that has taken place. *Past* is a noun or an adjective designating a former time.

The parade *passed* the reviewing stand at 10:30 A.M.

In the *past*, few people were concerned about the environmental effects of pesticides.

This *past* summer, I visited France.

patience, patients   *Patience* means "the ability to wait or endure without complaining." *Patients* are "people being treated by health-care professionals."

Thad's *patience* was exhausted by the slow service in the restaurant.

Following the tornado, doctors in the emergency room treated over sixty *patients.*

persecute, prosecute   *Persecute* means "to harass persistently because of race, religion, or belief." *Prosecute* means "to bring legal suit against."

Ethnic groups are often *persecuted.*

The company will *prosecute* anyone caught stealing.

personal, personnel   *Personal* is an adjective meaning "private, individual." *Personnel* are the people working in an organization.

Religious preference is a *personal* matter that you do not have to reveal during a job interview.

The *personnel* of the sanitation department will not be involved in the city workers' strike.

usage

plenty   When used as an adverb, *plenty* should be replaced by *very*.

Colloquial   That geology exam was *plenty* hard.

Standard   That geology exam was *very* hard.

precede, proceed   *Precede* means "to go before or ahead of." *Proceed* means "to go on" or "to go forward."

The ritual of sharpening his pencils always *preceded* doing his homework.

The guide then said, "If you will *proceed*, I will show you the paintings by da Vinci."

predominant, predominate   *Predominant* is an adjective meaning "chief, main, most frequent." *Predominate* is a verb meaning "to have authority over others."

The *predominant* European influence on South American culture was Spanish.

In America, the will of the people should *predominate*.

presently   *Presently* means "soon" rather than "at the present time." *Currently* is correct for the second meaning.

I will be there *presently*.

Currently, I am otherwise engaged.

principal, principle   *Principal*, which means "chief," "most important," or "the amount of money on which interest is computed," is used as both a noun and an adjective. *Principle* is used only as a noun and means "truths, beliefs, or rules generally dealing with moral conduct."

The *principal* suspect in the case was arrested last Friday by the police.

The *principal* of Lewiston High School is Alison Cooperstein.

At this interest rate, your *principal* will double in ten years.

His *principles* are unconventional.

proceed   See *precede, proceed*.

prosecute   See *persecute, prosecute*.

quiet, quite   *Quiet* is an adjective meaning "silent, motionless, calm." *Quite* is an adverb meaning "entirely" or "to a considerable extent or degree."

The class grew *quiet* when the teacher walked in.

He is *quite* wrong.

The movie was *quite* good.

raise, rise   *Raise* is a transitive verb and therefore requires a direct object. *Rise*, its intransitive counterpart, takes no direct object.

We plan to *raise* horses on our new farm.

The temperature is expected to *rise* to 75°F tomorrow.

Raise can also be a noun meaning "an increase in pay."

Tammy received a 25 percent *raise* last week.

real, really   *Real* is an adjective; *really* is an adverb.

She had *real* plants decorating the bedroom.

usage

533

When used as an adverb, *real* is a colloquialism and should be replaced with *really*.

Colloquial   We had a *real* good time at the party.

Standard   We had a *really* good time at the party.

reason is because, reason is that   The *reason is because* is colloquial and unacceptable in formal writing; the *reason is that* is the correct usage.

Colloquial   The *reason is because* I love her.

Standard   The *reason is that* I love her.

respectfully, respectively   *Respectfully* means "with respect." *Respectively* indicates that the items in one series are related to those in a second series in the order given.

Joseph should treat his parents *respectfully*.

Tom, Anna, and Susan were assigned *Bleak House*, *Great Expectations*, and *Dombey and Son*, *respectively*, for their reports.

rise   See *raise, rise.*

sensual, sensuous   *Sensual* refers to bodily or sexual sensations. *Sensuous* refers to impressions experienced through the five senses.

Singles bars offered *sensual* pleasures without emotional commitments.

The Tivoli Garden provides many *sensuous* delights for visitors.

set, sit   Generally, *set* means "to place" and takes a direct object. *Sit* means "to be seated" and does not take a direct object.

Alice *set* her glass on the mantel.

May I *sit* in this chair?

When it refers to the sun, however, *set* is used without a direct object.

As the sun *set*, we turned homeward.

shall, will   *Shall* is used in first-person questions and in specialized forms of writing such as military orders and laws. Otherwise, *will* is generally used.

Shall we go to the movies tonight?

The company *shall* fall into formation at precisely twelve noon.

No family home *shall* be assessed at more than 50 percent of its actual value.

should have, should of   *Should of* is an unacceptable substitute for *should have* because a preposition cannot substitute for a verb.

Nonstandard   I *should of* gone to the lake.

Standard   I *should have* gone to the lake.

[sic]   This Latin word, always enclosed in brackets, follows quoted errors in grammar, spelling, or information. Inclusion of [sic] indicates that the error appeared in the original, which is being quoted exactly.

sight   See *cite, sight, site.*

sit   See *set, sit.*

usage

site   See *cite, sight, site.*

so   *So* is an acceptable coordinating conjunction but tends to add an informal effect to writing and should therefore be used sparingly. For example, "Tom said he was divorcing me, *so* I began to cry" would be more effective if restated as follows: "When Tom said he was divorcing me, I began to cry." Do not use *so* as a substitute for *extremely* or *very* except with adverb clauses beginning with *that.*

Colloquial	You are *so* careless in what you say.
	The discussion was *so* informative that I took many notes.
Standard	You are *very* careless in what you say.
	The discussion was *extremely* informative.

some   *Some* is colloquial and unacceptable in writing when used as an intensifier (We had *some* time of it!) or an adverb (He'll probably pout *some* after you leave).

sometime, some time, sometimes   *Sometime* means "at a future unspecified time," *some time* means "a span of time," and *sometimes* means "occasionally."

We should get together *sometime* and play bridge.

The weather has been hot for *some time.*

Sometimes I go to dinner with Ethel.

sort of   See *kind of, sort of.*

specially   See *especially, specially.*

stationary, stationery   *Stationary* means "not moving" or "fixed." *Stationery* means "paper for writing letters."

The circular part in the center must remain *stationary,* or the machine will not function.

Sue always writes on scented *stationery.*

such, such . . . that   The use of *such* when it means "very" or "extremely" is unacceptable unless it is followed by a *that* clause completing the thought.

Colloquial	They were *such* good cookies.
Standard	They were *such* good cookies *that* I asked Steve for his recipe.

suppose to, supposed to   *Suppose to* is the nonstandard form of *supposed to.* In speech, it is difficult to hear the final *d* on *supposed,* and one may say *suppose to* without being detected; however, the correct written form is always *supposed to.*

sure, surely   *Sure* is colloquial for the adverb *surely.*

Colloquial	You *sure* know how to make good coffee, Mrs. Olsen.
Standard	You *surely* know how to make good coffee, Mrs. Olsen.

Although *surely* is correct, it may sound too formal and insincere. Therefore, *certainly* is often a better word to use.

take and, try and   Avoid these expressions. Simply eliminate them from the sentence or substitute *try to* for *try and.*

Unacceptable	If you *take and* cover the tomato plants, they probably won't freeze. I think you should *try and* settle your differences.
Standard	If you cover the tomato plants, they probably won't freeze. I think you should *try to* settle your differences.

than, then   *Than* is used to make comparisons; *then* means "at that time, in that case," or "after that."

Jill is taller *than* her brother.

First we will eat, and *then* we will discuss business.

that, which   These two words have the same meaning. *That* may refer both to things and groups of people; *which*, only to things. When referring to things, *that* is generally used with clauses that distinguish the things they modify from others in the same class (restrictive clauses). *Which* is generally used with clauses that add information about the things they modify (nonrestrictive clauses). Note that clauses starting with *which*, unlike those starting with *that*, are generally preceded by a comma.

Any book *that* she likes is certain to be trashy. (restrictive clause)

The Winthrop Building, *which* cost two million dollars to construct, could not now be duplicated for ten times that much. (nonrestrictive clause)

their, there, they're   These three separate words are often confused because they sound alike. *Their* is the possessive form of *they*. *There* is an expletive that appears at the beginning of a sentence and introduces the real subject, or it is an adverb meaning "in or at that place, at that point." *They're* is a contraction of *they are*.

It is *their* basketball.

There are many reasons why I cannot come.

Put the sofa down *there*.

They're going to be here soon.

theirself, theirselves   See *hisself, theirself, theirselves*.

then   See *than, then*.

there   See *their, there, they're*.

thorough, through   *Thorough* means "careful, complete, exact, painstaking." *Through* means "in one side and out the other, from end to end, from start to finish, over the whole extent of, finished."

Brenda has done a *thorough* job.

Let's run *through* the plan again.

thusly   *Thusly* is a nonstandard form of *thus*.

to, too, two   *To* is a preposition meaning "as far as, toward, until, onto." *Too* is an adverb meaning "excessively" or "also." *Two* is a number.

I'm going *to* the store.

Are you going *too?*

This car is *too* expensive for me.

There are *two* characters in the play.

toward, towards   Both forms are correct. *Toward* generally is used in the United States and *towards* in England.

try and   See *take and, try and.*

two   See *to, too, two.*

uninterested   See *disinterested, uninterested.*

unique   *Unique* means "without an equal" or "extremely unusual" and thus should not be modified by an adverb such as *very.*

use to, used to   *Use to* is the nonstandard form of *used to.* In speech it is difficult to hear the *d* on *used,* and one may say *use to* without being detected; however, the correct written form is always *used to.*

used to could   This phrase is nonstandard for *used to be able to.*

> *Nonstandard*   I *used to could* run ten miles.
>
> *Standard*   I *used to be able to* run ten miles.

very definite   See *definite, very definite.*

wander, wonder   *Wander* is a verb meaning "to move about without a plan or set destination." *Wonder* is a noun meaning "something causing surprise, admiration, or awe" or a verb meaning "to be curious about."

> Some people like to *wander* through shopping malls for recreation.
>
> That child is a *wonder* at mathematics.
>
> I *wonder* whether I have received an *A* on that test.

way, ways   *Ways* may be used to refer to two or more means or methods but not to time or distance.

> *Unacceptable*   Timbuktu is a long *ways* from the United States.
>
> *Standard*   There are two *ways* of thinking about that issue.
> Timbuktu is a long *way* from the United States.

well   See *good, well.*

were, where   *Were* is the past form of the verb *to be. Where* is an adverb or a pronoun meaning "in, at, to, from a particular place or situation" or "which or what place."

> I'm sorry that you *were* ill yesterday.
>
> Mr. Morris will show you *where* to register.

where . . . at, to, from   *At, to,* and *from* are unnecessary after *where.*

> *Wordy*   *Where* are you taking the car *to?*
> *Where* does she live *at?*
> *Where* did you get the book *from?*
>
> *Standard*   *Where* are you taking the car?
> *Where* does she live?
> *Where* did you get the book?

usage

whether   See *if, whether.*

which   See *that, which.*

who, whom   In formal writing, *who* should be used only as a subject in clauses and sentences and *whom* only as an object.

Unacceptable	*Who* are you taking to dinner on Friday?
	I know *who* the boss will promote.
	John is the candidate *whom* I think will be elected.
Standard	*Whom* are you taking to dinner on Friday?
	I know *whom* the boss will promote.
	John is the candidate *who* I think will be elected.

See the Handbook for a fuller discussion of *who* and *whom.*

who's, whose   *Who's* is a contraction of *who is* or *who has,* and *whose* is the possessive form of *who.*

Who's coming to see us tonight?

I would like to know *who's* been dumping trash in my yard.

Whose book is that?

will   See *shall, will.*

wise   Do not randomly add *wise* to the ends of nouns. Such word coinings are ineffective.

Ineffective	Personality *wise,* Sheila is ideal for the job.
Standard	Sheila has an *ideal personality* for the job.

wonder   See *wander, wonder.*

would have, would of   *Would of* is an unacceptable substitute for *would have.* A preposition cannot substitute for a verb.

Nonstandard	I *would of* enjoyed seeing the Picasso exhibit.
Standard	I *would have* enjoyed seeing the Picasso exhibit.

would have been, had been   When *would* occurs in the main part of a sentence, use *had been* (not *would have been*) in an "if" clause.

Nonstandard	If the engine *would have been* lubricated, the bearing *would not have* burned out.
Standard	If the engine *had been* lubricated, the bearing *would not have* burned out.

your, you're   *Your* is a possessive form of *you; you're* is a contraction of *you are.*

Where is *your* history book?

Tell me when *you're* ready to leave.

usage